A CENTURY OF AVIFAUNAL CHANGE IN WESTERN NORTH AMERICA

Joseph R. Jehl, Jr. and Ned K. Johnson, editors

Proceedings of an International Symposium at the
Centennial Meeting of the
COOPER ORNITHOLOGICAL SOCIETY
Sacramento, California,
April 17, 1993

Studies in Avian Biology No. 15

A PUBLICATION OF THE COOPER ORNITHOLOGICAL SOCIETY

STUDIES IN AVIAN BIOLOGY

Edited by

Joseph R. Jehl, Jr.
Hubbs-Sea World Research Institute
1700 South Shores Road
San Diego, California 92109

Editorial Assistants for this issue

Suzanne I. Bond, Jill T. Dye, and Donna McDonald

Studies in Avian Biology is a series of works too long for *The Condor,* published at irregular intervals by the Cooper Ornithological Society. Manuscripts for consideration should be submitted to the editor. Style and format should follow those of previous issues.

Price $40.00 including postage and handling. All orders cash in advance; make checks payable to Cooper Ornithological Society. Send orders to Assistant Treasurer, Cooper Ornithological Society, Western Foundation of Vertebrate Zoology, 439 Calle San Pablo, Camarillo, CA 93010.

ISBN: 0-935868-72-0

Library of Congress Catalog Card Number: 94-070897
Printed at Allen Press, Inc., Lawrence, Kansas 66044
Issued: 5 May 1994

CONTENTS

LIST OF AUTHORS   v

SYMPOSIUM OVERVIEW

A century of avifaunal change in western North America: overview . . . .
. . . . Ned K. Johnson and Joseph R. Jehl, Jr.   1

REGIONAL AVIFAUNAL CHANGE

A century of avifaunal change in Alaska . . . .
. . . . Brina Kessel and Daniel D. Gibson   4
The unlikely 18th century naturalists of Hudson's Bay . . . .
. . . . C. Stuart Houston   14
Pioneering and natural expansion of breeding distributions in western
North American birds . . . . Ned K. Johnson   27
Avifauna of the wetlands of Baja California, México: Current status . . .
. . . . Barbara W. Massey and Eduardo Palacios   45
Trends in nocturnal migrant landbird populations at Southeast Farallon
Island, California, 1968–1992 . . . .
. . . . Peter Pyle, Nadav Nur, and David F. DeSante   58
Avifaunal change on California's coastal islands . . . . Dennis M. Power   75
A chronology of ornithological exploration in the Hawaiian Islands, from
Cook to Perkins . . . . Storrs L. Olson and Helen F. James   91
Avifaunal change in the Hawaiian Islands, 1893–1993 . . . .
. . . . H. Douglas Pratt 103

POPULATION TRENDS

Seabird population trends along the west coast of North America: causes
and the extent of regional concordance . . . .
. . . . David G. Ainley, William J. Sydeman,
Scott A. Hatch, and Ulrich W. Wilson 119
A century of population trends of waterfowl in western North America
. . . . Richard C. Banks and Paul F. Springer 134
Shorebirds in western North America: late 1800s to late 1900s . . . .
. . . . Gary W. Page and Robert E. Gill, Jr. 147
Population trends and current status of selected western raptors . . . .
. . . . Clayton M. White 161
Population trends in the landbirds of western North America . . . .
. . . . David F. DeSante and T. Luke George 173
Changes in distribution patterns of select wintering North American birds
from 1901 to 1989 . . . . Terry L. Root and Jason D. Weckstein 191
Historical changes in populations and perceptions of native pest bird
species in the West . . . . John M. Marzluff, Randall B. Boone,
and George W. Cox 202
Population trends of introduced birds in western North America . . . . . .
. . . . Richard F. Johnston and Kimball L. Garrett 221

THE EFFECTS OF HUMAN-INDUCED ENVIRONMENTAL CHANGE ON AVIAN POPULATIONS

Human-induced changes in bird populations in coniferous forests in western North America during the past 100 years .... Sallie J. Hejl 232

Avian assemblages on altered grasslands .... Fritz L. Knopf 247

Changes in saline and alkaline lake avifaunas in western North America in the past 150 years .... Joseph R. Jehl, Jr. 258

The effects of human-induced changes on the avifauna of western riparian habitats .... Robert D. Ohmart 273

CASE HISTORIES

Evidence of changes in populations of the Marbled Murrelet in the Pacific Northwest .... C. John Ralph 286

Changes in the distribution and abundance of Spotted Owls during the past century .... R. J. Gutiérrez 293

The Cowbird's invasion of the Far West: history, causes and consequences experienced by host species .... Stephen I. Rothstein 301

Endemic Song Sparrows and Yellowthroats of San Francisco Bay ......
.... Joe T. Marshall and Kent G. Dedrick 316

Endangered small landbirds of the western United States ....
.... Jonathan L. Atwood 328

PROSPECTS

Preserving and restoring avian diversity: a search for solutions ....
.... J. Michael Scott 340

RECOMMENDED CITATIONS

BOOK:

Jehl, J. R., Jr., and N. K. Johnson (eds.). 1994. A century of avifaunal change in western North America. Studies in Avian Biology No. 15.

INDIVIDUAL CONTRIBUTIONS:

Kessel, B., and D. D. Gibson. 1994. A century of avifaunal change in Alaska. Pp. 4–13 *in* J. R. Jehl, Jr., and N. K. Johnson (eds.), A century of avifaunal change in western North America. Studies in Avian Biology No. 15.

LIST OF AUTHORS

DAVID G. AINLEY
Point Reyes Bird Observatory
4990 Shoreline Highway
Stinson Beach, CA 94970

JONATHAN L. ATWOOD
Manomet Bird Observatory
P.O. Box 1770
Manomet, MA 02345

RICHARD C. BANKS
National Biological Survey
National Museum of Natural History
Washington, D.C. 20560

RANDALL B. BOONE
Marine Cooperative Fish and
    Wildlife Research Unit
University of Maine
Orono, ME 04469

GEORGE W. COX
Department of Biology
San Diego State University
San Diego, CA 92182

KENT G. DEDRICK
1360 Vallejo Way
Sacramento, CA 95818

DAVID F. DeSANTE
The Institute for Bird Populations
P.O. Box 1346
Point Reyes Stations, CA 94956-1346

KIMBALL L. GARRETT
Section of Ornithology
Los Angeles County Museum of
    Natural History
900 Exposition Boulevard
Los Angeles, CA 90007

T. LUKE GEORGE
Department of Wildlife
Humboldt State University
Arcata, CA 95521

DANIEL D. GIBSON
University of Alaska Museum
907 Yukon Drive
Fairbanks, AK 99775

ROBERT E. GILL, JR.
National Biological Survey
1011 East Tudor Road
Anchorage, AK 99503

R. J. GUTIÉRREZ
Department of Wildlife
Humboldt State University
Arcata, CA 95521-8299

SCOTT A. HATCH
Point Reyes Bird Observatory
4990 Shoreline Highway
Stinson Beach, CA 94970

SALLIE J. HEJL
USDA Forest Service
Intermountain Research Station
P.O. Box 8089
Missoula, MT 59807

C. STUART HOUSTON
863 University Drive
Saskatoon, Saskatchewan
S7N 0J8

HELEN F. JAMES
Department of Vertebrate Zoology
National Museum of Natural History
Smithsonian Institution
Washington, D.C. 20560

JOSEPH R. JEHL, JR.
Hubbs-Sea World Research Institute
1700 South Shores Road
San Diego, CA 92109

NED K. JOHNSON
Museum of Vertebrate Zoology
University of California
Berkeley, CA 94720

RICHARD F. JOHNSTON
Museum of Natural History and Department
    of Systematics and Ecology
602 Dyche Hall
The University of Kansas
Lawrence, KS 66045-2454

BRINA KESSEL
University of Alaska Museum
907 Yukon Drive
Fairbanks, AK 99775

FRITZ L. KNOPF
National Biological Survey
Fort Collins, CO 80525-3400

JOE T. MARSHALL
National Biological Survey
Smithsonian Institution
Washington, D.C. 20560

JOHN M. MARZLUFF
Greenfalk Consultants
8210 Gantz Avenue
Boise, ID 83709

BARBARA W. MASSEY
pro esteros
1825 Knoxville Avenue
Long Beach, CA 90815

NADAV NUR
Point Reyes Bird Observatory
4990 Shoreline Highway
Stinson Beach, CA 94970

ROBERT D. OHMART
Center for Environmental Studies
Arizona State University
Tempe, AZ 85287-3211

STORRS L. OLSON
Department of Vertebrate Zoology
National Museum of Natural History
Smithsonian Institution
Washington, D.C. 20560

GARY W. PAGE
Point Reyes Bird Observatory
4990 Shoreline Highway
Stinson Beach, CA 94970

EDUARDO PALACIOS
CICESE
KM 107, Carretera Tijuana-Ensenada
APDO Postal 2732
Ensenada, B.C., Mexico

DENNIS M. POWER
Santa Barbara Museum of Natural History
2559 Puesta del Sol Road
Santa Barbara, CA 93105

H. DOUGLAS PRATT
Museum of Natural Science
Louisiana State University
Baton Rouge, LA 70803-3216

PETER PYLE
Point Reyes Bird Observatory
4990 Shoreline Highway
Stinson Beach, CA 94970

C. JOHN RALPH
Redwood Sciences Laboratory
U.S. Forest Service
1700 Bayview Drive
Arcata, CA 95521

TERRY L. ROOT
University of Michigan
School of Natural Resources and
    Environment
Ann Arbor, MI 48109-1115

STEPHEN I. ROTHSTEIN
Department of Biological Sciences
University of California
Santa Barbara, CA 93106

J. MICHAEL SCOTT
U.S. Fish and Wildlife Service
Department of Fish and Wildlife
University of Idaho
Moscow, ID 83843

PAUL F. SPRINGER
Wildlife Field Studies
Walter Warren House 38
Humboldt State University
Arcata, CA 95521

WILLIAM J. SYDEMAN
Point Reyes Bird Observatory
4990 Shoreline Highway
Stinson Beach, CA 94970

JASON D. WECKSTEIN
University of Michigan
School of Natural Resources and
    Environment
Ann Arbor, MI 48109-1115

CLAYTON M. WHITE
Department of Zoology
Brigham Young University
Provo, UT 84602

ULRICH WILSON
Point Reyes Bird Observatory
4990 Shoreline Highway
Stinson Beach, CA 94970

Nene (*Branta sandvicensis*). Painting by H. Douglas Pratt. Published courtesy of Dr. Pratt and its owner, Dr. John W. Fitzpatrick.

Studies in Avian Biology No. 15:1–3, 1994.

Symposium Overview

A CENTURY OF AVIFAUNAL CHANGE IN WESTERN NORTH AMERICA: OVERVIEW

NED K. JOHNSON AND JOSEPH R. JEHL, JR.

In 1992 a Centennial Committee established by the officers of the Cooper Ornithological Society planned a series of events to celebrate the organization's first one hundred years. Several of these events were inaugurated at the Society's 63rd Annual Meeting in Sacramento, California, April 13–18, 1993, and included a symposium organized by us. The topic, "A Century of Avifaunal Change in Western North America," seemed a fitting tribute to members of the Society and their associates who played such a seminal role in western North American ornithological research from the late 1890s to the present. The symposium also provided a challenge: to describe and analyze responses of birdlife to the unprecedented, human-induced environmental changes that have occurred during the 20th century in this vast and ecologically diverse region. Our intent was to ask specialists to provide concise but comprehensive overviews of topics. Insofar as possible we sought the participation of senior investigators because of the personal historical perspectives they could provide.

This Special Centennial Publication represents the fruition of that symposium. The 26 papers are divided into five sections: Regional Avifaunal Change, Population Trends of Major Groups of Birds, the Effects of Human-induced Environmental Change on Avian Populations, Case Histories, and Prospects. Our coverage is necessarily incomplete. There remain many geographic areas, habitats, or species for which a more complete accounting is needed. For example, essays on exploration and avifaunal change in western Canada and Mexico, including their offshore islands, could not be included. We must still await the long-needed, general treatment of avifaunal exploration in western North America, for which W. H. Behle's masterly *Utah birds: historical perspectives and bibliography* will serve as a template. Population trends of wetland species, exclusive of waterfowl and shorebirds, could not be treated for want of an available author. We also regret the lack of a comparative analysis of avifaunal responses to forest and woodland fragmentation between eastern and western North America, a topic of considerable current interest. Despite these admitted gaps, which we hope will be filled by future symposia, the included papers represent the most complete compilation to document the remarkable avifaunal change witnessed over the last century in western North America.

Brief comments on several of the most significant findings are in order. As anticipated, many authors concluded that population trends and adjustments in distributional boundaries often represent obvious responses to anthropogenic habitat modification. In contrast, some changes qualify instead as natural events. Especially perplexing are those trends that could have resulted from either human induction or natural causes or a complex combination of the two. In a troublingly large number of examples, the conclusion of change itself rests on unconvincing evidence, and a major finding of the volume is that baseline data typically are either too vague or incomplete to serve as a convincing basis for detecting change.

The most pervasive cause of negative population trends continues to be outright habitat destruction, with clear documentation of declines or extirpation of birds requiring riparian woodland, old-growth coniferous forest, grassland, saline lakes, marshes, and coastal

1

beaches. For example, an estimated 95% of riparian woodland, the richest ecologic formation for nesting birds in western North America, has either been degraded or destroyed in the past century by water management, agriculture, and domestic livestock grazing. The latter activity continues to be the most pervasive current threat to riparian habitats and their avifauna. Nest parasitism by the Brown-headed Cowbird (*Molothrus ater*), promoted by habitat destruction and the clumping or concentration of some hosts, is also implicated in the profound population losses of several riparian species. Public agencies and owners of private property must change their destructive land management practices if the avifauna of western North America is not to undergo further decline.

Direct human disturbance, especially of colonial species nesting in wetlands and on islands, has also exacted its toll. Introduced and domestic species have generally been detrimental to native birdlife. Predators, feral pigs, and disease have severely impacted the Hawaiian Islands' forest avifauna. Human overfishing of prey, coincident with severe climatic stress, appears to have played a major role in the decline of some seabirds. Habitat alteration and loss, exacerbated by hunting, has led to population reduction in some species of waterfowl, shorebirds, and raptors. In contrast, a large number of species show increasing population trends and expanding distributions, both during the breeding season and on the wintering grounds. Many more species expanded rather than contracted their winter ranges. Although the most striking enlargements of both nesting and wintering range are illustrated by introduced and managed species, native and non-managed birds are also well represented. Natural, ongoing climatic change is probably responsible for a significant number of distributional adjustments by native birds.

A few instances of conflicting interpretation vividly illustrate the problem of determining the validity of baselines against which change can be assessed. For example, one author reported severe declines in the Franklin's Gull (*Larus pipixcan*) and Cassin's Sparrow (*Aimophila cassinii*) in the Great Plains while another documents dramatic breeding range expansion in each. If either or both species are simply shifting populations among years, from deteriorating sites to favorable ones, then the easy conclusion of declines would be unjustified. The White-faced Ibis (*Plegadis chihi*) and American Avocet (*Recurvirostra americana*) clearly illustrate the phenomenon of geographic shifting of nesting distribution without demonstrable change in overall population size—the bane of population monitors!

Surprisingly, putatively detrimental habitat changes, for example, losses of old-growth forests and snags, have not universally led to declines expected in certain species apparently requiring such habitats. Therefore, either these species 1) do not really *require* old-growth forests and snags, 2) are somehow compensating for the loss of necessary resources or 3) have traits that mislead our population monitoring schemes, (in this example, Breeding Bird Surveys [BBS]). We suspect the latter reason and many authors share our view; indeed, a recurrent concern in the papers of this volume is the unreliability of current monitoring techniques, at least for particular species. Because this admission has far-reaching consequences for the allocation of precious financial resources, for management decisions by government and conservation agencies, and even for the creation of a National Biological Survey by the U.S. Department of the Interior, it calls for nothing less than a wholesale re-evaluation of methods by which population levels are assessed. Given these uncertainties, managers and conservationists should continue to focus their efforts at preservation 1) on endangered habitats, and 2) on those species whose deteriorating populations and distributions can be firmly documented (e.g., Spotted Owl [*Strix occidentalis*]), while simultaneously developing accurate and realistic methods for studying other taxa.

Without trustworthy temporal baselines, it is premature to invoke processes responsible for patterns of abundance. Although correlations can be relatively easy to find, causation remains as elusive as ever. Furthermore, because anthropogenic influences on natural biological processes are now global in scope, the separation of human from natural events in explaining fluctuating numbers and distributions will become increasingly difficult if not impossible.

It is time for biologists to face squarely the complexity of the natural world we attempt to interpret. A stochastic element, perhaps large and always of undefined dimensions, haunts every explanation for the population dynamics of birds.

Finally, a sobering note. Many authors properly lament the massive role played by humans in destroying natural landscapes and the birds they support. Recognition of this fact over the last decade or more has led to commendable conservation efforts, with some outstanding successes. We can be heartened by increasing public concern for the environment and expanded general efforts to protect biotic diversity. Despite these gains, however, the long-term prognosis is bleak. Incomprehensibly, national and international political leaders and the media either do not believe or will not discuss the connection between continued growth of the human population, with its attendant multitude of human social ills, and degradation of the world's resources. How ironic that overpopulation, the most pressing problem for ourselves and the earth's biota, is not only routinely ignored but its urgency is completely unappreciated. In company with many others, we conclude that *all* conservation efforts are doomed to eventual failure without prompt stabilization of the human population, which is now expanding at the rate of approximately one million every four days.

Studies in Avian Biology No. 15:4–13, 1994.

Regional Avifaunal Change

A CENTURY OF AVIFAUNAL CHANGE IN ALASKA

Brina Kessel and Daniel D. Gibson

Abstract. Avifaunal changes in Alaska have resulted from both natural and man-induced causes. The geographic ranges of eight North American species have expanded into Alaska, and the range of one (Barn Swallow) has contracted significantly—apparently all naturally. Most changes in distribution and numbers, however, have been man-induced, either through over-harvesting or through environmental alterations (Short-tailed Albatross, swans, geese, Peregrine Falcon, Bald Eagle). Through management efforts, declines in some species appear to have been stemmed, even reversed, but declines in others are only now being detected (two Beringian eiders and six Central Alaska passerines).

Key Words: Alaska; avian population changes; avian range expansions; albatrosses; cormorants; waterfowl; raptors; passerines.

Apparent changes in Alaska's avifauna in the last 100 years fall into several categories—those we believe are real changes; those that merely reflect our increased knowledge of the avifauna, especially over the last 30 years; those that may be natural long-term fluctuations; and those attributable to confused species identifications. It is almost impossible to distinguish, today, whether some perceived changes are real directional changes or just fluctuations, and some species seem to fall into more than one of the above categories.

The erratic pre-World War II history of exploration of Alaska's avifauna is well summarized in a 29-page introductory chapter of Gabrielson and Lincoln's (1959) *The Birds of Alaska.* Before the development of overland transportation in Alaska, exploration was largely by water. Hence, most early knowledge of the avifauna came from coastal areas and from the vicinity of the Yukon River (Fig. 1), and winter and spring observations were few, because ice blocked boat travel on the Yukon River and in the Bering, Chukchi, and Beaufort seas. Overland transportation was primitive until the Richardson Highway, between Valdez and Fairbanks, became regularly passable, after 1913, and until the Alaska Railroad, from Seward to Fairbanks, was completed in 1925. Even today, however,

ground transportation in Alaska is limited in extent. Air transportation, inaugurated in Alaska in 1924, has provided a critical platform for ornithological exploration, especially in the last 40–50 years.

A number of events 40–50 years ago contributed to the beginning of a real foundation against which future avifaunal changes could be compared: the stationing of World War II troops, including some ornithologists, in Southwestern Alaska in the 1940s; the opening of the Naval Arctic Research Laboratory at Barrow in 1949; the growth of biological disciplines at the University of Alaska Fairbanks, including, in 1950–1951, establishment of the Alaska Cooperative Wildlife Research Unit, and Kessel's arrival there; and the inauguration of U.S. Fish and Wildlife Service (USFWS) aerial Waterfowl Breeding Population Surveys in the mid-1950s. Interest in and knowledge of the avifauna has increased ever since, and in recent years it has been increasing almost exponentially.

Few databases are yet good enough, however, to use in detecting or measuring change—the exceptions being some species of waterfowl, seabirds, and raptors. For most species we have only either sporadic, often vague comments on status in the historical literature or data too recent or too incomplete to be a basis for evaluating change.

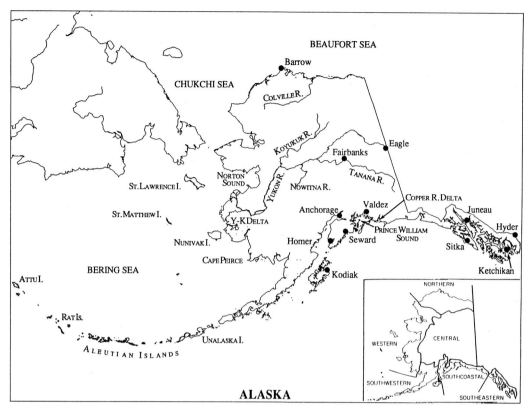

FIGURE 1. Alaska map showing selected place names and geographic features. The inset outlines Alaska's six biogeographic regions as recognized by Kessel and Gibson (1978).

Thus we have based our assessments of avifaunal change on information of variable quality from a variety of sources.

SEABIRDS: CONFUSED IDENTITIES?

ALBATROSSES

To an extent, problems of identification might be involved in the historic record of the abundance and distribution of the two white-bodied albatrosses in Alaska, Short-tailed (*Diomedea albatrus*) and Laysan (*D. immutabilis*). The precipitous decline of the Short-tailed Albatross during the 19th and in the early 20th century, at the hands of feather hunters on its breeding islands, from "over 100,000 birds on Torishima Island during the busiest time of feather gathering" to "at least 250 individuals" has been discussed recently by Hasegawa and DeGange (1982). Since the Laysan Albatross, which

superficially resembles the Short-tailed, was not described until 1893 (when the Short-tailed had been known to ornithology for 124 years), it is possible that some Laysan Albatrosses were present among the many Short-tailed Albatrosses in Alaska waters.

In June 1911 Bent (1922) saw so few white-bodied albatrosses in the Aleutians that he was unable to confirm that they were Short-tailed, the expected species. His estimate that the range of the Laysan Albatross did not extend north of 40°N was the last word on the subject for many years. The Laysan Albatross was first identified in Alaska from a specimen collected in the Aleutians in summer 1937 (Kenyon 1950). Today this species is an uncommon to fairly common summer visitant in the Aleutians (Kessel and Gibson 1978)—a conspicuous member of the avifauna. Yesner (1976) found that most of the (abundant) albatross remains in Aleutian archeological sites were of Short-tailed Albatrosses and that the remains of Laysan Albatrosses "were restricted to the upper levels" of these sites. We agree with his inference that increased reports of the Laysan are due to its recent expansion into the range formerly occupied by the Short-tailed Albatross.

CORMORANTS

Historically, there has been considerable confusion about the distribution and abundance of the several cormorant species in Alaska, apparently in part because of identification errors (see below; also Preble and McAtee 1923) and perhaps because of nomenclatorial confusion (Stejneger 1885). Cormorant populations have fluctuated over the years and breeding colonies have shifted, but we find no good basis for concluding that the overall status here of the Double-crested Cormorant (*Phalacrocorax auritus*), the Pelagic Cormorant (*P. pelagicus*), or the Red-faced Cormorant (*P. urile*) has changed significantly since the mid-1880s (contra Gabrielson and Lincoln 1959, Murie 1959, Sowl 1979).

Because not all information surfaces in a timely fashion, it can be hazardous to historical accuracy to infer from a few, contemporary data that a phenomenon itself is contemporary, e.g., the occurrence of Red-faced Cormorant in Southcoastal Alaska. As long ago as 1843 a Red-faced Cormorant was collected as far east as Kodiak (Russian Zoological Museum [ZIAN], St. Petersburg, list—*1*943 in Gabrielson and Lincoln [1959] is a typo), where the species also occurs today. For a complex of reasons, however, this information on the eastern extent of this bird's distribution in the North Pacific was not reflected in an AOU Check-list until 140 years later, in 1983.

In 1843–1844 the Russians (ZIAN list) also collected Red-faced Cormorants at Attu and at Unalaska islands; in 1873, Dall (1874) found them resident throughout the Aleutians; and in 1881–1883, Stejneger (1885) observed a population in the Commander

Islands. Fifty years later, in the 1930s, Murie (1959) also found them throughout the Aleutians. One must question, therefore, the identifications of Turner (1885), who did not list this species in the western Aleutians—its present center of abundance—in 1880–1881, but who reported Double-crested Cormorants to be abundant breeders there. (Like the Double-crested Cormorant, of course, Red-faced and Pelagic cormorants are also double-crested.)

Since no specimens were collected and no subsequent observers have reported the Double-crested Cormorant in the western Aleutians, early reports of them there (Turner 1885, Clark 1910) appear to be erroneous identifications. Turner (1886) also reported Double-crested Cormorants breeding abundantly on Besboro Island, Norton Sound, northeastern Bering Sea, although neither Dall and Bannister (1869) nor Nelson (1883, 1887) reported this species anywhere in the Bering Sea. Nelson (1883) reported Pelagic Cormorants nesting in large numbers toward the head of Norton Sound, however. Pelagic Cormorants currently breed on Besboro Island (Sowls et al. 1978), and Double-crested Cormorants are not known farther north than Cape Peirce and Nunivak Island.

Confusion was also caused by Nelson (1887:66), who outlined for the Red-faced Cormorant a wide distribution in the central and northern Bering Sea, including St. Matthew and St. Lawrence islands and both sides of the Bering Strait, an outline that reads remarkably like his earlier description (Nelson 1883:103) of the Pelagic Cormorant's range. Is this an error introduced during editing by H. W. Henshaw, after Nelson's retirement? Identity of bones from middens on St. Lawrence Island, ascribed to the Red-faced Cormorant by Friedmann (1934), is open to question.

And, finally, some recent work on Alaska cormorants by Siegel-Causey (1991)—work that described a new and contemporary species named "Kenyon's Shag (*Stictocarbo kenyoni*)"—must be viewed with skepti-

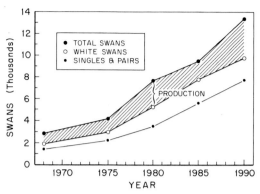

FIGURE 2. Trumpeter Swans recorded in Alaska during five statewide summer censuses 1968–1990 (from Conant et al. 1991).

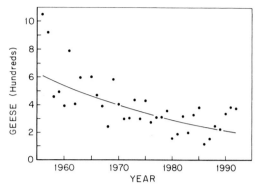

FIGURE 3. Decline of all geese recorded on the five segments of U.S. Fish and Wildlife Service Waterfowl Breeding Population Surveys within the coastal zone of the Yukon Delta (from Conant and Groves 1992). Species include the Emperor Goose, Greater White-fronted Goose, Brant, and Cackling Canada Goose, all of which have declined, mainly because of over-harvesting.

cism, in part because a number of the Red-faced Cormorant skeletons used in establishing a comparison for the diagnosis of "*S. kenyoni*" (for which no external characters are known) are from localities beyond the geographic range of *P. urile.*

WATERFOWL: UPS AND DOWNS

Swans

Early knowledge of the occurrence of Trumpeter Swans (*Cygnus buccinator*) in Alaska was hampered by identification problems, inaccessibility of their nesting marshes, and perhaps small numbers caused by hunting on portions of their wintering grounds. There is limited evidence of their presence, however, throughout most of the geographic area where they currently breed (Banko 1960, Hansen et al. 1971). Substantial breeding populations were "rediscovered" in several parts of Southcoastal Alaska between 1949 and 1957 and in Central Alaska—where the swans had been erroneously assumed to be Tundra Swans (*C. columbianus*)—in 1958–1960 (ibid.). Since then, the U.S. Fish and Wildlife Service has searched for and monitored through aerial surveys Alaska Trumpeter Swan populations. Five complete aerial censuses were flown from 1968 to 1990 (Fig. 2). During this period, the censuses showed a steady increase, from a total of 2847 in 1968 to 13,337 in 1990, and there is evidence that

available habitat in Southcoastal Alaska is now saturated and that peripheral habitat is being pioneered in Central Alaska (Conant et al. 1991).

In the past few years, too, Tundra Swans, previously thought to summer only on the coastal tundras along the Bering, Chukchi, and Beaufort seas, have also nested in some of the Yukon River drainages of Central Alaska. About 90% of swans in the lower Koyukuk river drainage and 50% in the lower Nowitna River are Tundra Swans (Loranger and Lons 1988), as are about 40% (11 pairs) in the upper Koyukuk drainages (Wilk 1989). In addition, up to four pairs have been identified at Minto Flats west of Fairbanks (K. S. Bollinger and R. J. King, USFWS unpubl.). The Tundra Swans in the lower Koyukuk and Nowitna rivers have probably been there for many years, but those on Minto Flats and in the upper Koyukuk apparently represent range expansion.

Geese

In contrast to swans, there has been a long-term population decline of geese, especially in Southwestern and Western Alaska, mainly because of varied human influences (King and Derksen 1986; also, Fig. 3). Except for the Aleutian Canada Goose

(*Branta canadensis leucopareia*), whose populations were nearly annihilated by Arctic Foxes (*Alopex lagopus*) introduced for fox farming numerous times between 1750 and 1930, most declines have occurred over the last 40 years and have ranged from 35% to over 90%.

The Emperor Goose (*Chen canagica*), an endemic form restricted primarily to the southern Chukchi and Bering sea region—Beringia—declined an estimated 34% between the 1960s (when 140,000–150,000 were reported by King and Lensink [1971]) and 1981 (Petersen and Gill 1982), and the population continued to decline through 1986 (USFWS 1988). The main cause was apparently "subsistence harvest," which was restricted beginning in 1984; also, fall hunting was reduced, and was closed completely in 1986 (ibid.). As a result, the population has begun to increase from its lows of about 50,000 adults and in 1991 was up again to 71,000–75,000 (USFWS 1992).

Other geese, especially those on the famous goose-producing Yukon-Kuskokwim Delta, have suffered from over-harvesting, including spring hunting, egging, and molt drives on their breeding grounds and fall hunting on their wintering grounds, mostly in Oregon, California, and western Mexico. Brant (*Branta bernicla*), Cackling Canada Geese (*B. c. minima*), and Greater White-fronted Geese (*Anser albifrons*) all declined significantly between the mid-1960s and the mid-1980s (King and Derksen 1986; USFWS 1986, 1987). The implementation in 1984 of a cooperative conservation program, known as the Yukon-Kuskokwim Delta Goose Management Plan (Pamplin 1986), seems to have allowed for some recovery, but population levels are still far below those of the 1940s–1960s (Migr. Bird Manage., USFWS unpubl.).

BERINGIAN EIDERS

Populations of two species of eiders endemic to Beringia, Spectacled Eider (*Somateria fischeri*) and Steller's Eider (*Polysticta stelleri*), have shown steep declines. The worldwide population of Steller's Eiders may have declined by 50–75% in the last 25 years; and on the Yukon–Kuskokwim Delta, where half of the world's population of Spectacled Eiders has nested, numbers may have dropped over 90%, from perhaps 47,700 pairs in the early 1970s to 2700 pairs today (Federal Register 57[90]:19852–19856, 8 May 1992). While the U.S. Fish and Wildlife Service agreed in 1992 that both eiders warranted listing as "threatened," listing for the Steller's Eider was "precluded by listing actions of higher priority" (ibid.), i.e., other species were in more imminent danger of extinction.

RAPTORS: RECOVERED POPULATIONS

PEREGRINE FALCON AND BALD EAGLE

Population changes in two falconiforms have occurred over the past 40 years. Those of the Peregrine Falcon (*Falco peregrinus*) have been well-documented (Cade et al. 1988, White 1994). Suffice it here to say, peregrines hit population lows along the Colville River in Northern Alaska and along the upper Yukon River in eastern Central Alaska in the early 1970s (Ambrose et al. 1988) as a result of pesticide contamination. Since then numbers have increased annually, with peak numbers reached in 1990, when there were 58 pairs, 37 of which produced 103 chicks, on the Colville River and 28 pairs, with 76 young, on the upper Yukon River (R. E. Ambrose and T. Swem, USFWS unpubl.). Ambrose and Swem's data for 1991 and 1992 suggest that the number of breeding birds is stabilizing at about 30 breeding pairs on the Colville and 25 on the upper Yukon.

Bald Eagle (*Haliaeetus leucocephalus*) numbers have increased in some regions of Alaska, especially in Southeastern Alaska, where their numbers were depressed by a predator-control bounty between 1917 and 1952. More than 128,000 Bald Eagles were destroyed for bounty during this period, over 100,000 of them from Southeastern Alaska (Robards and King 1966). Five aerial surveys of breeding eagles in Southeastern Alaska over a span of 25 years have shown a significant increase, from 7230 ± 896 adults in 1967 to 12,074 ± 2516 in 1987 and 13,341 ± 2348 in 1992 (Fig. 4). The total number of Bald Eagles in 1987, including immatures, was 14,000–16,000 (M. J. Jacobson, USFWS unpubl).

Especially since 1970, there also seem to have been increases in Central Alaska, where the current estimate is 525–725 nesting pairs (R. J. Ritchie and R. E. Ambrose, unpubl. MS), and in the Kodiak archipelago, where the current estimate is 600–800 nesting pairs (D. Zwiefelhofer, USFWS pers. comm.).

On the other hand, there has been a historical decline in westernmost Alaska. Formerly occupying a range that reached into the eastern Palearctic, the Bald Eagle was described in the mid-1880s as "not so abundant on Bering Island [Commander Islands] as it used to be" (Stejneger 1885), and by the 1930s it was "scarce in the Near Islands," the westernmost group of the Aleutians (Murie 1959). Today the Bald Eagle does not breed west of the Rat Islands, west-central Aleutians. Reasons for this range reduction are unknown.

PASSERINES: DECLINES AND FLUCTUATIONS

EMBERIZIDS AND TURDINAE

At least six of the common to abundant passerines in Central Alaska appear to have declined in numbers in recent years: Orange-crowned (*Vermivora c. celata*) and Yellow (*Dendroica petechia amnicola*) warblers and Fox (*Passerella iliaca zaboria*) and White-crowned (*Zonotrichia leucophrys gambelii*) sparrows—all shrub thicket birds—and the Yellow-rumped Warbler (*Dendroica coronata hooveri*) and Swainson's Thrush (*Catharus ustulatus incanus*), of deciduous and mixed deciduous-coniferous forests. It is difficult to detect declines in common species, partly because of well-known problems of percentage acoustical detections of numerous versus less numerous birds and partly because annual variations of 25–50% are not unusual in passer-

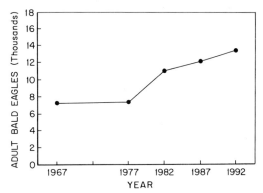

FIGURE 4. Population trend in adult Bald Eagles in Southeastern Alaska, 1967–1992 (from M. J. Jacobsen, USFWS unpubl.).

ines, at least in Central Alaska. But based on roadside counts that Kessel has run for over 20 years, and on casual observations of Fairbanks birders, including the authors, that the woods and thickets about our homes have been almost devoid of bird song since 1990, we believe that significant declines have occurred, at least in the above species. On the other hand, some species, such as the Alder Flycatcher (*Empidonax alnorum*) and American Robin (*Turdus m. migratorius*), do not appear to have declined.

Most of these declines have occurred since 1977. Of the shrub birds, the White-crowned Sparrow has shown a decline of over 50% since 1977, including a 52% drop from 1990 to 1992. Yellow Warbler populations declined more than 30% between 1977 and 1985, oscillated a few years, and then crashed another 45% between 1991 and 1992. The Orange-crowned Warbler declined 45% between 1980 and 1985 and has continued to decline since then, dropping 59% between 1987 and 1992. The Fox Sparrow has declined steadily since 1982, with a total loss of 77% by 1991 and 1992. The two deciduous forest birds have both shown sharp declines since 1989, the Yellow-rumped Warbler dropping 75% and the Swainson's Thrush at least 33%. As a result, the Swainson's Thrush, formerly the second most numerous passerine at Fairbanks, has slipped to third most numerous (behind Alder Flycatcher and American Robin) and has dropped from a relative abundance of "abundant" to "common."

The reasons for the population declines in these passerines remain obscure, and they may differ among species, since these birds have differing food habits, habitats, wintering grounds, and migration routes.

SWALLOWS

Changes in swallow populations in Alaska have been varied. The geographic range of the Cliff Swallow (*Hirundo pyrrhonota*), a species that, under natural conditions, usually affixes its nest to a rock cliff face, has probably not changed significantly over the years—its range apparently limited by environmental temperatures, especially the amount of summer warmth and availability of flying insects for food (Kessel 1989). Abundances have increased, however, with the availability of artificial nesting sites provided by human construction, e.g., buildings, mining dredges, and bridges. Colonies of 350–425 nests are known on bridges in Central Alaska.

Barn Swallow (*H. rustica*) populations, on the other hand, have declined dramatically since the early 1900s. The bird was common and widespread in the late 1800s–early 1900s (Dall and Bannister 1869, Turner 1886, McLenegan 1887, Nelson 1883, Grinnell 1900, McGregor 1902), but today it is largely restricted to Southeastern Alaska, where it is fairly common, and to Southcoastal Alaska, where it is uncommon as far west as Prince William Sound. The species is very rare or casual elsewhere. The cause of its decline since the turn of the century is unknown, but Western and Northern Alaska, with harsh environmental conditions, are at the extreme periphery of habitable range for this species. The increase of Cliff Swallows in these same regions in recent years is probably unrelated, since there appears to be no competition between the two species (McCann 1936, Samuel 1971).

Tree and Violet-green swallows (*Tachy-cineta bicolor* and *T. thalassina*) have shown unexplained long-term fluctuations. At Fairbanks, from 1951 to 1962, Violet-greens were more numerous than Trees, but in 1963 there was an increase in Trees to where they were about equal in numbers to Violet-greens. Numbers remained about equal through 1968, after which Tree Swallows began to predominate. By 1972 most swallows in the bird houses at Fairbanks were Trees. Violet-green Swallows increased somewhat in 1975, but were still outnumbered by Trees in 1976–1978. In 1979, however, even though Violet-green migration began early and continued normally through May, something severely affected Tree Swallow migration, and none was seen in Fairbanks until after 18 May. As a result, apparently, Violet-greens were more numerous than Trees in 1979, but numbers were again similar in 1980–1989. A major reversal occurred in 1990, however, when 80% of breeding *Tachycineta* in Fairbanks were again Violet-green Swallows.

SPECIES RANGE EXPANSIONS

INTO ALASKA

The first Alaska records of the Wilson's Phalarope (*Phalaropus tricolor*) were made in 1962, near Eagle (Kessel and Springer 1966) and at Barrow (Pitelka 1974). Its breeding range reached as far northwest as southwestern Yukon Territory by the late 1970s, when a pair appeared to be "defending the nest" near Haines Junction in 1977 (Am. Birds 31:1161, 1977) and as many as 14 adults, a nest with eggs, and two young were recorded near Whitehorse in 1978 (Am. Birds 32:1185, 1978). The species now occurs erratically and in small numbers in late spring and summer in Central, Southcoastal, Southeastern (and even Northern and Western) Alaska, and circumstantial evidence of local breeding has been recorded once each in the Anchorage and in the Fairbanks areas. In recent years the species has occurred as a casual fall migrant in Southeastern Alaska—perhaps birds that just moved due south from Yukon Territory.

The Caspian Tern (*Sterna caspia*) is a recent invader from lower latitudes via the eastern North Pacific coast (Gibson and Kessel 1992). The species was added to the Alaska avifauna in summer 1981, when up to four birds were seen at Ketchikan and two were seen in Sitka Sound. Since then the species has occurred annually in Southeastern and Southcoastal Alaska; adults feeding begging, flying juveniles pointed to probably breeding on the western Copper River Delta by 1989 (ibid.). Beyond Prince William Sound, Caspian Terns are now casual summer visitants as far west as Anchorage and Homer and in eastern Central Alaska.

The Band-tailed Pigeon (*Columba fasciata*) was unknown in Alaska until 1965 (Olson 1974). It occurs only at the southeastern periphery of the state, and in small numbers (Kessel and Gibson 1978). Despite sketchy information from adjacent sections of British Columbia (Campbell et al. 1990), it seems clear that the species is only a recent arrival in central British Columbia and in Southeastern Alaska.

The Barred Owl (*Strix varia*) was first recorded in Alaska in 1977, and its current status and distribution here—a scarce but conspicuous resident the length of the Southeastern Alaska mainland (Gibson and Kessel 1992)—is surely a development since that time, rather than an overlooked phenomenon. First noted in British Columbia in 1943, the species slowly expanded its range across that province, reaching the Pacific coast of Canada in 1966 (Campbell et al. 1990).

Anna's Hummingbird (*Calypte anna*) was unknown in Alaska until the late 1960s (Kessel and Gibson 1978), but it is possible that the paucity of observers, or the paucity of hummingbird feeders (since this species is unknown in Alaska away from sugar-water feeders), might account for the absence of records in Southeastern Alaska during the decade following the first certain records in coastal southern British Columbia, in 1958 (Guiguet 1959).

Known in Alaska prior to 1982 from a single sight report, the Least Flycatcher (*Empidonax minimus*) has been recorded all but annually since 1986 along a broad front, from the Interior to Southeastern Alaska, and the species is now regarded as a rare probable breeder at Hyder, the easternmost community in the state (Gibson and Kessel 1992).

Continuing the expansion of its North American range, the European Starling (*Sturnus vulgaris*) was first recorded in Alaska at Juneau in 1952 and was not known beyond Southeastern Alaska until 1960 (Kessel and Gibson 1978). We now consider it an uncommon to fairly common resident about towns and agricultural areas of Southeastern Alaska, and it is regular in small numbers in similar habitats in Southcoastal and Central Alaska east of about 149°W. It leaves Alaska's cold interior for the winter, and it is generally more numerous in Southcoastal Alaska in winter than summer, although it breeds regularly about farms in the Matanuska Valley, north of Anchorage.

It seems to have reached the limits of its breeding range at 65°N in the lower Tanana River Valley, where at Fairbanks in 1978 at least six successful nests were found and where a flock of up to 26 nonbreeders spent the summer (Kessel 1979). Since that time, however, while still of annual occurrence, only a few birds (including juveniles) have been recorded each season.

Note that all these range expansions have been by species from elsewhere in North America. We lack historical data on Asiatic taxa, because information from the western Aleutians was notably sparse until the 1970s, when the regular passage of Asiatic migrants in the Near Islands was discovered by Gibson (1981), and because most detailed information on the status and distribution of birds in northeasternmost Asia is also recent. Thus we have no basis from which to infer that any range expansion from Asia to Alaska has taken place in the last century.

WITHIN ALASKA

The Black Guillemot (*Cepphus grylle*) was first found breeding in Northern Alaska in 1966, in man-made debris at Point Barrow (MacLean and Verbeek 1968); a few years later, it was found breeding in man-made debris on barrier islands to the west and east of Barrow (Divoky et al. 1974). Subsequent expansion along the Beaufort Sea coast into Canada has been entirely man-effected, the result of guillemot "farming" by G. J. Divoky (pers. comm.) at Cooper Island, just east of Point Barrow, where he has provided nesting sites and where he has been able to study, by color-banding over 2000 Black Guillemots since 1976, the life cycle of these birds.

CONCLUSIONS

Some of the avifaunal changes outlined above, such as the Barn Swallow decline and the species that have recently expanded their ranges into Alaska, may just reflect the natural ebb and flow of mobile organisms. The changed status of all species for which we know causes, however, has been the result of human activities: over-harvesting; introduction of pesticides or predators into the environment; habitat changes; and, as in the starling, the introduction of an entirely new form into the biological community. Causes of the most recent precipitous declines in the Beringian eiders and the Fairbanks passerines are yet unknown.

LITERATURE CITED

AMBROSE, R. E., R. J. RITCHIE, C. M. WHITE, P. F. SCHEMPF, T. SWEM, AND R. DITTRICK. 1988. Changes in the status of Peregrine Falcon populations in Alaska. Pp. 73–82 *in* T. J. Cade, J. H. Enderson, C. G. Thelander, and C. M. White (eds.), Peregrine Falcon populations: their management and recovery. Peregrine Fund, Boise, ID.

BANKO, W. E. 1960. The Trumpeter Swan: its history, habits, and population in the United States. North American Fauna 63:1–214.

BENT, A. C. 1922. Life histories of North American petrels and pelicans and their allies. U.S. National Museum Bulletin 121. Washington, DC.

CADE, T. J., J. H. ENDERSON, C. G. THELANDER, AND C. M. WHITE (eds.). 1988. Peregrine Falcon populations: their management and recovery. Peregrine Fund, Boise, ID. 949 pp.

CAMPBELL, R. W., N. K. DAWE, I. MCTAGGART-

COWAN, J. M. COOPER, G. W. KAISER, AND M. C. E. MCNALL. 1990. The birds of British Columbia. Vol. 2. Royal British Columbia Museum, Victoria, BC.

CLARK, A. H. 1910. The birds collected and observed during the cruise of the United States Fisheries Steamer "Albatross" in the North Pacific Ocean and in the Bering, Okhotsk, Japan and Eastern Seas from April to December 1906. Proceedings U.S. National Museum 38:25–74.

CONANT, B., AND D. J. GROVES. 1992. Alaska-Yukon waterfowl breeding population survey, May 24 to June 21, 1992. Administrative report, Migratory Bird Management, U.S. Fish and Wildlife Service, Juneau, AK.

CONANT, B., J. I. HODGES, D. J. GROVES, AND J. G. KING. 1991. Alaska Trumpeter Swan status report. Administrative report, Migratory Bird Management, U.S. Fish and Wildlife Service, Juneau, AK.

DALL, W. H. 1874. Notes on the avifauna of the Aleutian Islands, especially those west of Unalashka. Proceedings California Academy Sciences 5:270–281.

DALL, W. H., AND H. M. BANNISTER. 1869. List of the birds of Alaska, with biographical notes. Transactions Chicago Academy Sciences 1, part 2:267–310.

DIVOKY, G. J., G. E. WATSON, AND J. C. BARTONEK. 1974. Breeding of the Black Guillemot in northern Alaska. Condor 76:339–343.

FRIEDMANN, H. 1934. Bird bones from Eskimo ruins on St. Lawrence Island, Bering Sea. Journal Washington Academy Sciences 24:83–96.

GABRIELSON, I. N., AND F. C. LINCOLN. 1959. The birds of Alaska. Stackpole Co., Harrisburg, PA, and Wildlife Management Institute, Washington, DC.

GIBSON, D. D. 1981. Migrant birds at Shemya Island, Aleutian Islands, Alaska. Condor 83:65–77.

GIBSON, D. D., AND B. KESSEL. 1992. Seventy-four new avian taxa documented in Alaska 1976–1991. Condor 94:454–467.

GRINNELL, J. 1900. Birds of the Kotzebue Sound region, Alaska. Pacific Coast Avifauna 1:1–80.

GUIGUET, C. J. 1959. Anna's Hummingbird (*Calypte anna*) at Victoria, British Columbia. Murrelet 40:13.

HANSEN, H. C., P. E. K. SHEPHERD, J. G. KING, AND W. A. TROYER. 1971. The Trumpeter Swan in Alaska. Wildlife Monographs 26:1–83.

HASEGAWA, H., AND A. R. DEGANGE. 1982. The Short-tailed Albatross, *Diomedea albatrus*, its status, distribution and natural history. American Birds 36:806–814.

KENYON, K. W. 1950. Distribution of albatrosses in the North Pacific and adjacent waters. Condor 52:97–103.

KESSEL, B. 1979. Starlings become established at Fairbanks, Alaska. Condor 81:437–438.

KESSEL, B. 1989. Birds of the Seward Peninsula, Alaska, their biogeography, seasonality, and natural history. University Alaska Press, Fairbanks, AK.

KESSEL, B., AND D. D. GIBSON. 1978. Status and distribution of Alaska birds. Studies in Avian Biology 1:1–100.

KESSEL, B., AND H. K. SPRINGER. 1966. Recent data on status of some Interior Alaska birds. Condor 68:185–195.

KING, J. G., AND D. V. DERKSEN. 1986. Alaska goose populations: past, present and future. Transactions North American Wildlife and Natural Resources Conference 51:464–479.

KING, J. G., AND C. J. LENSINK. 1971. An evaluation of Alaskan habitat for migratory birds. Administrative report, U.S. Bureau of Sport Fisheries and Wildlife, Washington, DC.

LORANGER, A., AND D. LONS. 1988. Relative abundance of sympatric Trumpeter and Tundra swan populations in west-central Interior Alaska. Pp. 92–98 *in* D. Compton (ed.), Proceedings and papers Eleventh Trumpeter Swan Society Conference. Everett, WA.

MACLEAN, S. F., JR., AND N. A. M. VERBEEK. 1968. Nesting of the Black Guillemot at Point Barrow, Alaska. Auk 85:139–140.

MCCANN, H. D. 1936. A colony of Cliff Swallows in Chester County, PA. Auk 53:84–85.

MCGREGOR, R. C. 1902. A list of birds collected in Norton Sound, Alaska. Condor 4:135–144.

MCLENEGAN, S. B. 1887. Exploration of the Noatak River, Alaska. Birds. Pp. 53–80 (Ornithology, Pp. 76–80) *in* M. A. Healy (ed.), Report of the cruise of the Revenue Marine Steamer *Corwin* in the Arctic Ocean in the year 1885. U. S. Government Printing Office, Washington, DC.

MURIE, O. J. 1959. Fauna of the Aleutian Islands and Alaska Peninsula. North American Fauna 61:1–406.

NELSON, E. W. 1883. Birds of the Bering Sea and the Arctic Ocean. Pp. 57–118 *in* Cruise of the Revenue-Steamer *Corwin* in Alaska and the N. W. Arctic Ocean in 1881. U. S. Government Printing Office, Washington, DC.

NELSON, E. W. 1887. Birds of Alaska. Pp. 35–222 *in* H. W. Henshaw (ed.), Report upon natural history collections made in Alaska between the years 1877 and 1881. No. III, Arctic Series, Signal Service, U.S. Army. U.S. Government Printing Office, Washington, DC.

OLSON, S. T. 1974. Bandtailed pigeons in southeast Alaska. Murrelet 55:27.

PAMPLIN, W. L. 1986. Cooperative efforts to halt population declines of geese nesting on Alaska's Yukon-Kuskokwim Delta. Transactions North American Wildlife and Natural Resources Conference 51:487–506.

PETERSEN, M. R., AND R. E. GILL. 1982. Population and status of Emperor Geese along the north side of the Alaska Peninsula. Wildfowl 33:31–38.

PITELKA, F. A. 1974. An avifaunal review for the Barrow region and North Slope of arctic Alaska. Arctic and Alpine Research 6:161–184.

PREBLE, E. A., AND W. L. MCATEE. 1923. A biological survey of the Pribilof Islands, Alaska. Part I. Birds and mammals. North American Fauna 46:1–255.

ROBARDS, F. C., AND J. G. KING. 1966. Nesting and productivity of Bald Eagles, Southeast Alaska—1966. Administrative report, Bureau of Sport Fisheries and Wildlife, Juneau, AK.

SAMUEL, D. E. 1971. The breeding biology of Barn and Cliff swallows in West Virginia. Wilson Bulletin 83:284–301.

SIEGEL-CAUSEY, D. 1991. Systematics and biogeography of North Pacific shags, with a description of a new species. Occasional Papers University Kansas Museum of Natural History 140:1–17.

SOWL, L. W. 1979. The historical status of nesting seabirds of the northern and western Gulf of Alaska. Pp. 47–71 *in* J. C. Bartonek and D. N. Nettleship (eds.), Conservation of marine birds of northern North America. Wildlife Research Report 11, U.S. Fish and Wildlife Service, Washington, DC.

SOWLS, A. L., S. A. HATCH, AND C. J. LENSINK. 1978. Catalog of Alaskan seabird colonies. FWS/OBS-78/78. Biological Services Program, U.S. Fish and Wildlife Service, Anchorage, AK.

STEJNEGER, L. 1885. Results of ornithological explorations in the Commander Islands and in Kamtschatka. U.S. National Museum Bulletin 29, Washington, DC.

TURNER, L. M. 1885. Notes on the birds of the Nearer Islands, Alaska. Auk 2:154–159.

TURNER, L. M. 1886. Birds, Part V. Pp. 115–196 *in* Contributions to the natural history of Alaska. No. II, Arctic Series, Signal Service, U.S. Army. U.S. Government Printing Office, Washington, DC.

U.S. FISH AND WILDLIFE SERVICE. 1986. Pacific Flyway management plan for the Cackling Canada Goose. U.S. Fish and Wildlife Service, Portland, OR.

U.S. FISH AND WILDLIFE SERVICE. 1987. Pacific Flyway management plan for the Pacific Flyway population of White-fronted Geese. U.S. Fish and Wildlife Service, Portland, OR.

U.S. FISH AND WILDLIFE SERVICE. 1988. Pacific Flyway management plan for Emperor Geese. U.S. Fish and Wildlife Service, Portland, OR.

U.S. FISH AND WILDLIFE SERVICE. 1992. Productivity surveys of geese, swans and brant wintering in North America 1991. Migratory Bird Management, U.S. Fish and Wildlife Service, Laurel, MD.

WHITE, C. M. 1994. Some trends and status of selected western raptors. Pp. 161–172 *in* J. R. Jehl, Jr. and N. K. Johnson (eds.), A century of avifaunal change in western North America. Studies in Avian Biology No. 15.

WILK, R. J. 1989. Status of Tundra and Trumpeter swans on the Kanuti National Wildlife Refuge and Todatonten Lake, Alaska, 1989. Administrative report, Kanuti National Wildlife Refuge, U.S. Fish and Wildlife Service, Fairbanks, AK.

YESNER, D. R. 1976. Aleutian Island albatrosses: a population history. Auk 93:263–280.

Studies in Avian Biology No. 15:14–26, 1994.

THE UNLIKELY 18TH CENTURY NATURALISTS OF HUDSON'S BAY

C. Stuart Houston

Abstract. The Hudson's Bay Territory, which included the entire drainage basin west to the Rocky Mountains, although one of the most thinly occupied areas in all of North America, was second only to South Carolina as the North American locality which contributed the most type specimens of birds. The collectors, fur traders of the Hudson's Bay Company, were Alexander Light, James Isham, Thomas Hutchins, Humphrey Marten, Andrew Graham, and Samuel Hearne. My researches in the Hudson's Bay Company Archives and the Royal Society library have solved the long-standing confusion about the relative contributions of Andrew Graham and Thomas Hutchins to the *Observations* published in 1969 by the Hudson's Bay Record Society. I have transcribed for publication the separate original "journals" of Graham and Hutchins and have compiled the largest dictionary of Cree Indian names of birds. Isham and Graham collected the most type specimens. Hearne was the best naturalist. Hutchins, the medical doctor and best scientist, was the only one to have a taxon named for him.

Key Words: Hudson's Bay Territory; Alexander Light; James Isham; Humphrey Marten; Andrew Graham; Samuel Hearne; Thomas Hutchins; type specimens.

From the Hudson's Bay Territory, one of the most thinly occupied areas in all of North America, came improbable but extremely important contributions to 18th-Century ornithology. Even though it included a large drainage basin that extended west to the Rocky Mountains (Fig. 1), it seems almost inconceivable today that Hudson's Bay should have been second only to South Carolina as the North American locality which contributed the most type specimens of birds. Even more unlikely were the men who made the collections, the literate but rugged fur traders of the Hudson's Bay Company. By sheerest chance their timing was perfect, involving them and their specimens in a revolutionary new scientific endeavour led by the Swede, Carolus von Linnaeus.

The fur traders were unaware of the system newly created by Linnaeus to give each species a unique binomial Latin name. Nor could they have guessed that their specimens would be hand-painted, page-size, in four large books by George Edwards, *A Natural History of Uncommon Birds,* between 1743 and 1751. Edwards, in turn, had no inkling of the fact that Linnaeus would give Latin names to the species illustrated in his book. But this improbable sequence of events put these fur traders at the very forefront of scientific ornithology and taxonomy.

Severn, with a year-round population of 20 white fur traders, and Albany with 33, became immortalized as type localities. The other five trading posts around Hudson's Bay, including York Factory with 42 employees, gave a total population of white people in the Hudson's Bay territory of under 250. Contributions from the settled, populated and more developed areas such as Pennsylvania, Massachusetts, New York and Florida lagged far behind those from the underpopulated wild reaches of Hudson's Bay. South Carolina, the leader thanks to Mark Catesby, had almost one-thousand-fold more people than did Hudson's Bay; in 1770, Charleston, Catesby's base, was the fourth largest city in British America with a population of 10,861.

When Linnaeus published his Tenth Edition of *Systema Naturae* in 1758, Mark Catesby's *Natural History of Carolina, Florida and the Bahama Islands* (1729–1747) was the sole source for 55 species, 43 of them from South Carolina. (Another 14 species, 11 from South Carolina, were added in Linnaeus' Twelfth Edition in 1766.) Edwards' *Natural History* was the next most important source, contributing 13 species described by Edwards from Hudson's Bay (McAtee 1957:291–300).

The Hudson's Bay Company was more than just a company with a charter for trade and an employer of fur traders; it acted as the government of its lands. As Harold A. Innis said in 1956, "The northern half of North America remained British because of the importance of fur as a staple product. . . . It is no mere accident that the present Dominion [of Canada] coincides roughly with the fur-trading areas of northern North America." As part of its assertion of its largely unstated hegemony, the Company undertook occasional forays into exploration and into science.

Each of the Company officers contributed primarily to the success of the fur trade; five of them also made direct or indirect contributions to geographic exploration. Natural history was at best an amusing sideline.

TYPE LOCALITY OF "HUDSON BAY"

Quite apart from the geographic ambiguity inherent in the citation of a vast inland sea, up to 1600 km in length and up to 1000 km in width, the general "type locality" of "Hudson Bay" used by the *American Ornithologists' Union Check-List* is inadequate or misleading for several species. Few ornithologists have appreciated that until 1870 the popular term "Hudson's Bay" (the possessive form Hudson's is no longer in official geographic use; modern maps show Hudson Bay rather than Hudson's Bay) designated an area of nearly 3.6 million km² extending west to the Rocky Mountains and draining into the bay (Rich 1958, Houston 1983). In this area, officially named "Rupert's Land" for 200 years, the people, as well as some of its birds and mammals, were often called "Hudsonians" (cf. Hearne 1795). For example, when Joseph Sabine described the North American form of the Black-billed Magpie, now *Pica pica hudsonia,* from a specimen collected by John Richardson and painted by Robert Hood at Cumberland House, over 1000 km by canoe from Hudson's Bay, he named it "*Corvus*

Hudsonius, Hudson's Bay Magpie" (Sabine 1823). The subspecies of Striped Skunk from "the Plains of the Saskatchewan" near Carlton, about 1500 km from the bay, was similarly named *Mephitis mephitis* var. *hudsonia,* the "Hudson's Bay Skunk" (Richardson 1829:55-56). Histories of the Hudson's Bay Record Society similarly spoke of the 1714 negotiations "settling the boundary between Hudson Bay and Canada" (Davies 1965).

The designation of Hudson Bay as the type locality for species such as the Marbled Godwit, American White Pelican and Purple Martin is thus somewhat misleading, since the overwhelming probability is that these specimens came from inland, within what is now Manitoba or eastern Saskatchewan.

Let us now look at the collectors.

ALEXANDER LIGHT

The first of the Hudson's Bay Company collectors was Alexander Light. A shipwright, he was sent to Churchill in 1733 for four years at £33 per annum. Light "was sent out, . . . by the Hudson's Bay Company, on account of his knowledge of Natural History" (Richardson 1832:ix–x).

Light collected five taxa of birds (all but one new), two mammals and a turtle, each illustrated by Edwards. New bird taxa included one new species, the Spruce Grouse (*Canachites canadensis*), and three new subspecies involving North American races which Linnaeus had correctly considered as belonging to the European species (McAtee 1950): Willow Ptarmigan (*Lagopus lagopus albus*); Northern Hawk-Owl (*Surnia ulula caparoch*); Gyrfalcon (*Falco obsoletus rusticolus*).

Light also collected specimens of the Snowy Owl and the Red-necked Phalarope. Linnaeus gave the name *Falco canadensis* to an eagle portrayed incorrectly by Edwards as having feathered tarsi but a white tail, obviously a composite of two eagle specimens. This eagle was said to have been brought alive to England by an unnamed

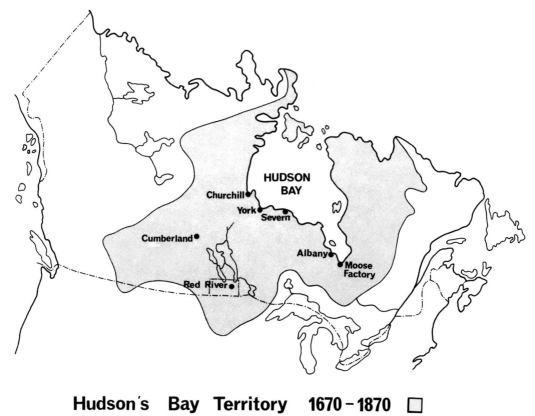

Hudson's Bay Territory   1670 – 1870 □

FIGURE 1.   Map of Hudson's Bay Territory, 1670–1870.

"Gentleman employ'd in the Hudson's-Bay Company's Service," in all probability Alexander Light. Not until the *Fourth AOU Check-List* in 1931 was this specimen designated on very questionable grounds as the type for the North American subspecies of the Golden Eagle, now *Aquila chrysaetos canadensis.*

In 1738, Light returned to begin his second term. Light told George Edwards (1750: 152) "there is a Goose which comes in Summer to *Hudson's-Bay,* having its Forehead as it were scorched with Heat, and the Natives firmly Believe, that these Geese to avoid the Winter's Cold, fly toward the Sun, and approach so near that it singes its Forehead against his Orb. It is hard to convince these Savages that there are Climates on this Earth warmer than their own, to which Birds may fly for Food and Shelter during their rigid Winters." Edwards presumed this to be the Blue colour phase of the Snow Goose.

There was a three-way connection between Alexander Light, George Edwards and Sir Hans Sloane. It was Sloane, the President of the Royal College of Physicians, to whom Edwards dedicated his second volume. Edwards was Keeper of the Royal College Library. Alexander Light brought live birds and mammals home from Hudson's Bay for Sloane's aviary-zoo and skinned specimens for the use of Edwards, who portrayed them in his book.

JAMES ISHAM

James Isham was the second Hudson's Bay collector of important natural history specimens. Unfortunately for Isham, although his specimens were among the first to receive binomial Latin names bestowed by Linnaeus himself, they were collected before it was fashionable to name new species after the collector. There are no species named *ishami*—and few modern ornithologists can remember his name.

Isham was a capable but plodding man who neither sought glory nor received much recognition. He is not listed in the *Canadian Encyclopedia* (1985, 1988) or its predecessor, *Encyclopedia Canadiana* (1957), nor has he received mention in the various compendia of ornithological biographies. More incredibly, his writings did not come to light in time for mention by that careful historian of early North American ornithology, Elsa Guerdrum Allen.

Isham was born in London, England, in 1716. He had a good general education for his time, but no special training in natural history. In 1732, at the age of 16, he was hired as a "writer" (and accountant) by the Hudson's Bay Company. When only 21 years old, he became the Chief at York Factory. Next he was Chief at the headquarters post of Fort Prince of Wales at Churchill. When he returned to England on his first furlough in 1745–1746, he took with him the specimens he had collected; large, interesting and edible birds were over-represented. These specimens he entrusted to George Edwards who depicted them in his splendid four-volume work. Edwards referred to Isham, who had "obliged me extremely by furnishing me with more than thirty different Species of Birds, of which we have hitherto had little or no Knowledge, the far greatest Part of them being non-descripts [not yet described to science]. . . . The Furs of the Beasts, and the Skins of the Birds were stuffed and preserved very clean and perfect . . . and brought to London in the Year 1745" (Edwards 1750:107).

Edwards painted Isham specimens that became the official "type specimens" for the following species: *Ardea herodias* (Great Blue Heron); *Anas caerulescens* (Snow Goose, blue morph)*; *Anas perspicillata* (Surf Scoter); *Tetrao canadensis* (Spruce

FIGURE 2. Whooping Crane, collected by James Isham, color painting by George Edwards (1750).

Grouse)*; *Tetrao phasianellus* (Sharp-tailed Grouse)*; *Ardea americana* (Whooping Crane) (Fig. 2)*; *Ardea canadensis* (Sandhill Crane)*; *Rallus carolinus* (Sora)*; *Scolopax fedoa* (Marbled Godwit); *Scolopax haemastica* (Hudsonian Godwit); *Tringa fulicaria* (Red Phalarope); *Tringa lobata* (Red-necked Phalarope); *Hirundo subis* (Purple Martin). (Only the six species with asterisks, above, were discussed by Isham in his *Observations*.)

Not until his 12th edition in 1776 did Linnaeus describe *Falco hudsonius,* now a subspecies of Northern Harrier, *Circus cyaneus hudsonius.*

Some of Isham's birds, especially the Marbled Godwit and possibly the Purple Martin and White Pelican, were in all likelihood collected inland. For these species, the best designation of the type locality would be "Hudson's Bay territory."

Isham provided Edwards with specimens of two species mentioned in the Isham manuscript, the White-fronted Goose and Black-billed Magpie. Another sixteen species were illustrated in the following sequence by Edwards: Three-toed Woodpecker, Belted Kingfisher, Pine Grosbeak (male and female), Snow Bunting, American Bittern, American Golden-Plover, Ruddy Turnstone, Horned Grebe, Arctic Loon, Parasitic Jaeger, Tundra Swan, King Eider and Harlequin Duck. Isham may also have contributed the Canada Goose, White-fronted Goose and Old-squaw, all from Hudson Bay, although no collector was named.

His last two years at York were miserable. His gout became worse. For two months he complained of "weakness & stoppage in his throat." He died on Monday 13 April 1761, and was buried with a 21-gun salute.

Not until 1949 were Isham's writings published in a 457-page book, *James Isham's Observations on Hudson's Bay, 1743–1749* (Rich and Johnson 1949). These included notes on 23 species of birds: the six with asterisks above and: Red-throated Loon, Common Loon, American White Pelican, Double-crested Cormorant, American Bittern, Tundra Swan, Greater White-fronted Goose, Brant, Canada Goose, Hutchin's Goose, Common Eider, Willow Ptarmigan, Rock Ptarmigan, Black Guillemot or "willock," Passenger Pigeon, Northern Flicker, Gray Jay, Black-billed Magpie, and eagle, owl, "kite" and swallow, unidentified as to species.

Isham described the American White Pelican as "a Large bird, with a great Bill Long neck't and short Legd. Carrying their neck Like a Swan . . . under the throat hangs a bag, which when fill'd wou'd hold 2 Gallons, the Substance of itt is a thin membrane, of a sky Colour, they fly Very heavy and Low, and fish is their Chiefest food, the Bouch, as well as stomach has fish found in itt. The Bouch or bag is purely to Keep their food in; they are Eat by some."

Concerning the Passenger Pigeon he said, "Its Very Rare to see any Pidgeons or doves, in these parts, or Downe by the sea side, tho in Land some hundred miles are Very Numerious, once in 12 Year I Did see some

millions of them, which Came from the Southw[d] flying in Ranges as the Geese does, &c.: they are of a Blew Grey and abou't as big as a dove pidgeon and Very Good Eating."

On the last page of his *Natural History,* published in 1750, Edwards paid tribute to Isham, "to whose Curiosity and good Nature I am beholden for the greatest Part of my *History of Birds*; and I believe the curious Part of the World will not think themselves less obliged to Mr. Isham than I acknowledge myself to be."

HUMPHREY MARTEN

Humphrey Marten contributed from Albany the type specimen of the Eskimo Curlew that was named as a new species by Johann Reinhold Forster in 1772. Marten is thus important as one of the first two natural history collectors (with Andrew Graham) in what is now Ontario, and the first person known to have put up bird boxes in what is now Canada. The boxes were immediately used by Tree Swallows. Marten also played a major role in planning the first inland fur trading posts of the Hudson's Bay Company.

Marten was born about 1729. An "unusually clear-headed man," he was engaged by the Company in the capacity of "writer" on 1 March 1750. He became acting chief at York Factory during James Isham's furlough in 1758–1759. He then founded Severn, acting as chief from 1759 to 1761. He served as chief at Albany for two terms, 1764–1768 and 1769–1774. Here he did his collecting. When in charge of the headquarters post, York Factory, in 1774–1775 he both supported and directed Samuel Hearne's founding of the Company's first inland fur trading post at Cumberland House, within present-day Saskatchewan.

Marten had in many ways a difficult life at the Bayside where journals could be written only after the ink thawed, and strong beer froze solid in bottles two feet from a stout fire. Yet he undertook some of the first farming northwest of the St. Lawrence river valley, maintaining at York Factory a flourishing breed of cattle and pigs and a fine garden.

During his second term as chief factor at Albany, 1769–1774, Marten was called upon to provide the Royal Society of London with natural history specimens and information. He sent back to England, as Samuel Hearne reported, several hundred specimens of animals and plants. Marten's initial shipment, sent with other specimens from Andrew Graham, contained 17 skins of seven species, including the skin of the Eskimo Curlew, described by Johann Reinhold Forster the next year as *Scolopax borealis.* Marten also sent home "a fine brace of Partridges a Cock & Hen," both alive, and a pair of snowshoe hares, only the male surviving the voyage.

Marten kept spring arrival dates for birds such as swallows, and reported late fall departure dates for snow buntings. He attempted unsuccessfully to have a domestic hen incubate eggs of the Sharp-tailed Grouse. For the 26 specimens of 21 species, Marten provided descriptions of the colors of soft parts that might fade before reaching England, described the color of the pupil of the eye (!), the Cree Indian name, and for all but the Snow Goose, which nested farther north, the number of eggs.

In 1949 and 1950, when Elsa G. Allen (Mrs. Arthur A. Allen) was writing her landmark history of early North American ornithology, her researches took her to the Royal Society offices in London. The librarian found for her a Marten manuscript, entitled "A Short Description of the Birds in a Box," in which Marten described 26 specimens by their native names. Mrs. Allen published Marten's description of the swallow (Allen 1951).

After his leave to Britain in 1781–1782 Marten returned to York Factory just in time to surrender York Factory to the French admiral, la Pérouse. Marten was taken back to France and held a prisoner for one year until the Treaty of Paris was signed.

ANDREW GRAHAM

Andrew Graham was born about 1733, probably near Edinburgh, Scotland. In 1749, as a lad of about 16, Graham joined the service of the Hudson's Bay Company. In 1753 he became assistant writer at York Factory under James Isham. Graham was so proficient as a clerk and accountant that he became Acting Chief at age 25 while Isham took a furlough to Britain in 1758–1759; thereafter, until 1761, Graham was second-in-command at York Factory. He was then promoted to Master at Severn House where he served until 1774, with three exceptions.

In 1770, on his return from his first English furlough and stimulated by Thomas Pennant, who had published the first three volumes of the second edition of his *British Zoology,* Graham began enthusiastically to collect natural history specimens at Severn. He encouraged Humphrey Marten at Albany to do the same.

At Severn, Graham became "the most industrious and systematic" collector (Williams 1968) among the Company factors. Among the 64 skins of 39 bird species he sent from Severn in 1771 were the type specimens for the Great Gray Owl (*Strix nebulosa*), Boreal Chickadee (*Parus hudsonicus*), Blackpoll Warbler (*Dendroica striata*), and White-crowned Sparrow (*Zonotrichia leucophrys*). These and one fish, the Longnose Sucker (*Catostomus catostomus*), were given their definitive Latin names by Johann Reinhold Forster in 1772, who gives his assessment of Graham as "a careful observer, and an indefatigable collector."

Forster failed to recognize the pelican as a species new to science. He mistakenly thought that the American White Pelican was the same as the Oriental Pelican described by Linnaeus and thus lost his opportunity to bestow a Latin name. His mistake was corrected when J. F. Gmelin in his 13th edition of *Systema Naturae,* 1789, bestowed the binomial of *Pelecanus erythrorhynchos.* Graham's natural history observations in HBC Archives manuscript E.2/ 12, published as *Observations,* included 41 mammals and 17 fish, as well as 92 species of birds. In the as yet unpublished manuscript E.2/5, Graham wrote of the Snow Bunting: ". . . we kill some of them with a net made for that purpose, which is put in a frame and set on the ground, one side being kept up by two sticks, and under it is scattered a little oatmeal or seeds of grass, and when they come to feed, the two sticks having a string fast to them is hawled out at pleasure, when the net falls down and all that are under made prisoners. They eat very fine in a pye."

Graham died at Prestonpans, Scotland, on 8 September 1815. Few authors have to wait 154 years after their death for their observations to be published and recognized. This was Andrew Graham's strange fate.

THOMAS HUTCHINS

Thomas Hutchins, surgeon, fur trader and meteorologist, whose name is perpetuated in Hutchins's Goose, *Branta canadensis hutchinsii,* was born somewhere in Great Britain about 1742. His first visit to Hudson's Bay was as surgeon on the *King George II,* the Hudson's Bay Company annual supply ship, which unloaded supplies and loaded the season's furs at York Factory in 1765. He returned the next summer and stayed as surgeon for the Company.

Hutchins had a scientific bent. He made his first careful measurements of temperature and atmospheric pressure during 1771–1772 when he was with Andrew Graham at York Factory. In 1774–1775 Hutchins added a set of observations on the dipping needle, and experimented with the congealing of mercury in severe cold. For the resulting publications in the *Philosophical Transactions* (1776, 1783), Hutchins was presented with the Copley gold medal by the Royal Society in December 1783, only the second Hudson's Bay man to be awarded one of the highest annual prizes in science in the 18th century.

Hutchins's detailed descriptions which accompanied the bird and mammal collections from York Factory in 1772, included careful notes of the colors of soft parts, which might subsequently fade, measurements, and Cree Indian names for a number of species. He made a greater effort than Graham to collect small songbirds such as warblers. Additional evidence of Hutchins's scientific approach is the notation by Pennant in the first edition of *Arctic Zoology* concerning the Burbot (*Gadus lota*), "Mr. Hutchins counted, in a single fish, 671,248 ovaria." However many hours or days this project required, it is evidence of the mindset and perseverance of Hutchins's scientific curiosity.

After Hutchins returned to London in 1783 to become Corresponding Secretary of the Hudson's Bay Company at £150 per annum, he gave further information to Pennant.

Concerning the Gray Jay, Hutchins said: "They feed on black moss, worms, and even flesh. When near habitations or tents, they are apt to pilfer every thing they can come at, even salt meat. They are bold, and come into the tents to eat victuals out of the dishes, notwithstanding they have their hoard of berries lodged in the hollows of trees. They watch persons baiting the traps for Martins, and devour the bait as soon as they turn their backs. These birds lay up stores for the winter; and are seldom seen in January, unless near habitations. . . . When caught, they pine away, and die, tho; their appetite never fails them. Detested by the natives of Hudson's Bay" (Pennant 1792, 2:290).

Concerning the Mourning Dove: "Mr. Hutchins informed me, a Pigeon with a reddish head, and orbits, was found far inland . . . ." (Pennant 1792, 3:7).

In 1969, almost 200 years after they were written, Hutchins's observations concerning 16 species of birds, 11 of which had not been listed by Andrew Graham, 14 species of fish, and seven species of mammals, were published as Appendix C of *Andrew Gra-*

ham's Observations on Hudson's Bay, 1767–1791 (Williams 1969).

For example, in his account of the Pectoral Sandpiper Hutchins tells of finding several bird-lice which he examined under his microscope, an instrument that even a surgeon was remarkably fortunate to own in 1772. The lice appeared like "very beautiful Tortoise-Shells." Hutchins, the surgeon-scientist, provides weights of birds, perhaps the first person to record this information in North America; 160 years later, Dr. T. S. Roberts could find only one reliable source, a taxidermist named Lano, for such weight information. Hutchins compiled Cree names for many additional species, something that Graham had initiated for about one-third (20) of the bird species in 1771.

Two new species are mentioned in the Hutchins Royal Society manuscript that do not appear in *Observations*: the Ruddy Turnstone and an unidentifiable gull. An additional species, the Chepethewuck, weight about 25 ounces, is unquestionably the Greater Prairie Chicken in E2/9: "*Pinnated Grous*: is found about Henley Settlement in Hudson's Bay, legs covered with soft brown feathers, toes naked & pecinated. The tufts which distinguish this species from all others are rooted high in the neck, not far from the hind part of the head . . . ."

Graham and Hutchins both had a firm understanding of bird migration, as Pennant had, in a time when Daines Barrington of the Royal Society was still claiming migration to be preposterous. Graham and Hutchins, knowing of Barrington's claim that swallows lie dormant during winter, made specific enquiries of Indians, both young and old, to confirm that none of them had observed such a phenomenon.

Hutchins at times kept a meteorological journal in which at York Fort in 1771–1772 he included spring migration dates and perhaps the first fall migration dates to be recorded in North America:

Sept. 12—Snow birds appear

Sept. 21—Snow birds & white geese plentiful.

Sept. 27—Snow birds increased today—geese almost gone

Oct. 4—ducks, geese & plover left us

Nov. 2—Snow birds taking their departure

Nov. 14—saw a flock of winter small birds like Tom Tits

Hutchins is the only one of the Hudson's Bay naturalists to have a bird named for him, *Branta canadensis hutchinsii.*

John Richardson wrote: "On Captain Parry's second voyage, several flocks of Geese were seen on Melville Peninsula, which were thought by the officers of the Expedition to be the *Anser leucopsis* or Barnacle. . . . A number of specimens were secured . . . I have since obtained information, which leads me to believe that they actually belong to a distinct species, hitherto confounded with the *A. Canadensis* [Canada Goose]. They are well known in Hudson's Bay by the Cree name of *Apistiskeesh,* and are generally thought by the residents to be merely a small kind of the Canada Goose, as they have the white kidney-shaped patch on the throat, which is deemed peculiar to that species. . . . We have designated the *Apistiskeesh* by the name of *Hutchinsii,* in honour of a gentleman from whom Pennant and Latham derived most of their information respecting the Hudson's Bay birds."

Richardson appended the following footnote: "Some mistake occurs in Forster's account of the Canada Goose (*Phil. Trans.,* lxii); the habits of *A. Hutchinsii* (Small Grey Goose of Graham) being ascribed to the *A. Canadensis*; while the Large Grey Goose, mentioned in the same passage, is undoubtedly the Canada Goose, which we know to be the only species that breeds abundantly about Severn River."

When P. A. Taverner (1931), ornithologist at the National Museum of Canada, undertook a revision of the Canada Geese, he confirmed the small size of the geese from

FIGURE 3. Portrait of Samuel Hearne, from the *European Magazine,* June 1797.

the arctic islands, and the "very small size and light breast and underbody . . . Weight . . . rarely as much as 5 pounds." Richardson's measurements were consistent except that he gave the culmen as 1 inch, 8½ lines or 43.5 mm., far too long. Taverner said "To anyone who has measured many Canada goose bills the solution is apparent. The feathering on the fore crown was worn away and did not give the true exposed culmen line . . . there can be no doubt that it was this little goose that Richardson designated *hutchinsii* and not its much larger relative to which the name has hitherto been attached. In order to avoid confusion with older references and to connect this bird with the man who first detected its distinctness I propose that it be known vernacularly as Richardson's goose."

Now that subspecies are no longer given vernacular names, but retain only their Latin name, "Richardson's goose" retains the single name of *hutchinsii,* and thereby honours the surgeon and naturalist who spent about 26 years on Hudson's Bay. It is highly probable that a future Check-List of the American Ornithologists' Union will accord it full specific status.

SAMUEL HEARNE

Samuel Hearne's exploits as an explorer, fur trader and author have been appreciated for more than two centuries. He is the only one of our six naturalists for whom a portrait has been found (Fig. 3). Hearne was the first European to reach the Arctic coast of North America, travelling on foot with a group of Chipewyan Indians from Churchill to the mouth of the Coppermine River. He founded in 1774 the first inland trading post of the Hudson's Bay Company at Cumberland House, now Saskatchewan's oldest settlement. This action kept the Hudson's Bay Company in competition with the much larger North West Company. As James Marsh has written, Hearne's "literary artistry . . . secured his fame in letters." Yet, modern naturalists rarely refer to Hearne's original and often incredibly apt observations. Ironically, only the historians appear to appreciate what a good naturalist he was.

Samuel Hearne was born in London, England, in 1745. He entered the navy at the age of 11, acting as servant to Admiral Hood, for six years. In 1766 he joined the Hudson's Bay Company as a seaman and mate of the *Charlotte,* a position he held for three years, sailing out of Churchill.

Hearne was chosen by Moses Norton for the Company's first major arctic exploration by land, to search for the fabled Neetha-san-san-dazey or "Far Off Metal River," now known as the Coppermine River. Hearne's first journey began from Churchill on 6 November 1769, but lasted only one month and five days, because Hearne was deserted by his Indian guide, Chawchina-haw. His second attempt, with an Indian guide named Conne-e-queese, began on 23 February 1770 and lasted 8 months and five days. Hearne was forced to return when he broke his quadrant, unable to make astronomical observations.

Not a man to be discouraged easily,

Hearne set out again on 7 December 1770, this time with Mattonabee, a skillful leader of great prestige among the Chipewyan Indians. His party reached the mouth of the Coppermine River on 16 July 1771 where Hearne was the first white man to view the Arctic Ocean from the northern shore of this continent.

Hearne was next assigned in 1774–1775 to found the first inland trading post of the Hudson's Bay Company, at Cumberland Lake. Occupied continuously ever since, Cumberland House celebrated its bicentenary in 1974.

Hearne also had a moment of ignominy, when he was compelled to surrender Prince of Wales's fort to a French force under the celebrated French navigator, Jean François de Galaup, Comte de la Pérouse, on 8 August 1782. La Pérouse found and claimed Hearne's journal as a fair prize, but then returned the manuscript, already under revision, "on the express condition that he publish it" (Glover 1958). If la Pérouse was responsible for the eventual publication, the world owes him a great debt; at the least, it was a gentlemanly gesture.

Hearne then made a brazen request: that la Pérouse let him take one of the fort's trading sloops which had been seized as a fair prize of war. La Pérouse acceded and Hearne sailed the little boat on a risky journey from Hudson Strait directly back to Stromness in the Orkney Islands, a big improvement over being taken prisoner back to Cadiz, Spain.

Hearne did not sulk over his defeat and waste his time in England, as others might have done. That winter he met Thomas Pennant and gave him a copy of his natural history observations, a dozen years in advance of their publication. As Glover has said, "the meeting of the two men was valuable to both." Pennant incorporated a number of Hearne observations into *Arctic Zoology,* which first appeared in print a little over a year after their meeting. Hearne in turn inserted a number of references to Pennant in his manuscript.

With the British again in possession, Hearne returned in 1783 to restore the fort and resume charge of Churchill. He was still working on his book. Ill-health forced him to retire and return to England in 1787. Following another five years of slow and "seemingly interminable" work on his manuscript, Hearne submitted it for publication in October 1792. He received the high price of £200 for it. A month later, when he died of "the dropsy," he was only 47. The book, *A Journey from Prince of Wales's Fort in Hudson's Bay to the Northern Ocean,* his greatest achievement, was published in 1795, three years after his death.

HEARNE'S JOURNAL

Hearne's journal, readily obtained from most libraries, is one of the greatest travel narratives ever written. His frank and often understated accounts of hardship and starvation are still well worth reading. Surprisingly few of Hearne's usages in reference to natural history observations are dated. The term "willick" for the guillemot, one of the smaller seabirds of the Auk family, is now obsolete. He used the word non-descript correctly to mean a species not yet described to science.

Hearne was a century ahead of his time in describing the habits of wild animals. He was an observer, not a collector. He was the first to give recognizable descriptions of the Ross's Goose, Musk-ox, and Wood Buffalo, and accounts of the habits of the Arctic Ground Squirrel and Arctic Hare. He was the first to describe the nesting of the White-crowned Sparrow, on the ground at the root of a dwarf willow or a gooseberry.

Hearne described the Ross's Goose as having the base of its bill studded with little knobs about the size of peas. This small goose was scarce at Churchill but more common 200 or 300 miles to the northwest. When another well-known fur trader and naturalist, Bernard Rogan Ross (1861), wrote about the mammals and birds used by the Chipewyan Indians, he listed the

"Horned-wavy Goose of Hearne" as a species still without a scientific name. The omission was quickly corrected that very year, when John Cassin gave the name of *Anser Rossii* to the specimen sent by Ross from Great Slave Lake. Cassin remarked that "this species has never again been noticed from the time of Hearne until the time of the receipt of the present specimens from Mr. Robert Kennicott, an enterprising young naturalist, now in the northern regions of British America, but has been constantly insisted on as a valid species in his letters to the Smithsonian Institution by Mr. Bernard R. Ross, an enthusiastic naturalist and careful observer in the service of the Hudson's Bay Company." Bernard Rogan Ross, "a tart Londonderry Irishman," was the chief trader at Fort Simpson, in charge of the entire Mackenzie district. Robert Kennicott had been the stimulus for men like Bernard Rogan Ross and Roderick Ross MacFarlane to collect specimens.

Hearne owned "an excellent microscope," a remarkable possession in that time and place. Being interested in the lice and other parasites on the Northern Lemming, he tried to examine them under the microscope. However the lens became damp with the moisture from his breath in his cold winter room, delaying further use until the busy summer season.

Richard Glover, in his introduction to the 1958 edition of Hearne's *Journey,* recognized that "Samuel Hearne was, of course, another first class observer and reporter—in fact, a much better naturalist than [Andrew] Graham . . . head and shoulders superior to every other North American naturalist who preceded Audubon." Glover singled out Hearne's accounts of the Whooping Crane and the beaver as especially well done.

Hearne understood sexual dimorphism, the male Willow Ptarmigan being larger. His description of the variable size of ptarmigan showed he had some understanding of what was later to be described as Gaussian distribution. Some of Hearne's observations

on the Ruffed Grouse were a century ahead of their time. He told how this species makes its nest on the ground, generally at the foot of a tree, and lays 12 or 14 eggs. He realized as many others did not, that the noise of "drumming" was made by "clapping their wings with such a force, that at half a mile distance it resembles thunder." He noted that the pouch at the base of the pelican's beak had a capacity of three quarts, and that, in the 1770s as today, muskrat houses were favorite nesting sites for Canada Geese. Hearne examined the "windpipes" of both the Whistling and Trumpeter Swan. Although he noted that the convoluted windpipe passed into the broad and hollow breast bone of the swan and after passing the length of the sternum, returned into the chest to join the lungs, he erroneously reported that both species had identical anatomy even though their notes were quite different in pitch. Pigeons, cranes and curlews were regularly shot for food. Hearne provided one of the earliest accounts of the Passenger Pigeon, flying in large flocks in the interior near Cumberland House, where he saw 12 killed at one shot. The Whooping Crane even then was not common, usually seen only in pairs and not very often. It was good eating. The wing bones were so long and large that they were sometimes made into flutes. Hearne was the first to recognize two different species of curlew, the Hudsonian Curlew and the Eskimo Curlew. He also gave important information concerning the northern edge of the Eskimo Curlew breeding range—Egg River, on the west coast of Hudson's Bay at 59 degrees, 30 minutes north, about 150 miles north of Churchill. But he did not restrict his attention to edible birds; he also described small birds such as the chickadee.

He understood well the concept of bird migration, but also recognized that other species such as the ptarmigan and Arctic Hare were year-round residents. He described the Trumpeter Swan as the first species of waterfowl to return in spring, sometimes as early as late March, before the ice of the rivers had broken up. At that time they frequented the open waters of falls and rapids.

Hearne provided valuable information concerning the numbers of some species of animals at the time when the fur trade reigned supreme. In January 1775 at Cumberland House the men brought back 26 grouse on one occasion and on another day brought 13 sledge loads of elk meat to the fort. Within half a mile of Churchill as many as 40 Arctic foxes could be killed in one night, while during one winter 120 foxes in the traps were destroyed by other foxes. In 1774 Hearne's men killed 11 black bears in one day of canoe travel between York Factory and Cumberland House. At Anawd Lake in the North West Territories 20 or 30 hares could be snared in a single night. One Indian could kill 20 Spruce Grouse in a day with his bow and arrow. Some Indians would kill upward of a 100 Snow Geese in a day, whereas the most expert of the English hunters would think it a good day's work to kill 30. At Albany Fort in one season 60 hogsheads of them were salted for winter consumption. Arctic Terns, ranked by Hearne among "the elegant part of the feathered creation," occurred in flocks of several hundreds; bushels of their eggs were taken on a tiny island.

Hearne once saw a flock of over 400 Willow Ptarmigan near the Churchill River. The Indians framed nets on stakes, placed over gravel bait, to entice ptarmigans to gather under the net. When the stake was pulled to drop the net on top of the birds, three people could catch up to 300 in one morning. In the winter of 1786 Mr. Prince at Churchill caught 204 ptarmigan with two separate pulls. Ptarmigan feathers made excellent beds and the feathers were sold at the rate of 3 pence per pound. The smaller Rock Ptarmigan would not go under nets but up to 120 could be shot in a few hours.

From our point of view Hearne's account of the large subspecies of the Canada Goose best reveals his scientific bent of mind. He met these very large geese on the barren grounds. Most naturalists who read Hearne appear to have walked right by this one. He did not call them the Barren Geese because they summered on the barren grounds, but rather because of the "exceeding smallness of their testicles."

The modern status of this large goose has been somewhat controversial. Hanson's book, *The Giant Canada Goose,* published in 1965, presents the results of recent research. Hanson believes that the Canada Geese nesting in Minnesota and Southern Manitoba and Saskatchewan belong to the giant race, *Branta canadensis maxima,* previously believed to be extinct. This race is characterized by a wing span of six feet or more in adult males, an unusually long neck, and frequently a white spot above the eye. They weigh anywhere from 8 pounds for an immature female to 18 pounds for an adult male, certainly reaching the 16 to 17 pounds weight cited by Hearne.

Hanson also tells about the capture of flightless Canada Geese on the tundra in Keewatin Territory. Some of these immature birds carried bands previously placed on them in Minnesota and Manitoba. They had journeyed about 1000 miles north in order to molt. Because they were not breeding they arrived in the far north later in the year than the other geese, as Hearne had said. Since they did not breed that summer, they had small testicles. Thus it took nearly two centuries to elucidate the precise scientific explanation for the phenomenon noted with such insight by Samuel Hearne, perhaps the most talented of the early naturalists on this continent.

CONCLUSION

The six fur traders from Hudson's Bay not only made contributions that must not be forgotten, but they set the stage for the arrival of Dr. John Richardson, surgeon and naturalist with the two arctic exploring expeditions led by Sir John Franklin in 1819–1822 and 1825–1827. Both expeditions, in whole or in part, came and left through the HBC depot of York Factory on Hudson Bay and relied extensively on the Company for supplies and for manpower. Richardson was assisted by Robert Hood on the first expedition and Thomas Drummond, who collected separately in the Canadian Rocky Mountains, on the second expedition. From Saskatchewan alone, Richardson, Hood and Drummond collected and/or named seven new species, Wilson's Phalarope, Franklin's Gull, Forster's Tern, Olive-sided Flycatcher, Chipping Sparrow, Smith's Longspur, and Rosy Finch, and seven subspecies. In the Rocky Mountains, Drummond took the type specimens of the White-tailed Ptarmigan and the Black-backed Three-toed Woodpecker, while the Trumpeter Swan was named from Hudson Bay. As a result of Richardson's observations, birds of the Saskatchewan River were better catalogued, before settlement, than any other region in North America.

ACKNOWLEDGMENTS

I wish to thank University of Toronto Press for permission to select, abridge and modify a portion of the text from my forthcoming book, co-authored by my wife, Mary Houston, *18th Century Naturalists of Hudson Bay*. The Hudson's Bay Company Archives, Provincial Archives of Manitoba, allowed permission to reproduce bird migration notes transcribed from the York Factory Journal of 1771–1772, HBCA B.239/a/ 66, by Dr. William B. Ewart. Glyndwr Williams and W. Earl Godfrey provided constructive criticism of portions of this material.

LITERATURE CITED

ALLEN, E. G. 1951. The history of American ornithology before Audubon. Transactions of the American Philosophical Society, new series, 41:386–591.

CATESBY, M. 1729–1747. The Natural History of Carolina, Florida, and the Bahama Islands. Published privately, London.

DAVIES, K. G. 1965. Letters from Hudson Bay, 1703–40. Hudson's Bay Record Society, London.

EDWARDS, G. 1750. A natural history of uncommon birds, Vol. 3. Published privately, London.

FORSTER, J. R. 1772. An account of the birds sent home from Hudson's Bay, with observations relative to their natural history; and Latin descriptions of some of the most uncommon. Philosophical Transactions 62:382–433.

GLOVER, R., ed. 1958. A Journey to the Northern Ocean, by Samuel Hearne. Macmillan, Toronto p. xi.

GLOVER, R. 1969. Introduction. Pp. xiii–lxxii *in* G. Williams (ed.), Observations on Hudson's Bay by Andrew Graham. Hudson's Bay Record Society, London.

GMELIN, J. F. 1789. Systema Naturae, Thirteenth Edition. J. B. Delamolliere, London.

HANSON, H. C. 1965. The Giant Canada Goose. Southern Illinois University Press, Carbondale.

HEARNE, S. 1795. A journey from Prince of Wales's Fort in Hudson's Bay to the Northern Ocean, 1769, 1770, 1771, 1772. A. Strahan & T. Cadell, London.

HOUSTON, C. S. 1983. Birds first described from Hudson Bay. Canadian Field-Naturalist 97:95–98.

HUTCHINS, T. 1776. An account of the success of some attempts to freeze quicksilver at Albany Fort, in Hudson's Bay, in the year 1775, with observations on the dipping needle. Philosophical Transactions 66:174–181.

HUTCHINS, T. 1783. Experiments for ascertaining the principle of mercurial congelation . . . Philosophical Transactions 73:305–306, 329, 341, 343.

INNIS, H. A. 1956. Pp. 391–392 *in* The fur trade in Canada: an introduction to Canadian economic history. University of Toronto Press, Toronto.

LINNAEUS, C. 1758. Systema Naturae, Tenth edition. L. Salvii, Stockholm.

LINNAEUS, C. 1766. Systema Naturae, Twelfth edition. L. Salvii, Stockholm.

McATEE, W. L. 1950. The North American birds of George Edwards. Journal of the Society for the Bibliography of Natural History 2:194–204.

McATEE, W. L. 1957. The North American birds of Linnaeus. Journal of the Society for the Bibliography of Natural History 3:291–300.

PENNANT, T. 1784–1785. Arctic zoology. Henry Hughs, London. 3 vols.

PENNANT, T. 1792. Arctic zoology, Second edition. Robert Faulder, London. 3 vols.

RICH, E. E. 1958. Pp. 52–60 *in* The history of the Hudson's Bay Company, 1670–1870. Vol. 1. Hudson's Bay Record Society, London.

RICH, E. E., AND A. M. JOHNSON. 1949. James Isham's observations on Hudson's Bay, 1743–49. Champlain Society, Toronto.

RICHARDSON, J. 1829. Fauna Boreali-Americana. Vol. 1, The Mammals. John Murray, London.

RICHARDSON, J., AND W. SWAINSON. 1832. Fauna Boreali-Americana. Vol. 2, The Birds. John Murray, London. [Introduction is by Richardson; all useful bird notes are by Richardson.]

ROSS, B. R. 1861. An account of the animals useful in an economic point of view to the various Chipewyan tribes. Canadian Naturalist & Geologist 6:433–434.

SABINE, J. 1823. Zoological appendix (V.). Pp. 647–703 *in* Narrative of a journey to the shores of the Polar Sea in the years 1819, 20, 21, and 22. John Murray, London.

TAVERNER, P. A. 1931. A study of *Branta canadensis* (Linnaeus), the Canada Goose. National Museum of Canada, Bulletin 67:28–40.

WILLIAMS, G. 1968. Hudson's Bay Record Society. [4 pp. pamphlet announcing the forthcoming publication in 1969 of Observations.]

WILLIAMS, G. 1969. Andrew Graham's observations on Hudson's Bay, 1767–91. Hudson's Bay Record Society, London. 423 + lxxii pp.

WILLIAMS, G. 1978. Andrew Graham and Thomas Hutchins: collaboration and plagiarism in 18th-century natural history. The Beaver 308:4–14.

Studies in Avian Biology No. 15:27–44, 1994.

PIONEERING AND NATURAL EXPANSION OF BREEDING DISTRIBUTIONS IN WESTERN NORTH AMERICAN BIRDS

NED K. JOHNSON

Abstract. Using as a baseline the distributional literature of the late 1950s–early 1960s, I compiled records for 24 species of birds from *Audubon Field Notes, American Birds,* and other sources which document massive pioneering and large-scale expansion of nesting distributions over the last three decades in the contiguous western United States. Four northern species have extended their ranges southward, three eastern species have expanded westward, 14 southwestern or Mexican species have moved northward, one Great Basin-Colorado Plateau species has expanded radially, and two Great Basin-Rocky Mountain subspecies have expanded westward. Breeding range expansions in migratory bird species are led predominantly by pioneering males. These range adjustments are not responses to anthropogenic influences. Instead, climatic change in the new regions of occupancy apparently has provided regimes of increased summer moisture and higher mean summer temperature typical of pre-expansion distributions.

Key Words: Birds; pioneering; distributional change; climatic change; western United States.

Because of unusual conspicuousness and mobility, birds are superior organisms for the documentation of rapid distributional change. Such change is often an obvious consequence of widespread, human-induced environmental modification. Given the pervasiveness of avian response to the direct and indirect activities of humans, small wonder that the simultaneous undercurrent of natural distributional change often passes unnoticed.

My purposes are (1) to review records of selected species that document apparently natural examples of pioneering and expanding breeding distributions in western North America, (2) to search for patterns among the taxa reviewed, (3) to discuss processes potentially responsible for any patterns discerned, and (4) to comment on the dynamics of range expansion.

METHODS

Documentation of avifaunal change requires a temporal baseline against which subsequent records can be compared and evaluated. For the western United States, such a baseline was lacking at the turn of the century because avian distributions were too poorly known. From the early 1900s through the 1950s, however, regional avifaunal surveys accompanied by mass collecting established reasonably precise breeding ranges for most species. Thus, the range for each species in the Fifth Edition of the *Check-list of North American Birds* (American Ornithologists' Union [= AOU] 1957) was chosen as the baseline in this study except where noted.

Distributional changes for selected species were identified by comparing this mid-century baseline with subsequently published regional avifaunal compilations, including AOU (1983). For detailed information on pioneers and extralimital nesting over the last three decades, I tallied nesting season records cited in *Audubon Field Notes* (1963–1970) and its successor, *American Birds* (1971–1992). I emphasize extralimital late spring records because they often point to pioneering and imminent summer residence. I define pioneering as the presence of a singing male or a pair in appropriate breeding habitat. Restriction of the tally to late spring vagrants ("overshoots") listed in nesting season reports reduced the chance of including true spring migrants typically listed in the spring migration reports. To save space, records are cited by year, journal abbreviation (either AFN or AB), volume, and page rather than by regional editor. References cited are neither geographically nor temporally exhaustive; instead, they provide an overview of the direction and relative timing of distributional change. Range expansions represented by abundant records are documented in an Appendix. Because my primary goal was to review natural range expansions, I deliberately excluded species whose distributional histories provided clear evidence of association with human-modified habitats. Scientific and vernacular nomenclature follow the American Ornithologists' Union (1983, 1989).

RESULTS

NORTHERN SPECIES EXPANDING SOUTHWARD

Four species of birds with basically northern distributions have expanded their nesting ranges southward over the last several decades. For a number of species, the pioneering and range expansions are continuing.

Larus pipixcan. Franklin's Gull. Alcorn (1988) reported nesting of this species at Carson Lake, Nevada in 1971 and 1975. Malheur Lake, Oregon (Littlefield 1990) and Great Salt Lake, Utah (Behle and Perry 1975), are the nearest persistent nesting colonies, either of which presumably served as the source of the Carson Lake birds. Nesting at Malheur Lake itself only dates from 1948 (Jewett 1949). An expansion of the breeding distribution in Montana is also indicated (Skaar et al. 1985), with either positive or circumstantial evidence of nesting in five and six latilongs, respectively. The American Ornithologists' Union (1957) listed only a single breeding record for Montana. Taylor (1992) documented widespread breeding sites and greater abundance in recent years in Idaho. Spring and summer nonbreeding records in Idaho also have increased. Moreover, the species also now nests in northwestern Wyoming (AOU 1983), a state not included in the breeding distribution outlined in AOU (1957). Finally, pioneering (without definite nesting) is strongly indicated for Colorado, where the species has increased dramatically since the 1920s and where non-breeders are uncommon in early summer (Andrews and Righter 1992). A broad pattern of expanded southerly nesting, spring and summer pioneering, and increased abundance in the northwestern United States is indicated.

Aegolius funereus. Boreal Owl. The AOU (1957) gave the southern limit of the breeding range of this species in western North America as northern British Columbia and central Alberta, with wintering birds spreading southward to southern British Columbia and northern Montana. As Figure 1 illustrates, in recent decades the Boreal Owl has been recorded during the breeding season from southern British Columbia (Campbell et al. 1990) southward through the subalpine forests of northern and eastern Washington, northern and eastern Idaho, western Montana (Hayward et al. 1987, Skarr et al. 1985, Stephens and Sturts 1991, Whelton 1989), to eastern and southern Wyoming (AB 34:917, AB 40:1235, AB 42:1323), Colorado (Andrews and Righter 1992), and northern New Mexico (Stahlecker and Rawinski 1990, AB 46:1163). Thus, the *entire* mapped nesting distribution in Figure 1 dates from August 1963, when Baldwin and Koplin (1966) discovered juveniles in north-central Colorado. Note that the current nesting distribution extends for hundreds of miles south of the previously known southern limits of the *winter* range.

Many new records were obtained through nocturnal surveys in remote regions in late winter and spring, when this elusive species is calling independently or can be induced to respond either to tape recordings or to whistled imitations of vocalizations. A significant number of summer records, however, surfaced without such surveys: one killed by car (AB 29:1012), one dead on ground (AB 30:984), one dead on road and another found in chimney (AB 33:885), a juvenile in campground (AB 40:1247), and a juvenile being mobbed by chickadees (AB 46:1158). Other owls have been discovered by hikers and forest workers. These records suggest that recent numbers are at least sufficient to have increased the probability of such random encounters.

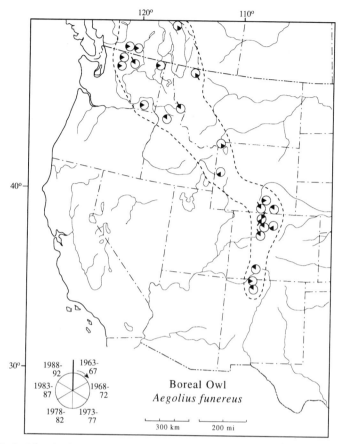

FIGURE 1.   The dashed line indicates the approximate border of the current nesting distribution of the Boreal Owl in southwestern British Columbia and the contiguous western United States. *All* symbols represent specific localities of summer presence since 1963. Blackened pie slices denote occurrence in the half-decade period indicated by the diagram in the lower left. A line protruding from the pie slice represents positive evidence of breeding.

Although it will never be possible to establish either former absence or rarity in regions where the species can now be found in numbers, the pattern of records at least suggests an explosive increase since the 1950s in the Cascades and Rocky Mountains. Even if uncommon, this owl would not have been overlooked by naturalists and others active throughout this region during the early part of this century. Whether current populations in the United States resulted from (1) a major southward incursion from Canadian nesting populations, (2) expansion from local and rare relictual distributions surviving in the western mountains since the Pleistocene, or (3) a combination of both sources, cannot be determined.

Seiurus noveboracensis. Northern Waterthrush. Contreras (1988) summarized summer records in the central Cascades of Oregon, where this warbler has been found since 1977. Formerly the species was known in the state only as a straggler (Gabrielson and Jewett 1940). Contreras also cites reports that indicate breeding in Washington, where Jewett et al. (1953) listed it as hypothetical, and recent range expansion and increase in abundance in British Columbia. With reference to Oregon, he states that, "The area was not often visited by observers prior to discovery of the waterthrushes, so the birds may have been present unobserved for many years." Nonetheless, the region of the Cascade Mountains where waterthrushes now occur regularly during the summer was not ignored by bird collectors and other naturalists in the first half of the present century. The large number of new records for Oregon, nesting in Washington, and expansion in British Columbia all point to a population increase and southerly extension of nesting range in the Pacific Northwest in the past 15 years or earlier.

Loxia leucoptera. White-winged Crossbill. AOU (1957) listed this species as breeding sporadically south to Washington, northeastern Oregon, and Montana. Records in the ensuing decades document more continuous summer presence at the southern edge of the known range as well as a major southward range expansion. Positive nesting records have been obtained in Utah in 1977 (Smith 1978), Colorado in 1987 (Groth 1992), and probable breeding either in New Mexico or (nearby) elsewhere in the southern Rockies (AB 36:207). Numbers began to swing upward in the mid-1970s. Widespread summer reports, sometimes of flocks of up to 100 individuals, which indicate extensive nomadism and at least occasional breeding in the subalpine forests of southwestern Canada and the western United States, are provided in the Appendix.

EASTERN SPECIES EXPANDING WESTWARD

In recent decades the following three species of birds of fundamentally eastern North American distribution have invaded western North America.

Strix varia. Barred Owl. Although by the middle of the present century the breeding range of this species reached only as far west as northern British Columbia and eastern Montana (AOU 1957), in recent decades this owl has dramatically expanded westward to the Pacific Coast from southeastern Alaska (AOU 1983) to southwestern British Columbia (Campbell et al. 1990), Washington (Taylor and Forsman 1976), western Oregon (1990, AB 44:1178; 1991, AB 45: 1152–1156), northwestern California (1990, AB 44:1182), southeastern Idaho (Stephens and Sturts 1991), and western Montana (Skaar et al. 1985). The speed with which the expansion occurred has been just as impressive as the distance traversed.

Several authors (Hejl 1994, Root and Weckstein 1994, and references cited therein) have opined that the westward incursion of the Barred Owl is a response to forest fragmentation and increased proportion of second-growth in the Northwest. I see no evidence for this. Indeed, in British Columbia, the region for which the best information on habitat use is available, the species is "primarily a bird of deep forests" (Campbell et al. 1990:374). Moreover, this owl has been recorded in pristine habitats in many regions, e.g., Glacier National Park (AFN 1969, 23:677) and, most recently, near Jackson, Wyoming (AB 1992, 46:1158). Finally, it is relevant to note that widespread logging in northwestern North America antedated the invasion of the Barred Owl by many decades. Until the possible role of human habitat modification is proved, I hypothesize that the range expansion in the Barred Owl has resulted from natural causes.

Empidonax minimus. Least Flycatcher. In the last two decades, a plethora of pioneers, mostly singing males, have moved westward and southwestward in North America from the previously known breeding range of this species (Fig. 2). Nesting has occurred at several sites in British Columbia (1966, AB 20:587; 1968, AB 22:630), northern Washington (1975, AB 29:1009; 1990, AB 44:1179), and at least once in northeastern California (1984, AB 38:1058). The majority of the records fall in the period 1973–1992. The Appendix documents presence and timing by province and state. Note that the distribution of records in space and time is most continuous near the margin of the former range.

Passerina cyanea. Indigo Bunting. From a status in the mid-1950s of rare vagrant, this species has massively invaded the southwestern United States in the last several decades; in several regions it breeds commonly (see map in Payne 1992). Al-

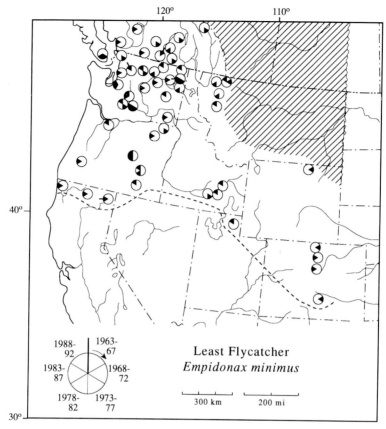

FIGURE 2. The pattern of diagonal lines indicates the approximate nesting range of the Least Flycatcher as of the mid-1950s in southwestern Canada, Montana, and Wyoming. The dashed line demarcates the approximate outline of occurrence of pioneers and new extralimital nesting localities of the species in southwestern British Columbia and the contiguous western United States. See legend to Figure 1 for explanation of symbols.

though some invaders have used thickets and secondary growth resulting from human habitat modification, many have occurred in undisturbed vegetation. Furthermore, secondary growth was available for decades prior to occupancy in much of the southwest and similar seral growth is still unoccupied over vast sections of the northwestern United States. These facts provide evidence that humans have played no obvious role in this expansion. I have not attempted to compile the abundant records.

SOUTHWESTERN SPECIES EXPANDING NORTHWARD

Fourteen species with traditional ranges in Mexico and the southwestern United States have moved northward since the mid-decades of the present century:

Buteogallus anthracinus. Common Black-Hawk. The AOU (1957) considered Central Arizona to be the northern nesting limit of this species, a status corroborated by Phillips (1968). By the early to mid-1960s it had nested in the Virgin River Valley in Utah and Arizona (Carter and Wauer 1965, Wauer and Russell 1967, Behle and Perry 1975). The AOU (1983) reported attempted breeding in southern Nevada, and Alcorn (1988) included reports from the 1970s and early 1980s from sites as far north as Elgin, Lincoln County. The first occurrence in California was of a spring vagrant in Riverside County, April 1985, reported by Daniels et al. (1989). In sum, the records indicate persistent recent pioneering and rare nesting at the northern limits of the Mojave Desert.

Buteo albonotatus. Zone-tailed Hawk. This species first appeared in the Santa Rosa Mountains, California, in 1978 and unsuccessfully attempted to nest in 1979–1981 (Weathers 1983). From 1986–1992, Zone-tailed Hawks either definitely or probably nested on Hot Springs Mountain, San Diego County, California (AB 1992, 46:1178). These localities extended the range from nearest known sites in the San Pedro Martír region, northern Baja California (AOU 1957), and at Bill Williams Delta, Lower Colorado River Valley (Rosenberg et al. 1991). Garrett and Dunn (1981) cited several spring records of nonbreeding birds in southern California. The increasing frequency of these records in the 1970s suggests persistent pioneering from the south and southeast. Spring and early summer sight records from southern Nevada from 1975–1980 (Alcorn 1988) also fit this pattern.

Caprimulgus vociferus. Whip-poor-will. Although extralimital breeding has not been reported because of the difficulty of finding nests, numerous late spring and summer records of calling birds document a clear pattern of northward pioneering in the southwestern United States (Fig. 3). Citations for specific records are listed in the Appendix.

Euptilotus neoxenus. Eared Trogon. Although rare in adjacent Mexico, this species has appeared irregularly in the summer months since 1977 in the mountains of southeastern Arizona (1989, AB 43:1350; 1991, AB 45:1146; 1992, AB 46:1161). Two reports for east-central Arizona in June 1992 (AB 46:1161) require confirmation.

Myiarchus tyrannulus. Brown-crested Flycatcher. Traditionally a Colorado Desert or Sonoran species, in recent decades this flycatcher has expanded northwestwardly to the limits of the Mojave Desert in California, Nevada, and Utah (Fig. 4). Documentation for the new mapped localities is given in the Appendix.

Dendroica graciae. Grace's Warbler. This warbler pioneered to appropriate habitat in California from 1974–1977 (Johnson and Garrett 1974, Garrett and Dunn 1981), and was established for breeding by the early 1970s in at least five mountain ranges in southern Nevada where previously unknown (Johnson 1965, 1973, 1974).

Cardellina rubrifrons. Red-faced Warbler. This is a weakly expanding species, with scattered records of pioneers from 1973–1978 in California (AB 27:920; AB 29:1036; Garrett and Dunn 1981) and Arizona (AB 29:1017; AB 31:1174; AB 32:1197) and an extralimital nesting in New Mexico in 1982 (AB 36:1007). New localities are plotted in Figure 5.

Setophaga picta. Painted Redstart. A pattern of irregular northern pioneering in this species is evidenced by repeated spring records of visitants and at least one nesting record in southern California (Johnson and Garrett 1974, Garrett and Dunn 1981), southern Nevada (Johnson 1965, Alcorn 1988), southwestern Utah (Behle and Perry 1975), central-western Colorado (Andrews and Righter 1992), Arizona (Monson and Phillips 1981), and New Mexico (Hubbard 1978).

Piranga flava. Hepatic Tanager. Recent decades have seen extralimital nesting of this tanager in California and Colorado and a scattering of late spring and summer pioneers (Fig. 6). Citations for these records are in the Appendix.

Piranga rubra. Summer Tanager. Reflecting their common preference for riparian habitats, this species and the Brown-crested Flycatcher show strikingly similar range expansions in southern California, southern Nevada, and southeastern Utah (Fig. 7). In contrast to the flycatcher, however, the tanager has also spread northward in New Mexico, apparently from the Rio Grande Valley. The Appendix lists specific citations for new records.

Guiraca caerulea. Blue Grosbeak. This species has expanded its summer range northward by several hundred miles over the last three decades (Fig. 8). A surprising

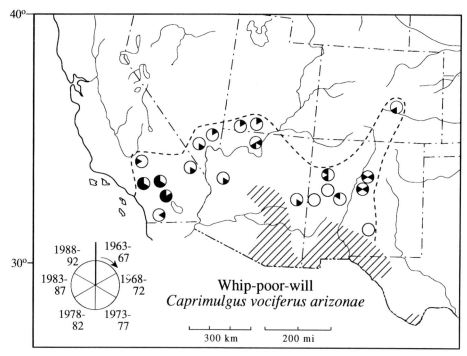

FIGURE 3. The pattern of diagonal lines indicates the approximate nesting range of the southwestern form of the Whip-poor-will as of the mid-1950s in Arizona, New Mexico, and Texas. The dashed line indicates the approximate northern limit of occurrence in the last three decades of extralimital summer birds without proof of nesting. Empty circles represent localities without specific dates in the literature. See legend to Figure 1 for explanation of other symbols.

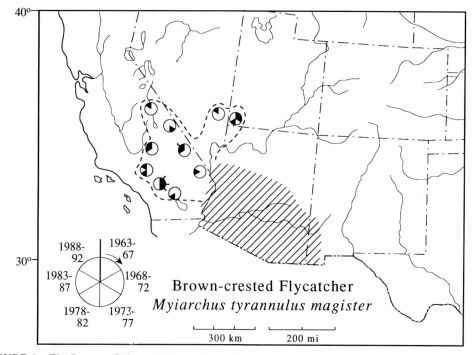

FIGURE 4. The Pattern of diagonal lines indicates the approximate nesting range of the northwestern form of the Brown-crested Flycatcher as of the mid-1950s in southeastern California, Arizona, and southwestern New Mexico. The dashed line indicates the approximate limits of pioneering and of nesting (symbols with protruding lines) in the last three decades. See legend to Figure 1 for explanation of symbols.

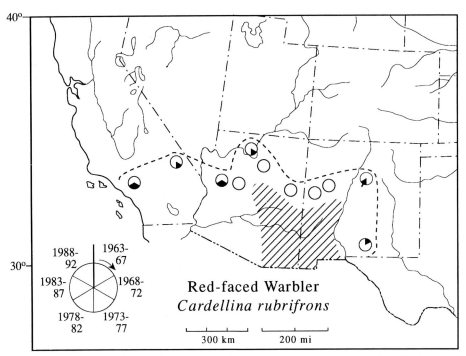

FIGURE 5. The pattern of diagonal lines indicates the approximate nesting range of the Red-faced Warbler as of the mid-1950s–early 1960s in Arizona and southwestern New Mexico. The dashed line shows the northern limit of the occurrence of pioneers and one extralimital nesting in northcentral New Mexico in the last three decades. See legend to Figure 1 for explanation of symbols.

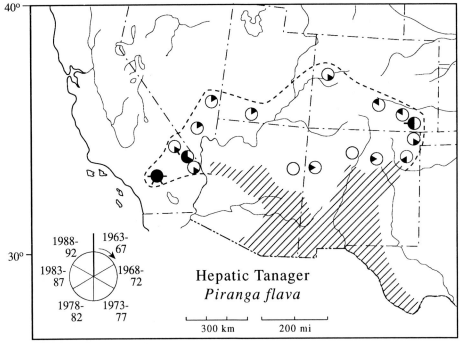

FIGURE 6. The pattern of diagonal lines indicates the approximate nesting range of the Hepatic Tanager as of the mid-1950s–early 1960s in Arizona, New Mexico, and western Texas. Symbols denote localities of westward and northward pioneers and colonists in the last three decades. See legend to Figure 1 for explanation of symbols.

number of positive nesting localities are plotted: southern Idaho (1981, AB 35:963; 1986, AB 40:1232), west-central Nevada (1969 [Alcorn 1988], Utah (1990, AB 44: 1163), Wyoming (1982, AB 36:1002; 1985, AB 39:944), and Colorado (1971, AB 25: 887; 1984, AB 38:1047; 1987, AB 41:1470). Specific references documenting these mapped records, and a few recent occurrences near the periphery of the former known range, are provided in the Appendix.

Icterus parisorum. Scott's Oriole. Since the 1960s, this oriole has steadily pioneered northward and colonized the interior of the contiguous western United States. Probable or certain nesting has been reported in southeastern Idaho (1972, AB 26:886), northern Nevada (1976, AB 30:985; 1980, Alcorn [1988]), central Utah (1963, AFN 17:474; 1965, AFN 19:568; 1971, AB 25: 887; 1980, AB 34:917), southwestern Wyoming (1982, AB 36:1002), and western Colorado (1980, AB 34:917; 1983, AB 37: 1012). Principal new late spring and summer localities are plotted in Figure 9. Citations of reports which document these mapped localities and other peripheral nesting season stations are given in the Appendix.

Aimophila cassinii. Cassin's Sparrow. Faanes et al. (1979:164) reported that "In a period of only 5 years [1974–1979], Cassin's Sparrow has apparently extended its breeding range into Wyoming, Nebraska and South Dakota. Maximum extension was the Wyoming record, a distance of 350 km." These authors also mention other reports from the same time period of range expansion in more southern regions of the western United States.

Amphispiza quinquestriata. Five-striped Sparrow. The first record of this species for the United States was from southern Arizona in June 1957. The next report (1969) was from Patagonia, Arizona where it had not been found previously despite repeated earlier visits by ornithologists, but where it has been found every year since. Mills (1977) reported a substantial number of local pop-

ulations in southern Arizona which held a combined minimum estimate of 57 adults in 1977. Monson and Phillips (1981:195) termed the species, "A presumed recent immigrant from Mexico."

Great Basin-Colorado Plateau Species Expanding Radially

Empidonax wrightii. Gray Flycatcher. This species has expanded its nesting range in all directions from the former stronghold in the Great Basin and Colorado Plateau (Fig. 10). Furthermore, it is now common or abundant at many of the new localities and nests to the periphery of the new distribution. Johnson and Garrett (1974) and Johnson and Cicero (1985) provided detailed records for new localities in southern and central California, and Cannings (1987) discussed the extension into Washington state and British Columbia. Documentation for additional mapped locality symbols is found in the Appendix.

Great Basin-Rocky Mountain Subspecies Expanding Westward

Vireo solitarius plumbeus. Solitary Vireo. Johnson (1965, 1973, 1974) documented the spread of this form in southern Nevada, and Johnson and Garrett (1974) reviewed records for westward colonization in California, where it was first detected in the summer of 1962. This major adjustment in breeding range continues, for in June 1988, *V. s. plumbeus* was found in Alpine County, California and recently it reached northern Lander County (June 1991), Pershing County (June 1992), and Humboldt County (June 1993), Nevada (NKJ ms).

Anthus rubescens. American Pipit. Miller and Green (1987) carefully chronicled the westward incursion of the form *A. r. alticola* into the alpine zone of the central and southern Sierra Nevada. The first breeding season reports date from 1971–1972, and the first nests were found in 1975. By the mid-1980s, the species was nesting commonly. Importantly, prior to the discovery of breeding pipits in the Sierra Nevada, many early or-

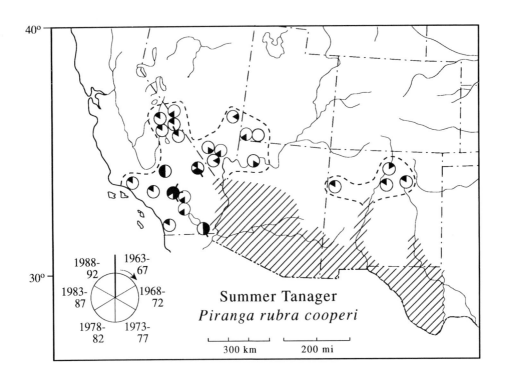

Summer Tanager
Piranga rubra cooperi

1988-92 | 1963-67
1983-87 | 1968-72
1978-82 | 1973-77

300 km   200 mi

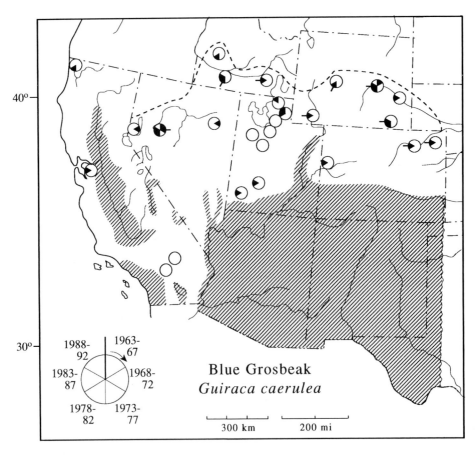

Blue Grosbeak
Guiraca caerulea

1988-92 | 1963-67
1983-87 | 1968-72
1978-82 | 1973-77

300 km   200 mi

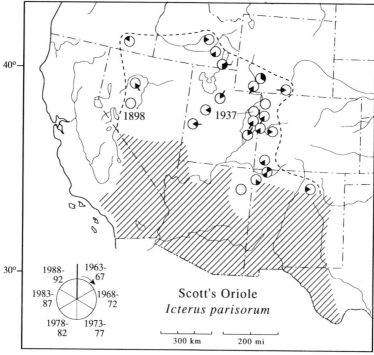

FIGURE 9. The pattern of diagonal lines shows the approximate nesting range of the Scott's Oriole in the Southwest as of the middle of the present century. The northern limit in Nevada is based in part on records in Linsdale (1936). The two dated locality symbols are documented in Oberholser (1918) and Twomey (1942). Records of the last three decades document pioneering and extralimital nesting to the extent of the dashed line. See legend to Figure 1 for explanation of symbols.

nithologists and other naturalists had spent extended periods in the alpine zone of that range without encountering this species as a summer resident.

DISCUSSION AND CONCLUSIONS

PATTERNS OF DISTRIBUTIONAL CHANGE

In common with ecologic niches, breeding distributions of birds are species-specific. Unique geographic ranges presumably reflect the unique spatial distribution of places which satisfy the innate requirements of each species. These needs include particular kinds of food, foraging and nesting sites, refuges, and innately selected habitats, all within preferred daily and seasonal regimes of temperature and humidity (Grinnell 1914, 1917; Salt 1952). Given these idiosyncratic requirements, broad distributional congruence among species is not to be expected. Nonetheless, four disparate taxa, a gull, an owl, a warbler, and a finch, demonstrated southwardly-expanding ranges. Similarly,

←

FIGURE 7. The pattern of diagonal lines shows the approximate breeding range of the western form of the Summer Tanager as of the mid-1950s–early 1960s in the Southwest. Localities of range expansion by pioneers and colonists in the last three decades are denoted by the symbols and dashed line. See legend to Figure 1 for explanation of symbols.

FIGURE 8. The pattern of diagonal lines demarks the approximate breeding regions of the Blue Grosbeak in the southwestern United States as of the mid-1950s–early 1960s. Symbols for the occurrence of pioneers and new nesting localities in the last 30 years are enclosed by a dashed line that indicates the approximate boundary of the range expansion. See legend to Figure 1 for explanation of symbols.

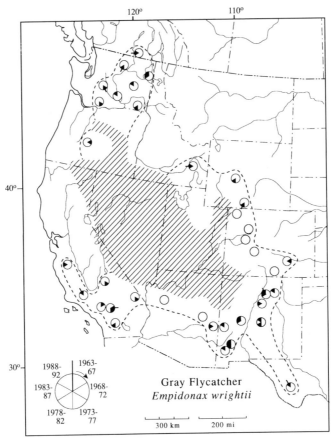

FIGURE 10. The pattern of diagonal lines shows the approximate breeding range of the Gray Flycatcher as documented by Johnson (1963). Localities of extralimital nesting and a few pioneers in the last 30 years are indicated. See legend to Figure 1 for explanation of symbols.

three species traditionally with eastern distributions, an owl, a flycatcher, and a bunting, have moved westward. Remarkably, an even more diverse group of species of southwestern distribution, two hawks, a nightjar, a trogon, a flycatcher, three species of warblers, two tanagers, a grosbeak, an oriole, and two sparrows, have enlarged their nesting distributions toward the north. (This pattern is not confined to birds. Davis and Callahan [1992] reported similar northward movement of 19 species of mammals in the Southwest.) Such broad-scale range adjustments that transcend taxonomic boundaries suggest that coincidental distributional barriers for groups of species have been lifted.

Are these expanding species reclaiming ground occupied in the past? Other "east-

ern" species, e.g., Ruffed Grouse (*Bonasa umbellus*), Veery (*Catharus fuscescens*), and Red-eyed Vireo (*Vireo olivaceus*), currently breed northwestward to British Columbia and Washington state or beyond. Perhaps the Barred Owl and Least Flycatcher, two species with broadly similar nesting ranges, are returning to regions of former occurrence. Their "expansions" could thus reflect the ebb and flow expected at range margins. Furthermore, some distributional "expansions" described here may actually be range *shifts* in which regions are evacuated in one part of the distribution as a wave of colonization advances elsewhere. The Franklin's Gull and Cassin's Sparrow, for example, may be retreating locally in the Great Plains (Knopf 1994) with simultaneous expansion elsewhere. For the southwestern species whose southern limits are in Mexico, data to answer this question are unavailable. For the Barred Owl and Least Flycatcher, however, possible population reduction and range shrinkage in the eastern United States concomitant with expansion in the northwest could be investigated.

SUGGESTED EXPLANATION FOR NATURAL RANGE EXPANSIONS

The 24 species dealt with here have enlarged their breeding ranges for reasons apparently unrelated to direct human modification of the environment. Instead, I propose that pervasive climatic change over the past several decades in the contiguous western United States is the most likely explanation. Although climatic warming is probably involved, especially for those southwestern species that are invading northward, it is probably neither the sole explanation nor even the primary cause for range adjustments among the expanding species as a group. First, despite an overall global trend in warming, parallel mean temperature increases for specific regions are not to be expected (Schneider 1993). Second, it is difficult to comprehend how climatic warming could assist either the southward expansions of northern species or the westward expansions of eastern species. Instead one must seek a regional common denominator of climatic change that could encourage movement into the western United States by clusters of species with pre-expansion ranges in either the north, east, or southwest.

Increased summer moisture is such a common denominator. Except for the Gray Flycatcher, whose radial expansion remains unexplained, most expanding species had former nesting distributions in regions with higher summer rainfall and humidity than in regions now being colonized. For example, wet summers and high humidity typify the eastern distributions of the Barred Owl and Least Flycatcher, and the northern distributions of the Boreal Owl and White-

winged Crossbill. Similarly, convective, monsoonal precipitation characterizes summer climatic regimes of the American southwest and northern Mexico, where many species are now advancing northward. I hypothesize that many of these species are responding primarily to a decades-long increase of summer rainfall in regions beyond their former ranges. A concomitant rise in mean temperature during the nesting season may have encouraged range adjustments of some species.

Climatic information for the contiguous western United States offers broad support for wetter and warmer summers in recent decades. Specifically, Diaz and Quayle (1980:259), in comparing rainfall patterns of the period 1921–1954 with 1956–1977, stated that "summer precipitation in the far western United States was greater in the recent period compared to the previous one." Moreover, summer patterns showed that "the West was much wetter while the East was generally drier" since the mid-1950s.

Selected climatic data from California provided by Goodridge (1992) are also in agreement. Both temperature and rainfall increased dramatically from the mid-1970s to mid-1980s over much of the state. (A reversal in total precipitation initiated a half decade of drought in the late 1980s and early 1990s.) Goodridge (1992) also documented the "strong heating trend" of 0.026 degrees per year for 10 stations on the southeastern deserts of California from 1909–1991, as well as an unspecified increase in rainfall at interior versus coastal California stations from 1889–1991. These trends could have promoted extralimital colonization of Brown-crested Flycatchers and Summer Tanagers, for example. At the base of the Santa Rosa Mountains, California, Weathers (1983:12–13) recorded sharp increases in rainfall in the period 1976–1980, over averages from 1961–1975, and specifically attributed to wetter summers the unprecedented nesting of Zone-tailed Hawks in 1978.

Climatic information from southern Nevada clearly conforms with the hypothesis of increased summer moisture in recent decades in the American Southwest. From 1965–1970, when the record ended, the Palmer Drought Index reflected a series of wet years which contrasted with a long span of relatively continuous drought from 1953–1964 (Houghton et al. 1975).

Thus, regional climatic trends agree broadly with the hypothesis that increased summer moisture, perhaps coupled with a higher mean temperature, has encouraged recent avian range expansions in the western United States. Nonetheless, detailed correlations of local climatic data with the temperature and moisture requirements of individual species will be necessary to establish causality. The classic research of Salt (1952), who demonstrated the close association of preferred ranges of temperature and vapor pressure with distribution and metabolic efficiency in three species of finches (*Carpodacus*), represents the approach ultimately necessary for a real understanding of the relationship between changing regional climatic patterns and major range expansions. The investigation of climatic adaptation in species of magpies (*Pica*) by Hayworth and Weathers (1984) represents a careful modern study of similar issues. Williamson (1975) and Brewer (1981) offered general discussion of the relationship of avian distributions to climatic change.

PIONEERING AND THE DYNAMICS OF EXPANDING NESTING DISTRIBUTIONS

Grinnell (1922) proposed that individuals occurring irregularly beyond the usual distributional limit of the species ("accidentals") are the chief instruments of range expansion. Such accidentals were hypothesized to typically emanate from peripheral or "frontier" populations, to be prone to pioneering, and to be adapted to marginal conditions. Such peripheral populations, with death rates exceeding birth rates, were thought to be sustained by the continual input of individuals from more successful, central populations where birth rates exceed death rates. Thus, nearly three-quarters of a century ago, Grinnell (1922) clearly captured the essence of the theoretical process known to modern ecology as the "Source-Sink hypothesis" (Pulliam 1988). Grinnell emphasized (1922:378) that the "great majority of these pioneers . . . [occur in the] autumnal season when the movement is most in evidence. . . ." Such accidentals typically represent strong flying, migratory species; some, however, include "the most sedentary of species" (Grinnell 1922:375).

In considering the role of the accidental as discussed by Grinnell, Newman (1976: 921) questioned how "*autumnal* straying leads to expansion of the *breeding* range" (italics his) and noted that, "no such explanation seems required in the case of summer rarities . . . the transformation from stray to breeder seems simple and direct."

Grinnell's and Newman's apparently contradictory views can be reconciled and refined. In support of Grinnell's position, I suggest that for *permanently resident species* it is easy to envision pioneering by fall immatures which eventually find extralimital sites in which to breed the following spring. But, as Newman suggests, spring vagrants, not fall accidentals, would serve more logically as colonists during the season when the nesting range is actually expanding. Although Newman does not explicitly identify *migratory species* as being more likely than resident species to produce such vagrants during the spring movement, I suggest that such a distinction is significant. Furthermore, increasing evidence on the nature of spring and summer vagrants, as documented by accumulated records in *American Birds* and other sources, points to *males* as the predominant sex of individuals leading the vanguard of spring-summer range expansion. Importantly, in many species males often preceed females in northward migration (Welty and Baptista 1988). These extralimital males are often discovered because they are singing and holding territories; witness the astounding numbers of vagrant eastern vireos and warblers singing on territories in several western states during the spring–summer of 1992 (AB 46:1159, 1162, 1175–1176, 1179–1180; Terrill et al. 1992). Although the initial discovery of males versus females is somewhat biased by the easier detectability of the former (singing and, in some species, more vivid coloration), I note that many of these birds defended territories for days or weeks without evidence of the presence of a female. This point is also vividly illustrated by the westwardly invading Indigo Bunting in which spring-summer vagrants are overwhelmingly males.

An especially illuminating example of the nature of breeding range expansion is provided by the American Redstart (*Setophaga ruticilla*). In 1981, this basically eastern species formed an unprecedented pioneering colony (evidently without nesting) at the mouth of the Klamath River, California (1981, AB 35:976–977). The first individual (sex unmentioned) was recorded on June 9. On June 21, *nine* singing males and *one* female were noted. By July 5, the number of males had decreased to four and the number of females had increased to five. None could be located on July 31. The species had nested twice before in the same region of northwestern California (1972, AB 26:898; 1980, AB 34:928).

THE BIOLOGICAL SIGNIFICANCE OF RAPID DISTRIBUTIONAL CHANGE IN BIRDS

Rapid natural adjustments over long distances in nesting distributions of birds must be dealt with by diverse kinds of biologists. For example, avian biogeographers (e.g., Mengel 1964 and others) who have proposed models of speciation in which avian distributions track the migration and disjunction of vegetation across vast distances and over millenia should be disconcerted by range shifts over equally great distances, but over decades, time spans too brief for significant vegetational change. Likewise, the concept of "indicator species" for particular regions should be reconsidered. How can we describe Scott's Oriole as an indicator of

upland Mojave Desert given that it nests in Idaho and Wyoming? Similarly, the Gray Flycatcher, now nesting from British Columbia to west Texas, should no longer be termed a "Great Basin-Colorado Plateau" species.

Community ecologists have long been impressed with invasions of plants and animals. Most examples of invasions, however, are in response to anthropogenic activity (Elton 1958). The natural range changes described here are thus of special interest. Several species (e.g., Barred Owl, Gray Flycatcher, Summer Tanager, Indigo Bunting) are now common or abundant in sections of their new ranges and would be expected to significantly alter local interspecific relationships. How could the addition of numbers of a large predator such as the Barred Owl not influence prey dynamics in the forests of southwestern British Columbia? The extralimital establishment of 32 territories of Gray Flycatchers in the Davis Mountains, Texas (1991, AB 45: 1137), of 60 Summer Tanagers along the South Fork of the Kern River, California (1991, AB 45:1162), and a minimum of 55 singing male Indigo Buntings in June–July 1977 at several sites along the Lower Colorado River Valley (Rosenberg et al. 1991), surely has also altered biotic relationships in those areas.

Finally, natural range extensions offer an important message to the conservationist. Namely, populations of at least some species of birds are healthy enough to provide sources for significant numbers of pioneers and potential colonists. However, as my conservationist colleague, Robert C. Stebbins, feared when informed of these data, this optimistic news may conceal a problem. Those either unaware of or oblivious to the deleterious effects of widespread environmental deterioration on many bird species may seize upon these few examples of range expansion as evidence that habitat destruction is not only inconsequential to bird populations but that it may actually benefit them. Whereas I anticipate such misrepresentations, they can readily be countered by a mounting body of evidence to the contrary.

ACKNOWLEDGMENTS

I appreciate the discussion, advice, and assistance of S. F. Bailey, C. Cicero, K. Dedrick, K. L. Garrett, T. Heindel, J. R. Jehl, and J. V. Remsen. K. Klitz prepared the final versions of the maps.

LITERATURE CITED

ALCORN, J. R. 1988. The birds of Nevada. Fairview West Publishing, Fallon, NV.

AMERICAN ORNITHOLOGISTS' UNION. 1957. Checklist of North American birds, 5th edition. Lord Baltimore Press, Inc., Baltimore, MD.

AMERICAN ORNITHOLOGISTS' UNION. 1983. Checklist of North American birds, 6th edition. Allen Press, Inc., Lawrence, KS.

AMERICAN ORNITHOLOGISTS' UNION. 1989. Thirty-seventh supplement to the American Ornithologists' Union Check-list of North American birds. Auk 106: 532–538.

ANDREWS, R., AND R. RIGHTER. 1992. Colorado birds, a reference to their distribution and habitat. Denver Museum of Natural History, Denver, CO.

BALDWIN, P. H., AND J. R. KOPLIN. 1966. The Boreal Owl as a Pleistocene relict in Colorado. Condor 68: 299–300.

BEHLE, W. H., AND M. L. PERRY. 1975. Utah birds: check-list, seasonal and ecological occurrence charts and guides to bird finding. Utah Museum of Natural History, University of Utah, Salt Lake City, UT.

BREWER, R. 1981. The changing seasons. American Birds 35:915–919.

BROWN, B. T., S. W. CAROTHERS, AND R. R. JOHNSON. 1987. Grand Canyon birds, historical notes, natural history, and ecology. The University of Arizona Press, Tucson, AZ.

CAMPBELL, R. W., N. K. DAWE, I. McTAGGART-COWAN, J. M. COOPER, G. W. KAISER, AND M. C. E. McNALL. 1990. The birds of British Columbia. Vol. II, Non-passerines. Royal British Columbia Museum, Victoria, British Columbia.

CANNINGS, R. J. 1987. Gray Flycatcher: a new breeding bird for Canada. American Birds 41:376–378.

CARTER, D. L., AND R. H. WAUER. 1965. Black Hawk nesting in Utah. Condor 67:82–83.

CONTRERAS, A. 1988. Northern Waterthrush summer range in Oregon. Western Birds 19:41–42.

DANIELS, B. E., L. HAYS, D. HAYS, J. MORLAN, AND D. ROBERSON. 1989. First record of the Common Black-Hawk for California. Western Birds 20:11–18.

DAVIS, R., AND J. R. CALLAHAN. 1992. Post-Pleistocene dispersal in the Mexican vole (*Microtos montanus*): an example of an apparent trend in the distribution of southwestern mammals. Great Basin Naturalist 52:262–268.

DIAZ, H. F., AND R. G. QUAYLE. 1980. The climate of the United States since 1895: spatial and temporal changes. Monthly Weather Review 108:249–266.

ELTON, C. S. 1958. The ecology of invasions by animals and plants. Methuen & Company, London.

FAANES, C. A., B. A. HANSON, AND H. A. KANTRUD.

1979. Cassin's Sparrow—first record for Wyoming and recent range extensions. Western Birds 10:163–164.

FINDHOLT, S. L., AND S. D. FITTON. 1983. Records of the Scott's Oriole from Wyoming. Western Birds 14:109–110.

GABRIELSON, I. N., AND S. G. JEWETT. 1940. Birds of Oregon. Oregon State College, Corvallis, OR.

GARRETT, K., AND J. DUNN. 1981. Birds of southern California, status and distribution. Los Angeles Audubon Society, Los Angeles, CA.

GOODRIDGE, J. D. 1992. Climate change in California. American Meteorological Society, 22nd Conference on Broadcast Meteorology, June 11–13, 1992, San Diego, CA.

GORDON, P., J. MORLAN, AND D. ROBERSON. 1989. First record of the White-winged Crossbill in California. Western Birds 20:81–87.

GRINNELL, J. 1914. Barriers to distribution as regards birds and mammals. American Naturalist 48:248–254.

GRINNELL, J. 1917. Field tests of theories concerning distributional control. American Naturalist 51:115–128.

GRINNELL, J. 1922. The role of the "Accidental." Auk 39:373–380.

GROTH, J. G. 1992. White-winged Crossbill breeding in southern Colorado, with notes on juveniles' calls. Western Birds 23:35–37.

HAYWARD, G. D., P. H. HAYWARD, E. O. GARTON, AND R. ESCANO. 1987. Revised breeding distribution of the Boreal Owl in the northern Rocky Mountains. Condor 89:431–432.

HAYWORTH, A. M., AND W. W. WEATHERS. 1984. Temperature regulation and climatic adaptation in Black-billed and Yellow-billed Magpies. Condor 86: 19–26.

HEJL, S. J. 1994. Human-induced changes in bird populations in coniferous forests in Western North America during the past 100 years. Pp. 232–246 *in* J. R. Jehl, Jr., and N. K. Johnson (eds.), A century of avifaunal change in western North America. Studies in Avian Biology No. 15.

HOUGHTON, J. G., C. M. SAKAMOTO, AND R. O. GIFFORD. 1975. Nevada's weather and climate. Nevada Bureau of Mines and Geology Special Publication 2:1–78.

HUBBARD, J. P. 1978. Revised check-list of the birds of New Mexico. New Mexico Ornithological Society Publication 6.

JEWETT, S. G. 1949. The Franklin's Gull in Oregon. Condor 51:189–190.

JEWETT, S. G., W. P. TAYLOR, W. T. SHAW, AND J. W. ALDRICH. 1953. Birds of Washington State. University of Washington Press, Seattle, WA.

JOHNSON, N. K. 1963. Biosystematics of sibling species of flycatchers in the *Empidonax hammondii-oberholseri-wrightii* complex. University of California Publications in Zoology 66:79–238.

JOHNSON, N. K. 1965. The breeding avifaunas of the Sheep and Spring ranges in southern Nevada. Condor 67:93–124.

JOHNSON, N. K. 1973. The distribution of Boreal avifaunas in southeastern Nevada. Occasional Papers Biological Society of Nevada 36:1–14.

JOHNSON, N. K. 1974. Montane avifaunas of southern Nevada: historical change in species composition. Condor 76:334–337.

JOHNSON, N. K., AND C. CICERO. 1985. The breeding avifauna of San Benito Mountain, California: evidence for change over one-half century. Western Birds 16:1–23.

JOHNSON, N. K., AND K. L. GARRETT. 1974. Interior bird species expand breeding ranges into southern California. Western Birds 5:45–56.

JONES, L. 1971. The Whip-poor-will in California. California Birds 2:33–36.

KNOPF, F. L. 1994. Avian assemblages on altered grassland. Pp. 247–257 *in* J. R. Jehl, Jr., and N. K. Johnson (eds.), A century of avifaunal change in western North America. Studies in Avian Biology No. 15.

LINSDALE, J. M. 1936. The birds of Nevada. Pacific Coast Avifauna 23:1–145.

LITTLEFIELD, C. D. 1990. Birds of Malheur National Wildlife Refuge, Oregon. Oregon State University Press, Corvallis, OR.

MENGEL, R. M. 1964. The probable history of species formation in some northern wood warblers (Parulidae). The Living Bird 3:9–43.

MILLER, J. H., AND M. T. GREEN. 1987. Distribution, status, and origin of Water Pipits breeding in California. Condor 89:788–797.

MILLS, G. S. 1977. New locations for the Five-striped Sparrow in the United States. Western Birds 8:121–130.

MONSON, G., AND A. R. PHILLIPS. 1981. Annotated checklist of the birds of Arizona, 2nd edition. University of Arizona Press, Tucson, AZ.

NEWMAN, R. J. 1976. The changing seasons. American Birds 30:920–925.

OBERHOLSER, H. C. 1918. The northernmost record of *Icterus parisorum*. Auk 35:481–482.

PAYNE, R. B. 1992. Indigo Bunting. *In* A. Poole, P. Stettenheim, and F. Gill (eds.), The birds of North America, No. 4. The Academy of Natural Sciences, Philadelphia; The American Ornithologists' Union, Washington, DC.

PHILLIPS, A. R. 1968. The instability of the distribution of land birds in the southwest. Pp. 129–162 *in* A. H. Schroeder (ed.), Collected papers in honor of Lyndon Lane Hargrave, Papers of the Archaeological Society of New Mexico: 1.

PHILLIPS, A., J. MARSHALL, AND G. MONSON. 1964. The birds of Arizona. University of Arizona Press, Tucson, AZ.

PULLIAM, H. R. 1988. Sources, sinks, and population regulation. American Naturalist 132:652–661.

ROOT, T. L., AND J. D. WECKSTEIN. 1994. Changes in distribution patterns of select wintering North American Birds from 1901 to 1989. Pp. 191–201 *in* J. R. Jehl, Jr., and N. K. Johnson (eds.), A century of avifaunal change in western North America. Studies in Avian Biology No. 15.

ROSENBERG, G. H., AND S. B. TERRILL. 1986. The avifauna of Apache County, Arizona. Western Birds 17:171–187.

ROSENBERG, K. V., R. D. OHMART, W. C. HUNTER, AND B. W. ANDERSON. 1991. Birds of the Lower Colorado River Valley. University of Arizona Press, Tucson, AZ.

SALT, G. W. 1952. The relation of metabolism to

climate and distribution in three finches of the genus *Carpodacus*. Ecological Monographs 22:121–152.

SCHNEIDER, S. H. 1993. Scenarios of global warming. Pp. 9–23 *in* P. M. Kareiva, J. G. Kingsolver, and R. B. Huey (eds.), Biotic interactions and global change. Sinauer Associates, Inc. Publishers, Sunderland, MA.

SKAAR, D., D. FLATH, AND L. S. THOMPSON. 1985. P. D. Skaar's Montana bird distribution. Montana Academy of Sciences Monograph No. 3, Supplement to the Proceedings.

SMITH, K. G. 1978. White-winged Crossbills breed in northern Utah. Western Birds 9:79–81.

STAHLECKER, D. W., AND J. J. RAWINSKI. 1990. First records for the Boreal Owl in New Mexico. Condor 92:517–519.

STEPHENS, D. A., AND S. H. STURTS. 1991. Idaho bird distribution. Special Publication No. 11, Idaho Museum of Natural History.

TAYLOR, A. L., JR., AND E. D. FORSMAN. 1976. Recent range extensions of the Barred Owl in western North America, including the first records for Oregon. Condor 78:560–561.

TAYLOR, D. M. 1992. The status of the Franklin's Gull in Idaho. Western Birds 23:39–40.

TERRILL, S., K. P. ABLE, AND M. A. PATTEN. 1992. The changing seasons, summer 1992. American Birds 46:1109–1111, 1182.

TWOMEY, A. C. 1942. The birds of the Uinta Basin, Utah. Annals of the Carnegie Museum 28:341–490.

WAUER, R. H., AND R. C. RUSSELL. 1967. New and additional records of birds in the Virgin River Valley. Condor 69:420–423.

WEATHERS, W. W. 1983. Birds of southern California's Deep Canyon. University of California Press, Berkeley, CA.

WELTY, J. C., AND L. BAPTISTA. 1988. The life of birds. 4th edition. Saunders College Publishing Co., New York, NY.

WHELTON, B. D. 1989. Distribution of the Boreal Owl in eastern Washington and Oregon. Condor 91:712–716.

WILLIAMSON, K. 1975. Birds and climatic change. Bird Study 22:143–164.

WORTHEN, G. L. 1973. First recorded specimens of the White-winged Crossbill from Utah. Wilson Bulletin 85:243–244.

APPENDIX I. (Sequence of species follows AOU 1983.)

Caprimulgus vociferus. Whip-poor-will. California (Jones 1971; 1968, AB 22:649; 1970, AB 24:717; 1971, AB 25:907; 1973, AB 27:919; 1974, AB 28:950; 1975, AB 29:1033; 1976, AB 30:1004; 1977, AB 31:1190; 1978, AB 32:1209; 1979, AB 33:897; 1980, AB 34:930; 1981, AB 35:979; 1982, AB 36:1016; 1983, AB 37:1028; 1984, AB 38:1062; 1985, AB 39:963; 1986, AB 40:1256; 1987, AB 41:1488; 1990, AB 44:1187; 1991, AB 45:1162); Nevada (Johnson 1965, Alcorn 1988); Utah (Behle and Perry 1975); Colorado (1981, AB 35:965; Andrews and Righter 1992); Arizona (Phillips et al. 1964; Brown et al. 1987; Rosenberg and Terrill 1986; 1973, AB 27:904; 1975, AB 29:1016); and New Mexico (1971, AB 25:890; 1972, AB 26:889; 1981, AB 35:967; 1982, AB 36:1006; 1983, AB 37:1015; 1990, AB 44:1168; 1992, AB 46:1163).

Empidonax minimus. Least Flycatcher. Alaska (1982,

36:1008); British Columbia (1966, AB 20:587; 1968, AB 22:630; 1969, AB 23:677; 1973, AB 27:895; 1974, AB 28:927; 1975, AB 29:1009 and 1023; 1978, AB 32: 1189; 1979, AB 33:882 and 892; 1982, AB 34:924; 1983, AB 37:1009; 1984, AB 38:1055; 1985, AB 39: 940 and 955; 1986, AB 40:1247); Washington (1968, AB 22:630; 1974, AB 28:927; 1975, AB 29:1009; 1976, AB 30:981 and 995; 1977, AB 31:1165; 1979, AB 33: 882; 1981, AB 35:962; 1983, AB 37:1021; 1984, AB 38:1043; 1985, 39:940; 1986, AB 40:1231; 1987, AB 41:1465 and 1480; 1988, AB 42:1320; 1989, AB 43: 1344; 1990, AB 44:1179; 1991, AB 45:1153; 1992, AB 46:1172); Oregon (1977, AB 31:1165; 1982, AB 36: 999; 1983, AB 37:1009; 1984, AB 38:1043 and 1055; 1985, AB 39:940; 1988, AB 42:1320; 1989, AB 43: 1344; 1990, AB 44:1179; 1991, AB 45:1153; 1992, AB 46:1172); California (1983, AB 37:1025; 1984, AB 38: 1058; 1986, AB 40:1252); Idaho (1977, AB 31:1165; 1989, AB 43:1344); Montana (1971, AB 25:886; 1978, AB 32:1189; 1989, AB 43:1344; 1990, AB 44:1160); Wyoming (1971, AB 25:886; 1986, AB 40:1235); Utah (1989, AB 43:1348); Colorado (1971, AB 25:886; 1972, AB 26:885; 1983, AB 37:1012; 1986, AB 40:1235).

Empidonax wrightii. Gray Flycatcher. British Columbia (1986, AB 40:1175, 1231); Washington (1973, AB 27:895; 1974, AB 28:927; 1975, AB 29:1009; 1976, AB 30:981; 1977, AB 31:1165; 1978, AB 32:1189; 1980, AB 34:913; 1985, AB 39:940; 1990, AB 44:1179; 1991, AB 45:1154; 1992, AB 46:1172); Oregon (1970, AFN 24:701); California (1968, AFN 22:649; 1969, AFN 23:696; 1975, AB 29:1033; 1979, AB 33:898; 1989, AB 43:1368–1369; 1990, AB 44:1188); Idaho (1985, AB 39:940); Montana (1990, AB 44:1160); Wyoming (1981, AB 35:963, 965; 1982, AB 36:1001; 1985, AB 39:944), Colorado (1971, AB 25:886); New Mexico (1977, AB 31:1173; 1978, AB 32:1196; 1982, AB 36: 1006; 1984, AB 38:1051; 1986, AB 40:1241; 1987, AB 41:1474; 1988, AB 42:1327; 1990, AB 44:1168; 1992, AB 46:1164); Arizona (1984, AB 38:1049); Texas (1991, AB 45:1137).

Myiarchus tyrannulus. Brown-crested Flycatcher. California (1964, AFN 18:536; 1965, AFN 19:578; 1967, AFN 21:605; 1970, AFN 24:718; 1971, AB 25: 907; 1973, AB 27:919; 1974, AB 28:950; 1978, AB 32: 1209; 1986, AB 40:1256; 1987, AB 41:1488; 1988, AB 42:1341; 1989, AB 43:1369; 1990, AB 44:1188; 1991, AB 45:1162; 1992, AB 46:1179); Nevada (Alcorn 1988, N. K. Johnson specimen in breeding condition from Meadow Valley Wash, Lincoln County, May 25, 1989); Utah (Behle and Perry 1975; 1978, AB 32:1193; 1981, AB 35:965 [record requires confirmation]).

Piranga flava. Hepatic Tanager. California (Johnson and Garrett 1974; 1971, AB 25:907; 1972, AB 26:907; 1973, AB 27:920; 1974, AB 28:951; 1975, AB 29:1036; 1976, AB 30:1005; 1977, AB 31:1191; 1978, AB 32: 1210; 1981, AB 35:980; 1982, AB 36:1017; 1983, AB 37:1028; 1984, AB 38:1063; 1985, AB 39:963; 1986, AB 40:1256; 1987, AB 41:1489; 1992, AB 46:1180); Nevada (Johnson 1965; one at Eureka [not plotted on map], June 19 [1977, AB 31:1170]); Utah (Behle and Perry 1975); Colorado (1973, AB 27:901; 1979, AB 33:886; 1983, AB 37:1012; 1985, AB 39:944; 1989, AB 43:1348; 1990, AB 44:1163); Arizona (Phillips et al. 1964; Rosenberg and Terrill 1986); New Mexico (1976, AB 30:989; 1980, AB 34:920; 1983, AB 37:

1017; 1984, AB 38:1051; 1985, AB 39:950; 1986, AB 40:1241).

Piranga rubra. Summer Tanager. California (1964, AB 18:536; 1966, AB 20:600; 1967, AB 21:605; 1968, AB 22:650; 1972, AB 26:907; 1973, AB 27:920; 1974, AB 28:951; 1977, AB 31:1191; 1978, AB 32:1210; 1979, AB 33:898; 1981, AB 35:980; 1985, AB 39:963; 1987, AB 41:1489; 1988, AB 42:1341; 1989, AB 43: 1369; 1991, AB 45:1162; 1992, AB 46:1180); Nevada (1977, AB 31:1170; 1982, AB 36:1002; Alcorn 1988); Utah (Behle and Perry 1975; 1978, AB 32:1193); Arizona (Brown et al. 1987); New Mexico (Hubbard 1978; 1992, AB 46:1164).

Guiraca caerulea. Blue Grosbeak. California (1977, AB 31:1187; 1979, AB 33:895; 1985, AB 39:960; 1992, AB 46:1176); Idaho (1981, AB 35:963; 1982 AB 36: 1000; 1986, AB 30:1232); Nevada (1969, AFN 23:680; 1984, AB 38:1047); Utah (1985, AB 39:944; 1986, AB 40:1236; 1987, AB 41:1470; 1989, AB 43:1348; 1990, AB 44:1163); Wyoming (1965, AFN 19:568; 1982 AB 36:1002; 1984, AB 38:1047; 1985, AB 39:944; 1987, AB 41:1470); Colorado (1971, AB 25:887; 1984, AB 38:1047; 1987, AB 41:1470).

Icterus parisorum. Scott's Oriole. Oregon (1991, AB 45:1155 [a female and, hence, perhaps not a pioneer); California (1975, AB 29:1036; 1977, AB 31:1191; 1992, AB 46:1176); Idaho (1972, AB 26:886; 1973, AB 27: 901; 1981, AB 35:963; 1986, AB 40:1232); Nevada (1976, AB 30:985); Utah (1963, AFN 17:474; 1965, AFN 19:568; 1971, AB 25:887; 1980, AB 34:917); Arizona (Rosenberg and Terrill 1986); Wyoming (Findholt and Fitton 1983; 1982, AB 36:1002; 1987, AB 41:1470); Colorado (1980, AB 34:917; 1982, AB 36:879 and 1002; 1983, AB 37:1012); New Mexico (1967, AFN 21:594; 1977, AB 31:1174; 1978, AB 32: 1197; 1980, AB 34:920; 1983, AB 37:1016; 1984, AB 38:1052; 1987, AB 41:1475; 1992, AB 46:1165).

Loxia leucoptera. White-winged Crossbill. British Columbia (1978, AB 32:1203; 1981, AB 35:972; 1985, AB 39:941 and 956; 1989, AB 43:1361); Washington (1977, AB 31:1182; 1978, AB 32:1203; 1981, AB 35: 972; 1984, AB 38:995, 1044; 1985, AB 39:941, 956; 1986, AB 40:1248; 1987, AB 41:1480; 1990, AB 44: 1180; 1992, AB 46:1173); Oregon (1981, AB 35:972; 1984 [Gordon et al. 1989]; 1986, AB 40:1232, 1248; 1987, AB 41:1480; 1989, AB 43:1361; 1990, AB 44: 1180); California (1978 [Gordon et al. 1989]); Idaho (1977, AB 31:1165; 1985, AB 39:941; also see records in Stephens and Sturts [1991], who denote, without dates, a breeding latilong in the far northern part of the state and records of "transients" from nine other latilongs); Nevada (1984, AB 38:995); Utah (1965 [Worthen 1973], 1977, AB 31:1170; 1982, AB 36:1003; 1985, AB 39:945; 1989, AB 43:1348); Montana (1984, AB 38:1044; also see Skaar et al. [1985] who present, without dates, records of probable breeding in nine latilongs and presence without evidence of breeding in 16 others); Wyoming (1977, AB 31:1170; 1980, AB 34:918; 1984, AB 38:995; 1987, AB 41:1470); Colorado (1976, AB 30:985; 1978, AB 32:1193; 1981, AB 35:966; 1982, AB 36:1003; 1983, AB 37:1012; 1987, AB 41:1470; 1988, AB 42:1323; 1989, AB 43:1348); and New Mexico (1982, AB 36:207; 1984, AB 38:995; 1985, AB 39:951).

Studies in Avian Biology No. 15:45–57, 1994.

AVIFAUNA OF THE WETLANDS OF BAJA CALIFORNIA, MÉXICO: CURRENT STATUS

Barbara W. Massey and Eduardo Palacios

Abstract. Although Baja California has not experienced loss of wetlands comparable in magnitude to that in California, some habitat changes have provoked changes in the abundance and distribution of wetland avifauna. The Osprey population has increased in the Vizcaíno wetlands, but at least three species of egrets and herons, and American Oystercatcher have declined due to human disturbance. The Elegant Tern is missing at Laguna Ojo de Liebre, but there is a new colony at Delta del Río Colorado. Several species have expanded their range into Baja California and have established breeding colonies, e.g., Little Blue Heron, Laughing Gull, Caspian, Royal, Forster's and Gull-billed terns, and Black Skimmer. Both number and variety of breeding birds have increased in Laguna San Ignacio. At least 52 species of water-associated birds breed in the several habitats of the wetlands, including five endangered or threatened species. The northernmost breeding colony of the Magnificent Frigatebird is located in Bahía Magdalena. Migratory birds use the wetlands in large numbers; the biggest concentrations of shorebirds are found in two wetlands—Laguna Ojo de Liebre and Delta del Río Colorado. The lagoons of Baja California are the primary wintering grounds for Brant. Mangroves in the southern wetlands have recently been identified as wintering habitat for passerines. Threats to the wetlands are primarily from resort and industrial developments being planned by international companies. Conservation of these vital avian habitats is a matter of concern to all ornithologists.

Key Words: México; Baja California; coastal wetlands; marsh avifauna; endangered species; distribution; conservation.

The peninsula of Baja California, México extends 1600 km south from Tijuana to Cabo San Lucas. Its diverse natural habitats include richly vegetated deserts, riparian valleys, rugged mountain ranges and the magnificent coastal wetlands whose avifauna is our subject. Long insulated from disturbance and development by lack of roads, the wetlands were also out of reach to all but the hardiest ornithologists prior to the opening of the peninsula-long highway in 1974. Post-highway changes have been gradual but inexorable and today some of the major wetlands are under threat, particularly from tourist-oriented development. However, most are still in near-pristine condition, and presumably have not experienced the changes in bird use that have characterized California's wetlands. Unfortunately, numerical baseline data are sketchy, as early ornithologists reported species' presence and breeding information, but seldom numbers.

The first checklist of the birds of Baja California appeared in 1889 (Bryant 1889), and in the 1920s Bancroft (1927a, b) and Grinnell (1928) added extensively to the scant literature. In 1987 Wilbur compiled an annotated checklist from the literature and from reliable field observers (Wilbur 1987); his bibliography was comprehensive and allows us to concentrate on data gathered subsequently. Recently there has been an accelerated interest in documenting numbers and species in Baja California, and much of the information presented here has not been published heretofore. Scientific names of species are given in Table 1.

The first attempt at estimating numbers of birds in Baja California was in 1949 when the U.S. Fish and Wildlife Service (USFWS) added the peninsular lagoons to its aerial surveys of Mexican waterfowl (Sanders and Sanders 1981). Since 1974 the surveys have been a cooperative project with the Mexican government. Brant have received special attention and have been censused every year even when the all-México surveys were reduced to every 3rd year (U.S. Fish and Wildlife Service unpublished reports on winter waterfowl surveys of the Mexican West Coast and Baja California, 1954–1992, available from J. Voelzer, USFWS, Portland, OR).

In 1977 the Osprey population of west coast mainland México and Baja California was censused (Henny and Anderson 1979). The survey was repeated in 1992–1993 (C. Henny, pers. comm.).

The first attempt at obtaining numerical data on a marsh bird was the 1981 census of the Light-footed Clapper Rail in the two northern wetlands, Estero de Punta Banda and Bahía San Quintín (Zembal and Massey 1981). Four more censuses were done in 1986–1988 (available from R. Zembal, USFWS, 2730 Loker Ave West, Carlsbad, CA 92008).

Regular shorebird censusing of the northern estuaries was begun in 1989 as part of the Point Reyes Bird Observatory (PRBO) Pacific Flyway Project in cooperation with *pro esteros,* a bi-national, non-profit group dedicated to protection of Baja California's wetlands and Centro de Investigación Científica y de Educación Superior de Ensenada, B.C. (CICESE), a Mexican research and teaching institution. Comprehensive counts have been done 2–3 times a year at the northern estuaries since 1989 (Page et al. 1992); in 1991 and 1992 all of the other major wetlands were visited by members of the above organizations, and numbers of wintering and breeding birds documented. Additional information on Ensenada de La Paz and Isla Margarita in Bahía Magdalena has come from studies by students at Universidad Autónoma de Baja California Sur (UABCS).

In 1992 the Canadian Wildlife Service (CWS) began a Mexican Shorebird Atlas Project in conjunction with the Mexican government. Estimates of wintering shorebird numbers in western México were made by aerial survey in early 1992, the first of a 3-yr series (Morrison et al. 1992).

All of the large estuaries in Baja California host thousands of migrating and wintering shorebirds and waterfowl. They also provide breeding habitat for raptors, rails, terns, gulls, cormorants, pelicans, frigatebirds, herons, egrets, shorebirds, and several passerines.

THE WETLANDS

Figure 1 shows the locations of the major wetlands; most are complexes of marshes with connecting waterways. We will focus on the seven largest: 1) Estero de Punta Banda, 2) Bahía San Quintín complex, 3) Ojo de Liebre complex, 4) Laguna San Ignacio complex, 5) Bahía Magdalena complex, 6) Ensenada de La Paz and 7) Delta del Río Colorado.

Small saltmarshes on the west coast not dealt with here are La Salina, La Misión, San Antonio del Mar, and San Gregorio. Laguna Percebú, a 5 km long, narrow saltmarsh on the northeast coast deserves special mention as it hosts many breeding birds including Wilson's Plover and California Least Tern (see Table 1). Freshwater marshes are extremely rare on the peninsula; examples are La Lagunita Formex-Ibarra in Ensenada, La Bocana de Santo Domingo, El Rosario, San Ignacio, Estero de San José del Cabo, La Poza de Todos Santos and Mulegé. Others are without names and known only to local residents, e.g., a series of ponds several kilometers inland from Puerto Lopez Mateos.

Estero de Punta Banda

Area: 2100 ha. A description of this northernmost estuary can be found in Ibarra-Obando (1990). Thousands of shorebirds winter here, the most important numerically is the Marbled Godwit (Palacios et al. 1991). Many species of wintering waterfowl have been documented; American Wigeon is the most numerous, numbering in the thousands (E. Palacios, pers. obs.). The California Least Tern and Light-footed Clapper Rail (U.S. and México endangered species), Snowy Plover (U.S. threatened species), and Belding's Savannah Sparrow (California endangered species) breed here.

Bahía de San Quintín complex

Area: 12,060 ha. Descriptions are given in Ibarra-Obando (1990) and Palacios and Alfaro (1991). Vast eel grass beds (*Zostera*

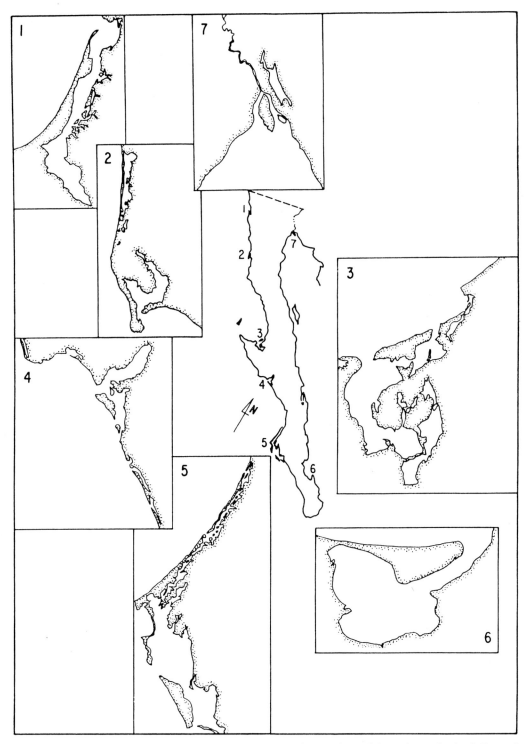

FIGURE 1. The peninsula of Baja California, México, showing locations of the major wetlands. 1) Estero de Punta Banda; 2) Bahía San Quintín complex (north to south—Laguna Figueroa, Bahía San Quintín); 3) Ojo de Liebre complex (Laguna Manuela, Guerrero Negro, Ojo de Liebre); 4) Laguna San Ignacio complex (La Bocana, El Coyote, San Ignacio, Estero el Delgadito); 5) Bahía Magdalena complex (Laguna Santo Domingo, Bahía Magdalena, Bahía Almejas); 6) Ensenada de La Paz; and 7) Delta del Río Colorado.

marina) in the channels attract >20,000 Brant in winter. On recent winter surveys up to 27,000 shorebirds have been counted on the extensive mudflats (Page et al. 1992). The above-mentioned four threatened or endangered species of birds also nest here. Salt ponds along the coast just north of the bay also attract shorebirds.

Approximately 15 km north of Bahía de San Quintín but not connected to it is Laguna Figueroa, a hypersaline flat 20 km long that lies behind very tall dunes and has no ocean outlet. After winter storms it is covered with water and attracts thousands of shorebirds, particularly Western Sandpipers (L. Stenzel, pers. comm.). The Snowy Plover, Caspian Tern, Forster's Tern, and California Least Tern have nested here (Palacios and Alfaro 1991). In 1992, however, the local community diverted three rivers to impound water in the basin, and heavy winter rains created a lake up to two meters deep, transforming shorebird habitat into waterfowl habitat. The future of this area as breeding habitat is uncertain.

Ojo de Liebre complex

Three lagoons are included in this group: Laguna Manuela (600 ha), Guerrero Negro (2100 ha), and Ojo de Liebre (36,600 ha) (Contreras 1988). All empty into Bahía Vizcaíno, all have vast areas of saltmarsh, mudflat and extensive barrier beaches. Several small islands in Laguna Ojo de Liebre provide breeding habitat for raptors and seabirds. Double-crested Cormorant, Osprey, Peregrine Falcon, American Oystercatcher, Wilson's Plover, Western Gull, California Least Tern, and several species of herons and egrets breed on Islote La Piedra; Isla Concha has breeding colonies of Double-crested Cormorant, Osprey, Western Gull, Caspian Tern, Royal Tern, and several species of herons and egrets. On the southeast side of Laguna Ojo de Liebre a huge saltworks is divided into cells, most of which are hypersaline, but several cells (close to Ocho Bombas, where sea water is pumped into the system) provide habitat for inver-

tebrates and fish and thus for birds. Caspian and Royal terns nest on an island in one of the cells; California Least Terns breed in scattered colonies around another. Snowy Plovers nest on saltpans throughout the saltworks. Thousands of Red-necked and Wilson's phalaropes are present during July and August in the saltworks close to Ocho Bombas; thousands of Eared Grebes and hundreds of Red Phalaropes are present in winter (F. Heredia, pers. comm.). Over 270,000 shorebirds (Morrison et al. 1992) and >35,000 Brant (Conant et al. 1992) winter here.

Laguna San Ignacio complex

Several small esteros lie north and south of Laguna San Ignacio, which covers approximately 28,000 ha (Contreras 1988), and lies in a NE/SW direction with the ocean entrance on the south end (Fig. 1). This lagoon complex marks the northern limit of red mangrove (Rhizophora mangle), which begins to replace saltmarsh as one moves south and becomes the dominant plant in Bahía Magdalena (Roberts 1989). White Ibis, Little Blue Heron and other species of wading birds nest in the mangroves. Two islands provide nesting habitat for Brown Pelican, Double-crested Cormorant, Osprey, Reddish Egret, Caspian and Royal terns, Snowy Plover, American Oystercatcher and others (Danemann and Guzmán Poo 1992; E. Palacios and L. Alfaro, pers. obs.). The bay is a major wintering site for Brant (>33,000) (Conant et al. 1992) and shorebirds (32,000) (E. Palacios, pers. obs.).

Bahía Magdalena complex

This vast complex of bays, dunes, islands and mangrove stands extends 250 km along the southwestern shore of Baja California. A series of long, narrow dune islands protects it against the sea for most of its length, with ocean openings between them. At the south end is the mountainous, 40 km long Isla Santa Margarita. A mangrove lagoon on its protected southwest side hosts the continent's northernmost breeding colony of Magnificent Frigatebirds. Brown Pelican and Brandt's Cormorant breed on Isla Santa Margarita in large numbers (Amador 1985, Everett and Anderson 1991); in winter their populations are further augmented by migrants. Other breeding birds in Bahía Magdalena are Double-crested Cormorant, several species of heron and egret, Snowy and Wilson's Plover, American Oystercatcher, and California Least Tern. A population of the Scrub Jay is resident in the mangroves (Pitelka 1951; M. Evans and S. Howell, pers. comm.; B. W. Massey, pers. obs.).

Ensenada de La Paz

This 4500 ha shallow lagoon is connected to Bahía de La Paz by a canal. Its mudflats, mangroves and recently created dredge-fill islands provide habitat diversity. Wilson's Plover, Yellow-footed Gull, California Least Tern and several species of heron and egret breed there. Brown Pelican, White Pelican, Yellow-footed Gull and a variety of shorebirds are abundant in winter (E. Palacios, pers. obs.).

Delta del Río Colorado

Once a vast wetland, the Colorado River delta (240,000 ha) has only a remnant stream emptying into the Gulf of California as the result of dams and water diversion along the river in both U.S. and México. There are, however, extensive mudflats at the land/gulf interface, which support >163,000 wintering shorebirds, principally small "peep" sandpipers (Morrison et al. 1992) and thousands of waterfowl, especially Pintail (Kramer and Migoya 1989). Estero Río Colorado and Marismas Nacionales on the mainland are the first sites in México to be designated reserves in the Western Hemisphere Shorbird Reserve Network. Isla Montague, a low, flat and sparsely vegetated island at the mouth of the delta, provides breeding habitat for herons and seabirds, including the California Least Tern (Palacios and Mellink 1992).

AVIFAUNA

The coastal wetland avifauna of Baja California is dominated, at least numerically, by large numbers of Anseriformes, Ciconiiformes, and Charadriiformes. Only at Bahía Magdalena is the dominant avifauna Pelecaniformes. At all sites, avian populations increase considerably in winter, when large numbers of waterfowl and shorebirds congregate to feed and rest in such areas.

Table 1 is a checklist of the birds of Baja California's wetlands as of January 1993, which includes all species seen within the past five years. Sources are recent publications (Danemann and Guzmán Poo 1992; Erickson 1992; Everett and Anderson 1991; Howell and Webb 1992, 1993; Morrison et al. 1992; Page et al. 1992; Palacios and Alfaro 1991, 1992a, b; Palacios et al. 1991; Palacios and Mellink 1992) and the observations of Lucía Alfaro, Edgar Amador, Jose Angel Sánchez, Michael Evans, Salvador González, Fernando Heredia, Steve Howell, Barbara Massey, Renato Mendoza, Leopoldo Moreno, Eduardo Palacios and Lynne Stenzel.

Breeding birds are designated by an asterisk and only recently documented breeding (since 1985) is acknowledged; several species that bred historically (e.g., Virginia Rail, Sora, and Common Yellowthroat) have no recent documentation. There may also be omissions of casually-occurring species.

Migratory Birds

Although the USFWS census of wintering waterfowl in México has included Baja California's wetlands for the past 40 years, the principal surveyors state that an aerial survey done every few years at different tide levels and under various weather conditions gives results far too variable to show statistically analyzable changes (James Voelzer, Bruce Conant, pers. comm.). While changes in waterfowl numbers may be undocumentable, survey data show that most waterfowl winter in the wetlands of mainland México rather than in Baja California, with the exception of Brant (Conant et al. 1992).

TABLE 1. CHECKLIST OF BIRDS OF THE BAJA CALIFORNIA WETLANDS

Scientific name	Common name	Where found†
Gavia stellata	Red-throated Loon	1
Gavia pacifica	Pacific Loon	2, 5
Gavia immer	Common Loon	1–3, 5
*Tachybaptus dominicus**	Least Grebe	10*
*Podilymbus podiceps**	Pied-billed Grebe	1, 2, 6, 10*
Podiceps auritus	Horned Grebe	2
Podiceps nigricollis	Eared Grebe	1–8, 10
Aechmophorus occidentalis	Western Grebe	1–7, 10
Aechmophorus clarkii	Clark's Grebe	2, 3, 5, 10
Fulmarus glacialis	Northern Fulmar	1–3
Sula dactylatra	Masked Booby	5, 6
Sula nebouxii	Blue-footed Booby	5, 6
Sula leucogaster	Brown Booby	6
Pelecanus erythrorhynchos	White Pelican	1, 3–7
*Pelecanus occidentalis**	Brown Pelican	1–3, 4*, 5*, 6–10
*Phalacrocorax auritus**	Double-crested Cormorant	1, 2, (3–5)*, 6, 7, 10
*Phalacrocorax penicillatus**	Brandt's Cormorant	1, 3, 4, 5*, 6, 7, 10
*Fregata magnificens**	Magnificent Frigatebird	4, 5*, 6, 8, 10
*Botaurus lentiginosus**	American Bittern	2, 4
*Ixobrychus exilis**	Least Bittern	4, 7*
*Ardea herodias**	Great Blue Heron	1, 2, (3–5)*, (7–9)*, 10
*Casmerodius albus**	Great Egret	1, 2, (3–6)*, 10
*Egretta thula**	Snowy Egret	1, 2, (3–7)*, 8–10
*Egretta caerulea**	Little Blue Heron	1–3, 4*, 5*, 6, 10
*Egretta tricolor**	Tricolored Heron	1, 2, (3–6)*, 8
*Egretta rufescens**	Reddish Egret	2, (3–6)*, 8
*Bubulcus ibis**	Cattle Egret	1, 2, 5, 6*, 7*, 10
*Butorides virescens**	Green Heron	1, (4–7)*, 9*
*Nycticorax nycticorax**	Black-crowned Night-Heron	1, 2, (3–7)*
*Nycticorax violaceus**	Yellow-crowned Night-Heron	(3–6)*
*Eudocimus albus**	White Ibis	(4–6)*
Plegadis chihi	White-faced Ibis	6, 10
Mycteria americana	Wood Stork	6
Anser albifrons	Greater White-fronted Goose	1–4
Anser caerulescens	Snow Goose	1, 2, 10
Branta bernicla	Brant	1–5, 8
Branta canadensis	Canada Goose	1
Anas platyrhynchos	Mallard	1–3, 6, 9, 10
Anas acuta	Northern Pintail	1–7, 10
Anas discors	Blue-winged Teal	1, 2
Anas cyanoptera	Cinnamon Teal	1–3, 5, 6, 9, 10
Anas clypeata	Northern Shoveler	1–3, 5, 6, 9, 10
Anas strepera	Gadwall	1–3, 5
Anas americana	American Wigeon	1–4, 9
Aythya valisineria	Canvasback	1–4
Aythya americana	Redhead	1–5, 10
Aythya collaris	Ring-necked Duck	1–4, 10
Aythya marila	Greater Scaup	1–4, 6, 10
Aythya affinis	Lesser Scaup	1–5, 6, 10
Melanitta nigra	Black Scoter	1, 2
Melanitta perspicillata	Surf Scoter	1–5
Melanitta fusca	White-winged Scoter	1–4
Bucephala albeola	Bufflehead	1–6, 10
Mergus merganser	Common Merganser	4, 5
Mergus serrator	Red-breasted Merganser	1–8, 10
*Oxyura jamaicensis**	Ruddy Duck	1–6, 9, 10*
Cathartes aura	Turkey Vulture	1–10
*Pandion haliaetus**	Osprey	1–10 (3, 4, 5, 6, 8)*
Elanus leucurus	White-tailed Kite	1, 2, 5
*Haliaeetus leucocephalus**	Bald Eagle	5*
Circus cyaneus	Northern Harrier	1–4, 9

TABLE 1. CONTINUED

Scientific name	Common name	Where found†
Buteo regalis	Ferruginous Hawk	1–3
Falco sparverius	American Kestrel	1, 2, 5, 6, 9
Falco columbarius	Merlin	1, 6
*Falco peregrinus**	Peregrine Falcon	1, 2, 3*, 4*, 5, 6, 9, 10
Laterallus jamaicensis	Black Rail	2
*Rallus longirostris**	Clapper Rail	(1–9)*
Rallus limicola	Virginia Rail	1, 2, 4, 7
Porzana carolina	Sora	2, 5, 7, 10
*Gallinula chloropus**	Common Moorhen	7*, 10*
*Fulica americana**	American Coot	2, 3, 6, 7*, 9, 10*
Pluvialis squatarola	Black-bellied Plover	1–10
*Charadrius alexandrinus**	Snowy Plover	(1–5)*, 6, 7, 9*, 10
*Charadrius wilsonia**	Wilson's Plover	1, 2, (3–6)*, 8*, 9*, 10
Charadrius semipalmatus	Semi-palmated Plover	(1–10)*
*Charadrius vociferus**	Killdeer	1–10
Charadrius montanus	Mountain Plover	1, 2
*Haemotopus palliatus**	American Oystercatcher	(3–6)*
*Haemotopus bachmani**	Black Oystercatcher	1, 2, 3*, 4*
*Himantopus mexicanus**	Black-necked Stilt	1, 2*, 3–6, 7*, 8, 9*, 10
*Recurvirostra americana**	American Avocet	1, 2*, 3–6, 7*, 8, 9*
Tringa melanoleuca	Greater Yellowlegs	1–10
Tringa flavipes	Lesser Yellowlegs	1–10
Catoptrophorus semipalmatus	Willet	1–10
Heteroscelus incanus	Wandering Tattler	1–6, 10
Actitis macularia	Spotted Sandpiper	1–6, 9, 10
Numenius phaeopus	Whimbrel	1–10
Numenius americanus	Long-billed Curlew	1–10
Limosa fedoa	Marbled Godwit	1–10
Arenaria interpres	Ruddy Turnstone	1–10
Arenaria melanocephala	Black Turnstone	1–5, 6, 10
Calidris canutus	Red Knot	1, 2, 5
Calidris alba	Sanderling	1–10
Calidris mauri	Western Sandpiper	1–10
Calidris minutilla	Least Sandpiper	1–10
Calidris bairdii	Baird's Sandpiper	3
Calidris melanotos	Pectoral Sandpiper	1, 2
Calidris alpina	Dunlin	1–10
Limnodromus griseus	Short-billed Dowitcher	1–10
Limnodromus scolopaceus	Long-billed Dowitcher	1–10
Phalaropus tricolor	Wilson's Phalarope	1–3
Phalaropus lobatus	Red-necked Phalarope	1–3
Phalaropus fulicaria	Red Phalarope	1–10
*Larus atricilla**	Laughing Gull	3, 5, 6, 7*, 8, 10
Larus philadelphia	Bonaparte's Gull	1–6, 10
Larus heermanni	Heermann's Gull	1–10
Larus canus	Mew Gull	1
Larus delawarensis	Ringed-billed Gull	1–10
Larus californicus	California Gull	1–6, 10
Larus argentatus	Herring Gull	1–3, 5
Larus thayeri	Thayer's Gull	1–3
*Larus livens**	Yellow-footed Gull	4, 5, 6*, 10
*Larus occidentalis**	Western Gull	1, 2, (3–5)*
Larus glaucescens	Glaucous-winged Gull	1
Larus hyperboreus	Glaucous Gull	1, 5
Xema sabini	Sabine's Gull	4, 10
*Sterna nilotica**	Gull-billed Tern	7*, 8
*Sterna caspia**	Caspian Tern	1, (2–4)*, 5–10
*Sterna maxima**	Royal Tern	1, 2, 3*, 4*, 5, 6, 7*, 8–10
*Sterna elegans**	Elegant Tern	1–6, 7*, 8–10
Sterna hirundo	Common Tern	10
*Sterna forsteri**	Forster's Tern	1, 2*, 3–10

TABLE 1. CONTINUED

Scientific name	Common name	Where found†
*Sterna antillarum**	Least Tern	(1–10)*
Chlidonias niger	Black Tern	1, 3
*Rynchops niger**	Black Skimmer	1–4, 6, 7*
*Zenaida asiatica**	White-winged Dove	6*, 10
*Zenaida macroura**	Mourning Dove	6*, 9, 10
*Athene cunicularia**	Burrowing Owl	(1–7)*
Asio flammeus	Short-eared Owl	1, 2
*Chordeiles acutipennis**	Lesser Nighthawk	6*
Ceryle alcyon	Belted Kingfisher	1–6, 10
*Eremophila alpestris**	Horned Lark	(1–4)*
*Aphelocoma coerulescens**	Scrub Jay	5*
Corvus corax	Common Raven	1–10
Anthus rufescens	American Pipit	1–4
Lanius ludovicianus	Loggerhead Shrike	2–6
*Dendroica petechia**	Yellow (Mangrove) Warbler	(4–6)*
Geothlypis trichas	Common Yellowthroat	2, 10
Geothlypis beldingi	Belding's Yellowthroat	10
*Passerculus sandwichensis**	Savannah Sparrow	(1–6)*

* Denotes recently documented breeding.
† Numbers in this column refer to the wetlands described in the section WETLANDS. Locations 1–7 are shown in Figure 1; locations 8–10 are noted in the text but not shown in the figure. 1 = Estero de Punta Banda, 2 = Bahía San Quintín complex, 3 = Laguna Ojo de Liebre complex, 4 = San Ignacio complex, 5 = Bahía Magdalena complex, 6 = Ensenada de La Paz, 7 = Delta del Río Colorado, 8 = Laguna Percebú, 9 = Small saltmarshes, 10 = freshwater ponds/marshes.

Brant receive special attention, as they winter almost exclusively on the Pacific coast of the U.S. and México. In 1952 an inventory that accounted for approximately 90% of the population showed that two-thirds of the birds were in Baja California, the rest in the U.S., mainly in the bays of California (Sanders and Sanders 1981); there were none on the Mexican mainland. In 1958 Brant were first seen in the wetlands of Sonora-Sinaloa and by 1990 represented 15% of the total in México (Conant et al. 1990). The California population declined concurrently as coastal wetlands were lost to development, and in 1990 85% of the total population was wintering in México, primarily in the Baja California lagoons. Brant numbers have shown wide fluctuations over the past 20 years, but "declines" were regularly followed by "recoveries," and in 13 of the 20 years the numbers were between 100,000 and 130,000 (USFWS winter waterfowl surveys of México).

Baja California's coastal wetlands are major wintering sites for shorebirds. Combining recent counts from three different sources, we estimate that 510,000 individuals winter in the wetlands of the peninsula (Morrison et al. 1992; Page et al. 1992; E. Palacios, pers. obs.). The first Canadian Wildlife Service aerial survey in 1992, which covered the west coast of mainland México and Baja California, documented the importance of the peninsular wetlands for shorebirds. The combined count at Laguna Ojo de Liebre complex and Delta del Río Colorado (434,000) was more than half of the total number (800,000) seen on the survey (Morrison et al. 1992).

The mangrove stands in the southern wetlands host many wintering passerines that nest in North America. The importance of this habitat throughout México has only been recognized recently (S. Howell, pers. comm.). Species seen in the mangroves at Bahía Magdalena are Solitary Vireo, Orange-crowned Warbler, Yellow-rumped Warbler, Black-and-white Warbler, Ovenbird, Northern Waterthrush, Painted Bunting, and Black-throated Sparrow (Amador 1985; M. Evans, S. Howell, pers. obs.).

BREEDING BIRDS

Fifty two species of birds now breed in the coastal wetlands of Baja California (Table 1). Six species, previously undocu-

TABLE 2.   ESTIMATED NUMBER OF PAIRS OF BIRDS BREEDING IN THE BAJA CALIFORNIA WETLANDS, 1985–1992

	Number of pairs in the wetlands						
	EPB*	BSQ	LOL	LSI	BM	ELP	DRC
Brown Pelican				1100	3000		
Double-crested Cormorant			3500	500	250		
Brandt's Cormorant					300		
Magnificent Frigatebird					20,000		
Great Blue Heron			5	12	<10	30	5
Great Egret			3	1			
Snowy Egret			20	68			100
Little Blue Heron				152	20		
Tricolored Heron			17	54		30	
Reddish Egret			50	95			
Cattle Egret						25	
Green Heron				20		10	
Black-crowned Night-Heron			50	30			20
Yellow-crowned Night-Heron				>4		>100	
White Ibis				50	20	5	
Osprey			76	146	12	3	
Bald Eagle					5		
Peregrine Falcon			6	2			
Clapper Rail	250	500					
Snowy Plover	30	>160	>190	>180	>45	1	
American Oystercatcher			28	30	20	6	
Laughing Gull							100
Yellow-footed Gull						25	
Western Gull			355	40	400		
Gull-billed Tern						200	
Caspian Tern		10	160	150			
Royal Tern			500	350			275
Elegant Tern							275
Forster's Tern		30					
California Least Tern†	90	97	>60	>30	30	150	20
Black Skimmer							250

* Abbreviations of the wetlands: EPB = Estero de Punta Banda, BSQ = Bahía San Quintín, LOL = Laguna Ojo de Liebre, LSI = Laguna San Ignacio, BM = Bahía Magdalena, ELP = Ensenada de La Paz, DRC = Delta del Río Colorado.
† California Least Terns also nested at Laguna Percebú (46–76 prs).

mented, have well established breeding colonies: Little Blue Heron, Cattle Egret, Laughing Gull, Gull-billed Tern, Forster's Tern and Black Skimmer. Table 2 shows the number of pairs and locations of all nesting species documented since 1985. Brandt's Cormorant was formerly known to breed only on offshore islands; there are now several small colonies (50–100 pairs each) on Santa Margarita Island in Bahía Magdalena (Amador 1985; E. Palacios, pers. obs.). The range of the Elegant Tern also appears to be shifting. Early in the century a few pairs were reported nesting in Laguna Ojo de Liebre (Bancroft 1927a), but there has been no recent nesting there. A new colony has recently formed on Isla Montague in the Colorado River Delta (Palacios and Mel-

link 1993). The bird's current status in the U.S. was recently summarized (Collins et al. 1991).

Two former breeding species, Northern Harrier and Sora, have not been documented recently; the harrier probably no longer nests in Baja California (Pete Bloom, pers. comm.); the Sora is presumably still present in freshwater marshes and has been overlooked. The uncommon Black Rail was a breeding bird in Bahía San Quintín in the 1920s (Wilbur 1987), but then not documented anywhere in Baja California until recently, when two or three individuals were heard calling in Bahía San Quintín in February 1991 (Erickson 1992). One endemic species, Belding's Yellowthroat, breeds exclusively in the freshwater marshes of the

TABLE 3. HABITAT PREFERENCES OF BREEDING BIRDS IN THE BAJA CALIFORNIA WETLANDS

	Beaches/saltflats	Saltmarsh vegetation	Freshwater marsh veg.	Mangroves	Islands
Least Grebe			X		
Pied-billed Grebe			X		
Brown Pelican†					X
Double-crested Cormorant†				X	X
Brandt's Cormorant†					X
Magnificent Frigatebird†				X	X
American Bittern			X		
Least Bittern			X		
Great Blue Heron				X	X
Great Egret				X	X
Snowy Egret				X	X
Little Blue Heron				X	
Tri-colored Heron				X	X
Reddish Egret				X	X
Cattle Egret				X	
Green Heron				X	X
Black-crowned Night-Heron				X	X
Yellow-crowned Night-Heron				X	X
White Ibis				X	
Ruddy Duck			X		
Osprey					X
Bald Eagle					X
Peregrine Falcon					X
Clapper Rail		X		X	
Common Moorhen			X		
American Coot			X		
Snowy Plover	X				X
Wilson's Plover	X				X
Killdeer	X				
American Oystercatcher	X				X
Black Oystercatcher	X				X
Black-necked Stilt	X	X			
American Avocet	X	X			
Laughing Gull†		X			
Yellow-footed Gull†					
Western Gull†					X
Gull-billed Tern†					X
Caspian Tern	X				X
Royal Tern†	X				X
Elegant Tern†	X				
Forster's Tern		X			X
Least Tern	X				
Black Skimmer	X				X
White-winged Dove				X	
Mourning Dove		X			
Burrowing Owl	X				
Lesser Nighthawk		X			
Horned Lark	X				
Scrub Jay				X	
Yellow (Mangrove) Warbler				X	
Belding's Yellowthroat			X		
Savannah Sparrow		X			

† Breeds only on islands in Baja California.

peninsula from Mulegé south (Howell and Webb 1992).

Breeding habitat in Baja California's wetlands generally falls into four categories: beaches and saltflats, saltmarsh vegetation, freshwater marsh vegetation, and mangrove stands. The islands in the lagoons often have several of these habitats; and some, e.g., Isla Ballena in Laguna San Ignacio, also have scrubby desert vegetation that provides nest sites for seabirds and wading birds. While some bird species are strictly island nesters, many others nest both on islands and the mainland, wherever there is suitable habitat. Table 3 categorizes the habitat preferences of the 52 breeding species.

DISCUSSION

Although Baja California has not experienced loss of wetlands comparable in magnitude to that documented for California, some habitat changes have occurred. The most altered wetland along Baja California's Pacific coast is Laguna Ojo de Liebre, site of the world's largest saltworks (20,000 ha). The area had previously been mostly saltmarsh and salt flats subject to periodic tidal inundation (Nelson 1921). The only preconstruction numerical baseline data are found in Bancroft (1927a) who estimated numbers of some of the breeding birds. The changes between 1927 and the present are: the American Oystercatcher declined from about 150 pairs in 1926 to 30 in 1991; the small Elegant Tern colony (6 pairs) is missing; the Snowy Egret decreased from >100 to 20 pairs; the Tricolored Heron declined from >75 to about 20 pairs; the Black-crowned Night-Heron dropped from 100 to 50 pairs. Herons and egrets that used to nest in the marshes are now found nesting only on islands, mainly due to increased human disturbance by fishermen and tourists. The populations of other breeding species have remained stable (Caspian, Royal and Least terns, Western Gull) or increased (Osprey and Double-crested Cormorant). Double-crested Cormorant numbers in Laguna Ojo de Liebre rose from 80 pairs in 1926 (Bancroft 1927a) to 3500 in 1984 (J. A. Sánchez, pers. comm.).

It is impossible to quantify changes in numbers of most migratory species over the past century for lack of baseline data. Some may have experienced changes due to loss of breeding grounds (e.g., Marbled Godwit and Willet); others may have shifted to Baja California when wintering habitat elsewhere was lost (Brant).

One species that has been reasonably well tracked is the Osprey, particularly in the Vizcaíno wetlands (Laguna Ojo de Liebre complex, Laguna San Ignacio complex). In 1927 Bancroft found a "dozen or more nests" restricted to the islands in the Laguna Ojo de Liebre complex (Bancroft 1927a); Kenyon (1947) visited the islands in May of 1946 and found 27 occupied nests; Jehl (1977) estimated the lagoon population at 25 pairs in 1957, 30 pairs in 1970, and 20 pairs in 1971. During the 1970s the population began to increase. In 1977 the population estimate was 27 pairs for the islands and 50 pairs for the whole complex (Henny and Anderson 1979); in 1980 Castellanos (1982) reported 71 active nests; and in 1984 Salinas-Zavala et al. (1991) reported 76 breeding pairs.

While several factors may be involved in the increase in Osprey numbers, including reduction of DDT in the environment, a major factor was a reversal in attitude by local residents. Protection of the Osprey is now an accepted fact in Guerrero Negro. Ospreys are no longer shot by fishermen, and dozens of nesting poles have been erected in the town and on islands in the lagoons. In 1992, at least 15 of these towers were in use (L. Alfaro, M. Evans, B. Massey, E. Palacios, pers. obs.).

Although tourism and commercial fishing have increased in recent years in Laguna San Ignacio, so have the number and variety of breeding birds (Danemann and Guzmán Poo 1992). Colonies of Brown Pelicans (1100 breeding pairs), Double-crested Cormorants (500 pairs), Caspian Terns (150 pairs) and Royal Terns (350 pairs) have become established on Isla Ballena, a site of little ornithological interest early in the century (Huey 1927).

Current plans to construct the world's largest solar salt evaporation pond system at Laguna San Ignacio (J. Bremer, pers. comm.) could increase the winter population size of several shorebird species in this area, since the plan calls mainly for the flooding of usually dry playa that has limited habitat value for shorebirds.

Several species have expanded their range into Baja California. The Black Skimmer has recently established nesting colonies in southern California, and at Isla Montague in Delta del Río Colorado, so nesting is likely also in Estero de Punta Banda and Bahía San Quintín, where the bird is a year-round resident (Palacios and Alfaro 1992b). The Cattle Egret is now found along the length of the peninsula and breeds at Ensenada de la Paz (E. Palacios, pers. obs.). The Pacific coast population of Caspian Terns has increased since the mid-1960s and they have colonized new nesting sites at Lagunas Figueroa and San Ignacio (Palacios and Alfaro 1992a). The Little Blue Heron colony in Laguna San Ignacio (150 pairs) is the first breeding record of this heron in Baja California, although it may also breed in the mangroves of Bahía Magdalena and Ensenada de La Paz.

The coastal wetlands of the peninsula lie within a transition zone between temperate and tropical climates, and draw species from both. The northern breeding limits of the Magnificent Frigatebird, Tricolored Heron, Reddish Egret, Yellow-crowned Night-Heron, White Ibis, Wilson's Plover and American Oystercatcher are found in Baja California (Table 1). On the Pacific coast, none of these species breeds north of the Ojo de Liebre Lagoon complex (28th parallel). Conversely, the peninsula is the southern end of the breeding range for Bald Eagle, Snowy Plover, Black Oystercatcher, American Avocet and Forster's Tern (Table 1).

The wetlands provide a portrait of California's coastal marshes as they were before their wholesale damage and destruction. They offer an opportunity to observe the behavior and breeding biology of water-associated birds in unaltered marsh habitat, such as the endangered Light-footed Clapper Rail and Belding's Savannah Sparrow. Equally unchanged are the islands in the lagoons that provide breeding sites for a great variety of species. The California Least Tern and Snowy Plover nest on ocean-fronting beaches and other natural habitats; in only a few instances have Least Terns been found on dredge-spoil islands or other man-made habitats in Baja California. In 1991–1992 a survey documented over 500 pairs at 28 breeding sites throughout the peninsula (E. Palacios and L. Alfaro, pers. obs.).

The recent surge of field work has filled many gaps in our knowledge, but there is still much to be learned. Shorebird censuses are continuing under the Pacific Flyway Project, and a year-long study of shorebird use of Bahía San Quintín will add data on seasonality in that important wintering and migratory ground. The use of mangroves by breeding and wintering Ciconiiformes and wintering Passeriformes needs further documentation, as does the importance of the small, scattered freshwater marshes to birds restricted to such habitat, e.g., Belding's Yellowthroat.

Conservation of natural habitat has become an increasingly important issue under the present Mexican government and cooperative programs between U.S. and Mexican wildlife agencies are expanding. Enforcement of the law, creation of reserves, and protection of endangered species are in their infancy. For example, the vast Viscaíno Biosphere Reserve extends across the peninsula and includes lagunas San Ignacio and Ojo de Liebre, but it is as yet a reserve in name only, there is neither headquarters nor personnel to implement protection.

Tourist developments have impacted some wetlands and there are new projects in the planning stage. At Estero de Punta Banda a resort development has destroyed two thirds of the barrier beach since 1987 and is encroaching on the remainder. In Bahía Magdalena, a foreign construction company has bought 80,000 ha of land with the purpose of building a hotel, golf course, marina, and other recreational facilities. Industrial development is another threat. At Bahía San Quintín exploitation of the volcanic rock from the cinder cones is under consideration by foreign investors. A phosphoric rock extraction plant and a thermoelectric plant have been constructed and are operational in Bahía Magdalena; their impacts on the bay have not been assessed.

The wetlands of Baja California are an ecological treasure of international importance. Their integrity is of concern to all ornithologists. A cooperative international effort to insure their conservation is an imperative.

ACKNOWLEDGMENTS

We thank all of those who contributed information about the birds of the wetlands, and especially F. Heredia and R. A. Mendoza. We are grateful also to C. T. Collins, R. A. Mendoza and G. W. Page for critical reading of the manuscript.

LITERATURE CITED

AMADOR, E. S. 1985. Avifauna de Isla Santa Margarita, Baja California Sur, México. Bachelor's Thesis, Universidad Autónoma de Baja California Sur, México. 42 pp.

BANCROFT, G. J. 1927a. Breeding birds of Scammons Lagoon, Lower California. Condor 29:29–57.

BANCROFT, G. J. 1927b. Notes on the breeding coastal and insular birds of central Lower California. Condor 29:188–195.

BRYANT, W. E. 1889. A catalogue of the birds of Lower California, México. Proceedings of the California Academy of Sciences, Series 2, 2:237–320.

CASTELLANOS, V. A. 1982. Distribución, abundancia y productividad del Aguila Pescadora. Biología 12: 11–16.

COLLINS, C. T., W. A. SCHEW, AND E. BURKETT. 1991. Elegant Terns breeding in Orange County, California. American Birds 45:393–395.

CONANT, B., J. F. VOELZER, AND J. C. DIAZ. 1990. Winter waterfowl survey México west coast and Baja California. U.S. Department of the Interior, Fish and Wildlife Service, Portland, OR.

CONANT B., J. F. VOELZER, AND S. T. MORALES. 1992. México winter waterfowl survey 1992. U.S. Department of the Interior, Fish and Wildlife Service, Portland, OR.

CONTRERAS, F. 1988. Las lagunas costeras Mexicanas. Centro de Ecodesarrollo. Secretaria de Pesca. México. 263 pp.

DANEMANN, G. D., AND J. R. GUZMÁN POO. 1992. Notes

on the birds of San Ignacio Lagoon, Baja California Sur, México. Western Birds 23:11–19.

ERICKSON, R. 1992. A recent Black Rail record for Baja California. The Euphonia 1:19–21.

EVERETT, W. T., AND D. W. ANDERSON. 1991. Breeding seabirds of Baja California and the Gulf of California. Pp. 115–139 *in* J. Croxall (ed.), Seabird status and conservation: a supplement. International Council Bird Preservation Technical Publication No. 11.

GRINNELL, J. 1928. A distributional summation of the ornithology of Lower California. University of California Publications in Zoology 32:1–300.

HENNY, C., AND D. W. ANDERSON. 1979. Osprey distribution, abundance, and status in western North America: III. The Baja California and Gulf of California population. Bulletin Southern California Academy of Sciences 78:98–106.

HOWELL, S. N. G., AND S. WEBB. 1992. Noteworthy bird observations from Baja California, México, October 1991. Western Birds 24:57–62.

HOWELL, S. N. G., AND S. WEBB. 1993. New and noteworthy bird observations from Baja California, México. Western Birds 23:153–163.

HUEY, L. 1927. The bird life of San Ignacio and Pond lagoons on the western coast of Lower California. Condor 29:239–243.

IBARRA-OBANDO, S. E. 1990. Lagunas costeras de Baja California. Ciencia y Desarrollo 16:39–49.

JEHL, J. R., JR. 1977. History and present status of Ospreys in northwestern Baja California. Transactions of the North American Osprey Research Conference, U.S. Department of Interior, National Park Service Transactions and Proceedings Series, No. 2.

KENYON, K. W. 1947. Breeding populations of the Osprey in Lower California. Condor 49:152–157.

KRAMER, G. W., AND R. MIGOYA. 1989. The Pacific coast of México. Pp. 507–528 *in* L. M. Smith, R. L. Pederson, and R. M. Kaminski (eds.), Habitat management for migrating and wintering waterfowl in North America. Texas Tech University Press.

MORRISON, R. I. G., R. K. ROSS, AND S. TORRES M. 1992. Aerial surveys of Nearctic shorebirds wintering in México: some preliminary results. Progress Notes. Canadian Wildlife Service, Canadian Ministry of the Environment.

NELSON, E. W. 1921. Lower California and its natural resources. Memoirs of National Academy of Sciences 16:1–94.

PAGE, G. W., W. D. SHUFORD, J. KJELMER, AND L. E. STENZEL. 1992. Shorebird numbers in wetlands of the Pacific flyway: a summary of counts from April 1988 to January 1992. A report of Point Reyes Bird Observatory, 4990 Shoreline Highway, Stinson Beach, CA 94970.

PALACIOS, E., AND L. ALFARO. 1991. Breeding birds of Laguna Figueroa and La Pinta Pond, Baja California, México. Western Birds 22:27–32.

PALACIOS, E., AND L. ALFARO. 1992a. First breeding records of the Caspian Tern in Baja California, (Norte), México. Western Birds 23:143–144.

PALACIOS, E., AND L. ALFARO. 1992b. Occurrence of Black Skimmers in Baja California. Western Birds 23:173–176.

PALACIOS, E., A. ESCOFET, AND D. H. LOYA-SALINAS. 1991. The Estero de Punta Banda, B.C., México as a link in the "Pacific Flyway": abundance of shorebirds. Ciencias Marinas 17:109–131.

PALACIOS, E., AND E. MELLINK. 1992. Breeding bird records from Montague Island, northern Gulf of California. Western Birds 23:41–44.

PALACIOS, E., AND E. MELLINK. 1993. Additional breeding bird records from Montague Island, northern Gulf of California. Western Birds 24:259–262.

PITELKA, F. A. 1951. Speciation and ecological distribution in American jays of the genus *Aphelocoma*. University of California Publications in Zoology 50(3):195–464.

ROBERTS, N. C. 1989. Baja California plant guide. Natural History Publishing Company, La Jolla, CA.

SALINAS-ZAVALA, C. A., J. LLINAS, AND R. RODRÍGUEZ-ESTRELLA. 1991. Aspectos biológicos del Aguila Pescadora. Pp. 265–293 *in* A. Ortega and L. Arriaga (eds.), La Reserva de la Biósfera El Vizcaíno en la Península de Baja California. Publication No. 4, CIB de Baja California Sur, A.C. La Paz, Baja California Sur.

SANDERS, G. B., AND D. C. SANDERS. 1981. Waterfowl and their wintering grounds in México, 1937–64. U.S. Department of Interior, Fish and Wildlife Service Resource Publication 138. Superintendent of Documents, I 49.66:138.

WILBUR, S. R. 1987. Birds of Baja California. University of California Press, Berkeley CA.

ZEMBAL, R., AND B. W. MASSEY. 1981. A census of the Light-footed Clapper Rail in California. Western Birds 12:87–89.

Studies in Avian Biology No. 15:58–74, 1994.

TRENDS IN NOCTURNAL MIGRANT LANDBIRD POPULATIONS AT SOUTHEAST FARALLON ISLAND, CALIFORNIA, 1968–1992

Peter Pyle, Nadav Nur, and David F. DeSante

Abstract. We examined trends in populations and age proportions of nocturnal migrant landbirds arriving on Southeast Farallon Island (SEFI), California during a 25-year period. Trends based on totals statistically adjusted for the effects of weather and lunar cycle on arrival were more precise than those detected with unadjusted annual totals. Significant linear trends were detected in 30 of 70 examined species and each of ten breeding or wintering bioregional groups. Within-season declines outnumbered increases 41 to 16; eight species and four groups showed declines in both seasons whereas only one species and no groups showed seasonally-consistent increases. Directions of slopes of linear trends concurred significantly with those determined with Breeding Bird Survey data, suggesting that both censusing methods may accurately reflect true population trends. Significant curvilinear trends were detected in 21 species and 5 bioregional groups; accelerating declines were detected in two species and no groups. Results based on age proportion suggested that declines in reproductive success could account for decreasing trends detected in four species. Our results of bioregional groups suggest that population declines may be influenced more by changes on the summer grounds than by those on the winter grounds, although changes in both areas are indicated. Increases in eastern "Neotropical migrants" at SEFI, combined with results of age proportion, may indicate that the likelihood of vagrancy in first-year birds of these species is increasing. Reductions of landbird populations breeding (and to a lesser extent wintering) on the Pacific North American coast were most consistent, and may warrant attention.

Key Words: Landbird; trend; population monitoring; migration; productivity.

Declines in North American landbird populations, particularly those that migrate to the Neotropics, have received considerable attention in recent years (Robbins et al. 1989, Hagan and Johnston 1992). Reasons for these declines likely include habitat destruction on the winter grounds (Robbins et al. 1989, Terborgh 1989), increased nest parasitism and predation resulting from forest fragmentation on the breeding grounds (Holmes and Sherry 1988, Askins et al. 1990, Wilcove and Robinson 1990), and other factors (Hagan and Johnston 1992). Population trends can vary geographically and/or according to habitat (Sauer and Droege 1992, James et al. 1992, Peterjohn and Sauer 1993), indicating that factors affecting trends are not biogeographically concordant. While many recent analyses have examined long-term trends among eastern North American landbirds (Robbins et al. 1989, Hill and Hagan 1991, papers in Hagan and Johnston 1992), only three recent analyses, each using Breeding Bird Survey (BBS) data, have statistically considered long-term trends in the west (Robbins et al. 1986, Sauer and Droege 1992, Peterjohn and Sauer 1993).

The BBS has provided an important database for analyses of population trends, however, some limitations and assumptions exist with this census technique (Hussell 1981, Hagan et al. 1992, Hejl 1994). In order to fully understand the causal components of trends, results derived from a variety of censusing methods should be synthesized. Counts of migrating birds (Dunn 1992), although strongly affected by fluctuation in weather (Richardson 1990), have revealed long-term population trends corresponding to those indicated by the BBS (Hagan et al. 1992), especially after effects of weather and other variables have been statistically controlled (Hussell 1981, Hussell et al. 1992). Migration counts also sample breeding or wintering populations that are difficult to monitor, thus providing additional information for consideration (see Dunn 1992).

For this paper we examined trends of nocturnal migrants recorded during daily censuses on Southeast Farallon Island (SEFI), California, over the 25-year period 1968–1992. Simple and polynomial regression techniques were applied to totals of 70 species and ten bioregional groups, statistically adjusted for the effects of date, weather, lunar cycle and/or age proportion. We hope that our results, in combination with those of the BBS and other investigations presented in this volume, will be useful in defining western species and biogeographical areas in need of conservation attention.

STUDY SITE AND METHODS

Topographical features and methods of censusing landbirds at SEFI were described by DeSante and Ainley (1980), DeSante (1983), and Pyle and Henderson (1991). Each day Point Reyes Bird Observatory (PRBO) biologists thoroughly censused all landbird migrants and banded as many as possible. Numbers of arrivals of each species and identifiable subspecies (hereafter referred to as "species") were calculated at the end of each day using all available information from banding and observations of plumage variation. If similar unmarked landbirds were encountered on successive days we assumed that a minimum number of individuals were involved (see DeSante and Ainley 1980). Because landbirds concentrated in a few restricted, vegetated areas of this small and barren island, censuses were virtually complete and little biased by variation in observer skills (DeSante and Ainley 1980). Habitat at SEFI remained relatively unchanged during the 25-year period (Pyle and Henderson 1991).

We examined trends in nocturnal migrants (as defined by Pyle et al. 1993) separately in spring (1 March–30 June) and fall (1 August–30 November). Our sample consisted of 77,633 individuals (19,515 in spring and 58,118 in fall) of 197 nocturnal migrant species (see Appendix I). We examined trends in 70 species represented by at least 125 recorded individuals (5/yr); within each season we analyzed trends only if at least 63 individuals (2.5/yr) were recorded. In all cases there were fewer than six years in which zero individuals of a species or group were recorded.

We categorized species into one each of five breeding and five wintering biogeographical groups for analyses of trends (Appendix I). We defined breeding groups as species breeding primarily in areas of the: 1) Pacific coast (PC), 2) lowland interior West (IW) including the Great Basin, 3) montane West (MW), 4) northern taiga or tundra (TT), and 5) eastern deciduous forests (EF). Winter groups included those species found wintering primarily in areas of the: 1) coastal Pacific (CP), 2) the United States (US) away from the Pacific coast, 3) western Mexico (WM), 4) eastern Mexico, the West Indies, and Central America (CA), and 5) South America (SA). Species of which breeding or wintering ranges substantially overlapped two or more bioregions were assigned the group geographically closest to SEFI (in the order of above listings; see DeSante and Ainley 1980).

We investigated temporal trends using linear and polynomial regression on both "unadjusted" and "weather-adjusted" forms of the dependent variable, summed by season and year. Unadjusted totals simply represent the annual number of arrivals of each species or group recorded within each season. These totals were log-transformed in order to normalize the data and because this allowed us to model number of arrivals in a multiplicative fashion rather than with an additive model. In other words, with $\log(Y)$ as the dependent variable (where Y = number of arrivals of a species in a given season and year), a constant slope represents a constant *proportional* change in number of arrivals.

Weather-adjusted indices represent annual totals (log-transformed), statistically adjusted for environmental effects on arrival numbers. These indices were calculated using statistical models, described in Pyle et al. (1993), that estimated the effects of date, weather and lunar variables on log-transformed arrival totals. For analyses of the ten biogeographical groups, we calculated daily arrivals for the appropriate group, adjusting for date, weather and lunar variables (Computing Resource Center 1992). Daily weather-adjusted values were summed over the appropriate season, for each year. Sample sizes of individual species were insufficient to adequately adjust for weather directly. Instead, we adjusted arrival totals for each species using the weather/date/lunar model developed for all nocturnal migrants (Pyle et al. 1993), with each species standardized ($\bar{X} = 0$, $sd = 1$). For each species, daily weather-adjusted values were back-transformed and summed over the appropriate season, for each year. Similar weather-arrival patterns were generally found among regional and taxonomic subgroups (Pyle et al. 1993), helping to justify this approach.

Our weather-adjustment procedure for biogeographical groups is very similar to the approach used by Hussell (1981); for individual species, direct adjustment was not possible. We recognize that daily arrival totals of each species may be affected by date-adjustment using overall migrants, but consider this point to be of negligible influence on the annual totals. To ensure that long-term changes in weather have not affected landbird arrival at SEFI we examined year–weather interaction terms as additions to our weather models and found no significant interactions between year and those variables that affected arrival (see Pyle et al. 1993). Weather-adjustment of arrivals appeared to reduce variability of arrival totals (see Results), presumably due to reduction of extraneous weather effects, and so we use weather-adjusted indices in analyses presented herein.

For biogeographical groups we examined trends using two different approaches. In "pooled" analyses, we pooled individuals of all representative species (Appendix I) within a defined biogeographical group and then examined trends in annual totals (weather-adjusted). For the second approach we included only the 70 species with

adequate sample sizes. The unit of observation is the annual total of each species, and group classification is represented as a categorical variable (see Kleinbaum et al. 1988, chapter 14). This second, "grouped-species" approach allowed us to test for heterogeneity of trends (slopes) within a biogeographical group as well as to examine heterogeneity among groups. Furthermore, an individual species was simultaneously classified according to wintering and summering group, and thus the effect of winter classification could be tested while controlling for summer classification, and vice versa.

We present two different approaches to analyzing the effects of biogeographical groups mainly in order to examine the robustness of our results. Pooling data has its pitfalls (Breslow and Day 1980); however, it also has the advantage that data are used from all representative individuals of each group rather than just those of species with higher samples.

To investigate interannual variation in productivity and its effects on trends in fall we calculated "adult indices" based on annual "HY-proportions" [(first-year birds)/(adults + first-years)] of nocturnal migrants on SEFI. We assume that HY-proportion provides an index of productivity (Bibby et al. 1992), although we also recognize that this relationship may be partially confounded by age-specific migration strategies (see Pyle et al. 1993). HY-proportions were based on a sample of 20,036 landbirds captured in fall and aged first-year or adult using skull pneumatization, plumage and other criteria (Pyle et al. 1987). Samples were limited to the months August–October (August–September for kinglets and gnatcatchers), when degree of skull pneumatization is a reliable indicator of the two age classes. HY-proportions based on annual samples of <3 individuals were excluded from analyses, and analyses were performed only on groups (all) and species (N = 41) with usable proportions in at least 18 of the 25 years. We investigated variation in productivity by examining linear regression on HY-proportion (arcsine square-root transformed), weighted by sample size. Trends of adults in fall were also estimated using adult indices (summed by year: weather-adjusted indices × adult proportion), and these were compared with trends of all birds in fall; insufficient sample sizes of aged birds (through 1985) prevented estimations of adult trends in spring.

Significant curvilinear effects indicated that a trend was accelerating or decelerating, and/or that there has been significant fluctuations in arrival within our 25-year period. These were estimated by examining the statistical significance of the highest-order trends of quadratic and cubic polynomial regressions. All statistical analyses were performed using the STATA statistics program (Computing Resource Center 1992). Significance was assumed at the $P < 0.05$ level. "Marginally-significant" linear trends are indicated when $0.05 < P < 0.10$.

RESULTS

Nocturnal migrant totals decreased overall between 1968 and 1992 (Fig. 1), significantly in spring using weather-adjusted indices ($\beta = -0.044$, SE $= 0.011$, $P = 0.001$) but not in fall ($\beta = -0.019$, SE $= 0.013$, $P = 0.162$). These trends were also detected but less precisely (see Fig. 1) using unadjusted totals ($\beta = -0.031$, SE $= 0.013$, $P = 0.025$ in spring, $\beta = -0.016$, SE $= 0.013$, t $= -1.20$, $P = 0.243$ in fall). No significant trend in HY-proportion of all nocturnal migrants was detected; however, the linear decline of adults in fall was "marginally-significant" ($\beta = -0.033$, SE $= 0.017$, $P = 0.072$).

Trends in Individual Species

Significant linear trends in at least one season were detected using weather-adjusted indices in 30 of 70 species (Table 1). Twenty species showed declines (six in both seasons), nine species increased (one in both seasons), and one showed a decline in spring but an increase in fall. Eight additional mar-

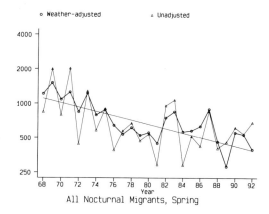

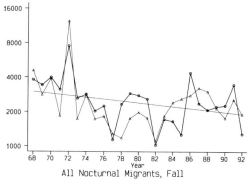

FIGURE 1. Trends in total number of nocturnal migrants recorded on SEFI, using unadjusted and weather-adjusted data, during spring and fall seasons, 1968–1992. For comparison, indices from both analysis types have been back-transformed, to reflect actual numbers of arrivals. Linear regression lines of best fit, derived from log-transformed weather-adjusted indices, are also presented; note the logarithmic scale.

ginally-significant trends were detected in one of the two seasons, five declining and three increasing. Including significant and marginally-significant results, more declines (20) than increases (2) were detected in spring, whereas in fall there were more increases (13) than declines (11). Two additional species that did not show trends within either season, Western Flycatcher and Ash-throated Flycatcher (see Appendix I for scientific names), showed significant declines when spring and fall totals were combined ($0.01 < P < 0.05$).

The use of weather-adjusted indices instead of unadjusted totals generally increased the resolution of trends. Of the 46

TABLE 1.   LINEAR AND CURVILINEAR TRENDS OF 70 SPECIES USING REGRESSION OF WEATHER-ADJUSTED INDICES; LINEAR TRENDS IN AGE PROPORTION ARE ALSO INCLUDED. SEE APPENDIX I FOR SCIENTIFIC NAMES AND SAMPLE SIZES OF EACH TAXON. SYMBOLS ARE AS FOLLOWS: nt = NOT TESTED DUE TO INSUFFICIENT SAMPLE SIZE WITHIN A SEASON; −ns, −ms, −, −−, −−− (OR WITH "+"), = INSIGNIFICANT (P > 0.1), MARGINALLY SIGNIFICANT (0.05 < P < 0.1), AND SIGNIFICANT (AT 0.010 < P < 0.050, 0.001 < P < 0.010, AND P < 0.001) DECLINES (OR INCREASES), RESPECTIVELY. NO DIRECTIONS ARE GIVEN FOR INSIGNIFICANT (ns) CURVILINEAR OR AGE PROPORTION TRENDS. ASTERISKS (*) IN FALL INDICATE THAT ANALYSES OF ADULTS (SEE TEXT) REVEALED DIFFERENT RESULTS THAN THOSE OF ALL INDIVIDUALS (INSIGNIFICANT VS. SIGNIFICANT AT P > 0.05, OR VICE VERSA). DIRECTIONS OF SLOPES OF ADULT TRENDS WERE THE SAME AS INDICATED FOR EACH OF THESE SPECIES EXCEPT ROSE-BREASTED GROSBEAK IN FALL, WHICH WAS SIGNIFICANTLY NEGATIVE. SIGNIFICANCE LEVELS OF HIGHEST-ORDER TERMS, LINEAR (LIN.), QUADRATIC (QUAD.) AND CUBIC (CUB.) ARE PRESENTED. SEE FIGURE 2 FOR ILLUSTRATIONS OF DIFFERENT LINEAR AND CURVILINEAR PATTERNS

Species	Spring			Fall			Age prop.
	Lin.	Quad.	Cub.	Lin.	Quad.	Cub.	
Band-tailed Pigeon	− −	ns	ns	−	ns	ns	nt
Mourning Dove	− − −	ns	ns	− −	ns	ns	nt
Red-shafted Flicker	nt	nt	nt	−ns	ns	ns	nt
Olive-sided Flycatcher	− − −	ns	ns	− −	ns	ns	nt
Western Wood-Pewee	− − −	ns	ns	−ns	ns	ns	ns
Willow Flycatcher	−ns	ns	ns	+ns	+ms	ns	ns
Hammond's Flycatcher	−ms	ns	−ms	nt	nt	nt	nt
Western Flycatcher	−ns	+	ns	−ns	ns	ns	−ms
Black Phoebe	nt	nt	nt	+ms	ns	ns	nt
Say's Phoebe	nt	nt	nt	−ns	ns	−	nt
Ash-throated Flycatcher	−ns	ns	ns	−ns	ns	ns	nt
Western Kingbird	nt	nt	nt	+ns	ns	ns	nt
Red-breasted Nuthatch	nt	nt	nt	−ns	ns	ns	nt
Brown Creeper	nt	nt	nt	−ns	ns	ns	nt
Rock Wren	nt	nt	nt	−ns	+ms	+ms	nt
House Wren	nt	nt	nt	+ns	+ms	ns	nt
Winter Wren	nt	nt	nt	−ns	ns	ns	nt
Golden-crowned Kinglet	+ns	−	ns	+ns	ns	ns	ns
Ruby-crowned Kinglet	−ns	ns	ns	+*	ns	ns	ns
Swainson's Thrush	− −	+ms	ns	+*	ns	ns	ns
Hermit Thrush	+ns	ns	ns	+ns	ns	ns	ns
American Robin	−ns	ns	ns	+ns	ns	ns	nt
Varied Thrush	−ns	ns	ns	+ +	ns	ns	nt
Northern Mockingbird	nt	nt	nt	−ns	ns	ns	nt
American Pipit	nt	nt	nt	+	ns	ns	nt
Cedar Waxwing	− −	ns	ns	+ns*	+ms	ns	−
Cassin's Solitary Vireo	nt	nt	nt	+ns	ns	−	ns
Warbling Vireo	+ns	+ +	ns	+ns*	ns	ns	− −
Tennessee Warbler	−ns	ns	ns	−ns	ns	ns	ns
Orange-crowned Warbler	−ms	+	ns	+ns	ns	ns	ns
Nashville Warbler	nt	nt	nt	+*	ns	ns	ns
Yellow Warbler	+ns	+	ns	+ns	+ms	ns	ns
Chestnut-sided Warbler	nt	nt	nt	−ns	ns	+ms	nt
Magnolia Warbler	+ns	−	ns	+	ns	ns	nt
Myrtle Warbler	+ns	ns	ns	+ +	ns	ns	ns
Audubon's Warbler	+ns	ns	ns	+ns	+ + +	ns	ns
Black-thr. Gray Warbler	nt	nt	nt	+ms	ns	ns	−ms
Townsend's Warbler	− −	ns	ns	+ns	ns	ns	ns
Hermit Warbler	−ns	ns	−ms	−ns	ns	ns	ns
Palm Warbler	nt	nt	nt	+*	ns	ns	ns
Blackpoll Warbler	nt	nt	nt	−ns	ns	ns	ns
American Redstart	+ns	ns	ns	−ns	ns	+	ns
Ovenbird	+ms	ns	ns	+ns*	ns	ns	− −
MacGillivray's Warbler	−	+ +	ns	−ns	ns	ns	ns
Common Yellowthroat	+ +	ns	ns	+ + +	ns	ns	ns
Wilson's Warbler	− −	+	ns	+ns	ns	ns	ns
Western Tanager	− −	+	ns	−ns	ns	ns	ns
Rose-breasted Grosbeak	+ns	ns	ns	+ns*	ns	+	+
Black-headed Grosbeak	−	ns	ns	− −	ns	−ms	ns

TABLE 1. CONTINUED

Species	Spring			Fall			Age prop.
	Lin.	Quad.	Cub.	Lin.	Quad.	Cub.	
Lazuli Bunting	−	+	ns	− −	ns	ns	−ms
Rufous-sided Towhee	nt	nt	nt	−ns	ns	ns	ns
Chipping Sparrow	− −	ns	ns	− −*	+ms	ns	−ms
Clay-colored Sparrow	nt	nt	ns	+++*	ns	ns	ns
Brewer's Sparrow	nt	nt	nt	+ns	ns	ns	nt
Vesper Sparrow	nt	nt	nt	+ns	ns	ns	nt
Lark Sparrow	nt	nt	nt	− − −	ns	ns	nt
Savannah Sparrow	−	ns	ns	−ns	ns	ns	ns
Fox Sparrow	−ns	ns	ns	−	ns	ns	ns
Lincoln's Sparrow	+ns	ns	− −	+ns	ns	ns	ns
White-throated Sparrow	nt	nt	nt	+ns	ns	ns	ns
Golden-crowned Sparrow	− −	+	ns	+ns	ns	ns	ns
White-crowned Sparrow	−ms	ns	ns	− −	−	ns	ns
Oregon Junco	−	ns	ns	−ns	ns	ns	ns
Lapland Longspur	nt	nt	nt	+ms	ns	ns	nt
Bobolink	nt	nt	nt	+ns	ns	ns	nt
Red-winged Blackbird	nt	nt	nt	+ns	+ms	−	nt
Western Meadowlark	−	ns	ns	−ms	ns	−ms	nt
Brewer's Blackbird	+ns	ns	+	+ns	++	ns	nt
Brown-headed Cowbird	−ns	ns	ns	+ns	ns	+ms	ns
Bullock's Oriole	−ns	ns	ns	−*	−	ns	ns

within-season trends detected with weather-adjusted indices, 39 were also detected, in the same direction, with analyses using unadjusted totals. Of these, 29 (74.3%) were more precise (as indicated by lower P values) using the weather-adjusted than the unadjusted analyses. For the remaining seven within-season trends (Orange-crowned Warbler, Lazuli Bunting, White-crowned Sparrow and Oregon Junco in spring; Bullock's Oriole in fall; and Western Meadowlark in both seasons), the unadjusted analyses indicated insignificant trends. By contrast only three fall trends (a significant increase in Rose-breasted Grosbeak and marginally-significant decreases in Blackpoll Warbler and Savannah Sparrow) were detected with the unadjusted totals but not with the weather-adjusted indices (see Table 1).

Trends in HY-proportion were detected in eight species (Table 1); seven proportions declined while only one increased. Trends in HY-proportion coincided with linear trends of migrants in four species (including Western Flycatcher; see above) and was opposite in two species (Table 1). Significance

levels of adult trends differed from those of all individuals in 11 species (Table 1). Significant non-linear trends within the 25-year period were detected in 21 species (Table 1). Fall trends of two species, White-crowned Sparrow and Bullock's Oriole, indicated accelerating population declines. Figure 2 illustrates four examples of linear and nonlinear trends among species.

A comparison of our linear trends with those detected with BBS data (Sauer and Droege 1992) indicated a significant degree of conformity between the two methods when directions of slopes were compared (Table 2). Of 42 within-season trends (in 24 species) detected using SEFI data, 32 had slopes in the same direction as detected by the BBS, including all 8 trends (6 species) that were at least marginally-significant according to both analyses. Results of both seasons at SEFI were consistent with those of the BBS, and the fall comparison was similar when adult trends at SEFI were used. Comparison of our results with those of Robbins et al. (1989) and Peterjohn and Sauer (1993) also indicated a high degree of consistency.

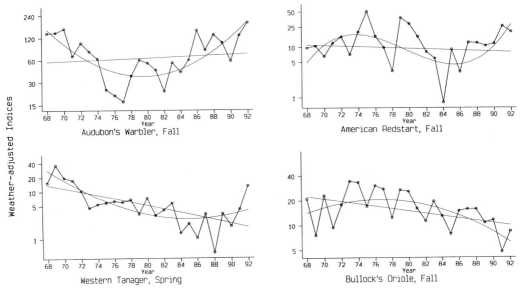

FIGURE 2. Four examples of within-season trends of species (see Table 1). Linear and, where significant, curvilinear regression lines based on regressions of log-transformed weather-adjusted indices are presented. Examples of trends include insignificant linear, positive quadratic (Audubon's Warbler); insignificant linear, positive cubic (American Redstart); decreasing linear, positive quadratic (Western Tanager), and decreasing linear, decreasing quadratic (Bullock's Oriole).

TRENDS IN BIOGEOGRAPHICAL GROUPS

Using pooled totals of all recorded species (Appendix I), significant linear trends were detected in at least one season in all ten breeding and wintering bioregional groups (Table 3, Figs. 3–4). Declines were indicated in seven groups in spring and one in fall, while increases occurred with three groups in fall. No significant trends in HY-proportions within groups were detected, and significant fall increases of two groups, eastern forest breeders and Central American winterers, became insignificant when adult indices were used (Table 3). Significant curvilinear trends were detected in six groups (Table 3). The most noteworthy trends occurred with Pacific coastal breeders, the only group to show consistent significant declines in both spring and fall. Trends in this group were also positively curvilinear in both seasons, indicating that most of the decline (within our 25-year period) occurred in the late 1960s and 1970s (see Figs. 3–4). Coastal

Pacific winterers also showed linear declines in both seasons, significant in spring and marginally-significant in fall.

The significant declines of Pacific coastal breeders were also evident using the analyses of grouped-species (Table 4), as were the positive curvilinear trends of this group (t = 3.97, P = 0.001 in spring; t = 3.82, P = 0.001 in fall estimated by quadratic year term). These analyses further indicated significant linear declines in interior western breeders and South American winterers in fall, not detected by pooled analyses. Most other group trends estimated with pooled indices were similarly detected with grouped-species analyses, particularly when number of representative species >10.

Tests for heterogeneity of slopes within bioregional groups indicated five within-season differences among breeding groups and eight among winter groups (Table 4). Differences tended to occur in the groups inhabiting more diverse geographic regions, e.g., most wintering areas and western

TABLE 2. COMPARISON OF SLOPE DIRECTIONS OF LONG-TERM TRENDS DETECTED ON SEFI WITH THOSE FOR NEOTROPICAL MIGRANTS DETECTED USING BREEDING BIRD SURVEY DATA FROM 1966 TO 1988 (SAUER AND DROEGE 1992), IN 24 SPECIES CONSIDERED IN BOTH ANALYSES. COMPARISONS ARE MADE WITH BBS RESULTS OF THE "WESTERN REGION" (P. 36), EXCEPT FOR THREE EASTERN SPECIES WHERE BBS ANALYSES WERE PERFORMED BY SAUER AND DROEGE ONLY ON POPULATIONS OF THEIR "EASTERN REGION" (PP. 32–33). MARGINALLY-SIGNIFICANT TRENDS (0.05 < P < 0.1) ARE CATEGORIZED AS SIGNIFICANT IN THIS TABLE. FREQUENCY TABLES DIRECTLY COMPARING SLOPE DIRECTIONS OF THE TWO METHODS INDICATED SIGNIFICANT CORRELATIONS IN BOTH SPRING (LIKELIHOOD RATIO (G) TEST; LRS = 6.49, P = 0.011) AND FALL (LRS = 8.46, P = 0.004). THE FALL COMPARISON WAS SIMILAR WHEN ADULT TRENDS AT SEFI WERE USED

Trend category using:		Direction of slopes			
		Spring		Fall	
SEFI data	BBS data	Same	Different	Same	Different
significant	significant	2	0	6	0
significant	insignificant	6	1	3	1
insignificant	significant	4	1	2	1
insignificant	insignificant	2	2	7	4
Total		14	4	18	6

breeding bioregions. When slopes of bioregional groups were compared, significant differences were found between breeding groups in both spring and fall, whereas slopes between wintering groups differed significantly in spring but not in fall (Table 5). This was true using both pooled and grouped-species data, and was also true after statistically controlling for trends in the opposite (breeding/wintering) class. In all four classification/season combinations, detected differences were greater after controlling for the opposite classification (Table 5).

DISCUSSION

Analyses of weather-adjusted arrival counts on SEFI revealed trends in total migrants, 30 of 70 species, and all ten biogeographical groups. DeSante and George (1994) examine in more detail possible explanations for these and other trends in western landbirds. Here we examine the validity of our results and interpret the relative strengths of inferred trends.

The separation of SEFI data into seasonal periods provides a measure with which to assess the relative importance of detected trends. Including both significant and "marginally-significant" (0.05 < P < 0.10) results, concordant linear trends in both seasons were detected in nine species (Table 1) and four bioregional groups (according to analyses of pooled totals and grouped-species, combined; Tables 3, 5). This independently-derived seasonal agreement suggests that true population changes may be occurring in these species and groups. Trends in one but not both seasons, detected in 12 species and six bioregional groups, are

TABLE 3. LINEAR AND CURVILINEAR TRENDS OF BIOGEOGRAPHICAL GROUPS AT SEFI USING POOLED, WEATHER-ADJUSTED INDICES; TRENDS IN AGE-PROPORTION ARE ALSO GIVEN. SEE APPENDIX 1 FOR GROUP CATEGORIZATION. SYMBOLS ARE AS DEFINED IN TABLE 1

Group	Spring			Fall			Age prop.
	Linear	Quadratic	Cubic	Lin.	Quad.	Cub.	
Breeding groups							
Pacific Coastal	− − −	+ +	ns	− −	+ +	ns	ns
Interior Western	−	ns	−	+ns	ns	ns	ns
Montane Western	−	ns	ns	−ns	ns	ns	ns
Taiga/Tundra	−	ns	ns	−ns	+ms	ns	ns
Eastern Forest	+ns	−	ns	+*	ns	ns	ns
Wintering groups							
Coastal Pacific	−	ns	ns	−ms	ns	ns	ns
United States	−ns	ns	ns	+	ns	+	ns
Western Mexico	−	+ +	−ms	+ns	ns	ns	ns
Central America	−ns	ns	ns	+*	−ms	ns	ns
South America	− −	ns	ns	+ns	−ms	ns	ns

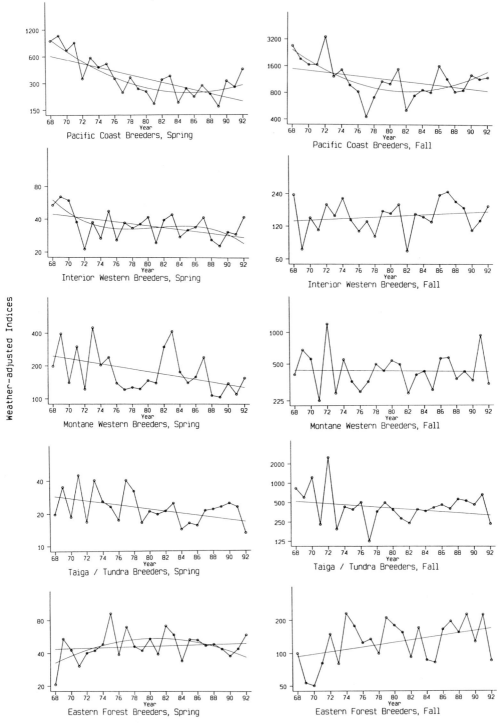

FIGURE 3. Significant trends in arrival of biogeographical breeding groups at SEFI, according to pooled, weather-adjusted totals. See Table 3 for significance values. Linear and, where significant, curvilinear regression lines based on regressions of log-transformed totals are presented.

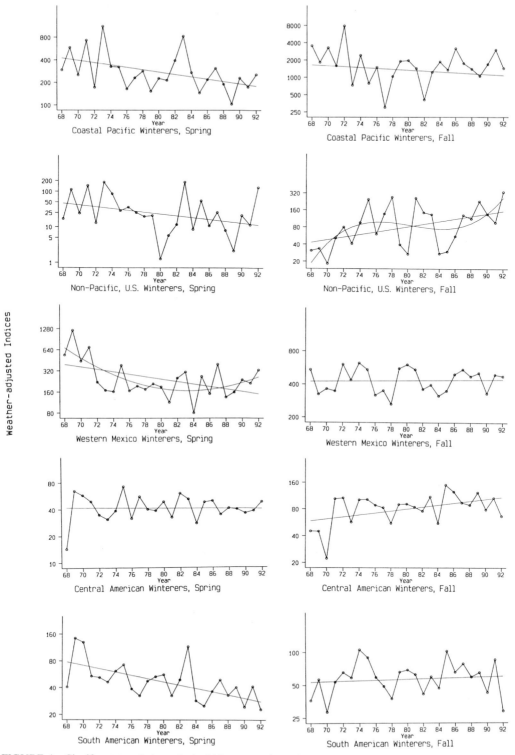

FIGURE 4. Significant trends in arrival of biogeographical wintering groups at SEFI, according to pooled, weather-adjusted totals. See Table 3 for significance values. Linear and, where significant, curvilinear regression lines based on regressions of log-transformed totals are presented.

TABLE 4. Sample Sizes of Species, Linear Trends, and Heterogeneity of Slopes (within Groups), in Breeding and Wintering Groups Using Analyses of Common Slopes on Weather-adjusted Indices. Linear Trends of Species are Summarized, and Indicated Positive and Negative Trends Include both Significant and Marginally-significant Results (Table 1)

Group	# of species			Linear trend		Within-group differences	
	Total	Positive	Negative	t	P	F	P
Spring							
Breeding							
Pacific Coast	25	1	11	−6.42	0.000	2.50	0.000
Interior West	6	0	2	−3.31	0.001	1.93	0.031
Montane West	13	0	6	−3.88	0.000	1.62	0.158
Taiga/Tundra	2	0	1	−1.49	0.141	3.46	0.003
Eastern Forest	6	1	0	0.48	0.635	0.83	0.532
Wintering							
Coastal Pacific	22	1	9	−4.28	0.000	4.12	0.048
United States	2	0	0	0.50	0.348	1.42	0.110
West Mexico	20	0	8	−5.00	0.000	3.03	0.001
Central America	6	1	1	−1.13	0.261	5.87	0.001
South America	2	0	2	−5.65	0.000	2.19	0.002
Fall							
Breeding							
Pacific Coast	29	4	7	−2.38	0.018	2.10	0.001
Interior West	12	0	3	−2.46	0.014	1.28	0.228
Montane West	13	3	1	0.63	0.531	2.95	0.001
Taiga/Tundra	5	3	0	1.48	0.143	0.66	0.619
Eastern Forest	10	3	0	2.84	0.005	1.33	0.246
Wintering							
Coastal Pacific	30	6	5	−1.94	0.053	7.50	0.000
United States	6	2	1	0.97	0.331	2.09	0.003
West Mexico	22	3	4	−0.13	0.898	1.84	0.095
Central America	7	2	0	1.45	0.149	3.01	0.003
South America	4	0	1	−2.13	0.036	1.51	0.045

more equivocal. For Swainson's Thrush we detected a significant decline in spring but a significant increase in fall. This may reflect occurrence patterns of different subpopulations on SEFI: arrival of western subpopulations may be declining in spring whereas more eastern subpopulations may be increasing in fall (see below and Marshall 1988).

The significant degree of consistency between SEFI and BBS results for populations in the west (Table 2) may provide validation of both censusing procedures, and suggests that migration counts, in general, can be used to detect population changes. Some of the species where opposite trends were indicated by the two analyses (e.g., Western Flycatcher, Swainson's Thrush, Wilson's

TABLE 5. Differences between Trends among Groups within Bioregional Classifications Using Linear Model Analyses on Pooled and Species-group Totals (See Text). Adjusted Species-group Figures Refer to Differences among Groups of Each Classification after Controlling for the Opposite (Breeding/Wintering) Classification

Bioregional class	Season	Pooled totals		Common slopes			
				Unadjusted		Adjusted	
		F	P	F	P	F	P
Breeding	Spring	3.92	0.005	2.84	0.023	3.64	0.006
Wintering	Spring	3.11	0.030	3.21	0.012	4.01	0.003
Breeding	Fall	2.48	0.048	5.00	0.001	5.32	0.000
Wintering	Fall	1.39	0.250	1.65	0.160	1.97	0.096

Warbler) have distinct subpopulations which may be unequally represented in the two analyses (see below). A more rigorous statistical comparison of SEFI and BBS data, partitioned taxonomically and geographically, is planned.

It is tempting to think that the greater and more consistent declines detected in spring than in fall reflected changes on the winter rather than the breeding grounds; however, declines in both seasons would be expected from changes at either location. The high proportion of first-year birds recorded in fall on SEFI (DeSante 1983) could be obscuring true population trends based on fall data, although fall and spring results were both consistent with those using BBS data (Table 2). Whether or not population changes were more accurately reflected by adult trends in fall is unclear at this time. Our data suggest that declines in Western Flycatcher, Cedar Waxwing, Lazuli Bunting, and Chipping Sparrow may be caused by decreased productivity on the breeding grounds, as indicated by concordant declines in HY-proportion. A significant increase in HY-proportion of Rose-breasted Grosbeak, coupled with a significant decline in the fall adult trend may indicate a population decrease due to changes on the winter grounds.

Our analyses of bioregional groups suggest that detected trends resulted from changes on both the breeding and the wintering grounds (Table 4). That slopes of group trends differed significantly from each other in three of the four classification/season categories (Table 5) implies that true differences occurred in the trends of populations among these groups. Differences were more evident between breeding groups (significant in both seasons) than wintering groups (significant in spring but not fall), even after controlling for trends in the opposite classification. This suggests that population trends detected at SEFI are caused more by events on breeding grounds than events on winter grounds, although trends due to changes in both areas are indicated.

The increases of eastern forest breeders and Central American winterers detected on SEFI are interesting, especially in light of the accelerating decreases in these Neotropical winterers detected on their breeding grounds by the BBS (Sauer and Droege 1992, Peterjohn and Sauer 1993, but see Hutto 1988). These combined results and the fact that fall adult trends in these groups were insignificant using SEFI data (Table 3) suggest that the proportion of vagrant individuals may be increasing among first-year birds of eastern forest species, as first suggested by DeSante (1983, see also DeSante and George 1994).

Clearly the strongest and most significant group trends indicated by SEFI data were the long-term decelerating declines in populations breeding (and to a lesser extent wintering) on the Pacific coast. Most of the declines in species of these groups occurred early within our 25-year period but populations have not recovered (see Fig. 3); similar decelerating trends were indicated with BBS data (Sauer and Droege 1992, DeSante and George 1994). Habitat loss due to coastal development and logging, particularly heavy in the 1960s and 1970s (see U.S. Forest Service 1988, Chapter 3), may be the primary cause of declines on SEFI in both breeding and wintering Pacific coast groups; unlike in dryer western bioregions, fire exclusion during this period may not have compensated for habitat loss on the wetter Pacific Slope (see Hejl 1994). Alternatively, the declines in Pacific coastal species may be representative of declines across North America, only appearing to be more significant on SEFI because of higher samples of these species.

The most consistent population declines in western species, as indicated by SEFI and BBS data, occurred in Band-tailed Pigeon, Mourning Dove, Olive-sided Flycatcher (see also Robbins et al. 1986, Marshall 1988), Western Wood-Pewee, Western Tanager, Black-headed Grosbeak, Lazuli Bunting, Chipping Sparrow, White-crowned Sparrow and Bullock's Oriole. Increased attention of these populations may be warranted.

On a brighter note, western populations of Nashville Warblers and Common Yellowthroats appear to be increasing in western North America.

ACKNOWLEDGMENTS

The research program on Southeast Farallon Island, part of the Farallon National Wildlife Refuge, is conducted with the cooperation and support of the U.S. Fish and Wildlife Service. The U.S. Coast Guard and the Farallon Patrol also provided logistic support. Farallon weather data for the years 1968–1970, used in weather-adjusted models, were provided by the National Climate Data Center, Asheville, North Carolina; subsequent data were collected by PRBO. The monitoring program for migrant birds has been carried out by numerous PRBO biologists and interns. We again acknowledge those listed in DeSante and Ainley (1980) and Pyle and Henderson (1991); we also thank L. Gilbert and M. Hart for help computerizing 1992 data for inclusion in these analyses. We especially acknowledge the long-term dedication of R. Philip Henderson to the landbird program on SEFI. The manuscript benefitted from comments by D. G. Ainley, E. H. Dunn, D. J. T. Hussell, C. Moore, and W. J. Sydeman. This is PRBO contribution #577.

LITERATURE CITED

ASKINS, R. A., J. F. LYNCH, AND R. GREENBERG. 1990. Population declines in migratory birds in eastern North America. Current Ornithology 7:1–57.

BIBBY, C. J., N. D. BURGESS, AND D. A. HILL. 1992. Bird census techniques. Academic Press, London.

BRESLOW, N. E., AND N. E. DAY. 1980. Statistical methods in cancer research. Vol. 1. The analysis of case-control studies. International Agency for Research on Cancer, Lyon, France.

COMPUTING RESOURCE CENTER. 1992. Stata reference manual: release 3. 5th ed. Santa Monica, CA.

DESANTE, D. F. 1983. Annual variability in the abundance of migrant landbirds on Southeast Farallon Island, California. Auk 100:826–852.

DESANTE, D. F., AND D. G. AINLEY. 1980. The avifauna of the South Farallon Islands, California. Studies in Avian Biology 4.

DESANTE, D. F., AND T. L. GEORGE. 1994. Population trends in the landbirds of Western North America. Pp. 173–190 in J. R. Jehl, Jr. and N. K. Johnson (eds.), A century of avifaunal change in western North America. Studies in Avian Biology No. 15.

DUNN, E. H. 1992. Using migration counts to monitor Canadian landbird populations: background and current status. Canadian Wildlife Service Report, Long Point Bird Observatory. 33 pp.

HAGAN, J. M., III, AND D. W. JOHNSTON (eds.). 1992. Ecology and conservation of neotropical migrant landbirds. Smithsonian Institution Press, Washington, DC.

HAGAN, J. M., III, T. L. LLOYD-EVANS, J. L. ATWOOD, AND D. S. WOOD. 1992. Long-term changes in migratory landbirds in the northeastern United States: evidence from migration capture data. Pp. 115–130 in J. M. Hagan, III and D. W. Johnston (eds.), Ecol-

ogy and conservation of neotropical migrant landbirds. Smithsonian Institution Press, Washington, DC.

HEJL, S. J. 1994. Human-induced changes in bird populations in coniferous forests in Western North America during the past 100 years. Pp. 232–246 in J. R. Jehl, Jr. and N. K. Johnson (eds.), A century of avifaunal change in western North America. Studies in Avian Biology No. 15.

HILL, N. P., AND J. M. HAGAN, III. 1991. Population trends of some northeastern North American landbirds: a half-century of data. Wilson Bulletin 103: 165–182.

HOLMES, R. T., AND T. W. SHERRY. 1988. Assessing population trends of New Hampshire forest birds: local vs. regional patterns. Auk 105:756–768.

HUSSELL, J. T. 1981. The use of migration counts for detecting population levels. Pp. 92–102 in C. J. Ralph and M. J. Scott (eds.), Estimating numbers of terrestrial birds. Studies in Avian Biology 6.

HUSSELL, J. T., M. H. MATHER, AND P. H. SINCLAIR. 1992. Trends in numbers of tropical- and temperate-wintering migrant landbirds in migration at Long Point, Ontario, 1961–1988. Pp. 101–114 in J. M. Hagan, III and D. W. Johnston (eds.), Ecology and conservation of neotropical migrant landbirds. Smithsonian Institution Press, Washington, DC.

HUTTO, R. L. 1988. Is tropical deforestation responsible for the reported declines in neotropical migrant populations? American Birds 42:375–379.

JAMES, F. C., D. A. WIEDENFELD, AND C. A. MCCOULLOCH. 1992. Trends in breeding populations of warblers: declines in the southern highlands and increases in the lowlands. Pp. 43–56 in J. M. Hagan III and D. W. Johnston (eds.), Ecology and conservation of neotropical migrant landbirds. Smithsonian Institution Press, Washington, DC.

KLEINBAUM, D. G., L. L. KUPPER, AND K. E. MULLER. 1988. Applied regression analysis and other multivariable methods. PWS-Kent Publ. Co., Boston, MA.

MARSHALL, J. T. 1988. Birds lost from a giant sequoia forest during fifty years. Condor 90:359–372.

PETERJOHN, B. G., AND J. R. SAUER. 1993. North American Breeding Bird Survey annual summary. Bird Populations 1:1–15.

PYLE, P., AND R. P. HENDERSON. 1991. The birds of Southeast Farallon Island: occurrence and seasonal distribution of migratory species. Western Birds 22: 41–84.

PYLE, P., S. N. G. HOWELL, R. P. YUNICK, AND D. F. DESANTE. 1987. Identification guide to North American passerines. Slate Creek Press, Bolinas, CA.

PYLE, P., N. NUR, R. P. HENDERSON, AND D. F. DESANTE. 1993. The effects of weather and lunar cycle on nocturnal migration of landbirds at Southeast Farallon Island, California. Condor 95:343–361.

RICHARDSON, W. J. 1990. Timing of bird migration in relation to weather: updated review. Pp. 78–101 in E. Gwinner (ed.), Bird migration: physiology and ecophysiology. Springer-Verlag, New York, NY.

ROBBINS, C. S., D. BYSTRAK, AND P. H. GEISSLER. 1986. The breeding bird survey: its first fifteen years, 1965–1979. U.S. Fish and Wildlife Service Resource Publication 157.

ROBBINS, C. S., J. R. SAUER, R. S. GREENBERG, AND S. DROEGE. 1989. Population declines in North American birds that migrate to the Neotropics. Proceedings of the National Academy of Science 86: 7658–7662.

SAUER, J. R., AND S. DROEGE. 1992. Geographic patterns in population trends of neotropical migrants in North America. Pp. 26–42 *in* J. M. Hagan, III and D. W. Johnston (eds.), Ecology and conservation of neotropical migrant landbirds. Smithsonian Institution Press, Washington, DC.

TERBORGH, J. 1989. Where have all the birds gone? Princeton University Press, Princeton, NJ.

U.S. FOREST SERVICE. 1988. Final supplement to the Environmental Impact Statement to the Pacific Northwest Regional Guide. Vol. 1. Spotted Owl guidelines. USDA GPO 1988-0-571-057/80700.

WILCOVE, D. S., AND S. K. ROBINSON. 1990. The impact of forest fragmentation in the temperate zone. Pp. 319–331 *in* A. Keast (ed.), Biogeography and ecology of forest bird communities. SPB Academic Publishers, The Hague, The Netherlands.

APPENDIX I. NOCTURNAL MIGRANT "SPECIES" USED IN ANALYSES OF TRENDS, INCLUDING SCIENTIFIC NAME, SPRING AND FALL SAMPLE SIZES, AND BREEDING AND WINTERING BIOGEOGRAPHICAL GROUPINGS. GROUP CODES ARE: BREEDING, PC = PACIFIC COASTAL, IW = INTERIOR WESTERN, MW = MONTANE WESTERN, TT = TAIGA/TUNDRA, EF = EASTERN FOREST; WINTERING, CP = COASTAL PACIFIC, US = UNITED STATES (AWAY FROM THE PACIFIC COAST), WM = WESTERN MEXICO, CA = EASTERN MEXICO AND CENTRAL AMERICA, SA = SOUTH AMERICA. A SMALL NUMBER OF RARER SPECIES WERE NOT CATEGORIZED, AS WERE HYBRIDS OF TAXA OF PARENT SPECIES FROM DIFFERENT BIOREGIONS

Taxon	Spring total	Fall total	Breeding group	Wintering group
Band-tailed Pigeon (*Columba fasciata*)	130	170	PC	CP
White-winged Dove (*Zenaida asiatica*)	0	13		WM
Mourning Dove (*Z. macroura*)	172	601	PC	CP
Black-billed Cuckoo (*Coccyzus erythropthalmus*)	0	2	EF	SA
Yellow-billed Cuckoo (*C. americanus*)	5	9	EF	SA
Lesser Nighthawk (*Chordeiles acutipennis*)	35	5	IW	WM
Common Nighthawk (*C. minor*)	1	2	IW	SA
Common Poorwill (*Phalaenoptilus nuttallii*)	0	7	IW	WM
Lewis' Woodpecker (*Melanerpes lewis*)	4	3	IW	US
Acorn Woodpecker (*M. formicivorus*)	0	8	PC	CP
Yellow-bellied Sapsucker (*Sphyrapicus varius*)	0	1	EF	US
Red-naped Sapsucker (*S. nuchalis*)	1	3	MW	US
Red-breasted Sapsucker (*S. ruber*)	2	19	IW	CP
Yellow-shafted Flicker (*Colaptes a. auritus*)	7	55	EF	US
Intergrade Flicker (*C. a. cafer × auritus*)	5	44		US
Red-shafted Flicker (*C. a. cafer*)	62	260	PC	CP
Olive-sided Flycatcher (*Contopus borealis*)	103	69	PC	SA
Western Wood-Pewee (*C. sordidulus*)	1081	450	PC	SA
Eastern Wood-Pewee (*C. virens*)	1	0	EF	SA
Willow Flycatcher (*Empidonax traillii*)	120	221	MW	WM
Yellow-bellied Flycatcher (*E. flaviventris*)	0	5	EF	CA
Least Flycatcher (*E. minimus*)	6	89	EF	CA
Hammond's Flycatcher (*E. hammondii*)	113	32	MW	WM
Dusky Flycatcher (*E. oberholseri*)	77	20	MW	WM
Gray Flycatcher (*E. wrightii*)	82	14	IW	WM
Western Flycatcher (*E. difficilis/occidentalis*)	256	700	PC	WM
Black Phoebe (*Sayornis nigricans*)	13	233	PC	CP
Eastern Phoebe (*S. phoebe*)	4	14	EF	US
Say's Phoebe (*S. saya*)	10	188	IW	US
Ash-throated Flycatcher (*Myiarchus cinerascens*)	66	116	IW	WM
Great Crested Flycatcher (*M. crinitus*)	0	9	EF	CA
Brown-crested Flycatcher (*M. tyrannulus*)	0	1	IW	WM
Tropical Kingbird (*Tyrannus melancholicus*)	1	11		WM
Cassin's Kingbird (*T. vociferans*)	1	1	IW	WM
Western Kingbird (*T. verticalis*)	61	95	IW	CA
Eastern Kingbird (*T. tyrannus*)	12	25	IW	SA
Scissor-tailed Flycatcher (*T. forficatus*)	1	1	IW	CA
Horned Lark (*Eremophila alpestris*)	10	97	IW	US
Red-breasted Nuthatch (*Sitta canadensis*)	32	909	MW	CP

APPENDIX I. CONTINUED

Taxon	Spring total	Fall total	Breeding group	Wintering group
White-breasted Nuthatch (*S. carolinensis*)	1	1	IW	US
Pygmy Nuthatch (*S. pygmaea*)	0	1	PC	CP
Brown Creeper (*Certhia americana*)	2	125	PC	CP
Rock Wren (*Salpinctes obsoletus*)	23	195	IW	CP
Bewick's Wren (*Thryomanes bewickii*)	0	3	PC	CP
House Wren (*Troglodytes aedon*)	36	116	IW	WM
Winter Wren (*T. troglodytes*)	18	120	PC	CP
Marsh Wren (*Cistothorus palustris*)	3	21	PC	CP
Dusky Warbler (*Phylloscopus fuscatus*)	0	2	TT	
Golden-crowned Kinglet (*Regulus satrapa*)	80	721	PC	CP
Ruby-crowned Kinglet (*R. calendula*)	1344	2290	MW	CP
Blue-gray Gnatcatcher (*Polioptila caerulea*)	7	14	IW	WM
Red-flanked Bluetail (*Tarsiger cyanurus*)	0	1	TT	
Northern Wheatear (*Oenanthe oenanthe*)	1	2	TT	CP
Western Bluebird (*Sialia mexicana*)	1	1	PC	US
Mountain Bluebird (*S. currucoides*)	4	10	MW	US
Townsend's Solitaire (*Myadestes townsendi*)	3	16	MW	SA
Veery (*Catharus fuscescens*)	1	2	EF	SA
Gray-cheeked Thrush (*C. minimus*)	2	8	TT	CA
Swainson's Thrush (*C. ustulatus*)	182	1160	PC	
Hermit Thrush (*C. guttatus*)	431	1746	PC	CP
American Robin (*Turdus migratorius*)	237	443	PC	CP
Varied Thrush (*Ixoreus naevius*)	132	324	PC	CP
Gray Catbird (*Dumetella carolinensis*)	3	4	EF	CA
Northern Mockingbird (*Mimus polyglottos*)	48	123	IW	CP
Sage Thrasher (*Oreoscoptes montanus*)	10	41	IW	US
Brown Thrasher (*Toxostoma rufum*)	6	10	EF	US
Bendire's Thrasher (*T. bendirei*)	3	2		WM
Yellow Wagtail (*Motacilla flava*)	0	1	TT	
White/Black-backed Wagtail (*M. alba/lugens*)	0	1	TT	CP
Red-throated Pipit (*Anthus cervinus*)	0	21	TT	
American Pipit (*A. rubescens*)	22	3077	TT	CP
Sprague's Pipit (*A. spragueii*)	0	3	IW	WM
Bohemian Waxwing (*Bombycilla garrulus*)	0	1	TT	US
Cedar Waxwing (*B. cedrorum*)	92	837	IW	CP
Phainopepla (*Phainopepla nitens*)	0	3	IW	US
Brown Shrike (*Lanius cristatus*)	0	1	TT	
Northern Shrike (*L. excubitor*)	0	1	TT	US
Loggerhead Shrike (*L. ludovicianus*)	5	6	IW	US
White-eyed Vireo (*Vireo griseus*)	1	1	EF	CA
Eastern Solitary Vireo (*V. s. solitarius*)	0	26	EF	CA
Plumbeous Solitary Vireo (*V. s. plumbeous*)	0	1	IW	WM
Cassin's Solitary Vireo (*V. s. cassinii*)	56	102	MW	WM
Yellow-throated Vireo (*V. flavifrons*)	1	0	EF	CA
Hutton's Vireo (*V. huttoni*)	12	35	PC	CP
Warbling Vireo (*V. gilvus*)	162	468	PC	WM
Philadelphia Vireo (*V. philadelphicus*)	2	8	EF	CA
Red-eyed Vireo (*V. olivaceus*)	47	26	EF	SA
Yellow-green Vireo (*V. flavoviridis*)	0	4		SA
Blue-winged Warbler (*Vermivora pinus*)	1	0	EF	CA
Brewster's Warbler (*V. pinus* × *chrysoptera*)	1	0	EF	CA
Golden-winged Warbler (*V. chrysoptera*)	2	2	EF	CA
Tennessee Warbler (*V. peregrina*)	145	159	EF	CA
Orange-crowned Warbler (*V. celata*)	1158	527	PC	WM
Nashville Warbler (*V. ruficapilla*)	57	215	MW	WM
Virginia's Warbler (*V. virginiae*)	6	26	IW	WM
Lucy's Warbler (*V. luciae*)	0	6		WM
Northern Parula (*Parula americana*)	31	7	EF	CA
Yellow Warbler (*Dendroica petechia*)	403	1444	PC	WM
Chestnut-sided Warbler (*D. pensylvanica*)	36	136	EF	CA

APPENDIX I. CONTINUED

Taxon	Spring total	Fall total	Breeding group	Wintering group
Magnolia Warbler (*D. magnolia*)	110	131	EF	CA
Cape May Warbler (*D. tigrina*)	29	26	EF	CA
Black-throated Blue Warbler (*D. caerulescens*)	0	78	EF	CA
Myrtle Warbler (*D. c. coronata*)	215	1551	TT	CP
Audubon's × Myrtle Warbler	12	62		CP
Audubon's Warbler (*D. c. auduboni*)	1236	1488	MW	CP
Black-throated Gray Warbler (*D. nigrescens*)	51	319	MW	WM
Townsend's Warbler (*D. townsendi*)	828	895	MW	CP
Townsend's × Hermit Warbler	1	2		WM
Hermit Warbler (*D. occidentalis*)	68	223	PC	WM
Black-throated Green Warbler (*D. virens*)	19	18	EF	CA
Golden-cheeked Warbler (*D. chrysoparia*)	0	1	IW	WM
Blackburnian Warbler (*D. fusca*)	5	64	EF	SA
Yellow-throated Warbler (*D. dominica*)	2	2	EF	US
Pine Warbler (*D. pinus*)	0	4	EF	US
Prairie Warbler (*D. discolor*)	0	38	EF	CA
Palm Warbler (*D. palmarum*)	31	883	EF	US
Bay-breasted Warbler (*D. castanea*)	29	27	EF	SA
Blackpoll Warbler (*D. striata*)	42	552	TT	SA
Cerulean Warbler (*D. cerulea*)	0	1	EF	SA
Black-and-white Warbler (*Mniotilta varia*)	52	47	EF	WM
American Redstart (*Setophaga ruticilla*)	85	367	EF	WM
Prothonotary Warbler (*Protonotaria citrea*)	0	2	EF	CA
Worm-eating Warbler (*Helmitheros vermivorus*)	6	2	EF	CA
Ovenbird (*Seiurus aurocapillus*)	172	123	EF	CA
Northern Waterthrush (*S. novaboracensis*)	6	68	TT	WM
Louisiana Waterthrush (*S. motacilla*)	1	0	EF	CA
Kentucky Warbler (*Oporornis formosus*)	17	3	EF	CA
Connecticut Warbler (*O. agilis*)	3	33	EF	SA
Mourning Warbler (*O. philadelphia*)	6	36	EF	SA
MacGillivray's Warbler (*O. tolmiei*)	84	288	MW	WM
Common Yellowthroat (*Geothlypis trichas*)	483	549	PC	CP
Hooded Warbler (*Wilsonia citrina*)	23	5	EF	CA
Wilson's Warbler (*W. pusilla*)	3012	969	PC	WM
Canada Warbler (*W. canadensis*)	11	28	EF	SA
Red-faced Warbler (*Cardellina rubrifrons*)	0	1	MW	WM
Yellow-breasted Chat (*Icteria virens*)	30	48	IW	WM
Hepatic Tanager (*Piranga flava*)	1	1	MW	WM
Summer Tanager (*P. rubra*)	13	8	EF	CA
Scarlet Tanager (*P. olivacea*)	1	5	EF	SA
Western Tanager (*P. ludoviciana*)	186	398	MW	WM
Rose-breasted Grosbeak (*Pheucticus ludovicianus*)	155	87	EF	CA
Rose-br. × Black-h. Grosbeak	1	3		
Black-headed Grosbeak (*P. melanocephalus*)	126	141	PC	WM
Blue Grosbeak (*Guiraca caerulea*)	10	50	IW	WM
Lazuli Bunting (*Passerina amoena*)	72	2442	IW	WM
Indigo Bunting (*P. cyanea*)	84	33	EF	CA
Painted Bunting (*P. ciris*)	0	7	IW	WM
Dickcissel (*Spiza americana*)	13	14	EF	SA
Green-tailed Towhee (*Pipilo chlorurus*)	8	21	MW	WM
Rufous-sided Towhee (*P. erythrophthalmus*)	30	455	PC	CP
Cassin's Sparrow (*Aimophila cassinii*)	3	6		WM
American Tree Sparrow (*Spizella arborea*)	16	49	TT	US
Chipping Sparrow (*S. passerina*)	274	1372	MW	WM
Chipping × Clay-c. Sparrow	0	1		WM
Chipping × Brewer's Sparrow	0	1		WM
Clay-colored Sparrow (*S. pallida*)	39	342	EF	WM
Brewer's Sparrow (*S. breweri*)	36	112	IW	WM
Field Sparrow (*S. pusilla*)	1	0	EF	US
Black-chinned Sparrow (*S. atrogularis*)	0	1	IW	WM

APPENDIX I. CONTINUED

Taxon	Spring total	Fall total	Breeding group	Wintering group
Vesper Sparrow (*Pooecetes gramineus*)	24	238	IW	US
Lark Sparrow (*Chondestes grammacus*)	29	240	IW	US
Sage Sparrow (*Amphispiza belli*)	5	3	IW	US
Black-throated Sparrow (*A. bilineata*)	7	17	IW	US
Lark Bunting (*Calamospiza melanocorys*)	1	58	IW	WM
Savannah Sparrow (*Passerculus sandwichensis*)	209	7068	PC	CP
Baird's Sparrow (*Ammodramus bairdii*)	0	2		WM
Grasshopper Sparrow (*A. savannarum*)	25	84	PC	WM
LeConte's Sparrow (*A. leconteii*)	0	7	EF	US
Sharp-tailed Sparrow (*A. caudacutus*)	0	1	IW	US
Fox Sparrow (*Passerella iliaca*)	98	1829	PC	CP
Song Sparrow (*Melospiza melodia*)	16	50	PC	CP
Lincoln's Sparrow (*M. lincolnii*)	495	1484	MW	WM
Swamp Sparrow (*M. georgiana*)	6	60	EF	US
White-throated Sparrow (*Z. albicollis*)	7	213	EF	US
Golden-crowned Sparrow (*Z. atricapilla*)	460	9185	TT	CP
Golden-c. × White-c. Sparrow	0	2		CP
White-crowned Sparrow (*Z. leucophrys*)	901	6771	PC	CP
Harris' Sparrow (*Z. querula*)	2	17	EF	US
Slate-colored Junco (*Junco h. hyemalis*)	35	66	TT	US
Oregon Junco (*J. h. oreganus*)	1236	3143	MW	CP
Lapland Longspur (*Calcarius lapponicus*)	5	204	TT	US
Chestnut-collared Longspur (*C. ornatus*)	2	47		US
Snow Bunting (*Plectophenax nivalis*)	0	18	TT	US
Bobolink (*Dolichonyx oryzivorus*)	10	149	EF	SA
Red-winged Blackbird (*Agelaius phoeniceus*)	37	554	PC	CP
Tricolored Blackbird (*A. tricolor*)	6	62	IW	CP
Western Meadowlark (*Sturna neglecta*)	58	1935	PC	CP
Yellow-headed Blackbird (*X. xanthocephalus*)	24	56	IW	WM
Rusty Blackbird (*Euphagus carolinus*)	3	8	TT	US
Brewer's Blackbird (*E. cyanocephalus*)	170	781	PC	CP
Brown-headed Cowbird (*Molothrus ater*)	477	1825	PC	US
Orchard Oriole (*Icterus spurius*)	1	36	EF	CA
Hooded Oriole (*I. cucullatus*)	1	12	IW	WM
Bullock's Oriole (*I. bullockii*)	124	434	IW	WM
Baltimore Oriole (*I. g. galbula*)	10	23	EF	CA
Intergrade Northern Oriole	1	3		
Scott's Oriole (*I. parisorum*)	0	1	IW	WM

Studies in Avian Biology No. 15:75–90, 1994.

AVIFAUNAL CHANGE ON CALIFORNIA'S COASTAL ISLANDS

DENNIS M. POWER

Abstract. I summarize the changes in status of breeding birds on California's Farallones and Channel Islands over the last 100 years. Several species have expanded their ranges, either colonizing from other islands or from the mainland. Other species, especially those with small populations, ceased to exist on certain islands. In many case these colonizations and losses seem due to normal species turnover. Several seabird species have declined due to human disturbance and are now increasing. Several raptor species have had significant losses. Several land bird populations have been lost, including endemic subspecies. Range expansions have come about naturally or as a result of protection and conservation efforts. Losses are almost all due to human influences, including direct disturbance and killing, DDT in the food chain, and predation and habitat destruction brought on by feral animals.

Key Words: California Channel Islands; extinction; range expansion; human influences; endemicity; conservation.

The breeding avifauna of the islands off California is unique. Hundreds of thousands of marine birds find resources just 20 or more miles from heavily populated metropolitan areas. Some resident land birds have evolved morphologically distinguishable populations, following, in a few cases, classic rules of island evolution (e.g., Johnson 1972, Power 1980a). Over the last 100 years there has been remarkable change. As with islands everywhere, there are natural processes at work. The numbers of bird species on islands are affected by plant species diversity and distances from sources of colonizing species [for the California Islands see Power (1972)]. Theoretically, immigration and extinction rates are also affected by island size and degree of isolation (MacArthur and Wilson 1967). Johnson (1972) describes several colonization scenarios specific to the Channel Islands.

In the shorter term, the balancing of extinction and immigration rates leads to a more-or-less constant number of species, but with the species composition subject to change, at least in theory (Diamond 1969). Diamond and Jones (1980), for example, record 56 species of land birds known to breed, or to have bred, on the eight Channel Islands, and found average annual turnover of island populations of 1–6% per year. For the avifauna of small Santa Barbara Island

(1.0 sq. mi.), Hunt and Hunt (1974) calculated turnover rates of 120% for birds of prey and 42% for songbirds over the period 1900–1972. That works out to 1.7% and 0.6% per year, respectively. Hunt and Hunt also compared calculated turnover rates to island area for the nine California Islands from San Miguel in the north to Los Coronados in the south. Turnover was inversely proportional to island area for raptors, but not for songbirds. [Regarding overestimating turnover see Lynch and Johnson (1974).] Climatic variation is another cause of natural avifaunal change. For example, El Niños raise the sea temperature, changing the abundance and distribution of some prey species on which many nesting birds have come to specialize.

Over the last 100 years the impact of humans has far exceeded the effects of natural causes. Marine birds have been victims of egging, oil pollution, overfishing, gill nets, and DDT contamination in the food chain (e.g., Ainley and Lewis 1974, Risebrough et al. 1970). Raptors and other land birds were shot, poisoned, preyed on by introduced mammals, and had nesting habitat destroyed (e.g., Kiff 1980, Howell 1917). An idea of the habitat degradation that took place on one small island can be found in Philbrick's (1972) account of Santa Barbara Island. He discusses farming, introduction of weeds and succulent plants, the spread of house cats, browsing by rabbits, and fire. Ainley and Lewis' (1974) account of the Farallones is as telling. Yet, if this paper had been written 20 years ago the situation would seem worse than today. Marine birds now are doing well, raptors may by reestablished soon, and habitat degradation has been reversed on many of the islands.

In this paper I review changes in the breeding populations of species that migrate to, or are resident on, the California Islands, from the Farallones in the north to San Clemente Island in the south (Fig. 1). I include only breeding species and populations that have changed. Space does not permit a review of nonbreeding birds or those populations that have been more-or-less stable over the last 100 years, nor am I treating changes in niche breadth or niche shifts (Yeaton 1974). I recognize four general categories: marine and shore birds, raptors, other land birds, and introduced birds. For a general overview of the state of our knowledge of the islands at three recent checkpoints, refer to the proceedings of symposia held in 1965, 1978, and 1987 (Philbrick 1967, Power 1980b, Hochberg 1993). There have been interesting changes on the Mexican islands off the Pacific Coast of Baja California as well, although they are not covered here. Among the useful papers to which readers can be referred are Abbott (1993), Dunlap (1988), Everett (1989), Everett and Anderson (1991), Friedmann et al. (1950), Jehl (1971, 1973, 1977a, b), Jehl and Everett (1985), and Kenyon (1947).

HISTORY OF BASELINE DATA

The first ornithological information on the Farallones dates to the 1850s and the U.S. Pacific Railroad Survey (Heermann 1859). H. R. Taylor (1887) reported on abundances of seabirds during a visit in 1886, and M. S. Ray (1904) and William Leon Dawson (1911) reported on longer stays. W. E. Bryant (1888) summarized information up to 1888 in a *Proceedings of the California Academy of Sciences* paper, and L. M.

Loomis (1895) referenced the Farallones in his historical study on California water birds. The period 1887–1903 was covered by W. O. Emerson (1904). In a 1974 paper, David Ainley and T. James Lewis of the Point Reyes Bird Observatory summarized the entire history of Farallon Island marine birds.

For the Channel Islands off southern California, C. P. Streator (1888) provided notes on birds of some of the islands, and is important because of the early date, rather than the extent of the information. Joseph Grinnell (1897) reported on his findings on Santa Barbara, San Nicolas, and San Clemente islands during the spring of 1897, in the first publication of the Pasadena Academy of Sciences. Charles H. Townsend (1890) collected on the islands in 1888 and 1889 as part of the scientific exploration by the U.S. Fish Commission steamer *Albatross*. Taxonomic status and mensural data appeared in Robert Ridgway's series *The Birds of North and Middle America,* published from 1901 to 1914 (Bulletin of the U.S. National Museum 50, various parts). George Willett (1910, 1933) recorded distributional data in the early 1900s. The first major summary of the Channel Islands was produced by A. B. Howell (1917). Both Willett and Howell published in early volumes of *Pacific Coast Avifauna,* a publication of the Cooper Ornithological Society and the predecessor of *Studies in Avian Biology.* Joseph Grinnell and Alden Miller (1944) synthesized what was known at the time in their important *Pacific Coast Avifauna* volume on the birds of California. Alden Miller (1951) compared the avifaunas of Santa Cruz and Santa Rosa islands. Jared Diamond and H. Lee Jones provided the most complete baseline data in recent time through extensive surveys in the late 1960s and early 1970s (Diamond 1969, Jones 1975, Jones and Diamond 1976).

MARINE AND SHORE BIRDS

There were very few serious surveys of breeding populations of marine birds until

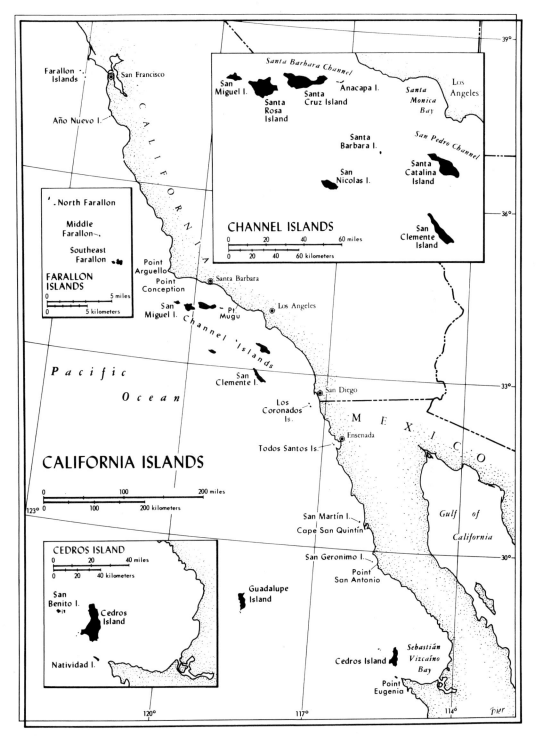

FIGURE 1.   Map of the California Islands. The area covered by this study is from the Farallon Islands in the north to San Clemente Island in the south.

TABLE 1. TRENDS IN BREEDING POPULATIONS OF CALIFORNIA CHANNEL ISLANDS MARINE AND SHORE BIRDS OVER THE LAST 100 YEARS

A. Increases on all or some islands
   Leach's Storm-Petrel (N)
   Ashy Storm-Petrel (N)
   Snowy Plover (N)
   Western Plover (H)
B. Declines followed by increases on most islands
   Brown Pelican (H)
   Brandt's Cormorant (N) (H)
   Pelagic Cormorant (N) (H)
   Common Murre (H)
   Pigeon Guillemot (H)
   Xantus' Murrelet (H)
   Rhinoceros Auklet (N)
C. Declines on all or some islands
   Double-crested Cormorant (N) (H)
   Tufted Puffin (N)
D. Increases followed by declines on most islands
   Cassin's Auklet (N)

(N) Presumed natural causes. (H) Presumed human-induced causes.

the 1960s. Following the DDT-induced decline of Brown Pelicans (*Pelecanus occidentalis*) and other seabirds in the late 1960s and early 1970s, surveying became more intense as money became available from federal and state agencies (e.g., Ingram 1992). Several seabird species underwent declines in the late 1800s and early 1900s, and others in the middle of the 1960s and 1970s (Table 1). In many cases populations have recovered.

Leach's Storm-Petrel (*Oceanodroma leucorhoa*) has remained steady or possibly increased in the last 100 years. On the Farallon Islands it was first discovered in 1896, but it may have been present earlier (Ainley and Lewis 1974). Fifty to 100 pairs were reported in 1959 and about 700 pairs were reported in 1972 up to the present (Ainley and Lewis 1974, Carter et al. 1992). On the Channel Islands, a few pairs were reported in the early 1970s (Hunt et al. 1980) and about 160 pairs in the late 1970s (Carter et al. 1992).

The Ashy Storm-Petrel (*Oceanodroma homochroa*) may have increased. On the Farallones it was rare in the mid-1800s, increased to about 1500–2000 pairs in 1959,

and stabilized at about 2000 pairs in 1972 up to the present (Ainley and Lewis 1974, Carter et al. 1992). On the other hand, Ainley et al. (1994) consider it less abundant on the Farallones than in the early 1970s. On the Channel Islands about 600 pairs of Ashy Storm-Petrels were reported throughout the 1970s, breeding on Castle Rock and Prince Island (islets near San Miguel Island), and on rocks and islets off Santa Cruz and Santa Barbara islands (Hunt et al. 1980, Carter et al. 1992). In 1991 about 1570 pairs were in the Channel Islands, with the greatest concentrations on Prince Island (about 580 pairs) and Santa Barbara Island (about 440 pairs) (Carter et al. 1992).

The episode of decline and recovery of the Brown Pelican on the California Islands is well known (e.g., Risebrough et al. 1970, 1971; Hom et al. 1974). The local subspecies *californicus* was classified as endangered under federal law in 1970 and under California law in 1971 (Carter et al. 1992). Brown Pelicans in the Southern California Bight raise more young when there is an abundance of northern anchovy (*Engraulis mordax*). Anderson et al. (1980) showed a relationship between northern anchovy biomass and pelican fledging rates at Anacapa and Los Coronados islands. Past pelican populations may have had a larger food base than they do today, feeding also on Pacific sardines (*Sardinops caerulea*) and Pacific mackerel (*Scomber japonicus*), species not now abundant. The pelican/anchovy relationship was disrupted by DDT residues in the Southern California Bight, contaminated anchovies being the major source of DDT for the pelicans (Anderson et al. 1980).

The pelican population in the California Current system had been declining since 1950 (Anderson and Anderson 1976). In historic times Anacapa Island had the largest breeding population in the region (Carter et al. 1992). Pelicans originally nested at both West and East Anacapa from 1884 to 1930 (Gress and Anderson 1983). By 1935 the entire colony existed only on West island. At Anacapa the estimated maximum breeding population during the first half of the 20th century was about 2000 pairs. While there were fluctuations from year to year owing to sea temperature and anchovy biomass, the mean annual rate of decrease was about 4% per year from 1949 to 1974. In 1969, five young at most hatched from 1272 nesting attempts on Anacapa Island (Risebrough et al. 1970).

In 1975 through 1977, Briggs et al. (1981) estimated between 1800 and 5000 pelicans in the Southern California Bight could be attributed to local breeders and immatures. By the mid-1980s Briggs et al. (1987) believed that pelicans had substantially recovered from the decline of the 1960s and early 1970s. Subsequent increases are documented in Carter et al. (1992). In 1975–1980 there were 1258 breeding pairs on West Anacapa and another 87 on Santa Barbara Island. In 1989–1991 there were 5340 breeding pairs on West Anacapa and another 618 on Santa Barbara. The increase on Santa Barbara Island is especially encouraging: Brown Pelicans recolonized there in 1980, when 97 pairs were reported. The year of highest numbers on Santa Barbara was 1986, when 1441 nests were active. Clearly the population has recovered.

The Double-crested Cormorant (*Phalacrocorax auritus*) also has gone through declines and recoveries. On the Farallones, it was abundant, breeding in the thousands in the mid- to late 1800s (Ainley and Lewis 1974). Nesting plummeted (e.g., 20 nests in 1904) as a result of egging in the mid-1800s [mostly for Common Murre (*Uria aalge*) eggs] and other human disturbance. By 1972, numbers were still low: 40 pairs. By the late 1970s numbers began to increase to about 90 pairs and by 1991 the breeding population was up to 570 pairs (Carter 1992). Yet the population remains smaller than in pre-egging days. On the Channel Islands the Double-crested Cormorant has gone from being a very common breeder to one in which only remnant populations exist (Hunt et al. 1980). The decline was probably due to a combination of factors, including the

disappearance of Pacific sardines owing to overfishing (Ainley and Lewis 1974) and increased human disturbance (Hunt et al. 1980). The most serious impact was reproductive failure due to eggshell thinning in the late 1960s (Gress et al. 1973). The largest breeding colonies were on Prince, Anacapa, and Santa Barbara islands. On West Anacapa in 1969, the year of greatest decline, there were only 76 nesting attempts and no young produced (Gress et al. 1973). In the mid-1970s population sizes began to increase, and in 1975 through 1977, the populations on Prince, West Anacapa, Santa Barbara, and Sutil (an islet near Santa Barbara Island) increased and adults fledged young in all colonies (Hunt et al. 1980). The total southern California island population was about 960 pairs in the late 1970s and about 1230 pairs in 1991 (Carter et al. 1992).

Brandt's Cormorant (*Phalacrocorax penicillatus*) on the Farallones suffered the same consequences as the Double-crested Cormorant, with numbers declining from about 15,000 birds around 1860 to a few thousand in the early 1900s (Ainley and Lewis 1974). By the late 1970s the number of breeding pairs increased to an estimated 14,000 and today there are 8450 (Carter et al. 1992). In 1980 the total population (individuals) may have been 64,900 birds, then the largest nesting colony of Brandt's Cormorant in the world (Briggs et al. 1987, Carter et al. 1992). However, numbers dropped after the 1982/1983 El Niño and have not recovered (see Ainley et al. 1994).

Hunt et al. (1980) reported that in the late 1970s Brandt's Cormorant bred at major historical colony sites on seven of the eight Channel Islands, but at reduced numbers: more than 350 breeding pairs on Santa Barbara Island in 1912 and a maximum of only 166 pairs in 1975–1977. They estimated 4000 pairs on Prince Island and Castle Rock as late as 1968, decreasing to no more than 1823 in 1970–1975. These authors believe human disturbance precipitating gull predation was the principal cause of decline, but also cite some evidence for eggshell thinning. More recently, Brandt's Cormorant has increased on the Channel Islands: the total breeding population in the late 1970s was about 3000 pairs and by 1990 was about 14,700 pairs (Carter et al. 1992). San Miguel had a total breeding population (all island and adjacent sites combined) of about 1850 pairs in the late 1970s and is up to 7850 now. Santa Rosa had 700 pairs in the late 1970s and has 2300 now. The Santa Cruz population jumped from 100 to 1570 pairs. Santa Barbara Island had about 130 pairs in the late 1970s and has 330 now. Finally, the San Nicolas population grew from about 200 to an estimated 2540 pairs in 1991. The species nests in small numbers on San Clemente Island (Jorgensen 1984).

The largest colony of the Pelagic Cormorant (*Phalacrocorax pelagicus*) in the study area is on South Farallon Island (Ainley and Lewis 1974). They reached their lowest numbers during the egging era, slowly increased until 1959, when 350–400 pairs were reported, and increased further to about 1000 pairs by 1972. Numbers seem to have held steady at 800–900 pairs in 1979, but then fell to only 400 pairs in 1987 (Carter et al. 1992). The decline occurred during the 1982/1983 El Niño. Ainley et al. (1994) show dramatic fluctuations in numbers between 1972 and 1992. On the Northern Channel Islands, both numbers of colonies and numbers of breeding birds have increased. Hunt et al. (1980) reported about 250 pairs throughout the Channel Islands in 1975–1977, and Carter et al. (1992) reported over 200 pairs in the same period. Breeding sites were San Miguel Island, Castle Rock, Prince, Santa Rosa, and Santa Cruz, and Santa Barbara and nearby Sutil islands. In 1991, Carter et al. (1992) reported about 1340 pairs at 46 active colonies (28 colonies were "newly discovered").

Spear (in Page and Stenzel 1981) summarized the status of the Snowy Plover (*Charadrius alexandrinus*) on the islands. On San Miguel it may have bred in the early 1900s, but breeding was only recently confirmed (35 pairs in 1979). On Santa Rosa, 21 pairs were recorded in 1980. On San Nicolas they have bred throughout the century (e.g., 74 pairs in 1978). Surveys in 1989 counted numbers of adults, and indicated smaller populations than in 1977–1980 on San Miguel and San Nicolas (36 vs. 84 and 90 vs. 133, respectively), and a larger population on Santa Rosa (91 vs. 43) (Page et al. 1991). The species was first recorded breeding on San Clemente in 1989 (Winchell 1990).

The Western Gull (*Larus occidentalis*) on the Farallon Islands fluctuated between 11,000 and 12,000 pairs from 1960 up to the 1982/1983 El Niño, when it declined slightly (Ainley et al. 1994). It then increased to about 14,000 pairs in 1986, dropped to less than 11,000 in 1987, and has declined gradually since then. On the Channel Islands the Western Gull has been ubiquitous throughout the century. It is one species that may have even benefited from human intrusion, feeding at dumps and taking offal from fishing vessels. Hunt et al. (1980) reported a maximum of about 5600 pairs in 1975–1977. Carter et al. (1992) counted over 13,800 pairs for the whole of the Channel Islands in 1991. Whether this represents a real increase or just more thorough censusing is not clear. On Santa Barbara Island, an excess of females and homosexual female pairing was reported (Wingfield, Martin et al. 1980). This behavior is not due to increased testosterone levels in females (Wingfield, Newman et al. 1980). Whether homosexual pairing is a recent phenomenon is not known.

The southernmost breeding point of the Common Murre is the Farallones (A.O.U. 1983). The population may have been as large as 200,000 pairs in the mid-1800s, but declined to only a few hundred to a few thousand in the early 1900s, after egging, human occupation of the islands, and oil spills (Ainley and Lewis 1974). It then grew to 3000–3500 pairs in 1959, and about 10,250 pairs by 1972 (Ainley and Lewis 1974). In the 1970s the population was estimated to be 55,770 pairs, but dropped to

34,000 pairs by the early 1990s, owing to a combination of gill net mortality, oil spills, and the 1982/1983 El Niño (Carter et al. 1992). In 1987, fishing regulation changes reduced mortality due to gill nets. The breeding population on the Farallones seems to be recovering at about 1–2% a year (Ainley et al. 1994). On the Channel Islands only one historic breeding site is known: about 11 pairs of Common Murres presumably bred on Prince Island between 1906 and 1912 (Garrett and Dunn 1981, Hunt et al. 1980).

Pigeon Guillemots (*Cepphus columba*) on the Farallones escaped egging because of their habit of nesting in crevices and burrows, but they did not escape the impact of oil pollution (Ainley and Lewis 1974). From 1900 into the 1940s oil tankers routinely flushed their tanks close to the island before entering San Francisco Harbor. The population was only about 100 pairs in 1911. After oil pollution lessened, the population reached about 500 pairs by 1959 and 1000 pairs by 1972, and it remains at about that number today (Carter et al. 1992). On the Channel Islands the Pigeon Guillemot breeds on San Miguel, Santa Rosa, Santa Cruz, Anacapa, and Santa Barbara islands. Hunt et al. (1980) reported about 850 pairs in 1975–1977. Carter et al. (1992) reported 770 pairs in 1975–1978 and about 1600 pairs in 1989. Carter et al. believe the higher numbers reflect both better census techniques and a true increase.

The Xantus' Murrelet (*Synthliboramphus hypoleucus*) is restricted to the Channel and Pacific Baja California islands, from San Miguel south to Natividad and Guadalupe (A.O.U. 1983). Hunt et al. (1980) and Carter et al. (1992) add San Clemente and Santa Catalina, at least as historical sites. There is some evidence of recent breeding on San Clemente Island (Jorgensen 1984). Hunt et al. (1980) reported about 1670 pairs on the Channel Islands in 1975–1977, the vast majority (1590 pairs) being on Santa Barbara Island and adjacent Sutil and Shag Rock. Carter et al. (1992) reported about 860 pairs

throughout the Channel Islands in 1991, with the majority (about 770 pairs) on Santa Barbara and adjacent islets. Carter et al. attributed the decline to differences in census techniques, loss of artificial habitat, loss of bush sites due to drought, and egg predation by deer mice (*Peromyscus maniculatus*). However, Carter et al. believed that in this century there has been a general increase in the population, which was presumed to be at a low in the early 1900s.

Cassin's Auklet (*Ptychoramphus aleuticus*) on the Farallones has increased tremendously over the last century (Ainley and Lewis 1974:438): "In the 1850s and 1860s they were rare and present only in the winter. . . . By the 1880s they were common and breeding, and by the 1890s they were abundant. In 1911 Dawson estimated 100,000–200,000 birds which includes the range of present estimates." Ainley and Lewis attribute the increase to a return of food-rich cold water following a warm-water period in the mid-1800s. Carter et al. (1992) estimate a breeding population of 67,500 pairs in the mid-1970s and about 19,140 in 1989. While Dawson's number may have been an overestimate, they attribute some real decline to the following possible factors: a decline in number of burrow sites, increased predation (especially by gulls), oil spills, and burrow collapses. (See also Ainley et al. 1994).

On the Channel Islands, Hunt et al. (1980) estimated at least 11,255 breeding pairs of Cassin's Auklets in 1975–1977, most from Prince Island and Castle Rock, both near San Miguel Island. Carter et al. (1992) reported 13,080 pairs in that period and a decrease to about 9150 pairs in 1991. They believe the decline was due to an overestimate of the Prince Island population in 1975–1977, but did not discount loss of burrow sites due to erosion and a die-back of vegetation. Cassin's Auklet bred within the last 100 years on Santa Barbara Island, but it is not there now and its loss is believed to be due to predation by feral house cats (Howell 1917).

TABLE 2.   TRENDS IN BREEDING POPULATIONS OF
CALIFORNIA CHANNEL ISLANDS RAPTORS OVER THE LAST
100 YEARS

A. Stable, increases, or turnover
      American Kestrel (N)
      Barn Owl (N)
      Burrowing Owl (N)
      Long-eared Owl (N)
      Short-eared Owl (N)
      Northern Saw-whet Owl (N)
B. Declines and increases (mixed)
      Red-tailed Hawk (N)
C. Declines or extirpations followed by increases
      Bald Eagle (H)
      Peregrine Falcon (H)
D. Declines or extirpations
      Osprey (H)

(N) Presumed natural causes. (H) Presumed human-induced causes.

The Rhinoceros Auklet (*Cerorhinca monocerata*) on the Farallones was present and breeding up to the mid-1860s and disappeared about that time (Ainley and Lewis 1974). It reestablished a breeding population in 1972 (Ainley et al. 1994). About 50 pairs were reported in the mid- to late 1970s. The population grew to 175 pairs by 1982, crashed during the 1982/1983 El Niño, and rebounded to about 260 pairs in 1989, where it remains today (Carter et al. 1992, Ainley et al. 1994). On Año Nuevo Island the population was estimated to have grown from zero in the mid-1970s to about 40 pairs in 1989 (Carter et al. 1992). On the Channel Islands the Rhinoceros Auklet was not known as a breeding bird until Carter et al. (1992) reported breeding behavior on Prince Island: 19 birds were observed. See Guthrie (1993) for fossil evidence of this species on San Miguel Island.

The Tufted Puffin (*Fratercula cirrhata*) on the Farallones did not decline during the egging years, but with the arrival of oil pollution their numbers dropped from an estimated several thousand in 1911 to 300 by 1933 (Ainley and Lewis 1974). In the early 1970s the numbers were apparently stable at 25–30 pairs. Numbers declined again owing to the 1982/1983 El Niño, but then recovered to about 35–50 pairs in 1985–1989 (Carter et al. 1992). On the Channel Islands

moderate numbers of Tufted Puffins bred from 1886–1912, mainly on the Northern Channel Islands and on Santa Barbara Island (Hunt et al. 1980). Smaller numbers may have bred into the mid 1900s, but none were reported during surveys in 1965, 1968, and 1975–1977. Ainley and Lewis (1974) argued that the decline in both the Farallones and the Channel Islands was due to the demise of the Pacific sardine. In 1991 Carter et al. (1992) discovered that five pairs had recolonized Prince Island, and observed courtship behavior and a possible nesting crevice.

RAPTORS

Several of the principal raptor species on the Channel Islands have had a history unlike that of marine birds or other land birds (Table 2). Some marine-feeding species have felt the impact of DDT; others have been hunted. Also, being top-level predators, many normally occurred in low numbers.

In the last century and early 1900s, the Osprey (*Pandion haliaetus*) was a breeding resident on the southernmost islands: San Nicolas, Santa Catalina, and San Clemente (Howell 1917, Grinnell and Miller 1944, Kiff 1980). San Clemente Island seemed to have the largest historic population, with 20 nests being reported in 1907 (Kiff 1980). Its decline was noticed in the 1920s and by 1930 it was presumed extirpated from the islands. Kiff believes shooting by fisherman was the principal cause.

The Bald Eagle (*Haliaeetus leucocephalus*) once nested on all the Channel Islands (Grinnell and Miller 1944). In the late 1800s and early 1900s Santa Rosa supported at least three pairs and Santa Cruz at least five, and eagles could have been even more abundant on Santa Catalina (Kiff 1980). San Miguel had at least three active nests in a single year. Kiff estimated that the highest number of active Bald Eagle nests in one year for the Channel Islands was 24. The Channel Islands were one of the last strongholds for the Bald Eagle in California; however, it eventually succumbed to persecution there as elsewhere (Kiff 1980). Declines were noted in the early 1900s. It was extirpated from Santa Barbara Island between 1927 and 1939, from San Miguel Island between 1939 and 1960, from San Nicolas between 1945 and 1959, and from Anacapa between 1959 and 1962. Kiff surmised that the eagle survived on Santa Catalina, Santa Cruz, and Santa Rosa until the late 1950s. Recorded causes of mortality include shooting, egg collecting, nest destruction and disturbance, trapping, and poisoning. Kiff (1980) believed that shooting, especially by sheepherders and visitors, was the most important factor leading to extirpation, but DDT likely contributed as well.

Attempts to reintroduce Bald Eagles to Santa Catalina began in 1980 (Garcelon et al. 1989, Garcelon and Roemer 1990), with introduction of eaglets. They were fed on carcasses of feral goats and pigs; later, as adults, they fed on their own, taking marine fish and birds. Hacking efforts ended in 1986, with 33 birds having been released. A pair of four-year-old birds built a nest in 1984 (D. Garcelon, pers. comm.). The first eggs were laid in 1987. Between 1987 and 1993, one to three pairs attempted nesting each year (three in 1992), but did not raise viable young until 1993 (one fledged), perhaps because DDT is too high for successful reproduction (D. Garcelon, pers. comm.). An attempt to reestablish the Bald Eagle on San Clemente Island was not successful (Jorgensen 1984).

The Red-tailed Hawk (*Buteo jamaicensis*) on the Channel Islands has not been subject to declines (Diamond and Jones 1980). It is present and breeds year round on Santa Rosa, Santa Cruz, and Santa Catalina islands, and has bred on more than one occasion, but not every year, on San Miguel, Anacapa, and San Clemente. Jones (pers. comm.) indicates that this species is probably relatively new to San Miguel Island: it was not recorded as a breeding bird before the late 1960s or early 1970s.

The American Kestrel (*Falco sparverius*) has been resident on Santa Rosa, Santa Cruz, Anacapa, Santa Catalina, and San Clemente, and the population on San Clemente seems to have increased (Jorgensen 1984). It has also bred, although not annually, on San Nicolas and Santa Barbara islands. Jones (pers. comm.) believes it did not breed on San Nicolas until 1976 and on Santa Barbara Island until after 1939, possibly as late as 1968 (see also Hunt and Hunt 1974). On San Miguel Island, the kestrel seems to have become an established breeder fairly recently (Diamond and Jones 1980). It was thought to be an occasional breeder or winter visitor in 1910, but presumed breeding was not documented there until 1968 (Jones, pers. comm.).

Peregrine Falcons (*Falco peregrinus*) were common residents on the islands into the first half of the 1900s (Kiff 1980). Throughout California, according to Herman et al. (1970), until the mid-1940s approximately 100 eyries were producing young annually, but in the two decades following 1945 there was a 95% decline of the total California population. Herman et al. believed the island populations were extirpated by 1955. Documented cases of mortality include shooting, collecting, and removal of young from nests for falconry. Reproductive failure associated with DDT was also important (Kiff 1980).

Peregrine Falcons now nest on the Channel Islands as a result of releases by the Predatory Bird Research Group, Santa Cruz, California (B. Walton, in litt.). The group began releases in Big Sur, in Los Padres National Forest, in the Santa Monica Mountains, and at two coastal locations in southern California. Because the birds wander they were likely visitors to the Channel Islands. The group also began releases on Santa Catalina Island in 1983 and on San Miguel Island in 1985. Today there is nesting on Anacapa, Santa Cruz, Santa Rosa, and San Miguel, and sightings are frequent on other islands. Along the California coast north of the Channel Islands, the density of Peregrine Falcons has returned to pre-DDT levels, but natural productivity is low, owing

TABLE 3. TRENDS IN BREEDING POPULATIONS OF CALIFORNIA CHANNEL ISLANDS LAND BIRDS OVER THE LAST 100 YEARS

A. Colonize new islands
Allen's Hummingbird (N)
Common Flicker (N)
Acorn Woodpecker (N)
Ash-throated Flycatcher (N)
Phainopepla (N)
Black-headed Grosbeak (N)
Rufous-crowned Sparrow (N)
Chipping Sparrow (N)
Western Meadowlark (N)
B. Declines and increases (mixed)
Orange-crowned Warbler (H) (N)
Dark-eyed Junco (H) (N)
C. Declines or one or more populations extirpated
Horned Lark (N)
Common Raven (H)
Bewick Wren
Loggerhead Shrike (H)
House Finch (H) (N)
Rufous-sided Towhee (H)*
Sage Sparrow (H)
Song Sparrow (H)*

(N) Presumed natural causes. (H) Presumed human-induced causes.
* Extinct subspecies.

to residual effects of DDT (Garcelon et al. 1989).

Barn, Burrowing, Long-eared, and Northern Saw-whet owls (*Tyto alba, Athene cunicularia, Asio otus,* and *Aegolius acadicus,* respectively) are residents or occasional breeders on one or more or the Channel Islands (Diamond and Jones 1980). However, we know little about their status. There is no evidence for decline, nor would this be expected in the absence of killing by humans and the fact that owls do not feed on DDT-contaminated marine food.

On Santa Barbara Island the Barn Owl was not recorded in early surveys (Howell 1917), but was present in 1968 and subsequently (Hunt and Hunt 1974). Jones (pers. comm.) states that the Burrowing Owl was not recorded before 1953 and may have colonized in this century. Also, on Santa Barbara Island, the Short-eared Owl (*Asio flammeus*) was present from 1980 through 1983, when numbers of deer mice (*Peromyscus maniculatus*) were high (Drost and Fellers 1991). Numbers of Barn Owls also track

mouse population size (Drost and Fellers 1991).

OTHER LAND BIRDS

Surveys of most land bird species have not been consistent over the last 100 years, and I know of no studies where population counts have been done over enough years to provide hard data. However, by noting presence or absence and casual comments some general trends can be discerned (Table 3). Some species have colonized new islands, and others, especially certain endemic races, have been extirpated, usually due to habitat degradation by introduced rabbits, goats, and sheep.

Costa's Hummingbird (*Calypte costae*) was recorded on Santa Barbara Island in 1911, but not subsequently (Hunt and Hunt 1974; Jones, unpub.). However, there is no firm data that it actually nested there (P. Collins, pers. comm.).

Allen's Hummingbird (*Selasphorus sasin*) probably has been a breeding resident on Santa Rosa, Santa Cruz, Anacapa, Santa Catalina, and San Clemente islands throughout this century. More recently it became an established breeder on San Miguel; the first record was in 1968, when it was common and nesting (Diamond and Jones 1980, Jones, pers. comm.). On Santa Barbara Island Allen's Hummingbird has been recorded sporadically, and may be subject to turnover (Hunt and Hunt 1974).

The Common Flicker (*Colaptes auratus*) is a common resident on Santa Cruz and Santa Catalina islands, but the lack of evidence of breeding before 1906 on Catalina suggests it may have colonized that island in this century (Diamond and Jones 1980, Jones, pers. comm.).

The Acorn Woodpecker (*Melanerpes formicivorus*) has immigrated and become an established breeder on Santa Cruz (1928–1929) and on Santa Catalina (1955) (Diamond and Jones 1980; Jones, pers. comm.). Johnson (1972) discusses these colonizations in detail. Although the colonizations were natural, they may have been enhanced by the presence of utility poles and trees planted by humans.

The Ash-throated Flycatcher (*Myiarchus cinerascens*) is an uncommon, summer resident on Santa Cruz Island (Diamond and Jones 1980), first recorded breeding there in 1968 (Jones, pers. comm.).

Horned Larks (*Eremophila alpestris*) are common residents on all of the Channel Islands, except Anacapa (Diamond and Jones 1980). It formerly bred on Anacapa but disappeared between 1941 and 1963 (Jones, pers. comm.). All Channel Island populations are considered a separate race, *E. a. insularis* [races of island land birds discussed here are given in A.O.U. (1957)]. On Santa Cruz cattle and feral sheep were taken off the island in the 1980s. In the absence of grazers, introduced sweet fennel (*Foeniculum vulgare*) is rapidly spreading through open grassland and may reduce habitat for larks.

The Common Raven (*Corvus corax*) is a common resident on the five largest Channel Islands. It was resident on San Miguel up to 1939, and may have been eliminated by poisoning or shooting by ranchers (Jones, pers. comm.). It is breeding again on San Miguel (B. Stewart, pers. comm.). Jones also reported that it may breed occasionally on Anacapa. It bred on Santa Barbara Island up to 1939, but in 1972 it was not recorded (Hunt and Hunt 1974).

The resident Bewick's Wren (*Thryomanes bewickii*) has differentiated sufficiently to have races identified for several island populations: *nesophilus* on Santa Rosa, Santa Cruz, and Anacapa; *catalinae* on Santa Catalina; and *leucophrys* was on San Clemente. *T. b. leucophrys* disappeared from San Clemente about 1941 (Diamond and Jones 1980; Jorgensen 1984; Jones, pers. comm.), probably owing to habitat destruction.

The Phainopepla (*Phainopepla nitens*) was known to breed only on Santa Catalina (Diamond and Jones 1980), until a pair was located on Santa Cruz in 1984 (Haemig 1986). Because Santa Cruz has been frequented by researchers for many years, this colonization is no doubt recent.

Two subspecies of Loggerhead Shrike (*Lanius ludovicianus*) occur on the Channel Islands, *anthonyi* on Santa Rosa, Santa Cruz, and Santa Catalina, and *mearnsi* on San Clemente. *L. l. mearnsi* was abundant in the early 1900s, but declined through the 1960s to 50 individuals in 1975 (U.S. Fish and Wildlife Service 1984), and ultimately to five pairs (Scott and Morrison 1990). The 1989 population estimate increased to 12–20 birds (Matthews 1990). The shrike seems to be affected in part by habitat degradation and resulting loss of prey. Predation by Common Ravens, feral cats, and island foxes (*Urocyon littoralis*) is also important, and mortality in young shrikes is higher than on the mainland (Scott and Morrison 1990).

The Orange-crowned Warbler (*Vermivora celata*) has long been a breeding resident on Santa Rosa, Santa Cruz, Anacapa, Santa Catalina and San Clemente islands (Diamond and Jones 1980). Island populations constitute a separate race, *V. c. sordida*. On San Miguel and San Nicolas it was not recorded as breeding until 1968 (Jones, pers. comm.). The population on Santa Barbara Island was absent for a time; Hunt and Hunt (1974) cite records for 1918, 1927, and 1939, but did not record it later, including during their 1972 survey. Hunt and Hunt surmise its loss may have been due to destruction of suitable nesting habitat by introduced rabbits and a fire in 1959. However, breeding has been recorded since 1972 (Jones, pers. comm.), so it has recovered on this island. Jones indicates variation in breeding from year to year.

The Black-headed Grosbeak (*Pheucticus melanocephalus*) occurs only on Santa Cruz Island, where the first confirmed breeding was in 1968 (Jones, pers. comm.).

The House Finch (*Carpodacus mexicanus*) occurred uninterruptedly on all eight of the Channel Islands until 20–25 years ago (Diamond and Jones 1980). On Santa Barbara Island, birds presumably of the island race *C. m. clementis* were last seen in 1968

TABLE 4. HUMAN-INDUCED INTRODUCTIONS TO THE BREEDING POPULATIONS OF THE CALIFORNIA CHANNEL ISLANDS OVER THE LAST 100 YEARS

A. Introductions followed by extirpation
    Common Peafowl
B. Successful introductions
    Chukar
    Wild Turkey
    Common [Ring-necked] Pheasant
    Gambel's Quail
    California Quail
    Rock Dove
    European Starling
    House Sparrow

(Hunt and Hunt 1974), the loss being attributed to destruction of nesting habitat by introduced rabbits. House Finches of an unknown subspecies have recolonized Santa Barbara Island and were again breeding by 1977.

The Rufous-sided Towhee (*Pipilo erythrophthalmus*) has differentiated into two recognizable races on the Channel Islands: *megalonyx* (the mainland race) on Santa Cruz and *clementae* on Santa Rosa, Santa Catalina, and San Clemente (Johnson 1972). The population on San Clemente was nearly extinct in 1968 (an immature bird was seen in 1975) and is presumed gone (Diamond and Jones 1980; Jorgensen 1984; Jones, pers. comm.).

The island race of the Rufous-crowned Sparrow (*Aimophila ruficeps obscura*) is a breeding resident on Santa Cruz Island (Diamond and Jones 1980), and seems to have colonized Anacapa in recent times (Johnson 1972). It was first recorded in 1940 and was common by 1963 (Jones, pers. comm.)

The Chipping Sparrow (*Spizella passerina*) is present only during the breeding season and occurs on Santa Rosa, Santa Cruz, Santa Catalina, and San Clemente islands (Diamond and Jones 1980). It colonized Anacapa Island about 1940 (Jones, pers. comm.).

The endemic San Clemente Sage Sparrow (*Amphispiza belli clementeae*) was common earlier in this century (Howell 1917). Owing to habitat destruction by feral goats and sheep, and increased predation by island fox, it is now a federally "threatened" subspecies (Anon. 1980, Jorgensen 1984). Recent population estimates range from 20–30 breeding adults in 1974 (Stewart et al. 1974), to 90–110 adults in 1976 (Byers 1976, Sward 1977), and 250–400 individuals in 1982 (U.S. Fish and Wildlife Service 1984).

The Song Sparrow (*Melospiza melodia*) is now a breeding resident only on San Miguel (*micronyx*) and Santa Rosa, and Santa Cruz (*clementae*) (Diamond and Jones 1980). Island populations on Santa Barbara (*graminea*) and San Clemente (*clementae*) have become extinct in this century (Jorgensen 1984); the form on Santa Barbara Island was last seen in 1967 (Hunt and Hunt 1974).

Dark-eyed Juncos (*Junco hyemalis*), winter visitors to the Channel Islands, were first recorded breeding on Santa Catalina in 1986 (Collins 1987).

The Western Meadowlark (*Sturnella neglecta*) is a breeding resident on all Channel Islands (Diamond and Jones 1980). It colonized San Nicolas Island in this century, being first recorded from in 1945 (Jones, pers. comm.).

INTRODUCTIONS IN THE LAST 100 YEARS

The final category of avifaunal change is species introduced directly onto the islands, such as for hunting, or of species introduced elsewhere in North America that subsequently reached the islands on their own (Table 4).

The Chukar (*Alectoris graeca*) was established in 1975 on San Nicolas Island after repeated introductions by the California Department of Fish and Game (Jones, pers. comm.). There was also a successful introduction on Santa Rosa Island in 1985–1986 (P. Collins, pers. comm.). Releases on Santa Catalina (year unknown) and on San Clemente (1960) were not successful.

A pair of Common (Ring-necked) Pheasants (*Phasianus colchicus*) was unsuccessfully introduced on Santa Rosa Island in 1988 (P. Collins, pers. comm.). A small flock of Common Peafowl (*Pavo cristatus*) occurs around the main ranch of Santa Cruz Island (pers. obs.); a release on Santa Catalina in the 1960s was not successful (Jones, pers. comm.). The Wild Turkey (*Meleagris gallopavo*) was introduced on Santa Cruz Island in 1877 but was never established; however, it was successfully reintroduced sometime before 1968 (Jones, pers. comm.). Jones also reports it was successfully introduced on Santa Catalina in 1969.

Gambel's Quail (*Callipepla gambelii*) was introduced on San Clemente Island about 1912 (Jorgensen 1984). The California Quail (*Callipepla californica*) on Santa Catalina Island (*catalinensis*) is larger and darker than its mainland counterpart (Johnson 1972), and may have been introduced by Native Americans, perhaps thousands of years ago. Quail from Santa Catalina were successfully introduced on Santa Rosa between 1935 and 1940, and on Santa Cruz in 1946 (Jones, pers. comm.). California Quail of an unknown race were introduced about 1890 on San Clemente, but eventually disappeared (Jorgensen 1984).

Rock Doves (*Columba livia*) are transient visitors to many of the Channel Islands (P. Collins, pers. comm.). They colonized the town of Avalon on Santa Catalina Island between 1917 and 1968 (Diamond 1969).

The European Starling (*Sturnus vulgaris*) was introduced in New York City in 1890 (A.O.U. 1983) and arrived in California about 1942 (Small 1974). The first record from the Channel Islands (Santa Cruz) came in 1964 (Jones, pers. comm.). It is now a common resident on all the Channel Islands.

The House Sparrow (*Passer domesticus*), introduced in New York City in 1850, with subsequent introductions elsewhere up to 1867 (A.O.U. 1983), was first seen on the Channel Islands (Santa Cruz) in 1915 (Jones, pers. comm.). In this century it became a breeding resident on Santa Rosa (first recorded in 1927), San Nicolas (colonized between 1945 and 1959), Santa Catalina (first recorded in 1928), and San Clemente (first

mentioned in 1915; well established in 1968) (Jones, pers. comm.). Interestingly, a breeding population was never firmly established on Santa Cruz and it is now extirpated on Santa Rosa, both islands with extensive ranching operations, at least until recently (Jones, pers. comm.).

DISCUSSION

Tables 1–4 summarize changes in the avifauna over the last 100 years. Groupings are only an approximation and are not used to summarize general trends. Also, the designation of whether changes are "natural" or "human-induced" are based on published opinions; only in a few cases are they truly documented.

Over the last 100 years, four species of marine birds seem to have increased in range or numbers, seven species first declined and later increased or recovered over at least part of their range, two species declined or are declining, and one species seems to have increased and is now declining.

Six species of raptors have stayed constant or expanded their ranges to new islands, and another increased on some of the islands and declined on another. Two species of raptors were first extirpated and have been reintroduced (the Bald Eagle and Peregrine Falcon). The Osprey is extirpated.

Up to nine species of land birds may have colonized new islands. Two species have gained populations on new islands and seen declines or total losses on others. Eight species have suffered losses or had individual island populations lost, or presumed so. Two endemic races are extinct: San Clemente Bewick's Wren and Santa Barbara Island Song Sparrow. Populations of more widespread island races that are extirpated on at least one island include the San Clemente Rufous-sided Towhee and San Clemente and Santa Barbara islands' populations of the Song Sparrow. One endemic island population was extirpated and was replaced with an unknown race: the Santa Barbara Island population of the House Finch. The Sage Sparrow on San Clemente decreased significantly in the first 75 years of this century and is increasing again. The San Clemente Loggerhead Shrike was on the brink of extinction.

Eight species have been introduced, or, after having been introduced to North America, have made their way to the islands.

A few of the changes are natural, having been caused by variation in food supply or the result of turnover. However, most of the changes are not. Declines and extirpations resulted from egging in the 1800s, oil pollution, human disturbance, overfishing, shooting, DDT in the food chain, conscious introductions by humans, and habitat alteration following introduction of predators, grazers, and browsers. Recent trends are encouraging: several species once in danger now have well-established populations. In other cases, the jury is still out. A few, morphologically differentiated populations have been lost forever.

ACKNOWLEDGMENTS

I am grateful for information provided by Trudy Ingram, Phil Unitt, Brian Walton, Grainger Hunt, Joseph Jehl, Jenifer Dugan, Jeff Lindgren, Dave Garcelon, and H. Lee Jones. Special thanks is due Paul Collins who reviewed a draft of this paper and provided several additional references and comments, and to the editors who carefully reviewed the manuscript.

LITERATURE CITED

ABBOTT, C. G. 1933. Closing history of the Guadalupe Caracara. Condor 35:10–14.

AINLEY, D. AND T. J. LEWIS. 1974. The history of Farallon Island marine bird populations, 1854–1972. Condor 76:432–446.

AINLEY, D. G., W. J. SYDEMAN, S. A. HATCH, AND U. W. WILSON. 1994. Seabird population trends along the west coast of North America: causes and the extent of regional concordance. Pp. 119–133 in J. R. Jehl, Jr. and N. K. Johnson (eds.), A century of avifaunal change in western North America. Studies in Avian Biology 15.

AMERICAN ORNITHOLOGISTS' UNION. 1957. Check-list of North American birds, 5th edition. American Ornithologists' Union, Washington, DC.

AMERICAN ORNITHOLOGISTS' UNION. 1983. Check-list of North American birds, 6th edition. American Ornithologists' Union, Washington, DC.

ANDERSON, D. W., AND I. T. ANDERSON. 1976. Distribution and status of Brown Pelicans in the California current. American Birds 30:3–12.

ANDERSON, D. W., F. GRESS, K. F. MAIS, AND P. R. KELLY. 1980. Brown Pelicans as anchovy stock indicators and their relationships to commercial fishing. CalCOFI Report 21:54–61.

ANONYMOUS. 1980. Selected vertebrate endangered species of the seacoast of the United States—San Clemente Sage Sparrow. Biological Services Program, U.S. Fish and Wildlife Service.

BRIGGS, K. T., D. B. LEWIS, AND W. B. TYLER. 1981. Brown Pelicans in southern California: habitat use and environmental fluctuations. Condor 83:1–15.

BRIGGS, K. T., W. B. TYLER, D. B. LEWIS, AND D. R. CARLSON. 1987. Bird communities at sea off California: 1975 to 1983. Studies in Avian Biology No. 11.

BRYANT, W. E. 1888. Birds and eggs from the Farallon Islands. Proceedings of the California Academy of Sciences, Second Series 1:25–50.

BYERS, S. J. 1976. Sage Sparrow population status survey, San Clemente Island. Report to the Natural Resources Program, Naval Undersea Center (unpubl.).

CARTER, H. R., G. J. McCHESNEY, D. L. JAQUES, C. S. STRONG, M. W. PARKER, J. E. TAKEKAWA, D. L. JORY, AND D. L. WHITWORTH. 1992. Breeding populations of seabirds in California, 1989–1991. U.S Fish and Wildlife Service unpublished report.

COLLINS, C. T. 1987. A breeding record of the Dark-eyed Junco on Santa Catalina Island, California. Western Birds 18:129–130.

DAWSON, W. L. 1911. Another fortnight on the Farallones. Condor 13:171–183.

DIAMOND, J. M. 1969. Avifaunal equilibria and species turnover rates on the Channel Islands of California. Proceedings of the National Academy of Science 64:57–63.

DIAMOND, J. M., AND H. L. JONES. 1980. Breeding land birds of the Channel Islands. Pp. 597–612 in D. M. Power (ed.), The California Islands. Santa Barbara Museum of Natural History, Santa Barbara, CA.

DROST, C. A., AND G. M. FELLERS. 1991. Density cycles in an island population of deer mice, Peromyscus maniculatus. Oikos 60:351–364.

DUNLAP, E. 1988. Laysan Albatross nesting on Guadalupe Island, Mexico. American Birds 42:180–181.

EMERSON, W. O. 1904. The Farallone Islands revisited, 1887–1903. Condor 6:61–68.

EVERETT, W. T. 1989. Historic and present distribution of breeding marine birds of Baja California's Pacific Coast. Pp. 97–106 in VII Simposio Biologia Marina.

EVERETT W. T., AND D. W. ANDERSON. 1991. Breeding seabirds of Baja California and the Gulf of California. ICBP Technical Publication No. 11:115–138.

FRIEDMANN, H., L. GRISCOM, AND R. T. MOORE. 1950. Distributional check-list of the birds of Mexico, part I. Cooper Ornithological Society, Berkeley, CA.

GARCELON, D. K., R. W. RISEBROUGH, W. M. JARMAN, A. B. CHARTRAN, AND E. E. LITTRELL. 1989. Accumulation of DDE by Bald Eagles Haliaeetus leucocephalus reintroduced to Santa Catalina Island in Southern California. Pp. 491–494 in B. U. Meyburg and R. D. Chancellor (eds.), Raptors in the modern world. WWGBP, Berlin.

GARCELON, D. K., AND G. W. ROEMER. 1990. The

reintroduction of Bald Eagles on Santa Catalina Island, California. Pp. 63–68 *in* P. J. Bryant and J. Remington (eds.), Endangered wildlife and habitats in Southern California. Memoirs Natural History Foundation of Orange County, Vol. 3.

GARRETT, K., AND J. DUNN. 1981. Birds of Southern California. Los Angeles Audubon Society, Los Angeles.

GRESS, F., AND D. W. ANDERSON. 1983. The California Brown Pelican recovery plan. U.S. Fish and Wildlife Service, Portland, OR.

GRESS, G., R. W. RISEBROUGH, D.W. ANDERSON, L. F. KIFF, AND J. R. JEHL, JR. 1973. Reproductive failures of Double-crested Cormorants in southern California and Baja California. Wilson Bulletin 85:197–208.

GRINNELL, J. 1897. Report on the birds recorded during a visit to the islands of Santa Barbara, San Nicolas and San Clemente, in the spring of 1897. Pasadena Academy of Science Publication No. 1.

GRINNELL, J., AND A. H. MILLER. 1944. The distribution and abundance of the birds of California. Pacific Coast Avifauna No. 27.

GUTHRIE, D. A. 1993. New information on the prehistoric fauna of San Miguel Island, California. Pp. 405–416 *in* F. G. Hochberg (ed.), Third California Islands symposium: recent advances in research on the California Islands. Santa Barbara Museum of Natural History, Santa Barbara, CA.

HAEMIG, P. D. 1986. Nesting of the Phainopepla on Santa Cruz Island, California. Western Birds 17:48.

HEERMANN, A. L. 1859. Report upon the birds collected on survey. U.S. Pacific Railroad Survey Reports 10:29–80.

HERMAN, S. G., M. N. KIRVEN, AND R. W. RISEBROUGH. 1970. The Peregrine Falcon decline in California. Audubon Field Notes 24:818–820.

HOCHBERG, F. G. (ed.) 1993. Proceedings of the third California Islands symposium: recent advances in research on the California Islands. Santa Barbara Museum of Natural History, Santa Barbara, CA.

HOM, W., R. W. RISEBROUGH, A. SOUTAR, AND D. R. YOUNG. 1974. Deposition of DDE and polychlorinated biphenyls in dated sediments of the Santa Barbara Basin. Science 184:1197–1199.

HOWELL, A. B. 1917. Birds of the islands off the coast of southern California. Pacific Coast Avifauna No. 12.

HUNT, G. L., JR., AND M .W. HUNT. 1974. Trophic levels and turnover rates: the avifauna of Santa Barbara Island, California. Condor 76:363–369.

HUNT, G. L., R. L. PITMAN, AND H. L. JONES. 1980. Distribution and abundance of seabirds breeding on the California Channel Islands. Pp. 443–459 *in* D. M. Power (ed.), The California Islands. Santa Barbara Museum of Natural History, Santa Barbara, CA.

INGRAM, T. 1992. Seabird monitoring in Channel Islands National Park 1990. Channel Islands National Park Science Report CHIS-92-001.

JEHL, J. R., JR. 1971. The status of *Carpodacus mcgregori*. Condor 73:375–376.

JEHL, J. R., JR. 1973. Studies of a declining population of Brown Pelicans in northwestern California. Condor 75:69–79.

JEHL, J. R., JR. 1977a. An annotated list of birds of Islas Los Coronados, Baja California, and adjacent waters. Western Birds 8:91–101.

JEHL, J. R., JR. 1977b. History and present status of Ospreys in northwestern Baja California. Pp. 141–145 *in* Transactions of the North American Osprey research conference. National Park Service Transactions and Proceedings Series No. 2.

JEHL, J. R., JR., AND W. T. EVERETT. 1985. History and status of the avifauna of Isla Guadalupe, Mexico. Transactions of the San Diego Society of Natural History 20:313–336.

JOHNSON, N. K. 1972. Origin and differentiation of the avifauna of the Channel Islands, California. Condor 74:295–315.

JONES, H. L. 1975. Studies of avian turnover, dispersal and colonization of the California Channel Islands. Ph.D. thesis, University of California, Los Angeles.

JONES, H. L., AND J. M. DIAMOND. 1976. Short-time-base studies of turnover in breeding bird populations of the California Channel Islands. Condor 78:526–549.

JORGENSEN, P. D. 1984. The birds of San Clemente Island. Western Birds 15:111–130.

KENYON, K. W. 1947. Breeding populations of the Osprey in Lower California. Condor 49:152–158.

KIFF, L. F. 1980. Historical changes in resident populations of California Islands raptors. Pp. 651–671 *in* D. M. Power (ed.), The California Islands. Santa Barbara Museum of Natural History, Santa Barbara, CA.

LOOMIS, L. M. 1895. California water birds. No. III. South Farallon Island in July, Proceedings of the California Academy of Sciences, Second Series 5:177–224.

LYNCH, J. F., AND N. K. JOHNSON. 1974. Turnover and equilibria in insular avifaunas, with special reference to the California Channel Islands. Condor 76:370–384.

MACARTHUR, R. H., AND E. O. WILSON. 1967. The theory of island biogeography. Princeton University Press, Princeton, NJ.

MATTHEWS, J. R. (ed.). 1990. The official World Wildlife Fund guide to endangered species of North America. Beacham, Washington, DC.

MILLER, A. H. 1951. A comparison of the avifaunas of Santa Cruz and Santa Rosa islands, California. Condor 53:117–123.

PAGE, G. W., AND L. W. STENZEL. 1981. The breeding status of the Snowy Plover in California. Western Birds 12:1–39.

PAGE, G. W., L. E. STENZEL, AND W. D. SHUFORD. 1991. Distribution and abundance of the Snowy Plover on its western North American breeding grounds. Journal of Field Ornithology 62:245–255.

PHILBRICK, R. N. (ed.). 1967. Proceedings of the symposium on the biology of the California Islands. Santa Barbara Botanic Garden, Santa Barbara, CA.

PHILBRICK, R. N. 1972. The plants of Santa Barbara Island California. Madroño 21:329–393.

POWER, D. M. 1972. Numbers of bird species on the California Islands. Evolution 26:451–463.

POWER, D. M. 1980a. Evolution of land birds on the California Islands. Pp. 613–649 *in* D. M. Power (ed.),

The California Islands. Santa Barbara Museum of Natural History, Santa Barbara, CA.

POWER, D. M. (ed.). 1980b. The California Islands: proceedings of a multidisciplinary symposium. Santa Barbara Museum of Natural History, Santa Barbara, CA.

RAY, M. S. 1904. A fortnight on the Farallones. Auk 21:425–442.

RISEBROUGH, R. W., J. DAVIS, AND D. W. ANDERSON. 1970. Effects of various chlorinated hydrocarbons. Pp. 40–50 in J. W. Gillett (ed.), The biological impact of pesticides in the environment. Oregon State University Press, Corvallis.

RISEBROUGH, R.W., F. C. SIBLEY, AND M. N. KIRVEN. 1971. Reproductive failure of the Brown Pelican on Anacapa Island in 1969. American Birds 25(1):8–9.

SCOTT, T. A., AND M. L. MORRISON. 1990. Natural history and management of the San Clemente Loggerhead Shrike. Proceedings of the Western Foundation of Vertebrate Zoology 4:23–57.

SMALL, A. 1974. The birds of California. Winchester Press, New York.

STEWARD, R. M., J. SMAIL, W. C. CLOW, AND R. P. HENDERSON. 1974. The status of the Song Sparrow and Bewick's Wren on San Clemente Island and Santa Barbara Island, California. Report to the U.S. Fish and Wildlife Service Office of Endangered Species (unpubl.).

STREATOR, C. P. 1888. Notes on the birds of the Santa Barbara islands. Ornithology and Oology 13:52–54.

SWARD, W. L. 1977. The status of the San Clemente Sage Sparrow and Loggerhead Shrike (unpubl.).

TAYLOR, H. R. 1887. A trip to the Farallone Islands. Ornithology and Oology 12:41–43.

TOWNSEND, C. H. 1890. Scientific results of explorations by the U.S. Fish Commission steamer Albatross. No. XIV. Birds from the coasts of western North American and adjacent islands, collected 1888–'89, with descriptions of new species. Proceedings of the National Academy of Sciences 13:131–142.

U.S. FISH AND WILDLIFE SERVICE. 1984. Recovery plan for the endangered and threatened species of the California Channel Islands. U.S. Fish and Wildlife Service, Portland, OR.

WILLETT, G. 1910. A summer trip to the northern Santa Barbara islands. Condor 12:170–174.

WILLETT, G. 1933. A revised list of the birds of southwestern California. Pacific Coast Avifauna No. 21.

WILLEY, D. W. 1990. Nesting success of San Clemente Sage Sparrows. Southwestern Naturalist 35:28–31.

WINCHELL, C. S. 1990. First breeding record of the Snowy Plover for San Clemente Island. Western Birds 21:39–40.

WINGFIELD, J. C., A. MARTIN, M. W. HUNT, G. L. HUNT, JR., AND D. S. FARNER. 1980. Origin of homosexual pairing of female Western Gulls on Santa Barbara Island. Pp. 461–466 in D. M. Power (ed.), The California Islands. Santa Barbara Museum of Natural History, Santa Barbara, CA.

WINGFIELD, J. C., A. NEWMAN, G. L. JUNT, JR., AND D. S. FARNER. 1980. Androgen in high concentrations in the blood of female Western Gulls, Larus occidentalis. Naturwissenschaften 67:514.

YEATON, R. I. 1974. An ecological analysis of chaparral and pine forest bird communities on Santa Cruz Island and mainland California. Ecology 55:959–973.

Studies in Avian Biology No. 15:91–102, 1994.

A CHRONOLOGY OF ORNITHOLOGICAL EXPLORATION IN THE HAWAIIAN ISLANDS, FROM COOK TO PERKINS

STORRS L. OLSON AND HELEN F. JAMES

Abstract. Although ornithological exploration of the Hawaiian archipelago began in 1778, more than a century elapsed before reasonably comprehensive avifaunal surveys were conducted in the 1880s and 1890s. We review the history of early bird collecting for each of the major islands, based on examination of specimen data, archives, and the published literature. An island-by-island approach shows that some islands were more favored for visits by early collectors, while others, especially Maui, were long neglected. Given the uneven collecting histories of individual islands, we speculate that additional species and populations may have become extinct after first European contact, but before specimens were preserved for science.

Key Words: Hawaiian Islands; history of ornithological collecting; historical extinctions; museum collections.

Compared to many parts of the world, ornithological exploration got an early start in the Hawaiian Islands, beginning with the third and final voyage of Captain James Cook in 1778, which expedition marked the first European contact with the islands. By way of contrast, the first bird to be collected for science in Panama, crossroads of world trade from the late 15th century onward, was not described until 65 years after Cook first landed in Hawaii (Gould 1843a). Despite this promising beginning, over a century elapsed before serious efforts were made to survey the Hawaiian avifauna.

We now know that human-caused degradation of Hawaiian ecosystems began with the arrival of Polynesians (Olson and James 1982, 1991; James and Olson 1991), and was only accelerated by the increased habitat destruction and introductions of animals, plants, and pathogens that followed with new waves of human settlers from abroad. The dominant theme in Hawaiian ornithology has therefore been a chronicle of extinction.

The present survey, based on an extensive literature search and on specimen data from most of the museums housing significant collections of Hawaiian birds, emphasizes the degree to which our perception of the number and kinds of birds known historically (as opposed to those known only from bones) in the islands may be biased by the manner and timing of ornithological collecting in the 19th century. Some species and island populations of birds probably survived undetected into the historic period but were overtaken by extinction before specimens could be collected. To identify possible biases of this nature, it is instructive to examine the history of ornithological collecting on an island-by-island basis.

In the century following Cook's arrival, ornithological exploration in the Hawaiian Islands was sporadic at best, so that an account of these years reads like a litany of missed opportunities, as noted a century ago by Newton (1892). Numerous exploring expeditions with naturalists aboard touched in the islands without adding much to ornithology. We have tried to list all those that brought back at least a few specimens (Table 1). Others that apparently did not may be found in Judd (1974). Explanations of museum acronyms are in the Acknowledgments.

In the late 1880s, Scott B. Wilson, motivated by the interest of his mentor Alfred Newton, of Cambridge University, undertook ornithological explorations of the major islands in 1887 and 1888. Wilson usually based himself in the mountain houses of island residents (Manning 1986:13), not necessarily in the best places for collecting. In several instances his activities on a given island were decidedly perfunctory, so that he overlooked numerous species. The results of Wilson's efforts were published over several years and summarized in his magnum opus (Wilson and Evans 1890–1899). His itinerary has been pieced together partly from that source but mainly from specimen data. Wilson visited the islands in the 1890s as well. Although Newton remarked on Wilson's apparent lack of interest in further collecting at that time (Manning 1986:18), a few of his specimens from this period are found scattered in various museums.

Wilson's original discoveries spurred Walter Rothschild to send his own collector, Henry Palmer, to the islands. The industrious Palmer, with assistants including George C. Munro and one Wolstenholme (? = Harry Wolstenholme—cf. Whittell 1954: 780), scoured the archipelago with such avidity that he was often accused by Rothschild's rival, Newton, of pillaging the avifauna during his sojourn from December 1890 to August 1893. An outline of Palmer's itinerary is given in Rothschild (1893) and Mearns and Mearns (1992).

Meanwhile, Newton and colleagues coordinated a Joint Committee for the Zoology of the Sandwich Islands that secured funding from the Royal Society, the British Association for the Advancement of Science, and eventually the Bishop Museum, to send another collector to the islands—R. C. L. Perkins, whose extensive labors in both ornithology and entomology spanned the period 1892 to 1897, after which his energies were devoted almost exclusively to the latter. The history of this cooperative effort and Perkins' itinerary are detailed by Manning (1986). Although Perkins' collections added only a single new species, the Black Mamo (*Drepanis funerea* Newton), to the then known avifauna, he was, fortunately, a very keen and intelligent observer who worked under field conditions of extreme deprivation and who left us with virtually all we will ever know about the habits of many now extinct species (Perkins 1893, 1895, 1901, 1903, 1913).

Although many of Wilson's specimens went initially to UMZC, he also sold specimens rather widely (e.g., to Rothschild and RMNH). Palmer's specimens went directly to Rothschild and the bulk was subsequently conveyed to AMNH with the purchase of the Rothschild collection, although a sizable portion went to BMNH with the Rothschild bequest. Perkins' specimens were divided mainly between UMZC, BMNH, and BPBM. Material of all three collectors has been extensively dispersed through exchange and may now be found in many museums around the world.

The itineraries of Wilson, Palmer, and Perkins are summarized in Table 1. What follows is a short account of collecting in the islands prior to their more organized efforts, with notice of a few significant subsequent collections.

HAWAII

Cook's third voyage brought back a number of birds from Hawaii upon which 11 new species were later based. The principal natural history forays of this expedition took place in January and February of 1779, when the vessels were anchored at Kealakekua Bay on the Kona (western) coast of the island of Hawaii. All Hawaiian specimens from the third voyage upon which new species were later founded came from this general area (Medway 1981, Olson 1989c). Most of what is known of the subsequent history of Cook voyage Hawaiian birds is dealt with in detail by Medway (1981). Of the 11 species named from this expedition, only the rail *Porzana sandwichensis* was never taken in the Kona district again.

Andrew Bloxam, naturalist of H.M.S. *Blonde* (see Oahu account), collected a single Elepaio (*Chasiempis sandwichensis*) on Hawaii in 1825 and reported the presence of what we now know to have been Dark-rumped Petrels (*Pterodroma phaeopygia*), but contributed little else to the island's ornithology (Bloxam 1827, 1925, MS notes).

Between 1825 and 1840, only a few specimens of birds, mostly geese (*Branta sandvicensis*) that presumably originated on the

TABLE 1. ISLAND-BY-ISLAND HISTORY OF COLLECTING IN THE HAWAIIAN ISLANDS MORE OR LESS CHRONOLOGICALLY ORDERED BY DATE OF FIRST SIGNIFICANT ORNITHOLOGICAL ACTIVITY. THESE HISTORIES COVER THE PERIOD THROUGH THE EXPLORATIONS OF R. C. L. PERKINS, BUT ALSO INCLUDE A FEW SUBSEQUENT COLLECTIONS OF NOTE. EACH ENTRY GIVES THE KNOWN TIME SPAN, COLLECTOR OR EXPEDITION, ANY PERTINENT LITERATURE, AND PRINCIPAL REPOSITORIES OF SPECIMENS (THE LAST TWO OMITTED FOR WILSON, PALMER, AND PERKINS). THIS SUPPLEMENTS THE TABULATION IN OLSON AND JAMES (1991:TABLE 1) IN WHICH THE ENDEMIC LAND BIRDS OF THE ISLANDS ARE LISTED CHRONOLOGICALLY BY DATE OF ORIGINAL DESCRIPTION (WHICH WAS SOMETIMES LONG AFTER THE SPECIMENS WERE COLLECTED)

HAWAII

1779 Jan. Cook's Third Voyage (Medway 1981, Olson 1989c; LIV, RMNH, NMW)

1825 June. H.M.S. *Blonde* (Bloxam 1827, Olson 1986; BMNH)

1832 Sept. David Douglas sends *Branta* (Olson 1989a; LIV, ANSP)

1834. Lord Derby's *Branta* received (Olson 1989a)

1836 Sept–Oct. *Bonite* (Eydoux and Souleyet 1841; MNHN)

Between 1837 and 1848. Rev. Forbes for J. K. Townsend (Peale 1848:107)

1840 Nov–1841 Mar. U.S. Exploring Expedition (Wilkes 1845, Peale 1848, Cassin 1858; USNM, ANSP, MCZ)

1846 Nov 2–12. *Galathea* (Steen Bille 1852; ZMUC, ZMB)

1851–1855. Jules Rémy (Wagner et al. 1990:table 8; MNHN, MCZ)

1856 Mar. U.S. North Pacific Surveying & Exploring Expedition (Cassin 1862; ANSP)

[1852–1863]. Andrew Garrett (present on Hawaii through years indicated—Thomas 1979; undated material at ANSP, 1857 and 1859 at MCZ)

1850s–1860s. J. D. Mills [arrived Hilo 1851, d. 1887, thought to have been most active collecting ca. 1859–1860] (Dole 1878, Manning 1978, 1979; BPBM, RMNH)

ca. 1863 or before. Specimens obtained for Ferdinand Gruber (Olson 1990; USNM, NMW)

1864 or 1865. William T. Brigham (Olson 1992; MCZ)

1872. Théodore Ballieu (Wagner et al. 1990:table 8; MNHN; Mearns and Mearns 1992)

1875 Aug 14–19. *Challenger* Expedition (Sclater 1878, 1881; BMNH)

1876–1878. Théodore Ballieu (Wagner et al. 1990:table 8; MNHN, also MCZ, BMNH, RMNH)

1887 May–1888 June. Wilson

1891 Apr, Aug. Wilson

1891 Sept. Palmer

1892 Jan–June. Palmer

1892 June–Oct. Perkins

1892 Apr, Nov. Wilson

1894 July–Aug. Perkins

1895 June–Sept. Perkins

TABLE 1. CONTINUED

1895 Apr 3, 8, May 29. Thos. C. White for Flood brothers (MCZ)

1895 Dec–1896 Jan. Perkins

1896 Mar, Aug–Sept, Nov–Dec. Perkins

1896 May, June. Wilson

1896. Schauinsland (UMB)

1897 Feb–Mar. Perkins

1898 Apr 9–1903 Aug 24. Henshaw (resident on Hawaii from Dec 1894 to Feb 1904—Henshaw 1919–1920, Nelson 1932; BPBM, USNM)

OAHU

1786 May–June. H.M.S. *Queen Charlotte* (Dixon 1789; BMNH)

1825 May. H.M.S. *Blonde* (Bloxam 1827, 1925, Olson 1986; BMNH)

1834 Sept. M. Botta (MNHN)

1835 Jan. Townsend and Nuttall (Townsend 1839; specimens not separable from those of 1837)

1837 Jan. Townsend (Townsend 1839; ANSP, LIV, USNM, FMNH)

1837 Jan. Deppe (ZMB, ZIL, NMW)

1837 July. *Venus* (Prévost and Des Murs 1849; MNHN, MCZ)

1837 July, 1839 June. HMS *Sulphur* (Gould 1843b; BMNH)

1840 Sept, Nov; 1841 Mar–Apr. U.S. Exploring Expedition (Midshipman Henry Eld; ROM)

1842. Specimens sent via Chile (Olson 1989b; SMF, BMNH)

1843. May *Danaïde* (M. Jaurès [or Jaurèr]; MNHN)

1843. Specimens obtained for I. G. Voznesensky (ZIL)

1845. Specimens obtained for I. G. Voznesensky (ZIL)

1846 Oct 7–31. *Galathea* (Steen Bille 1852; ZMUC, ZMB)

1849 May, 1850 Oct. H.M.S. *Herald* (Capt. Kellett; BMNH, ZIL)

1870 Feb 21–Mar 2. Austrian East Asian and American Expedition (Pelzeln 1873; NMW)

1873–1874. U.S. North Pacific Surveying Expedition (Streets 1877a, b; USNM)

1888 Apr, Oct–Nov. Wilson

1891 Oct. Wilson

1892 Aug, Sept. Wilson

1893 Jan. Wilson

1893 Mar–June. Palmer

1892 Mar–June, Oct–1893 May. Perkins

1895 Apr, June, Nov. Perkins

1895 Feb, May, June, July–Aug, Oct, Dec; 1896 Jan. M. J. Flood (especially Jul–Aug); some by John Seaburg, and James and Fred McGuire for Flood (MCZ)

1896 Feb, July, Aug, Sept, Nov. Perkins

1897 Jan, Feb, Mar. Perkins

1901 Nov, Dec. Perkins

1902 Oct, Nov. Perkins

KAUAI

1778 Jan. Cook's Third Voyage [no significant specimens]

TABLE 1. CONTINUED

1835 Feb. Townsend and Nuttall (Townsend 1839;
    ANSP, LIV, USNM)
1840 Oct. U.S. Exploring Expedition [no specimens]
    (Wilkes 1845, Peale 1848, Cassin 1858)
1866. Knudsen (Ridgway 1882, USNM)
1886–1893. Knudsen (Stejneger 1887a, b, 1888,
    1890; USNM, ZMUO, BMNH)
1888 Apr, Sept. Wilson
1890 Dec–1891 Jan–Apr. Palmer
1891 Apr 29. Wilson
1892 Feb, Nov. Wilson
1893 Jan, Nov. Hans Isenberg (UMB)
1893 Feb. Wilson
1893 June–Aug. Palmer
1894 May–June. Perkins
1895 Apr–May, Oct–Nov. Perkins
1895/1896. Hans Isenberg (UMB)
1896 Apr. Wilson
1896 July–Aug. Perkins
1897 Jan–Feb. Perkins

MOLOKAI

1864 or 1865. Brigham (Olson 1992; MCZ)
1888 June. Wilson
1892 Dec–1893 Feb. Palmer
1893 May–June, July–Sept, Oct–Nov. Perkins
1894. R. Meyer
1894 Dec–1895 Feb. M. J. Flood (MCZ)
1896 June. Perkins
1896. Meyer (UMB)
1898. Meyer (UMB)
1902 Feb. Perkins
1907 Apr–June. W. A. Bryan (Bryan 1908; BPBM)

MAUI

ca. 1850–1880. A single *Vestiaria* collected by a Mr.
    Chapin (CAS)
1879 June 30–July. Finsch (Finsch 1880; ZMB,
    BMNH)
1888 July. Wilson
1892 July–Oct. Palmer
1890s. Mathias Newell (Bryan 1901; BPBM, MCZ)
1894 spring. Mathias Newell (Henshaw 1900;
    BPBM)
1894 Mar, May. Perkins
1896 Feb–Mar, Apr–May, Sept–Oct, Dec. Perkins
1897 Jan. Perkins
1900 June, July. Henshaw (BPBM)
1901 June, Aug. Henshaw (BPBM)
1973 Sept. *Melamprosops* collected (Casey & Jacobi
    1974; BPBM, AMNH)

LANAI

1888 June. Wilson
ca. 1888. Hayselden (BPBM)
1892 Nov. Palmer
1893 Dec–1894 Feb. Perkins
1894 June–July. Perkins
[1911–1934] 1913 Feb 22. Munro [dates of residency
    and date *Dysmorodrepanis* collected] (Perkins
    1919; BPBM)

TABLE 1. CONTINUED

NIIHAU

1887 or 1888. Knudsen (Stejneger 1888; USNM)
1893 July 15–28. Palmer

KAHOOLAWE

1892 Oct. Palmer (Rothschild 1893)

NORTHWESTERN CHAIN

1889 Jan. Wilson's purchase of *Telespiza* (Wilson
    1890, Olson and James 1986; RMNH)
1891 May–June. Palmer
1916 Feb. 12. *Thetis* (Bryan 1917; CAS)
1923 June. *Tanager* Expedition (Wetmore 1924,
    1925; USNM, BPBM)

island of Hawaii, found their way to Europe (e.g., Olson 1989a). J. K. Townsend was on Hawaii briefly in 1837, where he remarked on the paucity of birds and apparently did not collect any himself (Townsend 1839). Specimens were later sent to him from there by a missionary, Rev. Forbes, including those used later by Peale (1848) in the original description of the Hawaiian Crow (*Corvus hawaiiensis*).

Vessels of the United States Exploring Expedition arrived in the islands in September 1840, some staying until April 1841. The expedition ornithologist, Titian Peale, was in the archipelago for a only a short period before being dispatched to the south (Wilkes 1845) and it is not clear to what extent the few Hawaiian bird specimens that have survived from this expedition were the result of his efforts or those of others. One of the expedition's two principal vessels, the *Peacock*, was wrecked at the mouth of the Columbia River, occasioning the loss of many specimens, including all those of the crow, as Peale (1848:107) later lamented. Although members of the expedition were on Kauai and Oahu, all of the birds that survive from the expedition (Peale 1848, Cassin 1858), save for a few from Oahu preserved by Midshipman Henry Eld and now in the ROM, are certainly or probably from the island of Hawaii.

Subsequent to the Exploring Expedition, collecting yielded little of interest for another 35 years. Although amateur taxidermist J. D. Mills was active in this period (Manning 1978, 1979), material from his important collections was not described until considerably later (Dole 1878).

In 1875, the brief visit of the British *Challenger* Expedition resulted in little other than securing the type of the Hawaiian Duck, *Anas wyvilliana,* though the species had been collected previously several times (at least on Oahu in 1837 and 1846). Théodore Ballieu, whose name has been almost invariably misspelled "Bailleu," including in the specific name of the Palila, which commemorates him (*Loxioides "bailleui"*), was French Consul at Honolulu from 1869 to 1878 (Mearns and Mearns 1992). By collecting at higher elevations in the Kona district of Hawaii, he was able to secure the first specimens of Palila in 1876 as well as what are the earliest extant examples of Akiapolaau (*Hemignathus wilsoni*), although the species was not recognized as new at the time.

The final few species to be added to the avifauna of Hawaii were collected by Wilson and by Palmer; no others were added by Perkins, or through the long residence of H. W. Henshaw, who collected extensively on the island at the turn of the century.

OAHU

The first vessels to visit the Hawaiian Islands after Cook, H.M.S.S. *King George* and *Queen Charlotte,* captains Nathaniel Portlock and George Dixon, called at various islands in 1786 and again in 1787. They returned with a few specimens of birds of which Dixon (1789) published a plate of what is clearly the Oahu Oo (*Moho apicalis*). The species was not recognized as distinct and named for another 70 years (Gould 1860), and it was even later that its island of origin was determined. Nevertheless, Dixon's plate is the earliest documentation of a bird specimen from Oahu.

The year 1825 saw the arrival of H.M.S. *Blonde* on a political mission, Lord Byron, successor to the poet, in command. Serving

as expedition naturalist was Andrew Bloxam, who at age 23 had recently graduated from Oxford, but with scant training in natural history. To judge from his diary (Bloxam 1925) and the journal of the expedition's horticulturalist (Macrae 1922), Bloxam did not exert himself unduly and collected birds on only a few days of his fairly lengthy stay on the island.

An account of the expedition was compiled by Maria Graham from various diaries and was published under Byron's name (see Bloxam 1827). The appendix on natural history was taken from Bloxam's manuscript notes and so heavily edited and misinterpreted that Newton (1892:466) dismissed it as "a disgrace . . . utterly unworthy of its reputed author." Nevertheless, several scientific names date from this publication with Bloxam as author. Bloxam's unpublished natural history notes (see Olson 1986) document that among the material that he turned over to the Lords of the Admiralty were 24 bird specimens from Oahu, all but two of which are present in the collections of the British Museum.

Bloxam was the only collector ever to find the Oahu thrush (*Myadestes*). His two specimens, an adult and an immature, were long thought to have been lost, but we have studied an immature in BMNH and an adult in ANSP that we believe most likely came from Oahu and that may well be Bloxam's specimens.

In 1835, John Kirk Townsend, accompanied by Thomas Nuttall, collected birds on Oahu (Townsend 1839). Townsend returned in December 1836 and linked up with Ferdinand Deppe, a renowned collector of Mexican birds. On 15 January 1837 he and Deppe hired a house in "Nuano" (= Nuuanu) Valley where they were "very successful" at procuring "birds, plants &c." (Townsend 1839:207).

The fate of Townsend's Hawaiian material was tangled and unfortunate (see Kauai account). Although none of his specimens from Oahu were ever described, new taxa based on Deppe's material were named over a span of years by Lichtenstein and Cabanis. Neither Townsend nor Deppe obtained any thrushes, despite their having collected in the same general area where Bloxam obtained them 12 years before. No collectors subsequent to Townsend and Deppe obtained either the Oahu Akialoa (*Hemignathus lichtensteini*) or the Oahu Oo (*Moho apicalis*), nor were any species discovered subsequently on Oahu that had not been taken by either Bloxam or Townsend and Deppe.

KAUAI

Specimens of *Vestiaria coccinea* were received in barter when Cook's ships stopped at Kauai in 1778, but there is no evidence of any other birds having come from Kauai prior to 1835. J. K. Townsend, accompanied by Thomas Nuttall, arrived on Kauai on 11 February of that year and made "several long excursions over the hills and through the deep valleys, without much success. The birds are the same as those we found and collected at Oahu, but are not so numerous. They are principally creepers (*Certhia*) and honey-suckers (*Nectarinia*) . . . and some species are very abundant" (Townsend 1839:207–208). Although Nuttall may have aided Townsend in collecting birds, he was mainly botanizing and his only published contribution to Hawaiian ornithology is his passing mention of the Short-eared Owl (*Asio flammeus*) (Nuttall 1840).

Townsend's specimens were later scattered and their significance never appreciated. Some went to ANSP but a large portion went to J. J. Audubon to try to sell in Europe. In June 1838, Audubon offered for sale to the 13th Earl of Derby a large selection of birds collected by Townsend, including 121 specimens of at least 13 species from the Sandwich Islands. The Earl made a manuscript list of the offering that was transcribed and discussed extensively by Medway (1981). The Earl selected only a handful, most of which are now in the Liverpool museum, and the others were dispersed. Such as still exist and can be identified as of Townsend origin may be found in diverse collections in Europe and North America.

Townsend's birds from Kauai were the first other than the Cook *Vestiaria* to be taken on that island and he brought back species that remained undescribed for decades afterwards. For example, there is a Townsend specimen of *Loxops parvus* in the collections of the Smithsonian Institution that had been received prior to 1841 by its predecessor, the National Institute. Yet the species was not named until 1887, from material supplied by Valdemar Knudsen (Stejneger 1887a).

The U.S. Exploring Expedition was on Kauai in 1840, where Peale (1848:149) mentions a bird that is certainly the endemic meliphagid *Moho braccatus,* although he confused it with *Certhia* (= *Drepanis*) *pacifica.* Although Peale says that some of these birds were killed at Hanalei, if they were preserved they must have been lost in the wreck of the *Peacock*.

Moho braccatus was clearly illustrated by Reichenbach (1853), although he erroneously regarded it as the female of *Moho nobilis.* In all likelihood this figure was based on one of the birds collected by Townsend. The species was finally recognized and named by Cassin in 1855, based on a Townsend specimen in ANSP.

Apart from the Exploring Expedition, which contributed nothing to knowledge of birds of the island, ornithology was essentially dormant on Kauai for the half century after Townsend, to be revived by Valdemar Knudsen, a Norwegian adventurer who settled on Kauai in 1857 (Peppin 1956). Knudsen forwarded birds to the Smithsonian Institution as early as 1866, though it was not until considerably later that any received attention (Ridgway 1886, 1888). These and additional specimens cataloged in 1886, 1887, 1888, and 1889, were described by Stejneger (1887a, b, 1888, 1890).

There is an interesting card in the biographical file of C. W. Richmond at USNM that was sent to Richmond, probably about

1912, by Augustus F. Knudsen, in which the latter states that he, too, "collected birds in 1885 & 86—specimens sent in with Mr. V. Knudsen's collection. Also in 1892–93–94. But again my father insisted on only his name going in as he had hoped to find new birds. I gave in. 4 new birds were found by me." A number of Knudsen specimens dated 1890 and 1893 were sent to Robert Collett in Norway (ZMUO), from which some were in turn sent to BMNH. Eleven specimens purchased 2 June 1887 by the Berlin Museum (ZMB) from a dealer, J. Wentscher, are of obvious Knudsen make and some bear label annotations in English that can only have come from Knudsen's original labels or notes. The most notable among this series is the holotype of Cabanis' name *Hemignathus procerus.*

In terms of ornithological knowledge, the Knudsen's efforts put Kauai ahead of the other Hawaiian islands for a time. Wilson collected on the island in 1888, securing and naming *Loxops caeruleirostris*, which had eluded previous collectors. Because of the better comparative material available to him, he was also able to distinguish as new both the akialoa and the amakihi of Kauai, naming them both for Stejneger, who had reported Knudsen specimens of each but, in the absence of comparative material, had no way to separate them from the previously described species from Hawaii. Palmer made his first visit to Kauai from December 1890 through April 1891, by which time there was but one new bird left for him to find, the small Kauai thrush, *Myadestes palmeri,* leaving no new ornithological discoveries for Perkins to make.

MOLOKAI

Strangely, the avifauna of the much smaller and less populous island of Molokai was better documented by collections than its larger neighbor of Maui. We know from Dole (1869) that William T. Brigham recorded and presumably collected a strange bird on Molokai in 1864 or 1865. What is believed to be Brigham's small, dateless col-

lection is in the MCZ and included two specimens of the extinct drepanidine *Ciridops anna,* which may have been Brigham's puzzling bird (Olson 1992).

Wilson visited Molokai in June 1888, but as on Maui, his activity must have been very limited and the number of specimens he procured were few, apparently including only *Phaeornis lanaiensis, Loxops virens,* and the types of *Paroreomyza flammea.*

Palmer made a much more thorough job of his visit from December 1892 through February 1893, adding *Palmeria dolei* to the Molokai list and obtaining the first specimens of *Moho bishopi.* Perkins followed hard on Palmer's heels in May and June of 1893 (he visited the island twice more during the same year), when he obtained the first specimen of *Drepanis funerea,* the only new species of Hawaiian bird that he personally was able to discover once Rothschild's collectors had been through the islands.

Milton J. Flood, who with his brother Oliver operated a commercial collecting business, was on Molokai from December 1894 to February 1895 and preserved very large series of specimens of the commoner birds, most of which are at MCZ. The more desirable rarities seem to have eluded him, however, probably because he was denied permission to collect on Bishop Estate lands because he did not represent a "reputable scientific society" (Manning 1986:16).

Perkins revisited Molokai in 1896. During this period, R. M. Meyer (Charles Bishop's ranch manager on Molokai—Manning 1986:15) and his family were host to most bird collectors visiting the island. Members of the Meyer family preserved birds about this time that are still in the possession of the family, including such rarities as *Drepanis funerea* and *Moho bishopi.* Six specimens of the former were taken by Theodore Meyer in 1894 according to Bryan (1908). Specimens in UMB are attributed to R. Meyer in 1896 and 1898, acquired through then director Hugo Schauinsland.

A substantial series of specimens was secured by William A. Bryan (1908) for the

Bishop Museum from 15 April to 15 June 1907. After great exertion, he was able to collect three specimens of *Drepanis funerea,* but did not encounter *Moho bishopi,* which by that time may already have been extinct. Based on specimens he took, he named the Molokai thrush as a distinct species, *Phaeornis rutha,* after his wife. This has usually been considered identical with *Phaeornis* (= *Myadestes*) *lanaiensis* of Lanai, although our comparisons indicate that it is probably subspecifically distinct.

MAUI

Maui is the second largest of the Hawaiian Islands and home to the once busy whaling port of Lahaina. As extraordinary as it may seem, with one unimportant exception, we have found no record of any specimen of bird having been preserved from Maui prior to 1879, exactly a century after the departure of Cook's expedition from the islands. Why this should be is unclear, but lack of convenient access to forest habitats in the steep mountains of West Maui that back Lahaina may have been a contributing factor. Regardless, the lack of early collecting has doubtless had an effect on our current perspective of the "historically" known avifauna of Maui.

In June and July 1879, Otto Finsch visited Maui and made desultory observations and collections in the lowlands and in forest near Olinda. Although he mentions several species that he did not collect (Finsch 1880), he brought back specimens of only 3 species of forest birds. He was thus the first collector to obtain specimens of *Paroreomyza montana,* which he misidentified as *Hemignathus obscurus* (!), and *Loxops coccinea ochracea,* which he accurately described but unfortunately under a previously used name that proved to be a synonym of *L. c. coccinea.*

Almost another decade then passed before Scott Wilson arrived on Maui in July 1888. His collecting effort seems to have been no more intense than that of Finsch and appears to have resulted in only a scant handful of specimens in the collections at UMZC, the only one of note being the single juvenile that became the type of what is now called *Palmeria dolei* (Wilson).

Thus, the avifauna of Maui was never adequately sampled until Palmer's sojourn from July through October 1892. Palmer obtained all the forest birds known historically from Maui (except *Melamprosops*) and because of his efforts the privilege of naming the most new forms from Maui fell to Lord Rothschild. The taxa include four valid subspecies of drepanidines, the genus *Palmeria,* and the singular Maui Parrotbill, *Pseudonestor xanthophrys.*

Brother Mathias Newell, who resided on Maui, preserved a number of birds in the 1890s, though these had minimal data (Bryan 1901). The most notable was the holotype of *Puffinus newelli* (Henshaw 1900). Perkins, followed by Henshaw, collected extensively on Maui, but neither discovered any new taxa there. No significant subsequent collections of birds were made on Maui until the surprising discovery of *Melamprosops phaeosoma* in 1973 (Casey and Jacobi 1974).

LANAI

The much smaller and less populated island of Lanai was neglected by ornithologists for even longer than Maui. Scott Wilson made the first bird collections we know of from the ornithologically depauperate island in June 1888. He stayed with F. H. Hayselden, who at about the same time supplied bird specimens from Lanai to the Bishop Museum. Henry Palmer visited Lanai in November 1892, when he obtained the only three specimens known of *Hemignathus lanaiensis.* Perkins collected birds on Lanai in 1893 and 1894.

The experienced naturalist and collector George C. Munro occasionally collected birds on Lanai during his residence from 1911 until 1934 (R. C. Munro 1957). Although the *Hemignathus* eluded him, he obtained the unique holotype of *Dysmorodrepanis munroi* (Perkins 1919) on 22 February 1913, the validity of which has recently been affirmed through anatomical studies (James et al. 1989).

NIIHAU

No native land birds have ever been recorded from Niihau. The first specimens of birds from the island are a few waterbirds taken by Knudsen in 1887 or 1888. Palmer collected there in 1893 and likewise found only shorebirds and introduced mynas (*Acridotheres tristis*). Only the fossil record of this paleontologically unexplored island can now tell us what species of native land birds once occurred here.

KAHOOLAWE

This smallest of the main Hawaiian Islands was ecologically degraded even in Cook's time. Subsequent ranching did nothing to improve the environment, after which the island was used as a bombing range, beginning in 1941. Palmer visited Kahoolawe briefly in October 1892, reporting that he found no land birds except introduced House Finches (*Carpodacus mexicanus*) and a few shorebirds (Rothschild 1893). Brief paleontological surveys of the island suggest that there is unfortunately little potential for obtaining much of a fossil record there.

NORTHWESTERN CHAIN

Extensive documentation of the history of ornithological collecting in the Northwestern Hawaiian Islands is available elsewhere (Amerson 1971, Amerson et al. 1974, Clapp 1972, Clapp and Kridler 1977, Clapp and Wirtz 1975, Clapp et al. 1977, Ely and Clapp 1973, Woodward 1972) and need not be repeated here. Only those expeditions or collectors obtaining new species are listed in Table 1. The first endemic bird reported from these islands was the Laysan Finch (*Telespiza cantans*), which was described from a specimen that Wilson purchased alive in Honolulu (Olson and James 1986). Palmer collected widely in the chain in 1891, obtaining all five endemic species of Laysan. He did not land at Nihoa, however, which held out its two endemic species until the

next century. The types of the Nihoa Finch (*Telespiza ultima*) were brought off by the *Thetis* in 1916, and the Nihoa Warbler (*Acrocephalus kingi*) was the prize of the *Tanager* expedition of 1923.

CONCLUSIONS

Vagaries in the history of ornithological collecting between different islands of the Hawaiian archipelago could have permitted a number of extinctions of species or island populations to have gone undetected during the historic period. Nowhere is this more likely to have been the case than on Maui, which was not adequately surveyed until 1892. By this time *Myadestes, Moho,* and the akialoa (*Hemignathus*) had long since vanished on Oahu, and flightless rails (*Porzana*) and the passerines *Chaetoptila angustipluma, Drepanis pacifica,* and *Ciridops anna* had disappeared on Hawaii. Representatives of all of these genera save *Ciridops* are known from late Holocene bones on Maui (Olson and James 1991, James and Olson 1991). Indeed, Perkins (1903:378) alludes to a report that thrushes existed on Maui some 30 years prior to the mid-1890s. Sabo (1982) refers to sight records of *Moho* on Maui from the early 1800s up to recent times. Perkins (1903:453) also reported native observations of flightless rails on Molokai in the 19th century.

In conclusion, although many species of birds, particularly the larger flightless species and raptors, were probably exterminated long before the arrival of Cook, we would emphasize that any assessment of the the distribution and extinction of the historically known avifauna of the Hawaiian Islands should also take into account the potentially great bias that has been introduced by the differences in timing and intensity of collecting efforts on the individual islands.

ACKNOWLEDGMENTS

We thank A. C. Ziegler for extensive comments on the manuscript. We are also especially grateful to the curators of the following institutions for providing access to collections or information about them. Acronyms generally follow those given by Leviton et al. (1985), with some departures, especially for institutions they did not include. AMNH, American Museum of Natural History, New York. ANSP, Academy of Natural Sciences of Philadelphia, Pennsylvania. BMNH, British Museum (Natural History), Sub-department of Ornithology, Tring, England. BPBM, Bernice P. Bishop Museum, Honolulu, Hawaii. CAS, California Academy of Sciences, San Francisco. FMNH, Field Museum of Natural History, Chicago, Illinois. LIV, Liverpool Museum, Liverpool, England. MCZ, Museum of Comparative Zoology, Harvard University, Cambridge, Massachusetts. MNHN, Museum National d'Histoire Naturelle, Paris, France. NMW, Naturhistorisches Museum, Wien (Vienna), Austria. RMNH, Rijksmuseum van Natuurlijke Historie, Leiden, Netherlands. ROM, Royal Ontario Museum, Toronto, Canada. SMF, Forschungsinstitut Senckenberg, Frankfurt/M, Germany. UMB, Übersee-Museum, Bremen, Germany. UMZC, University Museum of Zoology, Cambridge, England. USNM, National Museum of Natural History, Smithsonian Institution, Washington, D.C. ZIL, Academy of Sciences, Zoological Institute, St. Petersburg (Leningrad), Russia. ZMB, Universität Humboldt, Museum für Naturkunde, Berlin, Germany. ZMUC, Zoologisk Museum, University of Copenhagen, Denmark. ZMUO, Zoological Museum, University of Oslo, Norway.

LITERATURE CITED

AMERSON, B. 1971. The natural history of French Frigate Shoals, Northwestern Hawaiian Islands. Atoll Research Bulletin 150.

AMERSON, B., R. C. CLAPP, AND W. O. WIRTZ. 1974. The natural history of Pearl and Hermes Reef, Northwestern Hawaiian Islands. Atoll Research Bulletin 174.

BLOXAM, A. J. 1827. Of the natural history of the Sandwich Islands; selected from the papers of A. Bloxham [sic], esq. Of birds. Appendix 3, pp. 248–253 in Lord Byron, Voyage of H. M. S. Blonde to the Sandwich Islands, in the years 1824–1825. John Murray, London. [Dated 1826 but published in 1827.]

BLOXAM, A. J. 1925. Diary of Andrew Bloxam naturalist of the "Blonde." S. M. Jones (ed.), B. P. Bishop Museum Special Publication 10.

BRYAN, W. A. 1901. A list of the Hawaiian birds in the St. Louis College collection, Honolulu, H. I., including records of several North American species. Auk 18:382–387.

BRYAN, W. A. 1908. Some birds of Molokai. Occasional Papers of the B. P. Bishop Museum of Polynesian Ethnology and Natural History 4:133–176.

BRYAN, W. A. 1917. Description of Telespiza ultima from Nihoa Island. Auk 34:70–72.

CASEY, T. L. C., AND J. D. JACOBI. 1974. A new genus and species of bird from the island of Maui, Hawaii (Passeriformes: Drepanididae). Occasional Papers of the B. P. Bishop Museum 24:215–226.

CASSIN, J. 1855. Notices of some new and little known birds in the collection of the U.S. Exploring Expedition in the Vincennes and Peacock, and in the collection of the Academy of Natural Sciences of Phil-

adelphia. Proceedings of the Academy of Natural Sciences of Philadelphia 7:438–441.

CASSIN, J. 1858. United States Exploring Expedition during the years 1838, 1839, 1840, 1841, 1842. Under the command of Charles Wilkes, U.S.N. Mammalogy and ornithology. J. B. Lippincott & Co., Philadelphia, PA.

CASSIN, J. 1862. Catalogue of birds collected by the United States North Pacific Surveying and Exploring Expedition, in command of Capt. John Rodgers, United States Navy, with notes and descriptions of new species. Proceedings of the Academy of Natural Sciences of Philadelphia 1862:312–328.

CLAPP, R. B. 1972. The natural history of Gardner Pinnacles, Northwestern Hawaiian Islands. Atoll Research Bulletin 163.

CLAPP, R. B., AND E. KRIDLER. 1977. The natural history of Necker Island, Northwestern Hawaiian Islands. Atoll Research Bulletin 206.

CLAPP, R. B., E. KRIDLER, AND R. R. FLEET. 1977. The natural history of Nihoa Island, Northwestern Hawaiian Islands. Atoll Research Bulletin 207.

CLAPP, R. B., AND W. O. WIRTZ. 1975. The natural history of Lisianski Island, Northwestern Hawaiian Islands. Atoll Research Bulletin 186.

DIXON, G. 1789. A voyage round the world: but more particularly to the north-west coast of America: performed in 1785, 1786, 1787, and 1788, in the King George and Queen Charlotte, Captains Portlock and Dixon. Geo. Goulding, London.

DOLE, S. B. 1869. A synopsis of the birds hitherto described from the Hawaiian Islands. Proceedings of the Boston Society of Natural History 12:294–309.

DOLE, S. B. 1878. List of birds of the Hawaiian Islands. Corrected for the Hawaiian Annual, with valuable additions. Pp. 41–58 in Hawaiian Almanac and Annual for 1879. Thomas G. Thrum, Honolulu.

ELY, C. A., AND R. B. CLAPP. 1973. The natural history of Laysan Island, Northwestern Hawaiian Islands. Atoll Research Bulletin 171.

EYDOUX, F., AND F. L. A. SOULEYET. 1841. Voyage autour du monde exécuté pendant les années 1836 et 1837 sur la corvette "La Bonite" Zoologie. Vol. 1. Arthus Bertrand, Paris.

FINSCH, O. 1880. Ornithological letters from the Pacific. No. 1. Ibis series 4 4:75–81.

GOULD, J. 1843a. [Nine new birds collected during the voyage of H.M.S. Sulphur]. Proceedings of the Zoological Society of London 1843:103–106.

GOULD, J. 1843b. Birds. Pp. 39–50 in R. B. Hinds (ed.), The zoology of the voyages of H.M.S. Sulphur, under the command of Captain Sir Edward Belcher, R. N., C. B., F. R. G. S., etc. during the years 1836–42. Vol. 1. Smith, Elder and Co., London.

GOULD, J. 1860. Description of a new species of the genus Moho of Lesson. Proceedings of the Zoological Society of London 1860:381.

HENSHAW, H. W. 1900. Description of a new shearwater from the Hawaiian Islands. Auk 17:246–247.

HENSHAW, H. W. 1919–1920. Autobiographical notes. Condor 21:102–107, 165–171, 177–181, 217–222; 22:3–10, 55–60, 95–101.

JAMES, H. F., AND S. L. OLSON. 1991. Descriptions of thirty-two new species of birds from the Hawaiian

Islands. Part II. Passeriformes. Ornithological Monographs 46:1–88.

JAMES, H. F., R. L. ZUSI, AND S. L. OLSON. 1989. *Dysmorodrepanis munroi* (Fringillidae: Drepanidini), a valid genus and species of Hawaiian finch. Wilson Bulletin 101:159–179.

JUDD, B. 1974. Voyages to Hawaii before 1860. [enlarged and edited by H. Y. Lind]. University Press of Hawaii, Honolulu, HI.

LEVITON, A. E., R. H. GIBBS, JR., E. HEAL, AND C. E. DAWSON. 1985. Standards in herpetology and ichthyology: part I. Standard symbolic codes for institutional resource collections in herpetology and ichthyology. Copeia 1985:802–832.

MACRAE, J. 1922. With Lord Byron at the Sandwich Islands in 1825, being extracts from the MS diary of James Macrae, Scottish botanist. W. F. Wilson (ed.). Privately published, Honolulu, HI.

MANNING, A. 1978. James D. Mills: Hilo bird collector. Hawaiian Journal of History 12:84–98.

MANNING, A. 1979. Bishop Museum's first Hawaiian birds: the Mills collection. Elepaio 40:35–43.

MANNING, A. 1986. The Sandwich Islands Committee, Bishop Museum, and R. C. L. Perkins: cooperative zoological exploration and publication. Bishop Museum Occasional Papers 26:1–46.

MEARNS, B., AND R. MEARNS. 1992. Audubon to Xántus, the lives of those commemorated in North American bird names. Academic Press, London.

MEDWAY, D. G. 1981. The contribution of Cook's third voyage to the ornithology of the Hawaiian Islands. Pacific Science 35:105–175.

MUNRO, R. C. 1957. George C. Munro. Elepaio 17:82–86.

NELSON, E. W. 1932. Henry Wetherbee Henshaw—naturalist. Auk 49:399–427.

NEWTON, A. 1892. Ornithology of the Sandwich Islands. Nature 45:465–469.

NUTTALL, T. 1840. A manual of the ornithology of the United States and Canada. 2nd ed. Hilliard, Gray, and Co., Boston, MA.

OLSON, S. L. 1986. An early account of some birds from Mauke, Cook Islands, and the origin of the "Mysterious Starling" *Aplonis mavornata* Buller. Notornis 33:197–208.

OLSON, S. L. 1989a. David Douglas and the original description of the Hawaiian Goose. Elepaio 49:49–51.

OLSON, S. L. 1989b. Two overlooked holotypes of the Hawaiian flycatcher *Chasiempis* described by Leonhard Stejneger (Aves: Myiagrinae). Proceedings of the Biological Society of Washington 102:555–558.

OLSON, S. L. 1989c. Notes on some Hawaiian birds from Cook's third voyage. Bulletin of the British Ornithologists' Club 109:201–205.

OLSON, S. L. 1990. The supposed California record of Hawaiian Hawk *Buteo solitarius*. Elepaio 50:1–2.

OLSON, S. L. 1992. William T. Brigham's Hawaiian birds and a possible historical record of *Ciridops anna* (Aves: Drepanidini) from Molokai. Pacific Science 46:495–500.

OLSON, S. L., AND H. F. JAMES. 1982. Prodromus of the fossil avifauna of the Hawaiian Islands. Smithsonian Contributions to Zoology 365:1–59.

OLSON, S. L., AND H. F. JAMES. 1986. The holotype of the Laysan Finch *Telespiza cantans* Wilson (Drepanidini). Bulletin of the British Ornithologists' Club 106:84–86.

OLSON, S. L., AND H. F. JAMES. 1991. Descriptions of thirty-two new species of birds from the Hawaiian Islands. Part I. Non-passeriformes. Ornithological Monographs 45:1–88.

PEALE, T. R. 1848. United States Exploring Expedition during the years 1838, 1839, 1840, 1841, 1842. Under the command of Charles Wilkes, U.S.N. Vol. 8. Mammalia and ornithology. C. Sherman, Philadelphia, PA.

PELZELN, A. VON 1873. Ueber die von der österreichishen Mission nach Ost-asien und America (1869–1870) eingesendeten Säugethiere und Vögel. Verhandlungen der Kaiserlich-Königlichen Zoologisch-Botanischen Gesellschaft in Wien 23:153–164.

PEPPIN, H. 1956. Valdemar Knudsen. Elepaio 16:45.

PERKINS, R. C. L. 1893. Notes on collecting in Kona, Hawaii. Ibis series 6 5:101–112.

PERKINS, R. C. L. 1895. Notes on some Hawaiian birds. Ibis series 7 1:117–129.

PERKINS, R. C. L. 1901. An introduction to the study of the Drepanididae, a family of birds peculiar to the Hawaiian Islands. Ibis series 8 1:562–585.

PERKINS, R. C. L. 1903. Vertebrata. Pp. 365–466 *in* D. Sharp (ed.), Fauna Hawaiiensis or the zoology of the Sandwich (Hawaiian) Islands. Vol. 1, pt. 4. University Press, Cambridge, England.

PERKINS, R. C. L. 1913. Introduction. Pp. xv–ccxxviii *in* D. Sharp (ed.), Fauna Hawaiiensis or the zoology of the Sandwich (Hawaiian) Islands. Vol. 1, pt. 6. University Press, Cambridge, England.

PERKINS, R. C. L. 1919. On a new genus and species of bird of the family Drepanididae from the Hawaiian Islands. Annals and Magazine of Natural History series 9 3:250–252.

PRÉVOST, F., AND O. DES MURS. 1849. Notice sur le genre hemignathe (*Hemignathus*, Lichtenstein), (1837). *Heterorhynchus* (La Fresnaye), 1839. Pp. 183–193 *in* Oiseaux; pp. 177–284, *in* Abel du Petit-Thouars. Voyage autour du monde sur la frégate La *Venus* commandée par Abel du Petit-Thouars. Zoologie. Mammifères, oiseaux, reptiles et poissons. Gide et J. Baudry, Paris.

REICHENBACH, H. G. L. 1853. Handbuch der speciellen Ornithologie. Scansoriae. Tenuirostres. Icones ad Synopsis Avium. Number 11. Dresden and Leipzig: Expedition der Vollständigsten Naturgeschichte. Pp. 219–336. [The plate referred to was published as part of Die Vollständigste Naturgeschichte, issued in parts under various titles, to which the above reference was intended as a partial text.]

RIDGWAY, R. 1882. Description of a new fly-catcher and a supposed new petrel from the Sandwich Islands. Proceedings of the United States National Museum 4:337–338.

RIDGWAY, R. 1886. On *Aestrelata sandwichensis* Ridgw. Proceedings of the United States National Museum 9:95–96.

RIDGWAY, R. 1888. Note on *Aestrelata sandwichensis* Ridgw. Proceedings of the United States National Museum 11(693):104.

ROTHSCHILD, W. 1893 + 1900. The avifauna of Laysan and the neighbouring islands: with a complete history to date of the birds of the Hawaiian possessions. Part 1. Pp. i–xiv, 1–58, pl. 1–41. Part 2. Pp. 59–126, pl. 42–46, 48–52, 54–58. Part 3 [1900]. Pp. 126–317, pp. Di.1–21, i–xx, pl. 47, 53, 59–83. R. H. Porter, London.

SABO, S. R. 1982. The rediscovery of Bishop's O'o' [sic] on Maui. Elepaio 42:69–71.

SCLATER, P. L. 1878. Reports on the collections of birds made during the voyage of H. M. S. 'Challenger.'—no. VIII. On the birds of the Sandwich Islands. Proceedings of the Zoological Society of London 1878:346–351.

SCLATER, P. L. 1881. On the birds collected in the Sandwich Islands. Pp. 93–99 in Report on the birds collected during the voyage of H.M.S. Challenger in the years 1873–1876. The voyage of H.M.S. Challenger. Zoology. Vol. 8. Her Majesty's Gov't., London.

STEEN BILLE, A. 1852. Bericht über die Reise der Corvette Galathea um die Welt in den Jahren 1845, 46 und 47. 2 vols. C. U. Reitzel, Copenhagen; C. B. Lord, Leipzig.

STEJNEGER, L. H. 1887a. Birds of Kauai Island, Hawaiian Archipelago, collected by Mr. Valdemar Knudsen, with descriptions of new species. Proceedings of the United States National Museum 10:75–102.

STEJNEGER, L. H. 1887b. Notes on Psittirostra psittacea from Kauai, Hawaiian Islands. Proceedings of the United States National Museum 10:389–390.

STEJNEGER, L. H. 1888. Further contributions to the Hawaiian avifauna. Proceedings of the United States National Museum 11:93–103.

STEJNEGER, L. H. 1890. Notes on a third collection of birds made on Kauai, Hawaiian Islands, by Valdemar Knudsen. Proceedings of the United States National Museum 12 [for 1889]:377–386.

STREETS, T. H. 1877a. Description of a new moorhen from the Hawaiian Islands. Ibis series 4 1:25–27.

STREETS, T. H. 1877b. Contributions to the natural history of the Hawaiian and Fanning Islands and Lower California. Bulletin of the United States National Museum 7:1–172.

THOMAS, W. S. 1979. A biography of Andrew Garrett, early naturalist of Polynesia: part 1. Nautilus 93:15–28.

TOWNSEND, J. K. 1839. Narrative of a journey across the Rocky Mountains to the Columbia River and a visit to the Sandwich Islands, Chili, &c. with a scientific appendix. Henry Perkins, Philadelphia, PA.

WAGNER, W. L., JR., D. R. HERBST, AND S. H. SOHMER. 1990. Manual of the flowering plants of Hawai'i. Vol. 1. University of Hawaii Press, Honolulu, HI.

WETMORE, A. 1924. A warbler from Nihoa. Condor 26:177–178.

WETMORE, A. 1925. Bird life among lava rock and coral sand. National Geographic Magazine 48:76–108.

WHITTELL, H. M. 1954. The literature of Australian birds. Paterson Brokensha Pty. Ltd., Perth.

WILKES, C. 1845. Narrative of the United States' Exploring Expedition, during the years 1838, 1839, 1840, 1841, 1842. Condensed and abridged. Whittaker & Co., London.

WILSON, S. B. 1890. On a new finch from Midway Island, North Pacific. Ibis series 6, 2:339–341.

WILSON, S. B., AND A. H. EVANS. 1890–1899. Aves Hawaiienses: the birds of the Sandwich Islands. R. H. Porter, London.

WOODWARD, P. 1972. The natural history of Kure Atoll, Northwestern Hawaiian Islands. Atoll Research Bulletin 164.

Studies in Avian Biology No. 15:103–118, 1994.

AVIFAUNAL CHANGE IN THE HAWAIIAN ISLANDS, 1893–1993

H. Douglas Pratt

Abstract. The past century has witnessed more avifanal change in the Hawaiian Islands than in any other part of the United States. Two-thirds of the 68 species present in the main islands in 1893 are now extinct or endangered. Despite some early historical extinctions, a more or less intact native land and freshwater avifauna existed in 1893. The century began with rapid disappearances and declines of forest birds in large tracts of seemingly undisturbed habitat on the larger main islands, with a similar crash on Lanai following its settlement in 1920. A consensus has developed that these disasters resulted from alien bird diseases including avian pox and mosquito-borne avian malaria, although other causes such as the introduction of *Rattus rattus* have been suggested. Today, the presence of vectors of avian malaria is the most significant limiting factor in the distributions of native birds, which are restricted to higher elevations. Slow declines of species that survived the 1890–1910 crash resulted from a variety of factors including habitat alteration by man and feral pigs and predation by introduced mongooses. Kauai retained all of its 1893 species, some in reduced numbers, into the 1960s, but has since experienced still unexplained declines and extinctions. Two recent hurricanes may have wiped out the remnants of several species. Outside the main islands, Laysan lost 3 of its 5 endemic species as a result of the introduction of rabbits.

As a result of human disturbance, nesting seabirds had nearly disappeared from the main islands by 1893. With the decline of egg-gathering and legal protection of offshore islets, many colonies have been re-established. Those that attempt to nest on the main islands, including the endangered Hawaiian Petrel and threatened Newell's Shearwater, still suffer from predation by mongooses and feral pets. Seabird colonies in the Northwestern Hawaiian Islands have recovered from the depredations of feather hunters around the turn of the century and are now protected in a national wildlife refuge.

The Hawaiian Islands now harbor more alien bird species than any other place on earth, most of them introduced since 1893. They represent every zoogeographical realm and include game birds, ornamental species, common cage birds, and others. With the exception of freshwater birds, the lowland Hawaiian avifauna is now entirely artificial. Whether these aliens have a role in the restriction and decline of native birds is not known, but little direct competition has been documented for most species. They primarily inhabit areas no longer available to native birds due to the presence of disease vectors. However, the Japanese White-eye, now the most abundant bird in the islands, is widespread in montane forests and may compete with native birds and provide a disease reservoir.

Key Words: Avian disease; extinction; feral pig; Hawaiian Islands; introduced birds; mongoose.

The Hawaiian Islands have seen more change in their avifauna during the past century than any other part of the United States of America. In virtually every respect, the bird fauna that greets modern observers differs drastically from that described by researchers of the the 1880s and 1890s when the first thorough studies of Hawaiian birds were conducted. Because of the work of such observers as Valdemar Knudsen (Stejneger 1887, 1888, 1889), Scott Wilson (Wilson and Evans 1890–1899), Henry Palmer (Rothschild 1893–1900), R. C. L. Perkins (1903), Henry W. Henshaw (1902), Alvin Seale (1900), W. A. Bryan (1905, 1908), W. K. Fisher (1906), and George C. Munro (1960), we have a surprisingly complete picture of the Hawaiian avifauna as it existed a century ago. The ensuing years saw the extinction of many species, the reduction of others to tiny remnant populations, and the purposeful introduction of more alien birds than in any other place on earth. The willy-nilly destruction of the indigenous avifauna is particularly unfortunate because, as the world's most isolated archipelago, the Hawaiian Islands are singularly important in the study of evolution and island biology. [Note: Scientific nomenclature as given in Tables 1 and 2 follows Pyle (1992b) except for the Hawaiian Coot which follows Pratt (1987), and the akialoas which follow James and Olson (1991). English names follow Pratt et al. (1987) and Pratt (1992b).]

FIGURE 1. Above: Remnant montane ohia (*Metrosideros polymorpha*) rainforest at crest of ridge, eastern Molokai. Below: Lower elevation on south slope of same ridge showing a single ohia tree that has survived damage by feral goats, pigs, and deer.

THE HAWAIIAN AVIFAUNA IN 1893

Land birds

The forest and upland avifauna of the Hawaiian Islands was much degraded even a century ago. Although unknown to observers at the time, well over half of the archipelago's indigenous birds were already extinct. Henshaw (1902) attributed the absence of native forest birds from low elevations to the vagaries of island colonization, but recent fossil discoveries revealed that the first human inhabitants destroyed a rich and varied lowland forest avifauna (Olson and James 1982). New species described from skeletal remains, although undoubtedly an incomplete sample of the prehuman avifauna, more than doubled the recent species list for the islands (Olson and James 1982, 1991; James and Olson 1991). Following the first European contacts in the late 1700s, a new era of avifaunal change ensued, characterized by numerous extinctions on islands with the most contact with the outside world. Oahu, still the islands' political, economic, and population center, lost its oo, thrush, akialoa, and Nukupuu well before 1893 (Wilson and Evans 1890–1899, Henshaw 1901). Maui, site of the first capital of the Kingdom of Hawaii but not explored ornithologically until the 1880s, probably had already lost a thrush and the Black Mamo (James and Olson 1991); its oo and the Poo-uli also had become so rare that their existence was not even known at the time (Wilson and Evans 1890–1899, Henshaw 1902, Casey and Jacobi 1974). Hawaii, the first island to be affected by Europeans, had lost the large meliphagid Kioea and a flightless rail by the 1860s, and the Ula-ai-hawane barely survived in 1893 (Rothschild 1893–1900, Henshaw 1902). Nevertheless, with the exception of Oahu, the historically known terrestrial avifaunas of the Hawaiian Islands were still more or less intact in 1893 (Wilson and Evans 1890–1899, Rothschild 1893–1900). The original montane native forests still existed on most islands, although clearing for agriculture

FIGURE 2.   Hawaiian Stilt (*Himantopus mexicanus knudseni*) in taro patch, Hanalei, Kauai.

(Henshaw 1902) and grazing by feral cattle (Tomich 1986) were moving their lower limits inexorably upward (Fig. 1).

Freshwater birds

Freshwater habitats including marshes, taro farms, and fishponds were still an important part of the Hawaiian lowland landscape in 1893, and the native duck, coot, moorhen, and stilt (Fig. 2) were widespread and common (Henshaw 1902). On the other hand, the Nene or Hawaiian Goose, more of an upland bird than a waterfowl, had disappeared from Maui and was steadily declining on Hawaii as it had been since European contact (Baldwin 1945).

Breeding seabirds

Although most Hawaiian seabirds presumably bred throughout the archipelago in prehuman times, only those that nested in protected sites still nested on the larger islands in 1893. Hawaiian Petrels (usually considered a subspecies of *Pterodroma phaeopygia,* but see Tomkins and Milne 1991) nested in the alpine zone on several islands, and Newell's (Townsend's) Shearwaters on forested ridges. Cliff-nesting White-tailed Tropicbirds and Black Noddies still nested commonly throughout the main islands (Henshaw 1902, Perkins 1903). Others bred only on the uninhabited and still relatively undisturbed Northwestern Hawaiian Islands or on inaccessible off-shore islets (Munro 1960).

Introduced birds

By 1893, the indigenous Hawaiian species and the aboriginal Red Junglefowl had been joined by several imported ornamental and "game" species such as Wild Turkey, Common Peafowl, California Quail, Common Pheasant, feral pigeon, and Spotted Dove as well as such passerines as Eurasian Skylark, Common Myna, House Sparrow, House Finch, and Nutmeg Mannikin. Only the junglefowl penetrated far into native forests (Henshaw 1902).

CHANGES IN NATIVE BIRD POPULATIONS 1893–1993

Forest bird crashes

The past century in the Hawaiian Islands has been punctuated by sudden population crashes of native species. Unlike gradual declines that result from progressive events such as habitat alteration, these declines were rapid, obvious, and mysterious to contemporaneous observers (Warner 1968, Atkinson 1977). A wave of such extinctions occurred between 1893 and 1910. The Hawaii Oo was still common in 1893 but was "fast nearing extermination" (Henshaw 1902) a few years later. The Hawaii Akialoa, uncommon but still widespread in the 1890s (Henshaw 1902), was never reliably reported in the 20th century (Greenway 1967). During the same period several species already rare or with restricted distributions on Hawaii, including the Greater Amakihi, Hawaii Mamo, Ula-ai-hawane, both koa-finches, and the Kona Grosbeak disappeared. On Molokai, Bishop's Oo, Akohekohe, and Black Mamo, all of which existed in moderate numbers in the 1890s (Perkins 1903), were either extinct or nearly so by 1907 (Bryan 1908). Lanai lost its akialoa before 1900 and the Lanai Hookbill was last seen in 1918 (Munro 1960). On Maui, the once abundant Ou disappeared before 1900 and the Maui Parrotbill, Nukupuu, and Akohekohe became so rare that they were believed possibly extinct (Richards and Baldwin 1953, Banko 1968). Kauai lost no species, but its oo, akialoa, and Nukupuu were so reduced that their existence was uncertain until 1960 (Richardson and Bowles 1964). Lanai, which had been nearly uninhabited since 1900 experienced a wave of extinctions following the building of Lanai City in 1923. By 1940, seven of Lanai's original eight passerine species were extinct or very rare, with only the Apapane surviving in any numbers (Munro 1960). Table 1 lists species, subspecies, and populations that have become extinct or severely reduced since 1893.

Another aspect of this phenomenon was that huge tracts of seemingly pristine forest became devoid of native birds almost overnight (Henshaw 1902). Eventually, native birds withdrew entirely from forests below 600 m, and some disappeared from mid-elevation forests that even today appear nearly pristine (van Riper et al. 1986, pers. obs.). On eastern Molokai (Scott et al. 1977, pers. obs.), Kohala Mountain (van Riper 1973) and the east flank of Mauna Loa (Conant 1975) on Hawaii, and West Maui (Scott et al. 1986), forests that have experienced little apparent degradation have lost all but the most common native birds, and even those are scarce.

From the outset, disease had been hypothesized as a possible cause of the early 20th century avian disaster (Henshaw 1902, Perkins 1903, Munro 1960). Few other suggested causes could account for the rapidity of the declines. The obvious lesions and swellings of avian pox, a viral disease spread by physical contact, were noticed by every collector in the 1890s, and Henshaw (1902) remarked about the frequency with which dead birds were found in the forest. Nevertheless, evidence for epizootics remained circumstantial until Warner (1968) demonstrated not only that native birds are unusually susceptible to diseases such as pox and avian malaria, but that the distributions of native forest birds and mosquitoes are mutually exclusive. Both findings have been corroborated by more recent studies (Scott et al. 1986, van Riper et al. 1986). The mosquito *Culex quinquefasciatus,* introduced on Maui in 1826, provided the vector for avian malaria as well as a ready means of transmission of avian pox. Warner (1968) failed to show conclusively that the spread of mosquitoes was correlated with the observed population crashes of birds (Atkinson 1977) except on Lanai, and recent investigations (van Riper et al. 1986) revealed that avian malaria may not have been present in the islands during the turn-of-the-century wave of extinctions. But avian pox, which can spread by physical contact, could account entirely for that phenomenon (van Riper and van Riper 1985). Atkinson (1977) hypothesized that roof rats (*Rattus rattus*) were the main causative agent, but his hypothesis is based entirely on circumstantial evidence and suffers from a lack of contemporaneous observations of any unusual rat plague. In other examples of rat-caused population crashes of island birds, such as the one that occurred on Lord Howe Island, the cause was obvious at the time (McCulloch 1921). Although rats may have contributed to some extinctions, they are not now regarded as a primary cause of the 1890–1910 Hawaiian bird declines (Scott et al. 1986), which remain enigmatic. However, the second wave of extinctions on Lanai as well as the gradual declines of populations such as the Oahu Alauahio, Kakawahie, Maui Akepa, Kamao, Iiwi on Oahu and Molokai, and Ou, which survived the 1890–1910 plague in good numbers but were rare by the 1960s, probably resulted from the presence of avian malaria after 1920 (van Riper et al. 1986). Little doubt remains that avian malaria is today one of the most important limiting factors in the distribution of Hawaiian native birds (Scott et al. 1985, 1986).

The Laysan disaster

The avifaunal history of Laysan in the Northwestern Hawaiian Islands is independent of that of the main islands but equally disastrous. Its sad history has been recounted by numerous authors (for a detailed summary see Berger 1981). Previously undisturbed Laysan was leased to phosphate miners in 1890. The removal of guano was probably not detrimental to the breeding seabirds and five endemic land and freshwater birds, but the introduction of rabbits in 1903–1904 proved the island's undoing. By 1923, when the island was visited by the Tanager Expedition, the rabbits had destroyed all the vegetation; the Millerbird was extinct, and only two individuals of the Laysan Rail and three of the Laysan Apapane could be found (Wetmore 1925). The expedition witnessed the demise of the Apapane in a sandstorm and, even though the rabbits were exterminated, the rails disappeared before the island was visited again. Of the endemics, only the Laysan Finch and Laysan Duck survived. (The story that the latter was reduced to a single gravid female is apparently apocryphal.) Laysan's seabirds had been heavily harvested by Japanese feather collectors 1909–1910, but none were wiped out and these populations recovered following the designation of the Hawaiian Islands Bird Reservation (now National Wildlife Refuge) in 1909.

An interesting but tragic twist to the story is that the Laysan Rail might have been saved except for events associated with World War II. The rails had been introduced to Midway and became numerous there even as the parent population was disappearing. However, no attempt was made to reintroduce them to Laysan after its vegetation had recovered, and they succumbed quickly after rats got ashore at Midway in 1943. The last one was probably seen in June 1944 (Fisher and Baldwin 1946). The Laysan Rail is the only Hawaiian bird whose final demise can be unequivocally attributed to rat predation.

Effects of the mongoose

Small Indian mongooses (*Herpestes auropunctatus*) were introduced by sugar

TABLE 1. Extinctions, Near Extinctions, and Extirpations of Hawaiian Birds 1893–1993

Species	Range[1]	1893 status[2]	Last reported	1993 population estimate[4]
Laysan Rail				
Porzana palmeri	Ly/Md[3]	A	1923/1944[3]	0
Hawaiian Duck (populations)				
Anas wyvilliana	Mo	C	?	0
	Ma	C	?	0
Common Moorhen (populations)				
Gallinula chloropus sandvicensis	Mo	C	<1950	0
	Ma	C	<1950	0
	H	C	>1900	0
Hawaiian Crow				
Corvus hawaiiensis	Ko	C	1993	12[5]
Laysan Millerbird				
Acrocephalus f. familiaris	Ly	C	1912	0
Kamao				
Myadestes myadestinus	Ka	A	1989	<5
Lanai Olomao				
Myadestes l. lanaiensis	La	C	1931	0
Molokai Olomao				
Myadestes l. rutha	Mo	C	1988	<5
Puaiohi				
Myadestes palmeri	Ka	R	1991	<10
Hawaii Oo				
Moho nobilis	H	C	>1900	0
Bishop's Oo				
Moho bishopi	Mo	C	1904	0
	Ma	R	1980	<5
Ooaa (Kauai Oo)				
Moho braccatus	Ka	C	1987	0
Kona Grosbeak				
Chloridops kona	Ko	U	1896	0
Greater Koa-Finch				
Rhodacanthis palmeri	Ko	C	1896	0
Lesser Koa-Finch				
Rhodacanthis flaviceps	Ko	R	1891	0
Ou				
Psittirostra psittacea	Ka	A	1992?	<5
	La	C	ca. 1931	0
	Ma	C	ca. 1900	0
	H	A	1983	<10
Lanai Hookbill				
Dysmorodrepanis munroi	La	R	1918	0
Kakawahie				
Paroreomyza flammea	Mo	C	1963	0
Lanai Alauahio				
Paroreomyza m. montana	La	A	1937	0
Oahu Alauahio				
Paroreomyza maculata	O	C	1985	<5
Kauai Nakupuu				
Hemignathus lucidus hanapepe	Ka	U	1991?	<5
Maui Nakupuu				
Hemignathus l. affinis	Ma	U	1990[6]	<10
Kauai Akialoa				
Hemignathus stejnegeri	Ka	C	1969	0
Lanai Akialoa				
Hemignathus lanaiensis	La	U	1902	0
Hawaii Akialoa				
Hemignathus obscurus	H	C	>1900	0
Common Amakihi on Lanai				
Hemignathus virens	La	C	1976	0
Greater Amakihi				
Hemignathus sagittirostris	H	U	1901	0

TABLE 1. CONTINUED

Species	Range[1]	1893 status[2]	Last reported	1993 population estimate[4]
Maui Akepa				
Loxops coccineus ochraceus	Ma	R	1988	<10
Oahu Akepa				
Loxops c. wolstenholmei	O	R	1976?	0
Ula-ai-hawane				
Ciridops anna	H	R	1892	0
Laysan Apapane				
Himatione sanguinea freethii	Ly	A	1923	0
Akohekohe on Molokai				
Palmeria dolei	Mo	C	1907	0
Iiwi (populations)				
Vestiaria coccinea	La	A	1929	0
	Mo	A	1988	<50
Hawaii Mamo				
Drepanis pacifica	H	U	1898	0
Hoa (Black Mamo)				
Drepanis funerea	Mo	U	1907	0
Poo-uli				
Melamprosops phaeosoma	Ma	no data	1992?[6]	<5

[1] Abbreviations: H = Hawaii (whole island), Ka = Kauai, Ko = Kona Region of Hawaii, La = Lanai, Ly = Laysan, Ma = Maui, Md = Midway, Mo = Molokai, O = Oahu.
[2] Abbreviations: A = abundant, C = common, U = uncommon, R = rare. Sources: Berger (1981), Henshaw (1902), Munro (1960), Perkins (1903).
[3] Introduced population.
[4] Estimates based on Berger (1981); Scott et al. (1986); R. E. David, R. L. Pyle, pers. comm.; pers. obs., and recent publicity of various environmental organizations.
[5] Plus 11 in captivity.
[6] *Fide* R. L. Pyle.

planters during the 1880s on Hawaii, Maui, Molokai, and Oahu (Tomich 1986) and spread quickly throughout these islands. As a result, ground-nesting birds such as the Hawaiian Duck, Newell's Shearwater (King and Gould 1967), and Red Junglefowl disappeared except on Kauai. Mongooses were probably an important factor in the decline of the Nene (Baldwin 1945), and continue to be a limiting factor that may ultimately preclude the successful recovery of that species on Hawaii and Maui (Scott et al. 1986, Tomich 1986). Mongoose predation (along with that of feral cats) also has a significant negative impact on the nesting of Hawaiian Petrels on Maui (Simons 1985). Mongooses may also be one of several inimical factors contributing to the current plight of the Hawaiian Crow, the young of which spend several days on the ground after fledging (Johnston and Banko 1992).

Changes wrought by feral pigs

Pigs (*Sus scrofa*) arrived in the Hawaiian Islands with the first Polynesians. Aboriginal pigs were small and apparently did not penetrate far into native forests. Much larger and therefore more ecologically damaging pigs were introduced in historic times (Tomich 1986). Feral pigs are now the most significant modifiers of native forests (Scott et al. 1985). Their rooting destroys the shrub layer (Tomich 1986), spreads alien weeds into new areas (Scott et al. 1985), and facilitates the spread of mosquitoes (Scott et al. 1986). For reasons that are not entirely clear, feral pigs have within the past two decades penetrated into remote native rainforests not previously occupied where they may reach plague proportions locally (Lamoureux and Stemmermann 1976). As a result of one such ongoing plague, the Poouli, an understory bird of unknown affinities (Pratt 1992a) discovered in East Maui in 1973 (Casey and Jacobi 1974), by 1990 had disappeared from the type locality and survived only in a small portion of its original range not yet devastated by pigs (Engilis 1990). A thorough survey in August 1992 failed to find any Poo-uli (R. David, pers. comm.).

FIGURE 3. The recently-extinct Kauai Oo; Alakai Swamp, Kauai, July 1975.

The fall and rise of the Nene

The history of Hawaii's State Bird has been largely independent of that of other native land and freshwater birds because of its unique ecology. In historic times Nene were definitely known only from Hawaii but probably also lived on Maui before it was explored ornithologically. Fossil remains show that Nene once inhabited all the main Hawaiian Islands (Olson and James 1991). It was long a popular food item on Hawaii and was often hunted. In 1893, although it still existed "in fair numbers" in the remote upper lava flows of Kona, Wilson considered it "clearly doomed to extinction before many years are past" (Wilson and Evans 1890–1899).

Baldwin (1945) estimated a late 19th century population of 25,000 birds which dropped precipitously around the turn of the century. The Nene has been rare throughout the 20th century (Baldwin 1945). By 1951, the wild population may have been as low as 30 (Smith 1952). Fortunately, several flocks had been maintained in captivity, and a program of reintroduction of captive-reared birds was begun on Hawaii in 1960 and on Maui in 1963 (Kear and Berger 1980). Although successful in saving the species from extinction, this program has had only limited success in re-establishing self-sustaining Nene populations (Stone et al. 1983). Populations on Hawaii depend on continued release of captive-reared birds to maintain their numbers (Scott et al. 1985), but an apparently stable population of under 150 birds has been established in Haleakala National Park, Maui (Hodges 1991). Nene that escaped from captivity on mongoose-free Kauai in 1982 did so well that a second flock was purposely released at Kilauea Point National Wildlife Refuge in 1991 (Telfer 1991). The Kauai population now numbers over 100 and appears to be thriving even in totally artificial habitats (Telfer 1992). Reintroduction to the mongoose-free islands of Kauai and Lanai may be the key to long-term survival of the Nene.

Collapse of Kauai's avifauna

One of the most dismaying recent avifaunal events in the Hawaiian Islands is the ongoing collapse of the endemic avifauna of Kauai. Although several species had become greatly reduced in numbers and range at the turn of the century, Richardson and Bowles (1964) found that all of the island's historically known birds survived in 1960 and that, at least on the Alakai Plateau, an essentially intact native avifauna still existed. Thus Kauai was the only one of the main Hawaiian Islands not to have lost any bird species in historic times. It was not to remain so. The ensuing years witnessed a progressive withdrawal of native birds into the highest reaches of the Alakai (Scott et al. 1986). The Kauai Akialoa was last reliably reported in 1969 (P. L. Bruner, pers. comm.). The Kauai Oo, which had crashed shortly after 1900 but maintained a small population in the Alakai into the early 1970s, was reduced to a single known pair by 1981 (Scott et al. 1986). The female disappeared after Hurricane Iwa in 1982 (Pyle 1983b) and the male was last seen in 1985. Except for an unconfirmed voice-only report in 1987, subsequent searches have failed to find the oo (Pyle 1989b). Because its vocalizations are distinctive and audible at great distance (pers. obs.), the Kauai Oo must be presumed extinct (Fig. 3). The Kamao, once Kauai's most abundant bird and still common in the Alakai in 1960 (Richardson and Bowles 1964), declined to a few hundred individuals by 1973 (Sincock et al. 1984) and to about two dozen in 1981 (Scott et al. 1986). A 1989 survey in the heart of the bird's 1981 range located only a few individuals (Engilis and Pratt 1989, Pyle 1989b). The Ou maintained a population in the low hundreds in the heart of the Alakai into the mid-1970s (pers. obs.), but 1981 surveys estimated that fewer than ten remained (Scott et al. 1986). The 1989 survey observed only three. The Akikiki was still common to abundant in 1960, but declines were apparent by the mid-1970s (Scott et al. 1986, pers. obs.). Thousands remained in the heart of the Alakai in 1981 (Scott et al. 1986), but the species had disappeared from the Kokee area, where it could be found as recently as 1978 (pers. obs.). In the 1980s, it became increasingly difficult to find in the fringes of the Alakai region, and it is now uncommon to rare within it (pers. obs.). In contrast to these dismal trends, the Puaiohi, always considered rare (Richardson and Bowles 1964), still existed in 1989 at approximately its 1960 levels (Scott et al. 1986, Engilis and Pratt 1989). Likewise, the Nukupuu, very rare in 1960, continued to be reported occasionally (Pyle 1992a), and the more common species seemed to be holding their own into mid-1992 (pers. obs.).

The causes of Kauai's post-1960 bird declines are unknown. Pratt et al. (1987) speculatively attributed them to penetration of the Alakai by disease-bearing mosquitoes. Engilis and Pratt (1989) note that the Ou had disappeared from areas with high pig damage. By the 1980s, the severely stressed populations had become particularly vulnerable to natural disasters such as hurricanes. Montane forest birds in the islands historically moved to the lowlands in great numbers to ride out storms. Henshaw (1902) reported finding "scores" of forest birds dead or dying in the lowlands of Hawaii after severe weather. Now, however, lowland valleys that once were safe havens have become pestilential death traps. Hurricane Iwa in November 1982 may have delivered the *coup-de-grace* to the Kauai Oo (Pyle 1983a, b). The Ou and Kamao, though still extant after the storm, never regained even their modest numbers of the previous decade. Class 5 Hurricane Iniki in September 1992 caused even more serious island-wide devastation (Fig. 4). Populations of the common species appeared greatly reduced six weeks afterward (pers. obs.), and Apapane and Iiwi were reported from several low-elevation sites where they would not normally have been found. Surveys by state and federal biologists in the heart of the Alakai Plateau in early 1993 found much more serious damage to the habitat than had been apparent from aerial inspections. *All* remaining habitat for native birds was damaged more or less severely and none of the critically endangered species were found in 40 man-days of search (R. L. Pyle, pers. comm.). Only time will tell whether the Kamao, Puaiohi, Ou, and Nukupuu survived the ravages of Iniki. The prognosis is not hopeful.

Other native bird declines

In historic times, the Hawaiian Crow had an enigmatically restricted distribution in the Kona region and was absent from seemingly ideal habitats elsewhere on the island of Hawaii (Berger 1981). Crows were still common in 1892 (Perkins 1903) but declined thereafter at least partly as a result of active persecution by ranchers (Munro 1960). The population had reached dangerously low levels by the mid-1970s (Scott et al. 1986). A small captive flock established in the early 1970s is now highly inbred and has produced few young in the past decade. As of this writing, only 12 birds remain in the wild (Engbring 1992) and 11 in captivity (Duvall 1992). The Hawaiian Crow has recently been the center of considerable sometimes heated controversy with regard to how

FIGURE 4.   Former closed-canopy montane koa (*Acacia koa*) forest badly damaged by Hurricane Iniki: Kokee, Kauai, October 1992.

best to aid its recovery. A study by the National Research Council (1992) may bring some rationality to the effort, but prospects for the crow's survival are not good.

The Oahu Alauahio (= Oahu Creeper) is probably nearing extinction. Though common at the turn of the century (Bryan 1905), it has been regarded as rare ever since (Munro 1960, Berger 1981) and has received scant attention from ornithologists. The last reliable sighting was in 1985 (Bremer 1986), though one may have been seen in Halawa Valley in 1989 (Saito 1989). Surveys throughout the remaining habitat on Oahu in 1991 (Conry 1991) failed to find the alauahio, and also confirmed the recently suspected (Pyle 1990b, 1991, 1992a) near disappearance of the Oahu Elepaio, once the commonest native bird on the island (Henshaw 1902). The Elepaio was still widely distributed and relatively abundant in the 1960s (Conant 1977) and common in the 1970s (Berger 1981) but had been in a slow decline since the 1940s (Williams 1987). Its reduction is particularly troubling because the Elepaio had long been regarded as al-

most extinction-proof. Henshaw (1902) thought that it would survive in "scarcely diminished numbers" long after most Hawaiian birds were extinct "so long as any woodland at all is left." Berger (1981:103) stated that the Oahu Elepaio had adapted to man-made environmental changes "as no other endemic land bird has been able to do." Apparently even adaptable species can take only so much abuse. Because the Elepaio's decline on Oahu only recently received much notice, its specific causes have not even been hypothesized. The decline coincided with the spread into native forests and increase of several potentially competitive alien species (Williams 1987, pers. obs.), most noticeably the Japanese White-eye, Japanese Bush-Warbler, and Red-vented Bulbul, but whether these events are related is not known.

New natural arrivals

Successful natural colonizations of remote islands are exceedingly rare and few have been observed in historic times. However, in one of the few positive changes in the indigenous Hawaiian avifauna, two new freshwater birds have arrived in the last decade apparently unaided by man. Pied-billed Grebes (*Podilymbus podiceps*) were long regarded as only occasional stragglers to the islands (Berger 1981), but in the early 1980s at least one pair began breeding at Aimakapa Pond in Kona on the island of Hawaii. By 1989, 12 grebes were present on the pond and five active nests were recorded (Pyle 1989a). In a similar development, a small group of Fulvous Whistling-Ducks (*Dendrocygna bicolor*) appeared at James Campbell National Wildlife Refuge on Oahu in 1982. Although the operators of a nearby aquafarm have released a variety of ornamental waterfowl, they claim not to have brought in the whistling-ducks (R. L. Pyle, pers. comm.). This species has undergone recent "explosive" expansions in North America and the West Indies (Palmer 1976) so a natural colonization is plausible. In February 1990, ten adults and ten juveniles were seen at the aquafarm and an adult with 12 small chicks was found on the refuge (Pyle 1990a).

Resurgence of seabirds

In contrast to the dismal trends in native land birds, seabirds breeding in the Hawaiian Islands have rebounded from centuries of persecution and appear to be in better condition today than in 1893. Ancient Hawaiians and their commensals undoubtedly eliminated all but cliff-nesting seabirds from the lowlands of the main islands, and also raided offshore islets to capture birds for food (Harrison 1990). Since the turn of the century, several species have recolonized the main islands and colonies on islets have largely recovered (Berger 1981). Red-footed Boobies returned to mainland Kauai and Oahu in the 1940s (Berger 1981), Laysan Albatrosses (*Diomedea immutabilis*) recently established a now thriving (pers. obs.) colony at Kilauea Point National Wildlife Refuge on Kauai (Byrd and Telfer 1979), and Wedge-tailed Shearwaters (*Puffinus pacificus*) have established scattered colonies

on Kauai (Byrd and Boynton 1979). Relatively accessible Manana Island off Oahu had no seabird colonies by 1893 (Harrison 1990), but thousands of birds of five species nested there by the 1970s (Berger 1981). The Common Fairy-Tern (*Gygis alba*) was not known to have nested on the main islands in historic times (Munro 1960), but in 1961 colonized Koko Head, Oahu (Ord 1961) and subsequently expanded its range into the Honolulu area (Berger 1981) where it is now a common sight in urban parks (pers. obs.). Seabirds on Midway Atoll suffered greatly during the Second World War (Fisher and Baldwin 1946) and in subsequent years as a result of military activities. However, following destruction of antennas that killed many birds, the albatross colonies have recovered to previous levels (Berger 1981).

INTRODUCTIONS OF ALIEN BIRDS

The relatively few species of introduced birds present in the Hawaiian Islands a century ago have been joined by a vast array of additional alien species (Table 2). These fall into three basic categories: accidental escapes from captivity; birds purposely introduced by private individuals for a variety of reasons; and game birds introduced by government agencies. Most of those in the second category were brought in by the Hui Manu ("Bird Club"), an organization founded in 1930 for the sole purpose of introducing alien birds to the islands. Many introductions, such as those of bulbuls and estrildids in the 1960s, were illicit, but regulations were rarely enforced with any vigor until very recently. The enthusiasm for introduced birds in the Hawaiian Islands is difficult for mainlanders to understand, but can be appreciated in light of the near total absence of native birds from the lowland areas where most people live. Perhaps introduced birds are better than no birds at all. Fortunately, most species that have become established have filled unoccupied niches and, except as potential disease reservoirs, are probably of relatively benign

TABLE 2.   Birds Introduced and Established in the Hawaiian Islands 1893–1993[1]

Species	First introduced	Introduction site(s)[2]	Distribution 1992	In native forest?[3]
Cattle Egret				
Bubulcus ibis	1959	Ka, O, Mo, Ma, H	all main islands	no
Black Francolin				
Francolinus francolinus	1959	Ka, Mo, Ma, H	Ka, Mo, Ma, H	no
Gray Francolin				
Francolinus pondicerianus	1958	all main islands	O, Mo, Ma, H	no
Erckel's Francolin				
Francolinus erckelii	1957	all main islands	Ka, O, Mo, La, H	yes
Chukar				
Alectoris chukar	1923	all main islands	Mo, Ma, La, H	no
Japanese Quail				
Coturnix japonica	1921	all main islands	Ka, Ma, H	no
Kalij Pheasant				
Lophura leucomelana	1962	H	H	yes
Gambel's Quail				
Callipepla gambelii	1928	La, Kw, H	La, Kw, H	no
Chestnut-bellied Sandgrouse				
Pterocles exustus	1961	H	H	no
Zebra Dove				
Geopelia striata	1922	O	all main islands	no
Mourning Dove				
Zenaida macroura	1964	H	H	no
Rose-ringed Parakeet				
Psittacula krameri	?	Ka, O, H	Ka, O, H	no
Barn Owl				
Tyto alba	1958	Ka, O, Mo, H	all main islands	no
Island Swiftlet				
Aerodramus vanikorensis	1962	O	O	no
Red-vented Bulbul				
Pycnonotus cafer	1965	O	O	yes
Red-whiskered Bulbul				
Pycnonotus jocosus	1966	O	O	yes
Japanese Bush-Warbler				
Cettia diphone	1929	O	Ka, O, Mo, Ma, La	yes
White-rumped Shama				
Copsychus malabaricus	1931, 1940	Ka, O	Ka, O	yes
Greater Necklaced Laughing-thrush				
Garrulax pectoralis	1919[4]	Ka	Ka	no
Gray-sided Laughing-thrush				
Garrulax caerulatus	1947	O	O	yes
Melodious Laughing-thrush				
Garrulax canorus	1900	Ka, O, Mo, Ma, H	Ka, O, Mo, Ma, H	yes
Red-billed Leiothrix				
Leiothrix lutea	1918	Ka, O, Mo, Ma, H	Ka, O, Mo, Ma, H	yes
Northern Mockingbird				
Mimus polyglottos	1928	O, Ma	all main islands	no
Japanese White-eye				
Zosterops japonicus	1929	Ka, O, Ma, H	all main islands	yes
Northern Cardinal				
Cardinalis cardinalis	1929	Ka, O, H	all main islands	yes
Red-crested Cardinal				
Paroaria coronata	1928	O	Ka, O, Mo, Ma, La	no
Yellow-billed Cardinal				
Paroaria capitata	ca. 1930	H	H	no
Yellow-faced Grassquit				
Tiaris olivacea	ca. 1970	O	O	no
Saffron Finch				
Sicalis flaveola	>1960	O, H	O, H	no
Western Meadowlark				
Sturnella neglecta	1931	Ka, O	Ka	no

TABLE 2. CONTINUED

Species	First introduced	Introduction site(s)[2]	Distribution 1992	In native forest?[3]
Yellow-fronted Canary				
Serinus mozambicus	<1965	O, H	O, H	yes
Common Canary				
Serinus canaria	1910	Md	Md	no
Red-cheeked Cordonbleu				
Uraeginthus bengalus	<1965	O, H	H	no
Lavender Waxbill				
Estrilda caerulescens	<1965	O, H	H	no
Orange-cheeked Waxbill				
Estrilda melpoda	<1965	O, Ma, H	O, Ma	no
Black-rumped Waxbill				
Estrilda troglodytes	<1965	O, H	H	no
Common Waxbill				
Estrilda astrild	<1965	O	O	no
Red Avadavat				
Amandava amandava	1900	O, H	Ka, O, Ma, H	no
Warbling Silverbill				
Lonchura malabarica	>1960	H	all main islands	no
Chestnut Mannikin				
Lonchura malacca	1936	O	Ka, O	no
Java Sparrow				
Padda oryzivora	<1965	O	Ka, O, Ma, H	no

[1] Sources: Berger (1981), Hawai'i Audubon Society (1989), Moulton and Pimm (1983), Pyle (1992a, b), Williams (1983).
[2] Abbreviations as for Table 1 plus Kw = Kahoolawe.
[3] Sources: Berger (1981), Scott et al. (1986), Pratt et al. (1987).
[4] Probably misidentified at the time as *G. albogularis*.

influence on native ecosystems (Moulton and Pimm 1983). A few, however, have spread deep into native forests and may be competing with native birds or contributing to habitat degradation. The Japanese White-eye is now the most abundant bird in the Hawaiian Islands and is found at all elevations and in all habitats (Scott et al. 1986). White-eyes compete for food with several native species (Mountainspring and Scott 1985). The Red-billed Leiothrix and Melodious Laughing-thrush also are found throughout native rainforests at least on Maui and Hawaii, but they are understory birds that appear not to compete with any native species (Scott et al. 1986). The leiothrix and the Kalij Pheasant probably contribute to habitat degradation by spreading seeds of banana poka (*Passiflora mollisima,*), an aggressive vine that has overgrown large areas of native forest on Hawaii (Lewin and Lewin 1984, Scott et al. 1986). The Northern Cardinal occurs in a wide variety of habitats, including native rainforest, on the main Hawaiian Islands but is more common in disturbed areas (Scott et al. 1986). The Red-vented Bulbul has become ubiquitous on Oahu (Williams and Giddings 1984), including forests at the highest elevations (pers. obs.), and the Japanese Bush-Warbler, now abundant in Oahu forests, is also increasing on Molokai, Lanai, Maui, and Kauai (Scott et al. 1986, pers. obs.). The effects, if any, of cardinals, bulbuls, and bush-warblers on native birds are as yet undetermined.

THE MODERN HAWAIIAN AVIFAUNA

Today, the avifauna of the Hawaiian Islands includes only tattered remnants of the avian community present a century ago. Of the 68 native land and freshwater species or subspecies known to have been present in 1893, 29 are now extinct or nearly so (Table 1), and a further 17 are Endangered Species but not in immediate danger of extinction. Ongoing threats to endangered forest birds include habitat damage by feral pigs, upward expansion of the range of disease-bearing mosquitoes, and natural disasters. Some species (Olomao, Kamao, Bishop's Oo, Ou, Nukupuu, Oahu Alauahio, and Poo-uli), if still extant, may not survive the 20th century. The surviving indigenous birds have been joined by a host of alien species, several of which are now significant elements of forest bird communities. The Hawaiian lowlands now have an entirely artificial land avifauna.

The endemic freshwater birds are all Endangered Species that survive primarily in a few small refuges maintained for their benefit. The Hawaiian Duck has been successfully reintroduced on Oahu and Hawaii but interbreeding with feral Mallards (*Anas platyrhynchos*) poses a new threat to the species, at least on Oahu (Engilis and Pratt 1993). The Hawaiian moorhen no longer inhabits Maui or Hawaii, and 1983 reintroductions on Molokai apparently were not successful (Engilis and Pratt 1993). The Nene, although saved from imminent extinction, still depends on release of captive-reared birds to maintain its population, at least on Hawaii. On the positive side, the freshwater bird community has recently been augmented by two natural colonizations, and populations of the endemics appear to be more or less stable (Engilis and Pratt 1993).

Hawaiian seabirds have largely recovered from a series of challenges and have reoccupied a few nesting sites abandoned since ancient times. Laysan Albatrosses and Common Fairy-Terns now nest successfully on Kauai and Oahu respectively. Newell's Shearwaters and Hawaiian Petrels, though still imperiled, appear to be maintaining stable populations that benefit from protected nesting areas and active public programs to mitigate artificial losses. And nesting colonies in the Northwestern Hawaiian Islands are once again as large as they were in 1893. Seabirds provide the one bright spot in the rather pitiful present condition of the Hawaiian avifauna.

ACKNOWLEDGMENTS

I am grateful to P. L. Bruner, R. E. David, A. Engilis, D. Kuhn, and particularly R. L. Pyle, Regional Editor for *American Birds,* who shared unpublished information with me. D. Kuhn provided onsite information on Kauai forest birds immediately following Hurricane Iniki. J. V. Remsen and R. L. Pyle made helpful comments on the manuscript.

LITERATURE CITED

ATKINSON, I. A. E. 1977. A reassessment of the factors, particularly *Rattus rattus* L., that influenced the decline of endemic forest birds in the Hawaiian Islands. Pacific Science 31:109–133.

BALDWIN, P. W. 1945. The Hawaiian Goose, its distribution and reduction in numbers. Condor 47:27–37.

BANKO, W. E. 1968. Rediscovery of Maui Nukupuu, *Hemignathus lucidus affinis,* and sighting of Maui Parrotbill, *Pseudonestor xanthophrys,* Kipahulu Valley, Maui, Hawaii. Condor 70:265–266.

BERGER, A. J. 1981. Hawaiian birdlife. 2nd Edition. University Hawaii Press, Honolulu.

BREMER, D. 1986. Waipio, Oahu, Christmas bird count 1985. 'Elepaio 46:132–135.

BRYAN, W. A. 1905. Notes on the birds of the Waianae Mountains. Occasional Papers Bernice P. Bishop Museum 2:37–49.

BRYAN, W. A. 1908. Some birds of Molokai. Occasional Papers Bernice P. Bishop Museum 4:133–176.

BYRD, G. V., AND D. S. BOYNTON. 1979. The distribution and status of Wedge-tailed Shearwaters on Kauai. 'Elepaio 39:129–130.

BYRD, G. V., AND T. C. TELFER. 1979. Laysan Albatross is attempting to establish breeding colonies on Kauai. 'Elepaio 38:81–83.

CASEY, T. L. C., AND J. D. JACOBI. 1974. A new genus and species of bird from the Island of Maui, Hawaii (Passeriformes: Drepanididae). Occasional Papers Bernice P. Bishop Museum 24:216–226.

CONANT, S. 1975. Spatial distribution of bird species on the east flank of Mauna Loa. U. S. International Biological Program, Technical Report No. 74.

CONANT, S. 1977. The breeding biology of the Oahu 'Elepaio. Wilson Bulletin 89:193–210.

CONRY, P. 1991. Oahu forest bird survey indicates decline in native species. Hawaii's Forests and Wildlife 6:2.

DUVALL, F. 1992. Olinda 'Alala breeding season update. Hawaii's Forests and Wildlife 7:10–11.

ENGBRING, J. 1992. 'Alala surveyed on McCandless Ranch. Hawaii's Forests and Wildlife 7:1–2, 20.

ENGILIS, A., JR. 1990. Field notes on native forest birds in the Hanawi Natural Area Reserve, Maui. 'Elepaio 50:67–72.

ENGILIS, A., JR., AND T. K. PRATT. 1989. Kauai forest bird survey yields surprises and disappointments. Hawaii Wildlife Newsletter 4:1, 10.

ENGILIS, A., JR., AND T. K. PRATT. 1993. Status and population trends of Hawaii's native waterbirds, 1977–1987. Wilson Bulletin 105:142–158.

FISHER, H. I., AND P. H. BALDWIN. 1946. War and the birds of Midway Atoll. Condor 48:3–15.

FISHER, W. K. 1906. Birds of Laysan and the Leeward Islands, Hawaiian group. Bulletin U.S. Fish Commission 23:769–807 [For 1903].

GREENWAY, J. C., JR. 1967. Extinct and vanishing birds of the world. Dover Publications, Inc., New York, NY.

HARRISON, C. S. 1990. Seabirds of Hawaii: natural history and conservation. Cornell University Press, Ithaca and London.

HAWAI'I AUDUBON SOCIETY. 1989. Hawaii's birds. Hawai'i Audubon Society, Honolulu.

HENSHAW, H. W. 1902. Birds of the Hawaiian Islands being a complete list of the birds of the Hawaiian possessions with notes on their habits. Thos. G. Thrum, Honolulu, HI.

HODGES, C. S. N. 1991. Survey of Nene (*Nesochen sandvicensis*) at Haleakala National Park 1988 through 1990. 'Elepaio 51:38–39.

JAMES, H. F., AND S. L. OLSON. 1991. Descriptions of thirty-two new species of birds from the Hawaiian Islands: part II. Passeriformes. Ornithological Monographs No. 46.

JOHNSTON, S., AND P. BANKO. 1992. 'Alala monitoring continues. Hawaii's Forests and Wildlife 7:3, 11.

KEAR, J., AND A. J. BERGER. 1980. The Hawaiian Goose: an experiment in conservation. Buteo Books, Vermillion, SD.

KING, W. B., AND P. J. GOULD. 1967. The status of Newell's race of the Manx Shearwater. Living Bird 6:163–186.

LAMOUREUX, C. H., AND L. STEMMERMANN. 1976. Report of the Ki-pahulu Bicentennial Expedition June 26-29, 1976. Cooperative National Park Resources Studies Unit, University Hawaii, Technical Report No. 11.

LEWIN, V., AND G. LEWIN. 1984. The Kalij Pheasant, a newly established game bird on the island of Hawaii. Wilson Bulletin 96:634–646.

McCULLOCH, A. R. 1921. Lord Howe Island: a naturalist's paradise. Australian Museum Magazine 1:30–47.

MOULTON, M. P., AND S. L. PIMM. 1983. The introduced Hawaiian avifauna: biogeographic evidence for competition. American Naturalist 121:669–690.

MOUNTAINSPRING, S., AND J. M. SCOTT. 1985. Interspecific competition among Hawaiian forest birds. Ecological Monographs 55:219–239.

MUNRO, G. C. 1960. Birds of Hawaii. 2nd Edition. Charles E. Tuttle Co., Inc., Rutland, VT and Tokyo, Japan. [First published in 1944.]

NATIONAL RESEARCH COUNCIL. 1992. The scientific basis for the preservation of the Hawaiian Crow. National Academy Press, Washington, DC.

OLSON, S. L., AND H. F. JAMES. 1982. Prodromus of the fossil avifauna of the Hawaiian Islands. Smithsonian Contributions to Zoology 365.

OLSON, S. L., AND H. F. JAMES. 1991. Descriptions of thirty-two new species of birds from the Hawaiian Islands: part I. Non-Passeriformes. Ornithological Monographs No. 45.

ORD, W. M. 1961. White Terns at Koko Head, Oahu. 'Elepaio 22:17–18.

PALMER, R. S. (ed.). 1976. Handbook of North American birds. Vol. 2, part 1. Yale University Press, New Haven and London.

PERKINS, R. C. L. 1903. Fauna Hawaiiensis or the zoology of the Sandwich (Hawaiian) Isles. Vol. 1, Pt. IV, Vertebrata. University Press, Cambridge, England.

PRATT, H. D. 1987. Occurrence of the North American coot (*Fulica americana americana*) in the Hawaiian Islands, with comments on the taxonomy of the Hawaiian Coot. 'Elepaio 47:25–28.

PRATT, H. D. 1992a. Is the Poo-uli a Hawaiian honeycreeper (Drepanidinae)? Condor 94:172–180.

PRATT, H. D. 1992b. Systematics of the Hawaiian "creepers" *Oreomystis* and *Paroreomyza*. Condor 94: 836–846.

PRATT, H. D., P. L. BRUNER, AND D. G. BERRETT. 1987. A field guide to the birds of Hawaii and the tropical Pacific. Princeton University Press, Princeton, NJ.

PYLE, R. L. 1983a. The autumn migration: Hawaiian Islands region. American Birds 37:226–228.

PYLE, R. L. 1983b. The spring migration: Hawaiian Islands region. American Birds 37:914–916.

PYLE, R. L. 1989a. The autumn migration: Hawaiian Islands region. American Birds 43:172–174.

PYLE, R. L. 1989b. The winter season: Hawaiian Islands region. American Birds 43:369–371.

PYLE, R. L. 1990a. The winter migration: Hawaiian Islands region. American Birds 44:332–334.

PYLE, R. L. 1990b. The nesting season: Hawaiian Islands region. American Birds 44:1189–1190.

PYLE, R. L. 1991. The spring season: Hawaiian Islands region. American Birds 45:498–499.

PYLE, R. L. 1992a. The winter season: Hawaiian Islands region. American Birds 46:317–318.

PYLE, R. L. 1992b. Checklist of the birds of Hawaii—1992. 'Elepaio 52:53–62.

RICHARDS, L. P., AND P. H. BALDWIN. 1953. Recent records of some Hawaiian honeycreepers. Condor 55:221–222.

RICHARDSON, F., AND J. BOWLES. 1964. A survey of the birds of Kauai, Hawaii. Bulletin Bernice P. Bishop Museum No. 227.

ROTHSCHILD, W. 1893–1900. The avifauna of Laysan and the neighboring islands with a complete history to date of the birds of the Hawaiian possessions. R. H. Porter, London.

SAITO, R. 1989. Halawa Valley swiftlets. Hawaii Wildlife Newsletter 4:8.

SCOTT, J. M., D. H. WOODSIDE, AND T. L. C. CASEY. 1977. Observations of birds in the Molokai Forest Reserve, July 1975. 'Elepaio 38:25–27.

SCOTT, J. M., C. B. KEPLER, AND J. L. SINCOCK. 1985. Distribution and abundance of Hawai'i's endemic land birds: conservation and management strategies. Pp. 75–104 *in* C. P. Stone and J. M. Scott (eds.), Hawai'i's terrestrial ecosystems: preservation and management. Cooperative National Park Resources Studies Unit, University Hawaii, Honolulu, HI.

SCOTT, J. M., S. MOUNTAINSPRING, F. L. RAMSEY, AND C. B. KEPLER. 1986. Forest bird communities of the Hawaiian Islands: their dynamics, ecology, and conservation. Studies Avian Biology No. 9.

SEALE, A. 1900. Field notes on the birds of Oahu, H. I. Occasional Papers Bernice P. Bishop Museum 1:33–46.

SIMONS, T. R. 1985. Biology and behavior of the

endangered Hawaiian Dark-rumped Petrel. Condor 87:229–245.

SINCOCK, J. L., R. E. DAEHLER, T. TELFER, AND D. H. WOODSIDE. 1984. Kauai forest bird recovery plan. U.S. Fish and Wildlife Service, Portland, OR.

SMITH, J. D. 1952. The Hawaiian Goose (Nene) restoration program. Journal Wildlife Management 16: 1–9.

STEJNEGER, L. 1887. Birds of Kauai Island, Hawaiian Archipelago, collected by Mr. Valdemar Knudsen, with descriptions of new species. Proceedings U.S. National Museum 10:75–102.

STEJNEGER, L. 1888. Further contributions to the Hawaiian avifauna. Proceedings U.S. National Museum 11:93–103.

STEJNEGER, L. 1889. Notes on a third collection of birds made in Kauai, Hawaiian Islands, by Valdemar Knudsen. Proceedings U.S. National Museum 12:377–386.

STONE, C. P., R. L. WALKER, J. M. SCOTT, AND P. C. BANKO. 1983. Hawaiian Goose research and management—where do we go from here? 'Elepaio 44: 11–15.

TELFER, T. 1991. Nene successfully released on Kauai. Hawaii's Forests and Wildlife 6:9.

TELFER, T. 1992. Kauai Nene have cosmopolitan habits. Hawaii's Forests and Wildlife 7:10.

TOMICH, P. Q. 1986. Mammals in Hawai'i. 2nd Edition. Bishop Museum Press, Honolulu, HI.

TOMKINS, R. J., AND B. J. MILNE. 1991. Differences among Dark-rumped Petrel (Pterodroma phaeopygia) populations within the Galapagos Archipelago. Notornis 38:1–35.

VAN RIPER, C., III. 1973. Island of Hawaii land bird distribution and abundance. 'Elepaio 34:1–3.

VAN RIPER, C., III, S. G. VAN RIPER, M. L. GOFF, AND M. LAIRD. 1986. The epizootiology and ecological significance of malaria in Hawaiian land birds. Ecological Monographs 56:327–344.

VAN RIPER, S. G., AND C. VAN RIPER, III. 1985. A summary of known parasites and diseases recorded from the avifauna of the Hawaiian Islands. Pp. 298–371 in C. P. Stone and J. M. Scott (eds.), Hawai'i's terrestrial ecosystems: preservation and management. Cooperative National Park Resources Studies Unit, University Hawaii, Honolulu, HI.

WARNER, R. E. 1968. The role of introduced diseases in the extinction of the endemic Hawaiian avifauna. Condor 70:101–120.

WETMORE, A. 1925. Bird life among lava rock and coral sand. National Geographic Magazine 48:76–108.

WILLIAMS, R. N. 1983. Bulbul introductions on Oahu. 'Elepaio 43:89–90.

WILLIAMS, R. N. 1987. Alien birds on Oahu: 1944–1985. 'Elepaio 47:87–92.

WILLIAMS, R. N., AND L. V. GIDDINGS. 1984. Differential range expansion and population growth of bulbuls in Hawaii. Wilson Bulletin 96:647–655.

WILSON, S. B., AND A. H. EVANS. 1890–1899. Aves Hawaiiensis: the birds of the Sandwich Islands. R. H. Porter, London. [Reprint 1974, ARNO Press, New York.]

Studies in Avian Biology No. 15:119–133, 1994.

Population Trends

SEABIRD POPULATION TRENDS ALONG THE WEST COAST OF NORTH AMERICA: CAUSES AND THE EXTENT OF REGIONAL CONCORDANCE

David G. Ainley, William J. Sydeman, Scott A. Hatch, and Ulrich W. Wilson

Abstract. We compared trends in breeding population size among cormorants, gulls, alcids, and others, among the Farallon Islands, and sites in northern California and Washington, Gulf of Alaska, and Bering Sea, but in most cases only during the last two decades. For a given species, trends were usually concordant within the same oceanographic domain, except for the Rhinoceros Auklet which increased across all domains in its northeastern Pacific range. Overall, humans and their domestic animals have had severe negative impacts to individual islands, but recent restoration efforts have had spectacular results. On the other hand, the California Current and the eastern Bering Sea now seem unable to support historic populations of natural, top-trophic predators. The major factor responsible appears to be overfishing by humans of important seabird prey, especially, in a period when climate has been unstable. Notable trends indicating these general patterns were as follows: 1) The Ashy Storm-Petrel on the Farallon Islands, where 80% of this species breeds, may have decreased in response to the increase of gulls in the storm-petrel breeding habitat. 2) Brandt's and Pelagic cormorants in the central California Current declined radically owing to El Niño and anthropogenic factors in the early 1980s, and have since failed to recover, contrary to trends in the 1970s; farther north, populations fluctuated slightly but at low levels during this period. 3) Large *Larus* gulls have increased. 4) Common Murres in the central and northern portions of the California Current exhibited a marked decline during the early 1980s and have since failed to recover. 5) Most Common Murre populations in the Gulf of Alaska appear to be stable; whereas those in the eastern Bering Sea are decreasing. 6) Rhinoceros Auklet has increased throughout its range and has (re-)colonized new sites in the southern portion of it. 7) Tufted Puffin has ceased recovery in the California Current, but in Alaska it has continued to recover from former negative, anthropogenic impacts. 8) Cassin's Auklet has declined in the central California Current region.

Key Words: Alaska; California; climate stability; ecological scale; feral animals; Oregon; population trends; resource depletion; seabirds; Washington.

A review of trends in seabird populations of western North America is a difficult task due to the paucity of information. On the one hand, the avifaunal richness of the Farallon Islands, California, in close proximity to the large metropolis of San Francisco, has attracted the attention of ornithologists for over 100 years. Consequently, much is known of population trends for several species there since the 1850s (Ainley and Lewis 1974, Ainley and Boekelheide 1990). Because the Farallon populations contributed the majority of breeding birds to the marine avifauna of the central California Current, and to a lesser extent still do, their history takes on regional significance. On the other hand, such an historical perspective for a seabird fauna has few equals in western North America (Nisbet 1989, Wooller et al. 1992). Comparable is the information available for the Brown Pelican (*Pelecanus occidentalis*) in southern California, where long-term censusing and research has documented recent population growth (summarized in Ainley and Hunt 1991). Thus, comparison of seabird population trends elsewhere along the West Coast is difficult, at best, except for data collected during the past 20 years and discussed herein.

We will use the Farallon data as a focal point by first updating by ten years the information in Ainley and Boekelheide (1990) and by then making comparisons with populations of similar species in Northern California/Oregon, Washington, the Gulf of Alaska and Alaskan coast of the Bering Sea

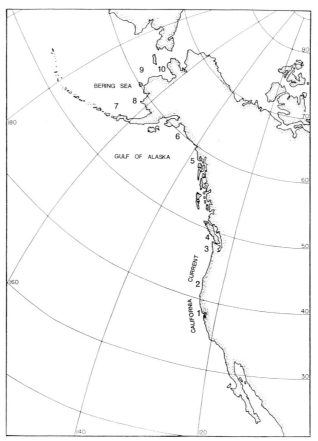

FIGURE 1.   Map of the northeastern Pacific Ocean and Bering Sea showing localities discussed in the text: 1, Farallon Islands; 2, Islands near California/Oregon border; 3, Outer coast islands in Washington; 4, Islands in the Strait of Juan de Fuca; 5, Forrester Island; 6, Middleton Island; 7, St. Paul and St. George islands; 8, Cape Peirce; 9, St. Matthew Island; 10, Bluff, Alaska.

(Fig. 1). Besides the review itself, another goal is to determine the degree and geographic scale of concordance in trends among sites and regions. If trends agree above the coarse or local scale, patterns may indicate responses to climate change or other large-scale factors. We will not elaborate on census methods, except as described in figure captions; interested readers may consult the original studies. The changing status of the Double-crested Cormorant (*Phalacrocorax auritus*) is being reviewed elsewhere by H. Carter and collaborators. In addition, the trends and status of this and several other species have been detailed recently in Vermeer et al. (1993). Hatch (1993) has reviewed historical information, mostly anecdotal accounts, in Alaska dating back to the 1800s.

SEABIRD POPULATION TRENDS IN THE CENTRAL CALIFORNIA CURRENT

Population growth among Farallon seabirds over the past two decades exhibits great annual variability, a pattern characteristic of marine avifaunas in eastern boundary currents (Duffy 1983, Ainley and Boekelheide 1990). At longer temporal scales other patterns are discernible. During the 1970s many species were showing recovery from human activities, such as disturbance from over-population of these islands (e.g., >200 persons housed in more than two dozen buildings during WW II), introduction of exotic vertebrates, oil spills, commercial egging, and changes in prey availability (Ainley and Lewis 1974). In the Gulf of the Farallones region many of these detrimental impacts had diminished significantly by the beginning of the 1970s, leading to increased numbers of virtually all Farallon species (Ainley and Boekelheide 1990). More recently, however, startling changes have occurred.

The Ashy Storm-Petrel (*Oceanodroma homochroa*), an endemic species to the California Current, is more abundant at the Farallones than elsewhere (80% of the world population) but is also at the extreme northern edge of its breeding range (Ainley and Boekelheide 1990). One line of evidence indicates a severe decline from the early 1970s to the late 1980s. Two mark-recapture, mistnetting studies showed a decrease in the adult population of about 50% (cf. Ainley and Lewis 1974, Carter et al. 1992). On the other hand, annual (semi-quantitative) observations in Monterey Bay, 80 km south, where perhaps the entire world population of Ashy Storm-Petrel congregates during autumn, have not indicated such a radical change, if any, during the past 15 years (R. Stallcup, pers. comm.).

In eastern boundary currents (e.g., the California Current), breeding populations of cormorants, especially, can fluctuate dramatically year-to-year in response to fish availability (Ainley and Boekelheide 1990). The Brandt's Cormorant (*P. penicillatus*) population at the Farallones, in the center of a range confined largely to the California Current, varied between 15,000 and 25,000 breeders until the early 1980s (Fig. 2A), when El Niño 1982–1983 severely restricted food resources, reproduction failed, and many birds died (Ainley et al. 1986, Ainley and Boekelheide 1990). To date, the breeding population has shown little recovery, and now ranges from 3000 to 10,000 birds.

An even more erratic pattern is evident in the Pelagic Cormorant (*P. pelagicus*; Fig. 2B), which at the Farallones is in the south-

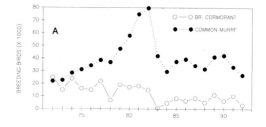

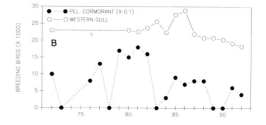

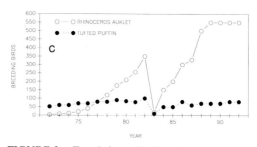

FIGURE 2. Trends in seabird breeding populations at the South Farallon Islands, 1972–1992; see Ainley and Boekelheide (1990) for details on census techniques. A) The number of breeding Brandt's Cormorants and Common Murres. The murre estimates for 1972–1979 are based on extrapolations from a single reference colony and back calculations of annual growth rate from the 1980 census figure when all murres on the island were counted (see Ainley and Boekelheide 1990, fig. 8.1). An island-wide census conducted in 1972 (see Ainley and Lewis 1974) counted 20,500 murres compared to the back-calculated estimate of 22,049. Counts after 1979 are based on island-wide censuses. B) The number of breeding Pelagic Cormorants and Western Gulls. Counts for cormorants are inflated by a factor of ten so that the scale, suitable for the gull numbers, does not hide fluctuations in the cormorant population. No gull censuses were made between 1972 and 1980; the population varied little during this period (Ainley and Boekelheide 1990). C) The number of Rhinoceros Auklets and Tufted Puffins breeding on the South Farallon Islands, 1972–1992.

ern portion of its distribution. In this species, the entire population may forgo breeding as a response to restricted food (Ainley and Boekelheide 1990). Maximum population size increased from about 1000 breeding birds in 1971 to 1600 by the early 1980s, then, following El Niño 1982–1983 dropped by half and is still decreasing.

The Farallon breeding population of the Western Gull (*Larus occidentalis*), another California Current endemic in the center of its range, was stable at about 23,000 birds from the 1960s until El Niño 1982–1983 (Ainley and Boekelheide 1990; Fig. 2B). Numbers then fluctuated until El Niño 1986, after which they began to decline. Overall in California, however, the population remained stable, because many small colonies have been newly founded in the San Francisco Bay Area (see Carter et al. 1992).

The Common Murre (*Uria aalge*), another species at the southern extreme of its range, showed the pattern similar to that exhibited by the cormorants (Fig. 2A). Murres in the PRBO census increased annually by 7.8% through the 1970s until 1982–1983 (Ainley and Boekelheide 1990). Suffering simultaneously from El Niño restrictions on food supply, oil spills, and intense gill netting, which was then greatly restricted (Salzman 1989), the murre breeding population crashed in 1983 to its 1972 level, and two small colonies south of the Farallones virtually disappeared (Takekawa et al. 1990). Since then the Farallon population has increased by only 1–2% per yr.

The Cassin's Auklet (*Ptychoramphus aleuticus*), a small, cavity-nesting species, which at the Farallones is within the southern third of its range, decreased by 50% between 1971 (Manuwal 1974) and 1989, when Carter et al. (1992) estimated 40,000 breeding birds. Because methods and personnel differed between the two estimates, we are uncertain about the magnitude of the decrease. That a significant decrease has occurred is indicated by a severe contraction in extent of nesting habitat used since the early 1970s (PRBO, unpub. data). This is significant because 30% of auklets in California nest on the Farallones, the only breeding population along a 600 km stretch of coast between San Miguel Island and is-

lands near the Oregon/California border (Carter et al. 1992).

Finally, contrasting rates of increase were exhibited by the two "puffins," Rhinoceros Auklet (*Cerorhinca monocerata*) and the Tufted Puffin (*Fratercula cirrhata*), both at the southern extreme of their breeding ranges. During the early 1970s, the Tufted Puffin increased gradually from 50 to 80 breeding birds (Fig. 2C), but after 1977, the population remained stable. The Rhinoceros Auklet recolonized the islands in 1972, following the extermination of cavity dwelling, feral hares (*Oryctolagus cuniculatus*) (Ainley and Lewis 1974). Subsequently, auklet numbers exploded at a rate of about 50% per yr, a pattern interrupted only by El Niño 1982–1983. Numbers stabilized at about 550 breeding birds by 1988.

TRENDS IN SEABIRD POPULATIONS OF THE NORTHERN CALIFORNIA CURRENT

Waters from northern California to central Washington comprise the northernmost portion of the California Current. Carter et al. (1992) suggested that Brandt's and Pelagic cormorant populations for northern California were slightly lower in 1989 than in 1980, but the lack of annual census data makes comparison risky. Wilson (1991, unpub. data) noted a slight increase among Brandt's Cormorants in Washington, in a series of censuses 1979–1992, but total population size is so small (153–265 nests, 1979–1985; 132–578 nests, 1986–1992) that the trend has little regional significance. Wilson's unpublished data for Pelagic Cormorants along Washington's outer coast indicate an increase from 1200 nests in 1985 to 2200 in 1992. On the inner coast (i.e., Strait of Juan de Fuca), numbers of Pelagics fluctuated between 800 and 1200 nests, 1983 to 1992. With a longer time scale, Speich and Wahl (1989) summarized all available census data in Washington over the past few decades, and found no consistent trends among Pelagic or Brandt's cormorants.

For Common Murres, five major California colonies near the Oregon border (ca. 550 km north of the Farallones) during five non-consecutive years 1979–1989, showed similar but less extreme trends as did Farallon murres (cf. Figs. 2, 3; Takekawa et al. 1990, Carter et al. 1992). Northern California populations did not experience oil spills or intense gill-netting, which probably explains why their decrease during El Niño 1982–1983 was minimal. The Farallon pattern of crash-and-no-recovery, however, was repeated farther north among all murre colonies in Washington (to 1000 km north of the Farallones). There, a series of oil spills coincided with El Niño 1982–1983 (Wilson 1991, unpub. data; Fig. 3).

Rhinoceros Auklet populations increased markedly in Oregon during the 1970s (Scott et al. 1974), and in central and northern California during the 1980s, including the founding of 22 new colonies (Carter et al. 1992). The increase was coincident with recolonization on the Farallones, indicating a regional expansion. In Washington, populations also increased to the extent that nesting habitat may have been saturated on Destruction Island (26,000–32,000 birds, Speich and Wahl 1989), though perhaps not Protection Island. Beginning in the late 1960s, the population on Protection Island increased 4–5 fold to about 31,400 birds by the late 1970s (Wilson and Manuwal 1986) and 40,600 birds by 1983 (Thompson et al. 1985). Unused nesting habitat remains (Wilson, unpub. data). During the same period, Tufted Puffins in Washington have been gradually declining (Speich and Wahl 1989); in the Juan de Fuca Strait and in the San Juan Islands the decline has been precipitous, from 1070 birds in the 1950s to about 100 at present (Wilson, unpub. data).

CAUSES OF SEABIRD POPULATION TRENDS IN THE CALIFORNIA CURRENT

The population trends at the Farallones and at other sites in the central and northern California Current were concordant for a number of species.

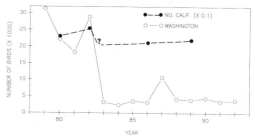

FIGURE 3. The number of breeding Common Murres in five California colonies near the Oregon border (data from Takekawa et al. 1990, Carter et al. 1992) and 28 colonies on the outer coast of Washington, 1979–1990 (data from Wilson 1991, unpub. data). California counts are reduced by a factor of 10 to complement the y-axis scale, fitted to the Washington counts.

The Rhinoceros Auklet was the only non-larid seabird species that significantly increased during the past 30 years. The increase in Washington (and farther north; see below) preceded that in California (see Speich and Wahl 1989), indicating that populations in the Pacific Northwest were the source of southward dispersal. The floating population (i.e., adults that do not breed because space is lacking; *sensu* Manuwal 1974), was so large near the Farallones, as evidenced by the remarkable rate of increase, the quick recovery from El Niño 1982–1983, and the high densities of this species at sea in central California (Briggs et al. 1987, Ainley and Allen 1992), that the species rapidly took over the deserted rabbit warrens. This invasion may have blocked, or at least severely slowed, the recovery of Tufted Puffins at the Farallones, as both "puffins" are cavity-nesting species of similar size and each is aggressive toward the other (Ainley and Boekelheide 1990). The Tufted Puffins at the Farallones were recovering from impacts attributed to humans, but recovery had been slow due to the presence of rabbits and, perhaps, changes in the food web, i.e., loss of an important prey, the Pacific sardine (*Sardinops coerulea*; Ainley and Lewis 1974). At the Farallones, the availability of cavities suitable for both puffins apparently reached saturation in 1988. In Washington, the decline of Tuft-

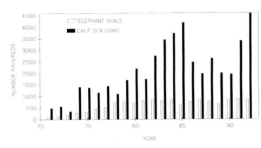

FIGURE 4. The number of California Sea Lions and Northern Elephant Seals hauling out on the South Farallon Islands during April and May, the seabird egg-laying and incubation periods, 1971–1992; data are based on censuses conducted weekly year round (PRBO, unpub. data).

ed Puffins is likely the result of human disturbance to nesting islands: farming, real estate development, Coast Guard activities, and feral animals.

In contrast, other factors affected trends in other seabird species. Predation and interference by Western Gulls may be responsible for the decrease among Ashy Storm-Petrels on the Farallones. In the early 1970s, few gulls nested in the optimal storm-petrel nesting habitat. Gulls are now spread everywhere and, besides eating storm-petrels, often nest in the sheltered positions at the entrance to petrel burrows. A dense, exotic grass introduced in the 1800s, appears to be spreading over the talus and also blocks crevice entrances.

By the early 1980s, the Western Gulls had colonized densely all available terrain on the island and a "floating" gull population was evident (Spear et al. 1987). The decrease in recent years, beginning about 1986, involves at least two factors: 1) a large increase in numbers of Elephant Seals (*Mirounga angustirostris*) and California Sea Lions (*Zalophus californianus*) along the seaward edges of the islands (Fig. 4; fig. 1.4 in Ainley and Boekelheide 1990), and 2) increased mortality due to disease (Spear et al. 1987; PRBO, unpub. data). The fact that the total California population did not change between 1980 and 1989 indicates that emigration from the huge population on the Farallones may also have increased.

The decrease in Cassin's Auklets on the Farallones may also involve several factors. 1) Different census methods could be involved, as discussed above, especially as cavity-nesting seabirds are difficult to estimate. Yet, auklets clearly nest less densely than they did in the early 1970s. 2) Predation by Western Gulls and Peregrine Falcons (*Falco peregrinus*) may have increased. Wintering falcons "recolonized" the island in the early 1970s, reaching maximum numbers (ca. 5) about 1980 (Pyle and Henderson 1990). Auklets are so numerous, however, that a measurable population effect seems unlikely, in contrast to effects among the many fewer auklets on Tatoosh Island, Washington (see Paine et al. 1990). 3) Most importantly, oceanographic factors may have changed food availability. In the early 1970s, a large floating population was evident (Manuwal 1972) and it may have been maintained by double-brooding, a rare phenomenon among seabirds. Since the mid-1970s, however, warm-water conditions have prevailed leading to a switch in diet composition, perhaps lower breeding success and certainly no second chicks fledged successfully (Ainley and Boekelheide 1990; PRBO, unpub. data). Ainley and Lewis (1974) noted that auklets were also much reduced in number during the late 19th century when another prolonged warm-water period occurred.

Populations of Pelagic and Brandt's cormorants and Common Murre at the Farallones and in Washington have recently begun to fluctuate within levels lower than those previous to El Niño 1982–1983. These species are largely piscivorous, feeding principally on juvenile rockfish (*Sebastes*) during the breeding season (Ainley and Boekelheide 1990). The principal prey that sustains *reproduction* is the juvenile shortbelly rockfish (*S. jordani*), which during mid-summer settles to depths beyond the foraging capabilities of seabirds. During the non-breeding season, these seabirds then feed on the early year-classes of other rockfish (those that settle to shallow depths) and of Pacific whiting (*Merluccius productus*), as well as all year-classes of anchovies (*Engraulis mordax*), Pacific herring (*Clupea harengus*), market squid (*Loligo opalescens*) and euphausiids (Baltz and Morejohn 1977, PRBO, unpub. data). Historically, when one prey species has been unavailable the seabirds have been able to switch to alternative species (Ainley and Boekelheide 1990). Seabird populations at the Farallones (and farther north) are depressed enough from historical levels (see Ainley and Lewis 1974, Ainley and Boekelheide 1990) that the spring surge in availability of rockfish juveniles is sufficient to produce high chick production (PRBO, unpub. data, see also Sydeman et al. 1991). Declines in reproductive success are too small to explain the trends (PRBO, unpub. data), in contrast to resource levels during the non-breeding season and effects on adult survival, juvenile recruitment or both.

The pattern exhibited by the three piscivores is closely similar to that shown by Peruvian guano birds before the crash of their prime prey species, the anchovetta (*Engraulis ringens*) (cf. Tovar et al. 1987). Documented since the time of the Incas, over a 30-year period beginning in the 1950s the guano birds recovered from successive El Niño events to lower and lower population levels concomitant with the increase in the commercial harvest of anchovetta. Ultimately, the anchovetta was lost due to over-fishing of a climatically stressed resource (Glantz and Thompson 1981). The birds and the fishery have yet to recover.

Similarly, commercial fisheries in California, except for anchovies and euphausiids, have been expanding greatly. In central and northern California, expansion of both pelagic (Fig. 5) and groundfish fisheries (Fig. 6) duplicates the pattern elsewhere in the California Current (see Pacific Fisheries Management Council 1992, and previous annual reports). Although the seabirds do not eat the adult groundfish (i.e., rockfish and whiting), reduction in spawning biomass of adults and curtailment of strong year-classes by the fisheries (or other factors), indirectly reduces the abundance of young fish available to seabirds and other predators. At present, no fishery exists for Shortbelly Rockfish, but proposals for development have been made. Among the pelagic fisheries, which compete directly with the birds, only the small one for anchovies has not greatly expanded (due to market conditions; Fig. 5A). Anchovies are abundant in southern California, where they are important to seabirds and other top-trophic predators (e.g., Anderson et al. 1982, Antonellis and Fiscus 1980, Hunt and Butler 1980); in central and northern California, anchovies are relatively unimportant to seabirds, except during summer (Ainley and Boekelheide 1990). In contrast, pelagic fisheries for Pacific herring (Fig. 5B) and market squid (Fig. 5C), centered in central California, have grown enormously.

We hypothesize that growth of fisheries for seabird prey species has been so dramatic, extensive, and coincident in time and region to the decrease in seabirds that a cause-effect process is involved. Prey switching may no longer be a viable alternative to seabirds (or individual fishermen) as virtually the entire suite of important prey species are now fished to their maximum. Annually extracting from this food web the amount and type of fish now accomplished by commercial fisheries cannot occur without consequences to the food web, and especially top carnivores (see Ludwig et al. 1993). Indeed, commercial catch rates for individual species have declined, specific fisheries in the California Current region recently have been closed (e.g., willow rockfish *S. entomelas,* Pacific Fishery Management Council 1992; Pacific herring, Calif. Dept. Fish and Game, results of 1993 Fish Commission hearings), and others have been severely restricted (e.g., rockfish, Pacific Fisheries Management Council 1992). For both reasons (fewer fish and more restrictions), commercial catches have declined (Fig. 6A). Moreover, as discussed above, the physical environment has been changing,

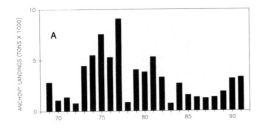

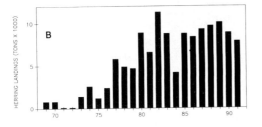

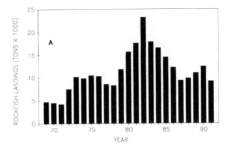

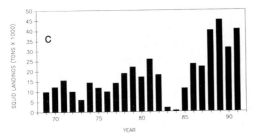

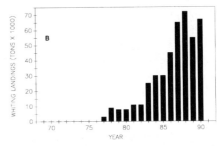

FIGURE 6. Annual landings (tons × 1000) of principal seabird prey by human fisheries in California waters over the previous few decades—groundfish whose juveniles are pelagic (although seabirds also eat year-old fish): A) rockfish, all species, with most of the catch taken in central and northern California; B) Pacific whiting, with most of the total taken in northern California (data from Calif. Dept. Fish and Game 1992); (McAllister 1975, 1976; Oliphant 1979; Oliphant et al. 1990; Pinkas 1974, 1977; Calif. Dept Fish & Game, R. Lea, pers. comm.).

FIGURE 5. Annual landings (tons × 1000) in central and northern California of principal seabird prey by human, "pelagic" fisheries (i.e., mid-water species) over the previous few decades: A) northern anchovy; B) Pacific herring; and C) market squid, with about 40% of the squid landings from central California and the remainder from the vicinity of the northern Channel Islands (data from McAllister 1975, 1976; Oliphant 1979; Oliphant et al. 1990; Pinkas 1974, 1977).

but fishery management has been too slow to respond to the change; since 1976, sea temperatures have been warmer and annual variability of climate has been more severe than at any period in historical times (Kerr 1985, 1992). Many of the fish prey species have a zooplankton diet similar to the Cassin's Auklet, whose diet and population size have changed likely in response to oceanographic anomaly. Thus, the same phenomena that wrecked the Peruvian anchovy fishery appear to be in place: intense fishing coincident with climatic stress.

The increase in California Sea Lions in the central and northern part of the Cali-

fornia Current (Fig. 4) may in a way represent still another "fishery" competing indirectly with seabirds. The sea lions feed heavily on Pacific whiting older than one year and, when such prey are not available, rockfish and anchovies (Jones 1981, Bailey and Ainley 1981/1982, Antonellis et al. 1983). Like the human fishery, the sea lions may reduce the spawning biomass and ultimately the availability of one-year-old and younger fish. Growth rates of this sea lion's population have changed in concert with harvest levels of whiting (Ainley et al. 1982). Overall population levels, however, may or may not have reached their historical levels, following recovery from persecution (Boveng 1988). In the 1800s, the same or a greater number of sea lions and, with the Farallon history as a gauge (Ainley and Lewis 1974), a population of seabirds an order of magnitude greater than now co-existed in the California Current. For what ever reason, the system no longer appears capable of supporting close to the former levels of upper trophic-level predators.

SEABIRD POPULATION TRENDS IN THE GULF OF ALASKA AND BERING SEA

The major oceanographic region north of the California Current is the Gulf of Alaska (Subarctic Current system) and father north, separated by a series of complex currents among the Aleutian Islands, is the Bering Sea Gyre (Favorite et al. 1977). As a result of the Outer Continental Shelf Environmental Assessment Program (OCSEAP) established in 1975, permanent plots at a number of sites in the Gulf of Alaska, Bering Sea and Chukchi Sea, have been censused periodically. The result is a time series of censuses spanning 15+ years for a few common and easily-studied species.

On Middleton Island, in the Gulf of Alaska, a large colony of Pelagic Cormorants (2000–4500 pairs) has fluctuated widely since 1974, but on average is much larger now than in 1956 (Rausch 1958, pers. comm). In Chiniak Bay (Kodiak Island), censuses of 13 mixed colonies of Pelagic and Red-faced cormorants (*P. urile*) between 1975 and 1991 indicate stable populations (D. R. Nysewander and D. B. Irons, unpub. data). No data are available in the Bering Sea, but at Cape Thompson, southeastern Chukchi Sea, Pelagic Cormorants decreased in the late 1970s to a level 20% lower than in the early 1960s (Springer 1993).

Among large *Larus* species north of the California Current, only the Glaucous-winged Gull (*L. glaucescens*) has been studied sufficiently. In Washington, at the transition between California Current and Gulf of Alaska systems, Glaucous-winged Gulls increased appreciably during the past few decades (Speich and Wahl 1989). Farther north, on the Alaid-Nizki island group (western Aleutians), the species increased from 200 to 1300 pairs within a few years

following eradication of feral foxes in 1976 (C. F. Zeillemaker and J. L. Trapp, unpub. data). The greatest documented change occurred on Middleton Island, where this species grew from none in 1956, to 500–700 pairs by the mid-1970s, to more than 7000 pairs by 1990 (S. A. Hatch, unpub. data). Thus, the increase is consistent among widely spaced sites in the region. A decline in the Glaucous-winged Gull population of Prince William Sound since the early 1970s (Vermeer and Irons 1991, Laing and Klosiewski 1993) probably reflects the local closure of some canneries and canning regulations that have reduced availability of offal (M. E. Isleib, pers. comm.).

In recent years Common Murres have been well studied in Alaska (Byrd et al. 1993), but historic data are rare. Elliot (1881) described "hundreds of thousands" of Common and Thick-billed murres (*U. lomvia*) on Walrus Island, Bering Sea. As recently as 1953, Peterson and Fisher (1955) estimated more than 1 million murres there; yet, by 1976 almost all had vanished (Hunt 1976). In partial explanation, Steller Sea Lions (*Eumetopias jubatus*) had moved onto the island's plateau, which had formerly been dominated by murres. At other sites in the Bering Sea monitored since the 1970s, most study colonies have declined (Fig. 7), but not due to competition with pinnipeds (see below). At Cape Thompson, in the southeastern Chukchi Sea, murres have declined as well (Springer 1993). Elsewhere in Alaska, trends among Common Murre populations have been inconsistent with those in the Bering Sea Gyre. For example, in 1956 on Middleton Island, Rausch (1958) counted only about 400 murres, mostly Thick-billed. Today the island supports a similar number of Thick-billed Murres but 6000–8000 Common Murres as well (Fig. 7).

Cassin's Auklets formerly nested in abundance on Sanak Island (Bendire 1895), but foxes were introduced and the auklets became scarce by the late 1930s (Murie 1959). Murie also learned of probable declines or

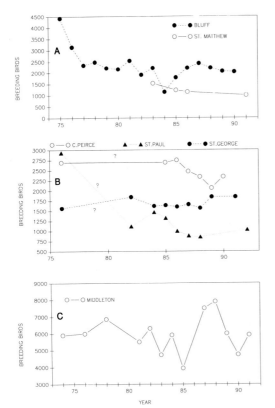

FIGURE 7. The number of breeding Common Murres at A) two reference colonies in the northeastern portion of the Bering Sea Gyre, Alaska, 1976–1991; B) three colonies in the southeastern Bering Sea Gyre, 1976–1992; and C) a colony in the Gulf of Alaska: Middleton Island, 1974–1991. Sources of the data are as follows: Middleton Island (Rausch 1958, Nysewander et al. 1986, S. Hatch, unpub. data); Cape Peirce (Haggblom and Mendenhall 1993); St. George Island (Dragoo et al. 1990, unpub. data); St. Paul Island (Dragoo et al. 1989, L. Climo, pers. comm.); St. Matthew Island (Murphy et al. 1987, A. L. Sowls, pers. comm.); Bluff (Murphy et al. 1986, Murphy 1993).

extirpations on other Aleutian Islands including Keegaloo, Adugak, Amlia (nearby islets) and Ilak.

Particularly susceptible to foxes is the Tufted Puffin. Murie (1937) recommended that Kaligagan Island should be managed as a fox farm because of the paucity of breeding seabirds (i.e., no impact evident). Foxes eventually died out, however, and today Kaligagan has one of the largest Tufted Puffin colonies in Alaska (>100,000 birds; Nysewander et al. 1982)!

Most of the Alaskan population of Rhinoceros Auklets breeds on Forrester Island, which is likely the world's largest colony of this species (>54,000 pairs; DeGange et al. 1977). The only site that has been closely censused, however, is Middleton Island where one of four small colonies located in 1976–1978 had increased from about 50 to more than 900 burrows by 1992 (Hatch et al. 1979, Hatch, unpub. data). Farther south in the Gulf of Alaska, in British Columbia, Rhinoceros Auklet populations also increased substantially during the past few decades (Rodway et al. 1992).

CAUSES OF SEABIRD POPULATION TRENDS IN THE GULF OF ALASKA AND BERING SEA

In Alaska, it is clear that many local populations of seabirds have undergone marked changes during recent decades. Given the enormity and environmental complexity of the region, we can rarely posit whether any species' population is changing throughout its range. An exception is the downward trend among murre colonies in the eastern Bering Sea, where changes are concordant among widely-spaced sites.

Alaskan seabirds are killed in large numbers in high seas gill nets (DeGange et al. 1993), although effects on local breeding populations are difficult to ascertain, and oil at sea poses a significant threat, as demonstrated by the *Exxon-Valdez* spill (Piatt et al. 1990, Nysewander et al. 1992). There is little doubt, however, that the introduction of exotic animals to islands—especially foxes, but other mammals as well—has been the most potent anthropogenic factor affecting Alaskan and other seabirds during recent centuries (Croxall et al. 1984). Introduced by Russian colonists late in the 1700s, the heyday of fox farming occurred between 1885 and 1930 and included 450 islands from southeastern Alaska to the western Aleutians (Bailey 1993). Fox trappers regarded seabirds as "feed," and not surprisingly, some of our richest seabird islands supported the most successful, if short-lived, fox farms (e.g., Middleton Island). Fox introductions were locally disastrous (Murie 1959, Bailey 1993), but this damage has been reversed in most cases. Fox farming ceased in the 1930s, and today, foxes remain on only about 50 islands (Bailey 1993). Some of these islands are large, however, and impossible to rid of foxes unless restrictions on the use of toxicants are lifted.

The trends among sites in the eastern Bering Sea indicate other than local, coarse-scale effects as with fox introductions. The regional decline in Common Murres, as well as in pup production of Northern Fur Seals (*Callorhinus ursinus*) and adult populations of Harbor Seals (*Phoca vitulina*) and Steller Sea Lions (York and Kozloff 1987, Merrick et al. 1987, Pitcher 1990), brings to issue whether fisheries are altering the marine ecosystem to the detriment of top-trophic predators (Murphy et al. 1986, Springer 1992). Since the 1960s, walleye pollock (*Theragra chalcogramma*) have supported the world's largest single-species fishery (Lloyd and Davis 1989; Fig. 8) and are also important to pinnipeds (Lowry et al. 1989) and piscivorous seabirds (Hunt et al. 1981, Dragoo 1991). Any cause-effect explanation, however, must address both the apparent increase of planktivorous auklets (*Aethia* spp.) in the region (Pribilof Islands, St. Lawrence Island; Springer 1993) and the decline of murres and kittiwakes (*Rissa* spp.) (Pribilof Islands, St. Matthew Island, etc.; Hatch et al. 1993). Auklets presumably compete with juvenile pollock for euphausiids and other zooplankton, whereas murres and kittiwakes take juvenile pollock, especially during the breeding season (Springer and Byrd 1989). The role of fishing in this scenario is unclear, because the adult pollock (age 2+) taken in the fishery are important predators on juvenile pollock and other seabird prey such as herring, myctophids, capelin (*Mallotus villosus*), and sandlance (*Ammodytes hexapterus*; Straty and Haight 1979, Livingston 1991, Springer 1992). Thus, this fishery could theoretically benefit piscivorous birds as was the case in

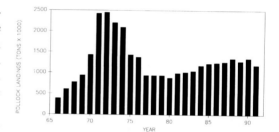

FIGURE 8. Annual landings of pollock from the eastern Bering Sea (data from Bakkala 1984; Pacific Fisheries Information Network, R. Kinoshita, pers. comm.).

the large-scale fisheries of the North Sea (Furness and Barrett 1991). The issue in Alaska, as in the California Current, requires critical information on seabird demography and trophic relationships during winter. Experience has shown us (e.g., Glantz and Thompson 1981) that understanding the whole system, both prey and predators, ultimately benefits man's commercial interests in the long-term perspective (see also Cairns 1992, Ludwig et al. 1993).

CONCLUSIONS

1. Trends in population size of seabirds at breeding sites along the western coast of North America have been concordant within different oceanographic regimes, e.g., the California Current or the eastern Bering Sea Gyre (continental shelf). The best example is given by the Common Murre, a species exhibiting two sets of concordant trends, one within the California Current and the other in the eastern Bering Sea Gyre.

2. At larger spatial scales (i.e., >1000 km) less concordance was apparent, although marked changes within one species, the Rhinoceros Auklet, was consistent across oceanographic boundaries. Its spectacular increase and southward colonization appear to have been fueled by factors initially operating in the Gulf of Alaska. From there, surplus breeders dispersed southward.

3. Seabird populations along the west coast of North America have been greatly affected by two general classes of factors: encroachment of humans and especially

their animals on breeding islands, and exploitation of the prey base by human fisheries (in concert with climatic stress).

ACKNOWLEDGMENTS

We thank the personnel of the Farallon Island National Wildlife Refuge and the Farallon Patrol of PRBO for logistical support. R. Hofman (Marine Mammal Commission), L. Jacobson (National Marine Fisheries Service), R. Lea (California Department of Fish and Game), and R. Kinoshita (Pacific Fisheries Information Network, NOAA) were helpful in obtaining fisheries data. G. L. Hunt, J. R. Jehl and L. B. Spear kindly provided clarifying comments on the manuscript. This is contribution no. 579 of PRBO.

LITERATURE CITED

AINLEY, D. G., AND S. G. ALLEN. 1992. Abundance and distribution of seabirds and marine mammals in the Gulf of the Farallones. Final Report, Environmental Protection Agency (Region IX), LTMS Study Group, San Francisco, CA.

AINLEY, D. G., AND R. J. BOEKELHEIDE (eds.). 1990. Seabirds of the Farallon Islands. Stanford University Press, Palo Alto, CA.

AINLEY, D. G., AND G. L. HUNT, JR. 1991. The status and conservation of seabirds in California. Pp. 103–114, in J. P. Croxall (ed.), Seabird status and conservation: a supplement. Technical Bulletin No. 11, International Council for Bird Preservation, Cambridge.

AINLEY, D. G., AND T. J. LEWIS. 1974. The history of Farallon Island marine bird populations 1843–1972. Condor 76:432–446.

AINLEY, D. G., H. R. HUBER, AND K. M. BAILEY. 1982. Population fluctuations of California sea lions and the Pacific whiting fishery off central California. U.S. Fishery Bulletin 80:253–258.

AINLEY, D. G., H. R. CARTER, D. W. ANDERSON, K. T. BRIGGS, M. C. COULTER, F. CRUZ, J. B. CRUZ, C. A. VALLE, S. I. FEFER, S. A. HATCH, E. A. SCHREIBER, R. W. SCHREIBER, AND N. G. SMITH. 1986. Effects on the 1982–83 El Niño-Southern Oscillation on Pacific Ocean bird populations. Pp. 1747–1758 in Proceedings XIX International Ornithological Congress, National Museum of Natural Science, Ottawa.

ANDERSON, D. W., F. GRESS, AND K. MAIS. 1982. Brown Pelicans: influence of food supply on reproduction. Oikos 39:23–31.

ANTONELLIS, G. A., JR., AND C. FISCUS. 1980. The pinnipeds of the California Current. California Cooperative Oceanic Fisheries Investigations, Reports 21:68–78.

ANTONELLIS, G. A., JR., C. H. FISCUS, AND R. L. DELONG. 1983. Spring and summer prey of California sea lions, Zalophus californianus, at San Miguel Island, California, 1978–79. U.S. Fishery Bulletin 82:67–76.

BAILEY, E. P. 1993. Introduction of foxes to Alaskan islands—history, effects on avifauna, and eradication. U.S. Department of the Interior, Fish and Wildlife Service, Anchorage. Resource Publication 13.

BAILEY, K. M., AND D. G. AINLEY. 1981/1982. The dynamics of California sea lion predation on Pacific hake. Fisheries Research 1:163–176.

BAKKALA, R. G. 1984. Research and commercial fisheries data bases for eastern Bering Sea groundfish. Pp. 39–66 in Biological interactions among marine mammals and commercial fisheries in the southeastern Bering Sea. Alaska Sea Grant Report 84-1, University of Alaska, Fairbanks, AK.

BALTZ, D. M., AND G. V. MOREJOHN. 1977. Food habits and niche overlap of seabirds wintering on Monterey Bay, California. Auk 94:526–543.

BENDIRE, C. 1895. Notes on the Ancient Murrelet (Synthliboramphus antiquus) by Chase Littlejohn with annotations. Auk 12:270–278.

BOVENG, P. 1988. Status of the California sea lion population on the U.S. West Coast. Administrative Report LJ-88-07, National Marine Fisheries Service, Southwest Fisheries Science Center, La Jolla, CA.

BRIGGS, K. T., W. B. TYLER, D. B. LEWIS, AND D. R. CARLSON. 1987. Bird communities at sea off California: 1975-1983. Studies in Avian Biology No. 11.

BYRD, G. V., E. C. MURPHY, G. W. KAISER, A. J. KONDRATYEV, AND Y. V. SHIBAEV. 1993. Status and ecology of offshore fish-feeding alcids (murres and puffins) in the North Pacific. Pp. 176–186, in K. Vermeer, K. T. Briggs, K. H. Morgan, and D. Siegel-Causey (eds.), The status, ecology and conservation of marine birds of the North Pacific. Special Publication, Canadian Wildlife Service, Ottawa.

CAIRNS, D. K. 1992. Bridging the gap between ornithology and fisheries science: use of seabird data in stock assessment models. Condor 94:811–824.

CALIFORNIA DEPARTMENT OF FISH AND GAME. 1992. Review of some California fisheries for 1991. California Cooperative Oceanic Fisheries Investigations, Reports 33:7–20.

CARTER, H. C., G. J. MCCHESNEY, D. L. JAQUES, C. S. STRONG, M. W. PARKER, J. E. TAKEKAWA, D. L. JORY, D. L. WHITWORTH, POINT REYES BIRD OBSERVATORY AND CHANNEL ISLANDS NATIONAL PARK. 1992. Breeding populations of seabirds on the northern and central California coasts in 1989–1991. U.S. Department of the Interior, Minerals Management Service, Los Angeles, CA.

CROXALL, J. P., P. G. H. EVANS, AND R. W. SCHREIBER (eds.). 1984. Status and conservation of the world's seabirds. Technical Bulletin No. 2, International Council for Bird Preservation, Cambridge.

DEGANGE, A. R., E. E. POSSARDT, AND D. A. FRAZER. 1977. The breeding biology of seabirds on the Forrester Island National Wildlife Refuge, 15 May to 1 September 1976. Unpublished Report, U.S. Department of the Interior, Fish and Wildlife Service, Anchorage, AK.

DEGANGE, A. R., R. H. DAY, J. E. TAKEKAWA, AND V. M. MENDENHALL. 1993. Losses of seabirds in gillnets in the North Pacific. Pp. 204–211, in K. Vermeer, K. T. Briggs, K. H. Morgan, and D. Siegel-Causey (eds.), The status, ecology and conservation of marine birds of the North Pacific. Special Publication, Canadian Wildlife Service, Ottawa.

DRAGOO, D. E. 1991. Food habits and productivity of kittiwakes and murres at St. George Island, Alaska. Unpublished M.Sc. Thesis, University of Alaska, Fairbanks, AK.

DRAGOO, D. E., B. E. BAIN, A. L. SOWLS, AND R. F. CHAUNDY. 1989. The status of cliff nesting seabirds in the Pribilof Islands, Alaska, 1976–1988: a summary. Unpublished Report, U.S. Department of the Interior, Fish and Wildlife Service, Homer, AK.

DRAGOO, D. E., S. D. SCHULMEISTER, AND B. K. BAIN. 1990. The status of Northern Fulmars, kittiwakes and murres at St. George Island, Alaska, in 1989. Unpublished Report, U.S. Department of the Interior, Fish and Wildlife Service, Homer, AK.

DUFFY, D. C. 1983. Environmental uncertainty and commercial fishing: effects on Peruvian guano birds. Biological Conservation 26:227–238.

ELLIOT, H. W. 1881. The seal-islands of Alaska. U.S. Department of the Interior, Government Printing Office, Washington, DC.

FAVORITE, F., T. LAEVASTU, AND R. R. STRATY. 1977. Oceanography of the northeastern Pacific Ocean and eastern Bering Sea, and relations to various living marine resources. Processed Report, U.S. Department of Commerce, Northwest and Alaska Fisheries Science Center, Seattle, WA.

FURNESS, R. W., AND R. T. BARRETT. 1991. Seabirds and fish declines. National Geographic Research 7:82–95.

GLANTZ, M. H., AND J. D. THOMPSON (eds.). 1981. Resource management and environmental uncertainty. Wiley, New York, NY.

HAGGBLOM, L., AND V. M. MENDENHALL. 1993. Cape Peirce. Pp. 14–59, *in* V. M. Mendenhall (ed.), Monitoring of populations and productivity of seabirds at Cape Peirce, Bluff, and Cape Thompson, Alaska, 1990. Final Report, OCSEAP Study 92-0047, U.S. Department of the Interior, Minerals Management Service, Anchorage, AK.

HATCH, S. A. 1993. Population trends of Alaskan seabirds. Pacific Seabird Group Bulletin 20:3–12.

HATCH, S. A., T. W. PEARSON, AND P. J. GOULD. 1979. Reproductive ecology of seabirds at Middleton Island, Alaska. U.S. Department of Commerce, National Oceanic and Atmospheric Administration, OCSEAP Annual Reports 2:233–308.

HATCH, S. A., G. V. BYRD, D. B. IRONS, AND G. L. HUNT, JR. 1993. Status and ecology of kittiwakes (*Rissa tridactyla* and *R. brevirostris*) in the North Pacific. Pp. 140–153, *in* K. Vermeer, K. T. Briggs, K. H. Morgan, and D. Siegel-Causey (eds.), The status, ecology and conservation of marine birds of the North Pacific. Special Publication, Canadian Wildlife Service, Ottawa.

HUNT, G. L., JR. 1976. Reproductive ecology, foods, and foraging areas of seabirds nesting on the Pribilof Islands. U.S. Department of Commerce, National Oceanic and Atmospheric Administration, OCSEAP Annual Reports 2:155–269.

HUNT, G. L., JR., AND J. BUTLER. 1980. Reproductive ecology of the Western Gulls and Xantus' Murrelets with respect to food resources in the Southern California Bight. California Cooperative Oceanic Fisheries Investigations, Reports 21:62–67.

HUNT, G. L., JR., B. BURGESON, AND G. A. SANGER. 1981. Feeding ecology of seabirds in the eastern Bering Sea. Pp. 629–647, *in* D. W. Hood and J. A.

Calder (eds.), The Eastern Bering Sea Shelf: oceanography and resources. University of Washington Press, Seattle, WA.

JONES, R. E. 1981. Food habits of smaller marine mammals from northern California. California Academy of Sciences, Proceedings 42:409–433.

KERR, R. A. 1985. Wild string of winters confirmed. Science 227:506.

KERR, R. A. 1992. Unmasking a shifty climate system. Science 255:1508–1510.

LAING, K. K., AND S. P. KLOSIEWSKI. 1993. Marine bird populations of Prince William Sound, Alaska, before and after the Exxon Valdez oil spill. Unpublished Report, U.S. Department of the Interior, Fish and Wildlife Service, Anchorage, AK.

LIVINGSTON, P. A. 1991. Walleye pollock. Pp. 9–30, *in* P. A. Livingston (ed.), Groundfish food habits and predation on commercially important prey species in the Eastern Bering Sea from 1984 to 1986. Technical Memorandum NMFS F/NWC-207, U.S. Department of Commerce, National Oceanic and Atmospheric Administration, Seattle, WA.

LLOYD, D. S., AND S. K. DAVIS. 1989. Biological information required for improved management of walleye pollock off Alaska. Pp. 9–31, *in* International symposium on the biology and management of walleye pollock. Alaska Sea Grant Report 89-1, Lowell Wakefield Fisheries Symposium 7, Fairbanks, AK.

LOWRY, L. F., K. J. FROST, AND T. R. LOUGHLIN. 1989. Importance of walleye pollock in the diets of marine mammals in the Gulf of Alaska and Bering Sea, and implications for fishery management. Pp. 701–726, *in* International symposium on the biology and management of walleye pollock. Alaska Sea Grant Report 89-1, Lowell Wakefield Fisheries Symposium 7, Fairbanks, AK.

LUDWIG, D., R. HILBORN, AND C. WALTERS. 1993. Uncertainty, resource exploitation and conservation: lessons from history. Science 260:17, 36.

MANUWAL, D. A. 1972. The population ecology of the Cassin's Auklet on Southeast Farallon Island, California. Unpublished Ph.D. Thesis, University of California, Los Angeles, CA.

MANUWAL, D. A. 1974. Effects of territoriality on breeding in a population of Cassin's Auklet. Ecology 55:1399–1406.

McALLISTER, R. 1975. California marine fish landings for 1973. California Department of Fish and Game, Fish Bulletin 163.

McALLISTER, R. 1976. California marine fish landings for 1974. California Department of Fish and Game, Fish Bulletin 166.

MERRICK, R. L., T. R. LOUGHLIN, AND D. G. CALKINS. 1987. Decline in abundance of the northern sea lion, *Eumetopius jubatus*, in Alaska, 1956–1986. U.S. Fishery Bulletin 85:351–365.

MURIE, O. J. 1937. Biological investigations of the Aleutians and southwestern Alaska. Unpublished field notes, U.S. Department of the Interior, Fish and Wildlife Service, Washington, DC.

MURIE, O. J. 1959. Fauna of the Aleutian Islands and Alaska Peninsula. North American Fauna 61: 1–406.

MURPHY, E. C. 1993. Population status of murres and kittiwakes at Bluff, Alaska, in 1990. Pp. 60–93, *in* V. M. Mendenhall (ed.), Monitoring of populations and productivity of seabirds at Cape Peirce, Bluff, and Cape Thompson, Alaska, 1990. Final Report, OCSEAP Study 92-0047, U.S. Department of the Interior, Minerals Management Service, Anchorage, AK. In press.

MURPHY, E. C., A. M. SPRINGER, AND D. G. ROSENEAU. 1986. Population status of Common Guillemots *Uria aalge* at a colony in western Alaska: results and simulations. Ibis 128:348–363.

MURPHY, E. C., B. A. COOPER, P. D. MARTIN, C. B. JOHNSON, B. E. LAWHEAD, A. M. SPRINGER, AND D. L. THOMAS. 1987. The population status of seabirds on St. Matthew and Hall Islands, 1985 and 1986. Final Report, OCSEAP Study MMS 87-0043, U.S. Department of the Interior, Minerals Management Service, Anchorage, AK.

NISBET, I. C. T. 1989. Long-term ecological studies of seabirds. Colonial Waterbirds 12:143–147.

NYSEWANDER, D. R., D. J. FORSELL, P. A. BAIRD, D. J. SHIELDS, G. J. WEILER, AND J. H. KOGAN. 1982. Marine bird and mammal survey of the eastern Aleutian Islands, summers of 1980–81. Unpublished Report, U.S. Department of the Interior, Fish and Wildlife Service, Anchorage, AK.

NYSEWANDER, D. R., B. ROBERTS, AND S. BONFIELD. 1986. Reproductive ecology of seabirds at Middleton Island, Alaska—summer 1985. Unpublished Report, U.S. Department of the Interior, Fish and Wildlife Service, Anchorage, AK.

NYSEWANDER, D. R., C. DIPPEL, G. V. BYRD, AND E. P. KNUDTSON. 1992. Effects of the T/V Exxon Valdez oil spill on murres: a perspective from observations at breeding colonies. Unpublished Report, U.S. Department of the Interior, Fish and Wildlife Service, Anchorage, AK.

OLIPHANT, M. S. 1979. California marine fish landings for 1976. California Department of Fish and Game, Fish Bulletin 170.

OLIPHANT, M. S., P. A. GREGORY, B. J. INGLE, AND R. MADRID. 1990. California marine fish landings for 1977–1986. California Department of Fish and Game, Fish Bulletin 173.

PACIFIC FISHERIES MANAGEMENT COUNCIL. 1992. Status of the Pacific Coast groundfish fishery through 1992 and recommended acceptable biological catches for 1993. Pacific Fisheries Management Council, Portland, OR.

PAINE, R. T., J. T. WOOTTON, AND P. D. BOERSMA. 1990. Direct and indirect effects of Peregrine Falcon predation on seabird abundance. Auk 107:1–9.

PETERSON, R. T., AND J. FISHER. 1955. Wild America. Weather Vane Books, New York, NY.

PIATT, J. F., C. J. LENSINK, W. BUTLER, M. KENDZIOREK, AND D. R. NYSEWANDER. 1990. Immediate impact of the 'Exxon Valdez' oil spill on marine birds. Auk 107:387–397.

PINKAS, L. 1974. California marine fish landings for 1972. California Department of Fish and Game, Fish Bulletin 161.

PINKAS, L. 1977. California marine fish landings for 1975. California Department of Fish and Game, Fish Bulletin 168.

PITCHER, K. W. 1990. Major decline in number of

harbor seals, *Phoca vitulina richardsi,* on Tugidak Island, Gulf of Alaska. Marine Mammal Science 6:121–134.

PYLE, P., AND R. P. HENDERSON. 1990. Birds of Southeast Farallon Island: occurrence and seasonal distribution of migratory species. Western Birds 22: 41–84.

RAUSCH, R. 1958. The occurrence and distribution of birds on Middleton Island, Alaska. Condor 60: 227–242.

RODWAY, M. S., K. J. MORGAN, AND K. R. SUMMERS. 1992. Seabird breeding populations in the Scott Islands on the west coast of Vancouver Island, 1982–1989. Pp. 52–59, *in* K. Vermeer, R. W. Butler, and K. H. Morgan (eds.), The ecology, status, and conservation of marine and shoreline birds on the west coast of Vancouver Island. Occasional Paper No. 75, Canadian Wildlife Service, Ottawa.

SALZMAN, J. E. 1989. Scientists as advocates: the Point Reyes Bird Observatory and gill netting in central California. Conservation Biology 3:170–180.

SCOTT, J. M., W. HOFFMAN, D. AINLEY, AND C. F. ZEILLEMAKER. 1974. Range expansion and activity patterns in Rhinoceros Auklets. Western Birds 5:13–20.

SPEAR, L. B., T. M. PENNIMAN, J. F. PENNIMAN, H. R. CARTER, AND D. G. AINLEY. 1987. Survivorship and mortality factors in a population of Western Gulls. Pp. 44–56, *in* J. L. Hand, W. E. Southern, and K. Vermeer (eds.), Ecology and behavior of gulls. Studies in Avian Biology No. 10.

SPEICH, S. M., AND T. R. WAHL. 1989. Catalog of Washington seabird colonies. U.S. Department of the Interior, Fish and Wildlife Service, Washington, DC.

SPRINGER, A. M. 1992. Walleye pollock in the North Pacific—how much difference do they really make? Fisheries Oceanography 1:80–96.

SPRINGER, A. M. 1993. Status and conservation concerns of seabirds in Alaska. Working Paper, Greenpeace, Seattle (July 1992). In press.

SPRINGER, A. M., AND G. V. BYRD. 1989. Seabird dependence on walleye pollock in the southeastern Bering Sea. Pp. 667–677, *in* International symposium on the biology and management of walleye pollock. Alaska Sea Grant Report 89-1, Lowell Wakefield Fisheries Symposium 7, Fairbanks, AK.

STRATY, R. R., AND R. E. HAIGHT. 1979. Interactions among marine birds and commercial fish in the eastern Bering Sea. Pp. 201–219, *in* J. C. Bartonek and D. N. Nettleship (eds.), Conservation of marine birds of northern North America. Research Report 11, U.S. Department of the Interior, Fish and Wildlife Service, Washington, DC.

SYDEMAN, W. J., J. F. PENNIMAN, T. M. PENNIMAN, P. PYLE, AND D. G. AINLEY. 1991. Breeding performance in the Western Gull: effects of parental age, timing of breeding and year in relation to food availability. Journal of Animal Ecology 60:135–149.

TAKEKAWA, J., H. C. CARTER, AND T. E. HARVEY. 1990. Decline of the Common Murre in central California, 1980–1986. Pp. 149–163, *in* S. G. Sealy (ed.), Auks at sea. Studies in Avian Biology No. 14.

THOMPSON, S. P., D. K. McDERMOND, U. W. WILSON,

AND K. MONTGOMERY. 1985. Rhinoceros Auklet burrow count on Protection Island, Washington. Murrelet 66:62–65.

TOVAR, H., V. GUILLEN, AND M. E. NAKAMA. 1987. Monthly population size of three guano birds species off Peru, 1953 to 1982. Pp. 208–219, *in* D. Paul and I. Tsukayama (eds.), The Peruvian Anchoveta and its upwelling ecosystem: three decades of change. Instituto del Mar Peru (IMARPE), Callao, Peru.

VERMEER, K., AND D. B. IRONS. 1991. The Glaucous-winged Gull on the Pacific coast of North America. Proceedings XX International Ornithological Congress 4:2378–2383.

VERMEER, K., K. T. BRIGGS, K. H. MORGAN, AND D. SIEGEL-CAUSEY (eds.). 1993. The status, ecology and conservation of marine birds of the North Pacific. Special Publication, Canadian Wildlife Service, Ottawa.

WILSON, U. W. 1991. Responses of three seabird species to El Niño events and other warm episodes on the Washington coast, 1979–1990. Condor 93:853–858.

WILSON, U. W., AND D. A. MANUWAL. 1986. The breeding biology of the Rhinoceros Auklet in Washington. Condor 88:143–155.

WOOLLER, R. D., J. S. BRADLEY, AND J. P. CROXALL. 1992. Long-term population studies of seabirds. Trends in Ecology and Evolution 7:111–114.

YORK, A. E., AND P. KOZLOFF. 1987. On the estimation of the numbers of northern fur seal, *Callorhinus ursinus,* pups born on St. Paul Island, 1980–86. U.S. Fishery Bulletin 85:367–375.

Studies in Avian Biology No. 15:134–146, 1994.

A CENTURY OF POPULATION TRENDS OF WATERFOWL IN WESTERN NORTH AMERICA

RICHARD C. BANKS AND PAUL F. SPRINGER

Abstract. In the mid-1800s waterfowl in the West, particularly in the Central Valley of California in winter, were said to have numbered in the millions. Because of hunting for urban markets, the killing of birds to protect crops, and the loss of habitat as a result of land use changes, local populations of some waterfowl species reportedly had been reduced to 1% or less of former numbers by the early 1900s. Midwinter population surveys indicate that the total duck population in the Pacific Flyway has declined from levels in 1955, when such surveys became standardized. The decline is led by reduced numbers of the Northern Pintail (*Anas acuta*). Hunting and habitat loss, compounded at times by drought, have been responsible for most of the decline. On the other hand, man has been the primary benefactor of waterfowl by restricting the harvest through regulations and by setting aside refuges in areas of good habitat. Case histories show that proper management has led to recovery of some species or subspecies that were greatly reduced in numbers, and provide hope for better days for all species.

Key Words: Waterfowl; Pacific Flyway; California; populations; habitat modification; *Aix sponsa*; *Anas acuta*; *Branta canadensis leucopareia*.

As Dawson (1923:1753) said, "It is difficult to convey . . . any accurate conception of the former abundance of waterfowl in America." We may be awed now by the number of birds in occasional flocks of geese or ducks flushed from a refuge or management area, but it is difficult to realize that once there were such flocks in appropriate habitat throughout the West, not just on isolated protected marshes. Anecdotal information in early writings about the western United States, particularly California, suggests that waterfowl occurred in numbers that we can hardly imagine today. In the mid-1800s, when the human population influx into California began in earnest, residents of the Sacramento Valley could complain about being "greatly annoyed by the almost deafening, tumultuous, and confused noises of the innumerable flocks of geese and ducks which were continually flying to and fro and at times blackening the very heavens with their increasing numbers . . ." (McGowan 1961:354). Most of the available information on early populations of waterfowl is from California, particularly the Central Valley, but we have no reason to believe that large flocks did not also exist originally in the great intermontane valleys of Oregon and Washington, along the coast,

and in the less continuous habitats of the Great Basin, with each region being of seasonally different importance. In 1824, when Jim Bridger drifted down the Bear River, he reported "millions of ducks and geese" at its marshy mouth along the shore of Great Salt Lake, Utah (Nelson 1966).

EARLY DECLINE

The abundance of waterfowl and other game was a mixed blessing to the settlers as California and the rest of the West began to develop in the 19th century. The rapid human population growth of the mid-century depended on it to some extent. Hunting for the urban market became a big business in the gold rush days, and increased through the last half of the 1800s. Ducks and geese reaching the market in San Francisco, and certainly the other growing cities, were measured by the thousands, wagonloads, and tons (McGowan 1961:365). Grinnell et al. (1918) presented data showing that hundreds of thousands of birds reached markets in San Francisco each year, with numbers not tapering off until after the first decade of the 1900s. Some market hunting continued into the mid-20th century.

Despite the large kill for the market, geese and ducks remained so numerous that with the development of agriculture in the Central Valley of California they became major crop depredators. Geese would land on a grain field at night and leave stubble in the morning. Men were hired as herders to keep geese off grain fields, mainly by shooting as many as they could. Often thousands of geese per year would be killed on a single farmer's holdings. Many of these birds, of course, found their way to the markets, as did hundreds of pounds of feathers for mattresses. Later, as rice replaced wheat as the main grain crop, ducks replaced geese as the major depredators (McGowan 1961).

Agricultural and other development did more than change prime waterfowl habitat to crop land where birds were unwelcome; it often changed it to land where waterfowl could not exist. More than 90% of California's historical natural wetlands have been lost by conversion to other land uses (Dahl 1990), although some converted land has alternative waterfowl values. Habitats for breeding, migrant and wintering birds have been affected.

Eventually, a major decline in the number of waterfowl was evident. Letters of inquiry to responsible observers throughout California in 1913 almost uniformly drew reports of a population decline of waterfowl, with estimates ranging from 25 to 99% in some areas. Snow Geese (*Chen caerulescens*) were particularly affected. According to Grinnell et al. (1918:214), "There has been a more conspicuous decrease in the numbers of [Snow] geese than in any other game birds in the state. Many observers testify that there is only one goose now for each hundred that visited the state twenty years ago, and some persons aver that in certain localities there is not more than one to every thousand which formerly occurred here."

MODERN DATA AND TRENDS

No one was making population counts in those early days and, except for the information on the number of birds reaching the markets tabulated by Grinnell et al. (1918), the figures on either the number of birds

present or the number killed are estimates and guesses, and cover only a small part of the range of the species involved. There were some Christmas Bird Counts in California and Oregon in the early 1900s, but we have not found any with sufficient continuity from appropriate localities to provide data on long-term trends. Some studies of individual species, such as the Brant (*Branta bernicla*), were made (Moffitt 1943), but over relatively short periods.

The U.S. Bureau of Biological Survey began inventorying winter waterfowl populations in 1935, and a private organization "More Game Birds in America" initiated a breeding census in prime prairie breeding habitat (Bellrose 1980:17). It took many years for reliable techniques to be developed and standardized. Since 1955, the U.S. Fish and Wildlife Service has provided comparably produced data-based indices of wintering and breeding populations over much of the United States, Canada and Mexico, and has conducted harvest surveys. These studies are conducted by federal, state, provincial, and Ducks Unlimited biologists, and the data are reported in various publications of these agencies.

For the purposes of revealing trends in western North America, we illustrate some of the population indices during January 1955–1992 as measured by the Midwinter Waterfowl Survey in the Pacific Flyway. Winter indices are obtained from coverage of most waterfowl concentration areas in states or portions of states west of the Continental Divide, exclusive of Alaska. Data are available by state and by species, but our analysis is limited to the broader picture of all ducks and geese and the few individual species numerically most important.

The Northern Pintail (*Anas acuta*) maintained relatively constant January population indices in 1955–1970 (Fig. 1). These indices increased to highs in the 1970s but declined in the 1980s, reaching record lows (see case study beyond). The trend for "total ducks" mirrors that for the pintail because that species comprised 36% of the 38-year-average index. This indicates that other duck species have generally fared better than the pintail. However, numbers of the Mallard (*Anas platyrhynchos*) have been lower than the long-term average for about 20 years, and American Wigeons (*Anas americana*) have been decreasing gradually over most of the survey period. Among important dabblers not shown, Northern Shovelers (*Anas clypeata*) have reflected pintail trends since about 1970.

Numbers of Canada Geese (*Branta canadensis*) decreased substantially after 1963, but have increased again since about 1984 (Fig. 1). Much of that increase is due to successful management of the western (*B. c. moffitti*) and cackling (*B. c. minima*) subspecies, as well as of the once-endangered Aleutian (*B. c. leucopareia*) subspecies (see case study beyond). Conversely, the dusky (*B. c. occidentalis*) subspecies has declined since 1979 due to a combination of negative habitat modification following the Alaskan earthquake in 1964, increased predation, and continued hunting. "White" geese, Snow and Ross' (*Chen rossii*) geese undifferentiated in aerial surveys, have fluctuated widely in the past 38 years but show no trend during the January surveys. Greater White-fronted Geese (*Anser albifrons*), on the other hand, declined markedly after about 1970 but have been recovering since 1985. Brant have decreased in winter along the coast of the United States, but greater numbers now winter along the west coast of Mexico and the combined total of birds has declined relatively slightly.

FACTORS LEADING TO DECLINES

Excessive harvests, epizootics, unusual long-term weather conditions, poor recruitment, and adverse alterations of habitat are usually blamed for declines of waterfowl populations. Although sport hunting is the most visible, readily measured, and easily controlled cause of mortality among fledged waterfowl, it is (perhaps surprisingly) the major mortality factor in only a few species. During the period 1950–1970 when hunting regulations ranged from restrictive to fairly liberal, about one in two deaths of adult Mallards was due to hunting, averaged over the entire country (Anderson 1975). Under restrictive regulations in 1988–1991, the mortality due to hunting in the Pacific Flyway ranged from about 1 in 3 to 1 in 8 deaths for adult Mallards and only 1 in 10 to 1 in 11 deaths for adult Northern Pintails (J. C. Bartonek, pers. comm.). These figures are based on recoveries of banded birds.

The estimated retrieved harvest (excludes birds shot and lost) of certain waterfowl species in the Pacific Flyway in 1955–1991 is shown in Figure 2. Waterfowl harvests tend to follow hunter numbers to a greater extent than either the abundance or availability of the species being hunted (Bartonek 1981). Hunter numbers, in turn, are influenced in large part by distribution, abundance and availability of birds, and by regulations. An exception occurs among some geese whose numbers have been adversely affected in the past not only by sport hunting along the Pacific Flyway but also by subsistence hunting on their breeding grounds in Alaska. Adoption of more restrictive regulations in the mid-1980s, however, has permitted increases in numbers of Greater White-fronted and Cackling Canada geese (Pamplin 1986).

The average number of ducks (all species) taken in California in the period 1961–1991 was close to 1.4 million; the highest annual take was about 2.5 million, in 1967, and the lowest was just over 0.5 million, in 1988 (Bartonek 1992). The number of birds sold in San Francisco markets in the 1910–1911 season was about 0.19 million (Grinnell et al. 1918: table 6), but adjusting that by a factor of ten (a factor with no basis outside of guess) to account for other California markets plus sport and subsistence harvest yields 1.9 million, not out of line with more recent average harvests. Despite the fact that total duck numbers were vastly greater 80 years ago, market hunting has been partly blamed for the major population decrease at the turn of the century. Perhaps the pre-

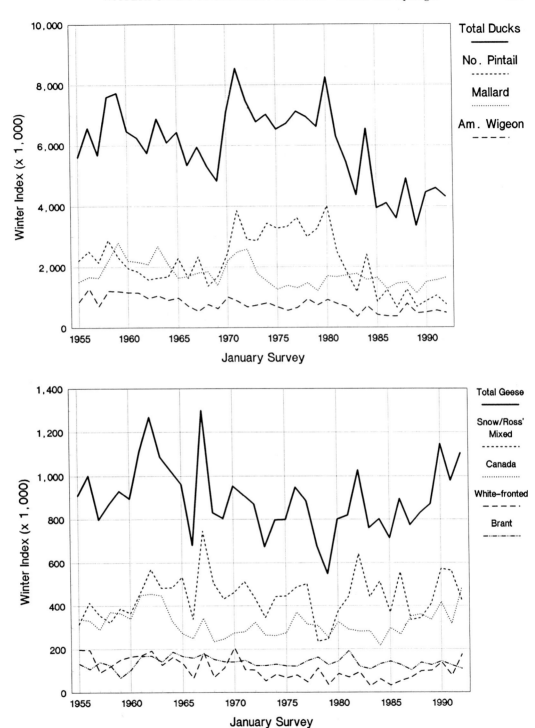

FIGURE 1. Top. Index of winter population trends of total ducks and selected species in the Pacific Flyway, 1955–1992. Bottom. Index of winter population trends of total geese and selected species in the Pacific Flyway, 1955–1992. Both from J. C. Bartonek.

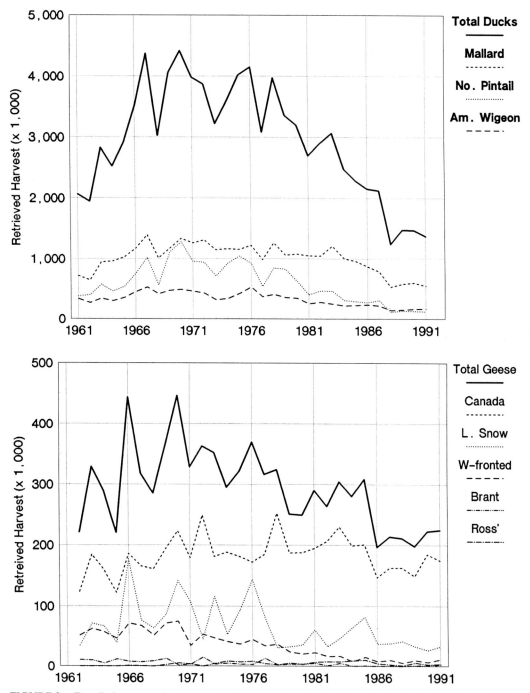

FIGURE 2. Top. Estimated retrieved harvest of total ducks and selected species in the Pacific Flyway, 1961–1991. Bottom. Estimated retrieved harvest of total geese and selected species in the Pacific Flyway, 1961–1991. Both from J. C. Bartonek.

sumed detrimental effects of market hunting should be reexamined, at least for perspective, as should the effects of modern sport hunting relative to less direct mortality factors.

Indirectly, man has been responsible for the loss of unknown numbers of waterfowl by poisoning or polluting their environment. One of the most pernicious pollutants has been lead. By using lead shot for hunting, and by shooting over favorable feeding areas, hunters seeded wetlands with pellets that waterfowl could ingest with food or as grit, with fatal or debilitating results. Lead poisoning in waterfowl has been known since the 1890s, affecting an estimated 2–3% of the fall and winter population (Bellrose 1980), but it has been only within the past decade that the use of non-toxic shot rather than lead has been mandated.

Man has also contaminated the environment with a wide variety of pesticides now known to have numerous, sometimes slowly accumulating biological effects on birds (White and Stickel 1975). Pesticide use increased enormously after World War II (San Joaquin Valley Drainage Program [SJVDP] 1990), the amount, type, and kind of application varying according to what crop was to be protected. In 1980, over 120 million pounds of pesticide were used in California, 70 million pounds in the Central Valley alone (SJVDP 1990). This is about 10 pounds for each of the 8–10 million waterfowl migrating through or wintering in the state (California Department of Fish and Game 1983). Recently, the accumulation of selenium in irrigation drain water has caused embryonic deformity in nesting waterfowl in some areas (Heitmeyer et al. *in* Smith et al. 1989).

Almost without a doubt, the most important factor influencing populations of most species of waterfowl in the West has been the modification or loss of suitable habitat as a result of human settlement and land use. Wetlands were drained or filled and levees and dams were constructed for agriculture, urbanization, and industrialization. Many of these activities destroyed the areas needed by nesting, migrant and wintering waterfowl. From the 1780s to the 1980s, wetland habitat loss within states in the Pacific Flyway ranged from 30% in Utah to 91% in California (Dahl 1990). However, some of the land use changes provided new habitat for waterfowl in the form of agricultural crops, ponds and reservoirs.

An extreme example of habitat modification that resulted in reduced waterfowl populations is found in the Tulare Basin at the southern end of the San Joaquin Valley of California. Tulare Lake, once the largest freshwater lake west of the Mississippi River, and three smaller lakes covered 1200 square miles and had 2100 miles of shoreline. With extensive associated marshes, the basin provided the largest single block of wetland habitat in California, and also stored abundant groundwater. It was an important breeding/migration/wintering area for waterfowl and other wildlife. Decline in the wetlands began early, well before the beginning of the present century. Water for irrigation was diverted from tributary streams in the 1850s, reducing flow to the basin. Land was converted to agricultural use, and ground water pumping began. With less standing water, more land could be converted to agriculture, which demanded more water for irrigation, in a vicious cycle. By the 1940s, Tulare Lake was reduced to 36 square miles. Today the lake is essentially gone and wetlands in the basin occupy only 6000 acres, less than 1% of the original extent. When flooded in the early fall, the former lake is still an important concentration area for ducks, especially Northern Pintails, but most of the wildlife value of the basin is gone (Jones and Stokes Assoc. 1987, U.S. Fish and Wildlife Service 1978).

Natural population regulating factors have been at work on waterfowl populations, also. These are not always easily differentiated from human-related mortality factors. Predation by other wild creatures was always a challenge for waterfowl, but a dynamic adaptive balance had evolved through millennia. Landscape and agricultural changes made by man have modified predator as well as waterfowl habitat, actually facilitating predation in some areas of formerly high waterfowl production by reducing cover and concentrating nesting birds. This has led to expanded predator research and management programs as well as programs to reestablish waterfowl habitat.

At times, disease can affect large numbers of waterfowl. In 1910, tremendous mortality among ducks, reputed to be in the millions, occurred in Utah and California (Bellrose 1980). Eventually the cause was determined to be botulism produced by a toxin from the bacterium *Clostridium botulinum,* type C. Outbreaks have occurred irregularly throughout the West. Conditions that favor the development of the bacterium are often the result of man-caused fluctuations of water level. Similarly, manipulation of water levels is a tool that can be used to fight outbreaks when they are detected. Another disease of increasing concern is avian cholera, which killed more than 70,000 waterfowl in California in outbreaks in the winter of 1965–1966 (Bellrose 1980).

Another influence on waterfowl is extremes of rainfall patterns resulting in drought or flooding. These have had periodic effects on productivity and may be related to some extent to man-invoked land use patterns. Drought can be especially important in the prairies and has been largely responsible for the recent decline in the dabbling duck populations there.

POSITIVE ACTIONS TO COUNTER MORTALITY FACTORS

One of the first positive actions taken by man was the passage of laws to regulate, or reduce, the number of birds killed. In California, the first legislation was passed in 1852 and established an open season for Mallards and Wood Ducks (*Aix sponsa*; see case study beyond) of 20 September to 1 March in some counties (Grinnell et al. 1918). With no laws providing open or closed seasons before that, the effect of that law would seem to be merely prohibiting the take of those two species for five and a half months and leaving the season open all the time for everything else. Other species of game bird and other counties were added to, or subtracted from, the list as the law was amended through the years. Aside from Brant, geese are not mentioned in the California legislation until 1915 (Grinnell et al. 1918). Other states also enacted protective regulations. Passage of the Federal Migratory Bird Law, which included waterfowl, came in 1913. The signing of the migratory bird treaty with Canada in 1916 and passage of the Migratory Bird Treaty Act in 1918 provided a new basis for protective regulations for game and nongame species alike. Seasons and bag limits are now based on the analysis of data obtained in waterfowl breeding and production surveys, midwinter population surveys, reports of harvest in previous years, and other factors, and are made by federal and state government interaction.

Another positive action was the establishment of refuges or protected areas where waterfowl could not legally be hunted or killed. Lake Merritt in Oakland and its shores were declared a bird sanctuary in 1867 and a game preserve in 1870. Twenty areas containing about 1.5 million acres were set aside as refuges in California between 1913 and 1921 (McGowan 1961). Gray Lodge state game refuge was established in 1931, the first in the Sacramento Valley, and Joice Island Refuge in the Suisun marshes was begun that same year. The first federal waterfowl refuges in the Pacific Flyway were Lower Klamath National Wildlife Refuge in California and Oregon, Malheur NWR in Oregon, both established in 1908. Now there are 88 national wildlife refuges encompassing 1.3 million acres in the Pacific Flyway (exclusive of Alaska) that have waterfowl as a primary management objective. These complement a greater number of state, provincial, and private refuges and management areas. Some of this land is purchased with funds from the sale of migratory bird hunting and conservation stamps (duck stamps) and other hunter-funded revenue sources.

CASE STUDIES

Wood Duck

Uniquely among waterfowl, the Wood Duck breeds primarily within the United States, hence its early name "summer duck." Its western nesting population, distinct from that to the east, was said to have extended from southern British Columbia and Alberta to California. Early writers reported it as common to abundant in California (Grinnell et al. 1918, Naylor 1960). In the Sacramento Valley "as many as a hundred" were shot in a single day. By the early 1900s, however, the species had become rare in California and in some areas to the north (Bellrose *in* Fredrickson et al. 1990). Whereas 440 birds were sold in the markets of San Francisco and Los Angeles in 1895–1896, only 6 were recorded in San Francisco in 1910–1911. One of the main reasons for the decline was excessive hunting. The birds were highly sought, not only as food by sport and market hunters, but also for use in millinery, taxidermy art, and fishing flies. Another cause of the bird's demise was habitat destruction. Clearing of woodlands adjoining streams and ponds for agricultural purposes and firewood, as well as dredging for gold along rivers in California, removed the cavity-bearing trees the Wood Ducks depended upon for nesting. In addition, drainage of swamps and marshes, accompanied by beaver trapping, destroyed or reduced the bird's feeding, brood rearing, and resting areas.

By 1913, the Wood Duck was reported to be on the verge of extinction in California (Dawson 1923). It was not until federal protection in 1918, which included regulations for complete prohibition of hunting of Wood Ducks (Lawyer 1919), that the bird's fortune changed. A marked increase was noted in California by the 1930s (Naylor 1960), and the species was said to have become exceedingly common along the wooded river bottoms of Oregon (Gabrielson and Jewett 1940). Hunting in states in the Pacific Flyway was not permitted again until 1942, when numbers had increased to the level that one bird was allowed in the daily bag and possession limit (Bartonek et al. *in* Fredrickson et al. 1990). There have been no special restrictions since 1967, with, depending on the year, 4–7 being allowed in the daily bag.

While cessation of hunting from 1913 until 1942 increased the Wood Duck population appreciably, destruction of its habitat continued through reservoir construction, timber harvest, livestock grazing, and stream channelization. By 1979 it was estimated that nearly 90% of the land originally covered by riparian vegetation in the Central Valley of California had been lost (Gilmer et al. 1982). In recognition of the unabated reduction of nesting sites a program of nest box construction was undertaken, beginning in Illinois in the late 1930s and spreading to other parts of the bird's breeding range (Soulliere *in* Fredrickson et al. 1990). Although nest box programs in the Pacific Flyway have been scattered and of various degrees of magnitude, studies have shown that they have been effective in expanding local breeding populations where there is a satisfactory food base but where shortage of natural nesting sites is a limiting factor.

Not only has the Wood Duck increased within its historical breeding range, but it apparently has expanded eastward in western Montana and into central Arizona and along the lower Colorado River (Bartonek et al. *in* Fredrickson et al. 1990). By the late 1980s the breeding population in the Pacific Flyway was estimated to range between 67,000 and 80,000 birds, an amazing recovery for a species that less than a century earlier was said to be on the verge of extinction there.

Aleutian Canada Goose

The Aleutian Canada Goose is an insular-nesting bird. Originally it bred in North

America from near Kodiak Island through the Semidi and Aleutian islands and wintered primarily in California (Byrd et al. 1991). A population in Asia that bred on the Commander and northern Kurile islands is thought to comprise the birds that wintered in Japan. No numerical records exist of former abundance, other than they nested in the thousands on Agattu Island in the western Aleutian Archipelago.

Starting as early as the 1750s, but principally between 1915 and 1939, Arctic foxes (*Alopex lagopus*) and, to a lesser extent, red foxes (*Vulpes vulpes*) were introduced on the larger Aleutian Islands for fur-farming purposes (Byrd et al. 1991). They preyed on the eggs and flightless geese. Additional birds were taken by Alaskan natives on the breeding and migration areas and by commercial and sport hunters on the wintering grounds. By the early 1930s only birds nesting on 5000-acre Buldir Island in the western Aleutians were thought to have survived. This island had been spared because of its isolation and lack of a good harbor. In 1967, the goose was placed on the federal endangered species list.

A program for fox eradication was undertaken on the Aleutian Islands National Wildlife Refuge in 1949 to benefit the depleted bird life (Byrd et al. 1991). This, supplemented by translocation of captive-reared geese initially and wild adults and their young later, beginning in 1971 and continuing to the present, resulted in the reestablishment of nesting geese on three islands. In addition, relict populations were found on two more islands, and geese pioneered to two other islands. Translocation apparently proved unsuccessful on one island, and one large and 14 small islands were rid of foxes but still await translocation or natural pioneering of wild geese.

Recoveries and resightings of geese banded on Buldir plus observations of unbanded birds revealed that the geese migrate east in the fall along the Aleutian Islands before apparently making a transoceanic flight to northern coastal California and sometimes southern coastal Oregon (Springer and Lowe 1994). Others bypass the coastal areas to stop in the central Sacramento Valley before wintering in the northern San Joaquin Valley. A relict subpopulation in the Semidi Islands south of the Alaskan Peninsula winters along the northern Oregon coast. Based on these findings, closures on all Canada Goose hunting were instituted in the Aleutian Islands west of Unimak in 1973, in the California areas in 1975, and in the Oregon coastal areas in 1982. These have continued to date with slight modification.

Concurrent with the restoration of breeding populations and establishment of hunting closures on key migration and wintering areas, about 18,000 acres of habitat have been acquired or protected as national wildlife refuges and state wildlife areas in California and Oregon. The Aleutian Islands and Semidi national wildlife refuges, now part of the Alaska Maritime National Wildlife Refuge, were established previously, in 1913 and 1932, respectively.

Counts of the Aleutian Islands population revealed a total of 790 geese in California in spring 1975 (Springer and Lowe 1994). Aided initially by protection afforded by the hunting closure areas and more recently by production from reestablished nesting islands, the population wintering in California rose to 7900 in spring 1992 (Ann Dahl and Roy Lowe, pers. comm.), a 10-fold increase. During the period from spring 1980 to spring 1992 the Semidi Island population wintering in Oregon doubled from 63 to 126 (Springer and Lowe 1994). In recognition of this growing population, the Aleutian Canada Goose was downlisted in 1991 from endangered to threatened.

The recovery plan (Byrd et al. 1991) calls for consideration of complete delisting if (1) the overall population includes at least 7500 geese and the long-term trend appears upward, (2) at least 50 nesting pairs are established in each of three geographic parts of the historic range in North America: western Aleutians other than Buldir, eastern Aleutians, and Semidi Islands, and (3) a total of 25,000–35,000 acres of migrating and wintering habitat have been secured and managed for the geese. To date the program has made good progress in attaining these goals, and the Aleutian Canada Goose appears well on its way to recovery.

Northern Pintail

The Northern Pintail is a species whose nesting habitat is characterized by short vegetation and shallow water (Ducks Unlimited 1990). Over half the pintails in North America migrate to the Pacific Flyway, with contributions extending from Alaska in the west to Saskatchewan in the east (Bellrose 1980). The species winters primarily in California, where it has been the most abundant duck during that season. Large numbers also winter on the west coast of the Mexican mainland. No one knows the historic Flyway wintering population, but it undoubtedly was much greater than the peak winter index of 4.6 million measured in January 1980 (J. C. Bartonek, pers. comm.).

The first real threat to the species in California was market hunting. Sport hunting also became a common activity, and duck clubs were organized beginning in California in 1879 (Heitmeyer et al. *in* Smith et al. 1989). Until 1901, when a daily limit of 50 ducks per day went into effect in California and spring and night hunting were prohibited (Grinnell et al. 1918), there were few restrictions, and many paired and breeding birds were shot. Unfortunately, law enforcement then was far from adequate. Market hunting and duck club records in California show that pintails were generally the most abundant duck (Grinnell et al. 1918, Moffitt 1938) out of the estimated 800,000 to 1 million taken annually (Phillips 1922–1923). By the late 1910s, Grinnell et al. (1918) stated of the pintail that "sportsmen have noted a distinct decrease in its numbers during the past ten years." According to Phillips (1922–1923), enactment of restrictive regulations following passage of the Migratory Bird Treaty Act perhaps resulted in a reduction of one-half in the annual waterfowl kill in the United States and probably benefitted the pintail more than any other species.

Habitat modification and destruction, predation, agricultural pollutants, lead poisoning and disease all have had effects on pintail populations. Agriculture has had both a positive and negative impact. On the one hand it provided food in the form of rice, barley, and wheat, as well as nesting cover in stubble and hay fields (Ducks Unlimited 1990). However, the monocultures of grain attracted hordes of birds, which in turn led to depredation control measures including shooting (formerly) and hazing (Heitmeyer et al. *in* Smith et al. 1989). In addition, tillage of summer fallow fields, harvest of crops, and mowing of hayfields destroyed nests and sometimes injured or killed incubating birds (Ducks Unlimited 1990). Mowing, burning of crop residues, and overgrazing made nests more visible and subject to predation, and these practices and fall plowing reduced early nesting cover for the following year. Conversion of native grasslands and aspen parklands to agriculture in prairie Canada and Montana have been significant factors in the population decline and likely will hinder recovery even in wet years. Construction of ponds for stock watering and of reservoirs for water supply, flood control, and power generation has likewise destroyed former pintail habitat but in turn has provided new sites for nesting, feeding, and roosting.

A third major factor in the life of the pintail is weather. Because its breeding is associated with shallow wetlands, it is strongly influenced by lack of precipitation and runoff. Major droughts occurred in the late 1920s and early 30s, late 50s to early 60s, and most recently in the late 70s extending to the present, with only an occasional year of relief (Heitmeyer et al. *in* Smith et al. 1989, Ducks Unlimited 1990). Pintail numbers have fluctuated with long term weather conditions in key nesting areas. Since inception of standardized midwinter surveys in 1955, they have achieved high levels only in the 1970s (Bartonek 1992). By 1992, the midwinter survey population in the Pacific

Flyway (excluding Mexico) was 774,000, 81% less than the 4.0 million in 1980 and 65% less than the 1955–1991 average of 2.2 million. In surveyed breeding areas contributing to the Pacific Flyway the population in 1992 had decreased 54% from the 1955–1991 average. As a result, the pintail has lost its title as the principal wintering duck in the Pacific Flyway and now ranks below the Mallard.

During periods of drought, some pintails have flown north to Alaska, the Yukon, and the Northwest Territories to breed where nesting success is less than that in the prairies in years of good water (Bellrose 1980, Ducks Unlimited 1990). This displacement has provided some production that probably would have been lower if the birds had remained and attempted to breed in the drought-stricken areas. Northern production areas provide a relatively stable base for pintail production, albeit not of the potential of the prairies and parklands during the best of conditions.

Modern-day hunting can also affect pintail numbers, but currently the harvest rate of adults is believed to be less than 3% (Bortner et al. 1992). Since 1988, federal regulations in the United States have allowed one pintail per day and two in possession. While further reduction in the harvest rate may increase survival, particularly at low population levels, the increase would be small (J. C. Bartonek, pers. comm.) and some biologists contend that any restriction has to be balanced against habitat conservation programs supported by the hunting public (Ducks Unlimited 1990).

In summary, the pintail population has decreased greatly since comprehensive breeding and wintering surveys were initiated in 1955. Habitat destruction compounded by drought has reduced numbers since the mid-1980s to their lowest recorded levels. Return to a period of greater precipitation and runoff will undoubtedly cause the pintail population to rise again. However, because of continuing loss and degradation of habitat, it is uncertain if it will ever attain the level of the 1970s.

WHAT OF THE FUTURE?

Waterfowl populations in the next century will, as in the past, be the product of opposing human forces—those leading to decline and those preventing decline and/or resulting in growth. There is likely to be at least one species in trouble at any given time, probably one that is relatively unimportant in the harvest and that will decline to precarious levels before anyone notices, as has happened recently to Spectacled (*Somateria fischeri*) and Steller's (*Polysticta stelleri*) eiders (Kessel and Gibson, 1994).

As the human population of the United States becomes more urban, waterfowl hunting pressure will decrease. There has been a decrease of 60% in the sale of duck stamps and of hunters in the Pacific Flyway since 1970 (Bartonek 1992). As a result, conservation and management activities by hunter-supported wildlife agencies and organizations may decline because of decreased financial and political support.

More of the already reduced wetland not in public ownership will be lost, polluted or converted because of need or greed. Breeding, migrant, and wintering habitats will be reduced. Breeding areas of the more northerly birds will be less affected than those of the Pacific coastal states or prairie provinces, but the more northerly birds will find a decrease in adequate wintering areas. More of the habitat they do find will be in refuges and other highly protected areas. There are likely to be fewer areas where waterfowl may be hunted, but more areas where they will be unwelcome because of the threat to crops or other human interests.

The authorization of the North American Waterfowl Management Plan in 1986 by the United States and Canada provided a new avenue to safeguard the continent's waterfowl and their significant habitats. The Joint Venture concept was adopted to foster partnerships among federal, state, provincial and local governments, conservation organizations, private corporations and individuals to carry out the program. Objectives include securing long-term protection for 11 million acres of habitat on public and private land in the most important breeding, staging and wintering areas, restoring waterfowl populations to levels of the 1970s and attaining specific population goals for geese and swans. The North American Wetlands Conservation Act in 1989 broadened the program to include Mexico and provided a federal funding base of about $35 million that was to generate a similar amount or more annually through matching fund requirements. In the first 5 years, total spending by all partners exceeded $500 million for waterfowl and wetland conservation projects affecting more than 2 million acres (H. K. Nelson, pers. comm.).

Although the populations of many species have declined during the last 100 years, waterfowl have a long evolutionary history and in all probability will be on earth at least as long as man. To a great extent, their future depends on how man treats them—and himself.

ACKNOWLEDGMENTS

The ready availability of data on waterfowl populations, more than for any other group of birds, is a result of the high degree of interest and dedicated work of hunters, conservationists and wildlife biologists, who are often interchangeable. Both the U.S. Fish and Wildlife Service and the Canadian Wildlife Service devote a high proportion of their resources to research and management of waterfowl, as do many state and provincial agencies and private organizations. J. C. Bartonek has been particularly helpful in providing information and graphic material for this report. We also thank F. C. Bellrose, G. V. Byrd, H. K. Nelson and H. M. Reeves for providing data and/or for reviewing and offering helpful comments on part or all of the manuscript.

LITERATURE CITED

ANDERSON, D. R. 1975. Population ecology of the Mallard. V. Temporal and geographic estimates of survival, recovery and harvest rates. U.S. Fish and Wildlife Service, Resource Publication 125.

BARTONEK, J. C. 1981. Stabilized and standardized regulations for waterfowl hunting in the United States. International Waterfowl Symposium 4:74–81.

BARTONEK, J. C. (comp.). 1992. 1992 Pacific Flyway briefing material. U.S. Fish and Wildlife Service, Portland, OR.

BELLROSE, F. C. 1980. Ducks, geese and swans of North America. 3rd ed. Stackpole Books, Harrisburg, PA.

BORTNER, J. B., D. F. CAITHAMER, J. A. DUBOVSKY, F. A. JOHNSON, G. W. SMITH, AND R. E. TROST. 1992. 1992 status of waterfowl and fall flight forecast. U.S. Fish and Wildlife Service.

BYRD, G. V., K. DURBIN, F. LEE, T. ROTHE, P. SPRINGER, D. YPARRAGUIRRE, AND F. ZEILLEMAKER. 1991. Aleutian Canada Goose recovery plan, 2nd rev. U.S. Fish and Wildlife Service, Anchorage, Alaska.

CALIFORNIA DEPARTMENT OF FISH AND GAME. 1983. A plan for protecting, enhancing, and increasing California's wetlands for waterfowl. Sacramento, California.

DAHL, T. E. 1990. Wetlands losses in the United States, 1780s to 1980s. U.S. Fish and Wildlife Service, Washington, D.C.

DAWSON, W. L. 1923. The birds of California. Students' edition, 3 vols. South Moulton Company, San Diego, California.

DUCKS UNLIMITED, INC. 1990. SPRIG: population recovery strategy for the Northern Pintail. Long Grove, IL.

FREDRICKSON, L. H., G. V. BURGER, S. P. HAVERA, D. A. GRABER, R. E. KIRBY, AND T. S. TAYLOR (eds.). 1990. Proceedings 1988 North American Wood Duck Symposium. St. Louis, MO.

GABRIELSON, I. N., AND S. G. JEWETT. 1940. Birds of Oregon. Oregon State College Corvallis, OR.

GILMER, D. S., M. R. MILLER, R. D. BAUER, AND J. R. LeDONNE. 1982. California's Central Valley wintering waterfowl: concerns and challenges. Transactions North American Wildlife and Natural Resources Conference 47:441–452.

GRINNELL, J., H. C. BRYANT, AND T. I. STORER. 1918. The game birds of California. University of California Press, Berkeley, CA.

JONES AND STOKES ASSOCIATES. 1987. Sliding toward extinction: the state of California's natural heritage. Sacramento, CA.

KESSEL, B., AND D. D. GIBSON. 1994. A century of avifaunal change in Alaska. Pp. 4–13 *in* J. R. Jehl, Jr. and N. K. Johnson (eds.), A century of avifaunal change in western North America. Studies in Avian Biology No. 15.

LAWYER, G. A. 1919. Federal protection of migratory birds. Pp. 303–316 *in* U.S. Department of Agriculture yearbook—1918.

McGOWAN, J. A. 1961. History of the Sacramento Valley. Vol. 1. Lewis Historical Publishing Co., New York, NY.

MOFFITT, J. 1938. Environmental factors affecting waterfowl in the Suisun area, California. Condor 40: 76–84.

MOFFITT, J. 1943. Twelfth annual Black Brant census in California. California Fish and Game 29:19–28.

NAYLOR, A. E. 1960. The Wood Duck in California with special reference to the use of nest boxes. California Fish and Game 46:241–269.

NELSON, N. F. 1966. Waterfowl hunting in Utah. Utah Department Fish and Game, Publication 66-10.

PAMPLIN, W. L., JR. 1986. Cooperative efforts to halt population declines of geese nesting on Alaska's Yukon and Kuskokwim Delta. Transactions North American Wildlife and Natural Resources Conference 51:487–506.

PHILLIPS, J. C. 1922–1923. A natural history of the ducks. Vols. 1–2. Houghton Mifflin Co., Boston. Reprinted 1986, Dover Publications, Inc., New York, NY.

SAN JOAQUIN VALLEY DRAINAGE PROGRAM. 1990. Fish and wildlife resources and agricultural drainage in the San Joaquin Valley, California. Vol. 1. Sacramento, CA.

SMITH, L. M., R. L. PEDERSON, AND R. M. KAMINSKI. 1989. Habitat management for migrating and wintering waterfowl in North America. Texas Tech University Press, Lubbock, TX.

SPRINGER, P. F., AND R. W. LOWE. 1994. Population, distribution, and ecology of migrating and wintering Aleutian Canada Geese. Proceedings International Canada Goose Symposium, Milwaukee, WI. In press.

U.S. FISH AND WILDLIFE SERVICE. 1978. Concept plan for waterfowl wintering habitat preservation. Central Valley California, Priority Category 4. U.S. Fish and Wildlife Service, Portland, OR.

WHITE, D. H., AND L. F. STICKEL. 1975. Impact of chemicals on waterfowl reproduction and survival. Pp. 138–142 in First international waterfowl symposium. Ducks Unlimited, Long Grove, IL.

Studies in Avian Biology No. 15:147–160, 1994.

SHOREBIRDS IN WESTERN NORTH AMERICA: LATE 1800s TO LATE 1900s

GARY W. PAGE AND ROBERT E. GILL, JR.

Abstract. Only anecdotal information is available to assess whether populations of the 47 shorebird species that breed or winter west of the Rocky Mountains changed in size or distribution during the past century. Unregulated hunting from 1870 to 1927 reduced populations of several species, at least temporarily, and was a factor in bringing the Eskimo Curlew (*Numenius borealis*) close to extinction. Large scale transformation of native grasslands and wetlands for agriculture and other purposes resulted in population declines and nesting range contractions of several temperate-zone breeders. In general, upland species were affected more than wetland species, breeding ranges contracted westward, and alteration of breeding habitat was the factor most responsible for range contractions and population declines. A ranking system assessing shorebird susceptibility to habitat alteration also predicted temperate breeders to be among the most vulnerable species to environmental change. The few estimates for current population sizes of western North American shorebirds range from fewer than 50 Eskimo Curlews to a few million Western Sandpipers (*Calidris mauri*), the most abundant species. Concentrations of at least 1000 shorebirds occur on migration at over 120 western North American sites and of 100,000 to 1,000,000 shorebirds at 18 sites. Whether populations are limited by conditions on breeding, wintering or migration ranges is unknown for most species. Expansion of ongoing programs coupled with economical new census efforts could be useful for monitoring the majority of western North American shorebirds during the next century.

Key Words: Shorebird; status; habitat; population; western North America; twentieth century.

The growth of human population in western North America has been accompanied by significant alteration of wetlands (Dahl 1990) and grasslands (Knopf 1994). Shorebird populations have undoubtedly been affected; however, because assessments of populations have only been initiated within the last 25 years most of what can be reported comes from anecdotal accounts. In this paper we describe western North American shorebird populations by geographical range and habitat preference. We outline the most apparent threats during the past century, and identify species most likely to have been affected. Finally, we summarize available information on their responses to these changes, and identify ongoing or upcoming census programs for measuring future population trends.

WESTERN NORTH AMERICAN SHOREBIRDS

We include all taxa with breeding or wintering populations in the Pacific Flyway (west of Rocky Mountains from Sinaloa, Mexico, north through the Yukon Territory to Alaska). Because this region includes a vast area of arctic and subarctic habitat, links North America to the east-Asian faunal region, and has over 75,000 km of coastline, it supports a large and diverse shorebird fauna (see Table 1 for scientific names). All but 3 of 50 shorebird species that breed regularly in North America occur commonly, and 8 breed only within this portion of the continent (Pitelka 1979).

Among the 47 species of western North American shorebirds, 32 (68%) breed only in arctic and subarctic habitats (Table 1). Eleven species (23%) are temperate breeders and 4 (9%) span both boreal and temperate zones. Wetlands are a key component of the breeding habitat of 11 of the 15 temperate breeders, including the Snowy Plover (*Charadrius alexandrinus*), Wilson's Plover (*C. wilsonia*) and American Oystercatcher (*Haematopus palliatus*), which nest primarily along sandy shores but feed in wetlands. Mountain Plovers (*C. montanus*), Long-billed Curlews (*Numenius americanus*), and Upland Sandpipers (*Bartramia longicauda*) nest primarily on uplands. The Black Oystercatcher (*H. bachmani*) is the only temperate breeder on rocky shores.

TABLE 1. SEASONAL USE OF HABITATS BY WESTERN NORTH AMERICAN SHOREBIRDS

Species	Breeding					Wintering						Habitat score[2]
	Arctic habitats[1]	Temperate				Interior		Coastal				
		Wetlands	Sand shore	Rock shore	Uplands	Wetlands	Uplands	Wetlands	Sand shore	Rock shore	Uplands	
North American wintering group[3]												
Haematopus bachmani				P[4]						P		6
Recurvirostra americana		P				P		P				12
Charadrius alexandrinus		S	P			S		P	P			14
Charadrius montanus					P		P				P	18
Numenius americanus					P		P	P	P		S	7
Limosa fedoa	P	S		P		O		P	P			14
Arenaria melanocephala	P							P	S	P		5
Calidris mauri	P					S		P	S			7
Calidris ptilocnemis	P							S	S	P		4
Calidris alpina pacifica	P					P		P			S	7
Limnodromus scolopaceus	P					P		P				7
Bicontinental wintering group												
Haematopus palliatus		S	P					P	P			4
Pluvialis squatarola	P					P	P	P	P	S	P	4
Charadrius semipalmatus	P					S		P	P			5
Charadrius wilsonia		S	P					P	P			15
Charadrius vociferus		P	S		S	P	P	P	S		P	15
Tringa melanoleuca	P					P		P				4
Tringa flavipes	P					P		P				4
Catoptrophorus semipalmatus		P			S	O		P	P	P		13
Actitis macularia	P	P			S	P		P	S	P		3
Aphriza virgata	P									P		4
Calidris canutus	P							P	P			4
Calidris pusilla	P					S		P	P			5
Calidris minutilla	P					P		P	S			7
Calidris himantopus	P					P		P				6
Limnodromus griseus	P							P	O			7
Gallinago gallinago	P	P				P	S	P			S	12
South American wintering group												
Pluvialis dominica	P					P	P	P	O		P	6
Tringa solitaria	P					P		P				4
Bartramia longicauda	S				P	O	O	P	O		O	11
Numenius borealis	P						P	S				6
Limosa haemastica	P					O		P	S			6
Calidris fuscicollis	P					P	O	P	O			6
Calidris bairdii	P					P		P			O	6
Calidris melanotos	P					P	P	S	O		S	6
Tryngites subruficollis	P					S	P				P	6
Phalaropus tricolor		P				P		S				10
Phalaropus lobatus	P							S	mostly pelagic			5
Phalaropus fulicaria	P							S	mostly pelagic			5
Oceania-Asia wintering group												
Pluvialis fulva	P							P	P	O	P	5
Numenius tahitiensis	P							P	P	P	S	5
Limosa lapponica baueri	P							P	P			5
Calidris alpina articola	P							P	P			5
Bicontinental/Oceania-Asia wintering group												
Himantopus mexicanus		P				P		P				12
Heteroscelus incanus	P							S		P		4
Numenius phaeopus	P							S	P	S		5
Arenaria interpres	P							P	P	P		4
Calidris alba	P					O		P	P	S		4

[1] Arctic habitats are as described by Kessel (1979); wetlands include fresh and brackish marsh, estuarine marsh, and intertidal flats [in part modified from Burger (1984), Myers (1980), Myers and Myers (1979), and Morrison and Ross (1989)]; sand and rock shores include those in or adjacent to littoral zone; uplands include pampas, grasslands, and agricultural lands.

Western North American shorebirds exhibit a wide array of wintering patterns (Table 1). Ten species (21%) winter primarily in North America and 12 (26%) in South America; 16 (34%) have bicontinental wintering ranges, 3 (6%) winter only in Oceania or Asia, and 5 (11%) have both bicontinental and Oceanic or Asiatic wintering distributions. The Dunlin (*Calidris alpina*) has discrete populations, one wintering in Asia and the other in North America (Gill and Handel 1990). While many species use a greater variety of habitats in winter than during summer, wetlands are of primary importance in winter to the majority (81%) of species. Rocky shorelines provide the primary winter habitat for 7 species, including Black Oystercatcher, Surfbird (*Aphriza virgata*), Wandering Tattler (*Heteroscelus incanus*) and Rock Sandpiper (*Calidris ptilocnemis*), which generally are not found elsewhere. Uplands provide important wintering habitat for 9 species, particularly Eskimo Curlew (*Numenius borealis*), Mountain Plover and Buff-breasted Sandpiper (*Tryngnites subruficollis*). All species use one or more coastal habitats in winter and 66% of the species also use interior habitats. Fourteen species (30%) are restricted to the coast and 2 species, *Phalaropus lobatus* and *P. fulicaria,* are primarily pelagic.

MAJOR FACTORS INFLUENCING POPULATION SIZE

HUNTING

Unregulated hunting between 1870 and 1927 significantly reduced populations of Red Knot (*Calidris canutus*) and species of the genera *Pluvialis, Numenius, Bartramia, Limosa,* and *Limnodromus* in eastern North America (Cooke 1910, Forbush 1912, Wetmore 1926). Faced with concomitant widespread loss of habitat along the spring migratory route some species, including Eskimo Curlew, Hudsonian Godwit (*Limosa haemastica*) and Lesser Golden Plover (*Pluvialis dominica*), have never recovered to their former abundance. All available evidence suggests shorebirds were also hunted heavily throughout the western United States. Whimbrels (*Numenius phaeopus*), Long-billed Curlews, Marbled Godwits (*Limosa fedoa*) and dowitchers (*Limnodromus* spp.) in particular were actively procured for the California markets and declined in numbers (Grinnell et al. 1918).

The unregulated killing of shorebirds in North America declined dramatically with the passage of the Migratory Bird Treaty Act in 1918 and subsequent conventions with Mexico, Japan and Russia. Currently only Woodcock (*Scolopax minor*) and Common Snipe (*Gallinago gallinago*) are legally hunted. About 500,000 of each species are shot annually (Banks 1979); 17% of the snipe are taken in the Pacific Flyway (USFWS, unpubl. data). Indigenous peoples of Alaska take small numbers of shorebirds and their eggs but this is not currently a threat to populations. Subsistence hunting of shorebirds south of the United States, however, may be more serious, but its extent and effects remain undocumented (Senner and Howe 1984).

HABITAT ALTERATION

The alteration of native wetlands and grasslands for agriculture and other purposes has had the most profound effect on shorebirds since North America was settled by Caucasians. Settlement has destroyed 35–89% (median = 48%) of the native wetlands in Great Plains states, including 57% of the pothole wetlands in North and South Dakota (Dahl 1990). West of the Rocky Mountains statewide wetland losses range from

---

←

[2] Higher score (range 3–18) indicates habitats used by species are more vulnerable to alteration or destruction given current conditions. See text for derivation and discussion of scores.
[3] Wintering group designations modified from Boland (1991).
[4] P = principal habitat used, S = secondary use, O = occasional use.

30–91% (median = 37%), including 51% of the wetlands associated with Pyramid Lake, Winnemucca Lake, and the Carson and Humboldt sinks in Nevada; 60% of the delta marshes and intertidal areas of Puget Sound; 30% of the estuarine flats, marshes and swamps in the Columbia River Estuary; 85% of similar habitats in Coos Bay; and 91% of the wetlands in California (Peters 1989, Dahl 1990). Conversion of native grasslands has been just as extensive (Knopf 1994). By contrast, over 99% of the wetlands in Alaska remain pristine (Dahl 1990).

It is difficult to outline the full response of shorebirds to wetland and grassland modification during the past century because of the complexity of the changes and the paucity of information on shorebird abundance. Many surviving wetlands have been degraded with toxic chemicals or the erection of power lines, which lower reproductive success or increase shorebird mortality. Not all wetland alterations have been detrimental. For example, the conversion of salt marsh to salt ponds has created habitat for phalaropes and stilts in San Francisco Bay (Harvey et al. 1992). Some shorebirds also benefit when uplands are turned into wetlands. In recent decades winter mortality and possibly population sizes of shorebirds may have fluctuated inversely with avian predator populations, which plummeted from the 1950s to 1970s due to organochlorine poisoning and recovered in the 1980s partly in response to conservation efforts (White 1994). A recent change of unknown consequence is the predominance of introduced invertebrates in shorebird diets in some west coast estuaries (Carlton 1979).

POPULATIONS AT RISK

Risk assessments are useful for ranking vulnerability of populations to environmental change. Ranking systems, which differ in variables selected, precision within variables and manner of computation, are often tailored to specific taxonomic or regional requirements (Mace and Lande 1991). Since habitat alteration has had the greatest

effect on shorebirds during the last century, we developed a habitat-based ranking system to assess the vulnerability of species.

For each species we first calculated a series of breeding (**B**) and wintering (**W**) area scores for each combination of habitat and region. For breeding areas $B = bn$ where b = breeding region score (Arctic = 1, Temperate = 3) and n = breeding habitat score (all arctic habitats = 1; temperate habitats include: uplands = 3, sandy shore = 3, wetlands = 2, rocky shore = 1); for wintering areas $W = ws$, where w = wintering region score (North America = 3, pelagic = 1, and all other regions = 2); and s = wintering habitat score (uplands = 3, wetlands = 2, sandy shore = 2, rocky shore = 1, pelagic = 1). For each species we then calculated an overall habitat ranking score $H = B + W$, where B = average breeding area score and W = average wintering area score.

We placed higher values on breeding habitats in temperate latitudes because they have been more altered than arctic habitats. For similar reasons, upland habitats (especially native prairies, grasslands and pampas) were assigned higher values than wetlands. Sandy shore in temperate regions was scored high because of extensive recreational use, particularly along the California coast. Habitat degradation was assumed to have been more extensive in North America than in other wintering regions.

Based on these criteria, habitat vulnerability scores ranged from 18 for the Mountain Plover to 3 for the Spotted Sandpiper (*Actitis macularia*, Table 1). The mean for all species was 7.0 (SD = 3.7). Species wintering in North America had the highest mean score (9.2, SD = 4.5) followed by the bicontinental group (7.0, SD = 4.2), South American group (6.3, SD = 2.2), Americas/Oceania-Asia group (5.8, SD = 3.5) and Oceania-Asia group (5.0, SD = 0.0). Species associated with uplands overall had higher rankings (e.g., Mountain Plover, Killdeer (*Charadrius vociferus*), Marbled Godwit, and Upland Sandpiper). We emphasize that this ranking system is limited to the selection of breeding and wintering habitats. If other factors were considered, such as extent of breeding and wintering areas, population size, and dependency on limited migratory staging areas, scores for arctic breeders such as the Eskimo Curlew and many of the calidridine sandpipers may have been higher.

CHANGES IN DISTRIBUTION AND ABUNDANCE

TEMPERATE BREEDERS

There have been notable changes in the abundance and distribution of several temperate breeders during the past 150 years. In general, upland species have been affected more than wetland species and breeding ranges have contracted westward. Alteration of nesting habitat is believed to have been the dominant factor for range contraction and population declines.

Mountain Plover

This species historically nested on short grass prairie where bison (*Bison bison*) and prairie dog (*Cynomys* spp.) activity kept vegetation sparse (F. Knopf, pers. comm.). Plovers were abundant enough to be an important game bird prior to 1900, but by 1914 were reported as declining due to hunting, eradication of bison and prairie dogs, cultivation of the prairies, and degradation of traditional wintering areas (Graul and Webster 1976, Knopf 1992). Mountain Plovers continue to breed in Alberta, Saskatchewan, Colorado, Montana, Wyoming, Kansas, Nebraska, Oklahoma, New Mexico and Texas, but have been extirpated from North and South Dakota. Their range has contracted in Colorado, Kansas and New Mexico, and numbers have declined in Alberta and Saskatchewan (Leachman and Osmundson 1990; Knopf 1992, pers. comm.). In California the decline has been marked by the disappearance of wintering plovers from most valleys of the central coastal ranges and by decreasing numbers on Christmas Bird Counts in the Sacramento Valley, Salton Sea and coastal Orange County (Jurek 1973, Leachman and Os-

mundson 1990). The continental population, currently between 5000–15,000 birds (F. Knopf, pers. comm.), has declined significantly during the past quarter century due primarily to habitat degradation on the wintering grounds (Knopf 1992, 1994).

Long-billed Curlew

Hunting in the late 19th and early 20th centuries, and cultivation of grasslands, caused the Long-billed Curlew population to decline and the breeding range to shrink (Bent 1929, Palmer 1967, Redmond 1984). Today Long-billed Curlews breed in short grass habitats, especially pastures and uncultivated range lands, from British Columbia to California in the west, and Saskatchewan to Texas in the east. Formerly their range extended farther east into Manitoba, Minnesota, Iowa, Wisconsin and Illinois (DeSante and Pyle 1986) and was more extensive in Saskatchewan (Renaud 1980), North Dakota (Johnsgard 1981), Colorado (McCallum et al. 1977), the Great Basin (Sugden 1933) and Washington (Yocom 1956). Long-billed Curlews ceased breeding in Illinois before 1880 (Bent 1929) and in Minnesota by 1900 (Roberts 1932). According to Palmer (1967), the Long-billed Curlew population was dangerously low for several decades but increased appreciably beginning in the 1950s. Data collected for the U.S. Fish and Wildlife Service Breeding Bird Survey during the past quarter century (credited hereafter as FWS, unpubl. data) suggest a declining population in the eastern portion of the range and an increasing one in the western portion.

Upland Sandpiper

Enormous numbers of Upland Sandpipers once bred on grasslands in the Great Plains. With conversion of forest to agricultural fields their range expanded east to the Atlantic coast (Bent 1929, Palmer 1967). Then extensive hunting in North and South America and cultivation of the prairies during the late 19th and early 20th centuries caused a steep and widespread population decline (Bent 1929, Roberts 1932, White 1983). Numbers increased after the prohibition of shorebird hunting in North America but expanded cultivation of grasslands probably has prevented full population recovery (Palmer 1967, White 1983). Upland Sandpipers now breed fairly commonly to commonly in the western Great Plains and uncommonly as far east as Maine and Virginia and as far west as Utah and eastern Oregon (DeSante and Pyle 1986). Disjunct populations also breed in Alaska and the Northwest Territories (Johnsgard 1981). In Illinois the population was estimated at 283,000 birds in 1907–1909 and 177,000–208,000 birds in 1957–1958 (Graber and Graber 1963). Stewart and Kantrud (1972) estimated 91,000–183,000 breeding pairs for North Dakota in 1976. Since numbers have increased during the past 25 years (Knopf 1994), and the species is currently a fairly common to common breeder in 10 states or provinces including North Dakota (DeSante and Pyle 1986), the North American population likely numbers between several hundred thousand and a few million birds.

Marbled Godwit

According to Palmer (1967) the Marbled Godwit had a larger breeding range and a much larger population before 1900. It no longer breeds in Wisconsin, Iowa and Nebraska and its range has shrunk in Minnesota (Roberts 1932, DeSante and Pyle 1986). Marbled Godwits now breed chiefly in the prairie pothole country of the U.S. and Canada, and have small isolated populations in Alaska, the Northwest Territories, Ontario and Colorado (Johnsgard 1981). Godwits depend on both grasslands and wetlands for breeding. Fire and grazing, formerly by bison and currently by cattle, are necessary to maintain the short upland vegetation and the open areas at wetland edges they prefer (Ryan et al. 1984). Godwits have suffered from conversion of native grasslands to agricultural crops. Additionally, wildlife management on the northern prairies is directed at producing tall, dense nesting cover for waterfowl and upland game — habitat not favored by nesting godwits (Ryan et al. 1984). Stewart and Kantrud (1972) estimated 37,000 pairs of breeding godwits in 1967 in North Dakota, one of six states or provinces where breeders are categorized as fairly common to common (DeSante and Pyle 1986). Surveys between 1990 and 1992 indicate around 100,000 wintering godwits along the Pacific coast of North America (Table 2). Since Marbled Godwits winter chiefly on the Pacific coast of North America (Palmer 1967, Root 1988), the continental population is probably currently fewer than 200,000 birds. There has been no evidence of a decline in breeding numbers during the past 25 years (FWS, unpubl. data).

Willet

The western subspecies of the Willet (*Catoptrophorus semipalmatus inornatus*) breeds in the prairie pothole and Great Basin regions of western North America (AOU 1983). On the prairies they exploit short, sparse cover in wetlands and grasslands. Their population has declined because of the conversion of wetlands and uplands to small grain and row crops (Ryan and Renken 1987). Willets no longer breed in Minnesota and Iowa (DeSante and Pyle 1986) and their range has shrunk in North Dakota (Ryan and Renken 1987). There were an estimated 41,000 breeding pairs in North Dakota in 1967 (Stewart and Kantrud 1972). The current winter population in the Pacific Flyway is at least 70,000 birds (Table 2). There has been no distinct trend in breeding numbers during the past 25 years (FWS, unpubl. data).

Snowy Plover

The subspecies west of the Rockies, *Charadrius alexandrinus nivosus,* breeds along coastal beaches and at interior saline and alkaline wetlands (Page et al. 1991). Surveys of Washington, California, Oregon and Nevada from 1977–1980 indicated 10,200 breeders; about 2300 were on the coast (Page

TABLE 2. POPULATIONS OF SELECTED SPECIES OF SHOREBIRDS FOR WHICH CURRENT ESTIMATES ARE AVAILABLE

Species	Population size[1]	Season	Area[2]	Source[3]
Charadrius montanus	5000–15,000	breeding	Continental	F. Knopf (pers. comm.)
C. alexandrinus nivosus	18,500	breeding	Western U.S.	Page et al. (1991), Paton and Edwards (1992)
Haemantopus bachmani	7600	breeding	Pacific Flyway	Carter et al. (1992), *in* Campbell et al. (1990)
Himantopus mexicanus	25,000	winter	Pacific Flyway	Page et al. (1992), Morrison et al. (1992), PRBO (unpubl. data), MBO (unpubl. data)
H. m. knudseni	1100	resident	Hawaiian Is.	HDFW (unpubl. data), Engilis and Pratt (1993)
Recurvirostra americana	100,000	winter	Pacific Flyway	Page et al. (1992), Morrison et al. (1992), PRBO (unpubl. data), MBO (unpubl. data)
Catoptrophorus semipalmatus	70,000+	winter	Pacific Flyway	Page et al. (1992), Morrison et al. (1992), PRBO (unpubl. data), MBO (unpubl. data)
Numenius borealis	25–50	breeding	Continental	*in* Alexander et al. (1991), Gollop (1988)
N. tahitiensis	7000	breeding	Alaska	Gill and Redmond (1992), C. Handel and R. Gill (unpubl. data)
Limosa lapponica	25,000–40,000	breeding	Alaska	Gill and Jorgensen (1979), Gill and Handel (1990), B. McCaffery (unpubl. data)
L. fedoa	100,000	winter	Pacific Flyway	Page et al. (1992), Morrison et al. (1992), PRBO (unpubl. data), MBO (unpubl. data)
Arenaria melanocephala	61,000–99,000	breeding	Alaska	Handel and Gill (1992)
Aphriza virgata	50,000–70,000	spring	Alaska	Norton et al. (1990), P. Martin (unpubl. data)
Calidris alpina pacifica	450,000–600,000	winter	Pacific Flyway	Page et al. (1992), Morrison et al. (1992), PRBO (unpubl. data), MBO (unpubl. data)
Phalaropus tricolor	1,500,000	autumn	Continental	Jehl (1988)

[1] Population size = estimated number of individual birds.
[2] Pacific Flyway as depicted on Figure 1, this report. Continental = North America.
[3] HDFW = Hawaii Division of Forestry and Wildlife, MBO = Manomet Bird Observatory, Manomet, Massachusetts, PRBO = Point Reyes Bird Observatory, Stinson Beach, California.

et al. 1991). Breeders were absent at 33 of 53 California coastal sites with records prior to 1970 (Page and Stenzel 1981). Christmas Bird Counts from the early 1960s to the mid-1980s also indicated declining numbers in winter along the southern California coast (Page et al. 1986, Butcher and Lowe 1990). The situation in the interior was unclear since breeding habitat had been lost at some locations, especially in the Central Valley, but gained elsewhere such as the Salton Sea (Page and Stenzel 1981). A repeat breeding season survey in the same states during 1988–1989 indicated only 7900 Snowy Plovers, a 20% decline from a decade earlier both on the coast and in the interior (Page et al. 1991). By 1990 the number of historical coastal breeding sites had declined from 29 to 6 in Oregon (C. Bruce, pers. comm.) and from 6 to 2 in Washington (E. Cummins, pers. comm.). Plants introduced to stabilize dunes, expanding recreational use of beaches, and heavy nest predation by feral foxes (*Vulpes vulpes*) threaten to reduce coastal nesting populations even further. The discovery of up to 10,000 breeding Snowy Plovers at Great Salt Lake in 1992 would put the current U.S. population west of the Rockies at about 18,500 birds (Page et al. 1991, Paton and Edwards 1992).

Black-necked Stilt (Himantopus mexicanus)

Stilts breed at ephemeral fresh to brackish water pools, salt meadows, rice fields, agricultural waste water ponds, coastal lagoons, and salt evaporation ponds (Johnsgard 1981). Their western North American range includes the western Great Plains, the Great Basin, California's Central Valley, the central and southern California coast, the Texas coast, Mexico, and the Hawaiian Islands (AOU 1983). During the last two decades stilts have expanded their western range, at least temporarily, northward into Washington, Montana, Alberta and Saskatchewan, in response to drought in their

traditional range (Rohwer et al. 1979, Salisbury and Salisbury 1989). Within the last century stilts have colonized the salt evaporation ponds of San Francisco Bay (Shuford et al. 1989) and the Salton Sea. The degree to which these gains offset losses in the Central Valley, where over 90% of the historic wetland habitat has been destroyed (Frayer et al. 1989), is unknown. Numbers of stilts breeding on the North American continent are probably much reduced over former times, based on the amount of wetland habitat lost during the past 200 years in western states where they currently breed (range for 11 states 27–91%; median = 38%; Dahl 1990). The population wintering in the Pacific Flyway has recently been estimated at about 25,000 birds (Table 2). Hunting and loss of lowland wetland habitat caused the Hawaiian population of stilts to decline to possibly as few as 200 birds in 1944 (Monroe 1976). Stilts were protected in 1939 following a prohibition on hunting. By 1949 the population had rebounded to 1000 birds (Swartz and Swartz 1949) and currently fluctuates around 1000 birds (Engilis and Pratt 1993).

American Avocet (Recurvirostra americana)

Avocets breed at alkaline lakes and ponds, coastal lagoons, and salt and waste water evaporation ponds over a range including the western Great Plains; the intermountain region of the U.S. west of the Rockies; California's Central Valley and central and southern coast; and Mexico (AOU 1983). Historically they bred farther north through Alberta to the Northwest Territories (AOU 1983). Wetland loss has been extensive during the past 200 years in states where avocets currently breed (range 27–91%; median = 42%; Dahl 1990). Such losses must have caused a shrinkage of population size (Grinnell and Miller 1944) despite habitat gains such as creation of the salt ponds in San Francisco Bay and the Salton Sea. Currently, about 100,000 avocets winter in the Pacific Flyway (Table 2). Unless there are substantially more avocets throughout the remainder of the winter range in southern Texas and Mexico (Palmer 1967, Root 1988), the continental population must be in the low hundreds of thousands. Although breeding bird surveys indicate a decline in the western breeding population during the past 10 years (FWS, unpubl. data), lower numbers may only reflect fluctuations in response to a recent widespread drought in the west (Alberico 1993).

Wilson's Phalarope *(Phalaropus tricolor)*

Wilson's Phalaropes breed abundantly in ephemeral wetlands and are able to respond to droughts with large population shifts (M. Colwell, pers. comm.). Because of the high rate of wetland loss during the past two centuries on the phalarope's Great Plains and Great Basin breeding grounds (Dahl 1990), the continental population most likely has declined. During the past 50 years, however, the breeding range has expanded north into the Yukon Territory; south into Arizona, New Mexico, Oklahoma and Texas; and east into the Canadian maritime provinces and Maine (Jehl 1988, McAlpine et al. 1988). An abundant breeder in Minnesota prior to 1900, the Wilson's Phalarope inexplicably nearly disappeared for 20 years beginning in 1900. Although numbers increased steadily thereafter, by 1930 it was still not nearly as abundant as in the pre-1900s (Roberts 1932). Wilson's Phalaropes are now described as fairly common breeders in Minnesota (DeSante and Pyle 1986). Jehl (1988) makes a gross estimate of 1.5 million birds for the current size of the continental population in fall. Breeding bird surveys indicate a decline in numbers in the Great Plains over the past 10 years, a period too short to reveal much about population trends (FWS, unpubl. data). Jehl (pers. comm.) has not noted any overall decline in Wilson's Phalarope numbers at major fall staging areas during the past decade, although local reductions have been large at some localities.

Other temperate breeders

Little has been reported on other temperate breeders to indicate a change in population size or breeding range. The Common Snipe likely has lost breeding habitat and declined in the west because its breeding range includes the Great Plains and Great Basin, where there have been significant wetland losses. The continental population showed a decline over the last 10 years but not over the past 25 years of breeding bird surveys (FWS, unpubl. data). Spotted Sandpipers and Killdeers are likely to have been less affected by change on their breeding grounds than most other temperate breeders because of their broad ranges, diverse nesting habitats and affinity for altered habitats (Grinnell et al. 1918, Johnsgard 1981). Spotted Sandpipers have shown no evidence of decline over the past 25 years in the central or western portions of their U.S. breeding range. Killdeers, in contrast, have declined over the past 25 years in the western range and over the past 10 years in the western and central range (FWS, unpubl. data). The range of the Black Oystercatcher is restricted to the rocky shoreline of the Pacific coast, where there is minimal human impact. The only other temperate breeders in western North America are the American Oystercatcher and Wilson's Plover, which nest in the extreme southern part of the Pacific Flyway. The beaches and wetlands that they use are likely little altered and disturbed compared to those farther north.

ARCTIC BREEDERS

Our ability to assess change in arctic and subarctic shorebird populations is extremely limited. Remoteness of breeding areas, broad distributions, and limited life history observations have resulted in a paucity of information on which to assess population trends, with one notable exception, the Eskimo Curlew. As of 1989 the Eskimo Curlew population was thought to be about two dozen individuals (Alexander et al. 1991). There have been no authenticated sightings in North America since 1989 or in South America since 1939 (Wetmore 1939). Eskimo Curlews formerly nested in the McKenzie District, Northwest Territories eastward to Hudson Bay and possibly westward throughout northern Alaska (Banks 1977, Gollop et al. 1986, Houston 1994). Aside from reference to the species as a common spring and fall migrant in western Alaska (Nelson 1883, Murdoch 1885, McLenegan 1887), there are no records west of the Rocky Mountains (Gollop et al. 1986).

Although anecdotal accounts suggest a historic population of millions of Eskimo Curlews (Gollop et al. 1986), numbers may not have exceeded hundreds of thousands of birds (Gollop 1989). Although the curlew's decline was dramatic and well documented, the causes are still uncertain (Banks 1977, Gollop et al. 1986). Market hunting from 1880–1890 on both the South American wintering grounds and on migration staging areas in North America is frequently mentioned as the most important factor. Concomitantly, however, there was widespread conversion of curlew habitat from native grasslands to croplands and pasture. Banks (1977) speculated that a combination of factors was responsible for the decline including: hunting, habitat alteration, mortality during autumn migration caused by severe Atlantic storms in the 1880s, and volcanic eruptions between 1883 and 1907, which produced extensive atmospheric dust and prolonged winter conditions on the breeding grounds. Still lacking, however, is an explanation for why other species such as Lesser Golden Plover and Hudsonian Godwit, which nested at the same latitudes, shared the same migration routes and wintering areas, and were excessively hunted, rebounded from suppressed population levels whereas the curlew did not.

Changes in populations of other arctic breeders during the past century are not readily apparent because of the absence of data on historical abundance. Fortunately, recent studies are beginning to generate baseline information on population sizes. The population of Black Turnstones (*Arenaria melanocephala*) breeding in Alaska was estimated at about 95,000 birds in the early 1980s (Handel and Gill 1992) and the Bristle-thighed Curlew (*Numenius tahitiensis*) population in the early 1990s was estimated at about 7000 breeding birds (Gill and Redmond 1992; C. Handel and R. Gill, unpubl. data). Less precise information has also been obtained for the Surfbird. The 50,000–70,000 birds that stage in western Prince William Sound, Alaska, during spring migration are suspected to include the majority of the continental population (Norton et al. 1990). Studies on a more regional level include those of Troy (1992), who has amassed a 10-year data set on population trends of breeding shorebirds on the arctic coastal plain of Alaska; Connors and Risebrough (1978), who studied shorebird dependency on littoral habitats in Alaska; and Gill and Handel (1981, 1990) and Woodby and Divoky (1983), who studied postbreeding shorebird concentrations along the coast of western Alaska.

POPULATION SIZES AND LIMITING FACTORS

The few crude population estimates available for North American shorebirds range widely in size from a handful of Eskimo Curlews to 1.5 million Wilson's Phalaropes (Table 2). Probably the most abundant western North American species is the Western Sandpiper (*Calidris mauri*). Over 6 million reportedly passed through the Copper River Delta during the 1973 spring migration (Isleib 1979), but this estimate may be too high since it assumed complete population turnover every three tidal cycles. About 1.3 million were counted in Pacific Flyway wetlands south of Alaska over a week-long period at the peak of spring migration in late April 1991 (PRBO, unpubl. data).

Very little is known about the factors that have affected population size in shorebirds. The anecdotal information on temperate breeders suggests the amount and quality of available breeding habitat may have been the most important limiting factor in the

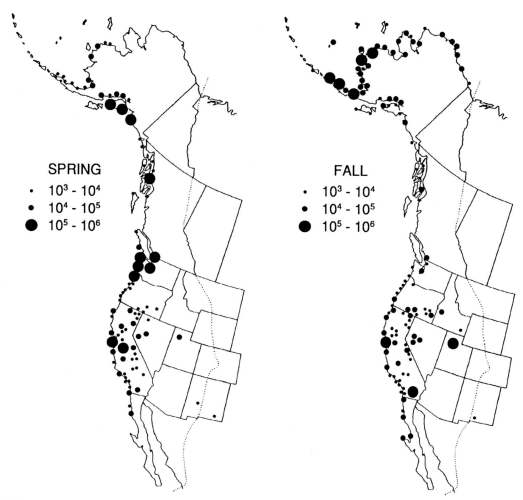

FIGURE 1. Sites of concentrations of shorebirds in spring and fall throughout the Pacific Flyway. Numbers represent total birds of all species (after Page et al. 1992; Morrison et al. 1992; Gill, unpubl. data).

recent past. Ranges have shrunk and populations have declined as grasslands and wetlands have been converted to croplands, or as beaches have been engulfed by urban and recreational development. Mountain Plover populations are believed to be declining now, however, due to deteriorating conditions on their wintering grounds (Knopf 1994). Eskimo Curlews have not been able to recover from the excessive hunting and habitat alteration around the turn of the century. Whether other arctic breeders are limited by conditions on their breeding, staging or wintering grounds is unknown. Information emerging from long-term studies in Europe suggests that some arctic species may be limited by conditions on the wintering grounds and others by conditions on the breeding grounds (Goss-Custard and Moser 1988, Moser 1988).

CAPACITY TO DETECT FUTURE POPULATION CHANGE

While there is little precise information on changes in western North American shorebird populations during the past century, expansion of ongoing programs, coupled with new efforts, could provide the information needed to monitor some populations during the next century (Table

TABLE 3. MONITORING SCHEMES BEST SUITED FOR DETECTING TRENDS IN POPULATION OF SELECTED SPECIES OF SHOREBIRDS DURING THE NEXT CENTURY

	Monitoring scheme[1]			
Species	BBS	CBC	ISS	SSS
Pluvialis squatarola			x (W[2], S)	
Charadrius alexandrinus		x		x
C. semipalmatus			x (F, S)	
C. vociferus	x	x		
C. montanus	x			x
Haematopus bachmani		x		x
Himantopus mexicanus	x		x (F)	
Recurvirostra americana	x		x (F, W)	
Catoptrophorus semi-palmatus	x		x (F, W)	
Actitis macularia	x			
Bartramia longicauda	x			
Numenius phaeopus			x (S)	
N. tahitiensis				x
N. americanus	x		x (F, W)	
Limosa fedoa	x		x (W, S)	
Arenaria melanocephala		x		x
Aphriza virgata				x
Calidris alba		x		
C. mauri			x (W, S)	
C. minutilla			x (F, W)	
C. alpina			x (W, S)	
Limnodromus griseus			x (S)	
Gallinago gallinago	x	x		
Phalaropus tricolor			x (F)	

[1] BBS = U.S. Fish and Wildlife Service Breeding Bird Survey, CBC = National Audubon Society Christmas Bird Count, ISS = International Shorebird Survey (Howe et al. 1989), SSS = Species Specific Survey.
[2] S = spring, F = fall, W = winter.

3). The Breeding Bird Survey of the U.S. Fish and Wildlife Service could prove useful for identifying future population trends of 10 temperate breeders. Christmas Bird Counts of the National Audubon Society could be used for wintering populations of at least six species. Recently completed species-specific breeding season surveys could be periodically replicated for six species. At least eight additional species that breed in the arctic could be monitored by adapting the methods of the International Shorebird Survey (Howe et al. 1989) to the Pacific Flyway. New information on the key staging and wintering areas for shorebirds in western North America (Fig. 1) could be used to identify monitoring sites that would be representative of the total Pacific Flyway population. Work still needs to be done to develop economical monitoring methods for the remaining species.

ACKNOWLEDGMENTS

We thank B. Peterjohn and the U.S. Fish and Wildlife Service for supplying population trends from the Breeding Bird Survey and C. M. Handel and J. R. Jehl, Jr. for reviewing the manuscript.

LITERATURE CITED

ALBERICO, J. A. R. 1993. Drought and predation cause avocet and stilt breeding failure in Nevada. Western Birds 24:43–51.

ALEXANDER, S. A., R. S. FERGUSON, AND K. J. MC-CORMICK. 1991. Key migratory bird terrestrial habitat sites in the Northwest Territories. 2nd ed. Canadian Wildlife Service Occasional Paper No. 71, Ottawa, Canada.

AMERICAN ORNITHOLOGISTS' UNION. 1983. Checklist of North American birds. 6th ed. American Ornithological Union, Washington, D.C.

BANKS, R. C. 1977. The decline and fall of the Eskimo Curlew, or why did the curlew go extaille? American Birds 31:127–134.

BANKS, R. C. 1979. Human related mortality of birds in the United States. United States Fish and Wildlife Service Special Scientific Report on Wildlife No. 215, Washington, D.C.

BENT, A. C. 1929. Life histories of North American shorebirds. Vol. 2. United States National Museum Bulletin No. 146.

BOLAND, J. M. 1991. An overview of the seasonal distribution of the North American shorebirds. Wader Study Group Bulletin 62:39–42.

BURGER, J. 1984. Shorebirds as marine animals. Pp. 17–81 in J. Burger and B. Olla (eds.), Behavior of marine animals. Vol. 5. Shorebirds: breeding behavior and populations. Plenum Press, New York.

BUTCHER, G. S., AND J. D. LOWE. 1990. Population trends of twenty species of migratory birds as revealed by Christmas bird counts, 1963–87. Unpublished Report Cornell Laboratory of Ornithology, Ithaca, N.Y.

CAMPBELL, R. W., N. K. DAWE, L. MC-TAGGART-COWAN, J. M. COOPER, G. W. KAISER, AND M. C. E. MCNALL. 1990. The birds of British Columbia. Vol. 2. Mitchell Press, Vancouver, B.C.

CARLTON, J. T. 1979. Introduced invertebrates of San Francisco Bay. Pp. 427–444 in T. J. Conomos (ed.), San Francisco Bay: the urbanized estuary. Pacific Division of the American Association for the Advancement of Science, San Francisco, CA.

CARTER, H. R., G. J. McCHESNEY, D. L. JAQUES, C. S. STRONG, M. W. PARKER, J. E. TAKEKAWA, D. L. JORY, AND D. L. WHITWORTH. 1992. Breeding populations of seabirds in California. Vol. 1. Population estimates, 1989–1991. Unpublished Fish and Wildlife Service Report, Northern Prairie Wildlife Research Center, Dixon, CA.

CONNORS, P. G., AND R. W. RISEBROUGH. 1978. Shorebird dependence on arctic littoral habitats. Pp. 84–166 in Environmental assessment of the Alaska continental shelf. Final Report of principal investigators. Vol. 18. Outer Continental Shelf Environmental Assessment Program, National Oceanic and Atmospheric Administration, Boulder, CO.

COOKE, W. W. 1910. Distribution and migration of

North American shorebirds. United States Biological Survey Bulletin No. 35.

DAHL, T. E. 1990. Wetlands of the United States 1780's to 1980's. Unpublished Report of the Fish Wildlife Service, Washington, D.C.

DeSANTE, D., AND P. PYLE. 1986. Distributional checklist of North American birds. Artemisia Press, Lee Vining, CA.

ENGILIS, A., JR., AND P. K. PRATT. 1993. Status and population trends of Hawaii's native waterbirds, 1977–1987. Wilson Bulletin 105:142–158.

FORBUSH, E. H. 1912. A history of the game birds, wildfowl, and shore birds of Massachusetts and adjacent states. Massachusetts Board of Agriculture.

FRAYER, W. E., D. D. PETERS, AND H. R. PYWELL. 1989. Wetlands of the California Central Valley: status and trends 1939 to mid 1980s. Unpublished Report of the U.S. Fish Wildlife Service, Portland, OR.

GILL, R. E., JR., AND C. M. HANDEL. 1981. Shorebirds of the eastern Bering Sea. Pp. 719–738 *in* D. W. Hood and J. A. Calder (eds.), The eastern Bering Sea shelf: oceanography and resources. Vol. 2. University of Washington Press, Seattle, WA.

GILL, R. E., JR., AND C. M. HANDEL. 1990. The importance of subarctic intertidal habitats to shorebirds: a study of the central Yukon-Kuskokwim Delta, Alaska. Condor 92:709–725.

GILL, R. E., JR., AND P. D. JORGENSEN. 1979. A preliminary assessment of the timing and migration of shorebirds along the northcentral Alaska Peninsula. Studies in Avian Biology 2:113–123.

GILL, R. E., JR., AND R. L. REDMOND. 1992. Distribution, numbers, and habitat of Bristle-thighed Curlews (*Numenius tahitiensis*) on Rangiroa Atoll. Notornis 39:17–26.

GOLLOP, J. B. 1989. The Eskimo Curlew. Pp. 583–595 *in* W. J. Chandler (ed.), Audubon wildlife report 1988/1989. Academic Press, San Diego, CA.

GOLLOP, J. B., T. W. BERRY, AND E. H. IVERSON. 1986. Eskimo Curlew: a vanishing species? Saskatchewan Natural History Society Special Publication No. 17.

GOSS-CUSTARD, J. D., AND M. E. MOSER. 1988. Rates of change in the numbers of Dunlin, *Calidris alpina* wintering in British estuaries in relation to the spread of *Spartina anglica*. Journal of Applied Ecology 25:95–109.

GRABER, R. R., AND J. W. GRABER. 1963. A comparative study of bird populations in Illinois, 1906–1909 and 1956–1958. Illinois Natural History Survey Bulletin 28.

GRAUL, W. D., AND L. E. WEBSTER. 1976. Breeding status of the Mountain Plover. Condor 78:265–267.

GRINNELL, J., H. C. BRYANT, AND T. I. STORER. 1918. The game birds of California. Univ. Calif. Press, Berkeley, CA.

GRINNELL, J., AND A. H. MILLER. 1944. The distribution of the birds of California. Pacific Coast Avifauna No. 27.

HANDEL, C. M., AND R. E. GILL, JR. 1992. Breeding distribution of the Black Turnstone. Wilson Bulletin 104:122–135.

HARVEY, T. E., K. J. MILLER, R. L. HOTHEM, M. J. RAUZON, G. W. PAGE, AND R. A. KECK. 1992. Status and trends report on wildlife of the San Francisco estuary. Unpublished Report, San Francisco Bay Estuary Project, United States Environmental Protection Agency, San Francisco, CA.

HOUSTON, C. S. 1994. The unlikely 18th century naturalists of Hudson's Bay. Pp. 14–26 *in* J. R. Jehl, Jr. and N. K. Johnson (eds.), A century of avifaunal change in western North America. Studies in Avian Biology No. 15.

HOWE, M. A., P. H. GEISSLER, AND B. A. HARRINGTON. 1989. Population trends of North American shorebirds based on the international shorebird survey. Biological Conservation 49:185–199.

ISLEIB, M. E. P. 1979. Migratory shorebird populations on the Copper River Delta and eastern Prince William Sound, Alaska. Studies in Avian Biology 2:125–129.

JEHL, J. R., JR. 1988. Biology of the Eared Grebe and Wilson's Phalarope in the non-breeding season: a study of adaptations to saline lakes. Studies in Avian Biology No. 12.

JOHNSGARD, P. A. 1981. The plovers, sandpipers and snipes of the world. University of Nebraska Press, Lincoln, NB.

JUREK, R. M. 1973. California shorebird study: accelerated research program for shore and upland migratory game birds. Unpublished Project Final report California Department of Fish and Game, Sacramento, CA.

KESSEL, B. 1979. Avian habitat classification for Alaska. Murrelet 60:86–94.

KNOPF, F. L. 1992. Status and conservation of Mountain Plovers. Unpublished Report of United States Fish and Wildlife Service, National Ecological Research Center, Fort Collins, CO.

KNOPF, F. L. 1994. Avian assemblages on altered grassland. Pp. 247–257 *in* J. R. Jehl, Jr. and N. K. Johnson (eds.), A century of avifaunal change in western North America. Studies in Avian Biology No. 15.

LEACHMAN, B., AND B. OSMUNDSON. 1990. Status of the Mountain Plover: a literature review. Unpublished Report of United States Fish Wildlife Service, Fish and Wildlife Enhancement, Golden, CO.

MACE, G. M., AND R. LANDE. 1991. Assessing extinction threats: toward a reevaluation of IUCN Threatened Species Categories. Conservation Biology 5:148–157.

McALPINE, D. F., M. PHINNEY, AND S. MAKEPEACE. 1988. New Brunswick breeding of Wilson's Phalarope confirmed. Canadian Field-Naturalist 102:77–78.

McCALLUM, D. A., W. D. GRAUL, AND R. ZACCAGNINI. 1977. The status of the Long-billed Curlew in Montana. Auk 94:599–601.

McLENEGAN, S. B. 1887. Ornithology. Exploration of Noatak River, Alaska. Pp. 53–80 *in* Report of the cruise of the Revenue Marine Steamer, *Corwin,* in the Arctic Ocean in the year 1885. Government Printing Office, Washington, D.C.

MONROE, G. C. 1976. Birds of Hawaii. Charles E. Tuttle Company, Incorporated, Rutland, VT.

MORRISON, R. I. G., AND R. K. ROSS. 1989. Atlas of Nearctic shorebirds on the coast of South America. Vol. 1 and 2. Special Publication of Canadian Wildlife Service, Ottawa, Canada.

MORRISON, R. I. G., R. K. ROSS, AND S. TORRES. 1992. Aerial surveys of Nearctic shorebirds wintering in Mexico: some preliminary results. Canadian Wildlife Service Progress Notes, Ottawa, Ontario.

MOSER, M. E. 1988. Limits to the numbers of Grey Plovers *Pluvialis squatarola* wintering on British estuaries: an analysis of long-term population trends. Journal of Applied Ecology 25:473–485.

MURDOCH, J. 1885. Birds. Pp. 104–128 *in* Report of the International Polar Expedition to Point Barrow, Alaska. Government Printing Office, Washington, D.C.

MYERS, J. P. 1980. The Pampas shorebird community: interactions between breeding and nonbreeding members. Pp. 37–49 *in* A. Keast and E. S. Morton (eds.), Migrant birds in the Neotropics: ecology, behavior, distribution, and conservation. Smithsonian Institute Press, Washington, D.C.

MYERS, J. P., AND L. P. MYERS. 1979. Shorebirds of coastal Buenos Aires Province, Argentina. Ibis 121:186–200.

NELSON, E. W. 1883. Birds of Bering Sea and the Arctic Ocean. Pp. 55–118 *in* Cruise of the Revenue Marine Steamer, *Corwin*, in Alaska and the N.W. Arctic Ocean in 1881. Government Printing Office, Washington, D.C.

NORTON, D. W., S. E. SENNER, R. E. GILL, JR., P. D. MARTIN, J. M. WRIGHT, AND A. K. FUKUYAMA. 1990. Shorebird and herring roe in Prince William Sound, Alaska. American Birds 44:367–371, 508.

PAGE, G. W., AND L. E. STENZEL (eds.). 1981. The breeding status of the Snowy Plover in California. Western Birds 12:1–40.

PAGE, G. W., F. C. BIDSTRUP, R. J. RAMER, AND L. E. STENZEL. 1986. Distribution of wintering Snowy Plovers in California and adjacent states. Western Birds 17:145–170.

PAGE, G. W., W. D. SHUFORD, J. E. KJELMYR, AND L. E. STENZEL. 1992. Shorebird numbers in wetlands of the Pacific Flyway: a summary of counts from April 1988 to January 1992. Unpublished Report of Point Reyes Bird Observatory, Stinson Beach, CA.

PAGE, G. W., L. E. STENZEL, W. D. SHUFORD, AND C. R. BRUCE. 1991. Distribution and abundance of the Snowy Plover on its western North American breeding grounds. Journal of Field Ornithology 62:245–255.

PALMER, R. S. 1967. The shorebirds of North America. G. D. Stout (ed.), The Viking Press, NY.

PATON, P. W. C., AND T. C. EDWARDS, JR. 1992. Nesting ecology of the Snowy Plover at Great Salt Lake, Utah—1992 breeding season. Unpublished Report of Utah Coop. Fish Wildlife Research Unit, Department of Fisheries and Wildlife, Logan, UT.

PETERS, D. D. 1989. Status of wetland habitats in the western U. S. Proceedings of Western Raptor Manag. Symposium and Workshop. National Wildlife Federation Science and Technical Series No. 12.

PITELKA, F. A. 1979. Introduction: Pacific coast shorebird scene. Studies in Avian Biology 2:1–11.

REDMOND, R. L. 1984. The behavioral ecology of Long-billed Curlews *Numenius americanus* breeding in western Idaho. Ph.D. thesis, University of Montana, Missoula.

RENAUD, W. E. 1980. The Long-billed Curlew in

Saskatchewan: status and distribution. Blue Jay 38:221–237.

ROBERTS, T. S. 1932. The birds of Minnesota. McGill Lithography Company, Minneapolis, MN.

ROHWER, S., D. F. MARTIN, AND G. G. BENSON. 1979. Breeding of Black-necked Stilt in Washington. Murrelet 60:67–71.

ROOT, T. L. 1988. Atlas of wintering North American birds: analysis of Christmas bird count data. University Chicago Press, Chicago, IL.

RYAN, M. R., AND R. B. RENKEN. 1987. Habitat use by breeding Willets in the northern Great Plains. Wilson Bulletin 99:175–189.

RYAN, M. R., R. B. RENKEN, AND J. J. DINSMORE. 1984. Marbled Godwit habitat selection in the northern prairie region. Journal of Wildlife Management 48:1206–1218.

SALISBURY, C. D. C., AND L. D. SALISBURY. 1989. Successful breeding of Black-necked Stilts in Saskatchewan. Blue Jay 47:154–156.

SENNER, S. E., AND M. A. HOWE. 1984. Conservation of Nearctic shorebirds. Pp. 379–421 *in* J. Burger and B. Olla (eds.), Behavior of marine animals. Vol. 5. Shorebirds: breeding behavior and populations. Plenum Press, New York.

SHUFORD, W. D., G. W. PAGE, J. G. EVENS, AND L. E. STENZEL. 1989. Seasonal abundance of waterbirds at Point Reyes: a coastal California perspective. Western Birds 20:137–265.

STEWART, R. E., AND H. A. KANTRUD. 1972. Population estimates of breeding birds in North Dakota. Auk 89:766–788.

SUGDEN, J. W. 1933. Range restriction of the Long-billed Curlew. Condor 35:3–9.

SWARTZ, C. W., AND E. R. SWARTZ. 1949. The game-birds in Hawaii. Board of Agriculture and Forestry, Territory of Hawaii, Honolulu.

TROY, D. 1992. Trends in bird use of the Pt. McIntyre reference area, 1981–1991. Unpublished report, Troy Ecological Associates and BP Exploration (Alaska), Incorporated, Anchorage, AK.

WETMORE, A. 1926. Observations of the birds of Argentina, Paraguay, Uruguay, and Chile. United States National Museum Bulletin No. 133.

WETMORE, A. 1939. Recent observations on the Eskimo Curlew in Argentina. Auk 56:475–476.

WHITE, C. M. 1994. Population trends and current status of selected western raptors. Pp. 161–172 *in* J. R. Jehl, Jr. and N. K. Johnson (eds.), A century of avifaunal change in western North America. Studies in Avian Biology No. 15.

WHITE, R. P. 1983. Distribution and habitat preference of the Upland Sandpiper *Bartramia longicauda* in Wisconsin. American Birds 37:16–22.

WOODBY, D., AND G. DIVOKY. 1983. Bird use of coastal habitats in Norton Sound. Pp. 353–704 *in* Environmental assessment of the Alaska continental shelf. Final report principal investigators. Vol. 18. Outer Continental Shelf Environmental Assessment Program, National Oceanic and Atmospheric Administration, Boulder, CO.

YOCOM, C. F. 1956. Re-establishment of breeding populations of Long-billed Curlews in Washington. Wilson Bulletin 68:228–231.

Studies in Avian Biology No. 15:161–172, 1994.

POPULATION TRENDS AND CURRENT STATUS OF SELECTED WESTERN RAPTORS

Clayton M. White

Abstract. The term status can reflect either numbers or inherent biological characteristics (e.g., sensitivity to environmental conditions). The Ferruginous Hawk (*Buteo regalis*), for example, may undergo wide fluctuations that may follow, in part, changes in prey abundance. Thus, numbers of breeders change annually, although this indicates little about the hawk's future population size. Brief case studies are given for selected raptors, e.g., Bald Eagle (*Haliaeetus leucocephalus*), Peregrine Falcon (*Falco peregrinus*), several species of hawks (*Buteo* and *Accipiter*), and the Saw-whet Owl (*Aegolius acadicus*) and Flammulated Owl (*Otus flammeolus*). A few species are stable, some are declining for various reasons, and several are increasing mainly due to human-caused habitat alterations. In the future conservation efforts should emphasize species that can co-exist with humans.

Key Words: Raptors; birds of prey; population trends; status; habitat alteration.

Status goes beyond population size at any particular moment; it also includes trends in abundance. For raptors, a confounding effect is the fact that tens of thousands were shot during the first half of this century. It is not known what effect this had on the population structure of these largely "K-selected" species, the very sort of species that lend themselves to rarity or endangerment. Another complication is that we do not fully understand the ecological relationships that may drive status change, although one seemingly well documented case is that of the Bald Eagle (*Haliaeetus leucocephalus*) in Glacier National Park (Spencer et al. 1991). Eagles had been studied for more than two decades as they gathered there during migration. Apparently, the introduced opossum shrimp (*Mysis relecta*) reduced or eliminated zooplankton necessary to sustain a reproductive population of kokanee salmon (*Oncorhynchus nerka*). Dying salmon, the principal food for eagles, attracted several hundred eagles annually since their first record in 1939. There was a cascading interaction and once the salmon were gone so were the eagles, which did not decline but simply shifted to new locations. By contrast, non-breeding Bald Eagles are increasing in southeast Alaska (Hansen and Hodges 1985) but the reasons for this change are not clear.

Some species undergo natural numerical oscillations over time and this may affect our judgment of their status. For example, in the Ferruginous Hawk (*Buteo regalis*), numbers appear outwardly to be related to cyclicity of prey (e.g., rabbits, ground squirrels). Overall, however, hawk numbers may change but not in accordance with prey numbers. Thus, focussing on current numbers or directional trends does not necessarily provide an accurate understanding of the species.

Some species are stable but have reached that point following historical increases or declines. Others are stable and have "always" been so historically. In many cases, however, we know little about change because a historical baseline is essentially nonexistent. Most recent authors (e.g., Johnsgard 1988, 1990; Voous 1988; Snyder and Snyder 1991) summarize population status, but there were earlier and more detailed attempts at assessing numbers of some western diurnal raptors (Porter and White 1975, Evans 1982). More thorough reviews of current trends and status are in Ladd and Schempf (1982), Glinski et al. (1988), and National Wildlife Federation (1989). In the latter, trends are listed for five medium-sized owls in nine western states. In general, species were stable except for the Burrowing Owl [*Athene* (*Speotyto*) *cunicularia*], which tended to be declining. Of 36 western raptors summarized (National Wildlife Federation 1989), 13 were too poorly studied to reveal trends. Eleven were recorded as stable, six were increasing, and five were either decreasing or decreasing/stable. From one decade to the next the status of some raptors is likely to change quickly, even by several orders of magnitude [see comments under Peregrine Falcon (*Falco peregrinus*)]. Thus, current allocation to categories is tentative. In Table 1, I evaluate 48 species of western raptors based on the literature, personal communications and observations. Note that 24 (50%) are considered to be either in jeopardy or potentially so (Table 2). Interestingly, the percentage of those listed changed little over the past two decades (cf. White 1974, LeFranc and Millsap 1984).

HISTORICAL FRAMEWORK

Raptors have been revered as emblems of justice, power, and nations and appear on coinage; athletic teams carry their names. At the same time, they have been persecuted and abused for economic gain or for other human "needs". In fact, our national emblem, the Bald Eagle, was subject to a bounty for several decades. Until the 1960s raptors were generally viewed as "vermin", even in North America (cf. White 1990). To detect changes in perceptions I reviewed a sample of 54 papers in *The Condor* over the past century (see Table 3). The most personally-exciting paper, in Volume 1, reported eggs of the Peregrine Falcon taken from an eyrie on a very small 11 m cliff in northern Utah (Johnson 1899), about 20 km from my home. The small cliff of easy access was of a type often used by Peregrines at the turn of the century, and indicated a large and numerically healthy population. Today, such nest sites, except in arctic and sub-arctic regions, would be viewed as marginal or unacceptable.

The "vermin" image of raptors in the first half of this century was not portrayed in any of the articles (Table 3), which simply reflected the sort of science conducted at that time. One article in 1955 even anticipated the forthcoming conservation movement by heralding the rarity of the White-tailed Kite

(*Elanus leucurus*) in California. In the 1950s such names as "chicken hawk", Big and Little Blue Darter, Bullet Hawk and Prairie Falcon (*Falco mexicanus*) appeared as unprotected species on the hunting proclamation in Utah. Attitudes have changed dramatically, even to the extent that raptors are sometimes considered to be environmental barometers (see Morrison 1983, and Temple and Wiens 1989 for a discussion). The Bald Eagle represents an excellent example of this shift in attitude. Up to 1952, over $133,000 was spent on bounty payments (about 130,000 eagles killed). Following the eagle's protection and its declaration as an endangered species, millions of dollars have been spent on protection and restoration.

APPARENT TRENDS AND PATTERNS

Most species of western raptors declined, independent of agricultural biocides, as a simple consequence of human encroachment and use of the landscape. Prime examples are the Bald Eagle (also affected by biocides), Swainson's Hawk (*Buteo swainsoni*), and Golden Eagle (*Aquila chrysaetos*) (locally). For example, early in this century flocks of over 2000 Swainson's Hawks were still together when they reached the northern tier of states during spring migration (Cameron 1907, see also Bendire 1877). Today such large single aggregations are only seen in autumn as they reach the lower part of the U.S. or Latin America. Contemporary declines in local breeding areas also have been extensive, such as in California with a 90% loss (Risebrough et al. 1989) and Oregon (Littlefield et al. 1984). These changes seem to be related to breeding ground habitat alterations, although changes in the Latin American non-breeding habitat cannot be ruled out (cf. White et al. 1989).

Notable exceptions to earlier general declines may be the Red-tailed Hawk (*Buteo jamaicensis*), American Kestrel (*Falco sparverius*) and perhaps the Great-horned Owl (*Bubo virginianus*). All seem to have benefited from landscape modifications be-

TABLE 1. SUMMARY OF SOME EVENTS CAUSING OR REFLECTED IN THE CURRENT STATUS OF WESTERN RAPTOR SPECIES OVER THE PAST CENTURY. DATA ON MOST SPECIES ARE CURRENT ONLY TO 1990

Species	Status/trend	Event/condition
Black Vulture (*Coragyps atratus*)	Stable/increasing	Range expansion; increased in west in past century.
Turkey Vulture (*Cathartes aura*)	Increasing	Unknown cause of response; perhaps weather related? Expansion of livestock industry?
California Condor[1] (*Gymnogyps californianus*)	Extinct in wild	Last wild condor taken into captivity 1987. Captive breeding for reintroduction into wild.[1]
Osprey (*Pandion halieatus*)	Variable by region, fluctuating?	Increasing in response to regional habitat alterations (newly created habitat); was affected by agricultural biocides.
White-tailed Kite (*Elanus leucurus*)	Increasing	Severe population loss in first third of century and current recovery and range expansion; perhaps recurring local losses?
Mississippi Kite[2] (*Ictinia mississippiensis*)	Increasing	Range expansion.[2]
Bald Eagle (*Haliaeetus leucocephalus*)	Increasing	Earlier depression of populations because of bounty shooting, habitat alterations or loss, and agricultural biocides.
Northern Harrier (*Circus cyaneus*)	Variable, may be decreasing?	Populations may be impacted because of habitat alterations (wetlands loss).
Sharp-shinned Hawk (*Accipiter striatus*)	Undetermined—stable?	Information unclear; possible recent (post 1980) increases as suggested from migration data.
Cooper's Hawk (*Accipiter cooperi*)	Undetermined	Information unclear; earlier in century heavily persecuted and affected by agricultural biocides. Migration data suggest increases.
Northern Goshawk (*Accipiter gentilis*)	Undetermined	Recently (1990) said to be seriously declining locally because of habitat alterations (see text for discussion); earlier heavily persecuted.
Common Black-Hawk[2,3] (*Buteogallus anthracinus*)	Stable	Status appears stable; sensitive riparian habitats mandate close monitoring.[2,3]
Harris Hawk[2,3] (*Parabuteo unicinctus*)	Stable/increasing	May be affected by habitat alterations (urbanization) but no clear trend; highly adaptable; probably lost some range earlier in century; increasing locally in Arizona thornscrub.[2,3]
Gray Hawk[2,3] [*Buteo (Asturina) nitidus*]	Increasing	Riparian habitats becoming increasingly protected; may have increased locally early in century due to habitat alteration.[2,3]
Red-shouldered Hawk (*Buteo lineatus*)	Increasing	Positive local adjustments to urbanization.
Broad-winged Hawk (*Buteo platypterus*)	Increasing?	Newly determined migration patterns; western occurrence recently clarified and expanding range westward.
Swainson's Hawk (*Buteo swainsoni*)	Declining[4]	Apparent significant (regional) reductions perhaps related to habitat alterations; agricultural chemicals often suggested as reason for decline; status in question.
Zone-tailed Hawk[3,5] (*Buteo albonotatus*)	Stable?	Apparent habitat loss locally but may also be undergoing local range expansion.[3,5]
Hawaiian Hawk[4] (*Buteo solitarius*)	Currently stable?	Earlier loss of range; now breeds on only one island.
Red-tailed Hawk (*Buteo jamaicensis*)	Stable—increasing?	May be increasing locally.
Ferruginous Hawk (*Buteo regalis*)	Variable	Recently petitioned for U.S. Fish and Wildlife threatened listing (see text for discussion); range expanding eastward.
Rough-legged Hawk (*Buteo lagopus*)	Not analyzed—stable?[4]	No historical data.
Golden Eagle (*Aquila chrysaetos*)	Stable?	Earlier heavily persecuted (mainly by domestic livestock owners); local losses; currently stable(?) in some areas, declining(?) in others.

TABLE 1. CONTINUED

Species	Status/trend	Event/condition
Crested Caracara[3] (*Polyborus plancus*)	Stable?	Some local losses early in century, probably not affecting populations in southwest.[3]
American Kestrel (*Falco sparverius*)	Stable/increasing[4]	Increases seem to be regional or local.
Merlin (*Falco columbarius*)	Increasing	Recent positive effects of habitat alterations and responses to reduced agricultural chemicals. Local positive responses to urbanization.
Peregrine Falcon (*Falco peregrinus*)	Increasing	Drastic decrease by 1950 because of agricultural chemicals. Subsequent and remarkable recovery aided by human manipulation and captive breeding for release to wild (see text).
Aplomado Falcon (*Falco femoralis*)	Declining[6]	Essentially extirpated from U.S. range. Habitat alterations in Mexican range.[6]
Prairie Falcon (*Falco mexicanus*)	Stable[4]	Perhaps very local losses?
Gyrfalcon (*Falco rusticolus*)	Stable[4]	Wide fluctuations in breeding numbers with food cycles.
Common Barn-Owl (*Tyto alba*)	Stable?[4]	Heavy local and temporary winter loss but no declining trend.
Flammulated Owl (*Otus flammeolus*)	Stable?	Recent advances in population knowledge; common and widespread with "clumped" breeding populations.
Western Screech-Owl (*Otus kennicottii*)	Stable[4]	Recent clarification of systematic status; separation from Eastern Screech Owl.
Whiskered Screech-Owl (*Otus trichopsis*)	Not analyzed	Status unknown?
Great Horned Owl (*Bubo virginianus*)	Stable/increasing	Occupies wide variety of habitats.
Snowy Owl (*Nyctea scandiaca*)	Not analyzed—stable?	No census data; undergoes wide fluctuations following food cycles.
Northern Hawk Owl (*Surnia ulula*)	Not analyzed	No census data.
Northern Pygmy-Owl (*Glaucidium gnoma*)	Stable?	No reported losses; inadequate surveys.
Ferruginous Pygmy-Owl (*Glaucidium brasilianum*)	Declined[3]	Severe declines in U.S. range since early in century.[3]
Elf Owl[3] (*Micrathene whitneyi*)	Not analyzed	Appears to have decreased in extreme western part of range.[3]
Burrowing Owl [*Athene* (*Speotyto*) *cunicularia*]	Declining[4]	Habitat alterations and other human impacts; human intervention and manipulation (nest site improvements) locally.
Spotted Owl (*Strix occidentalis*)	Declining/uncertain?	Treated elsewhere in this volume (Gutiérrez 1994).
Barred Owl (*Strix varia*)	Increasing?	Recent range expansion.
Great Gray Owl (*Strix nebulosa*)	Not analyzed	Reportedly vulnerable in Canada; at risk to habitat alterations in southern part of range in U.S.
Long-eared Owl (*Asio otus*)	Stable?[4]	Some local losses in far west.[3]
Short-eared Owl (*Asio flammeus*)	Declining?[4]	Apparent recent reductions because of habitat loss; difficult to assess because of large oscillations in numbers.
Boreal Owl (*Aegolius funereus*)	Increasing	Recent southern range expansions (Johnson, this volume).
Saw-whet Owl (*Aegolius acadicus*)	Stable	Apparent recent population increase and range expansions in north (see text).

[1] Snyder and Snyder 1989; [2] R. L. Glinski, pers. comm., 1993; [3] Glinski et al. 1988; [4] National Wildlife Federation 1989; [5] Snyder and Snyder 1991; [6] Hector 1987.

TABLE 2. STATUS OF WESTERN NORTH AMERICAN RAPTORS SUGGESTED BY DIFFERENT ORGANIZATIONS. CATEGORY 2 IS GIVEN TO SPECIES FOR WHICH THERE ARE NOT ENOUGH DATA TO INDICATE A THREATENED OR ENDANGERED DESIGNATION

Species	List/organization	Status
Northern Harrier	1. Blue List, American Birds[1]	"Down"
Bald Eagle	1. T&E List, U.S. Fish and Wildlife Service[2]	Endangered
Northern Goshawk	1. Candidate List, U.S. Fish and Wildlife Service[3]	Category 2
	2. Sensitive List, U.S. Forest Service[4]	Sensitive
Cooper's Hawk	1. Blue List	"Down"
	2. Jeopardy List, Canadian Wildlife Service[5]	Vulnerable
Sharp-shinned Hawk	1. Blue List	"Down"
Harris' Hawk	1. Sensitive List	Sensitive
Ferruginous Hawk	1. Blue List	"Down"
	2. Sensitive List	Listed
	3. Jeopardy List	Threatened
	4. Candidate List	Category 2
Swainson's Hawk	1. Blue List	"Down"
	2. Sensitive List	Sensitive
Zone-tailed Hawk	1. Sensitive List	Sensitive
Gray Hawk	1. Candidate List	Category 2
Hawaiian Hawk	1. T&E List	Endangered
Crested Caracara	1. Sensitive List	Sensitive
Merlin	1. Blue List	"Down"
Aplomado Falcon	1. T&E List	Endangered
Prairie Falcon	1. Sensitive List	Sensitive
Peregrine Falcon		
race *pealei*	1. Sensitive List	Sensitive
	2. Jeopardy List	Vulnerable
race *tundrius*	1. Jeopardy List	Vulnerable
	2. T&E List	Threatened
race *anatum*	1. Jeopardy List	Endangered
	2. T&E List	Endangered
Common Barn-Owl	1. Blue List	"Down"
Burrowing Owl	1. Blue List	Declining
	2. Sensitive List	Sensitive
	3. Jeopardy List	Vulnerable
Spotted Owl	1. Blue List	In trouble
	2. Sensitive List	Sensitive
	3. Jeopardy List	Threatened
	4. T&E List	Threatened
Great Gray Owl	1. Sensitive List	Sensitive
	2. Jeopardy List	Vulnerable
Ferruginous Pygmy-Owl	1. Sensitive List	Sensitive
Elf Owl	1. Sensitive List	Sensitive
Flammulated Owl	1. Sensitive List	Sensitive
	2. Jeopardy List	Vulnerable
Boreal Owl	1. Sensitive List	Sensitive

[1] Tate 1986; [2] U.S. Department of Interior 1992c; [3] U.S. Department of Interior 1991; [4] Rath, M., U.S. Forest Service, Region 4, Threatened and Endangered Species program, pers. comm. 1993; [5] Steenhof 1993.

cause they are so ecologically versatile, and all adapt well to urbanization. Other raptors, such as the Merlin (*Falco columbarius*) in Canada (Oliphant and Haug 1985, James 1988), have recently adapted to urbaniza-tion. With the general protection of raptors over the past three decades, there is some suggestion of increase in most species ana-lyzed in Breeding Bird Surveys from 1965 to 1979 (Robbins et al. 1986). Migration

TABLE 3. SURVEY OF *Condor* RAPTOR ARTICLES BY PERIODIC INTERVALS

Year	Total articles in volume	Raptor articles (%)	General content
1899	83	8 (10)	Mainly egg collecting or occurrence records (including capture methods for the California Condor).
1925	90	4 (4)	Mainly notes on food habits, distribution or status, and behavior (does not include the bird banding section or "Birds of . . . " articles).
1955	89	8 (9)	Taxonomic, status/records of occurrence, physiology, ecology (including one lengthy annotated list "Birds of Mexico" with extensive raptor data), rare species.
1975	109	13 (12)	Several were notes, physiology (2), ecology (2), behavior (3), rare species, general biology, distribution.
1991	181	11 (6)	Migration, energetics, behavior, ecology, environment/conservation, molecular systematics, distribution.

data for the west started being collected some two decades ago (Hoffman 1985) and may prove valuable in detecting trends (Hussell 1985). To date most of the 15 species analyzed from migration data between 1977 and 1991 either were stable or showed an upward trend (Hoffman et al. 1992).

Generally, grassland and wetland species may have been more severely impacted than woodland species because of greater habitat loss. A decline in the Burrowing Owl may also reflect the loss of prairie dog towns. With alterations of wetlands one would also expect the Northern Harrier (*Circus cyaneus*) to have declined but current migration numbers do not indicate this. The White-tailed Kite's post-settlement decline in California (May 1935) was a classic example of the multiple negative effects of landscape alterations (Waian and Stendell 1970, Pruett-Jones et al. 1980). Reasons for the decline were not fully documented but

shooting, habitat alterations and subsequent reductions in the food base for this food specialist seem to have been involved. The kite represents an even more interesting example since currently, in the face of continued habitat alterations from native habitats to agriculture, it has conspicuously increased in the west in the past several decades and is also expanding its range (cf. Palmer 1988). Agricultural lands that replaced native habitats provided, however, stable habitats and their stability in turn seemingly provided the necessary elements for the increase of kites (Pruett-Jones et al. 1980).

CASE HISTORIES

To follow are sketches of population trends and changes in status of selected raptors over the past century. Most statements rely on data from the past three to four decades since intensive studies were not generally available prior to that time. These examples illustrate the diversity of factors affecting status.

Saw-whet Owl (Aegolius acadicus)

Early in this century the Saw-whet Owl was found only in the southeastern portion of Alaska (Gabrielson and Lincoln 1959). In adjacent British Columbia the species is still little known (perhaps rare) outside the southern half of the province (Campbell et al. 1990). Kessel and Gibson (1978) listed it as a probable breeder in the vicinity of Anchorage, Alaska. Over the past eight years Ted Swem (pers. comm. 1992) erected 110 owl nest boxes around Anchorage of which 25 different boxes were used by Saw-whet Owls. Annual use gradually increased over the eight years and 11 boxes were occupied in 1992.

Flammulated Owl (Otus flammeolus)

This owl, once thought to be rare, has proven to be rather common in appropriate habitats (see Johnsgard 1988). Its apparent increase probably resulted from greater search effort and better techniques. There is no evidence for a real population change and numbers can be sporadic. Marshall (1957), for example, found five singing males one season and 14 the next in the same area. Fortunately, they respond well to playback of recorded calls of their own and other species. While using playback calls and searching for Spotted Owls (*Strix occidentalis*) on the Dixie National Forest, Utah in 1990–1991, S. E. Rinkevich (pers. comm.) found that six owl species gave 280 independent responses. Flammulated Owls responded 116 times (41%) of the total, indicating their commonness.

Osprey, eagles and falcons

Several taxa, among them the Osprey (*Pandion haliaetus*), Bald Eagle, and at least three falcons, of which the Merlin and Peregrine are mentioned here, were all affected to some degree by synthetic agricultural biocides in the 1950s–1970s. All are now showing increases (Bird 1983, Cade et al. 1988). In western North America the Osprey was least affected, especially in Baja California (Henny and Anderson 1979) where, on the other hand, the Peregrine suffered severe declines (Cade et al. 1988). Ospreys responded well to artificial nest platforms, a fact that aided in their recovery and expansion (Poole 1989). Their increase in the west is reflected in migration counts at several observation stations between 1983–1991 (Hoffman et al. 1992).

The Bald Eagle suffered large losses from habitat alterations, bounties in Alaska, and biocide poisoning. The recovery plan for the "Pacific" population set a goal of 800 pairs (Steenhof 1990). Over the decade of the 1980s the numbers of pairs doubled in many states (e.g., Washington 99 to 398 pairs, Wyoming 19 to 49), and by 1990 there were 861 pairs (Steenhof 1990).

While the Merlin may be contracting from the southern portion of its range (e.g., Wyoming, pers. obs.) it has increased in some other areas (e.g., Alberta, R. Fyfe, pers. comm.) and spread into urban situations

(Oliphant and Haug 1985). With populations having been somewhat depressed because of biocides (Cade 1982), their increase was detectable in migration data at western localities (Hoffman et al. 1992). This increase was also seen on the nonbreeding grounds. In Utah, for example, the western prairie-parkland subspecies (*F. c. richardsoni*) (see Temple 1972) was represented by only three or four specimens before 1968. Many Merlins were seen or trapped each winter by competent observers between 1945 and 1968 (pers. obs.). None was *richardsoni*. Then in 1968, an adult female was found near Salt Lake City. Now, about 30% of all observations or specimens in Utah (1975–1992) are *richardsoni*. This may be a function of increasing populations, or may reflect a shift in the non-breeding range. Such shifts are not unknown and the occurrence and subsequent increase in wintering Bald Eagles in Utah since the 1930s represents an example (Palmer 1988, J. R. Murphy, pers. comm.).

The Peregrine Falcon may represent the best documented case of a decrease and subsequent increase. The species' decline in North America (Hickey 1969, Cade and Fyfe 1970) and recovery (White 1984, Cade et al. 1988) is well chronicled. Because pre-decline numbers were not known (cf. Bond 1946, Beebe 1960, and Cade 1960) several studies have tried to reconstruct that baseline (cf. Enderson 1965, Beebe 1969, Herman et al. 1970, Porter and White 1973, and Henny and Nelson 1981). However, their success in determining accurate numbers against which to measure recovery is debated.

The following numbers reflect the recovery: California, 38 pairs (1981) to 123 (1992) aided by reintroduction (Kirven and Walton 1992); Arizona, 17 (1980) to 179 (1992) by natural increase but also reflecting more extensive survey coverage (T. Tibbits, pers. comm.); and Colville River, arctic Alaska, 15 (1973) to 57 (1992) by natural increase (T. Swem, pers. comm.). Numbers have not increased proportionately in Alberta (Western Raptor Technical Committee 1988) and perhaps interior British Columbia (Campbell et al. 1990).

In addition to a residual wild population in the west, the recovery was aided by releasing captive bred falcons by The Peregrine Fund, the Canadian Wildlife Service, and other peregrine breeders. The Peregrine Fund (1992) released over 2200 young peregrines in the west between 1974 and 1991. There are approximately 550 known or suspected pairs currently (1992) in 12 western states (Recovery Team 1992) representing nearly 150 more pairs than thought necessary for down listing and about 100 more than had been documented historically for this same region.

Hawks

Three western hawks allegedly showed sufficient declines in the past two decades to receive special attention by the U.S. Fish and Wildlife Service. The Swainson's Hawk, mentioned earlier in connection with local declines in California and Oregon, was listed by a special designation in 1982 (U.S. Department of Interior 1982). It was not, however, on any U.S. Fish and Wildlife list in 1991 (U.S. Department of Interior 1991) because insufficient data indicated that it was threatened.

The Ferruginous Hawk, which also appeared on the 1982 list, was petitioned in May 1991 for listing as endangered. Widespread declines were believed to be human-caused: 1) by increased disturbance, 2) direct mortality, and 3) habitat alterations that reduced prey or nesting substrate (cf. Olendorff 1993). Some local populations have been entirely lost in the last two decades (Woffinden and Murphy 1989). However, almost 2000 more pairs than had been estimated for the species in 1979 were found recently (U.S. Department of Interior 1992a). The increase seems to be accounted for by denser populations in Canada (especially Alberta but also Manitoba) that more than offset losses elsewhere (U.S. Department of Interior 1992a).

In 1991 the Northern Goshawk (*Accipiter gentilis*) was believed to be seriously declining in Arizona, New Mexico, and southern Utah because of habitat loss or alteration and was petitioned for emergency listing (Silver 1991). Much of the petition was based on Crocker-Bedford (1990) who claimed a decline greater than 80% over presettlement populations. But goshawk populations, especially in the northern part of their range, fluctuate widely with oscillations of prey (e.g., rabbits, ground squirrels and grouse). There may have been local declines (cf. U.S. Department of Interior 1992b) and slight reductions generally over pre-settlement times, but increasing data suggest that the species is stable over most of its southern range.

Broad-winged Hawk (Buteo platypterus)

Although generally a species of the midwest and east, prior to the 1960s it was known to extend westward into Alberta (Salt and Wilk 1958, Godfrey 1966). It was neither recorded in Washington (Jewett et al. 1953), Oregon (Gabrielson and Jewett 1940), nor California (Grinnell and Miller 1944) nor mentioned in raptor literature for Nevada (Herron et al. 1985), Utah (Eyre and Paul 1973) and Wyoming (Williams and Matteson 1948). The first records for Arizona (1956), New Mexico (1951), and Nevada (1973) were of single specimens (Phillips et al. 1964, Hubbard 1970, Alcorn 1988). It was first recorded on the west coast in 1966 (McCaskie 1968) and was found with increasing frequency through the 1980s on Great Basin migration routes (Hoffman et al. 1992). This increase corresponded with an apparent population upswing in British Columbia, where first recorded in 1965, and by the 1980s was seen regularly in local areas (Campbell et al. 1990).

THE FUTURE

Senner et al. (1986) and Jehl (1986) attempted to predict future trends for North American birds, a difficult task. Some trends, however, seem likely. Some taxa may go extinct in the face of human impact and landscape use, as happened with the Guadalupe Caracara (*Caracara lutosus*) at the turn of the century. We know well the fate of the California Condor (*Gymnogypus californianus*). One wonders about the security of the Hawaiian Hawk (*Buteo solitarius*) if the brown tree snake (*Boiga irregularis*), which has caused havoc with birds in Guam, successfully reaches Hawaii. Perhaps most species will show declines because of continued habitat alterations. Habitat alterations may also increase the risk of predation by mammals (e.g., foxes and raccoons which increase as a result of those alterations). Burrowing and Short-eared Owls (*Asio flammeus*) may be especially vulnerable. In spite of the recovery of the Bald Eagle, continued habitat deterioration may cause another decline (K. Steenhof, pers. comm.). Habitat alterations are viewed as the main threat to the Northern Goshawk and Spotted Owl (Gutiérrez 1994). The Peregrine Falcon, Osprey, Bald Eagle and White-tailed Kite are examples of significant recovery, following very severe declines, even to the point of expanding their ranges and overshooting their presumed historical levels (e.g., Peregrine). Some raptors viewed as real "wilderness" species are adapting to human use of the environment; Prairie Falcons use power transmission towers and Gyrfalcons (*Falco rusticolus*) occupy oil pipelines for nesting (Roppe et al. 1989, Ritchie 1991).

An optimistic future, however, seems to lie with raptors that can adapt to urbanization within the human matrix (e.g., American Kestrels, Red-tailed Hawk, Merlins [in Canada] and Red-shouldered Hawks (*Buteo lineatus*) [in California]). The latter example has involved behavioral changes and smaller territory sizes in highly urbanized areas (Bloom et al. 1993) beyond those reported by Wiley (1975). In addition to breeding of Peregrine Falcons in many major cities in North America, the Cooper's Hawk (*Accipiter cooperii*) now nests in a busy city park in the center of Salt Lake City, Utah. If these two species can breed in cities, then we can expect others to follow. There is no reason why raptors could not be as "common" in urban situations as reported by Galushin (1971), who found an average density in Delhi, India to be approximately 19.3 pairs/km^2. For this to happen, however, the most important ingredient, in addition to food and nesting sites, will be, as Galushin found, the good will of people toward raptors.

ACKNOWLEDGMENTS

I thank the many people who suggested material, especially R. R. Olendorff, M. R. Fuller and R. L. Glinski who sent unpublished data.

LITERATURE CITED

ALCORN, J. R. 1988. The birds of Nevada. Fairview West Press, Fallon, NV.

BEEBE, F. L. 1960. The marine peregrines of the northwest Pacific coast. Condor 62:145–189.

BEEBE, F. L. 1969. The known status of the Peregrine Falcon in British Columbia. Pp. 53–60 *in* J. J. Hickey (ed.), Peregrine Falcon populations: their biology and decline. The University of Wisconsin Press, Madison, WI.

BENDIRE, C. 1877. Notes on some of the birds found in southeastern Oregon, particularly in the vicinity of Camp Harney, from November 1874 to January 1877. Biological Society of Natural History, Proceedings 19:109–149.

BIRD, D. M. (chief ed.). 1983. Biology and management of Bald Eagles and Ospreys. Harpell Press, Ste. Anne de Bellevue, Quebec, Canada.

BLOOM, P. H., D. M. MCCRAARY, AND M. J. GIBSON. 1993. Red-shouldered Hawk home-range and habitat use in southern California. Journal of Wildlife Management 57:258–265.

BOND, R. M. 1946. The peregrine population in western North America. Condor 48:101–116.

CADE, T. J. 1960. Ecology of the peregrine and Gyrfalcon populations in Alaska. University of California Publications in Zoology 63:151–290.

CADE, T. J. 1982. The falcons of the world. Comstock, Cornell University Press, Ithaca, NY.

CADE, T. J., AND R. W. FYFE. 1970. The North American peregrine survey, 1970. Canadian Field-Naturalist 84:231–247.

CADE, T. J., J. H. ENDERSON, C. G. THELANDER, AND C. M. WHITE (eds.). 1988. Peregrine Falcon populations: their management and recovery. The Peregrine Fund, Boise, ID.

CAMERON, E. S. 1907. The birds of Custer and Dawson counties, Montana. Auk 24:241–270.

CAMPBELL, R. W., N. K. DAWE, I. MCTAGGART-COWAN, J. M. COOPER, G. W. KAISER, AND C. E. MCNALL. 1990. The birds of British Columbia, Vol. II nonpasserines. Royal British Columbia Museum, Victoria, B.C.

CROCKER-BEDFORD, D. C. 1990. Goshawk reproduction and forest management. Wildlife Society Bulletin 18:262–269.

ENDERSON, J. H. 1965. A breeding and migration

survey of the Peregrine Falcon. Wilson Bulletin 77: 327–339.

EYRE, L., AND D. PAUL. 1973. Raptors of Utah. Utah Division of Wildlife Resources Publication No. 73-7, 2nd edition.

EVANS, D. L. 1982. Status reports on twelve raptors. U.S. Fish and Wildlife Service, Special Scientific Report—Wildlife No. 238.

GABRIELSON, I. N., AND S. G. JEWETT. 1940. Birds of Oregon. Oregon State College, Corvallis, OR.

GABRIELSON, I. N., AND F. C. LINCOLN. 1959. The birds of Alaska. Stackpole Co. and Wildlife Management Institute, Washington, D.C.

GALUSHIN, V. M. 1971. A huge urban population of birds of prey in Delhi, India (preliminary note). Ibis 113:522.

GLINSKI, R. L., B. G. PENDLETON, M. B. MOSS, M. N. LEFRANC, JR., B. A. MILLSAP, AND S. W. HOFFMAN (eds.). 1988. Proceedings of the Southwest raptor management symposium and workshop, Technical Series No. 11. National Wildlife Federation, Washington, D.C.

GODFREY, W. E. 1966. The birds of Canada. National Museum of Canada Bulletin 203. Ottawa, Canada.

GRINNELL, J., AND A. H. MILLER. 1944. The distribution of the birds of California. Pacific Coast Avifauna No. 27.

GUTIÉRREZ, R. J. 1994. Changes in the distribution and abundance of Spotted Owls during the past century. Pp. 293–300 in J. R. Jehl, Jr. and N. K. Johnson (eds.), A century of avifaunal change in western North America. Studies in Avian Biology No. 15.

HANSEN, A. J., AND J. I. HODGES, JR. 1985. High rates of nonbreeding adult Bald Eagles in southeastern Alaska. Journal of Wildlife Management 49:454–458.

HECTOR, D. P. 1987. The decline of the Aplomado Falcon in the United States. American Birds 41:4381–4389.

HENNY, C. J., AND D. W. ANDERSON. 1979. Osprey distribution, abundance, and status in western North America: III. The Baja California and Gulf of California populations. Bulletin of the Southern California Academy of Sciences 78:89–106.

HENNY, C. J., AND M. W. NELSON. 1981. Decline and present status of breeding Peregrine Falcons in Oregon. Murrelet 62:43–53.

HERMAN, S. G., M. N. KIRVEN, AND R. W. RISEBROUGH. 1970. The Peregrine Falcon decline in California: I. A preliminary review. Audubon Field Notes 24:609–613.

HERRON, G. B., C. A. MORTIMORE, AND M. S. RAWLINGS. 1985. Nevada raptors: their biology and management. Biological Bulletin No. 8, Nevada Department of Wildlife, Reno, NV.

HICKEY, J. J. (ed.). 1969. Peregrine Falcon populations: their biology and decline. The University of Wisconsin Press, Madison, WI.

HOFFMAN, S. W. 1985. Raptor movements in inland western North America: a synthesis. Pp. 325–338 in M. Harwood (ed.), Proceedings of the Hawk Migration Conference IV. Hawk Migration Association of North America, Bothell, WA.

HOFFMAN, S. W., W. R. DERAGON, AND J. C. BEDNARZ. 1992. Patterns and recent trends in counts of mi-grant hawks in western North America. Unpubl. ms. HawkWatch International, Albuquerque, NM.

HUBBARD, J. P. 1970. Check-list of the birds of New Mexico. New Mexico Ornithological Society Publication No. 3.

HUSSELL, D. T. 1985. Analysis of hawk migration counts for monitoring population levels. Pp. 243–254 in M. Harwood (ed.), Hawk migration conference IV. Proceedings of the Hawk Migration Association of North America, Bothell, WA.

JAMES, P. C. 1988. Urban Merlins in Canada. British Birds 81:274–277.

JEHL, J. R., JR. 1986. Status and trends in the birdlife of the United States. President's Council on Environmental Quality, Washington, D.C. Annual Report, No. 17, pp. 1–64.

JEWETT, S. G., W. P. TAYLOR, W. T. SHAW, AND J. W. ALDRICH. 1953. Birds of Washington State. University of Washington Press, Seattle, WA.

JOHNSGARD, P. A. 1988. North American owls, biology and natural history. Smithsonian Institution Press, Washington, D.C.

JOHNSGARD, P. A. 1990. Hawks, eagles and falcons of North America. Smithsonian Institution Press, Washington, D.C.

JOHNSON, H. C. 1899. A successful day with the Duck Hawk. Condor 1:45–46.

KESSEL, B., AND D. D. GIBSON. 1978. Status and distribution of Alaskan birds. Studies in Avian Biology 1:1–100.

KIRVEN, M. N., AND B. J. WALTON. 1992. The Peregrine Falcon population recovery in California from 1981 to 1992. Report to U.S. Bureau of Land Management State Office, Sacramento, CA.

LADD, W. H., AND P. F. SCHEMPF (eds.). 1982. Proceedings of a symposium, raptor management and biology in Alaska and western Canada. U.S. Fish and Wildlife Service, Anchorage, AK, FWS/AK/PROC-82.

LEFRANC, M. N., JR., AND B. A. MILLSAP. 1984. A summary of state and federal agency raptor management programs. Wildlife Society Bulletin 12:274–282.

LITTLEFIELD, C. D., S. P. THOMPSON, AND B. D. EHLERS. 1984. History and present status of Swainson's Hawk in southeast Oregon. Raptor Research 18:1–5.

MARSHALL, J. T., JR. 1957. Birds of pine-oak woodland in southern Arizona and adjacent Mexico. Pacific Coast Avifauna, No. 32.

MAY, J. B. 1935. The hawks of North America. National Audubon Society, New York.

McCASKIE, R. G. 1968. A Broad-winged Hawk in California. Condor 70:93.

MORRISON, M. L. 1983. Bird populations as indicators of environmental change. Current Ornithology 3:429–451.

NATIONAL WILDLIFE FEDERATION. 1989. Proceedings of the Western raptor management symposium and workshop, Technical Series No. 12, National Wildlife Federation, Washington, D.C.

OLENDORFF, R. R. 1993. Status, biology and management of Ferruginous Hawks (Buteo regalis): a review. Raptor Research and Technical Assistance Center Occasional Paper No. 1, Bureau of Land Management, Boise, ID.

OLIPHANT, L. W., AND E. HAUG. 1985. Productivity, population density and rate of increase of an expanding Merlin population. Raptor Research 19:56–59.

PALMER, R. S. (ed.). 1988. Handbook of North American birds, Vols. 4 and 5. Diurnal raptors, Parts 1 and 2. Yale University Press, New Haven, CT.

PHILLIPS, A., J. MARSHALL, AND G. MONSON. 1964. The birds of Arizona. University of Arizona Press, Tucson, AZ.

POOLE, A. F. 1989. Ospreys, a natural and unnatural history. Cambridge University Press, Cambridge, UK.

PORTER, R. D., AND C. M. WHITE. 1973. The Peregrine Falcon in Utah, emphasizing ecology and competition with the Prairie Falcon. Brigham Young University Science Bulletin, Biological Series 18(1): 1–74.

PORTER, R. D., AND C. M. WHITE. 1975. Status of some rare and lesser known hawks in western North America. Pp. 31–57 *in* R. D. Chancellor (ed.), Proceedings, First World Conference Birds of Prey, International Council for Bird Preservation, Vienna, Austria.

PRUETT-JONES, S. G., M. A. PRUETT-JONES, AND R. L. KNIGHT. 1980. The White-tailed Kite in North and Middle America: current status and recent population changes. American Birds 34:682–688.

RECOVERY TEAM. 1992. Addendum to the Pacific Coast and Rocky Mountain/Southwest Peregrine Falcon recovery plan, (Draft). Typed report August 1992 to U.S. Fish and Wildlife Service Regions 1,2,6, by the Western Peregrine Falcon Recovery Team.

RISEBROUGH, R. W., R. W. SCHLORFF, P. H. BLOOM, AND E. L. LITTRELL. 1989. Investigations of the decline of Swainson's Hawk populations in California. Raptor Research 23:63–71.

RITCHIE, R. J. 1991. Effects of oil development on providing nesting opportunities for Gyrfalcons and Rough-legged Hawks in northern Alaska. Condor 93:180–183.

ROBBINS, C. S., D. BYSTRAK, AND P. H. GEISSLER. 1986. The breeding bird survey: its first fifteen years, 1965–1979. Resource Publication 157, U.S. Fish and Wildlife Service, Washington, D.C.

ROPPE, J. A., S. M. SIEGEL, AND S. E. WILDER. 1989. Prairie Falcon nesting on transmission towers. Condor 91:711–712.

SALT, W. R., AND A. L. WILK. 1958. The birds of Alberta. The Queen's Printer, Edmonton, Canada.

SENNER, S. C., C. M. WHITE, AND J. R. PARRISH (eds.). 1986. Raptor conservation in the next 50 years. Raptor Research Report No. 5, Raptor Research Foundation, Inc.

SILVER, R. D. 1991. Formal petition to list the isolated regional population of Northern Goshawk (*Accipiter gentilis*) in the southwestern United States. Correspondence to Mr. Secretary, Manuel Lujan, Department of Interior, Washington, D.C.

SNYDER, N. F. R., AND H. A. SNYDER. 1989. Biology and conservation of the California Condor. Current Ornithology 6:175–276.

SNYDER, N., AND H. SNYDER. 1991. Birds of prey; natural history and conservation on North American raptors. Voyageur Press, Stillwater, MN.

SPENCER, C. N., B. R. MCCLELLAND, AND J. A. STANFORD. 1991. Shrimp stocking, salmon collapse and eagle displacement. BioScience 41:14–21.

STEENHOF, K. 1990. The status of Bald Eagles in the Pacific Recovery Region in relation to recovery goals, 1990. Unpubl. ms., Bureau of Land Management, Boise, ID.

STEENHOF, K. (ed.). 1993. Wingspan 2(1). Raptor Research & Technical Assistance Center, Boise, ID.

TATE, J., JR. 1986. The blue list for 1986. American Birds 40:227–236.

TEMPLE, S. A. 1972. Systematics and evolution of the North American Merlin. Auk 89:325–338.

TEMPLE, S. A., AND J. A. WIENS. 1989. Bird populations and environmental changes: can birds be bioindicators. American Birds 43:260–270.

THE PEREGRINE FUND, INC. 1992. Peregrine Falcon recovery program, status and recommendations. The Peregrine Fund, Boise, ID.

U.S. DEPARTMENT OF INTERIOR. 1982. Endangered and threatened wildlife and plants; review of vertebrate wildlife for listing as endangered or threatened, Part II. Federal Register 47:58454–58460.

U.S. DEPARTMENT OF INTERIOR. 1991. Endangered and threatened wildlife and plants; animal candidate review for listing, proposed rule: Part VIII. Federal Register 56:58804–58836.

U.S. DEPARTMENT OF INTERIOR. 1992a. Endangered and threatened wildlife and plants; notice of findings on petition to list the Ferruginous Hawk. Federal Register 57:37507–37513.

U.S. DEPARTMENT OF INTERIOR. 1992b. Endangered and threatened wildlife and plants; notice of 90 day finding on petition to list the Northern Goshawk as endangered or threatened in the southwestern United States. Federal Register 57:546–548.

U.S. DEPARTMENT OF INTERIOR. 1992c. Endangered and threatened wildlife and plants. 50 CFR 17.11 & 17.12, August 29, 1992.

VOOUS, K. H. 1988. Owls of the northern hemisphere. The MIT Press, Cambridge, MA.

WAIAN, L., AND R. E. STENDELL. 1970. The White-tailed Kite in California with observations on the Santa Barbara population. California Fish and Game 56:188–198.

WESTERN RAPTOR TECHNICAL COMMITTEE. 1988. *Anatum* Peregrine Falcon recovery plan. Canadian Wildlife Service, Ottawa, CW-66-97/1988E.

WHITE, C. M. 1974. Current problems and techniques in raptor management and conservation. Transactions of the 39th North American Wildlife Natural Resource Conference, pp. 301–312.

WHITE, C. M. 1984. The beginning of an endangered species' comeback: the Peregrine Falcon. American Biological Teacher 46:212–220.

WHITE, C. M. 1990. Reflections on time and attitudes. The Eyas 13:47–49.

WHITE, C. M., D. A. BOYCE, JR., AND R. STRANECK. 1989. Observations on *Buteo swainsoni* in Argentina, 1984 with comments on food, habitat alterations and agricultural chemicals. Pp. 79–87 *in* B-U Meyburg and R. D. Chancellor (eds.), Raptors in the modern world. World Working Group, Birds of Prey, London, UK.

WILEY, J. 1975. The nesting and reproductive success

of Red-tailed Hawks and Red-shouldered Hawks in Orange County, California. Condor 77:133–139.

WILLIAMS, R. B., AND C. P. MATTESON, JR. 1948. Wyoming hawks. Wyoming Fish and Game Department Bulletin No. 5, Cheyenne, WY.

WOFFINDEN, N. D., AND J. R. MURPHY. 1989. Decline of a Ferruginous Hawk population: a 20-year summary. Journal of Wildlife Management 53:1127–1132.

Studies in Avian Biology No. 15:173–190, 1994.

POPULATION TRENDS IN THE LANDBIRDS OF WESTERN NORTH AMERICA

DAVID F. DeSANTE AND T. LUKE GEORGE

Abstract.   We examined avifaunal literature of the states and provinces of western North America to gather evidence of population changes in landbirds over the past 100 years, and we analyzed population trend ranks (PTRs) developed by Carter and Barker for migratory landbirds from 26 years of North American Breeding Bird Survey (BBS) data for western states. We identified 75 native landbird species whose breeding populations decreased substantially in at least one state or province in the past 100 years and 65 species that increased. Destruction of riparian habitat, destruction of grasslands, shooting, overgrazing, logging and clearing of forests, and cowbird parasitism were the major factors responsible for the decreases, while increased agricultural, suburban, and urban development and irrigation were the major factors responsible for the increases. We identified 58 species of migratory landbirds that showed decreasing population trends in either the past 26 or past 13 years, 44 species that showed increasing trends, and 35 species that showed no trends. Significantly more short-distance migrants decreased during the past 26 years than increased (P < 0.001) but no such relationship existed for long-distance migrants, which generally showed fewer and smaller decreasing trends and more increasing trends than short-distance migrants. Populations of most short- and long-distance migrants generally fared better during the past 13 years than during the past 26 years. Our results qualitatively agree with other analyses of BBS data that do not include information on the magnitude or uncertainty of the population trends, but quantitatively tend to show more and stronger negative trends. Finally, we discuss limitations of BBS data and suggest key elements for an integrated population monitoring system for western landbirds.

Key Words: Population trends; landbirds; western North America; BBS.

The Centennial Year of the Cooper Ornithological Society, 1993, marks the milestone of 100 years of organized study of birds in western North America. As such, it is a fitting time to review what is known of the population changes in the landbirds of western North America, particularly in light of the extensive human-caused environmental changes that have occurred over the past century. Moreover, attention has been focused recently on populations of Neotropical migratory landbirds that appear to be declining, at least in eastern North America (Robbins et al. 1989, Terborgh 1989, Askins et al. 1990). The Neotropical Migratory Bird Conservation Program, "Partners in Flight," was established in 1991 to reverse these apparent population declines. Many federal and state agencies and private organizations have become involved with this program and are committed to its goal.

In this paper, western North America is defined as all states west of Montana, Wyoming, Colorado, and New Mexico inclusive, along with Alberta, British Columbia, Yukon Territory, and Alaska. This area thus includes all of continental North America west of and including the Rocky Mountains (except for the mountains of western Texas and a portion of the Black Hills of South Dakota and Nebraska), along with the western edge of the Great Plains.

Despite the fact that this huge area includes much of the least populated portions of North America, the human-caused environmental changes wrought on this region have been enormous. Most of the watersheds have been dammed, diverted, or otherwise managed; most of the grasslands and even much of the forests, scrublands, and deserts have been grazed (or overgrazed) by cattle, sheep, and horses, and a great proportion of the native perennial grasses has been replaced by introduced annuals; virtually all of the forests have been harvested at least once and most have undergone many years of attempted fire suppression; and the natural habitats of the valleys and surrounding hills of many areas have been converted to agriculture, industry, and housing.

Two basic types of avifaunal changes could accompany these human-induced environmental changes. First are population changes in which the numbers of birds of any given species increase or decrease during the breeding season, nonbreeding season, or migration periods; second are distribution (range or habitat) changes in which species appear or disappear from certain areas or habitats. Both types are intimately related: when population size for a given species in a given area decreases to (or increases from) zero, a distributional change has taken place. Despite this inter-relatedness, the two types of changes do not always occur in parallel. It is possible, for example, for a species to be undergoing major population declines over much of its range and still be expanding its range elsewhere.

Here we concentrate on population changes in western landbirds, especially those changes that may be anthropogenically caused. Distributional changes in western landbirds, particularly those caused by "natural" climatic changes, are the focus of a paper by Johnson (1994). Population changes were assessed by two methods. First, we perused the avifaunal literature for general evidence of population changes over the past 100 years. Second, for quantitative evidence, we analyzed population trend ranks developed by Carter and Barker (1993) from 26 years of data from the North American Breeding Bird Survey (BBS) (Robbins et al. 1986) and compared our results to those obtained recently by Sauer and Droege (1992) and Peterjohn and Sauer (1993). We discuss these population changes in terms of their possible causes, general population dynamic considerations, and the adequacy of the data. Finally, we suggest key elements for an integrated population monitoring scheme for western landbirds.

METHODS

We reviewed major state-level literature on the distribution and abundance of birds in western North America for evidence of population changes in landbirds (Gabrielson and Jewett 1940, Grinnell and Miller 1944, Munro and McTaggert-Cowan 1947, Jewett et al. 1953, Gabrielson and Lincoln 1959, Ligon 1961, Phillips et al. 1964, Bailey and Niedrach 1967, Burleigh 1971, Behle and Perry 1975, Salt and Salt 1976, Alcorn 1988, Campbell et al. 1990). In general, these sources provided information on landbird population changes only when the distribution of a given species expanded or contracted over a substantial portion of the state or when population changes were so pronounced as to command attention. Very little mention was made of more subtle population trends, simply because no quantitative data existed from which such trends could be extrapolated. We also compared abundance designations provided by these sources with those compiled by DeSante and Pyle (1986) for each state and province for additional evidence of population changes, as well as the USFWS list of species of management concern (Office of Migratory Bird Management 1987).

The BBS, begun in 1965 (1968 in western North America), is the only quantitative source of information regarding regional changes in the breeding populations of western landbirds. The BBS consists of more than 2000 randomly located permanent survey routes established along secondary roads throughout the continental United States and southern Canada that are surveyed annually during the height of the breeding season, usually in June (Robbins et al. 1986). Each route is 39.4 km long and consists of 50 stops spaced at 0.8-km intervals. Observers start 0.5 hr before local sunrise and at each stop count all birds detected within a 0.4-km radius circle during a 3-min period. For each species, the total number of individuals recorded at all stops along the route is used as an index of relative abundance. Long-term population trends for each of about 370 species are provided by the BBS for every state and province in North America by a route-regression method. Route trends are estimated using a linear regression of the log-transformed counts on year, with observer data included as covariables. The slope of the year variable, when back-transformed, provides the estimate of route trend for a species. Regional trends are estimated from weighted averages of the route trends (Sauer and Droege 1992, Peterjohn and Sauer 1993).

Using these population trend data, Carter and Barker (1993) derived a population trend rank (PTR) and population trend uncertainty rank (PTUR) for each migratory landbird species in each of the 11 western states. The PTUR was based on the number of routes in a state on which a species was recorded, the number of routes with a statistically significant trend for the species, and the proportion of routes with trends that agreed with the overall state trend for the species. The PTR was based upon the magnitude and direction of the trend and the associated PTUR. Carter and Barker's PTR indices are as follows: 1 = definite increase—moderate increase (>1% but <5% annually) with very low uncertainty, or large increase (>5% annually) with low or very low uncertainty; 2 = increasing trend—small increase (<1% annually) with low or very low uncertainty, moderate increase with moderate or low uncertainty, or large increase with moderate uncertainty; 3 = trend unknown—small increase or decrease (<1% annually) with moderate uncertainty or any increase or decrease with high uncertainty; 4 = decreasing trend—small decrease with low or very low uncertainty, moderate decrease (>1% but <5% annually) with moderate or low uncertainty, or large decrease (>5% annually) with moderate uncertainty; and 5 = definite decrease—moderate decrease with very low uncertainty or large decrease with low or very low uncertainty. Carter and Barker calculated these PTRs separately for the entire 26-year period that the BBS has been in operation (1966–1991; actually only 1968–1991 in western North America) and for the most recent 13 years (1979–1991).

We examined Carter and Barker's PTRs and identified those species that exhibited consistently decreasing (more than 50% of the states for which data were sufficient to calculate trends showed decreasing trends or definite decreases, and no more than 25% of the states showed increasing trends or definite increases) or increasing (vice versa) trends in either time period. We then examined these lists for overall patterns with regard to the migratory status of the species. Because the data from the 13-year period are included within the 26-year data set, the two data sets are not independent. Thus, it is invalid to use inferential statistics to analyze differences in trends between these periods (Sauer and Droege 1992). Therefore, we compared the trends between the 26-year and 13-year periods in a qualitative manner to determine whether or not there were consistent changes between the two periods. Finally, we compared these results to other analyses of BBS data and to other data sets and to the general historical information that we assembled.

RESULTS

A review of the major state-level avifaunal literature produced a list of 75 native landbird species whose breeding populations were known to have decreased substantially in at least one state or province in western North America in the past 100 years (Table 1; see Appendix for scientific names). Although these species were nearly equally divided between passerines (41, 55%) and non-passerines (34, 45%), the most severe and widespread declines were generally among the larger non-passerine species, particularly various grouse (especially grassland species), Yellow-billed Cuckoo, and Burrowing Owl. Except for (Masked) Northern Bobwhite in Arizona, these were the only landbird species to have been extirpated from any of the western states or provinces. Shooting was a major contributor to the decline of some of these larger non-passerines, although habitat loss and overgrazing were probably more important and pervasive factors. Some of these species have mostly recovered or at least stabilized since shooting was regulated earlier in this

TABLE 1. NATIVE SPECIES OF LANDBIRDS KNOWN TO HAVE DECREASED IN WESTERN NORTH AMERICA OVER THE PAST 100 YEARS, STATES (OR PROVINCES) WHERE THEY HAVE DECREASED, AND PROBABLE CAUSES FOR THEIR DECREASES. UNDERLINED STATES (OR PROVINCES) ARE AREAS WHERE MAJOR DECREASES (>50% POPULATION DECLINES) HAVE OCCURRED; * = EXTIRPATED

Species	Where decreased	Probable causes
Spruce Grouse	AK AB WA	Shooting, clearing of forests
Blue Grouse	BC WA OR CA NV ID CO AZ NM	Shooting, clearing of forests
White-tailed Ptarmigan	WY NM	Unknown
Ruffed Grouse	WA OR CA	Shooting
Sage Grouse	BC* AB WA OR CA NV ID MT UT NM*	Shooting, overgrazing, destruction of grasslands
Greater Prairie-Chicken	AB* MT* CO	Shooting, destruction of grasslands
Lesser Prairie-Chicken	CO NM	Shooting, destruction of grasslands
Sharp-tailed Grouse	AK BC AB WA OR* CA* NV* ID MT WY UT CO NM*	Shooting, overgrazing, destruction of grasslands
Wild Turkey	CO AZ NM	Shooting
Montezuma Quail	AZ NM	Overgrazing
Northern Bobwhite	WY AZ* NM	Overgrazing, hunting
Scaled Quail	AZ NM	Overgrazing, destruction of grassland
California Quail	CA	Shooting (essentially recovered at present)
Mountain Quail	CA	Shooting (mostly recovered at present)
Band-tailed Pigeon	WA OR CA	Shooting (mostly recovered at present)
Yellow-billed Cuckoo	BC* WA* OR* CA NV ID UT AZ	Destruction of riparian habitat
Greater Roadrunner	CA	Agricultural development, urbanization
Northern Hawk-Owl	AB	Clearing of forests
Ferruginous Pygmy-Owl	AZ	Destruction of riparian habitat
Elf Owl	CA	Destruction of riparian habitat
Burrowing Owl	BC AB* CA NV ID MT CO AZ NM	Destruction of grasslands, elimination of fossorial mammals, agricultural development, urbanization
Spotted Owl	BC CA AZ	Logging, particularly of old-growth forests
Long-eared Owl	CA NV	Destruction of riparian habitat
Short-eared Owl	CA NM	Destruction of grasslands
Lesser Nighthawk	NM	Pesticide use?
Common Nighthawk	AB	Pesticide use?
White-throated Swift	CA AZ	Unknown
White-eared Hummingbird	AZ	Unknown
Belted Kingfisher	OR CA AZ	Shooting by fisherman (entirely recovered at present)
Lewis' Woodpecker	BC OR CA UT	Cutting of old oak woodlands and snags, competition with starlings
Gila Woodpecker	CA	Destruction of riparian habitat
Ladder-backed Woodpecker	AZ	Unknown (destruction of mesquite woodlands?)
Northern (Gilded) Flicker	CA AZ	Destruction of riparian habitat
Pileated Woodpecker	CA	Logging (partially recovered because of increasing adaptation to second-growth forests)
Olive-sided Flycatcher	CA	Destruction of wintering habitat?
Willow Flycatcher	CA AZ	Destruction of riparian habitat, cowbird parasitism
Buff-breasted Flycatcher	AZ	Overgrazing of woodland habitat
Vermillion Flycatcher	CA NV	Destruction of riparian habitat
Cassin's Kingbird	CA	Unknown
Horned Lark	AZ	Destruction of grasslands
Purple Martin	WA OR CA AZ	Competition with starlings, snag removal (some increases recorded early in the century)

TABLE 1. CONTINUED

Species	Where decreased	Probable causes
Bank Swallow	CA	Channelization and bank stabilization of rivers
Chihuahuan Raven	CO	Unknown
Common Raven	OR CA	Unknown (local reductions, now increasing?)
Cactus Wren	CA	Urbanization
California Gnatcatcher	CA	Urbanization
Western Bluebird	NV AZ	Competition with starlings, overgrazing of woodland habitat
Mountain Bluebird	AB NV	Competition with starlings
Crissal Thrasher	CA	Destruction of riparian mesquite habitat
LeConte's Thrasher	CA AZ	Loss of habitat to agriculture?
Sprague's Pipit	AB	Destruction of grasslands
Loggerhead Shrike	CA	Pesticides?
Bell's Vireo	CA AZ	Cowbird parasitism, destruction of riparian habitat
Gray Vireo	CA AZ	Cowbird parasitism?
Lucy's Warbler	CA AZ	Destruction of riparian mesquite habitat
Yellow Warbler	OR CA AZ	Cowbird parasitism, destruction of riparian habitat
Common Yellowthroat	CA AZ	Drainage of marshes and loss of riparian habitat, cowbird parasitism?
Yellow-breasted Chat	CA NV	Destruction of riparian habitat, cowbird parasitism?
Summer Tanager	CA AZ	Destruction of riparian habitat
Lazuli Bunting	UT	Unknown
Painted Bunting	AZ	Unknown
Dickcissel	AZ	Degradation of wintering habitat?
Botteri's Sparrow	AZ	Overgrazing, destruction of grasslands
Rufous-winged Sparrow	AZ	Overgrazing
Chipping Sparrow	BC WA OR	Unknown (cowbird parasitism?)
Vesper Sparrow	WA OR	Destruction of grasslands?
Black-throated Sparrow	NV	Unknown
Lark Bunting	CA NV	Destruction of grasslands
Baird's Sparrow	AB AZ	Destruction of grasslands
Grasshopper Sparrow	BC WA NV UT CO	Unknown
Song Sparrow	AZ	Destruction of marshes and riparian habitat
McCown's Longspur	AB AZ NM	Destruction of grasslands
Chestnut-collared Longspur	AB AZ NM	Destruction of grasslands
Tricolored Blackbird	CA	Drainage of marshes, pesticides?
Yellow-headed Blackbird	CA	Drainage of marshes

century, although Burrowing Owls and grassland grouse continue to decline and Yellow-billed Cuckoos only persist in very small numbers.

Destruction of riparian habitat was implicated as a cause of decline for the largest number of species (16); destruction of grassland habitat was a close second (15 species), followed by shooting (13), overgrazing (9), logging and clearing of forests (7), cowbird parasitism (7), destruction of marshes (4), urbanization (4), competition with starlings for nest holes (4), possible pesticide use (4), possible degradation of tropical wintering habitat (2), agricultural development of desert habitat (2), streambank channelization and stabilization (1), and elimination of fossorial mammals (1). Permanent resident species comprised the largest proportion (38.7%) of the 75 decreasing species, followed by short-distance (32.0%) and long-distance (29.3%) migrants.

A list of 65 landbird species whose breeding populations were known to have in-

TABLE 2. Species of Landbirds Known to Have Increased in Western North America over the Past 100 Years, States (or Provinces) Where They Have Increased, and Probable Causes for Their Increases. Underlined States (or Provinces) Are Areas Where Major Increases (>50% Population Increases) Have Occurred

Species	Where increased	Probable causes
Rock Dove	BC AB WA OR CA NV ID MT WY UT CO AZ NM	Range expansion, urbanization, agricultural practices, development
Band-tailed Pigeon	BC	Northward range expansion
Mourning Dove	BC WA OR	Clearing of forests, agricultural practices, urbanization
Inca Dove	NV AZ NM	Urbanization, range expansion
Common Ground-Dove	CA AZ	Agricultural practices, irrigation
Barn Owl	BC CA	Agriculture, increased nesting sites, range expansion
Western Screech-Owl	CA	Logging, settlement of grassland (recent decreases have occurred)
Barred Owl	BC WA OR CA ID	Westward and southward range expansion
Whip-poor-will	CA NV UT	Northward range expansion
White-throated Swift	BC OR	Range expansion
Berylline Hummingbird	AZ	Northward range expansion
Violet-crowned Hummingbird	AZ	Northward range expansion
Magnificent Hummingbird	CO	Northward range expansion
Black-chinned Hummingbird	BC	Flower gardens and feeders
Anna's Hummingbird	BC WA OR CA	Flower gardens and feeders
Allen's Hummingbird	CA	Flower gardens and feeders
Red-headed Woodpecker	NM	Westward range expansion (following telephone poles?)
Williamson's Sapsucker	BC	Westward range expansion
Hammond's Flycatcher	AK	Northward range expansion
Black Phoebe	NM	Agricultural practices, irrigation
Brown-crested Flycatcher	NV UT	Northward range expansion
Tropical Kingbird	AZ	Northward range expansion
Thick-billed Kingbird	AZ	Northward range expansion
Western Kingbird	WA	Settlement of grasslands
Scissor-tailed Flycatcher	NM	Settlement of grasslands
Rose-throated Becard	AZ	Northward range expansion
Cliff Swallow	AK AB WA OR CA	Increased nesting sites
Cave Swallow	AZ NM	Northward range expansion, increased nesting sites
Barn Swallow	AK AB WA OR CA	Increased nesting sites
Blue Jay	MT WY CO	Westward range expansion
Black-billed Magpie	AK AB	Range expansion following development
American Crow	AB WA OR CA NV NM	Increased agriculture and urbanization
Common Raven	AK AB	Range expansion following development
Verdin	AZ	Increase in brushlands
Bushtit	BC CA	Increased development and urbanization
White-breasted Nuthatch	AB	Northward range expansion
American Robin	CA	Increased development and urbanization
Northern Mockingbird	AB OR CA NV	Increased development and urbanization, northward range expansion
Brown Thrasher	AB	Northward range expansion
Bendire's Thrasher	AZ	Agricultural practices and development
Curve-billed Thrasher	AZ	Development and urbanization
White Wagtail	AK	Range expansion
American Pipit	CA NV	Westward range expansion
European Starling	AK BC AB WA OR CA NV ID MT WY UT CO AZ NM	Range expansion, agricultural practices, development, urbanization
Warbling Vireo	BC AB WA OR	Increased adaptation to towns
Townsend's Warbler	OR	Unknown
Grace's Warbler	NV CO	Northward range expansion
Red-faced Warbler	AZ	Northward range expansion

TABLE 2. Continued

Species	Where increased	Probable causes
Painted Redstart	NV	Northward range expansion
Hepatic Tanager	CA NV	Northward range expansion
Northern Cardinal	AZ	Range expansion
Indigo Bunting	AZ	Range expansion
California Towhee	CA	Development and urbanization
Song Sparrow	CA	Agricultural practices (irrigation)
Bobolink	AB WA OR CA	Westward range expansion, agricultural practices, irrigation (more recently, numbers have decreased)
Red-winged Blackbird	CA	Agricultural practices, irrigation
Western Meadowlark	AB WA OR CA	Agricultural practices, irrigation
Brewer's Blackbird	CA	Development, urbanization
Great-tailed Grackle	CA NV UT CO AZ NM	Range expansion, agricultural practices, development
Bronzed Cowbird	AZ	Range expansion, livestock, agricultural practices
Brown-headed Cowbird	BC WA OR CA NV AZ	Livestock, agricultural practices, range expansion
Hooded Oriole	CA AZ	Planting of palm trees, urbanization, range expansion
House Finch	BC AB WA OR CA	Development, urbanization, agricultural practices
American Goldfinch	WA	Development, spread of agriculture
House Sparrow	BC AB WA OR CA NV ID MT WY UT CO AZ NM	Range expansion, urbanization, agricultural practices, development

creased substantially in at least one state or province in western North America in the past 100 years is presented in Table 2. In contrast to the decreasing species, the majority (47, 72%) were passerines; moreover, six of the 18 increasing non-passerine species were hummingbirds. The most frequent cause for population increase was range expansion (38 species), particularly northward range expansion (18 species; see also Johnson 1994).

Increased agriculture was implicated as a cause for the next largest number of increasing species (17), followed by increased development (14), urbanization (14), irrigation (5), increases in nesting sites (4), settlement of grassland (3), flower gardens and hummingbird feeders (3), clearing of trees (2), livestock practices (2), increases in brushland (1), planting of palm trees (1), and adaptation to towns (1). Three introduced species that arrived by range expansion from the east, Rock Dove, European Starling, and House Sparrow, showed the largest and most widespread increases. The next largest and

most widespread increases were shown by American Crow, Great-tailed Grackle, Brown-headed Cowbird, House Finch, Barn and Cliff swallows, and the rapidly expanding Barred Owl. All but the owl are closely tied to agricultural practices and urban development and adapt well to human modification of the environment. In contrast to decreasing species, long-distance migrants comprised the largest proportion (40.0%) of increasing species, followed by permanent residents (32.3%) and short-distance migrants (27.7%).

We used data on population trends for 130 migratory landbird species in western United States, as compiled by Carter and Barker (1993), to investigate recent population changes. An additional 56 migratory landbird species that have bred in the western states but are too local or rare to be sampled effectively by the BBS and another 91 primarily resident species were not included in this analysis. We identified 58 migratory species that decreased in either the past 26 or 13 years (Table 3), 44 that in-

TABLE 3. SPECIES OF MIGRATORY LANDBIRDS FOR WHICH OUR ANALYSIS OF BBS DATA INDICATES A DECREASING POPULATION TREND IN THE WESTERN UNITED STATES DURING EITHER THE PAST 26 OR PAST 13 YEARS (SEE TEXT)

Species	Mig. status[1]	Past 26 yrs (1966–1991)			Past 13 yrs (1979–1991)		
		Trend[2]	Number states	Mean PTR[3]	Trend[2]	Number states	Mean PTR[3]
Band-tailed Pigeon	S	D	3	4.00	D	3	4.00
Mourning Dove	S	d	11	3.27	D	11	3.73
Black-billed Cuckoo	L	D	1	4.00	D	1	4.00
Burrowing Owl	S	d	5	3.40	d	5	3.20
Short-eared Owl	S	D	1	4.00	d	4	3.25
Common Poorwill	S	D	1	4.00	—	3	3.00
Vaux' Swift	L	D	3	4.33	—	3	3.33
White-throated Swift	S	—	3	3.67	D	4	3.75
Black-chinned Hummingbird	L	D	1	5.00	—	4	3.75
Anna's Hummingbird	S	D	1	4.00	—	1	3.00
Rufous Hummingbird	L	D	2	5.00	D	2	4.50
Allen's Hummingbird	L	D	1	5.00	—	1	3.00
Belted Kingfisher	S	D	6	3.67	—	7	3.43
Lewis' Woodpecker	S	D	1	4.00	—	2	3.50
Williamson's Sapsucker	S	D	1	5.00	D	1	5.00
Northern Flicker	S	—	10	3.70	d	11	3.36
Olive-sided Flycatcher	L	D	4	4.25	D	6	4.00
Say's Phoebe	S	D	10	3.70	—	10	3.10
Eastern Kingbird	L	—	5	2.80	D	6	3.67
Horned Lark	S	D	11	3.73	D	11	3.91
North. Rough-winged Swallow	L	—	9	2.78	d	11	3.36
Bank Swallow	L	d	4	3.25	—	6	3.00
Rock Wren	S	D	11	4.18	D	11	3.55
Golden-crowned Kinglet	S	(D)	4	4.00	—	4	3.50
Veery*	L	I	3	2.00	D	4	3.75
Swainson's Thrush	L	D	5	3.80	—	6	2.83
Sprague's Pipit	S	D	1	4.00	D	1	4.00
Loggerhead Shrike	S	—	9	3.11	D	9	4.00
Bell's Vireo	L	—	1	3.00	D	2	4.00
Red-eyed Vireo*	L	I	2	1.50	D	2	4.00
Nashville Warbler*	L	d	4	3.25	I	4	2.00
Lucy's Warbler	L	D	1	4.00	—	1	3.00
Yellow-rumped Warbler	S	d	7	3.43	—	8	2.88
Black-throated Gray Warbler*	L	D	3	3.67	I	3	1.67
American Redstart*	L	I	1	2.00	D	1	4.00
MacGillivray's Warbler	L	D	5	3.60	—	7	3.14
Wilson's Warbler	L	D	5	4.40	—	6	2.83
Lazuli Bunting	L	—	7	2.86	d	8	3.50
Chipping Sparrow	S	D	10	4.30	D	11	4.36
Brewer's Sparrow	S	D	7	4.57	D	7	4.00
Black-chinned Sparrow	L	D	1	5.00	D	1	5.00
Black-throated Sparrow	S	D	5	4.60	—	5	3.40
Baird's Sparrow*	S	I	1	2.00	D	1	5.00
Grasshopper Sparrow	L	(D)	6	3.67	—	6	3.17
Fox Sparrow	S	D	1	4.00	—	2	2.50
Song Sparrow	S	D	8	3.88	—	8	3.50
White-crowned Sparrow	S	d	5	3.40	d	7	3.43
Dark-eyed Junco	S	D	5	3.80	D	7	4.00
Bobolink	L	D	1	4.00	D	1	5.00
Eastern Meadowlark	S	D	1	4.00	D	1	4.00
Western Meadowlark	S	D	10	3.90	—	11	3.27
Brewer's Blackbird	S	D	8	4.12	—	9	3.56
Bronzed Cowbird	S	—	—	—	D	1	4.00
Hooded Oriole	L	D	1	4.00	—	2	2.50
Scott's Oriole*	L	D	4	4.25	I	4	2.25
Pine Siskin	S	—	7	3.71	D	8	4.00
Lesser Goldfinch	S	D	4	4.00	—	6	3.17
Lawrence's Goldfinch	S	D	1	5.00	D	1	4.00

creased in either of the two time periods (Table 4), and 35 for which trends could be identified in neither of the two time periods (Table 5).

The mean (±SD) PTR of all 125 species under consideration during the 26-year period (1966–1991) was 3.20 ± 0.85, suggesting a small decreasing trend. Sixty-eight of these 125 species (54.4%) showed evidence of decreasing or increasing population trends over the 26 years. Of these 68 species, the proportion of decreasing species (66%) was significantly greater than the proportion of increasing species (34%, P = 0.01, binomial test). When we examined the 130 species under consideration during the 13-year period (1979–1991), we found that the mean PTR (3.01 ± 0.81) indicated virtually no trend whatsoever. Of the 64 species that showed evidence of population trends over these 13 years, the proportion of decreasing species (50%) was the same as the proportion of increasing species (50%, P ≫ 0.95). Thus, when all species are considered, there was a declining trend in the abundance of migratory birds in the western United States over the past 26 years, but no trend over the past 13 years.

We next divided the species into two groups based on the location of their major wintering grounds: short-distance migrants that winter extensively in the temperate areas of North America and long-distance migrants that winter primarily in the tropics (Tables 3, 4, and 5). Of the 34 short-distance migrants that showed evidence of population trends over the past 26 years, 27 (79%) declined while only seven (21%) showed in-

creasing trends (P = 0.0008); their mean PTR over this period was 3.31 ± 0.78. This pattern was still evident, but was not statistically significant, for short-distance migrants during the the past 13 years, when 20 (59%) of 34 declined and 14 (41%) increased (P = 0.39); their mean PTR for this period was 3.09 ± 0.77. The proportion of decreasing and increasing species did not differ among the long-distance migrants for either time period (proportion of declining species = 53% for last 26 years [P = 0.86] and 40% for last 13 years [P = 0.36]), suggesting that these species as a group did not undergo any significant population trends in the western United States in the past 26 or 13 years. Their mean PTRs over these two periods were 3.07 ± 0.92 and 2.93 ± 0.77.

The mean PTRs for most species groups generally decreased somewhat between the past 26 years and the past 13 years (Table 6). For decreasing species, there was a consistent tendency for the rate of decline to be lower over the past 13 years than over the entire 26 years. For increasing species, there was a tendency for the rate of increase to be higher over the past 13 years than over the past 26 years, at least for short-distance migrants. For species that showed no trends in the past 26 or 13 years, there was also a tendency for the mean PTRs to be more positive. Thus, there is no evidence for an increasing rate of decline in western migratory landbirds as has been observed in many species of Neotropical migrants in the eastern United States (Robbins et al. 1989, Sauer and Droege 1992).

←

[1] Migration status: S = short-distance migrant; substantial numbers winter in temperate North America. L = long-distance migrant; virtually all individuals winter in the tropics.

[2] D = strong decreasing trend; more than 50% of the states showed decreasing trends (PTR = 4) or definite decreases (PTR = 5), not more than 25% of the states showed increasing trends (PTR = 2) or definite increases (PTR = 1), and the mean PTR was greater than 3.50. d = weak decreasing trend; same as D except mean PTR not greater than 3.50. (D) = local decreasing trend; less than 50% of the states showed decreasing trends or definite decreases, or more than 25% of the states showed increasing trends or definite increases, but the mean PTR was greater than 3.50. I = strong increasing trend; more than 50% of the states showed increasing trends or definite increases, not more than 25% of the states showed decreasing trends or definite decreases, and the mean PTR was less than 2.50. i = weak increasing trend; same as I except mean PTR not less than 2.50. (I) = local increasing trend; less than 50% of the states showed increasing trends or definite increases, or more than 25% of the states showed decreasing trends or definite decreases, but the mean PTR was less than 2.50.

[3] Mean PTR = mean population trend ranking (see text).

* Included on both the decreasing and increasing lists.

TABLE 4. Species of Migratory Landbirds for which Our Analysis of BBS Data Indicates an Increasing Population Trend in the Western United States during Either the Past 26 or Past 13 Years (See Text)

Species	Mig. status[1]	Past 26 yrs (1966–1991)			Past 13 yrs (1979–1991)		
		Trend[2]	Number states	Mean PTR[3]	Trend[2]	Number states	Mean PTR[3]
Lesser Nighthawk	L	I	2	1.50	I	2	2.00
Costa's Hummingbird	S	—	1	3.00	I	1	2.00
Red-naped Sapsucker	S	I	3	1.33	—	5	2.40
Red-breasted Sapsucker	S	I	3	2.00	I	3	1.00
Western Wood-Pewee	L	I	9	2.44	—	10	3.20
Willow Flycatcher	L	—	6	3.17	I	7	2.14
Least Flycatcher	L	—	1	3.00	I	1	2.00
Hammond's Flycatcher	L	—	4	3.00	I	4	2.25
Dusky Flycatcher	L	—	6	2.50	I	7	2.00
Gray Flycatcher	L	—	2	3.00	I	2	2.00
Ash-throated Flycatcher	L	I	6	2.17	I	6	2.17
Brown-crested Flycatcher	L	I	1	1.00	I	1	1.00
Western Kingbird	L	—	11	2.91	I	11	2.36
Violet-green Swallow	L	(I)	11	2.36	—	11	3.00
Cliff Swallow	L	I	11	2.45	I	11	2.45
House Wren	S	—	7	2.86	I	8	2.12
Blue-gray Gnatcatcher	L	—	2	3.00	I	4	2.00
Townsend's Solitaire	S	—	4	2.75	I	5	2.00
Veery*	L	I	3	2.00	D	4	3.75
Hermit Thrush	S	—	5	2.60	(I)	6	2.33
Cedar Waxwing	S	—	5	3.40	I	5	2.40
Phainopepla	S	—	2	2.50	I	2	1.50
Solitary Vireo	L	I	6	2.33	—	9	3.00
Warbling Vireo	L	I	7	2.29	I	7	2.29
Red-eyed Vireo*	L	I	2	1.50	D	2	4.00
Orange-crowned Warbler	S	i	4	2.75	—	4	3.25
Nashville Warbler*	L	d	4	3.25	I	4	2.00
Black-throated Gray Warbler*	L	D	3	3.67	I	3	1.67
American Redstart*	L	I	1	2.00	D	1	4.00
Northern Waterthrush	L	—	—	—	I	1	2.00
Common Yellowthroat	S	—	7	2.86	(I)	7	2.43
Yellow-breasted Chat	L	I	6	2.33	—	6	3.17
Black-headed Grosbeak	L	I	9	1.78	I	10	2.40
Blue Grosbeak	L	I	4	2.25	I	5	2.20
Rufous-sided Towhee	S	—	10	3.30	i	11	2.64
Cassin's Sparrow	L	I	2	2.00	—	2	3.00
Clay-colored Sparrow	L	I	2	1.50	—	2	2.50
Savannah Sparrow	S	—	6	3.00	i	7	2.50
Baird's Sparrow*	S	I	1	2.00	D	1	5.00
Lincoln's Sparrow	S	I	1	2.00	I	3	2.33
McCown's Longspur	S	I	1	1.00	I	2	1.50
Chestnut-collared Longspur	S	I	1	2.00	I	1	2.00
Scott's Oriole*	L	D	4	4.25	I	4	2.25
Purple Finch	S	—	3	3.00	I	3	2.33

[1] See Table 3 for definitions.
[2] See Table 3 for definitions.
[3] See Table 3 for definitions.
* Included on both the decreasing and increasing lists.

Table 6 also indicates that the mean PTRs of short-distance and long-distance migrants did not differ much or were lower for short-distance migrants for increasing species and for species with no trends. Mean PTRs for short-distance migrants, however, tended to be higher than those for long-distance migrants for decreasing species and for total species, again confirming the tendency for greater decreases among short-

TABLE 5. SPECIES OF MIGRATORY LANDBIRDS FOR WHICH OUR ANALYSIS OF BBS DATA INDICATES A DECREASING OR INCREASING POPULATION TREND IN THE WESTERN UNITED STATES DURING NEITHER THE PAST 26 OR PAST 13 YEARS (SEE TEXT)

Species	Mig. status[1]	Past 26 yrs (1966–1991)			Past 13 yrs (1979–1991)		
		Trend[2]	Number states	Mean PTR[3]	Trend[2]	Number states	Mean PTR[3]
White-winged Dove	L	—	2	2.50	—	1	3.00
Common Nighthawk	L	—	10	3.10	—	11	2.91
Black Swift	L	—	—	—	—	2	3.50
Calliope Hummingbird	L	—	3	3.33	—	4	2.75
Broad-tailed Hummingbird	L	—	2	3.50	—	4	3.00
Cassin's Kingbird	L	—	4	3.50	—	4	3.00
Purple Martin	L	—	1	3.00	—	2	3.50
Tree Swallow	L	—	8	2.75	—	8	2.75
Barn Swallow	L	—	10	3.30	—	11	3.00
Brown Creeper	S	—	3	3.33	—	3	3.00
Marsh Wren	S	—	2	3.00	—	2	3.00
Ruby-crowned Kinglet	S	—	7	2.71	—	7	2.71
Western Bluebird	S	—	5	3.20	—	6	2.83
Mountain Bluebird	S	—	10	2.70	—	10	2.60
American Robin	S	—	11	3.00	—	11	2.91
Gray Catbird	L	—	3	2.67	—	4	3.50
Northern Mockingbird	S	—	6	2.67	—	6	2.67
Sage Thrasher	S	—	6	2.83	—	6	2.83
Bendire's Thrasher	L	—	—	—	—	3	3.33
Virginia's Warbler	L	—	—	—	—	1	3.00
Yellow Warbler	L	—	8	3.00	—	8	3.12
Townsend's Warbler	S	—	2	3.00	—	2	2.50
Hermit Warbler	L	—	2	3.00	—	2	2.50
Western Tanager	L	—	7	3.00	—	11	2.64
Green-tailed Towhee	L	—	5	2.80	—	8	2.50
Vesper Sparrow	S	—	10	3.00	—	10	3.00
Lark Sparrow	S	—	9	3.22	—	11	3.18
Sage Sparrow	S	—	4	2.75	—	4	2.50
Lark Bunting	S	—	3	3.00	—	4	3.25
Red-winged Blackbird	S	—	11	3.18	—	11	3.09
Yellow-headed Blackbird	S	—	8	3.00	—	8	3.12
Brown-headed Cowbird	S	—	11	3.00	—	11	2.64
Northern Oriole	L	—	10	3.00	—	11	3.18
Cassin's Finch	S	—	7	3.43	—	8	2.88
American Goldfinch	S	—	7	3.14	—	7	3.00

[1] See Table 3 for definitions.
[2] See Table 3 for definitions.
[3] See Table 3 for definitions.

distance than among long-distance migrants. None of the differences, however, were significant.

There was relatively little comparability between the decreasing species found on lists generated from BBS data versus those generated from long-term avifaunal information on population changes in the various states. Of 58 migratory landbird species identified as decreasing from relatively recent BBS data, 20 also occurred on the long-term decreasing list while 13 occurred on the long-term increasing list. The situation was even more disparate for the 44 migratory species identified as increasing from BBS data, as only five were on the long-term increasing list while seven were on the long-term decreasing list. This suggests that the major factors affecting populations of migratory landbirds are different today than they were more than half a century ago.

DISCUSSION

Our indices of population trends from BBS data involve three factors: the magnitude of the trend over the census period in a par-

TABLE 6. MEAN PTR[1] VALUES FOR WESTERN MIGRATORY SPECIES IN THE WESTERN UNITED STATES FOR THE PAST 26 YEARS (1966–1991) AND THE PAST 13 YEARS (1979–1991)

	Past 26 years		Past 13 years	
	Number species	PTR[1] (mean ± SD)	Number species	PTR[1] (mean ± SD)
Decreasing species[2]				
Short-distance migrants	32	3.88 ± 0.55	33	3.65 ± 0.54
Long-distance migrants	25	3.66 ± 0.97	25	3.38 ± 0.84
Total	57	3.78 ± 0.76	58	3.53 ± 0.69
Increasing species[3]				
Short-distance migrants	17	2.49 ± 0.67	17	2.34 ± 0.85
Long-distance migrants	26	2.45 ± 0.73	27	2.47 ± 0.71
Total	43	2.47 ± 0.70	44	2.44 ± 0.76
Species with no trends[4]				
Short-distance migrants	18	3.01 ± 0.22	18	2.87 ± 0.23
Long-distance migrants	14	3.03 ± 0.30	17	3.01 ± 0.32
Total	32	3.02 ± 0.25	35	3.94 ± 0.28
Total species[5]				
Short-distance migrants	66	3.31 ± 0.78	67	3.09 ± 0.77
Long-distance migrants	59	3.07 ± 0.92	63	2.93 ± 0.77
Total	125	3.20 ± 0.85	130	3.01 ± 0.77

[1] PTR = population trend ranking: 5.00 = definite decrease, 4.00 = decreasing trend, 3.00 = no trend or trend unknown, 2.00 = increasing trend, 1.00 = definite increase (see text).
[2] Species identified as decreasing in either the past 26-year or 13-year period.
[3] Species identified as increasing in either the past 26-year or 13-year period.
[4] Species showing a decreasing or increasing trend in neither the past 26-year or 13-year period.
[5] Total species does not equal the sum of the decreasing, increasing, and no trend species because seven species (identified by * in Tables 3 and 4) decreased in one period and increased in the other and, consequently, were placed on both the decreasing and increasing species lists.

ticular state, the uncertainty of the trend within the state, and the consistency of the trend across all western states (see Carter and Barker [in press] for a discussion of the first two factors). Thus, our index only allows us to detect changes that are more or less consistent in most of the western states.

Peterjohn and Sauer (in press) provide a summary of 26 years (1966–1991) of BBS data for North America as a whole, for three major geographical regions (Eastern, Central, Western), and for various species guilds based on migratory status, breeding habitat, and nest location. They found that the proportion of increasing species among all species with sufficient sample size was higher in the Western Region (56.5%; differs from the expected value of 50.0% at P < 0.10) than in either the Eastern (52.7%; P > 0.10) or Central (36.8%; P < 0.01) regions. They also found that the proportion of increasing species in the Western Region was exactly 50.0% for both permanent resident and short-distance migrant species, but was

62.1% (differs from the expected value of 50.0% at P < 0.10) for long-distance migrants. Their results echo those of Sauer and Droege (1992) who found that 65% (P < 0.05) of 48 long-distance migrant species had increasing trends in the Western Region over the long-term (1966–1988), whereas 68% (P < 0.05) of 47 species had increasing trends in a more recent time period (1978–1988). Moreover, they also found differences in the proportion of increasing species among the Eastern, Central, and Western regions in the latter time period (P < 0.06), primarily because of a higher proportion of increasing species in the West.

Our analyses of BBS data from the western states, based upon Carter and Barker's (1993) population trend ranks (PTRs), provide qualitatively similar but quantitatively different results. Like Peterjohn and Sauer (1993), we suggest that long-distance migrant species fared better in the West during the last quarter-century than did short-distance migrants. But, in contrast to their results, we suggest that long-distance migrants as a whole showed no trend while short-distance migrants showed a decreasing trend. Peterjohn and Sauer suggest that long-distance migrants showed an increasing trend (as did Sauer and Droege [1992]), while short-distance migrants (and permanent residents) showed no trend. Like Sauer and Droege (1992), however, our results suggest that population trends for long-distance migrants (and short-distance migrants) improved somewhat during the more recent 13 years compared to the entire 26-year period.

We explain differences between our results and those of Peterjohn and Sauer (1993) and Sauer and Droege (1992) by our use of data (PTRs generated by Carter and Barker [1993]), which included measures of both the magnitude and the uncertainty of the trends, rather than data limited only to the number of species undergoing decreasing or increasing trends. The results of analyses that include information on the magnitude and uncertainty of the trends appear to be less optimistic than the results of analyses that do not include this information.

Our results also agree well with data on passage migrants from Southeast Farallon Island (SEFI) over the past 25 years (Pyle et al. 1994). They showed that nocturnal migrant arrivals to SEFI decreased overall between 1968 and 1992, and that this decrease was significant in spring but not in fall. They also showed that species and groups of species showing declines outnumbered those showing increases 28 to 16, and that significant decelerating declines during the 25-year period were detected in 21 species and 5 groups, whereas accelerating declines were detected in only one species and no group. Virtually all analyses of BBS data, including ours, also show smaller decreases (or larger increases) over the last 12–13 years than over the entire 25–26 year period in western North America.

Some major points emerge from these results. First, the most important cause of the decline of landbird species in western North America has been the destruction of riparian habitat. Because the key to human activity in arid lands is water, the most important management strategy that should be implemented immediately in western North America is the complete protection and, as possible, the restoration of riparian habitats. Such areas provide critical breeding habitat for a number of declining species, important habitat for wintering populations of many species, and stop-over locations for most long- and short-distance migrants.

A second point is that short-distance migrants, particularly species associated with grasslands and shrublands, appear to be declining in western North America. The historical record implicates the destruction of grasslands and overgrazing as the second and fourth most important causes of population declines of western landbirds during the past century, and BBS data suggest that the declines are continuing. Arguments to stop the extensive grazing of public lands in western United States deserve a fair hearing. The possibility that the declines in a number of western sparrows (Table 3) may be linked to habitat degradation on their wintering grounds in southwestern United States and northwestern Mexico also deserves study. Moreover, a probable connection between grazing on public lands and increased cowbird parasitism is obvious.

A third point is that accelerating declines in forest-inhabiting, long-distance migrant species, recently documented from eastern and central North America (Robbins et al. 1989, Terborgh 1989, Askins et al. 1990, Sauer and Droege 1992), do not seem to be occurring in western North America. This is *not* to say that western populations of such species are not being affected by deforestation and forest fragmentation on both their temperate breeding grounds and tropical wintering grounds; rather, the effects are not yet as acute as in eastern North America.

Forest-inhabiting long-distance migrants from eastern North America winter primarily in the Caribbean Basin (eastern Mexico, Central America, extreme northern South America, and the West Indies), a very small land area compared to the area of their breeding grounds. In contrast, forest-inhabiting long-distance migrants from western North America winter primarily in western and southern Mexico, an area that equates to a relatively larger proportion of their breeding grounds. As a result, eastern species may winter in higher densities so that degradation of winter habitat may have a relatively greater effect on eastern than on western species. Moreover, the wintering habitat for forest-inhabiting Neotropical migrants is likely more intact overall for western species than for eastern ones (Hutto 1988). Still, it should be noted that significant declines were found on SEFI, at least in spring, for species wintering in western Mexico (Pyle et al. 1994). A similar situation may also exist on the breeding grounds. Despite massive deforestation, forest fragmentation, and destruction of old-growth forests in the past quarter-century, the forests of western North America are still more intact than those over much of eastern North America, where both old growth and large tracts of forested land are becoming vanishingly small.

Another change is the increased occurrence rates of vagrant, out-of-range species in western North America. From 10 years of unbiased data from SEFI (1968–1978), DeSante (1983) suggested that the increase in vagrants was a real phenomenon and not an artifact of increased observation. This was confirmed by Pyle et al. (1994) who showed that eastern forest-inhabiting species had increasing trends on SEFI over the past 25 years in both spring and fall. This is especially noteworthy because 1) most other landbird species showed decreasing trends on SEFI and 2) overall populations of eastern forest-inhabiting species appear to be decreasing, particularly in the past 10–12 years. These results suggest that the proportion of vagrant individuals is increasing in populations of these eastern forest-inhabiting species. DeSante (1983) hypoth-

esized that this increase could be caused by a selective increase in both the proportion of dispersing individuals and the dispersal distances of those individuals (vagrants being merely the extremes of dispersal) in response to increased rates of habitat change and disturbance.

Inferences about population trends in western landbirds are constrained by the limited and anecdotal nature of historical data and by deficiencies of BBS data (Hagan et al. 1992). First, the quarter-century from which BBS data are now available is very short. It is possible that patterns in landbird populations are much more cyclic than we believe and reflect weather phenomena (and associated changes in food supply, breeding success, and survivorship) that are not well understood and that may be changing because of natural or human-caused changes in global climate. It may not be a coincidence that the proportion of increasing species among all long-distance migrants decreased significantly in eastern North America from the decade of the seventies to the eighties, when it tended to increase in western North America (Sauer and Droege 1992; see also DeSante 1992, 1993 for further discussion).

Second, the BBS can provide reliable information only for relatively common species. Of the 75 species that we identified from historical accounts as decreasing in the past century and the 65 species we identified as increasing, 23 (31%) and 20 (31%), respectively, were too rare or local in the west to be sampled effectively by the BBS. Indeed, the Monitoring Working Group (1992) suggested that the BBS was unable to monitor effectively 31% (79 of 256 species) of Neotropical migratory species.

Third, BBS data are limited to roadsides, which often include a large proportion of fragmented and edge habitats. This may cause biases both in the kinds of species that are detected on BBS routes and in the counts of these species (O'Connor 1992). Furthermore, roadside biases could be positive for some species and negative for others. A related problem with BBS data is that they are not habitat specific, thereby making it difficult to relate population trends to specific habitat changes in any particular habitat type or to large-scale habitat changes in general.

A final shortcoming of BBS data, and of all census or survey data, is that they only provide information on secondary population parameters (e.g., population size, density, age structure) and not on primary parameters (e.g., productivity, fecundity, survivorship, dispersal). Primary parameters may be more useful than secondary parameters in determining the causes of population change because environmental variation affects primary parameters directly and can be observed over a short time period (Hutto 1988, Temple and Wiens 1989). Because of buffering effects of floater individuals and density-dependent responses of populations, there may be substantial time lags between changes in primary parameters and resulting changes in population size or density as measured by census or survey methods (Temple and Wiens 1989). Thus, a population could be in trouble long before it becomes evident from survey data. Finally, because of the vagility of most bird species, local variations in secondary population parameters may often be masked by recruitment from a wider region (George et al. 1992) or accentuated by lack of recruitment from a wider area (DeSante 1990).

Substantially greater monitoring and research efforts than are currently underway will be required to obtain the data necessary to manage western landbird populations effectively in the face of the challenges that will be presented by human population growth and development in the twenty-first century. We recommend the establishment of a continent-wide "integrated avian population monitoring system," patterned after the scheme pioneered in Great Britain (Baillie 1990), that should include the following elements:

1. Increased coverage of existing and proposed BBS routes, especially in the West where coverage in many areas is inconsistent and incomplete.

2. Implementation of a systematic program of habitat-specific, off-road surveys, perhaps concentrating on public lands.

3. Implementation of a program of intensive surveys of rare species that cannot be surveyed adequately by large-scale, broad-based programs.

4. Increased and improved analyses of existing population trend data. Few analyses of BBS data at a local or regional scale exist for western North America, and only cursory analyses of trends within habitat types have been attempted (Carter and Barker 1993, Peterjohn and Sauer 1993). Moreover, most analyses of BBS data, including ours, have used relatively long time periods. James et al. (1990, 1992) showed that exploratory analyses of short-term trends using nonparametric, nonlinear route regression may provide insights that are not evident from linear route regression that is used in most BBS analyses.

5. Increased efforts to monitor primary demographic parameters through programs such as the Monitoring Avian Productivity and Survivorship (MAPS) program, coordinated by The Institute for Bird Populations, and the Breeding Biology Research Database (BBIRD) program, coordinated by T. E. Martin.

6. A concerted effort, using DNA fingerprinting and increased analysis of banding recoveries, to determine, on as fine a scale as possible, the wintering localities for local populations of breeding migratory landbirds. Marshall (1988) suggested that the disappearance of certain populations of long-distance migratory birds in California may have been caused by the destruction of their wintering grounds in a relatively limited area of Central America.

We further recommend that the operation of an effective integrated avian population monitoring system should: (1) allow the standardized collection of data on both primary and secondary population parameters; (2) allow the interpretation of these data using population-modelling techniques capable of describing interrelationships between population variables and readily-measured environmental covariables; (3) assist in establishing action thresholds for management and/or further research; (4) facilitate identification of changes caused by anthropogenic factors by comparing observed population trends with those predicted from environmental data and from preceding population levels; and (5) lead to the testing and refining of current models for population processes and the development of new ones.

In summary, the past 100 years have witnessed pronounced changes in the characteristics of avian habitats in western North America, substantial changes in the populations of landbirds associated with those habitats, the beginning of effective efforts to monitor and understand the causes of those changes, and the first coordinated resolve to prevent further decreases in landbird populations. Today, western landbird populations are facing a growing number of environmental problems of ever increasing severity, including accelerating habitat loss, global climate change, and widespread toxic pollution. It is generally agreed that these threats could bring about rates of avian extinction and avian range change that could exceed the highest rates ever recorded in the fossil record. Indeed, the next 100 years (or considerably less) will provide a real test of the resolve to prevent further decreases in landbird populations.

ACKNOWLEDGMENTS

We thank the hundreds of able volunteers who collected BBS data for western North America during the past quarter-century, M. Carter and K. Barker for the use of their population trend ranking system, and the editors of this volume for their helpful comments. This is Contribution No. 13 of The Institute for Bird Populations.

LITERATURE CITED

ALCORN, J. R. 1988. The birds of Nevada. Fairview West Publishing, Fallon, NV.

ASKINS, R. A., J. F. LYNCH, AND R. GREENBERG. 1990. Population declines in migratory birds in eastern North America. Current Ornithology 7:1–57.

BAILEY, A. M., AND R. J. NIEDRACH. 1967. Pictorial checklist of Colorado birds. Denver Museum of Natural History, Denver, CO. 168 pp.

BAILLIE, S. R. 1990. Integrated population monitoring of breeding birds in Britain and Ireland. Ibis 132: 151–166.

BEHLE, W. H., AND M. L. PERRY. 1975. Utah birds: checklist, seasonal and ecological occurrence charts and guides to bird finding. Utah Museum of Natural History, Salt Lake City, UT. 143 pp.

BURLEIGH, T. D. 1971. Birds of Idaho. Caxton Printers, Caldwell, ID.

CAMPBELL, W. W., N. K. DAWE, I. McTAGGERT-COWAN, J. M. COOPER, G. W. KAISER, AND M. C. E. McNALL. 1990. The birds of British Columbia, Vol. 2: Non-passerines. Royal British Columbia Museum, Victoria, BC.

CARTER, M., AND K. BARKER. In press. Setting conservation priorities for western neotropical migrants. In D. M. Finch and P. W. Stangel (eds.), Status and management of neotropical migratory birds. USDA Forest Service. Rocky Mountain Forest and Range Experimental Station, Fort Collins, CO. General Technical Report.

DeSANTE, D. F. 1983. Annual variability in the abundance of migrant landbirds on Southeast Farallon Island, California. Auk 100:826–852.

DeSANTE, D. F. 1990. The role of recruitment in the dynamics of a Sierran subalpine bird community. The American Naturalist 136:429–445.

DeSANTE, D. F. 1992. Monitoring Avian Productivity and Survivorship (MAPS): a sharp, rather than blunt, tool for monitoring and assessing landbird populations. Pp. 511–521 in D. C. McCullough and R. H. Barrett (eds.), Wildlife 2001: populations. Elsevier Applied Science, London, U.K.

DeSANTE, D. F. In press. The Monitoring Avian Productivity and Survivorship (MAPS) program: overview and progress. In D. M. Finch and P. W. Stangel (eds.), Status and management of neotropical migratory birds. USDA Forest Service. Rocky Mountain Forest and Range Experimental Station, Fort Collins, CO. General Technical Report.

DeSANTE, D., AND P. PYLE. 1986. Distributional checklist of North American birds, Vol. I: U.S. and Canada. Artemisia Press, Lee Vining, CA. 442 pp.

GABRIELSON, I. N., AND S. G. JEWETT. 1940. Birds of Oregon. Oregon State College, Corvallis, OR. 650 pp.

GABRIELSON, I. N., AND F. C. LINCOLN. 1959. The birds of Alaska. Stackpole Co., Harrison, PA and Wildlife Management Institute, Washington, D.C. 922 pp.

GEORGE, T. L., A. C. FOWLER, R. L. KNIGHT, AND L. C. McEWEN. 1992. Impacts of a severe drought on grassland birds in western North Dakota. Ecological Applications 2:275–284.

GRINNELL, J., AND A. H. MILLER. 1944. The distribution of the birds of California. Pacific Coast Avifauna No. 27. Cooper Ornithological Society, Berkeley, CA. 608 pp.

HAGAN, J. M., III, T. L. LLOYD-EVANS, J. L. ATWOOD, AND D. S. WOOD. 1992. Long-term changes in migratory landbirds in the northeastern United States: evidence from migration capture data. Pp. 115–130 in J. M. Hagan, III and D. W. Johnson (eds.), Ecology and conservation of neotropical migrant landbirds. Smithsonian Institution Press, Washington, D.C. 609 pp.

HUTTO, R. L. 1988. Is tropical deforestation responsible for the reported decline in neotropical migrant populations? American Birds 42:375–379.

JAMES, F. C., C. E. MCCULLOCH, AND L. E. WOLF. 1990. Methodological issues in the estimation of trends in bird populations with an example: the Pine Warbler. Pp. 84–97 *in* J. R. Sauer and S. Droege (eds.), Survey designs and statistical methods for the estimation of avian population trends. U.S. Fish and Wildlife Service, Biological Report 90(1). 166 pp.

JAMES, F. C., D. A. WIEDENFELD, AND C. E. MC-CULLOCH. 1992. Trends in breeding populations of warblers: declines in the southern highlands and increases in the lowlands. Pp. 43–56 *in* J. M. Hagan, III and D. W. Johnson (eds.), Ecology and conservation of neotropical migrant landbirds. Smithsonian Institution Press, Washington, D.C. 609 pp.

JEWETT, S. G., W. P. TAYLOR, W. T. SHAW, AND J. W. ALDRICH. 1953. Birds of Washington state. University of Washington Press, Seattle, WA. 767 pp.

JOHNSON, N. K. 1994. Pioneering and natural expansion of breeding distributions in western North America birds. Pp. 27–44 *in* J. R. Jehl, Jr. and N. K. Johnson (eds.), A century of avifaunal change in western North America. Studies in Avian Biology No. 15.

LIGON, J. S. 1961. New Mexico birds and where to find them. University of New Mexico Press, Albuquerque, NM.

MARSHALL, J. T. 1988. Birds lost from a giant sequoia forest during fifty years. Condor 90:359–372.

MONITORING WORKING GROUP OF PARTNERS IN FLIGHT. 1992. Needs assessment: monitoring neotropical migratory birds. Neotropical Migratory Bird Conservation Program, Arlington, VA.

MUNRO, J. A., AND I. MCTAGGERT-COWAN. 1947. A review of the bird fauna of British Columbia. British Columbia Provincial Museum, Victoria, BC.

O'CONNOR, R. J. 1992. Population variation in relation to migrancy status in some North America birds. Pp. 46–74 *in* J. M. Hagan, III and D. W. Johnson (eds.), Ecology and conservation of neotropical migrant landbirds. Smithsonian Institution Press. Washington, D.C. 609 pp.

OFFICE OF MIGRATORY BIRD MANAGEMENT. 1987. Migratory nongame birds of management concern in the United States: the 1987 list. U.S. Fish and Wildlife Service, Washington, D.C.

PETERJOHN, B. G., AND J. R. SAUER. 1993. North American Breeding Bird Survey: annual summary 1990–1991. Bird Populations 1:52–67.

PHILLIPS, A., J. MARSHALL, AND G. MONSON. 1964. The birds of Arizona. University of Arizona Press, Tucson, AZ. 220 pp.

PYLE, P., N. NUR, AND D. F. DESANTE. 1994. Trends in nocturnal migrant landbird populations at Southeast Farallon Island, California, 1968–1992. Pp. 58–74 *in* J. R. Jehl, Jr. and N. K. Johnson (eds.), A century of avifaunal change in western North America. Studies in Avian Biology No. 15.

ROBBINS, C. S., D. BYSTRAK, AND P. H. GEISSLER. 1986. The breeding bird survey: its first fifteen years,

1965–1979. U.S. Fish and Wildlife Service Research Publication 157, Washington, D.C. 196 pp.

ROBBINS, C. S., J. R. SAUER, R. S. GREENBERG, AND S. DROEGE. 1989. Population declines in North American birds that migrate to the neotropics. Proceedings of the National Academy of Sciences (USA) 86:7658–7662.

SALT, W. R., AND J. R. SALT. 1976. The birds of Alberta with their ranges in Saskatchewan and Manitoba. Hurtig Publishers, Edmonton, AB. 498 pp.

SAUER, J. R., AND S. DROEGE. 1992. Geographic patterns in population trends of neotropical migrants in North America. Pp. 26–42 *in* J. M. Hagan, III and D. W. Johnson (eds.), Ecology and conservation of neotropical migrant landbirds. Smithsonian Institution Press, Washington, D.C. 609 pp.

TEMPLE, S. A., AND J. A. WIENS. 1989. Bird populations and environmental changes: can birds be bioindicators? American Birds 43:260–270.

TERBORGH, J. 1989. Where have all the birds gone? Essays on the biology and conservation of birds that migrate to the American tropics. Princeton University Press, Princeton, NJ.

APPENDIX. Scientific names of species mentioned in the text or tables.

Spruce Grouse (*Dendragapus canadensis*), Blue Grouse (*Dendragapus obscurus*), White-tailed Ptarmigan (*Lagopus leucurus*), Ruffed Grouse (*Bonasa umbellus*), Sage Grouse (*Centrocercus urophasianus*), Greater Prairie-Chicken (*Tympanuchus cupido*), Lesser Prairie-Chicken (*Tympanuchus pallidicinctus*), Sharp-tailed Grouse (*Tympanuchus phasianellus*), Wild Turkey (*Meleagris gallopavo*), Montezuma Quail (*Cyrtonyx montezumae*), Northern Bobwhite (*Colinus virginianus*), Scaled Quail (*Callipepla squamata*), California Quail (*Callipepla californica*), Mountain Quail (*Oreortyx pictus*), Rock Dove (*Columba livia*), Band-tailed Pigeon (*Columba fasciata*), White-winged Dove (*Zenaida asiatica*), Mourning Dove (*Zenaida macroura*), Inca Dove (*Columbina inca*), Common Ground-Dove (*Columbina passerina*), Black-billed Cuckoo (*Coccyzus erythropthalmus*), Yellow-billed Cuckoo (*Coccyzus americanus*), Greater Roadrunner (*Geococcyx californianus*), Barn Owl (*Tyto alba*), Western Screech-Owl (*Otus kennicottii*), Northern Hawk-Owl (*Surnia ulula*), Ferruginous Pygmy-Owl (*Glaucidium brasilianum*), Elf Owl (*Micrathene whitneyi*), Burrowing Owl (*Athene cunicularia*), Spotted Owl (*Strix occidentalis*), Barred Owl (*Strix varia*), Long-eared Owl (*Asio otus*), Short-eared Owl (*Asio flammeus*), Lesser Nighthawk (*Chordeiles acutipennis*), Common Nighthawk (*Chordeiles minor*), Common Poorwill (*Phalaenoptilus nuttallii*), Whippoor-will (*Caprimulgus vociferus*), Black Swift (*Cypseloides niger*), Vaux's Swift (*Chaetura vauxi*), White-throated Swift (*Aeronautes saxatalis*), White-eared Hummingbird (*Hylocharis leucotis*), Berylline Hummingbird (*Amazilia beryllina*), Violet-crowned Hummingbird (*Amazilia violiceps*), Magnificent Hummingbird (*Eugenes fulgens*), Black-chinned Hummingbird (*Archilochus alexandri*), Anna's Hummingbird (*Calypte anna*), Costa's Hummingbird (*Calypte costae*), Calliope Hummingbird (*Stellula calliope*), Broad-tailed Hummingbird (*Selasphorus platycercus*), Rufous Hummingbird (*Selasphorus rufus*), Allen's Hummingbird (*Selasphorus sasin*), Belted Kingfisher (*Ceryle alcyon*), Lewis' Woodpecker (*Melanerpes lewis*), Red-headed Woodpecker (*Melanerpes erythrocephalus*), Gila Woodpecker (*Melanerpes uropygialis*), Red-naped Sapsucker (*Sphyrapicus nuchalis*), Red-breasted Sapsucker (*Sphyrapicus ruber*), Williamson's Sapsucker (*Sphyrapicus thyroideus*), Ladder-backed Woodpecker (*Picoides scalaris*), Northern (Gilded) Flicker (*Colaptes auratus*), Pileated Woodpecker (*Dryocopus pileatus*), Olive-sided Flycatcher (*Contopus borealis*), Western Wood-Pewee (*Contopus sordidulus*), Willow Flycatcher (*Empidonax traillii*), Least Flycatcher (*Empidonax minimus*), Hammond's Flycatcher (*Empidonax hammondii*), Dusky Flycatcher (*Empidonax oberholseri*), Gray Flycatcher (*Empidonax wrightii*), Buff-breasted Flycatcher (*Empidonax fulvifrons*), Black Phoebe (*Sayornis nigricans*), Say's Phoebe (*Sayornis saya*), Vermilion Flycatcher (*Pyrocephalus rubinus*), Ash-throated Flycatcher (*Myiarchus cinerascens*), Brown-crested Flycatcher (*Myiarchus tyrannulus*), Tropical Kingbird (*Tyrannus melancholicus*), Cassin's Kingbird (*Tyrannus vociferans*), Thick-billed Kingbird (*Tyrannus crassirostris*), Western Kingbird (*Tyrannus verticalis*), Eastern Kingbird (*Tyrannus tyrannus*), Scissor-tailed Flycatcher (*Tyrannus forficatus*), Rose-throated Becard (*Pachyramphus aglaiae*), Horned Lark (*Eremophila alpestris*), Purple Martin (*Progne subis*), Tree Swallow (*Tachycineta bicolor*), Violet-green Swallow (*Tachycineta thalassina*), Northern Rough-winged Swallow (*Stelgidopteryx serripennis*), Bank Swallow (*Riparia riparia*), Cliff Swallow (*Hirundo pyrrhonota*), Cave Swallow (*Hirundo fulva*), Barn Swallow (*Hirundo rustica*), Blue Jay (*Cyanocitta cristata*), Black-billed Magpie (*Pica pica*), American Crow (*Corvus brachyrhynchos*), Chihuahuan Raven (*Corvus cryptoleucus*), Common Raven (*Corvus corax*), Verdin (*Auriparus flaviceps*), Bushtit (*Psaltriparus minimus*), White-breasted Nuthatch (*Sitta carolinensis*), Brown Creeper (*Certhia americana*), Cactus Wren (*Campylorhynchus brunneicapillus*), Rock Wren (*Salpinctes obsoletus*), House Wren (*Troglodytes aedon*), Marsh Wren (*Cistothorus palustris*), Golden-crowned Kinglet (*Regulus satrapa*), Ruby-crowned Kinglet (*Regulus calendula*), Blue-gray Gnatcatcher (*Polioptila caerulea*), California Gnatcatcher (*Polioptila californica*), Western Bluebird (*Sialia mexicana*), Mountain Bluebird (*Sialia currucoides*), Townsend's Solitaire (*Myadestes townsendi*), Veery (*Catharus fuscescens*), Swainson's Thrush (*Catharus ustulatus*), Hermit Thrush (*Catharus guttatus*), American Robin (*Turdus migratorius*), Gray Catbird (*Dumetella carolinensis*), Northern Mockingbird (*Mimus polyglottos*), Sage Thrasher (*Oreoscoptes montanus*), Brown Thrasher (*Toxostoma rufum*), Bendire's Thrasher (*Toxostoma bendirei*), Curve-billed Thrasher (*Toxostoma curvirostre*), Crissal Thrasher (*Toxostoma crissale*), LeConte's Thrasher (*Toxostoma lecontei*), White Wagtail (*Motacilla alba*), American Pipit (*Anthus rubescens*), Sprague's Pipit (*Anthus spragueii*), Cedar Waxwing (*Bombycilla cedrorum*), Phainopepla (*Phainopepla nitens*), Loggerhead Shrike (*Lanius ludovicianus*), European Starling (*Sturnus vulgaris*), Bell's Vireo (*Vireo belli*), Gray Vireo (*Vireo vicinior*), Solitary Vireo (*Vireo solitarius*), Warbling Vireo (*Vireo gilvus*), Red-eyed Vireo (*Vireo olivaceus*), Orange-crowned Warbler (*Vermivora celata*), Nashville Warbler (*Vermivora ruficapilla*), Virginia's Warbler (*Vermivora virginiae*), Lucy's Warbler (*Vermivora luciae*), Yellow Warbler (*Dendroica petechia*), Yellow-rumped Warbler (*Dendroica coronata*), Black-throated Gray Warbler (*Dendroica nigrescens*), Townsend's Warbler (*Dendroica townsendi*), Hermit Warbler (*Dendroica occidentalis*), Grace's Warbler (*Dendroica graciae*), American Redstart (*Setophaga ruticilla*), Northern Waterthrush (*Seiurus noveboracensis*), MacGillivray's Warbler (*Oporornis tolmiei*), Common Yellowthroat (*Geothylpis trichas*), Wilson's Warbler (*Wilsonia pusilla*), Red-faced Warbler (*Cardellina rubrifrons*), Painted Redstart (*Myioborus pictus*), Yellow-breasted Chat (*Icteria virens*), Hepatic Tanager (*Piranga flava*), Summer Tanager (*Piranga rubra*), Western Tanager (*Piranga ludoviciana*), Northern Cardinal (*Cardinalis cardinalis*), Black-headed Grosbeak (*Pheucticus melanocephalus*), Blue Grosbeak (*Guiraca caerulea*), Lazuli Bunting (*Passerina amoena*), Indigo Bunting (*Passerina cyanea*), Painted Bunting (*Passerina ciris*), Dickcissel (*Spiza americana*), Green-tailed Towhee (*Pipilo chlorurus*), Rufous-sided Towhee (*Pipilo erythrophthalmus*), California Towhee (*Pipilo crissalis*), Botteri's Sparrow (*Aimophila botterii*), Cassin's Sparrow (*Aimophila cassinii*), Rufous-winged Sparrow (*Aimophila carpalis*), Chipping Sparrow (*Spizella passerina*), Clay-colored Sparrow (*Spizella pallida*), Brewer's Sparrow (*Spizella breweri*), Black-chinned Sparrow (*Spizella atrogularis*), Vesper Sparrow (*Pooecetes gramineus*), Lark Sparrow (*Chondestes grammacus*), Black-throated Sparrow (*Amphispiza bilineata*), Sage Sparrow (*Amphispiza belli*), Lark Bunting (*Calamospiza melanocorys*), Savannah Sparrow (*Passerculus sandwichensis*), Baird's Sparrow (*Ammodramus bairdii*), Grasshopper Sparrow (*Ammodramus savannarum*), Fox Sparrow (*Passerella iliaca*), Song Sparrow (*Melospiza melodia*), Lincoln's Sparrow (*Melospiza lincolnii*), White-crowned Sparrow (*Zonotrichia leucophrys*), Dark-eyed Junco (*Junco hyemalis*), McCown's Longspur (*Calcarius mccownii*), Chestnut-collared Longspur (*Calcarius ornatus*), Bobolink (*Dolichonyx oryzivorus*), Red-winged Blackbird (*Agelaius phoeniceus*), Tricolored Blackbird (*Agelaius tricolor*), Eastern Meadowlark (*Sturnella magna*), Western Meadowlark (*Sturnella neglecta*), Yellow-headed Blackbird (*Xanthocephalus xanthocephalus*), Brewer's Blackbird (*Euphagus cyanocephalus*), Great-tailed Grackle (*Quiscalus mexicanus*), Bronzed Cowbird (*Molothrus aeneus*), Brown-headed Cowbird (*Molothrus ater*), Hooded Oriole (*Icterus cucullatus*), Northern Oriole (*Icterus galbula*), Scott's Oriole (*Icterus parisorum*), Purple Finch (*Carpodacus purpureus*), Cassin's Finch (*Carpodacus cassinii*), House Finch (*Carpodacus mexicanus*), Pine Siskin (*Carduelis pinus*), Lesser Goldfinch (*Carduelis psaltria*), Lawrence's Goldfinch (*Carduelis lawrencei*), American Goldfinch (*Carduelis tristis*), House Sparrow (*Passer domesticus*).

Studies in Avian Biology No. 15:191–201, 1994.

CHANGES IN DISTRIBUTION PATTERNS OF SELECT WINTERING NORTH AMERICAN BIRDS FROM 1901 TO 1989

Terry L. Root and Jason D. Weckstein

Abstract. Range and abundance patterns of birds change with time. We used National Audubon Society's Christmas Bird Count data and similar census data recorded in the *Canadian Field Naturalist* to examine such changes in select birds by comparing distribution and maps from 1901–1940 with those from 1960–1989. For both time periods, we plotted average winter abundances within each of the 48 conterminous United States and eight southern-most provinces in Canada for all species examined. Many more birds exhibit range expansions than contractions. Introduced and managed species show the most dramatic expansions. Although changes are less extensive, native non-managed birds also show expansions that apparently are linked to environmental modifications by humans. For example, water management programs provide winter habitat for the prey of Bald Eagles, and, coincidentally, the eagle expanded its winter range into these areas. In addition, abundance patterns changed over time for most species. The locations of the highest abundances shifted and the number of states and provinces with maximum abundance changed. Due to extensive habitat alterations over the past century, most of the observed avian distributional changes appear to be linked either directly or indirectly to human causes.

Key Words: Conservation biology; Christmas Bird Counts; landscape ecology; range expansions; range contractions; abundance shifts.

Biogeographic patterns of species are dynamic, not static; ranges expand and contract, and abundance patterns shift over time. Such changes can be precipitated by factors intrinsic to populations (e.g., dispersal of juveniles), by factors extrinsic to populations (e.g., habitat modification), or by a combination of both. Species exist in habitats where the environment provides at least minimum requirements for survival. Ranges and abundances can expand when suitable new habitat develops, or when surplus individuals from nearby areas continually immigrate into habitats unsuitable for sustained survival (Pulliam 1988, Pulliam and Danielson 1991). Ranges can contract when population sizes decline and individuals abandon less-than-ideal habitats (Fretwell 1972), which are often at the edges of ranges. Environmental modifications can render habitats unsuitable for survival, causing localized extirpations, which along with stochastic, demographic, or genetic changes can also result in range contractions. Abundance patterns can shift when less extreme cases of any of the above situations occur inside the ranges of species.

In addition, changes in species abundances can have cascading effects on abundances of other species, by changing, for example, competitive or predator/prey interactions (e.g., Terborgh 1986, Spencer et al. 1991, Flecker 1992). Introductions of exotic species can have a similar effect, thereby reducing abundances of native species (e.g., Savage 1987, Coblentz 1990). Hunting can also reduce abundances, but the enactment and enforcement of various laws (e.g., Migratory Bird Act) have ameliorated its impact in most cases (Williams and Novak 1987). Management of species for hunting, however, has dramatically changed the ranges and abundance patterns of game species by changing the carrying capacities of habitats (see below). Therefore, changes in distributional patterns of birds wintering throughout North America can be due to habitat modifications, immigration among populations, and indirect effects such as changing competitive interactions.

The purpose of this paper is to compare historical and recent distributional patterns of selected wintering North American birds to determine if shifts occurred in the ranges and abundance patterns, and, if so, what type of changes they were and to speculate on possible causes. We found that the majority of birds examined exhibit range changes; most species expanded their ranges and only a very few showed range contractions. Some shift in abundance patterns occurred in almost all species.

METHODS

We used data collected by volunteers for the National Audubon Society's Christmas Bird Counts and similar census data recorded in the *Canadian Field Naturalist* from 1924 through 1939. Wing (1947) summarized data from 1901 to 1940 (from winter 1900/1901 to winter 1939/1940), which included 6853 censuses. We obtained data for 32,167 censuses from U.S. Fish and Wildlife Service for 1960 through 1989, excluding those for 1969, which were missing. All data were collected on a day around Christmas and, for each species, observers recorded all individuals seen. Count effort was recorded as total number of census hours (total census hours) for the earlier (1901 to 1940) data, and as total number of census hours per censusing party (total party hours) for the later (1960 to 1989) data.

For each species Wing (1947) calculated the average number of individuals seen per total census hour in each state or province. We attempted to analyze the later data in a similar manner: for each species we calculated the average number of individuals seen per total party hour in each state or province. The absolute abundances from the two time periods cannot be compared directly because count efforts were recorded in two different ways. Consequently, we converted all state and province averages for each species into proportions of the maximum averages for each time period. This normalization forced the value to run between 0 and 1, which we then plotted by state or province. The use of political boundaries is not biologically meaningful, but is unfortunately necessary due to the way Wing

compiled the earlier data. Because we used states and provinces as plotting units, ranges appear larger than they actually are; we plotted species as "present" in an entire state or province, even if its distribution was limited to a small portion of that unit. This is of little consequence in this comparative study, given that we plotted data for both time periods similarly. More census sites and more participants with better equipment during the later time period, however, may have biased the observed distributional patterns. For example, our analysis could indicate an apparent range expansion if a bird occurred only in a part of a state or province, and a census site was not established at that location until after 1940. Consequently, we noted expansions only when individuals were recorded in states and provinces beyond those neighboring the earlier range.

Because we were looking for shifts in distributions, we identified 58 wintering North American species or subspecies that we expected would show such changes. This included 27 non-passerines and 31 passerines. Very rare or extremely gregarious species are poorly represented by these types of censuses (Bock and Root 1981). Thus, we ignored those taxa. Additionally, we disregarded difficult to distinguish species (e.g., Black-capped and Carolina chickadees, *Parus atricapillus* and *P. carolinensis,* respectively). Although House Sparrows (*Passer domesticus*) and European Starlings (*Sturnus vulgaris*) are gregarious, we included them in our analysis because the range and abundance patterns of these introduced birds have not only changed dramatically (Forbush 1929, Robbins 1973), but those changes have affected greatly the patterns of native birds (Zeleny 1976, Robbins et al. 1986, Ehrlich et al. 1988:459–463).

RESULTS

As we expected, given the biased manner in which we selected the species examined, most of these birds exhibit some type of change in their winter ranges and abundance patterns.

RANGE CHANGES

Range expansions were much more common than contractions. This is true even though we recorded expansions only when individuals were present in states beyond those neighboring their 1901–1940 range. The most extreme expansions are evident in introduced and managed species. These include Mute Swan (*Cygnus olor*), Wild Turkey (*Meleagris gallopavo*; Fig. 1), European Starling (*Sturnus vulgaris*), and House Finch (*Carpodacus mexicanus*). Several birds moved into the northeastern region: Northern Harrier (*Circus cyaneus*), Mourning Dove (*Zenaida macroura*; Fig. 1), Tufted Titmouse (*Parus bicolor*), and Northern Cardinal (*Cardinalis cardinalis*). A couple of species expanded into the northwestern region: Ferruginous Hawk (*Buteo regalis*) and Barred Owl (*Strix varia*; Fig. 1). No species expanded south except irruptive species (see below), perhaps because most wintering North American species have southerly ranges. The Golden Eagle (*Aquila chrysaetos*; Fig. 2) and red-shafted race of the Northern Flicker (*Colaptes auratus*) moved east, whereas the yellow-shafted race expanded west. The Bald Eagle (*Haliaeetus leucocephalus*; Fig. 2) expanded its range into the center of the continent.

Irruptive species irregularly expand their winter ranges south (Bock and Lepthien 1976, Widrlechner and Dragula 1984). Consequently, we expected differences in these species' southern range limits between the two different time periods. Red Crossbill (*Loxia curvirostra*) and Evening Grosbeak (*Coccothraustes vespertinus*; Fig. 2) fit this expectation. The other irruptive species we examined, Boreal Chickadee (*Parus hudsonicus*), Pine Siskin (*Carduelis pinus*), Common Redpoll (*Carduelis flammea*; Fig. 3), White-winged Crossbill (*Loxia leucoptera*), and Pine Grosbeak (*Pinicola enucleator*), do not.

We found relatively few species with contracted ranges. Of these, most associate with water and only one is a passerine: Pied-billed Grebe (*Podilymbus podiceps*), Northern Pintail (*Anas acuta*), Common Merganser (*Mergus merganser*), and Brown-headed Cowbird (*Molothrus ater*; Fig. 3). The cowbird, which benefits from habitat fragmentation (Brittingham and Temple 1983, May and Robinson 1985, Ehrlich et al. 1988:495–501), has expanded its winter range into the northeastern region (Maine and Nova Scotia), but has contracted its range elsewhere, particularly along its northern border (Pennsylvania, Michigan, Wisconsin, Iowa, Montana and Washington).

SHIFTING ABUNDANCE PATTERNS

Abundance patterns of most species changed. The areas of peak abundances for many species shifted into the northeastern region. These include: Bufflehead (*Bucephala albeola*), Hairy Woodpecker (*Picoides villosus*), Blue Jay (*Cyanocitta cristata*), Brown Creeper (*Certhia americana*), White-breasted Nuthatch (*Sitta carolinensis*), Red-breasted Nuthatch (*S. canadensis*), and Evening Grosbeak (Fig. 2). Other species have become more abundant toward the center of the continent in recent years. Some of these are managed and/or introduced; Northern Bobwhite (*Colinus virginianus*; Fig. 3), Ring-necked Pheasant (*Phasianus colchicus*), House Sparrow (*Passer domesticus*); others are native and non-managed; Northern Harrier, Ferruginous Hawk, and Red-headed Woodpecker (*Melanerpes erythrocephalus*). The data, unfortunately, do not allow us to know if these shifts were due to increases or decreases in absolute abundances.

Another measure of changing abundance patterns is a difference in the absolute number of states and provinces with very high abundances. This number decreased in roughly three times as many species (e.g., Fig. 3, bottom) as it increased (e.g., Fig. 1, middle). About half of the birds examined have the same number of states and provinces with maximum abundance peaks (e.g., Figs. 1–3).

DISCUSSION

North America has experienced dramatic changes over the last 100 years that have strikingly altered its natural resources and environment. The human population in Canada and the United States has increased from about 150 million at the end of World War II to around 280 million in 1991 (Ehrlich et al. 1992). Along with habitat fragmentation (Wilcove et al. 1986), air and water pollution have greatly degraded the environment by affecting the productivity of our forests, lakes and streams (Bormann 1985). Furthermore, we have been draining our wetlands at an alarming rate (WRI 1992), and climatic change has the potential to disrupt communities due to differential relocation of species' ranges (Peters 1992, Root and Schneider 1993). All of these alterations have had and will probably continue to have major impacts on the biogeographic patterns of birds.

RANGE EXPANSIONS

Along with introduced species that have strong dispersal abilities (e.g., House Sparrow and European Starling), successfully managed birds show extensive range expansions. Up to 1940 the Mute Swan was recorded only in Pennsylvania and Michigan. Since that time, programs to introduce and establish it—primarily in parks—have allowed it to spread to 19 states and three provinces. The Wild Turkey (Fig. 1) shows even a more dramatic change. Its original range covered all the states east of the 100th meridian, except for North Dakota and most of Minnesota. Additionally, Merriam's subspecies (*M. g. merriami*) ranged throughout New Mexico, Texas and Arizona (Schorger 1966). Hunting pressures, habitat loss, and disease spread by domestic poultry all contributed to a dramatic range contraction (Schorger 1966, Hewitt 1967, Lewis 1973). From 1901 to 1940 it was recorded in only ten states. According to Schorger (1966), turkeys were reintroduced into all but three states within its original range, and introduced into all the states outside its original range. Additionally, individuals were introduced into Alberta, Saskatchewan, Manitoba and probably Ontario (AOU 1983). Obviously, management has had a major impact on the distribution of the Wild Turkey, because it is now found in 52 states and provinces.

Supplemental feeding of birds by humans has also contributed to a change in both the presence and abundances of various seed-eating birds in the northeastern region. On average, a third of the households in North America provide about 60 pounds of supplemental feed a year, with the average being even higher in New England (Ehrlich et al. 1988:349). Feeders apparently have contributed strongly to both the expansion of winter ranges (e.g., Mourning Dove, Fig. 1) and increased winter densities (e.g., Blue Jay; White-breasted Nuthatch; Tufted Titmouse; Northern Cardinal; and Evening Grosbeak, Fig. 2). Birds that frequent feeders are attracted to a steady food supply at feeders, and by urbanized habitats with thickets and shrubbery that ornamental plantings often provide (Eaton 1959, Beddall 1963, Kircher 1981, Ehrlich et al. 1988: 349–353).

Habitat manipulation, albeit of another sort, may have contributed to the extensive distributional changes of the Barred Owl (Fig. 1). This owl has moved into the north-

→

FIGURE 1. Top: Map showing distributional pattern of Wild Turkey. The data from 1901 to 1940 are provided on the left-hand side of the rectangle, while those from 1960 to 1989 (except 1969) are on the right-hand side. The six different symbols (open squares with dashed margins, open square, diagonal line, crossed lines, asterisk, and filled square) correspond respectively with the following proportion of the maximum value: 0.0, 0.01 to 0.10, 0.11 to 0.25, 0.26 to 0.45, 0.46 to 0.70, and 0.71 to 1.00. Question marks indicate that no data were available. Middle: Mourning Dove. Bottom: Barred Owl.

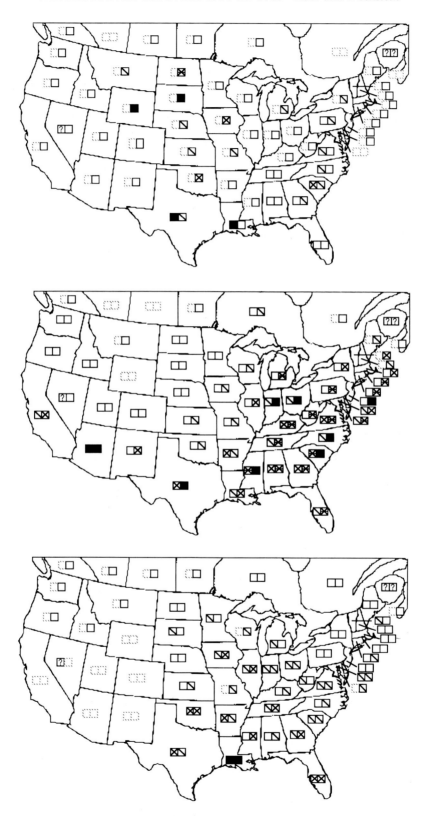

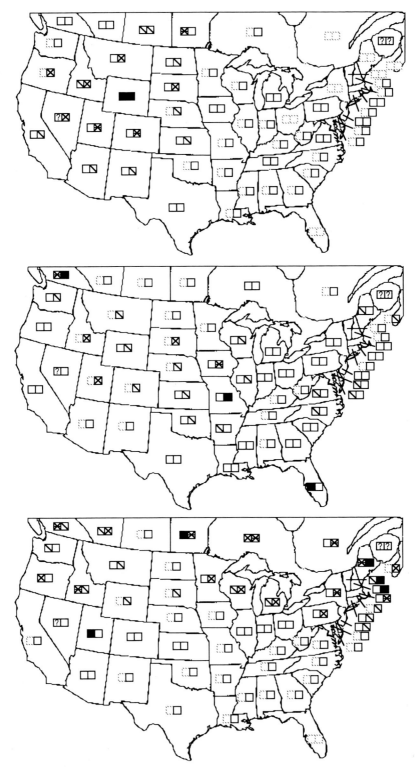

FIGURE 2.   Top: Map showing distributional pattern of Golden Eagle. Middle: Bald Eagle. Bottom: Evening Grosbeak. See Figure 1 for key.

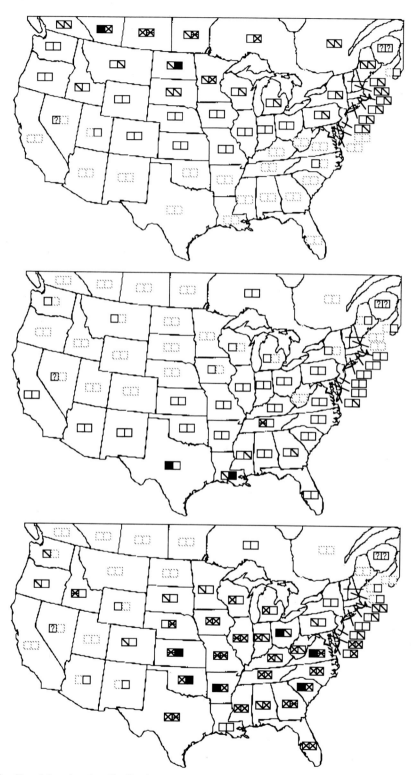

FIGURE 3.   Top: Map showing distributional pattern of Common Redpoll. Middle: Brown-headed Cowbird. Bottom: Northern Bobwhite. See Figure 1 for key.

western region relatively recently (Holt and Hillis 1987, Sharp 1989, Taylor and Forsman 1976). From 1963 to 1972 no northern populations were reported west of the 100th meridian, and only one individual was recorded north of the 50th parallel—in Pinawa, Manitoba (Root 1988). Logging and associated activities in the northwestern region may have facilitated invasions (T. E. Hamer, unpubl. data).

The Barred Owl expansion is of major interest, because its range is now partly sympatric with that of the endangered Northern Spotted Owl (*Strix occidentalis occidentalis*). The consequences of interspecific competition between these two species have not yet been quantified, but nesting sites, foraging activities, and diet are similar, particularly in the Northwest (Taylor and Forsman 1976). Anecdotal evidence suggests that the larger, more aggressive Barred Owl may be able to displace the smaller Spotted Owl; on the Olympic Peninsula in Washington, territories previously held by Spotted Owls, which have strong territory fidelity, have been taken over by Barred Owl pairs (Sharp 1989). This range expansion provides an excellent opportunity to quantify the effects of invasion. Given the endangered status of the Northern Spotted Owl, such research will not only help us understand basic biological problems but it could help in the assessment of different forestry policies.

Other raptors, specifically the two North American eagles, have significantly expanded their ranges; the Golden Eagle (Fig. 2) has moved east, while the Bald Eagle (Fig. 2) has spread into the center of the continent. The Golden Eagle is uncommon throughout its newly established range in the east. Higher abundances occur in the west, even though ranchers previously hunted them from small planes. This practice began in the late 1930s and for over 20 years people killed between 1000 and 2000 individuals each year in west Texas and southeastern New Mexico (Spofford 1969). The location of peak abundance, Wyoming, remained unchanged (Fig. 2).

Over the years humans have strongly influenced the expansion of the Bald Eagle's range by implementing various water management programs. Historically, birds were forced to move south during unusually cold winters because they need open water for hunting. This could help explain the high abundance recorded in Florida in 1901–1940. Large lakes and impoundments built in the 1930s, locks placed on major waterways, and numerous hydroelectric plants built with cooling ponds provide open water in winter. For example, core wintering areas adjacent to parts of the Mississippi, Illinois, and Missouri rivers accounted for 30% of the sightings in Millsap's study (1986). Dams on these and other rivers create sloughs and are therefore indirectly responsible for the open water used by eagles for feeding (Southern 1963). The turbines in the dams also kill or stun fish, thereby allowing the eagle easy access to food (Spencer 1976).

The winter abundance of the Bald Eagle throughout most of the contiguous United States dropped by about a third from 1957 to 1970 due to the use of persistent insecticides (e.g., DDT) and habitat destruction (Brown 1975). Since World War II, population declines in the East have been blamed on habitat destruction due to human disturbances in the form of waterfront housing and outdoor recreation (Sprunt 1969). Shooting by ranchers from small planes from the late 1930s to the early 1960s could have depressed the abundance during this time period, and for sometime after (Sprunt 1969).

Winter distributions of irruptive, boreal, seed-eating birds are highly variable from year to year (Benkman 1987, Bock and Lepthien 1976). The availability of seeds is assumed to be the primary factor driving the movements of the irruptive fringillids (Bock and Lepthien 1976) and perhaps even the Boreal Chickadee (Root 1988). For most species that we examined, however, long-term averages show little change, even when censuses are separated by 30 years (e.g., Common Redpoll, Fig. 3). This implies that the response of these birds, and perhaps the factors driving their irruptive behavior, have been fairly constant over the past century. The average ranges of two species (Red Crossbill and Evening Grosbeak; Fig. 2) are quite different between the early and later part of the century; both species expanded their ranges much farther south. Dietary preferences might help explain why we found distributional changes in some species, but not in others.

RANGE CONTRACTIONS

Given the amount of habitat modification that has occurred over the past century, we expected the ranges of many birds to contract significantly. Of the species examined, fewer than 10% showed such a pattern. This low percentage could have been partly an artifact of our sample, because we avoided species that have very restricted ranges. The plotting unit (state or province) may also have artificially decreased the instances of detectable range contractions, because individuals had to vacate entire states, not just part of them, before a contraction would be recorded. Of the four species showing range contractions, three of them depend on open water: Pied-billed Grebe, Northern Pintail and Common Merganser. The contraction of the Northern Pintail is particularly disconcerting. This game species has been extensively managed, yet estimates of its breeding population have shown a five-fold decrease since the mid-1900s (Migratory Bird Management Office 1992; also Banks and Springer 1994). The reasons for this large decline are not yet understood.

The fourth species with a contracted winter range is the Brown-headed Cowbird (Fig. 3). This result was unexpected, because this cowbird has reportedly expanded its range due to clearing of eastern forests and increased cattle grazing (Mayfield 1965, May and Robinson 1985, Ehrlich et al. 1988:495–497). Indeed, the percentage of Christmas Bird Counts east of Texas, and south of the 37th parallel reporting Brown-headed Cow-

birds, increased from near zero to over 80%, suggesting this bird has been steadily increasing its numbers in this area (Brittingham and Temple 1983). Maps of average winter abundance do not show this large increase, except perhaps in Louisiana, and small increases in Mississippi and Georgia. This is because relative, not absolute, abundances are plotted in this study. A comparison of the relative data suggests that the absolute abundances throughout most of its range may have increased. This is not the case in the upper mid-west where the cowbird range has contracted. The reasons for this are undoubtedly complex, but one contributing factor may be that during the breeding season the U.S. Fish and Wildlife Service and Michigan Department of Natural Resources trap and remove cowbirds from Michigan. Its parasitism on the endangered Kirtland's Warbler (*Dendroica kirtlandii*) is extensive (over 70% in the 1960s) (Mayfield 1978). By 1980 they had removed over 40,000 cowbirds (Walkinshaw 1983).

SHIFTING ABUNDANCE PATTERNS

Shifts in abundance patterns could indicate whether changes in habitats had significantly increased or decreased the carrying capacity of species in various areas. If an increase in carrying capacity occurred, then more individuals could survive in the area, thereby forming a new peak. A new peak could also be formed by decreasing carrying capacity in areas around a particular habitat.

Due to feeders, the carrying capacity in the northeastern region has presumably increased. Besides ranges of species expanding into this region, abundance patterns of birds attracted to feeders also have shifted so that higher relative densities are reported in this region (e.g., Evening Grosbeak, Fig. 2). Consequently, feeding stations have apparently had major impact on the winter distribution patterns of select wintering birds.

Another common change in abundance pattern is toward the center of the country, which corresponds to regions where the most winter wheat is grown (USGS 1970). Species such as Northern Bobwhite (Fig. 3) are apparently attracted to waste grain, unharvested areas along fence rows, and open fields. In the Great Plains, populations have increased as humans suppressed fires and brushy cover became established, and as farmers built more fence rows (De Vos 1964).

CONCLUSION

The National Audubon Society's Christmas Bird Count data and similar census data recorded in the *Canadian Field Naturalist* provide an excellent source for examining distribution patterns of wintering North American birds over both broad-spatial and long-temporal scales. We found extensive changes in the ranges and abundance patterns of the birds we examined. The primary cause of these shifts, directly or indirectly, was human activity. Although these include activities specifically designed to manifest a change (e.g., management of the Wild Turkey), most were not purposeful (e.g., water management programs and the Bald Eagle). Subsequent studies are needed to focus on possible factors regulating the distributional shifts we begin to explore here. One obvious approach would be to include more species, examine breeding-season data, and investigate directly possible effects of climate.

ACKNOWLEDGMENTS

We are grateful for Larry McDaniel's competent and tireless help in analyzing the data from 1960 to 1989. We appreciate helpful comments on earlier drafts of this paper by Stephen Schneider, J. R. Jehl, Jr., Ned Johnson, Michael Burger, Thomas Dietsch, Betsy Daub, Jeff Goldsmith, Yonat Swimmer, and particularly Thomas Jones. This project was partially funded by the National Science Foundation (Presidential Young Investigator Award #IBN-9058031) and U.S. Fish and Wildlife Service.

LITERATURE CITED

AMERICAN ORNITHOLOGISTS' UNION (AOU). 1983. Checklist of North American Birds. 6th ed. Allen Press, Lawrence, KS.

BANKS, R. C., AND P. F. SPRINGER. 1994. A century of population trends of waterfowl in western North America. Pp. 134–146 *in* J. R. Jehl, Jr. and N. K.

Johnson (eds.), A century of avifaunal change in western North America. Studies in Avian Biology No. 15.

BEDDALL, B. G. 1963. Range expansion of the Cardinal and other birds in the northeastern states. Wilson Bulletin 75:140–158.

BENKMAN, C. W. 1987. Food profitability and the foraging ecology of crossbills. Ecological Monographs 57:251–267.

BOCK, C. E., AND L. W. LEPTHIEN. 1976. Synchronous eruptions of boreal seed-eating birds. American Naturalist 110:559–571.

BOCK, C. E., AND T. L. ROOT. 1981. The Christmas Bird Count and avian ecology. Pp. 17–23 *in* C. J. Ralph and J. M. Scott (eds.), Estimating numbers of terrestrial birds. Studies in Avian Biology No. 6.

BORMANN, F. H. 1985. Air pollution and forests: an ecosystem perspective. BioScience 35:434–441.

BRITTINGHAM, M. C., AND S. A. TEMPLE. 1983. Have cowbirds caused forest songbirds to decline? BioScience 33:31–35.

BROWN, W. H. 1975. Winter population trends in the Bald Eagle. American Birds 29:12–14.

COBLENTZ, B. E. 1990. Exotic organisms: a dilemma for conservation biology. Conservation Biology 4:261–265.

DE VOS, A. 1964. Range changes of birds in the Great Lake Regions. American Midland Naturalist 71:489–502.

EATON, S. W. 1959. The Tufted Titmouse invades New York. The Kingbird 9:59–62.

EHRLICH, P. R., D. S. DOBKIN, AND D. WHEYE. 1988. The birder's handbook. Simon and Shuster, New York.

EHRLICH, P. R., D. S. DOBKIN, AND D. WHEYE. 1992. Birds in jeopardy. Stanford University Press, Stanford, CA.

FLECKER, A. S. 1992. Fish trophic guilds and the structure of a tropical stream: weak direct vs strong indirect effects. Ecology 73:927–940.

FORBUSH, E. H. 1929. Birds of Massachusetts and other New England states. Part III. Commonwealth of Massachusetts, Boston.

FRETWELL, S. D. 1972. Populations in a seasonal environment. Princeton University Press, Princeton.

HEWITT, O. H. 1967. The Wild Turkey and its management. Wildlife Society, Washington, D.C.

HOLT, D. W., AND J. M. HILLIS. 1987. Current status and habitat associations of forest owls in western Montana. Pp. 281–288 *in* R. W. Nero, R. J. Clark, R. J. Knapton, and R. H. Hamre (eds.), Biology and conservation of northern forest owls. USDA Forest Service General Technical Report RM-142, Fort Collins, CO.

KIRCHER, J. C. 1981. Range expansion of the Tufted Titmouse (*Parus bicolor*) in Massachusetts. American Birds 35:750–753.

LEWIS, J. C. 1973. The world of the Wild Turkey. J. B. Lippincott Co., Philadelphia.

MAY, R. M., AND S. K. ROBINSON. 1985. Population dynamics of avian brood parasitism. American Naturalist 126:475–494.

MAYFIELD, H. F. 1965. The Brown-headed Cowbird with old and new hosts. Living Bird 4:13–28.

MAYFIELD, H. F. 1978. Brood parasitism: reducing

interactions between Kirtland's Warblers and Brown-headed Cowbirds. Pp. 85–91 *in* S. A. Temple (ed.), Symposium on endangered birds: management techniques for endangered species. University of Wisconsin Press, Madison.

MIGRATORY BIRD MANAGEMENT OFFICE. 1992. Status of waterfowl and fall flight forecast. U.S. Fish and Wildlife Service.

MILLSAP, B. A. 1986. Status of wintering Bald Eagles in the conterminous 48 states. Wildlife Society Bulletin 14:434–440.

PETERS, R. L. 1992. Conservation of biological diversity in the face of climate change. Pp. 3–26 *in* R. L. Peters and T. E. Lovejoy (eds.), Global warming and biological diversity, Yale University Press, New Haven.

PULLIAM, H. R. 1988. Source, sinks, and population regulation. American Naturalist 132:652–661.

PULLIAM, H. R., AND B. J. DANIELSON. 1991. Sources, sinks and habitat selection: a landscape perspective on population dynamics. American Naturalist 137: S50–S66.

ROBBINS, C. S. 1973. Introduction, spread, and present abundance of the House Sparrow in North America. Ornithological Monographs 14:3–9.

ROBBINS, C. S., D. BYSTRAK, AND P. H. GEISSLER. 1986. The Breeding Bird Survey: its first fifteen years, 1965–1979. U.S. Fish and Wildlife Service Resource Publication 157. Washington, D.C.

ROOT, T. L. 1988. Atlas of wintering North American birds. University of Chicago Press, Chicago.

ROOT, T. L., AND S. H. SCHNEIDER. 1993. Can large-scale climatic models be linked with multiscale ecological studies? Conservation Biology 7:256–270.

SAVAGE, J. A. 1987. Extinction of an island forest avifauna by an introduced snake. Ecology 68:660–668.

SCHORGER, A. W. 1966. The Wild Turkey: its history and domestication. University of Oklahoma Press, Norman.

SHARP, D. V. 1989. Range extension of the Barred Owl in western Washington and first breeding record on the Olympic Peninsula. Journal of Raptor Research 23:179–180.

SOUTHERN, W. E. 1963. Winter populations, behavior, and seasonal dispersal of Bald Eagles in northwestern Illinois. Wilson Bulletin 75:42–55.

SPENCER, D. A. 1976. Wintering of the migrant Bald Eagle in the lower 48 states. National Agricultural Chemical Association, Washington, D.C.

SPENCER, C. N., B. R. MCCLELLAND, AND J. A. STANFORD. 1991. Shrimp stocking, salmon collapse, and eagle displacement. BioScience 41:14–20.

SPOFFORD, W. R. 1969. Problems of the Golden Eagle in North America. Pp. 345–347 *in* J. J. Hickey (ed.), Peregrine Falcon populations: their biology and decline. University of Wisconsin Press, Madison.

SPRUNT, A., IV. 1969. Population trends of the Bald Eagle in North America. Pp. 347–351 *in* J. J. Hickey (ed.), Peregrine Falcon populations: their biology and decline. University of Wisconsin Press, Madison.

TAYLOR, A. L., AND E. D. FORSMAN. 1976. Recent range extensions of the Barred Owl in western North America, including the first records for Oregon. Condor 78:560–561.

TERBORGH, J. 1986. Keystone plant resources in the tropical forest. Pp. 330–344 *in* M. E. Soule (ed.), Conservation biology. Sinauer Press, Sunderland, MA.

U.S. GEOLOGICAL SURVEY (USGS). 1970. The national atlas of the United States of America. U.S. Government Printing Office, Washington, D.C.

WALKINSHAW, L. H. 1983. Kirtland's Warbler: the natural history of an endangered species. Cranbrook Institute of Science, Bloomfield Hills, MI.

WIDRLECHNER, M. P., AND S. K. DRAGULA. 1984. Relationship of cone-crop size to irruptions of four seed-eating birds in California. American Birds 38:840–846.

WILCOVE, D. S., C. H. MCLELLAN, AND A. P. DOBSON. 1986. Habitat fragmentation in the temperate zone. Pp. 237–256 *in* M. E. Soule (ed.), Conservation biology. Sinauer Press, Sunderland, MA.

WILLIAMS, J. D., AND R. M. NOVAK. 1987. Vanishing species in our own backyard: extinct fish and wildlife of the United States and Canada. Pp. 107–139 *in* L. Kaufman and K. Mallory (eds.), The last extinction. MIT Press, Cambridge, MA.

WING, L. 1947. Christmas census summary 1900–1939. State College of Washington, Pullman Mimeograph.

WORLD RESOURCES INSTITUTE (WRI). 1992. World resources 1992–1993. Oxford University Press, New York.

ZELENY, L. 1976. The bluebird. Indiana University Press, Bloomington.

Studies in Avian Biology No. 15:202–220, 1994.

HISTORICAL CHANGES IN POPULATIONS AND PERCEPTIONS OF NATIVE PEST BIRD SPECIES IN THE WEST

John M. Marzluff, Randall B. Boone, and George W. Cox

Abstract. A wide variety of native bird species are considered pests because they damage agriculture, present health hazards, damage structures, create a nuisance, or damage natural resources. Damage to agriculture is the most costly and most frequently reported pest problem. However, nuisance problems and damage to natural resources, especially endangered species, are becoming increasingly common. Review of the literature and analysis of BBS, BBC, and CBC survey data showed that wintering and breeding populations of most pests have increased over the last century, despite frequent eradication campaigns against them. Great-tailed Grackles have increased most rapidly and have spread throughout the west. Gulls have increased rapidly, but have shown only minor range expansions. Corvids have increased moderately, and invaded agricultural and urban habitats. Woodpecker, Golden Eagle, Red-winged and Yellow-headed Blackbird, and Northern Mockingbird populations have remained steady or increased slightly. Tri-colored Blackbirds have declined in abundance. A key to the development of pest problems is the initial removal or conversion of natural habitat to urban or agricultural sites. These changes displace native birds and provide supplemental feeding and nesting locations for those species destined to become pests. Flocking and generalized diets are important traits that may have preadapted pest species to exploit humans.

Key Words: Distribution; abundance; pest; agriculture; breeding bird survey; Christmas Bird Count.

When humans began to manage their environment to provide food and shelter the animals that successfully competed with them became known as "pests." To the student of avian populations, familiar pests are introduced exotics like the European Starling (*Sturnus vulgaris*) and House Sparrow (*Passer domesticus*; Johnston and Garrett 1994). However, native species also are serious competitors with humans, inflicting heavy monetary losses on societies in industrialized nations and threatening human survival in some underdeveloped countries (DeGrazio 1989).

Native birds are considered pests if they: 1) damage agricultural products, 2) present health hazards, 3) damage human structures, 4) create a nuisance or reduce aesthetics, or 5) damage natural resources.

Damage to agriculture is the most frequent and most costly complaint. Fifteen native birds are commonly cited as agricultural pests in the west and many others are occasionally implicated (Table 1). Most of these species eat a variety of mature crops and newly sprouted seeds. However, the larger corvids and Golden Eagles (*Aquila*

chrysaetos) also prey upon poultry and livestock. A few notable examples include American Crows (*Corvus brachyrhynchos*) consuming $85,000 worth of almonds in California in 1965 (Simpson 1972), Red-winged Blackbirds (*Agelaius phoeniceus*), Yellow-headed Blackbirds (*Xanthocephalus xanthocephalus*), and Common Grackles (*Quiscalus quiscula*) damaging $7.9 million worth of sunflowers in North Dakota, South Dakota and Minnesota in 1980 (Hothem et al. 1988), House Finches (*Carpodacus mexicanus*) damaging $3 million worth of California wine grapes in 1974 (DeHaven 1974), Golden Eagles killing $48,000 worth of lambs in Montana in 1975 (O'Gara 1978), and Black-billed Magpies (*Pica pica*) destroying $10,000 worth of pollination bees in Idaho in 1989 (United States Department of Interior 1989). California leads all western States in total agricultural damage caused by birds (an estimated $12.75 million in 1976; DeGrazio 1978).

Three health hazards are created by native birds; neurosis, spread of disease, and collisions with aircraft. Aggregation of many individual birds, especially at communal

TABLE 1. NATIVE BIRD SPECIES IN THE WESTERN U.S. THAT ARE CONSIDERED IMPORTANT AGRICULTURAL PESTS

Species	Type of product damaged[a]
Primary pests	
House Finch	Grain, fruit, sunflower, grapes, sugar beets, truck crops, buds/flowers
American Crow	Grain, fruit, peanuts, tree nuts, feedlots, poultry
Black-billed Magpie	Grain, fruit, tree nuts, feedlots, potatoes, poultry, livestock, apiary
Red-winged Blackbird	Grain, sunflower, peanuts, feedlots
Brown-headed Cowbird	Grain, peanuts, feedlots
Scrub Jay	Grain, fruit, tree nuts, grapes
Common Grackle	Grain, sunflower, peanuts
Yellow-headed Blackbird	Grain, sunflower, feedlots
Brewer's Blackbird	Grain, fruit, feedlots
Common Raven	Grain, poultry, livestock
Great-tailed Grackle	Grain, fruit
Tri-colored Blackbird	Grain, feedlots
Mallard	Grain
Northern Pintail	Grain
Golden Eagle	Livestock
Secondary pests	
Western Meadowlark	Peanuts, feedlot
Franklin's Gull	Peanuts, feedlot
Blue Jay	Peanuts, feedlot, grapes
Killdeer	Feedlot
Water Pipit	Feedlot
Mourning Dove	Feedlot, grapes
Western Bluebird	Wine grapes
American Goldfinch	Sunflower, grapes, buds/flowers
American Robin	Grapes
California Quail	Grapes
White-crowned Sparrow	Grain, fruit, grapes, flowers
Horned Lark	Truck crops, buds/flowers, sugar beets
Acorn Woodpecker	Tree nuts, grapes
Lewis' Woodpecker	Tree nuts, grapes
Northern Flicker	Tree nuts, grapes
White-winged Dove	Grain
Sandhill Crane	Grain, potatoes
Northern Mockingbird	Grapes
California Thrasher	Grapes
Catbird	Grapes
Rufous-sided Towhee	Grapes
Turkey Vulture	Grapes
Western Kingbird	Grapes
Western Tanager	Grapes
Great-blue Heron	Fish
Great Egret	Fish
Double-crested Cormorant	Fish
California Gull	Fruit

TABLE 1. CONTINUED

Species	Type of product damaged[a]
Canada Goose	Grain
Snow Goose	Grain
White-fronted Goose	Grain

[a] References: Cottam 1935, Stockdale 1967, Larsen and Dietrich 1970, Palmer 1970, DeHaven 1971, 1974, Mott et al. 1972, Simpson 1972, Clark 1975, Crase and DeHaven 1976, Crase et al. 1976, Knittle and Guarino 1976, DeGrazio 1978, O'Gara 1978, Avery and DeHaven 1982, Besser and Brady 1982, Besser 1985, Hothem et al. 1988, Knittle and Porter 1988, Phillips and Blom 1988, Stickley and Andrews 1989, Pochop et al. 1990.

roosts, is a common denominator. The noises associated with large roosts of several million blackbirds have been known to drive humans crazy, and fecal deposits under roosts can act as a vector for disease transmission and promote the growth of other local pathogens, such as *Histoplasmosis capsulatum* (Garner 1978).

Bird collisions with aircraft are typically local, but deadly and expensive problems. The first human fatality occurred in San Diego, CA in 1910, but research into this problem began in earnest in 1960 when a small plane collided with a flock of starlings and killed 62 people (Pearson 1967). In 1965 the U.S. Air Force estimated that 839 collisions caused $10 million of damage to their aircraft (Pearson 1967). Large birds or flocking species that feed, or roost near airfields pose the greatest problems; these include Snow Geese (*Chen caerulescens*), Tundra Swans (*Cygnus columbianus*), Common Loons (*Gavia immer*), Red-tailed Hawks (*Buteo jamaicensis*), gulls, waterfowl and blackbirds.

Human structures, principally buildings, transmission lines, and utility poles, are damaged by several species of woodpeckers and communally roosting gulls, blackbirds, and corvids. Red-headed Woodpeckers (*Melanerpes erythrocephalus*), Northern Flickers (*Colaptes auratus*) and Pileated Woodpeckers (*Dryocopus pileatus*) damaged $250,000 worth of utility poles in Missouri from 1981–1982 (Stemmerman 1988). Acorn Woodpeckers (*Melanerpes formicivorus*) use utility poles in the southwest as graneries, causing extensive damage (Pope 1974). Lewis' Woodpeckers (*Melanerpes lewis*), Acorn Woodpeckers and Northern Flickers damage buildings, water tanks and fence posts in California (Clark 1975). Damage to house siding by woodpeckers is typically a local problem, but can cause substantial monetary loss to individual landowners ($1000 to one Idaho home in 1982). Fecal deposition by Common Ravens (*Corvus corax*) roosting above transmission line insulators enables electricity to arc between lines and cause expensive power outages (Young and Engel 1988). Feces from blackbirds, gulls, or Cliff Swallows (*Hirundo pyrrhonota*) damage houses and automobiles (e.g., Gorenzel and Salmon 1982).

Nuisance complaints against native birds are diverse. Defecation by waterfowl, notably Mallards (*Anas platyrhynchos*), Canada Geese (*Branta canadensis*), and American Coots (*Fulica americana*), on lawns, golf courses, and water treatment plants is a problem in the eastern U.S. and in parts of the west (Conover and Chasko 1985, Woronecki et al. 1990). The noise associated with urban corvids and blackbird roosts is often objectionable, as is the nocturnal singing of Northern Mockingbirds (*Mimus polyglottos*; Fitzwater 1988). Mississippi Kites (*Ictinia mississippiensis*) vigorously defend their nests and occasionally harm humans walking nearby (Peterson and Brown 1985).

Complaints of damage to natural resources have typically implicated nest predators, particularly corvids. In the late 1800s and early 1900s "jay shoots" were organized by sportsmen in California to kill the "vermin" that were believed to be lowering the productivity of California Quail (*Callipepla californica*; Erickson 1937). More recently, avian nest predators have been implicated in the decline of other native animals. For example, Pinyon Jay (*Gymnorhinus cyanocephalus*) productivity has declined in Flagstaff, AZ, partly because of increased predation by crows and ravens (Marzluff and Balda 1992). Several endangered species [Marbled Murrelet (*Brachy-*

ramphus marmoratus), Desert Tortoise (*Xerobates agassizii*) and California Least Tern (*Sterna antillarum*)] may be suffering similar fates at the hands of corvids and other predators [e.g., American Kestrel (*Falco sparverius*) and Burrowing Owl (*Athene cunicularia*); Butchko 1990, Singer et al. 1991].

Most pests present more than one problem. Blackbirds, for example, consume agricultural crops, spread disease and disturb residents near their roosts, choke airplane engines, and damage structures with their feces. Gulls and corvids present hazards near airfields, damage structures with their feces, prey upon the eggs and nestlings of a variety of species, and consume large quantities of agricultural products.

HISTORICAL DEVELOPMENT OF PEST PROBLEMS

As soon as Europeans began to settle North America they encountered problems with some of the abundant, granivorous native birds. The first documented problem was in 1717, when blackbirds in Connecticut destroyed settlers' crops (DeHaven 1971). The problem must have been substantial because all men were required to kill 12 birds per day during the summer to curb the damage. They were fined if their quota was not met! The first settlers moving west met with similar problems (Stockdale 1967), but most problems in the western U.S. began after the transcontinental railway was completed in the 1860s and settlement of the west grew at exponential rates.

The development of early pest problems followed a consistent three phase pattern; 1) human settlement and agriculture increased, 2) native foods or nest sites were reduced, then supplemented or replaced by human agricultural crops and structures, and 3) locally abundant birds capitalized upon new feeding or nesting opportunities. The drainage of the wetlands and establishment of agribusiness in California is a classic example. Currently less than 10% of the state's historical wetlands remain (Cowan 1970).

Gone with them are traditional breeding and nesting sites for blackbirds and waterfowl. However, man has provided abundant food and habitat in the irrigated croplands of the state's interior valleys. Red-winged, Yellow-headed, and Tri-colored Blackbirds (*Agelaius tricolor*), Mallards, and Canada Geese have taken advantage of this bounty and wreaked havoc on agriculture (Knittle and Porter 1988).

A key to the development of such a pest problem is the initial removal or conversion of natural habitat. Damage rarely develops if natural resources are abundant. For example, losses of sheep to Golden Eagles and peanuts to corvids were greatly reduced in years of abundant native prey (jackrabbits and acorns, respectively; Mott et al. 1972, O'Gara 1978).

Pest problems appear to have persisted once native species began to exploit human agriculture because large populations of pests were sustained and they could quickly switch to feed on each new crop. Blackbirds surviving on cereal grains quickly became pests on sunflower crops (Hothem et al. 1988). House Finches, sustained by a variety of agricultural crops in the early 1900s, quickly adapted to blueberries in 1958, figs in 1970, wine grapes in 1973, and sunflowers in 1982 (Palmer 1970, DeHaven 1974, Avery and DeHaven 1982).

CHANGING PERCEPTIONS OF NATIVE BIRD PESTS

As human settlement of the west increased and our uses of the land multiplied, conflicts with native birds diversified (Fig. 1). From the late 1800s to approximately 1960, most concerned consumption of agricultural products. This has continued to be the major complaint, expanding greatly from 1960 to 1990 as many new crops were planted (e.g., wine grapes, sunflowers, and wild rice). However, during the last 30 years, birds have come into conflict with man increasingly for nonagricultural reasons, especially as nuisances in urban settings and as predators on threatened species (Fig. 1).

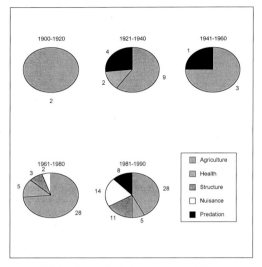

FIGURE 1. Historical changes in problems caused by native bird pests. Each pie diagram covers a specific range of dates (listed above each pie) and presents the percentage of published papers addressing the five major types of damage caused by pests (see text for definition of types and key for corresponding shading). The actual number of papers in each damage category is listed outside the pie. All issues of *The Condor* and *Proceedings of the Vertebrate Pest Conference* through 1992 were surveyed.

CHANGES IN THE ABUNDANCE AND DISTRIBUTION OF NATIVE BIRD PESTS

METHODS

We searched the ornithological literature for documentation of avian populations early in the century and discussions of recent changes in populations of native bird pests. General trends in population size and distribution can be obtained from such accounts, but quantification is difficult. Therefore, we supplemented our literature review by examining annual Breeding Bird Surveys (BBS) and Christmas Bird Counts (CBC). These counts have been conducted each year and the results have been computerized for most of the past three decades (e.g., Droege 1990).

We used BBS surveys from 1966–1990. Only "type 1" surveys, those with no known problems and experienced observers, were used. We avoided biases in raw trends, caused by variable observers and missing censuses, by calculating Bailey indices. This index (Bailey 1967) only uses censuses surveyed in successive years by the same observer. Changes from year to year are therefore proportional and unbiased. We assessed the occurrence of "random walk" error in Bailey indices with a test developed by Moss (1985). Nonsignificant correlations between raw census counts and the Bailey indices indicate random walk (a rare event in our analyses; only three correlations were not significant and the maximum P-value was only 0.25). Each index was truncated to remove annual indices for years with few paired censuses (Boone 1991).

We used CBC surveys from 1961–1989. We treated census circles that overlapped in area by 50% or more as replicates of the same circle with center coordinates equal to the center of the most frequently used circle. Counts were adjusted for variable observer effort by using several modifications of the Butcher and McCulloch (1990) procedure: 1) The exponent relating survey party-hours to the number of birds counted was calculated on a state-by-state, rather than "national", scale. 2) The effect of observer effort was calculated without including counts derived from fewer than 30 party-hours. 3) Each count's contribution to the total variance between observed and predicted counts was computed. If this contribution exceeded 10%, the modified count was considered suspect and the unmodified count was used in its place.

To understand which factors influenced changes in the numbers of birds counted we used a nonparametric classification and regression tree (CART) approach (Breiman et al. 1984) to relate the natural log of the count total to the following variables: 1) Year; 2) Long-term (1966–1990) means of January temperatures, July temperatures, and precipitation; 3) Annual deviations in mean January temperatures, July temperatures, and precipitation from the long-term mean temperatures and precipitation; 4) Distance from the start of the route to the nearest

coastline (± 25 km); 5) Latitude and longitude for the start of the route; 6) USFWS physiographic stratum assigned to each route or circle (Robbins et al. 1986); 7) Proportion of farmland in the county containing most of the route determined by the 1987 Census of Agriculture; 8) People per square mile in the county containing most of the route determined by the 1990 population census; and 9) Total number of species observed on the route for the year surveyed.

We used breeding bird census (BBC) data to investigate changes in corvids in California. We selected surveys for single years from each of the available locations to reduce bias due to the peculiar characteristics of individual survey sites, procedures, or observers. We considered 196 survey areas covering the period from 1937 through 1990 (54 years).

For sites with breeding surveys in more than one year, we selected the one year that overlapped least with annual coverage by other surveys to minimize bias from any unusual weather conditions. Nevertheless, in 28 cases, two or more sites were surveyed by the same observers in the same year; 17 of these cases involved two sites, 11 others from three to six sites. Many of these multiple surveys were in desert habitats, where observer differences were probably less extreme than in closed vegetation types.

Ten independent variables were used in statistical analyses: 1) Year in which the survey was carried out; 2) Latitude of the survey site to the nearest 0.1 degree; 3) Direct eastward distance of the site from the Pacific Ocean; 4) Altitude of the site in meters; 5) Plot area in hectares; 6) Number of non-raptorial breeding land bird species recorded; 7) Number of pairs of non-raptorial breeding land birds per 40.5 ha; 8) Moisture/temperature Index; 9) Vegetation Structure Index; 10) Human Impact Index.

The three index variables were ratings of survey plot conditions on a 10-point scale. These ratings were assigned on the basis of information given in the description of the survey site, or determined from the geographical location of the survey plot. The moisture-temperature ranking ranged from an index of 1.0 for Sonoran Desert sites with 2–8 inches of annual precipitation and 280–345 frost-free days to 10.0 for alpine tundra sites with 25–35 inches of annual precipitation and possible freezing conditions any time. The vegetation structure ranking ranged from an index of 1.0 for low, homogeneous, herbaceous, seasonal vegetation types, such as annual grassland, to 10.0 for tall, heterogeneous, arboreal, aseasonal vegetation types, such as mixed hardwood-conifer riparian forest. The human impact ranking ranged from 1.0 for sites with negligible direct human influences, such as ecological preserves with controlled access and non-manipulative research and monitoring practices, to 10.0 for sites with intensive urban, agricultural, industrial, or vehicular use characteristics.

We used stepwise multiple regression to test whether year was correlated with bird abundance after the variability in the dependent variable due to geographical, climatic, vegetational, and human impact differences among the locations had been considered. Power, root, and logarithmic transformations were examined for certain variables. Number of species and number of breeding pairs were considered indices of general productivity or "richness" of habitat conditions. In these analyses, we set the critical F-value for inclusion or retention of an independent variable in the multiple regression analysis to 4.0. For resulting regression equations that contained year, we estimated the long-term change in numbers of pairs per 40.5 ha by examining the slope of the regression of year on the residuals of multiple regression analyses with the remaining independent variables.

Results

Pest species can be characterized by the change in abundance within their historic ranges and the shifts in their distribution (Fig. 2). Most pests are increasing within their historic ranges and invading nearby

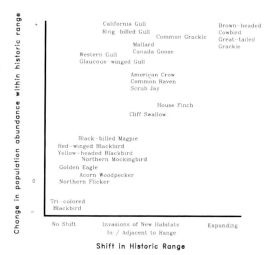

FIGURE 2. Changes in the abundance and distribution of native bird pests in the west. The position of each species is indicated by the start of its name and is plotted relative to other pests. The x-axis presents a continuum from no shift in range to large shifts in range. The y-axis presents a continuum from declines in population size (−) through stable population size (0) to progressively larger increases in population size (+).

urban or agricultural developments. However, some species are not or have declined; others have expanded their ranges significantly across the west. Several case histories illustrate this variety.

The only pest species that appears to be declining throughout its historic range is the Tri-colored Blackbird. It was extremely abundant in California and southern Oregon during the late 1800s and early 1900s, although patchily distributed because of its colonial habits (Grinnell 1915, Neff 1937). Tri-colored Blackbird populations suffered from market hunting and marsh draining in the late 1800s, but they capitalized on increased habitat and food created in the extensive rice farms of California's Central Valley beginning in 1910 (Neff 1942). They were considered a serious pest in the Sacramento Valley in the 1930s. Yet, despite poisoning campaigns (McCabe 1932), the populations flourished through the 1950s.

Colonies including 25,000 or more pairs were frequently noted early in the century, but rarely late in the century. Extensive surveys from 1969–1972 indicated that the distribution of the breeding colonies remained unchanged for 35 years, but that the population size began to decline in the 1960s, perhaps reducing the Central Valley population by as much as 50% (DeHaven et al. 1975). Populations declined to perhaps 10% of their historic levels during the 1970s and 1980s (Beedy et al. 1991), prompting the species' removal from the pest list in 1989 and addition to the California list of species of special concern and the federal endangered species candidate list. Surveys in 1992 revealed many birds in nontraditional upland habitats, suggesting that the population may not have declined as greatly as thought (R. Bowen, pers. comm.).

A group of pests including Black-billed Magpies, Red-winged and Yellow-headed Blackbirds, Northern Mockingbirds, Golden Eagles, Acorn Woodpeckers and Northern Flickers have changed only slightly in abundance and distribution (Fig. 2). Flickers, mockingbirds and Acorn Woodpeckers have maintained abundant and constant breeding populations. However, their wintering populations have all tended to increase, especially in the Rocky Mountain States (e.g., Fig. 3). Wintering populations of Golden Eagles have also increased throughout the west, possibly by as much as 29% (Phillips and Blom 1988).

Black-billed Magpies maintained high populations during the 20th century. They expanded their range east in the early 1900s into Oklahoma and Kansas (Tate 1927) and increased in abundance in western riparian locations that border agriculture (Rickard 1959). Recently, populations of breeding birds remained relatively stable (Robbins et al. 1986), but wintering populations, especially in Texas and Utah, have increased. CART analyses of BBS counts suggested that populations were declining in the Plains States, and least abundant in human dominated habitats. However, in the Coastal and Mountain States, magpies were positively correlated with human density and farmland. Winter densities were positively correlated with farmland.

Red-winged and Yellow-headed Blackbirds were noted as common by the earliest explorers of the western marshes (Grinnell 1915). They have both changed their abundance and distribution slightly by invading agriculture whenever breeding sites were close to human population centers (e.g., Howell 1922). As with all marsh dwelling birds, Red-winged and Yellow-headed Blackbird populations in the west declined periodically during the 1930s in response to urban sprawl and the draining of marshes (Davis 1935). Population growth also was checked from the 1850s–1930s by market hunters who killed hundreds of thousands of them (Neff 1942). Red-wings remained common throughout the western U.S. and Canada into the 1960s (e.g., Gullion 1951), and were first observed breeding in Alaska in the late 1950s (Shepherd 1962).

Recently, breeding populations of both species have remained stable or increased slightly throughout the western U.S. and Canada (Twedt et al. 1991, Erskine et al. 1992) while increasing significantly in the Plains States (Robbins et al. 1986). However, Red-wings in the Dakotas declined by as much as 41% from 1965–1981 due to drought and tilling of wetlands (Besser et al. 1984). Winter population trends are difficult to interpret.

Two species, Cliff Swallows and House Finches, have exhibited moderate range expansions and increases in population size. Cliff Swallows have increased throughout the west, but the major change has been in California, where increases in foraging and nesting habitat provided by irrigation and bridge building have facilitated the spread

→

FIGURE 3. Recent trends in the population size of Northern Flickers throughout the western U.S. Counts during the breeding season (BBS) are given on the left half of the graph and counts during the winter (CBC) are

Northern Flicker   AOU: 412.0

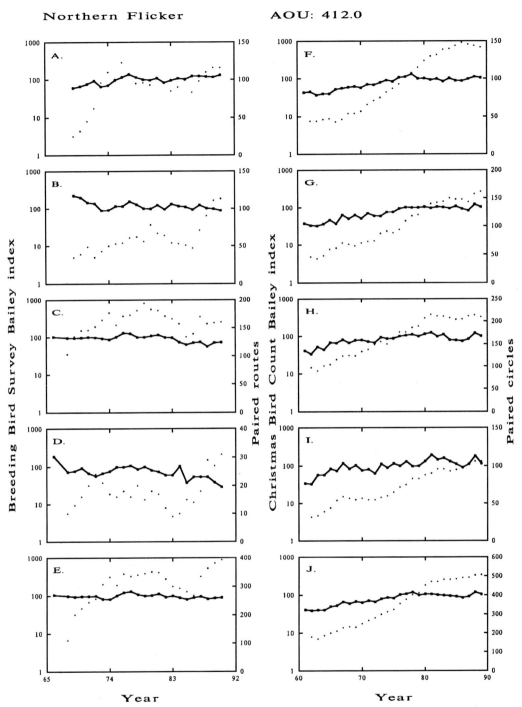

given on the right half. A solid line connects the squares representing the value of the Bailey index of population size in each year. This index is scaled to 100 in 1979 to allow relative comparisons between the years. The number of surveys (routes or circles) used to create each index is indicated by the solid circles without a line. Trends are presented separately for the Pacific Coast States (A, F), Rocky Mountain States (B, G), Plains States (C, H), Texas, Louisiana, and Utah (D, I), and all of the United States west of the Mississippi (E, J). Indices were not calculated when sample sizes of paired counts were very small, but the number of counts is still plotted.

of a large population throughout the Central Valley since the late 1950s (Gorenzel and Salmon 1982).

House Finches spread to the north from their center of abundance in California and the southeastern deserts (Edwards and Stirling 1961, Paul 1964). In 1910, they only occurred from Oregon, Idaho, and Wyoming south. By 1928 they were common in California, central Idaho and central Washington and began to spread into British Columbia in 1935, reaching 130 km north of the U.S. border by 1948. In the early 1960s, they were common throughout the lower half of British Columbia. They also spread west to coastal Oregon in 1940 and east to Montana in 1968 (Hand 1969). Recently, the numbers of breeders have remained stable for the west as a whole, but declined slightly in the Mountain West and Great Plains (Fig. 4; Robbins et al. 1986). Wintering populations have increased (Fig. 4).

The four principal species of gulls in the western U.S. have exhibited large increases in population size, with modest changes in range. Western and Glaucous-winged gulls bred on islands off the Pacific Coast early in the century (Grinnell 1915, Dickey and Van Rossem 1925). Both species are now much commoner in coastal urban areas. CBC surveys indicate that wintering populations of Western Gulls have increased approximately 10× in the last 30 years. Glaucous-winged Gulls began to increase in British Columbia in the 1930s (Woodberry and Knight 1951) and have increased by 2.6% per year from 1960–1980 (Vermeer 1982). In the last 30 years, CBC data do not suggest that winter populations of Glaucous-winged Gulls in the U.S. are increasing.

California and Ring-billed gulls increased 2.7× and 22×, respectively, from approximately 1930–1980 (Conover 1983). The expansion of California Gulls came principally from increased colony establishment in Washington, Montana and North Dakota (Conover 1983), and Canada. A similar pattern, but with greater expansion of colonies in Idaho and Oregon, was noted for Ring-billed Gulls (Conover 1983). Both species have continued to increase into the 1990s (Fig. 5; Blokpoel and Tessier 1986, Yochem et al. 1991).

Spring (BBS) and winter (CBC) surveys conducted over the last 30 years have detected sustained increases in California Gulls. Counts during the breeding season have increased more consistently in the Coastal States than in the Mountain States. Moreover, CART analyses indicated that populations in the Mountain States were more closely associated with agriculture than coastal populations. Wintering populations were greatest in areas of high human density and were less closely correlated with farmland.

CBC and BBS surveys suggest that Ring-billed Gulls have increased dramatically in the spring and winter throughout the western U.S. (Fig. 5). Counts in Plains States were strongly, positively associated with farmland and deviations from mean January temperature, and negatively correlated with the abundance of humans. Coastal counts were more strongly associated with plot species richness. Wintering populations throughout the west were positively associated with farmland and human density.

The principal waterfowl and corvid pests have sustained large increases in population size and moderate shifts in density within their historic ranges (Fig. 2). Waterfowl populations likely declined during the first third of the century in response to increased wetland drainage and severe droughts in the Prairie States (Banks and Springer 1994). Populations were lowest in the mid-1930s, but during the last 30 years, the principal pest species (Canada Geese and Mallards) increased substantially in the Plains States (Fig. 6; Conover and Chasko 1985, Robbins et al. 1986). Increases during the winter are partially due to overwintering in the breeding range by many urban and suburban populations that were once migratory.

Ravens were conspicuous but sparsely distributed permanent residents in the early

House Finch   AOU: 519.0

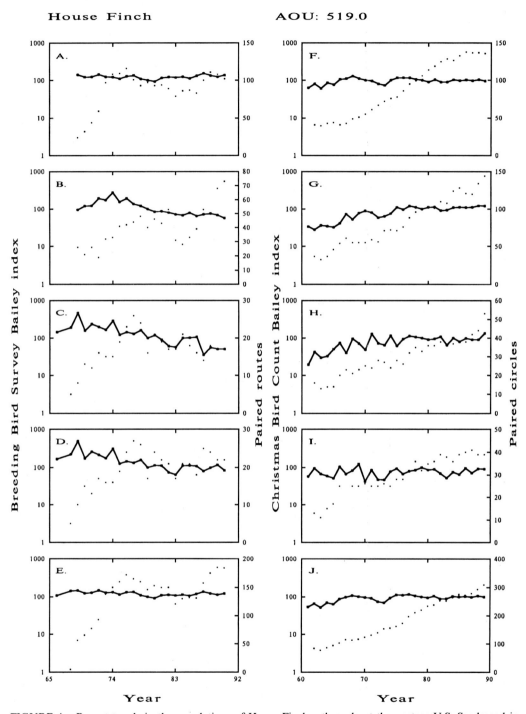

FIGURE 4.   Recent trends in the populations of House Finches throughout the western U.S. See legend in Figure 3 for details.

Ring–billed Gull AOU: 054.0

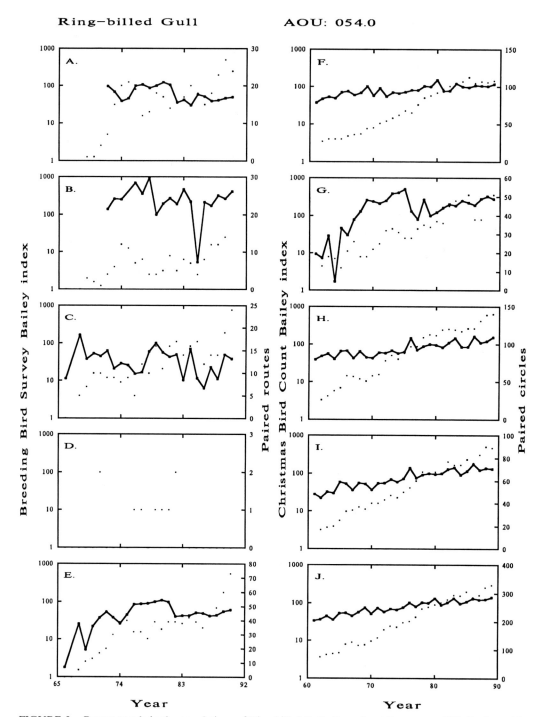

FIGURE 5. Recent trends in the populations of Ring-billed Gulls throughout the western U.S. See legend in Figure 3 for details.

Canada Goose   AOU: 172.0

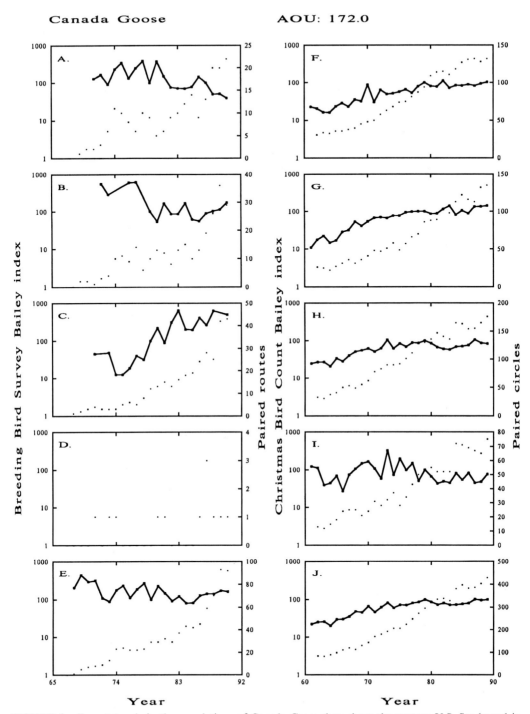

FIGURE 6. Recent trends in the populations of Canada Geese throughout the western U.S. See legend in Figure 3 for details.

1900s (Grinnell 1915). Their numbers remained fairly constant from the 1920s–1960s, except for a reduction in highly settled areas (Grinnell and Miller 1944) and local increases in response to new feeding opportunities (e.g., Santa Barbara Island in response to sheep farming; increases around garbage dumps in rural villages (Pemberton 1929, Cahn 1947).

Recently, breeding and, more notably, wintering ravens have increased in the Far Western States (Robbins et al. 1986). Ravens in southwestern deserts have increased by 5–15× in the last 20 years (Boarman in press), and moderate-sized towns in the Rocky Mountains have seen explosions in wintering populations (e.g., a 9-fold increase from the mid-1970s to the late 1980s in Flagstaff, Arizona [Marzluff 1988]). BBS counts of ravens were positively correlated with plot species richness and farmland, but negatively associated with human density. The negative influence of high human density was least important in the Coastal States and most important in the Mountain States. The positive influence of farmland was greatest in the Plains States, suggesting that the breeding populations on the edge of the range were more closely associated with agriculture than in the dense center of the range. Farmland was the most important variable used in CART analyses to explain variation in wintering populations.

American Crows were uncommon in most parts of the west through the early 1900s, except along riparian corridors (Monson 1946, Richards 1971). However, populations increased with the arrival of agriculture and irrigation in the interior of California, Oregon, and Washington. Brooks (1925) estimated a regional increase of 30× over much of the west from 1900–1920 (see also Robertson 1931). Emlen (1940) suggested that numbers in California changed little from the late 1800s to the 1930s, except along the northern coast and in the Sacramento Valley, where abundance increased substantially. Crows were uncommon throughout the Great Basin until the 1930s, after which they increased slowly with

spreading agriculture (Pitelka 1942, Richards 1971). They were rare at Las Vegas Hot Springs, New Mexico in 1882, but were one of the commonest species in 1959 (Rickard 1959).

Over the last 30 years, BBS and CBC surveys indicated steady, but slight, increases in breeding and wintering populations of crows (Robbins et al. 1986). BBS counts were correlated positively with plot species richness and human density, and correlated negatively with mean January temperature and farmland. CBC surveys also were correlated positively with human density. Apparently crows are invading urban areas to a greater extent than agricultural areas. In contrast, ravens appear to be invading agricultural areas to a greater extent than urban areas (although they are common in many urban areas as well). CART analyses suggest that the importance of urban areas to crows was greatest in the Mountain and Coastal States.

During the first half of the century, Scrub Jay (*Aphelocoma coerulescens*) populations evidently remained stable throughout most of the west (Hargrave 1932, Stoner 1934), then increased slightly in lowland areas of California (Grinnell and Miller 1944), and in Arizona and Texas where overgrazing increased the spread of scrub vegetation into former grassland (Phillips et al. 1964). Breeding populations were stable from the mid-1960s to the late 1980s, increasing significantly only in Oregon and California (Robbins et al. 1986). Wintering populations have gradually increased in all areas over the last 30 years (Fig. 7). Scrub Jays appear to be invading most human dominated landscapes because BBS counts were positively correlated with human density and farmland. Colonization of farmland appears to be especially important in the Mountain States.

Results from our analysis of BBC data from California support the observations of recent increases in corvids. We found a significant increase in total corvids (per 40.5 ha) through years ($F_{1,182} = 5.24$) in combination with a significant positive relation-

Scrub Jay   AOU: 481.0

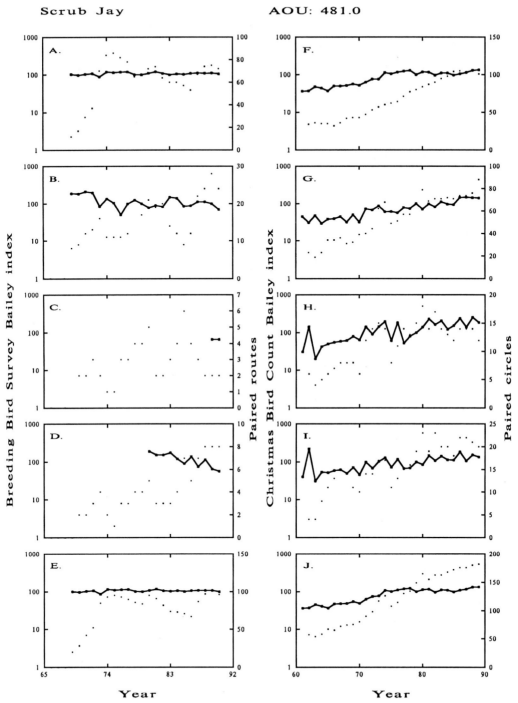

FIGURE 7. Recent trends in the populations of Scrub Jays throughout the western U.S. See legend in Figure 3 for details.

ship to number of species ($F_{1,182} = 11.85$) and a significant negative relationship to census plot size ($F_{1,182} = 32.07$). These relationships largely reflected population trends in jays (Scrub Jay, Steller's Jay [*Cyanocitta stelleri*], Gray Jay [*Perisoreus canadensis*]), which made up 96.5% of all corvids recorded in censuses.

The increases have occurred only in certain habitats. Of the 17 censuses with jays, showing residuals of more than +10 pairs per 40.5 ha, 12 were upland or riparian woodlands with a major component of oaks. Of the remaining five censuses, three were riparian woodlands, one a wooded urban park, and one a chaparral habitat. Of these 17 census sites, 13 were at elevations below 500 m.

Common Grackles, Great-tailed Grackles (*Quiscalus mexicanus*) and Brown-headed Cowbirds (*Molothrus ater*) have experienced the greatest rates of increase within their historic range and largest expansions of any native pest birds in the western U.S. (Fig. 2). Common Grackles were relatively rare in the west until recently. They were first observed in the 1940s in Nevada (Alcorn 1946) and the late 1950s in Utah (Talley 1957). Recently, they were mostly confined to the Great Plains, where populations increased slightly, especially in Oklahoma (Robbins et al. 1986). Although breeding populations are small in the Rocky Mountain States, they appear to be rapidly increasing. Winter population trends are erratic and difficult to interpret (Bock and Root 1981).

In the mid-1800s Great-tailed Grackles were locally abundant, but restricted to the northern Plateau of Mexico and extreme southern Texas (Selander and Giller 1961). They remained there until approximately 1913, when they began a slow northern invasion into Arizona, New Mexico, and inland Texas (Phillips 1950). Colonization proceeded north along the Rio Grande so that by the early 1940s grackles were in central and northern New Mexico, and followed the conversion of grassland to brushland north in Texas up to the panhandle

(Compton 1947, Phillips 1950, Selander and Giller 1961). Grackles were resident in Arizona along the Salt and Gila Rivers north and west to Phoenix by the 1950s, and expanded west and north in the 1960s into California, all of New Mexico, and Colorado (McCaskie et al. 1966, Phillips 1968). Breeding was confirmed in Colorado in 1973 (Stepney 1975). Populations exploded in the Great Plains during the late 1960s and 1970s, especially on the Osage Plains of Kansas, Oklahoma, and southern Nebraska (Robbins et al. 1986).

Wintering and breeding populations have continued to increase, especially in the Rocky Mountain States. CART analyses of BBS counts indicated that grackles, though primarily confined to the Southwest, are increasing faster than any other pest species. Abundance was positively correlated with farmland, especially in the Plains States. Winter populations were also increasing rapidly and were associated with areas of high human density, and to a lesser extent with areas of abundant farmland.

WHY ARE MOST PESTS SUCCESSFUL?

In this era of widespread endangerment and extinction of species, most native bird pests in the west have stable or increasing populations (Fig. 2), owing to their ability to take advantage of feeding and nesting sites provided by man.

Three characteristics shared by many pests may be especially important in preadapting them to exploit humans. First, many pests forage in flocks (McAtee 1946), a common adaptation to patchily distributed, but locally abundant foods (Marzluff and Balda 1992), such as agricultural crops. Second, flocking and non-flocking pests are usually generalist foragers. This ability has likely been a key to recent increases in the abundance of many larids and corvids, which can exploit human refuse when other foods are scarce. Third, suitable breeding habitat has been expanded by human impoundment of rivers and creation of wildlife refuges (for waterfowl and larids), construction of bridges (swallows), irrigation of farmland (icterids), and creation of urban parks (corvids). Widespread geographic distribution may be of secondary importance because the one pest with a declining population, the Tricolored Blackbird, also has a very restricted range.

Our CART analyses of factors correlated with the abundance of pests indicated that large human populations were more beneficial to pest species in the winter than during the breeding season. Food provided at feeders, parks, marinas, and refuse dumps may have increased survival or changed wintering distribution of pests, or both.

Although agricultural and urban areas are important refuges for pests, increases have not been limited to sites of extensive human disturbance. For example, our results suggest that small corvids in California have increased in abundance in low- to mid-elevation woodland habitats since the early 1960s. This is most clearly shown in broadleaf woodland habitats, but is not restricted to sites internally impacted by human disturbance. Evidently, small corvids have been favored by general landscape changes such as the spread of suburban residential developments, vehicular campgrounds, and other human activities into the more accessible portions of extra-urban California. Spillover from areas of strong human impact may have increased populations of small corvids even in lightly impacted habitats.

LIMITATIONS OF RESULTS

We have relied upon the published literature and recent standardized surveys to assess changes in the population sizes of a variety of birds. A few caveats should be noted. Trends in some bird species or groups are not easily identified in BBS or CBC census data. In addition to the enormous variation in the structure of the bird communities themselves, differences among observer practices often make results difficult to compare. Data from BBC, BBS and CBC censuses may also be poor at characterizing trends in abundance of large corvids, primarily because of the small size of most census plots relative to their home ranges, and colonial larids and icterids, because census plots may only rarely fall within historically used colonies (Bock and Root 1981).

FORECAST

Native species of birds will continue to plague humans. A recent nationwide survey of Animal Damage Control needs reported that six of the top ten research needs concerned native birds (Packham and Connolly 1992). Ways to control blackbird and waterfowl populations were the top two priorities, ranking above coyote, fox and dog control. Control of wading birds, cormorants, gulls, woodpeckers, crows and ravens was considered more pressing than bear, skunk, raccoon, or rat control.

The survey results reflect current perceptions of species that will be pests in the immediate future. Many will likely continue to be problems into the indefinite future because new crops and settlements will encroach upon native habitats, forcing birds to adapt, move, or go extinct. Each new crop planted will be exploited by native birds, principally blackbirds, finches, and corvids. Indeed, any species that adapts to human encroachment is certain to be considered a pest by a portion of the human population.

Among species not considered above, cormorants and herons will be problems for western aquaculture, as is currently the case in the southeastern and southwestern U.S. Ducks and geese will gain prominence for fouling the urban environments. Problems with corvids and cowbirds (Rothstein 1994) will increase, through predation on the eggs and nestlings of endangered species, as forested areas become increasingly fractured and utilized by humans for recreation.

Safety-related problems with native birds should lessen during the next century. Relocation and closing of many landfills will reduce the concentrations of gulls, blackbirds and corvids that pose hazards to aircraft. Communal roosts, however, are likely to persist in urban areas and may increase as humans occupy more land. Disease transmission and neurosis may therefore continue to be minor problems.

At the Bicentennial meeting of the Cooper Society, participants should not be surprised to learn that the western avifauna has become dominated by generalized, flocking species.

ACKNOWLEDGMENTS

The analyses of CBC data would not have been possible without the helpful guidance of M. T. Jones. R. O'Connor provided access to computerized CBC and BBS databases. L. Kiff and the staff of the Western Foundation of Vertebrate Zoology kindly provided many reprints of the historical literature. E. Knittle, G. Connolly, M. Collinge, the Staff of the Denver Wildlife Research Center, and M. Conover freely discussed their ideas about avian pests and introduced us to the wealth of literature about pests contained in the A.D.C. publications. J. R. Jehl, Jr. critically reviewed the manuscript. N. Hendley retrieved, copied, and returned many volumes of journals.

LITERATURE CITED

ALCORN, J. R. 1946. The birds of Lahontan Valley, Nevada. Condor 48:129–138.

AVERY, M. L., AND R. DeHAVEN. 1982. Bird damage to sunflowers in the Sacramento Valley, California. Pp. 197–200 in R. E. Marsh (ed.), Proceedings Tenth Vertebrate Pest Conference. University of California, Davis, CA.

BAILEY, R. S. 1967. An index of bird population changes on farmland. Bird Study 14:195–209.

BANKS, R. C., AND P. F. SPRINGER. 1994. A century of population trends of waterfowl in Western North America. Pp. 134–146 in J. R. Jehl, Jr. and N. K. Johnson (eds.), A century of avifaunal change in western North America. Studies in Avian Biology No. 15.

BEEDY, E. C., S. D. SANDERS, AND D. A. GLOOM. 1991. Breeding status, distribution and habitat associations of the tricolored blackbird (*Agelaius tricolor*), 1850–1989. Jones & Stokes Associates, Inc., Sacramento, CA.

BESSER, J. F. 1985. A growers guide to reducing bird damage to U.S. agricultural crops. U.S. Department of the Interior, Denver, CO.

BESSER, J. F., AND D. J. BRADY. 1982. Bird damage to ripening field corn in the United States, 1981. U.S. Department of the Interior, Denver, CO.

BESSER, J. F., J. W. DeGRAZIO, J. L. GUARINO, D. F. MOTT, D. L. OTIS, B. R. BESSER, AND C. E. KNITTLE. 1984. Decline in breeding Red-winged Blackbirds in the Dakotas, 1965–1981. Journal of Field Ornithology 55:435–443.

BLOKPOEL, H., AND G. D. TESSIER. 1986. The Ring-billed Gull in Ontario: a review of a new problem species. Occasional Papers of the Canadian Wildlife Service. No. 57.

BOARMAN, W. I. In press. When a native predator becomes a pest: a case study. Pp. 186–201 in S. K. Majumdar, E. W. Miller, D. E. Miller, J. R. Pratt, R. F. Schmalz, and E. K. Brown (eds.), Conservation and resource management. The Pennsylvania Academy of Science, Easton, Pennsylvania.

BOCK, C. E., AND T. L. ROOT. 1981. The Christmas bird count and avian ecology. Studies in Avian Biology 6:17–23.

BOONE, R. B. 1991. Avian population changes in agricultural areas. M.S. Thesis. University of Maine, Orono, ME.

BREIMAN, L., J. FRIEDMAN, R. OLSHEN, AND C. STONE. 1984. Classification and regression trees. Wadsworth, Pacific Grove, CA.

BROOKS, A. 1925. Ament the crow. Condor 27:83–84.

BUTCHER, G. S., AND C. E. McCULLOCH. 1990. Influence of observer effort on the number of individual birds recorded on Christmas Birds Counts. Pp. 5–13 in J. R. Sauer and S. Droege (eds.), Survey designs and statistical methods for the estimation of avian population trends. U.S. Fish and Wildlife Service Biological Report No. 90, Washington, DC.

BUTCHKO, P. H. 1990. Predator control for the protection of endangered species in California. Pp. 237–240 in L. R. Davis and R. E. Marsh (eds.), Proceedings 14th Vertebrate Pest Conference. University of California, Davis, CA.

CAHN, A. R. 1947. Notes on the birds of the Dutch Harbor area of the Aleutian Islands. Condor 49:78–82.

CLARK, D. O. 1975. Vertebrate Pest Control Handbook. California Department of Food and Agriculture, Sacramento, CA.

COMPTON, L. V. 1947. The Great-tailed Grackle in the upper Rio Grande Valley. Condor 49:35–36.

CONOVER, M. R. 1983. Recent changes in Ring-billed and California Gull populations in the western United States. Wilson Bulletin 95:362–383.

CONOVER, M. R., AND G. G. CHASKO. 1985. Nuisance Canada Goose problems in the eastern United States. Wildlife Society Bulletin 13:228–233.

COTTAM, C. 1935. Unusual food habits of California Gulls. Condor 37:170–171.

COWAN, J. B. 1970. The role of the wildlife refuge in relief of vertebrate pest damage in agriculture. Pp. 150–155 in R. H. Dana (ed.), Proceedings Fourth Vertebrate Pest Conference. University of California, Davis, CA.

CRASE, F. T., AND R. W. DeHAVEN. 1976. Bird damage to sunflowers in the Sacramento Valley, California. Pp. 46–50 in C. C. Siebe (ed.), Proceedings Seventh Vertebrate Pest Conference. University of California, Davis, CA.

CRASE, F. T., C. P. STONE, R. W. DeHAVEN, AND D. F. MOTT. 1976. Bird damage to grapes in the United States with emphasis on California. U.S. Department of the Interior, Washington, D.C.

DAVIS, W. B. 1935. An analysis of the bird population in the vicinity of Rupert, Idaho. Condor 37:233–238.

DeGRAZIO, J. W. 1978. World bird damage problems. Pp. 9–24 in W. E. Howard and R. E. Marsh (eds.), Proceedings Eighth Vertebrate Pest Conference. University of California, Davis, CA.

DeGRAZIO, J. W. 1989. Pest birds—an international

perspective. Pp. 1–8 *in* R. L. Bruggers and C. C. H. Elliot (eds.), *Quelea quelea* Africa's bird pest. Oxford University Press, Oxford.

DeGrazio, J. W., and J. F. Besser. 1970. Surfactants as blackbird stressing agents. Pp. 162–167 *in* R. H. Dana (ed.), Proceedings Fourth Vertebrate Pest Conference. University of California, Davis, CA.

DeHaven, R. W. 1971. Blackbirds and the California rice crop. The Rice Journal 74:1–4.

DeHaven, R. W. 1974. Bird damage to wine grapes in central California, 1973. Pp. 248–252 *in* W. V. Johnson (ed.), Proceedings Sixth Vertebrate Pest Conference. University of California, Davis, CA.

DeHaven, R. W., F. T. Crase, and P. P. Woronecki. 1975. Breeding status of the Tricolored Blackbird, 1969–1972. California Fish and Game 61:166–180.

Dickey, D. R., and A. J. Van Rossem. 1925. A revisionary study of the Western Gull. Condor 27:162–164.

Droege, S. 1990. The North American breeding bird survey. Pp. 1–4 *in* J. R. Sauer and S. Droege (eds.), Survey designs and statistical methods for the estimation of avian population trends. U.S. Fish and Wildlife Service Biological Report No. 90, Washington, DC.

Edwards, R. Y., and D. Stirling. 1961. Range expansion of the House Finch into British Columbia. The Murrelet 42:38–42.

Emlen, J. T., Jr. 1940. The midwinter distribution of the crow in California. Condor 42:287–294.

Erickson, M. M. 1937. A jay shoot in California. Condor 39:111–115.

Erskine, A. J., B. T. Collins, E. Hayakawa, and C. Downes. 1992. The cooperative breeding bird survey in Canada, 1989–91. Canadian Wildlife Service Progress Notes, No. 199.

Fitzwater, W. D. 1988. Solutions to urban bird problems. Pp. 254–259 *in* A. C. Crabb and R. E. Marsh (eds.), Proceedings 13th Vertebrate Pest Conference. University of California, Davis, CA.

Garner, K. M. 1978. Management of blackbird and starling winter roost problems in Kentucky and Tennessee. Pp. 54–59 *in* W. E. Howard and R. E. Marsh (eds.), Proceedings Eighth Vertebrate Pest Conference. University of California, Davis, CA.

Gorenzel, W. P., and T. P. Salmon. 1982. The Cliff Swallow—biology and control. Pp. 179–185 *in* R. E. Marsh (ed.), Proceedings Tenth Vertebrate Pest Conference. University of California, Davis, CA.

Grinnell, J. 1915. A distributional list of the birds of California. Cooper Ornithological Club, Berkeley, California, USA.

Grinnell, J., and A. H. Miller. 1944. The distribution of the birds of California. Cooper Ornithological Club, Berkeley, California, USA.

Hand, R. L. 1969. House Finches (*Carpodacus mexicanus*) in Montana. Condor 71:115–116.

Hargrave, L. L. 1932. Woodhouse Jays on the Hopi Mesas, Arizona. Condor 34:140–141.

Hothem, R. L., R. W. DeHaven, and S. D. Fairaizl. 1988. Bird damage to sunflower in North Dakota, South Dakota, and Minnesota, 1979–1981. U.S. Department of the Interior, Washington, DC.

Howell, A. B. 1922. Red-wings of the Imperial Valley, California. Condor 24:60–61.

Johnston, R. F., and K. L. Garrett. 1994. Populations trends of introduced birds in Western North America, 1890–1991. Pp. 221–231 *in* J. R. Jehl, Jr. and N. K. Johnson (eds.), A century of avifaunal change in western North America. Studies in Avian Biology No. 15.

Knittle, C. E., and J. L. Guarino. 1976. A 1974 questionnaire survey of bird damage to ripening grain sorghum in the United States. Sorghum Newsletter 19:93–94.

Knittle, C. E., and R. D. Porter. 1988. Waterfowl damage and control methods in ripening grain: an overview. U.S. Department of the Interior, Washington, DC.

Larsen, K. H., and J. H. Dietrich. 1970. Reduction of a raven population on lambing grounds with DRC-1339. Journal of Wildlife Management 34:200–204.

Marzluff, J. M. 1988. Do pinyon jays alter nest placement based on prior experience? Animal Behaviour 36:1–10.

Marzluff, J. M., and R. P. Balda. 1992. The Pinyon Jay: behavioral ecology of a colonial and cooperative corvid. T. & A. D. Poyser, London.

McAtee, W. L. 1946. The economic status of flocking birds. Condor 48:29–31.

McCabe, T. T. 1932. Wholesale poison for the Red-wings. Condor 34:49–50.

McCaskie, G., R. Stallcup, and P. DeBenedictis. 1966. Notes on the distribution of certain Icterids and Tanagers in California. Condor 68:595–597.

Monson, G. 1946. Notes on the avifauna of the Rio Grande Valley, New Mexico. Condor 48:238–241.

Moss, D. 1985. Some statistical checks on the BTO Common Bird Census Index—20 years on. Pp. 175–179 *in* K. Taylor, R. J. Fuller, and P. C. Lack (eds.), Bird census and atlas studies: Proceedings VIII International Conference of Bird Census and Atlas Work. British Trust for Ornithology, London.

Mott, D. F., J. F. Besser, R. R. West, and J. W. DeGrazio. 1972. Some approaches to control depredations by crows and jays in Tulare County. Pp. 118–120 *in* R. E. Marsh (ed.), Proceedings Fifth Vertebrate Pest Conference. University of California, Davis, CA.

Neff, J. A. 1937. Nesting distribution of the Tricolored Red-wing. Condor 39:61–81.

Neff, J. A. 1942. Migration of the Tricolored Red-wing in central California. Condor 44:45–53.

O'Gara, B. W. 1978. Sheep depredation by golden eagles in Montana. Pp. 206–213 *in* W. E. Howard and R. E. Marsh (eds.), Proceedings Eighth Vertebrate Pest Conference. University of California, Davis, CA.

Packham, C. J., and G. Connolly. 1992. Control methods research priorities for animal damage control. Pp. 12–16 *in* J. E. Borrecco and R. E. Marsh (eds.), Proceedings 15th Vertebrate Pest Conference. University of California, Davis, CA.

Palmer, T. K. 1970. House finch (linnet) control in California. Pp. 173–178 *in* R. H. Dana (ed.), Proceedings Fourth Vertebrate Pest Conference. University of California, Davis, CA.

Paul, A. 1964. More range expansion of the House Finch. The Murrelet 45:11.

Pearson, E. W. 1967. Birds and airports. Pp. 79–86

in M. W. Cummings, R. H. Dana, and R. E. Marsh (eds.), Proceedings Third Vertebrate Pest Conference. University of California, Davis, CA.

PEMBERTON, J. R. 1929. Some new records for Santa Barbara Island. Condor 31:37.

PETERSON, B. R., AND C. S. BROWN. 1985. Aggressive behavior of Mississippi Kites in suburban areas. Pp. 92–95 *in* D. B. Fagre (ed.), Proceedings Seventh Great Plains Wildlife Damage Control Workshop. Texas A&M University, College Station, Texas.

PHILLIPS, A. R. 1950. The Great-tailed Grackles of the Southwest. Condor 52:78–81.

PHILLIPS, A. R. 1968. The instability of the distribution of land birds in the Southwest. Papers of the Archaeological Society of New Mexico 1:129–162.

PHILLIPS, R. L., AND F. S. BLOM. 1988. Distribution and magnitude of eagle/livestock conflicts in the western United States. Pp. 241–244 *in* A. C. Crabb and R. E. Marsh (eds.), Proceedings 13th Vertebrate Pest Conference. University of California, Davis, CA.

PHILLIPS, A., J. MARSHALL, AND G. MONSON. 1964. The birds of Arizona. The University of Arizona Press, Tucson.

PITELKA, F. A. 1942. High population of breeding birds within an artificial habitat. Condor 44:172–174.

POCHOP, P. A., R. J. JOHNSON, D. A. AGUERO, AND K. M. ESKRIDGE. 1990. The status of lines in bird damage control—a review. Pp. 317–324 *in* L. R. Davis and R. E. Marsh (eds.), Proceedings 14th Vertebrate Pest Conference. University of California, Davis, CA.

POPE, R. L. 1974. Urbanized wildlife. Pp. 20–22 *in* W. V. Johnson (ed.), Proceedings Sixth Vertebrate Pest Conference. University of California, Davis, CA.

RICHARDS, G. L. 1971. The Common Crow, *Corvus brachyrhynchos,* in the Great Basin. Condor 73:116–118.

RICKARD, W. H. 1959. Changes in winter bird species of two habitats in San Miguel County, Mexico, after three-fourths of a century. Condor 61:438.

ROBBINS, C. S., D. BYSTRAK, AND P. H. GEISSLER. 1986. The breeding bird survey: its first fifteen years, 1965–1979. U.S. Department of the Interior, Washington, DC.

ROBERTSON, J. M. 1931. Some changes in the bird life of western Orange County, California. Condor 33:204–205.

ROTHSTEIN, S. I. 1994. The Cowbird's invasion of the far west: history, causes and consequences experienced by host species. Pp. 301–315 *in* J. R. Jehl, Jr. and N. K. Johnson (eds.), A century of avifaunal change in western North America. Studies in Avian Biology No. 15.

SELANDER, R. K., AND D. R. GILLER. 1961. Analysis of sympatry of Great-tailed and Boat-tailed Grackles. Condor 63:29–86.

SHEPHERD, P. E. K. 1962. A breeding record of the Red-winged Blackbird in Alaska. Condor 64:440.

SIMPSON, G. 1972. Some approaches to control dep-

redations by crows and jays in Tulare County. Pp. 112–117 *in* R. E. Marsh (ed.), Proceedings Fifth Vertebrate Pest Conference. University of California, Davis, CA.

SINGER, S. W., N. L. NASLUND, S. A. SINGER, AND C. J. RALPH. 1991. Discovery and observations of two tree nests of the Marbled Murrelet. Condor 93:330–339.

STEMMERMAN, L. A. 1988. Observation of woodpecker damage to electrical distribution line poles in Missouri. Pp. 260–265 *in* A. C. Crabb and R. E. Marsh (eds.), Proceedings 13th Vertebrate Pest Conference. University of California, Davis, CA.

STEPNEY, P. H. R. 1975. First recorded breeding of the Great-tailed Grackle in Colorado. Condor 77:207–210.

STICKLEY, A. R., AND K. J. ANDREWS. 1989. Survey of Mississippi catfish farmers on means, effort and costs to repel fish-eating birds from ponds. Eastern Wildlife Damage Control Conference Proceedings 4:105–108.

STOCKDALE, T. M. 1967. Blackbirds-depredation, research and control in Ohio and the midwest. Pp. 47–49 *in* M. W. Cummings, R. H. Dana, and R. E. Marsh (eds.), Proceedings Third Vertebrate Pest Conference. University of California, Davis, CA.

STONER, E. A. 1934. The jay as a benefactor of man. Condor 36:112–113.

TALLEY, G. M. 1957. Common Grackle in Utah. Condor 59:400.

TATE, R. C. 1927. The American Magpie in the Oklahoma panhandle. Condor 29:244–245.

TWEDT, D. J., W. J. BLEIER, AND G. M. LINZ. 1991. Geographic and temporal variation in the diet of Yellow-headed Blackbirds. Condor 93:975–986.

UNITED STATES DEPARTMENT OF INTERIOR. 1989. Annual Report of Bureau of Sport Fisheries and Wildlife. Idaho Division of Wildlife Services, Boise, Idaho.

VERMEER, K. 1992. Population growth of the Glaucous-winged Gull *Larus glaucescens* in the Strait of Georgia, British Columbia, Canada. Ardea 80:181–185.

WOODBURY, A. M., AND H. KNIGHT. 1951. Results of the Pacific gull color-banding project. Condor 53:57–77.

WORONECKI, P. P., R. A. DOLBEER, AND T. W. SEAMANS. 1990. Use of alpha-chloralose to remove waterfowl from nuisance and damage situations. Pp. 343–349 *in* L. R. Davis and R. E. Marsh (eds.), Proceedings 14th Vertebrate Pest Conference. University of California, Davis, CA.

YOCHEM, P. K., J. R. JEHL, JR, AND B. S. STEWART. 1991. Distribution and history of California Gull colonies in Nevada. Western Birds 22:1–12.

YOUNG, L. S., AND K. A. ENGEL. 1988. Implications of communal roosting by Common Ravens to operation and maintenance of Pacific Power and Light Company's Malin to Midpoint 500 kV transmission line. U.S. Department of Interior, Boise, ID.

Studies in Avian Biology No. 15:221–231, 1994.

POPULATION TRENDS OF INTRODUCED BIRDS IN WESTERN NORTH AMERICA

RICHARD F. JOHNSTON AND KIMBALL L. GARRETT

Abstract. Introduced birds are those captured, transported, and released elsewhere, either intentionally or accidentally. Eighty-three species of birds have been introduced into western North America; about 43 of these now have reproductively competent populations. Nearly half the introductions into western North America have been of gamebirds. Feral pigeons, European Starlings, and House Sparrows are at numerical stasis; Spotted Doves, Ringed Turtle-Doves, and Crested Mynas show major decreases, partly owing to urban environmental succession. Successful introduced species tend to have had multiple introductions, a large area of natural distribution, ability to exploit resources generated and dominated by humans, and high fecundity. Results of avian introductions are difficult to predict, but knowing this means we are not necessarily doomed to repeat the past.

Key Words: Distribution; abundance; anthropogenic ecology; colonizing species.

Humans have been modifying the distribution and abundance of birds for thousands of years. In some instances species have been extirpated, in some their numbers increased or decreased, and in others their distributions changed. Causes for increases in range or numbers are several, and include the introduction by humans of individuals from one place to another. It is some population consequences of the latter concerning western North America that is the focus of this review.

Introduced birds are defined as those captured and transported by humans and released elsewhere. Release sites may be where the species has never occurred, no longer occurs, or occurs at low density; an introduction may be accidental or intentional. Instances of human-mediated dispersal of birds are known for most regions of the world. More than 200 pertain to North America (Long 1981), and 84 of them have affected the American west. Currently, about 43 of these have self-replicating populations (Table 1).

The fraction for western North America is small if numbers of species are considered, and even smaller if restricted to viable species. But that is not the only point of reference, or else this chapter would not have been written. In fact, a few introductions have resulted in enormously abundant populations that command our interest because they tell something about population biology, perhaps certain ecological asymmetries, and the initial stages of the evolutionary process, as well as being possible sources of recreational, public health, agricultural, and economic concerns. The degree to which these concerns are realized varies from place to place, but this examination for western North America probably represents the world in microcosm.

SPECIES ACCOUNTS

In the accounts below, a few species or groups of species listed in Table 1 are discussed; records of winter population trends at some stations of western occurrence are from Christmas Bird Counts (CBCs; see citations to Bird-Lore, Audubon Magazine, Audubon Field Notes, and American Birds).

*Peregrine Falcon (*Falco peregrinus*)*

Decline in population sizes throughout North America in the 1960s, a response to chlorinated hydrocarbon pesticides, almost exterminated Peregrine Falcons. In the west in the early 1970s, just two pairs were known in California, six in Colorado, one in Oregon, three in Washington, and "a few" in New Mexico and Texas (Burnham and Cade 1992). In 1973, private organizations, including the Peregrine Fund, and State and Federal wildlife agencies, began releasing captive-reared peregrines in regions where

TABLE 1. SUCCESSFULLY INTRODUCED BIRDS OF WESTERN NORTH AMERICA[1]

Family/species	Locality and date[1]	References
Anatidae		
Olor buccinator	USA: OR, NV 1957, WA 1964	Johns and Erickson 1970
	CAN: BC	Godfrey 1966
Cygnus olor	USA: OR	Wing 1956
	CAN: BC	Long 1981
Branta canadensis	USA: AZ 1966	Palmer 1976
	CAN: BC 1931	Carl and Guiguet 1972
Cathartidae		
Gymnogyps californianus	USA: CA 1991	Snyder and Johnson 1992
Falconidae		
Falco peregrinus	Western USA: 1973–	Burnham and Cade 1992
Phasianidae		
Perdix perdix	USA: 1877. CA, OR, WA, ID, UT, MO	Guiguet 1961
	CAN: 1904. BC, Alta., Sask.	Carl and Guiguet 1972
Francolinus pondicerianus	USA: CA 1959, NV	Christensen 1963, Bohl 1968, Bump and Bohl 1964
Tetraogallus himalayensis	USA: 1962. NV	Christensen 1963, Bump and Bohl 1964
Alectoris chukar	USA: 1893. CA, OR, WA, MN, WY, ID, CO, NV, AZ, NM, UT	Bump 1968, Whitney 1971, Gottschalk 1967
	CAN: 1940. BC, Alta.	Carl and Guiguet 1972
	MEX: Baja	Long 1981
Phasianus colchicus	USA: 1730. CA 1889, OR 1882, MN 1895, UT 1900, and all other western states	Roberts 1960, Allen 1962
	CAN: 1882. BC, Alta.	Carl and Guiguet 1972
	MEX: Baja	AOU 1983
Pavo cristatus	USA: CA	Hardy 1973
Dendragapus canadensis	USA: AK 1957	Long 1981
Dendragapus obscurus	CAN: BC 1970	Carl and Guiguet 1972
Bonasa umbellus	USA: NV	McColm 1970
	CAN: BC	Carl and Guiguet 1972
Lagopus leucurus	USA: CA, UT	Gaines 1988, Behle et al. 1985
Meleagris gallopavo	USA: 1925–. CA, OR, WA, MD, ID, NV, AZ, NM, UT, CO, WY	Walker, E. 1949
Colinus virginianus	USA: 1865–. OR, WA, ID, MN, WY, CO, AZ	Goodrum 1949
	CAN: 1900–. BC	Carl and Guiguet 1972
Callipepla californica	USA: 1865–. CA, OR, WA, ID, UT	Phillips 1928, Johnsgard 1973
	CAN: 1860–. BC	Carl and Guiguet 1972
Callipepla squamata	USA: NV 1960s, WA 1913	AOU 1957, Johnsgard 1973
Oreortyx pictus	USA: WA 1860s, NV, ID	Carl and Guiguet 1972
	CAN: BC 1860s	Guiguet 1961
Columbidae		
Columba livia	USA: 1621. now in all western states	Schorger 1952
	CAN: 1606. BC, Alta., Yukon	Schorger 1952
	MEX:	Peterson and Chalif 1973
Streptopelia risoria	USA: CA 1930s	Cooke and Knappen 1941
Streptopelia chinensis	USA: CA 1917?	Reuther 1951, Storer 1934
Psittacidae		
Aratinga mitrata	USA: CA 1980s	CBCs, Los Angeles region
Melopsittacus undulatus	USA: CA 1930s	Cooke and Knappen 1941, Hardy 1973
Psittacula krameri	USA: CA 1956	Hardy 1964
Myiopsitta monachus	USA: CA 1972	Hardy 1973, Davis 1974
Nandayus nenday	USA: CA 1968	Hardy 1973

TABLE 1. CONTINUED

Family/species	Locality and date[1]	References
Rhynchopsitta pachyrhyncha	USA: AZ 1986, 87, 91	Snyder and Johnson 1992
Brotogeris versicolurus	USA: CA 1971	Hardy 1973
Amazona viridigenalis	USA: CA 1980s	CBCs, Los Angeles region
Amazona finschi	USA: CA 1977–1981?	CBCs, Los Angeles region
Amazona autumnalis	USA: CA 1968	Hardy 1973
Amazona oratrix	USA: CA 1962	Hardy 1973
Alaudidae		
Alauda arvensis	CAN: BC 1903	Scheffer 1935, Carl and Guiguet 1972
Pycnonotidae		
Pycnonotus jocosus	USA: CA 1968	Hardy 1973
Mimidae		
Mimus polyglottos	USA: CA 1891, OR 1892	Phillips 1928, Jewett and Gabrielson 1929
	CAN: BC, Alta.	Godfrey 1966
Mimus gilvus	PANAMA: 1932	Ridgeley 1976
Sturnidae		
Sturnus vulgaris	USA: 1890. CO 1938, NV 1938, MN 1939, UT 1939, ID 1941, CA 1942, OR 1943, WA 1943, AK 1952	Long 1981; Kessel 1953
	CAN: 1914. BC 1945, Yukon 1962, NW Terr. 1969	Godfrey 1966, Carl and Guiguet 1972
	MEX: Tamps. 1935, Coah. 1939, Nuevo L. 1948, Yucatan >1973	Coffey 1959, Yocum 1963, Long 1981
Acridotheres cristatellus	USA: WA 1920s	Jewett et al. 1953
	CAN: BC 1894–1897	Wood 1924, Carl and Guiguet 1972
Emberizidae		
Cardinalis cardinalis	USA: CA 1880	Hardy 1973
Passeridae		
Passer domesticus	USA: 1852. CA 1871, UT 1873	Robbins 1973
	CAN: BC 1886	Godfrey 1966, Carl and Guiguet 1972
	MEX: SLP 1930, Isthmus of Tehuan. 1947, Chiapas 1950	Coffey 1959, Wagner 1959, Peterson and Chalif 1973
	COSTA RICA: 1974–1975	Reynolds and Stiles 1982
Estrildidae		
Estrilda melpoda	USA: 1965. CA	Hardy 1973

[1] For western North American localities unless otherwise stated.

they had formerly nested. This program has been successful, and peregrines now occur again in most regions of the west. A discussion of details is presented by White (1994).

Galliform birds (Phasianidae)

Some 19, or 44%, of the successful avian introductions to western North America are of birds important in recreational hunting. These species have been extensively studied, propagated in confinement, transported, and released into habitat likely to support free-living populations. Management of game species has commanded significant fractions of State fish and game department budgets, and the resultant gamebird populations can be important to local human economies. The literature is enormous and cannot be covered here in any depth, but the ecology and behavior of many introduced species has been treated at book length a number of times.

One species, the Ring-necked Pheasant, *Phasianus colchicus,* has had multiple introductions of a variety of genetic stocks for more than 200 years in North America, for more than 100 years in many places in the west beginning in Alberta, British Columbia, Montana, and Oregon, and ultimately in all western states. Introductions have been made by both private and governmental agencies, and continue to the present time (Long 1981).

In a few places in the west, such as the Central Valley of California, the Ring-necked Pheasant is wholly successful as a free-living bird, despite human predation each autumn, and needs little except population monitoring and adjustment of hunting seasons and bag limits to maintain itself. Other populations need occasional augmentation, and others, in rapidly urbanizing regions such as southern California, have almost entirely disappeared.

Introductions of genetic stocks from populations different from those used historically, namely *P. c. colchicus* and *P. c. torquatus,* are still underway. Recent work has featured birds from the Near and Middle East, taken from populations identified as *P. c. talischensis, P. c. persicus,* their hybrids, and their hybrids with other named stock; for introductions into western dryland habitats (as well as others) see Long (1981).

The White-tailed Ptarmigan (*Lagopus leucurus*) was introduced from Colorado to the Sierra Nevada of California, near Yosemite National Park, in the early 1970s; it has spread within the alpine zone along some 75 km of range (Gaines 1988). It has also been introduced into Utah (Behle et al. 1985).

The Wild Turkey (*Meleagris gallopavo*) is another species of intense management interest, and provides as good a case history of the efficacy of modern wildlife management policies as one could wish. Subsequent to essentially unrestricted hunting and degradation of forest habitats following European colonization of North America, turkeys were markedly reduced in numbers and distribution, a condition that persisted until perhaps 65 years ago (E. Walker 1949). But introductions, reintroductions, restocking, and transplants since then have been successful, and turkeys are now found in southwestern Canada and nearly throughout the lower 48 states of the U.S.A., at localities where they had never historically occurred (AOU 1983). Distribution is disjunct, in accord with distribution of woodlands, and some populations may depend on restocking for their maintenance. Seasonal and bag limits are monitored relative to population numbers wherever hunting is feasible.

Feral Pigeon (Rock Dove, Columba livia)

Feral pigeons developed in the west following introductions of domestic pigeons by settlers and merchants, presumably to most localities at a relatively early time; there is, however, no documentation of any such activity. Ferals today occur commonly in urban centers, smaller towns, cattle feedlots, grain storage facilities, and family farms. Colonies in large cities and elsewhere, as along the Front Range in Colorado (R. Ryder, pers. comm.), have served as foraging foci for Peregrine Falcons being reintroduced to their former range.

Numbers of feral pigeons are small where few humans live, as in the Great Basin and in high montane sites, but the birds occur in low density at all seasons of the year in central Utah, southwestern Wyoming, southeastern Colorado, and central montane New Mexico. In such regions the pigeons behave much more like wild *C. livia* of the Old World than urban pigeons; they nest in canyon cliffsides (vertical limestone rimrock above steep talus slopes) and commute to cattle feeding stations in tight, high-speed flocks only a few meters above ground level.

CBCs at four western cities (Table 2) show larger numbers in the 1980s than earlier,

TABLE 2. TOTALS AND YEARLY MEANS OF ROCK DOVES ON WINTER BIRD COUNTS IN FIVE-YEAR PERIODS FOR FOUR STATIONS IN WESTERN NORTH AMERICA[1]

Period	El Paso		Salt Lake City		Spokane		Oakland	
	N	X̄	N	X̄	N	X̄	N	X̄
1972–1976	304	101	nc[2]	—	1457	486	2365	788
1977–1981	3248	650	1518	304	3208	642	5709	1142
1982–1986	4890	978	2094	419	3024	605	6371	1274
1987–1991	3136	1568	1321	330	2497	624	5299	1419

[1] Data from American Birds.
[2] No counts.

but the most recent counts suggest little yearly increase. Pigeons are frequently the target of population control programs, usually with limited success (Murton et al. 1972). Only if availability of food is severely restricted can feral pigeon populations be kept within acceptable limits (e.g., Haag 1987).

*Ringed Turtle-Dove (*Streptopelia risoria*)*

The Ringed Turtle-Dove was established in the Los Angeles region, from captive escapes in the early 1900s, but apparently spread little beyond the urban core of the city of Los Angeles. As with many exotic species, the geographic limits and population parameters of established populations of these doves have been confounded by ongoing escapes or releases of caged individuals; escaped Ringed Turtle-Doves are reported widely, but generally singly, from much of the urban west.

A representative CBC from Los Angeles, CA (Table 3), shows that numbers increased to a peak in the 1940s and 1950s and subsequently declined, probably reflecting some consequences of urban succession there. At present, the population of Ringed Turtle-Doves around downtown Los Angeles has almost completely disappeared.

*Spotted Dove (*Streptopelia chinensis*)*

The Spotted Dove was introduced into southern California in the early 1900s, and became established from the Los Angeles area northwest to Santa Barbara County, south to San Diego and immediately adjacent Baja California Norte, and east to the Coachella Valley by the 1960s (Long 1981).

Outlying populations in the Central Valley, centered in Bakersfield, may have been part of this range expansion or the result of separate introduction events. This dove appeared on Santa Catalina Island some time after the mid-1970s, probably through a secondary introduction from the mainland, and is regularly noted in a recently-established CBC from the island. CBCs at Pasadena-San Gabriel and at Los Angeles (Table 3) suggest that numbers peaked from the early 1950s to the early 1970s; the subsequent decline at both CBC sites probably is due to urban succession. Current dynamics of the species' distribution in California appear to include a degree of range contraction in Santa Barbara County, after having become "fairly common" by the early 1980s (Lehman 1982), and in the San Diego re-

TABLE 3. TOTALS AND YEARLY MEANS OF *Streptopelia* DOVES ON WINTER BIRD COUNTS IN FIVE-YEAR PERIODS FOR FOUR STATIONS IN WESTERN NORTH AMERICA[1]

	Spotted Dove				Ringed Turtle-Dove	
	Pasadena, CA		Los Angeles, CA		Los Angeles, CA	
Period	N	X̄	N	X̄	N	X̄
1938–1941	0	0	274	69	54	14
1942–1946	—	—	423	85	47	9
1947–1951	444	89	534	107	542	108
1952–1956	982	196	1041	208	575	115
1957–1961	596	119	366	73	386	77
1962–1966	862	172	952	190	277	55
1967–1971	323	65	480	120	243	49
1972–1976	431	86	999	200	210	42
1977–1981	297	59	625	125	94	24
1982–1986	368	74	417	83	48	10
1987–1991	117	29	287	72	80	20

[1] Data from Bird-Lore, Audubon Magazine, Audubon Field Notes and American Birds.

gion. But they seem also to include continued expansion in the San Joaquin Valley.

Parrots (Psittacidae)

Reproductive populations of several species of exotic parrots have developed from escapes in southern California in the past 30 years (Table 1). Information on population status and reproductive ecology of these exotic psittacids remains sketchy, in part because standard monitoring schemes, such as the USFWS Breeding Bird Survey and Christmas Bird Counts, fail to provide relevant data, the former because of poor coverage in urban and suburban habitats, and the latter because of selective and erratic treatment of exotics. Difficulties in field identification, especially in the genera *Amazona* and *Aratinga*, also contribute to the confusion about the current status of feral parrots in the region. Information on the ecology of feral parrots in southern California is provided by Froke (1981) and Hall (1988).

Of the psittacids noted by Hardy (1973) to have established feral populations in southern California, several (*Nandayus nenday, Psittacula krameri, Amazona oratrix,* and *A. viridigenalis*) have maintained or increased their populations; it is not clear, however, whether the specific populations mentioned by Hardy are still extant, because current populations may not have descended from those established in the 1960s and early 1970s.

Specimen evidence (Los Angeles County Museum of Natural History) shows that the populations of "Canary-winged Parakeets" noted from coastal Los Angeles County by Hardy (1973) were of the nominate subspecies, *Brotogeris versicolurus versicolurus.* By the 1980s, the species had spread over much of the Los Angeles basin, but more recent specimen samples are of *B. v. chiriri,* the "Yellow-chevroned Parakeet," whose native South American range lies to the south of that of the nominate form, from which it may be specifically distinct (Sibley and Monroe 1990). This temporal replacement of *versicolu* ~~~~ *by chiriri* in the 1980s exactly duplicates their history in southern Florida (Robertson and Woolfenden 1992), and probably represents a shift in the source regions of the birds imported into the U.S.A.

The Mitred Parakeet (*Aratinga mitrata*) increased throughout the Los Angeles basin in the 1980s and now appears to be the most numerous feral psittacid in the region; the regional population probably has reached several hundred thousand individuals (CBC data; Garrett, unpubl. data). Other species of *Aratinga,* especially *A. acuticaudata* and *A. erythrogenys,* are sporadically seen, often with flocks of *mitrata.*

Noteworthy is the failure of the Monk Parakeet (*Myiopsitta monachus*) and Budgerigar (*Melopsittacus undulatus*) to have established long-lived populations in southern California. Both species are present in numbers elsewhere in North America and, while mentioned by Hardy (1973) as having nested, appear not to be established in southern California at present.

Concerning a non-exotic introduction: Thick-billed Parrots became extinct in the United States some time after 1938 (Monson and Phillips 1981). The birds are locally common in the Sierra Madre Occidental of Mexico, and are caught there for sale as captives. Releases of federally confiscated Thick-billed Parrots illegally sold in the U.S.A. were made in 1985 in the Chiricahua Mts. of Arizona, and in 1987 and 1991 of cage-reared birds (Snyder and Johnson 1992). Although pairing and nesting of some of the confiscated birds was seen in 1988 and 1989, none of the released birds are thought to be alive in the wild as of 1992.

European Starling (Sturnus vulgaris)

European Starlings were introduced to North America in the 1870s and reached the west coast through natural dispersal by 1942 (Howard 1959). Winter populations seem to have stabilized at El Paso and Salt Lake City, and have perhaps declined from peaks reached in the 1970s in Spokane and Oakland (Table 4). Counts for the latter two

ERRATA

...column, second paragraph, first sentence beginning with; "The Mitred ...itrata)..." should read; "...has reached several hundred individuals..." ...thousand individuals..."

TABLE 4. TOTALS AND YEARLY MEANS OF EUROPEAN STARLINGS ON WINTER BIRD COUNTS IN FIVE-YEAR PERIODS FOR FOUR STATIONS IN WESTERN NORTH AMERICA[1]

Period	El Paso		Salt Lake City		Spokane		Oakland	
	N	X̄	N	X̄	N	X̄	N	X̄
1947–1951	939	188	30,856	6171	0	0	0	0
1952–1956	1052	210	39,333	9833	5	1	0	0
1957–1961	2811	718	nc[2]	—	376	75	241	48
1962–1966	7602	1520	56,373	11,275	1063	213	14,948	2989
1967–1971	273	55	65,157	13,031	1132	226	27,311	9140
1972–1976	609	122	77,566	15,513	2524	504	61,026	12,205
1977–1981	976	195	71,553	14,311	7990	1598	38,312	7662
1982–1986	1051	210	72,224	14,245	4786	957	20,483	4097
1987–1991	570	143	59,260	14,815	2195	1544	14,810	3703

[1] Data from Audubon Field Notes and American Birds.
[2] No counts.

cities were in force prior to the arrival of starlings, so the totals provide a summary of how this successful invader fared numerically in two climatically distinctive regions. Starlings appeared in Alaska 40 years ago and currently overwinter; CBCs for 1991 showed Sitka with 66 individuals, Mitkoff Is. 100, the Matanuska Valley (61°36′N) 125, Wrangell Is. 12, and Juneau 69. They appeared in Yellowknife, NWT, 24 years ago. To the south, starlings were found in Yucatan 20 years ago, and their breeding occupancy of Middle American highlands may not be far off.

Crested Myna (Acridotheres cristatellus)

Crested Mynas were introduced to the Vancouver, B.C. region in the period 1894–1897. The population increased until about 1927, when approximately 20,000 birds were estimated to live in the region; num-

bers then decreased and were estimated at 2000 to 3000 birds in 1960 (Mackay and Hughes 1963). CBCs were not taken (or, not published in *Audubon Field Notes*) until 1957. The species had its CBC peak in the period 1960–1972 (Table 5) and since then has gradually decreased in abundance on counts at Vancouver and Ladner, B.C. Mynas in 1989 were considered to be close to extinction in Vancouver (Weber and Cannings 1990).

House Sparrow (Passer domesticus)

House Sparrows were introduced into western North America in 1871 or 1872 at San Francisco, California, perhaps from North American sources, and in 1873 or 1874 at Salt Lake City, Utah, from European sources (Robbins 1973). Numbers of sparrows have apparently declined from a high that was reached around 100 yrs ago in eastern North America (Robbins 1973, who suggested the decline of family farming and of the horse as transportation as possible causes of population decreases), but are stable in the west at present (Table 6). Breeding Bird Survey data show House Sparrows living in all parts of the western USA and Canada, but at low densities in eastern Oregon, southern Idaho and Montana, western Wyoming, Colorado, and Arizona, and most of Utah, which is to say desert, montane, and basin and range sectors of the west (Robbins et al. 1986). Even so, local densities may be appreciable, and

TABLE 5. TOTALS AND YEARLY MEANS OF CRESTED MYNAS ON WINTER BIRD COUNTS IN FIVE-YEAR PERIODS IN SOUTHERN BRITISH COLUMBIA[1]

Period	Vancouver		Ladner	
	N	X̄	N	X̄
1957–1961	2941	588	200	67
1962–1966	3347	669	504	126
1967–1971	3777	775	281	70
1972–1976	1190	238	96	24
1977–1981	709	142	80	20
1982–1986	317	79	63	16
1987–1991	70	18	12	3

[1] Data from Audubon Field Notes and American Birds.

TABLE 6. TOTALS AND YEARLY MEANS OF HOUSE SPARROWS ON WINTER BIRD COUNTS IN FIVE-YEAR PERIODS FOR FOUR STATIONS IN WESTERN NORTH AMERICA[1]

Period	El Paso		Salt Lake City		Spokane		Oakland	
	N	X̄	N	X̄	N	X̄	N	X̄
1947–1951	8101	1636	24,965	4993	1276	255	1679	336
1952–1956	2427	485	32,000	8000	2572	514	4136	827
1957–1961	2773	555	nc[2]	—	7626	1525	3189	638
1962–1966	1616	323	10,618	2124	5312	1062	2353	471
1967–1971	2329	466	12,702	2540	1132	226	879	293
1972–1976	2787	558	9006	1801	2928	586	6533	1307
1976–1981	6669	1334	4485	897	3655	731	3342	668
1982–1986	4250	850	4129	826	4298	860	2430	486
1987–1991	2536	1268	4556	1139	4786	1197	1475	369

[1] Data from Audubon Field Notes and American Birds.
[2] No counts.

populations at Salt Lake City are sometimes extremely large, to judge by CBCs from 1938 to 1990.

Maximum recorded densities on the Breeding Bird Survey have been in the San Joaquin Valley, California, and the vicinity of Portland, Oregon, almost certainly reflecting the intensely agricultural habitats of those regions (Robbins et al. 1986). Over the past 20 yrs of CBC information (Table 6), House Sparrows have been at relatively stable numbers per count area, averaging around 500 (Oakland), 1000 (El Paso and Spokane), or 1500 (Salt Lake City).

Exotic finches (Ploceidae and Estrididae)

Occasional, apparently ephemeral, populations of exotic finches have appeared since the 1960s in the Los Angeles region and elsewhere in the urban west. The population of *Estrilda melpoda* mentioned by Hardy (1973) appears to be no longer extant, but other species of *Estrilda* and *Lonchura* are seen frequently, sometimes in flocks, in rank, weedy areas of the Los Angeles basin. The Northern Red Bishop (*Euplectes franciscanus*) also is seen frequently in similar habitats and was documented as breeding along the Los Angeles River, Los Angeles County, California, in 1991 (Garrett, unpubl. data). The frequent appearance of small, "incipient" populations underscores the need for tracking and documenting occurrences of exotic species as well as for incorporating carefully identified exotics into standard census efforts such as CBCs.

DISCUSSION

Approximately half the 84 avian species introduced to western North America can now be found there, which means that the probability of success is modest. The survivors of course include some of the world's most gifted colonizing species–the House Sparrow, the European Starling, and the Rock Dove. These three have occupied an important part of the anthropogenic ecology of the west in the past century. We may ask, given that humans keep caged birds and modify habitats, was this inevitable—would even these top-level colonizing species have persisted without intentional human-mediated dispersal?

Colonizing species are those for which environments provide little or no reproductive or demographic constraints. Thus, a species predisposed toward colonizing will inevitably be assisted by deliberate multiple releases. Lapses in keeping caged birds confined eventually would have allowed sparrows and starlings to have had their opportunities in the west, if we are to judge by what happened to domestic pigeons, which had relatively few intentional releases. Successful invasions require a range of conditions, however, and these occur unpredictably for any species. Additionally, no single characteristic of birds themselves guarantees their colonizing capability.

In a comprehensive examination of cause and effect in introduced or invading species, Smallwood (1990) identifies a complex of variables that help explain success or failure of an introduced species. These include 1) the size of the initial introduction, 2) the ultimate number of introductions, 3) the area of natural range of the introduced species, 4) the ability to exploit resources generated and dominated by humans, and 5) the fecundity of the species. This requires us to think of a multivariate world, with interacting causes and effects. We have in the past handled such a complexity by conceiving of the "empty niche," an ecologic hyperspace waiting to be occupied. But it is only when a colonizing species is found to succeed that a niche is identified.

The niche may be a difficult abstraction, but humans have never had difficulty visualizing habitat components of niche, and have persistently maintained a confrontational attitude toward natural habitats. Some habitats are powerfully affected, with some destroyed (and thus some created); others are not changed so dramatically. At one extreme, urban habitat for exotic doves and psittacids currently is being subtly changed in parts of southern California occupied by humans at high density; at the other, the woodland habitat formerly occupied by Passenger Pigeons (*Ectopistes migratorius*) was strongly modified and largely destroyed over a century of heavy human use.

This is to say that humans do not sensitively react to important aspects of their natural environment. Whether by intention, as with House Sparrows and gamebirds, or by indirection, as with Rock Doves, we do not keenly anticipate the consequences of our ecologic behavior. We still lack the ability to make high-probability predictions concerning introductions (although we are getting close); for now we know only enough to avoid repeating earlier mistakes. Thus, providing potentially colonizing species a foothold in a new region is something we can avoid. Nevertheless, we will almost certainly continue to foster

introductions, one way or another. The small size and ephemeral nature of many of these introductions in western North America suggests that most will be biologically insignificant. But, so were the initial stages in the colonization of North America by House Sparrows and Eurasian Collared-Doves.

The accelerating urbanization of the west, with modification of native habitats and addition of non-native life forms, virtually guarantees that exotics of many taxa will constitute an increasing percentage of the avifauna of western North America. Careful monitoring of all free-flying exotics will help insure that important early stages of population development are understood and will also aid in the development of strategies for control of exotics when such action is deemed necessary.

LITERATURE CITED

ALLEN, G. 1962. Birds and their attributes. Dover Press, New York.

AMERICAN BIRDS. 1971–1992 (Vols. 25–46). Christmas bird counts. National Audubon Society, New York.

A.O.U. CHECK-LIST COMMITTEE. 1957. Check-list of North American birds. 5th Ed. Lord Baltimore Press, Baltimore, MD.

A.O.U. CHECK-LIST COMMITTEE. 1983. Check-list of North American birds. 6th Ed. Allen Press, Lawrence, KS.

AUDUBON FIELD NOTES. 1948–1970 (Vols. 1–24). Christmas bird counts. National Audubon Society, New York.

AUDUBON MAGAZINE. 1942–1946 (Vols. 44–48). Christmas bird counts. National Audubon Society, New York.

BEHLE, W. H., E. D. SORENSEN, AND C. M. WHITE. 1985. Utah birds: a revised checklist. Occasional Paper Number 4, Utah Museum of Natural History.

BIRD-LORE. 1900–1941 (Vols. 2–43). Christmas bird counts. National Audubon Society, New York.

BOHL, W. H. 1968. Results of foreign game introductions. Transactions North American Wildlife Conference 33:389–398.

BUMP, G., AND W. H. BOHL. 1964. Summary of foreign game bird propagation and liberations. United States Fish and Wildlife Service Special Scientific Report 80:1–48.

BURNHAM, W. A., AND T. J. CADE. 1992. Peregrine Falcon recovery program: status and recommendations. The Peregrine Fund, Boise, ID.

CARL, G. C., AND C. J. GUIGUET. 1972. Alien animals in British Columbia. British Columbia Provincial Museum Department of Recreation Conservation Handbook 14:1–103.

CHRISTENSEN, G. C. 1963. Exotic game bird introductions into Nevada. Nevada Fish Game Commission Biological Bulletin 3.

COFFEY, B. 1959. The starling in eastern Mexico. Condor 61:299.

COOKE, M. T., AND P. KNAPPEN. 1941. Some birds naturalized in North America. Transactions, North American Wildlife Conference 5:176–183.

DAVIS, L. R. 1974. The Monk Parakeet: a potential threat to agriculture. Proceedings, Vertebrate Pest Control Conference 6:253–256.

FROKE, J. B. 1981. Population, movements, foraging and nesting of feral *Amazona* parrots in southern California. MS thesis, Humboldt State University, Arcata, California.

GAINES, D. 1988. Birds of Yosemite and the east slope. Artemesia Press, Lee Vining, California.

GODFREY, W. E. 1966. The birds of Canada. Bulletin, National Museum of Canada 203.

GOODRUM, P. 1949. The status of the bobwhite in the United States. Transactions, North American Wildlife Conference 14:359–367.

GOTTSCHALK, J. S. 1967. The introduction of exotic animals into the United States. Proceedings, Tenth Technical Meeting, International Union for the Conservation of Nature, pt. 3.

GUIGUET, C. J. 1961. The birds of British Columbia, 4: upland game birds. Handbook Series 10, Department of Recreation and Conservation, British Columbia Provincial Museum, Victoria.

HAAG, D. 1987. Regulationmechanismen bei der Strassentaube *Columba livia* forma *domestica* (Gmelin). Verhandlung Natur Gesellschaft Basel 97:31–41.

HALL, L. A. 1988. Habitat variables which influence the dissemination and colonization of introduced psittacines in southern California. MS thesis, San Diego State University, San Diego.

HARDY, J. W. 1964. Ringed parakeets nesting in Los Angeles, California. Condor 66:445–447.

HARDY, J. W. 1973. Feral exotic birds in southern California. Wilson Bulletin 85:506–512.

JEWETT, S. G., AND I. N. GABRIELSON. 1929. Birds of the Portland area, Oregon. Pacific Coast Avifauna 19:1–54.

JEWETT, S. G., W. P. TAYLOR, W. T. SHAW, AND J. W. ALDRICH. 1953. Birds of Washington state. University of Washington Press, Seattle.

JOHNS, J. E., AND C. W. ERICKSON. 1970. Breeding of free-living Trumpeter Swans in northeastern Washington. Condor 72:377–378.

JOHNSGARD, P. 1973. Grouse and quails of North America. University of Nebraska Press, Lincoln.

JOHNSTON, R. 1992. Rock Dove. The birds of North America No. 13. Academy of Natural Sciences, Philadelphia and The American Ornithologists' Union, Washington, D.C.

KESSEL, B. 1953. Distribution and migration of the European Starling in North America. Condor 55:49–67.

LEHMAN, P. E. 1982. The status and distribution of the birds of Santa Barbara County, California. MS thesis, University of California at Santa Barbara.

LONG, J. 1981. Introduced birds of the world. Universe Books, New York.

MACKAY, V. M., AND W. M. HUGHES. 1963. Crested

Mynah in British Columbia. Canadian Field Naturalist 77:154–162.

MCCOLM, M. 1970. Ruffed Grouse. Nevada Outdoors 4:27.

MONSON, G., AND A. PHILLIPS. 1981. The birds of Arizona. University of Arizona Press, Tucson.

MURTON, R., R. THEARLE, AND J. THOMPSON. 1972. Ecological studies of the feral pigeon *Columba livia* var. I. Population, breeding biology and methods of control. Journal of Applied Ecology 9:835–874.

PALMER, R. S. 1976. Handbook of North American birds. Vols. 2 and 3. Yale University Press, New Haven.

PETERSON, R. T., AND E. L. CHALIF. 1973. A field guide to Mexican birds. Houghton Mifflin, Boston.

PHILLIPS, J. C. 1928. Wild birds introduced and transplanted into North America. United States Department of Agriculture Technical Bulletin 61:1–63.

REUTHER, R. T. 1951. The Chinese Spotted Dove at Bakersfield, California. Condor 53:300–301.

REYNOLDS, J., AND G. STILES. 1982. Distribucion y densidad de poblaciones del gorrion comun (*Passer domesticus*; Aves: Ploceidae) en Costa Rica. Revista Biologia Tropical 30:65–71.

RIDGELEY, R. S. 1976. A guide to the birds of Panama. Princeton University Press, Princeton, NJ.

ROBBINS, C. S. 1973. Introduction, spread and present abundance of the House Sparrow in North America. Ornithological Monographs 14:3–9.

ROBBINS, C. S., D. BYSTRAK, AND P. GEISLER. 1986. The breeding bird survey: its first fifteen years, 1965–1979. United States Fish and Wildlife Service Research Report 157.

ROBERTS, T. S. 1960. Bird portraits in color. University of Minnesota Press, Minneapolis.

ROBERTSON, W. B., AND G. E. WOOLFENDEN. 1992. Florida bird species: an annotated list. Florida Ornithological Society Special Publication No. 6.

SCHEFFER, T. H. 1935. The English Skylark on Vancouver Island. Condor 37:256–257.

SCHORGER, A. W. 1952. Introduction of the domestic pigeon. Auk 69:462–463.

SIBLEY, C. G., AND B. L. MONROE, JR. 1990. Distribution and taxonomy of the birds of the world. Yale University Press, New Haven.

SMALLWOOD, K. S. 1990. Turbulence and ecology of invading species. Ph.D. dissertation, University of California, Davis.

SNYDER, N. F. R., AND T. B. JOHNSON. 1992. Reintroduction of the Thick-billed Parrot in the Chiricahua Mountains. Manuscript of March, 1992, for Chiricahua Mountains Research Symposium.

STORER, T. I. 1934. Economic effects of introducing alien animals to California. Proceedings, 5th Pacific Science Congress 1:779–784.

WAGNER, H. O. 1959. Die Einwanderung des Haussperlings in Mexiko. Zeitschrift für Tierpsychologie 16:584–592.

WALKER, A. 1949. The starling reaches the Pacific. Condor 57:271.

WALKER, E. 1949. The status of the Wild Turkey west of the Mississippi River. Transactions, North American Wildlife Conference 14:336–354.

WEBER, W. C., AND R. J. CANNINGS. 1990. British

Columbia and Yukon region. American Birds 44: 144–149.

WHITE, C. M. 1994. Some trends and status of selected western raptors. Pp. 161–172 *in* J. R. Jehl, Jr. and N. K. Johnson (eds.), A century of avifaunal change in western North America. Studies in Avian Biology No. 15.

WHITNEY, C. 1971. Chukar Partridge. Pp. 175–179 *in* T. W. Mussehl and F. W. Howell (eds.), Game management in Montana. Montana Fish and Game Department, Helena.

WING, L. 1956. Natural history of birds. Ronald Press, New York.

WOOD, C. A. 1924. The starling family at home and abroad. Condor 26:123–136.

YOCUM, C. F. 1963. The Hungarian Partridge, *Perdix perdix* L., in the Palouse region, Washington. Ecological Monographs 13:167–201.

Studies in Avian Biology No. 15:232–246, 1994.

The Effects of Human-Induced Environmental
Change on Avian Populations

HUMAN-INDUCED CHANGES IN BIRD POPULATIONS IN CONIFEROUS FORESTS IN WESTERN NORTH AMERICA DURING THE PAST 100 YEARS

SALLIE J. HEJL

Abstract. Data on population trends for bird populations in coniferous forests in western North America over the past 100 years are few and mostly from the United States during the breeding season. The few community and species-specific studies do not indicate similar historic population changes for any one species across habitats. West-wide 24-year trends (Breeding Bird Surveys [BBS]) were noted for 21 species; some of these changes may be caused by fire suppression or logging, the two primary ways humans have affected coniferous forests.

Because most old-growth forests are gone, snag numbers are probably lower than they were historically, and fire patterns have changed, species associated with old-growth forests, snags, and burns are probably less abundant today than they were 100 years ago. Yet, such trends were not substantiated by BBS or other studies. Regional and local changes due to fire suppression and logging have occurred for many species, but many of these changes might be partially compensatory for some species when looked at from a larger scale. Uncommon species, many of which (woodpeckers, nuthatches, creeper) are likely to be those most affected by logging and fire suppression, are not sampled well by BBS. Five of the seven declining species are long- and short-distance migrants. Human-induced changes on wintering grounds may have caused these declines.

If current patterns of forest use continue, species associated with old-growth, snags, burns, and interior forests will continue to decline. Allowing natural disturbance patterns (especially fire) to return to these ecosystems and retaining all ages, components, and landscape patterns of natural forests will help maintain avian populations and diversity.

Key Words: Population change; permanent residents; neotropical migrants.

Humans have changed the coniferous forests of western North America during the past 100 years. Some forests have been converted to fields or housing tracts, but most changes have been more subtle (Norse 1990, Hejl 1992). The age-class distribution of forests, the structure and composition of forest stands, and the pattern of forests across the landscape are a direct result of logging, fire exclusion, and forest restoration. This paper considers how such changes have affected bird populations. I defined Western North America as the region west of and including the Rocky Mountains and Sierra Madre Occidental in Canada, United States, and Mexico. Unfortunately, few studies directly address this subject; most consider only the past few decades and most have been conducted in the United States.

I assessed changes in bird populations by four approaches. First, I searched the general avifaunal literature for community and species-specific studies examining historic changes in bird populations in coniferous forests. Second, I examined U.S. Fish and Wildlife Service's Breeding Bird Survey data (BBS) for the past 24 years (1968–1991). Third, I inferred population trends from our current knowledge of the transformation of western coniferous forests over the past 100 years and our knowledge of bird-habitat relations in natural and treated forests. For these inferences, I assumed that changes in bird populations are a direct result of habitat changes, and that population trends can be estimated based on habitat changes. Fourth, I compared estimates of population change made by researchers in two specific regions of the western United States.

Finally, I discuss limitations of each approach, compare implications for past population trends, predict future trends, and

TABLE 1. CHANGES IN DISTRIBUTION AND ABUNDANCE IN SELECTED BIRD SPECIES BETWEEN HISTORIC AND MORE RECENT TIMES IN "LONG-TERM" COMMUNITY STUDIES IN CONIFEROUS FORESTS IN WESTERN NORTH AMERICA. SPECIES WERE ARBITRARILY SELECTED. SYMBOLS ARE + = INCREASING TREND, − = DECREASING TREND, NT = NO TREND, AND ? = NOT OBVIOUS TREND

Species	Oregon, juniper 1899–1983[1]	Sierra Nevada, burn 1966–1985[2]	Sierra Nevada old growth				Sierra Nevada, logged 1930s–1986[4]	San Benito, CA 1936–1984[5]	Grape-vines, NV 1939–1973[6]	Spring Ranges, NV 1936–1963[7]
			Pon-derosa Pine	Mixed Conifer	Red Fir	Lodge-pole Pine				
Band-tailed Pigeon							NT			+
Hairy Woodpecker		NT	+	NT	NT	+	−	NT		?
Olive-sided Flycatcher		+ burn	+	NT	−	+	−	+		+
Western Wood-Pewee	+	NT	−	NT	−	−	NT	+		+
Dusky Flycatcher		+ burn	NT	−	NT	+		+	+	+
Mountain Chickadee	+	+ burn	NT	NT	NT	−	NT			NT
Red-breasted Nuthatch		+ forest	NT	NT	+	+	+			
Brown Creeper		+ forest	+	NT	+	+	NT			?
Golden-crowned Kinglet		− forest	+	+	+	+	+			
Ruby-crowned Kinglet			−	−	−	NT			+	+
Mountain Bluebird	+	− burn							+	
Swainson's Thrush			−	−			−			
Solitary Vireo		NT	−	NT			NT	NT	+	+
Black-throated Gray Warbler	+		−	−				−		+
Chipping Sparrow	+	− burn	−	NT	−	−				?
Fox Sparrow	+	+ burn	−	−	−					
Brown-headed Cowbird	+	+ burn				+	+			

[1] Sharp (1985).
[2] Raphael et al. (1987). Trend occurred in the indicated habitat.
[3] Beedy (1982).
[4] Marshall (1988).
[5] Johnson and Cicero (1985).
[6] Johnson (1974).
[7] Johnson (1965).

note management options that will help maintain these species.

HISTORICAL CHANGES IN CONIFER BIRD POPULATIONS

COMMUNITY STUDIES

Researchers in seven community studies in coniferous forests (Johnson 1965, Johnson 1974, Beedy 1982, Johnson and Cicero 1985, Sharp 1985, Raphael et al. 1987, Marshall 1988) compared bird populations in four habitats and three mountain ranges between at least two different points in time. No common trends for individual species were seen across all studies, although some species varied in parallel in a few studies (Table 1; scientific names in Appendix I). The studies differed, however, in methods, habitat, scale, time period, and in the degree to which human-induced and natural changes had occurred. Therefore, it is difficult to compare results or to know if they represented local or regional trends.

The greatest strength of these studies might be in allowing us to better understand natural and human-induced changes in bird populations. In studies from several mountain ranges in the southwestern United States, Johnson (1974) suggested that a natural factor, short-term global cooling, was contributing to increases of boreal species. Johnson and Cicero (1985) similarly proposed that changes in bird populations at San Benito, California were caused by the recent shift toward cooler, moist summer climates. Sharp (1985) and Raphael et al. (1987) linked changes in bird populations to changes in vegetation. Sharp (1985) attributed increases in Chipping Sparrows to the increase of juniper in an Oregon grassland. Raphael et al. (1987) concluded that the changes in abundance on burned and unburned plots were due to changing vegetation structure, not variations in weather. Shrub cover and the density of overstory trees increased on the burned plot, as did the numbers of birds that foraged on the ground or searched for food in the brush or in foliage. When the density of snags left after the fire decreased so did the numbers of bark-gleaning birds.

Beedy (1982) and Marshall (1988) attributed bird population changes to human-induced factors. In four old-growth habitats in Yosemite National Park, Beedy (1982) concluded that many changes were likely caused by the effects of fire exclusion on forest structure and composition. For example, Golden-crowned Kinglets, which prefer dense, shaded forests, probably increased due to the encroachment of fir saplings. Numbers of Fox Sparrows and Green-tailed Towhees decreased, possibly because shading reduced shrub habitat. In a virgin and a second-growth forest in the Sierra Nevada, Marshall (1988) ascribed declines in six species (e.g., Flammulated Owl and Hairy Woodpecker) and increases of two species to logging and declines of Olive-sided Flycatcher and Swainson's Thrush to the loss of winter habitat.

Burns and fire exclusion appear to have the opposite effect on some forest birds. Seventy percent of the species common in burned habitat in the eastern Sierra Nevada (Raphael et al. 1987) have become less abundant in at least one old-growth habitat in the western Sierra Nevada, where fire had been excluded (Beedy 1982). Calliope Hummingbird, Green-tailed Towhee, and Fox Sparrow were less abundant in all old-growth habitats in which they were found. On the other hand, 66% of the species common in unburned, forested habitat in the eastern Sierra Nevada (e.g., Red-breasted Nuthatch, Brown Creeper, Golden-crowned Kinglet) (Raphael et al. 1987) have increased in at least one old-growth habitat in the western Sierra Nevada (Beedy 1982).

INDIVIDUAL SPECIES TRENDS

I searched the literature for population trends for individual species, excluding the most well-documented—Marbled Murrelet, Spotted Owl, and Brown-headed Cowbird, which are covered by Ralph (1994), Gutiérrez (1994), and Rothstein (1994), respectively.

Regional or local changes are indicated for some species during the last half of this century. Northern Goshawk may have declined on the North Kaibab in northern Arizona, especially between 1972 and 1988 (Crocker-Bedford 1990, but see Reynolds et al. 1992) and Hairy Woodpecker in Washington and Oregon between 1953 and 1982 (Morrison and Morrison 1983). The Barred Owl has recently expanded its range southwestward into the Northern Rockies and Pacific Northwest (Taylor and Forsman 1976). Chestnut-backed Chickadee expanded southward in the Sierra Nevada over 40 years ago, and populations have seemed stable since (Brennan and Morrison 1991). Since 1960, Hermit Warblers may have declined in the Puget Sound region and expanded in the northern Cascades (Chappell and Ringer 1983). Red-breasted Sapsuckers may have extended their range in the last 50 years in coastal California (Shuford 1986). No population changes were recorded for woodpeckers between 1953 and 1982 along the entire Pacific Coast (Morrison and Morrison 1983) or for Black-capped and Mountain chickadees in the Pacific Northwest from 1944 to 1985 (Brennan and Morrison 1991).

American Birds uses information from active birders to create "Blue Lists" of species that show local or widespread population declines or range contractions. The most recent (Tate 1986) indicates decline in only three coniferous forest birds (Cooper's Hawk, Hairy Woodpecker, and Purple Martin) in one or two subregions of the West.

The causes of any of these apparent changes are unknown. Moreover, the status of some species may have since changed, and most have not been intensively studied over large geographic areas. Woodpecker (Morrison and Morrison 1983) and chickadee (Brennan and Morrison 1991) trends, however, were based on the Christmas Bird Count (CBC) data, which are widespread and relatively long-term (>30–40 yr).

TABLE 2. Significant Breeding Bird Survey Trends for the Western United States and Canada for Coniferous Forest Bird Species with Average Abundance Greater than 1.00 per Route When More than 50 Routes Were in the Sample. Species Are Listed in Ascending Order from Most Negative 24-yr Trend

Species	24-yr trend[1] (1968–1991)		10-yr trend (1982–1991)		Migratory status[2]
	%	N	%	N	
Olive-sided Flycatcher	−3.5*	343	−2.7*	281	long
Band-tailed Pigeon	−3.2*	186	−9.0*	138	long
Rufous Hummingbird	−3.1*	182	−3.9*	136	long
Golden-crowned Kinglet	−2.8*	229	−1.5	192	permanent
Chipping Sparrow	−2.7*	527	−0.5	407	long
Plain Titmouse	−2.5*	174	−2.6*	131	permanent
Western Bluebird	−2.2*	229	−2.0	161	short
Lark Sparrow	−1.2	395	−2.6*	283	long
Orange-crowned Warbler	−0.6	325	+2.7*	265	long
Black-capped Chickadee	−0.1	293	+2.4*	247	permanent
Wilson's Warbler	+0.4	332	−3.5*	246	long
Acorn Woodpecker	+0.9	137	+3.1*	96	permanent
Scrub Jay	+1.2*	244	+0.5	198	permanent
Winter Wren	+1.2*	157	−2.6*	129	permanent
Hermit Thrush	+1.9*	301	+1.7	238	short
Nashville Warbler	+2.0*	156	−2.0	134	long
Varied Thrush	+2.2*	140	−1.8	109	permanent
Black-throated Gray Warbler	+2.2*	188	−1.2	150	long
Red-breasted Nuthatch	+2.2*	341	+6.2*	290	permanent
Cedar Waxwing	+2.3*	274	+5.5*	224	short
Warbling Vireo	+2.3*	469	+2.8*	377	long
House Wren	+2.3*	475	+3.6*	380	long
Tree Swallow	+2.4*	493	+1.2	393	short
Solitary Vireo	+2.5*	351	+5.2*	276	long
Red-tailed Hawk	+2.6*	676	+1.1	563	short
Common Raven	+3.2*	623	+1.5	524	permanent

[1] Trend = the rate of change in the population, expressed as percent annual change; * denotes a significant trend (P < 0.10).
[2] Migratory status: long = long-distance migrant species that breed in North America and spend their nonbreeding period primarily south of the United States, short = short-distance migrants that breed and winter extensively in North America, permanent = permanent resident species that primarily have overlapping breeding and nonbreeding areas.

BREEDING BIRD SURVEYS FROM 1968 TO 1991

I examined U.S. Fish and Wildlife Service Breeding Bird Surveys (BBS) for Western Northern America, using their weightings and statistical tests. John Sauer performed the analyses using the methods described by Geissler and Sauer (1990) and Sauer and Geissler (1990). I listed the "coniferous forest" species (broadly defined) with average abundance greater than 1.0/route, when more than 50 routes were included in a sample that had statistically significant (P < 0.10) 24- or 10-year trends (Table 2).

Of 113 western coniferous forest species detected, only 57 (50%) met the abundance and number of routes criteria (Appendix I). Seven had significant declining trends over the past 24 years, seven had significant declining trends over the past 10 years, and four species declined significantly over both periods (Table 2). Fourteen species had significant increasing trends in the past 24 years, and eight had significant increasing trends in the past 10 years. Three species with nonsignificant or increasing trends over 24 years had significant declining 10-year trends.

Many coniferous forest species are not sampled well enough by the BBS routes in the West to discern trends. In general, these were raptors (especially owls), grouse, woodpeckers, "eastern" warblers, and birds peculiar to the southwestern and northern

United States and Canada, but also included a few widespread birds of coniferous forests (e.g., White-breasted Nuthatch, Pygmy Nuthatch, and Brown Creeper).

Extrapolating from 24-year BBS trends to 100-year trends presents problems, even for the best-sampled species. The number of survey routes changes each year, continues to increase, and emphasizes roadside birds, whose trends do not necessarily apply to forest birds, especially "interior" forest species (but see Hutto et al. in press). Coverage is spotty, especially in Alaska, Canada, and Mexico. Roadsides, and thus species composition, are also likely to change due to local plant succession and fragmentation of the surrounding area. Since BBS routes do not just cover conifer habitats and since some "conifer" species breed in other habitats as well, changes in BBS data may not be caused by changes in coniferous forest habitats.

INFERENCES ABOUT HISTORICAL CHANGES IN BIRD POPULATIONS IN CONIFEROUS FORESTS

TRANSFORMATION OF WESTERN CONIFEROUS FORESTS

The six major ways in which humans have changed forest composition and structure in the past 100 years are: fire exclusion, logging, grazing, introduction of foreign organisms (diseases, insects, and plants), residential development, and chemical applications. Fire exclusion and logging have had the greatest effects, and are the best studied.

The exclusion of fire for the past 50 or more years has been the most significant factor affecting today's western forests. Almost all wildfires have been fought, even in wilderness areas. Only since the 1960s have federal agencies allowed some fires to burn (Taylor and Barmore 1980). The result of past fire control is usually a decrease in frequency and increase in intensity of fires (see Weatherspoon et al. 1992).

Logging practices and silvicultural recommendations have changed frequently for specific forest types and geographic areas. In general, the most accessible forests (i.e., near railroad construction camps, mining camps, or cities) and commercially valuable tree species were logged first. Early on, land was often stripped either of all trees or of the favored species and size classes ("high-grading"). Small trees and defective trees were often not harvested.

In the late 1800s and early 1900s, both clearcutting and selective logging were used in many forest types throughout the west. Sanitation logging (the removal of dead, damaged, or susceptible trees to prevent the spread of insects and diseases) and salvage logging (the removal of dead, dying, or deteriorating trees before the timber becomes "worthless") occurred in many areas after World War I and have continued as important practices to the present (Wellner 1984, McKelvey and Johnston 1992).

Timber harvest increased as technologies improved, especially after World War II (McKelvey and Johnston 1992). Large clearcuts separated by small strips of standing trees were the norm in some areas on public land [e.g., Douglas-fir in Rocky Mountains (Wellner 1984) and Pacific Northwest (Norse 1990)], whereas in other areas, clearcutting was infrequent (e.g., mixed-conifer forests in Sierra Nevada, McKelvey and Johnston 1992). Higher elevation forests, such as spruce-fir, were rarely logged before 1950 (Alexander 1986; but see Losensky 1990). Pinyon-juniper has been chained for the past 40 years to convert areas either to grassland for livestock or to shrubland for game management (Evans 1988). In the 1970s and 1980s, logging treatments became more varied as federal agencies and the public attained a broader knowledge of the multiple uses of forests.

Fire exclusion across the west has allowed many forests to change from open to closed stands and has altered fire regimes which naturally differed among forest types (Weatherspoon et al. 1992). The effects of logging varied. High-grading took the healthiest, largest, usually shade-intolerant, trees, leaving stands of inferior, usually shade-tolerant, trees. After fires, windstorms, or insect or disease damage, snags and dying trees were salvaged for lumber or firewood. If artificial regeneration were used, planting usually involved one or a few economically valuable species rather than the natural diversity of the prelogging forest.

Fire exclusion and logging have opposite effects on the age-class distribution of forests. Little is left of the original old-growth forests in the West (e.g., less than 13–37% in Pacific Northwest Douglas-fir forests, Hejl 1992). Because of logging, the proportion of young forests is greater today than 100 years ago in some of the Pacific Northwest (Raphael et al. 1988). In contrast, because of fire exclusion and in spite of logging, the proportion of early successional forests is often similar or smaller today in the Northern Rocky Mountains (Gruell 1983). The age-class distribution in specific forest types in the Northern Rockies may have changed more than the proportion of forests considered young or old growth (Hejl 1992). For example, in one area on the Bitterroot National Forest, the amount of mature and older ponderosa pine stands had decreased due to logging, but older Douglas-fir stands had increased because of fire exclusion, with the result that the total amount of older forests is the same today as in 1900.

Current landscape patterns are different from those of 100 years ago and reflect the combined effects of logging, fire, and other factors. Large expanses of continuous forest with relatively little diversity once covered the moist areas of Pacific Northwest and the Sierra Nevada (Rosenberg and Raphael 1986, Norse 1990, Laudenslayer and Darr 1990). Further inland, as in the drier Rocky Mountains, forests were more heterogeneous due to topographic, climatic, and fire effects (Gruell 1983, Hejl 1992). Grasslands, shrubsteppes, and deserts create forest islands in the Great Basin and southeast Arizona; yet, northern Arizona has the largest continuous stand of ponderosa pine (Brawn and Balda 1988).

Patterns of habitat fragmentation have varied among forest types. For example, cutting regimes in the Rocky Mountains have tended to vary from large clearcuts that are often densely spaced in moist forests (e.g., spruce-fir and cedar-hemlock forests) to repeated entries of selective cutting in drier forests (e.g., ponderosa pine, western larch, or Douglas-fir forests; S. Arno, pers. comm.). Staggered clearcuts result in a patchwork of uncut "old growth" and new plantations or young forests, increasing landscape heterogeneity (Franklin and Forman 1987). Selectively logged forests can result in even-aged stands and decreased landscape heterogeneity (McKelvey and Johnston 1992).

DIFFERENCES IN BIRDS AMONG NATURAL YOUNG, MATURE, AND OLD-GROWTH STANDS

Douglas-fir forest birds were studied extensively and intensively in the Pacific Northwest from 1984 to 1986 (Ruggiero et al. 1991). Bird populations were compared in three age-classes of natural forests: young (42–75 years), mature (105–165), and old-growth (250–500). Eight breeding species were clearly associated with old-growth forests: Allen's Hummingbird (California only), Vaux's Swift (Oregon and Washington only), Hairy Woodpecker, Pileated Woodpecker, Red-breasted Sapsucker (Oregon and Washington only), Western (Pacific-slope) Flycatcher, Chestnut-backed Chickadee, and Brown Creeper. Brown Creeper was the only species often associated with mature forests and Black-throated Gray Warbler was the only species often associated with young forests. All ages of natural stands may also be important winter habitat for resident species (Raphael 1984, Manuwal and Huff 1987, Ruggiero et al. 1991).

Other comparisons of bird species in different age-classes of natural forests include three studies in the Rocky Mountains (Catt 1991, Hallock 1989–1990, Moore 1992) and one in the Pacific Northwest (Kessler and Kogut 1985). Whereas several species were associated with particular age classes, none was associated with a particular forest age class in all studies.

The reasons for the differences among studies are unknown. Indeed, one might not expect many differences within any one study, since natural young and mature forests often contain a number of structural characteristics typical of old-growth forests, such as snags and logs.

LOGGING EFFECTS ON BIRDS

Most studies of the effects of logging have compared clearcuts to control forests (presumably uncut or lightly cut), or various partially logged areas to control forests. Hejl et al. (in press) made both comparisons across conifer forests in the Rocky Mountains. Thirteen species (Three-toed Woodpecker, Black-capped Chickadee, Mountain Chickadee, Red-breasted Nuthatch, Brown Creeper, Winter Wren, Golden-crowned Kinglet, Ruby-crowned Kinglet, Swainson's Thrush, Varied Thrush, Solitary Vireo, Townsend's Warbler, Evening Grosbeak) were always less abundant in recent clearcuts than in uncut forest. In contrast, the Mountain Bluebird was always more abundant in recent clearcuts. Differences were less dramatic between partially logged forests and unlogged forests. Brown Creeper, Pygmy Nuthatch, and Pine Grosbeak were always less abundant in partially logged forests than in unlogged forests. Calliope Hummingbird was always more abundant in partially logged forests. In general, forest species were found less often in clearcuts, and species that frequent open forests or open habitats were found more often in clearcuts. Resident species tended to decrease after any kind of harvesting, while only about half of the migrants decreased. In contrast, almost all the species that increased after partial cutting or soon after clearcutting were migrants, and most on the recent clearcuts were short-distance migrants. Similar patterns have been documented in chained pinyon-juniper areas (O'Meara et al. 1981, Sedgwick and Ryder 1987) as in clearcuts from other forest types.

Hejl et al. (in press) also compared differences in bird populations between old-growth and mature second-growth forests (intensively logged 60–120 years ago) in the Rocky Mountains. No species was consistently more abundant in either situation. When there were differences, woodpeckers and nuthatches, in general, were more abundant in old-growth than in mature second-growth. At least three owl species (Flammulated Owl, Spotted Owl, and Boreal Owl) also seemed to be associated with old-growth habitats.

Studies elsewhere have produced similar results. Raphael et al. (1988) compared birds in three stages of forest development following logging, fire, windthrow, or landslide in northwestern California: brush/sapling, pole/sawtimber, and mature Douglas-fir forests. Eleven species found in forests greater than 100 years of age were never found in shrub/sapling stands which are primarily less than 20 years old. Seventeen species were either much more abundant or found only in shrub/sapling stands. Migrants predominated in the shrub/sapling stages; most species were ground or brush foragers. Most species associated with forests were permanent residents. All but one of the bole-foraging species were forest obligates. A majority of forest species were canopy or air foragers.

For many species, snags are important for nesting, foraging, perching, and roosting. Cavity-nesting bird density varied in proportion to snag density in logged, burned, and natural forests (Cunningham et al. 1980, Raphael and White 1984, Zarnowitz and Manuwal 1985). In two studies, cavity-nesting bird density declined 53–77% after snags were removed (Scott and Oldemeyer 1983, Raphael and White 1984). Cavity-nesting birds are more likely to nest in large snags or trees and thus are common in old growth (Mannan et al. 1980). In some areas, certain tree species (e.g., western larch) are preferred (McClelland et al. 1979).

FIRE AND FIRE SUPPRESSION EFFECTS ON BIRDS

Fire affects bird communities differently depending on its intensity. High intensity fires often create habitat for primary cavity nesters, secondary cavity nesters, and shrub users (Taylor and Barmore 1980, Raphael et al. 1987), whereas low intensity fires create habitats for birds that prefer open forests. Some species (Black-backed Woodpecker, Olive-sided Flycatcher, and Mountain Bluebird) even seem relatively restricted to conditions after fires (R. L. Hutto, pers. comm.). The benefits of fires are sometimes short-term.

Six species were more abundant in high intensity burns than in unburned forests in the Sierra Nevada (Raphael et al. 1987) and Rockies (Taylor and Barmore 1980): Hairy Woodpecker, Black-backed Woodpecker, Northern Flicker, Western Wood-Pewee, House Wren, and Mountain Bluebird. Three species were more abundant in unburned forests in both areas: Red-breasted Nuthatch, Golden-crowned Kinglet, and Western Tanager. The shrub-nesting species present after the Sierra Nevada burn (e.g., Green-tailed Towhee and Fox Sparrow) were notably absent from severely burned areas in the Rockies.

Moderate and low intensity burns show less dramatic immediate effects than high intensity burns. For the first few years after a moderate burn in the Rockies, birds characteristic of severely burned forests as well as unburned forests were present (Taylor and Barmore 1980). In the Sierra Nevada, Granholm (1982) found that Hairy Woodpecker, Black-backed Woodpecker, Steller's Jay, and Cassin's Finch responded positively to surface burns. Northern Flicker, typically associated with high intensity burns, was as abundant in unburned forests as in surface burns. Hammond's Flycatcher, Mountain Chickadee, Hermit Thrush, and Golden-crowned Kinglet consistently responded negatively to surface burns.

Open forest species may be lost with fire suppression. In pine-oak forests of southern Arizona and northern Mexico (Sonora and Chihuahua), Marshall (1963) found marked differences in bird populations due to different fire regimes (suppressed in Arizona, unchecked fires in Mexico). Many open forest species (e.g., Purple Martin and Western Bluebird) were more abundant in Mexico or often found only in lowlands in Arizona. Several brush or dense forest species were more abundant in Arizona (e.g., Black-throated Gray Warbler).

Logged burns probably benefit fewer burn-associated species than unlogged burns. Overturf (1979) described bird communities on three severely burned ponderosa pine forests that were later logged in Arizona. Nine species that had been abundant in at least one of the unlogged high intensity burns (Taylor and Barmore 1980, Raphael et al. 1987) were also present in the logged burns. However, three of these species were equally abundant in an "unlogged," unburned area and the other six species were only present in one of the three burns.

IMPORTANCE OF LANDSCAPE PATTERNS TO BIRDS

The greatest effects of logging and fire exclusion on bird populations may be through changes in landscape patterns, but this is difficult to isolate (Dobkin 1992). Concerns about human-induced changes in western landscapes include forest fragmentation, juxtaposition of various habitats, and loss of landscape elements. Forest fragmentation is difficult to quantify since most western forests are not isolated patches surrounded by nonforested habitats but are interconnected with other forests of different ages and species composition.

Several studies (Rosenberg and Raphael 1986, Lehmkuhl et al. 1991, Hejl 1992, Keller and Anderson 1992, Hejl and Paige in press) have addressed relationships between birds and various landscape patterns. Our knowledge on these issues is rudimentary. Some species are associated with continuous forest (Winter Wren). Others seem to avoid edges (Band-tailed Pigeon). Some species may be less abundant in insular forests (Golden-crowned Kinglet) and in more fragmented landscapes (Brown Creeper). Certain species (Acorn Woodpecker) may be more abundant in conifer stands with adjacent hardwoods. As in the east (Askins et al. 1990), changes in western forest landscapes may negatively affect nest productivity for these species and others through an increase in nest predation or nest parasitism (Verner and Ritter 1983, Hejl and Paige in press).

Because we have little knowledge, no experimental studies, and the effects of changing landscapes are likely cumulative and may have a time-lag associated with them, we cannot estimate how much current bird populations are different from historical populations due to landscape changes.

ESTIMATED HISTORICAL TRENDS BASED ON FOREST CHANGES AND BIRD-HABITAT RELATIONS

Because we do not know the current or historical acreages of natural and logged forests of different ages, and thus cannot ascertain changes in total acres of forest today from the past, we can only guess how bird numbers might have changed in the past 100 years. We do know, however, that most old-growth habitats are gone, that snag numbers are probably much lower, and that the intensity (usually higher) and frequency (usually lower) of fires have changed. Because our understanding of the effects of forestry practices on birds is based mostly on recent, short-term studies, any generalizations must be tentative. However, strong evidence suggests that: 1) some species clearly associate with old-growth forests, even when those forests are compared to natural younger forests that contain a legacy of "old-growth" characteristics; 2) logging treatments generally decrease the abundance of almost all permanent residents and half the migrants; 3) density of cavity-nesters is directly related to snag density, with cavity-nesters selecting large snags of cer-

tain preferred species; 4) fire suppression causes changes in populations in old-growth and other forests, especially among species that forage in shrubs or on the ground; and 5) fire creates habitat for Three-toed Woodpeckers, Black-backed Woodpeckers, other primary and secondary cavity nesters, and shrub-nesters. Therefore, I hypothesize that those species associated with burns, old-growth forests, or snags are less abundant today than they were 100 years ago. The greatest declines have probably occurred for snag-users that preferentially live in burned areas or old-growth forests. Other scientists (Brawn and Balda 1988, Raphael et al. 1988) made similar suggestions.

BIRD TRENDS IN THE PACIFIC NORTHWEST AND THE SOUTHWEST

Raphael et al. (1988) used current bird populations of three seral stages, and estimates of past and current forest area in each seral stage, to hypothesize historic trends in bird populations in Douglas-fir forests in northwest California (Table 3). With a change of 20% considered significant, twenty-two species have probably declined and 18 species have probably increased. Historic populations were likely dominated by migrants that foraged in the forest canopy and air. Current populations have increased and are also dominated by this group, although some individual species (e.g., Hammond's Flycatcher) have declined. Ground and brush foragers are found more abundantly in the current avifauna. Resident species that forage in canopy and air have declined. Seven bole-foraging species likely have decreased. This group of birds apparently has been most adversely affected by shifts from forested to nonforested land.

Brawn and Balda (1988) speculated on the reasons for long-term changes in the ponderosa pine avifauna in the southwestern United States. Purple Martin and Lark Sparrow may have been nearly extirpated because of snag removal and fire exclusion. Declines in 13 other species may be due to

TABLE 3. Hypothesized Population Changes for Coniferous Forest Birds from Presettlement Times in Southwestern Ponderosa Pine (Modified from Brawn and Balda 1988) and in Northwestern Douglas-fir (Modified from Raphael et al. 1988). Percentage Change Are Only Indicated for Douglas-fir Forests

Species	Ponderosa pine[1]	Douglas-fir
Sharp-shinned Hawk		+19
Cooper's Hawk		−19
Blue Grouse		−34
Mountain Quail		+84
Band-tailed Pigeon		−25
Calliope Hummingbird		+243
Broad-tailed Hummingbird	−	
Acorn Woodpecker	−	−42
Red-breasted Sapsucker		−15
Hairy Woodpecker	NT	−36
Three-toed Woodpecker	−	
Northern Flicker	NT	−4
Pileated Woodpecker		−38
Olive-sided Flycatcher		+2
Western Wood-Pewee	NT	+78
Hammond's Flycatcher		−43
Dusky Flycatcher		+216
Western (Pacific-slope) Flycatcher		−39
Western (Cordilleran) Flycatcher	+	
Purple Martin	−	
Violet-green Swallow	−	
Steller's Jay	NT	−5
Scrub Jay		+243
Common Raven		−42
Mountain Chickadee	−	
Chestnut-backed Chickadee		−36
Red-breasted Nuthatch		−37
White-breasted Nuthatch	−	−42
Pygmy Nuthatch	−	
Brown Creeper	−	−35
House Wren	+	+228
Winter Wren		−47
Golden-crowned Kinglet		−45
Western Bluebird	−	+236
Mountain Bluebird	−	
Townsend's Solitaire	+	−36
Hermit Thrush	+	−32
American Robin	−	−22
Solitary Vireo	+	−26
Hutton's Vireo		−39
Warbling Vireo		−19
Orange-crowned Warbler		+190
Nashville Warbler		+129
Virginia's Warbler	+	
Yellow-rumped Warbler	+	+41
Black-throated Gray Warbler		+87
Hermit Warbler		−40
Grace's Warbler	+	
MacGillivray's Warbler		+162
Wilson's Warbler		+67
Red-faced Warbler	−	
Olive Warbler	?	
Western Tanager	+	−28
Green-tailed Towhee		+200

TABLE 3. Continued

Species	Ponderosa pine[1]	Douglas-fir
Chipping Sparrow	−	+241
Lark Sparrow	−	
Fox Sparrow		+243
Dark-eyed Junco	NT	+18
Brown-headed Cowbird		+5
Purple Finch		+76
Red Crossbill		−37
Pine Siskin	?	+2
Lesser Goldfinch		+84
Evening Grosbeak		−17

[1] "+" = increased population, "−" = decreased population, "NT" = no trend, and "?" = no data.

loss of the herbaceous layer, reduction in old trees and snags, and decline in Gambel's oaks. Increases in nine species may be due to more dense thickets, more productive foliage, more shrubby understory and the presence of downed slash, changes resulting from logging and fire exclusion.

Comparing estimates of trends from the Northwest and Southwest, only 18 of 64 bird species that were speculated to have increased or decreased were present in both ponderosa pine and Douglas-fir (Brawn and Balda 1988, Raphael et al. 1988; Table 3). Nine had similar trends (using the 20% criterion). Acorn Woodpecker, White-breasted Nuthatch, Brown Creeper, and American Robin had declined; Northern Flicker, Steller's Jay, and Dark-eyed Junco were unchanged; and House Wren and Yellow-rumped Warbler had increased. Six species had opposite trends in the two areas.

SYNTHESIS

No data substantiate human-induced, 100-yr, west-wide trends for any species of bird in western coniferous forests. Regional and local changes, however, were seen for many species (e.g., range contraction of Swainson's Thrush and extension of Chestnut-backed Chickadee), and short-term, west-wide trends were shown by BBS. I suggest that birds associated with burns, old-growth forests, and snags have probably declined (see also Brawn and Balda 1988,

Raphael et al. 1988), although this has not been confirmed by BBS, individual or community studies.

Perhaps no trends exist. It is possible, for example, that logging and burning create similar habitat for many birds, that a similar number of acres have been logged as would have burned under "natural" fire regimes, and that fire exclusion compensates for any differences between logged habitats and unburned habitats. Or, because many species are found in many different coniferous forests, regional changes may counter one another at the large, half-a-continent scale. For example, the Western Bluebird and Chipping Sparrow were speculated to have increased in Douglas-fir in the Northwest (Raphael et al. 1988) and to have decreased in ponderosa pine in the Southwest (Brawn and Balda 1988). These seemingly contradictory trends may have been due to the increase of early successional habitats created by logging in the Northwest and the closing in of habitats due to fire exclusion in the Southwest.

Sources of information on population trends of coniferous forest birds are poor. BBS currently is our best source of quantitative data on large-scale trends in breeding birds. Unfortunately, many coniferous forest habitats and species have not been sampled adequately, especially those (woodpeckers, nuthatches, Brown Creeper) that are negatively affected by logging and fire suppression. While greater coverage would be beneficial, adding routes will not improve the sampling for all 51 species that had low abundances (the "poorer" and "poorest" classifications in Appendix I) and probably only help us examine trends for species whose optimum habitat has been missed. It will not improve sampling for those species that are sampled poorly due to low density, time-of-year, or time-of-day problems. If "interior" forest species exist or if species are more or less successful in forests than they are along roadsides, it would be useful to supplement BBS with a systematic program of habitat-based, off-road surveys (DeSante and George 1994). Special surveys are needed for rare and nocturnal species.

Sources of information on the effects of human activities on western forest birds are limited; there are few studies on the effects of silviculture, fire, fire suppression, or of changing landscape patterns, and even fewer on the effects of other human-induced changes. Most studies are based on a few study sites, are short-term, are based on secondary population parameters, and in most cases the data are not adequate for statistical tests. In three studies in which sample sizes were sufficient, researchers only analyzed the most common species individually (from 28% [Hejl et al. 1988] to 38% [Hejl and Woods 1991] to 63% [Tobalske et al. 1991]), making inferences tentative for the other species.

Many of the species with recent and significant declines according to BBS are long- and short-distance migrants. Pyle et al. (1994) identify three additional species that breed in coniferous forests. Human-induced changes on wintering grounds should be considered as a possible cause of these declines.

Predicting the future is even more difficult than understanding the past. Raphael et al. (1988) expect bird species associated with young timber in Douglas-fir in California to increase most in the future and those associated with mature forest or the brush/sapling stage to decrease. Species that prefer old-growth forests will remain in reduced numbers and may decline even further. Resident birds that forage in the forest canopy or in the air will continue to decline as a whole. Raphael et al. (1988) concluded that future avian communities in Californian Douglas-fir will become more similar to the original communities than to those of the present. Brawn and Balda (1988) predicted that secondary cavity nesters in Southwest ponderosa pine forests will decline as snags and other trees are removed, especially for fuelwood. Birds in general, however, may increase due to improved forest vigor resulting from more frequent natural and managed fires. If current patterns of forest use across the west continue, I predict species associated with old-growth forests, snags, burns, and interior forests will continue to decline.

Allowing natural disturbance patterns (especially fire) to return to these ecosystems and retaining all ages, components, and landscape patterns of natural forests (especially old-growth, snags, and all tree species) will help maintain avian populations and diversity in western landscapes. While we do not know all of the specifics of bird-habitat relations, we understand many principles that would help maintain healthy forests for most bird species: retain old growth, encourage old-growth characteristics in logged forests, leave snags and replacement trees to become snags, leave or plant the natural diversity of trees (including hardwoods) found in an area, burn and allow fires to happen in a manner similar to natural fire regimes, and mimic natural landscape patterns and patch dynamics. Many wildlife managers are currently adhering to these principles.

ACKNOWLEDGMENTS

Many thanks to L. C. Paige for help with obtaining and understanding BBS trends; to U.S. Fish and Wildlife Service (especially S. Droege, B. Peterjohn, and J. R. Sauer) for the use and understanding of BBS and to all of the volunteers who conducted the surveys; to E. C. Beedy, R. L. Hutto, J. R. Jehl, Jr., N. K. Johnson, P. B. Landres, L. J. Lyon, B. Peterjohn, M. G. Raphael, and J. R. Sauer for reviewing the manuscript; and to B. Lindler and J. R. Jehl, Jr. for editing the manuscript.

LITERATURE CITED

ALEXANDER, R. R. 1986. Silvicultural systems and cutting methods for old-growth spruce-fir forests in the Central and Southern Rocky Mountains. USDA Forest Service, General Technical Report RM-126.

ASKINS, R. A., J. F. LYNCH, AND R. GREENBERG. 1990. Population declines in migratory birds in eastern North America. Current Ornithology 7:1–57.

BEEDY, E. C. 1982. Bird community structure in coniferous forests of Yosemite National Park, California. Ph.D. diss., Univ. California, Davis.

BRAWN, J. D., AND R. P. BALDA. 1988. The influence of silvicultural activity on ponderosa pine forest bird communities in the southwestern United States. Bird Conservation 3:3–21.

BRENNAN, L. A., AND M. L. MORRISON. 1991. Long-term trends of chickadee populations in western North America. Condor 93:130–137.

CATT, D. J. 1991. Bird communities and forest succession in the subalpine zone of Kootenay National Park, British Columbia. M.S. thesis, Simon Fraser Univ., British Columbia.

CHAPPELL, C. B., AND B. J. RINGER. 1983. Status of the Hermit Warbler in Washington. Western Birds 14:185–196.

CROCKER-BEDFORD, D. C. 1990. Goshawk reproduction and forest management. Wildlife Society Bulletin 18:262–269.

CUNNINGHAM, J. B., R. P. BALDA, AND W. S. GAUD. 1980. Selection and use of snags by secondary cavity-nesting birds of the ponderosa pine forest. USDA Forest Service, Research Paper RM-222.

DESANTE, D. F., AND T. L. GEORGE. 1994. Population trends in the landbirds of Western North America. Pp. 173–190 *in* J. R. Jehl, Jr. and N. K. Johnson (eds.), A century of avifaunal change in western North America. Studies in Avian Biology No. 15.

DOBKIN, D. S. 1992. Neotropical migrant landbirds in the Northern Rockies and Great Plains. USDA Forest Service Northern Region. Publication No. R1-93-34. Missoula, MT.

EVANS, R. A. 1988. Management of pinyon-juniper woodlands. USDA Forest Service, General Technical Report INT-249.

FRANKLIN, J. F., AND R. T. FORMAN. 1987. Creating landscape patterns by forest cutting: ecological consequences and principles. Landscape Ecology 1:5–18.

GEISSLER, P. H., AND J. R. SAUER. 1990. Topics in route-regression analysis. Pp. 54–57 *in* J. R. Sauer and S. Droege (eds.), Survey designs and statistical methods for the estimation of avian population trends. U.S. Fish and Wildlife Service, Biological Report 90 (1).

GRANHOLM, S. L. 1982. Effects of surface fires on birds and their habitat associations in coniferous forests of the Sierra Nevada, California. Ph.D. diss., Univ. California, Davis.

GRUELL, G. E. 1983. Fire and vegetative trends in the Northern Rockies: interpretations from 1871–1982 photographs. USDA Forest Service, Intermountain Forest and Range Experiment Station, General Technical Report INT-158.

GUTIÉRREZ, R. J. 1994. Changes in the distribution and abundance of Spotted Owls during the past century. Pp. 293–300 *in* J. R. Jehl, Jr. and N. K. Johnson (eds.), A century of avifaunal change in western North America. Studies in Avian Biology No. 15.

HALLOCK, D. 1989–1990. A study of breeding and winter birds in different age-classed lodgepole pine forests. Colorado Field Ornithological Journal 24:2–16.

HEJL, S. J. 1992. The importance of landscape patterns to bird diversity: a perspective from the Northern Rocky Mountains. Northwest Environmental Journal 8:119–137.

HEJL, S. J., AND L. C. PAIGE. In press. A preliminary assessment of birds in continuous and fragmented forests of western redcedar/western hemlock in northern Idaho. *In* D. M. Baumgartner and J. E. Lotan (eds.), Proceedings of a symposium on interior cedar-hemlock-white pine forests: ecology and management. Pullman: Washington State University.

HEJL, S. J., AND R. E. WOODS. 1991. Bird assemblages in old-growth and rotation-aged Douglas-fir/ponderosa pine stands in the northern Rocky Mountains: a preliminary assessment. Pp. 93–100 in D. M. Baumgartner and J. E. Lotan (eds.), Proceedings of a symposium on interior Douglas-fir: the species and its management. Pullman: Washington State University.

HEJL, S. J., J. VERNER, AND R. P. BALDA. 1988. Weather and bird populations in true fir forests of the Sierra Nevada, California. Condor 90:561–574.

HEJL, S. J., R. L. HUTTO, C. R. PRESTON, AND D. M. FINCH. In press. The effects of silvicultural treatments on forest birds in the Rocky Mountains. In T. E. Martin and D. M. Finch (eds.), Population ecology and conservation of neotropical migratory birds. Oxford Univ. Press, New York.

HUTTO, R. L., S. J. HEJL, J. F. KELLY, AND S. M. PLETSCHET. In press. A comparison of bird detection rates derived from on-road versus off-road point counts in northern Montana. In C. J. Ralph, J. R. Sauer, and S. Droege (eds.), Proceedings of a symposium on monitoring bird population trends by point counts. USDA Forest Service, General Technical Report PSW.

KELLER, M. E., AND S. H. ANDERSON. 1992. Avian use of habitat configurations created by forest cutting in southeastern Wyoming. Condor 94:55–65.

KESSLER, W. B., AND T. E. KOGUT. 1985. Habitat orientations of forest birds in southeastern Alaska. Northwest Science 59:58–65.

JOHNSON, N. K. 1965. The breeding avifaunas of the Sheep and Spring ranges in southern Nevada. Condor 67:93–124.

JOHNSON, N. K. 1974. Montane avifaunas of southern Nevada: historical change in species composition. Condor 76:334–337.

JOHNSON, N. K., AND C. CICERO. 1985. The breeding avifauna of San Benito Mountain, California: evidence for change over one-half century. Western Birds 16:1–23.

LAUDENSLAYER, W. F., JR., AND H. H. DARR. 1990. Historical effects of logging on the forests of the Cascade and Sierra Nevada Ranges of California. Transactions of the Western Section of the Wildlife Society 26:12–23.

LEHMKUHL, J. F., L. F. RUGGIERO, AND P. A. HALL. 1991. Landscape-scale patterns of forest fragmentation and wildlife richness and abundance in the southern Washington Cascade range. Pp. 425–442 in L. F. Ruggiero, K. B. Aubry, A. B. Carey, and M. H. Huff (tech. coords.), Wildlife and vegetation of unmanaged Douglas-fir forests. Portland, OR: USDA Forest Service, General Technical Report PNW-285.

LOSENSKY, B. J. 1990. Historical uses of whitebark pine. Pp. 191–197 in W. C. Schmidt and K. J. McDonald (comps.), Proceedings—symposium on whitebark pine ecosystems: ecology and management of a high-mountain resource. USDA Forest Service, General Technical Report INT-270.

MANNAN, R. W., E. C. MESLOW, AND H. M. WIGHT. 1980. Use of snags by birds in Douglas-fir forest, western Oregon. Journal of Wildlife Management 44:787–797.

MANUWAL, D. A., AND M. H. HUFF. 1987. Spring and winter bird populations in a Douglas-fir forest sere. Journal of Wildlife Management 51:586–595.

MARSHALL, J. T., JR. 1963. Fire and birds in the mountains of southern Arizona. Pp. 135–141 in Proceedings of the Tall Timbers fire ecology conference, Tall Timbers Research Station, Tallahassee, Florida.

MARSHALL, J. T. 1988. Birds lost from a giant sequoia forest during fifty years. Condor 90:359–372.

McCLELLAND, B. R., S. S. FRISSELL, W. C. FISCHER, AND C. H. HALVORSON. 1979. Habitat management for hole-nesting birds in forests of western larch and Douglas-fir. Journal of Forestry 77:480–483.

McKELVEY, K. S., AND J. D. JOHNSTON. 1992. Historical perspectives on forests of the Sierra Nevada and the Tranverse Ranges of southern California: forest conditions at the turn of the century. Pp. 225–246 in J. Verner, K. S. McKelvey, B. R. Noon, R. J. Gutiérrez, G. I. Gould, Jr., and T. W. Beck (tech. coords.), The California Spotted Owl: a technical assessment of its current status. USDA Forest Service, General Technical Report PSW-GTR-133.

MOORE, R. L. 1992. Breeding birds in old-growth forests and snag management for birds. Technical report available through Bozeman Ranger District, Gallatin National Forest, Bozeman, MT 59715.

MORRISON, M. L., AND S. W. MORRISON. 1983. Population trends of woodpeckers in the Pacific coast region of the United States. American Birds 37:361–363.

NORSE, E. A. 1990. Ancient forests of the Pacific Northwest. The Wilderness Society, Island Press, Washington, D.C.

O'MEARA, T. E., J. B. HAUFLER, L. H. STELTER, AND J. G. NAGY. 1981. Nongame wildlife responses to chaining of pinyon-juniper woodlands. Journal of Wildlife Management 45:381–389.

OVERTURF, J. H. 1979. The effects of forest fire on breeding bird populations of ponderosa pine forests of northern Arizona. M.S. thesis, Northern Arizona Univ., Flagstaff.

PYLE, P., N. NUR, AND D. F. DeSANTE. 1994. Trends in nocturnal migrant landbird populations at Southeast Farallon Island, California, 1968–1992. Pp. 58–74 in J. R. Jehl, Jr. and N. K. Johnson (eds.), A century of avifaunal change in western North America. Studies in Avian Biology No. 15.

RALPH, C. J. 1994. Evidence of changes in populations of the Marbled Murrelet in the Pacific Northwest. Pp. 284–292 in J. R. Jehl, Jr. and N. K. Johnson (eds.), A century of avifaunal change in western North America. Studies in Avian Biology No. 15.

RAPHAEL, M. G. 1984. Wildlife populations in relations to stand age and area in Douglas-fir forests of northwestern California. Pp. 259–274 in W. R. Meehan, T. R. Merrell, and T. A. Hanley (eds.), Proceedings of a symposium on fish and wildlife relationships in old-growth forests. American Institute of Fisheries and Resource Biology.

RAPHAEL, M. G., AND M. WHITE. 1984. Use of snags by cavity-nesting birds in the Sierra Nevada. Wildlife Monographs 86:1–66.

RAPHAEL, M. G., M. L. MORRISON, AND M. P. YO-

DER-WILLIAMS. 1987. Breeding bird populations during twenty-five years of postfire succession in the Sierra Nevada. Condor 89:614–626.

RAPHAEL, M. G., K. V. ROSENBERG, AND B. G. MARCOT. 1988. Large-scale changes in bird populations of Douglas-fir forests, northwestern California. Bird Conservation 3:63–83.

REYNOLDS, R. T., R. T. GRAHAM, M. H. REISER, R. L. BASSETT, P. L. KENNEDY, D. A. BOYCE, JR., G. GOODWIN, R. SMITH, AND E. L. FISHER. 1992. Management recommendations for the Northern Goshawk in the southwestern United States. USDA Forest Service, General Technical Report RM-217.

ROSENBERG, K. V., AND M. G. RAPHAEL. 1986. Effects of forest fragmentation on vertebrates in Douglas-fir forests. Pp. 263–272 *in* J. Verner, M. L. Morrison, and C. J. Ralph (eds.), Wildlife 2000: modeling habitat relationships of terrestrial vertebrates. Madison: University of Wisconsin Press.

ROTHSTEIN, S. I. 1994. The Cowbird's invasion of the far west: History, causes and consequences experienced by host species. Pp. 301–315 *in* J. R. Jehl, Jr. and N. K. Johnson (eds.), A century of avifaunal change in western North America. Studies in Avian Biology No. 15.

RUGGIERO, L. F., L. L. C. JONES, AND K. B. AUBRY. 1991. Plant and animal habitat associations in Douglas-fir forests of the Pacific Northwest: an overview. Pp. 447–462 *in* L. F. Ruggiero, K. B. Aubry, A. B. Carey, and M. H. Huff (tech. coords.), Wildlife and vegetation of unmanaged Douglas-fir forests, USDA Forest Service, General Technical Report PNW-285.

SAUER, J. R., AND P. H. GEISSLER. 1990. Annual indices from route regression analyses. Pp. 58–62 *in* J. R. Sauer and S. Droege (eds.), Survey designs and statistical methods for the estimation of avian population trends. U.S. Fish and Wildlife Service, Biological Report 90 (1).

SCOTT, V. E., AND J. L. OLDEMEYER. 1983. Cavity-nesting bird requirements and response to snag cutting in ponderosa pine. Pp. 19–23 *in* J. W. Davis, G. A. Goodwin, and R. A. Ockenfels (tech. coords.), Proceedings of a symposium on snag habitat management. USDA Forest Service, General Technical Report RM-99.

SEDGWICK, J. A., AND R. A. RYDER. 1987. Effects of chaining pinyon-juniper on nongame wildlife. Pp. 541–551 *in* R. L. Everett (comp.), Proceedings—pinyon-juniper conference. USDA Forest Service, General Technical Report INT-215.

SHARP, B. 1985. Avifaunal changes in central Oregon since 1899. Western Birds 16:63–70.

SHUFORD, W. D. 1986. Have ornithologists or breeding Red-breasted Sapsuckers extended their range in coastal California? Western Birds 17:97–105.

TATE, J., JR. 1966. The Blue List for 1986. American Birds 40:227–236.

TAYLOR, A. L., JR., AND E. D. FORSMAN. 1976. Recent range extensions of the Barred Owl in western North America, including the first records for Oregon. Condor 78:560–561.

TAYLOR, D. L., AND W. J. BARMORE, JR. 1980. Postfire succession of avifauna in coniferous forests of Yellowstone and Grand Teton National Parks, Wyoming. Pp. 130–145 *in* R. M. DeGraff and N. G. Tilghman (comps.), Management of western forests and grasslands for nongame birds. USDA Forest Service, General Technical Report INT-86.

TOBALSKE, B. W., R. C. SHEARER, AND R. L. HUTTO. 1991. Bird populations in logged and unlogged western larch/Douglas-fir forest in northwestern Montana. USDA Forest Service, Intermountain Research Station, Research Paper INT-442.

VERNER, J., AND L. V. RITTER. 1983. Current status of the Brown-headed Cowbird in the Sierra National Forest. Auk 100:355–368.

WEATHERSPOON, C. P., S. J. HUSARI, AND J. W. VAN WAGTENDONK. 1992. Fire and fuels management in relation to owl habitat in forests of the Sierra Nevada and southern California. Pp. 247–260 *in* J. Verner, K. S. McKelvey, B. R. Noon, R. J. Gutierrez, G. I. Gould, Jr., and T. W. Beck (tech. coords.), The California Spotted Owl: a technical assessment of its current status. USDA Forest Service, General Technical Report PSW-GTR-133.

WELLNER, C. A. 1984. History and status of silvicultural management in the interior Douglas-fir and grand fir forest types. Pp. 3–10 *in* D. M. Baumgartner and R. Mitchell (comps.), Proceedings of a symposium on silvicultural management strategies for pests of the interior Douglas-fir and grand fir forest types. Washington State Univ., Pullman.

ZARNOWITZ, J. E., AND D. A. MANUWAL. 1985. The effects of forest management on cavity-nesting birds in northwestern Washington. Journal of Wildlife Management 49:255–263.

APPENDIX I. Ability of current Breeding Bird Survey routes to sample individual coniferous forest bird species in western United States and Canada. Four categories are listed: 1) good: average abundance ≥ 1.0/route and ≥ 50 routes, 2) poor: average abundance ≥ 1.0/route but < 50 routes, 3) poorer: < 1.0/route but ≥ 50 routes, and 4) poorest: < 1.0/route and < 50 routes.

GOOD: AVERAGE ABUNDANCE ≥ 1.0/route and ≥ 50 routes:

Red-tailed Hawk (*Buteo jamaicensis*), American Kestrel (*Falco sparverius*), Mountain Quail (*Oreortyx pictus*), Band-tailed Pigeon (*Columba fasciata*), Broad-tailed Hummingbird (*Selasphorus platycercus*), Rufous Hummingbird (*Selasphorus rufus*), Acorn Woodpecker (*Melanerpes formicivorus*), Olive-sided Flycatcher (*Contopus borealis*), Western Wood-Pewee (*Contopus sordidulus*), Hammond's Flycatcher (*Empidonax hammondii*), Dusky Flycatcher (*Empidonax oberholseri*), Tree Swallow (*Tachycineta bicolor*), Violet-green Swallow (*Tachycineta thalassina*), Steller's Jay (*Cyanocitta stelleri*), Scrub Jay (*Aphelocoma coerulescens*), Pinyon Jay (*Gymnorhinus cyanocephalus*), Common Raven (*Corvus corax*), Black-capped Chickadee (*Parus atricapillus*), Mountain Chickadee (*Parus gambeli*), Chestnut-backed Chickadee (*Parus rufescens*), Plain Titmouse (*Parus inornatus*), Red-breasted Nuthatch (*Sitta canadensis*), House Wren (*Troglodytes aedon*), Winter Wren (*Troglodytes troglodytes*), Golden-crowned Kinglet (*Regulus satrapa*), Ruby-crowned Kinglet (*Regulus calendula*), Western Bluebird (*Sialia mexi-*

cana), Mountain Bluebird (*Sialia currucoides*), Swainson's Thrush (*Catharus ustulatus*), Hermit Thrush (*Catharus guttatus*), American Robin (*Turdus migratorius*), Varied Thrush (*Ixoreus naevius*), Cedar Waxwing (*Bombycilla cedrorum*), Solitary Vireo (*Vireo solitarius*), Warbling Vireo (*Vireo gilvus*), Orange-crowned Warbler (*Vermivora celata*), Nashville Warbler (*Vermivora ruficapilla*), Black-throated Gray Warbler (*Dendroica nigrescens*), Townsend's Warbler (*Dendroica townsendi*), Hermit Warbler (*Dendroica occidentalis*), American Redstart (*Setophaga ruticulla*), MacGillivray's Warbler (*Oporornis tolmiei*), Wilson's Warbler (*Wilsonia pusilla*), Western Tanager (*Piranga ludoviciana*), Green-tailed Towhee (*Pipilo chlorurus*), Chipping Sparrow (*Spizella passerina*), Lark Sparrow (*Chondestes grammacus*), Fox Sparrow (*Passerella iliaca*), White-throated Sparrow (*Zonotrichia albicollis*), White-crowned Sparrow (*Zonotrichia leucophrys*), Brown-headed Cowbird (*Molothrus ater*), Purple Finch (*Carpodacus purpureus*), Cassin's Finch (*Carpodacus cassinii*), Red Crossbill (*Loxia curvirostra*), Pine Siskin (*Carduelis pinus*), Lesser Goldfinch (*Carduelis psaltria*), Evening Grosbeak (*Coccothraustes vespertinus*).

POOR: AVERAGE ABUNDANCE ≥ 1.0/route but <50 routes:

Marbled Murrelet (*Brachyamphus marmoratus*), Virginia's Warbler (*Vermivora virginiae*), Grace's Warbler (*Dendroica graciae*), Red-faced Warbler (*Cardellina rubrifrons*), Yellow-eyed Junco (*Junco phaeonotus*).

POORER: <1.0/route but ≥50 routes:

Sharp-shinned Hawk (*Accipiter striatus*), Cooper's Hawk (*Accipiter cooperii*), Northern Goshawk (*Accipiter gentilis*), Blue Grouse (*Dendragapus obscurus*), Ruffed Grouse (*Bonasa umbellus*), Great Horned Owl (*Bubo virginianus*), Northern Pygmy-Owl (*Glaucidium gnoma*), Vaux's Swift (*Chaetura vauxi*), Calliope Hummingbird (*Stellula calliope*), Lewis' Woodpecker (*Melanerpes lewis*), Williamson's Sapsucker (*Sphyrapicus thyroideus*), Hairy Woodpecker (*Picoides villosus*), White-headed Woodpecker (*Picoides albolarvatus*), Pileated Woodpecker (*Dryocopus pileatus*), Gray Flycatcher (*Empidonax wrightii*), Purple Martin (*Progne subis*), Gray Jay (*Perisoreus canadensis*), Clark's Nut-

cracker (*Nucifraga columbiana*), White-breasted Nuthatch (*Sitta carolinensis*), Pygmy Nuthatch (*Sitta pygmaea*), Brown Creeper (*Certhia americana*), Townsend's Solitaire (*Myadestes townsendi*), Hutton's Vireo (*Vireo huttoni*), Tennessee Warbler (*Vermivora peregrina*), Magnolia Warbler (*Dendroica magnolia*), Pine Grosbeak (*Pinicola enucleator*).

POOREST: <1.0/route and <50 routes:

Harlequin Duck (*Histrionicus histrionicus*), Spruce Grouse (*Dendragapus canadensis*), Wild Turkey (*Meleagris gallopavo*), Flammulated Owl (*Otus flammeolus*), Northern Hawk-owl (*Surnia ulula*), Spotted Owl (*Strix occidentalis*), Barred Owl (*Strix varia*), Great Gray Owl (*Strix nebulosa*), Long-eared Owl (*Asio otus*), Northern Saw-whet Owl (*Aegolius acadicus*), Magnificent Hummingbird (*Eugenes fulgens*), Allen's Hummingbird (*Selasphorus sasin*), Three-toed Woodpecker (*Picoides tridactylus*), Black-backed Woodpecker (*Picoides arcticus*), Greater Pewee (*Contopus pertinax*), Yellow-bellied Flycatcher (*Empidonax flaviventris*), Boreal Chickadee (*Parus hudsonicus*), Bohemian Waxwing (*Bombycilla garrulus*), Gray Vireo (*Vireo vicinior*), Blackpoll Warbler (*Dendroica striata*), Painted Redstart (*Myioborus pictus*), Olive Warbler (*Peucedramus taeniatus*), Hepatic Tanager (*Piranga flava*), Golden-crowned Sparrow (*Zonotrichia atricapilla*), White-winged Crossbill (*Loxia leucoptera*).

SPECIES NOT LISTED IN THE BREEDING BIRD SURVEY DATABASE. Most were not listed because of recent taxonomic changes; data on some of the earlier species' names were listed.

Thick-billed Parrot (*Rhynchopsitta pachyrhyncha*), Boreal Owl (*Aegolius funereus*), Whip-poor-will (*Caprimulgus vociferus*), Yellow-bellied Sapsucker (*Sphyrapicus varius*), Red-naped Sapsucker (*Sphyrapicus nuchalis*), Red-breasted Sapsucker (*Sphyrapicus ruber*), Northern Flicker (*Colaptes auratus*), Pacific-slope Flycatcher (*Empidonax difficilis*), Cordilleran Flycatcher (*Empidonax occidentalis*), Mexican Chickadee (*Parus sclateri*), Siberian Tit (*Parus cinctus*), Gray-cheeked Thrush (*Catharus minimus*), Yellow-rumped Warbler (*Dendroica coronata*), Dark-eyed Junco (*Junco hyemalis*).

Studies in Avian Biology No. 15:247–257, 1994.

AVIAN ASSEMBLAGES ON ALTERED GRASSLANDS

FRITZ L. KNOPF

Abstract. Grasslands comprise 17% of the North American landscape but provide primary habitat for only 5% of native bird species. On the Great Plains, grasslands include an eastern component of tall grasses and a western component of short grasses, both of which have been regionally altered by removing native grazers, plowing sod, draining wetlands, and encouraging woody vegetation. As a group, populations of endemic bird species of the grasslands have declined more than others (including neotropical migrants) in the last quarter century. Individually, populations of the Upland Sandpiper and McCown's Longspur have increased; the wetlands-associated Marbled Godwit and Wilson's Phalarope appear stable; breeding ranges are shifting for the Ferruginous Hawk, Mississippi Kite, Short-eared Owl, Upland Sandpiper, Horned Lark, Vesper, Savannah, and Henslow's sparrows, and Western Meadowlark; breeding habitats are disappearing locally for Franklin's Gull, Dickcissel, Henslow's and Grasshopper sparrows, Lark Bunting, and Eastern Meadowlark; and populations are declining throughout the breeding ranges for Mountain Plover, and Cassin's and Clay-colored sparrows. Declines of these latter three species, and also the Franklin's Gull, presumably are due to ecological phenomena on their respective wintering areas. Unlike forest species that winter in the neotropics, most birds that breed in the North American grasslands also winter on the continent and problems driving declines in grassland species are associated almost entirely with North American processes. Contemporary programs and initiatives hold promise for the conservation of breeding habitats for these birds. Ecological ignorance of wintering habits and habitats clouds the future of the endemic birds of grasslands, especially those currently experiencing widespread declines across breeding locales.

Key Words: Grasslands; Great Plains; biological diversity; *Larus pipixcan*; *Charadrius montanus*; *Aimophila cassinii*; *Calamospiza melanocorys*.

Native grasslands represent the largest vegetative province of North America. Almost 1.5×10^6 km² of grasslands historically covered the continent on the Great Plains from south central Saskatchewan to central Texas, plus in the Central Valley of California and Palouse region of eastern Washington and Oregon (Knopf 1988). The continental grasslands of the Great Plains evolved in the rainshadow of the Rocky Mountains; seasonal precipitation falls mostly in spring or summer. These grasslands are characterized by warm-season grasses of the shortgrass prairie on the west and fire-maintained, cool- and warm-season grasses that grow much taller on the east. The mediterranean grasslands of the west coast states evolved with fall/winter precipitation and the historical composition of especially the California grasses is uncertain. This paper focuses specifically on the Great Plains landscape and major patterns of avifaunal metamorphosis over the last 100 years.

THE NATIVE GRASSLAND LANDSCAPE

Inferences about the historical landscapes of the Great Plains are available in the writings of nineteenth century adventurers as Irving (1835), explorers as Frémont (1845) and Stansbury (1852), and civilian travelers along the Platte River Road (Mattes 1988). Read collectively, one envisions the short and taller grass prairies intergrading just east of an irregular line from El Reno, Oklahoma, through Fort Hays, Kansas, and North Platte, Nebraska, northwestward into the west-central Dakotas. The landscapes of eastern Oklahoma, Kansas, and Nebraska were heavily wooded stream bottoms in uplands of fire-maintained grasses of a meter or more in height. Wapiti (*Cervus canadensis*) and white-tailed deer (*Odocoileus virginiana*) were abundant. The grasses, however, do not cure well (i.e., lose their nutritive value when dried) and these ungulates survived the season of vegetative dormancy by grazing or browsing within the wooded stream bottoms. Native Americans of this region, such as the Pawnee, hunted these species, but generally raised vegetables in relatively permanent villages along eastern prairie streams then journeyed west into the shortgrass province semiannually to hunt plains bison (*Bison bison bison*), for meat (Hyde 1974).

The shortgrass prairie landscape was one of relatively treeless stream bottoms and uplands dominated by blue grama (*Bouteloua gracilis*) and buffalo grass (*Buchloe dactyloides*), two warm-season grasses that flourish under intensive grazing pressure by reproducing both sexually and by tillering. Unlike the more eastern species, short grass species remain highly digestible and retain their protein content when dormant. This character supported the evolution of a major herbivore assemblage dominated by bison, pronghorn (*Antilocapra americana*) and prairie dogs (*Cynomys* spp.). Native Americans, including the Sioux and Cheyenne of shortgrass landscapes, tended to be semi-nomadic, following the massive bison herds upon which their lifestyle was specifically dependent in the late 1870s.

THE NATIVE GRASSLAND BIRDS

As is the case for most biogeographic provinces, pre-settlement information on native bird assemblages of Great Plains grasslands is limited. Ornithological study on the Great Plains commenced in 1832 when John Kirk Townsend (1839, the first trained zoologist to cross the continent) accompanied by the prominent naturalist Thomas Nuttall traveled with the Wyeth expedition along the Rocky Mountain Road to the Columbia River. Later, the surveys by Hayden (1862), Allen (1871, 1874), Coues (1878) and others provided additional insights into the regional avifauna. Generally, however, these earlier works were all exploratory, tended to emphasize avifaunas along stream courses (Allen 1874), and provided few perspectives of avian species densities or assemblages relative to lo-

cal geographic features or vegetative associations.

Although the Great Plains played a major role in the evolution of the North American avifauna (Mengel 1970), the grassland avifauna itself is relatively depauperate. Only 5% of all North American bird species are believed to have evolved within the Great Plains (Udvardy 1958, Mengel 1970). Mengel (ibid.) listed 12 species of birds endemic to the grasslands along with 25 others that he considered to be secondarily evolved to grasslands (Table 1). Two of the endemics frequent wetland habitats within the grasslands, with the others being upland species. Species that are secondarily evolved to the grasslands typically occur in more widespread geographic areas and are found primarily in landscapes where brush or trees have invaded grasslands on the periphery of the Great Plains. None of the secondary species are wetland associates, although the breeding biology of the White Pelican (*Pelecanus erythrorhynchos*) suggests that it also is a member of this more widespread group (Knopf 1975). Five of the secondary species (Sage Grouse, Sage Thrasher, Green-tailed Towhee, Sage Sparrow, and Brewer's Sparrow) are really species of the Great Basin shrubsteppe.

The endemic birds evolved with specific ecological niches within the grasslands. Wetland species obviously occur locally at moist-soil sites. Species of taller grasses as the Greater Prairie-chicken and Dickcissel nest in habitats of standing residual vegetation from a preceding growing season and are dependent upon stand rejuvenation by periodic fires (e.g., Kirsch 1974). Many of the endemic species of shortgrass and mixed grass landscapes such as the Baird's Sparrow, McCown's and Chestnut-collared longspurs coevolved with grazing ungulates, whereas others such as the Ferruginous Hawk, Prairie Falcon, and Burrowing Owl are strongly associated with prairie-dog towns. Evolutionarily, drought tolerance appears to be the principal ecological process influencing grassland-bird assemblages locally (Wiens 1974), with grazing (Hobbs and Huenneke 1992) and wildfire (Zimmerman 1992) having major, secondary roles.

THE CONTEMPORARY LANDSCAPE

The landscape of the Great Plains has undergone significant alteration from descriptions provided in early accounts. The impacts have been varied, with many (e.g., urbanization, mineral exploration, defense installations) having primarily local impacts on the native avifauna. Activities with more universal impacts on the landscape have included 1) transformation of the native grazing community, 2) cultivation of grains and tame grasses, 3) draining of wetlands, and 4) woody development in the form of tree plantings and ecological invasions.

Removal of native grazers

An estimated historical population of 30 million plains bison was systematically reduced to 281 by 1889 (Hornaday 1887, Roe 1951), with most of this reduction coming in the Great Slaughters of 1870–1873 south of the Platte River and 1880–1883 north of the Platte River. Beginning in the 1860s, cattle were quickly moved into locales as soon as bison were removed, but probably had little immediate impact as they were grazed over broad expanses. Homesteading of the grasslands commenced with the Homestead Act of 1862 and progressively resulted in grasslands being fenced into smaller parcels. The great blizzards of 1885 and 1886 killed 85% of the cattle in Colorado (Badaracco 1971) and blizzards of 1886 and 1887 locally killed 30–80% of the cattle in the northern plains states (Fedkiw 1989). The evolving cattle industry then began fencing also and switched from "open-range" grazing to a ranching industry to grow supplemental winter feeds. Subsequent homesteading acts of the early 20th century increased parcel size from 0.65 km² to 2.6 km² and resulted in the remaining (arably more marginal) public lands on the western

TABLE 1. THE NORTH AMERICAN GRASSLANDS AVIFAUNA (AFTER MENGEL 1970).

Non-passerines	Passerines
I. Primary species (endemic)	
1. *Buteo regalis* Ferruginous Hawk	1. *Anthus spragueii* Sprague's Pipit
2. *Charadrius montanus* Mountain Plover	2. *Aimophila cassinii* Cassin's Sparrow
3. *Numenius americanus* Long-billed Curlew	3. *Ammodramus bairdii* Baird's Sparrow
4. *Limosa fedoa* Marbled Godwit	4. *Calamospiza melanocorys* Lark Bunting
5. *Phalaropus tricolor* Wilson's Phalarope	5. *Calcarius mccownii* McCown's Longspur
6. *Larus pipixcan* Franklin's Gull	6. *C. ornatus* Chestnut-collared Longspur
II. Secondary species (more widespread)	
1. *Ictinia mississippiensis* Mississippi Kite	1. *Eremophila alpestris* Horned Lark
2. *Buteo swainsoni* Swainson's Hawk	2. *Oreoscoptes montanus* Sage Thrasher
3. *Circus cyaneus* Northern Harrier	3. *Sturnella magna* Eastern Meadowlark
4. *Falco mexicanus* Prairie Falcon	4. *S. neglecta* Western Meadowlark
5. *Tympanuchus cupido* Greater Prairie-chicken	5. *Spiza americana* Dickcissel
6. *T. pallidicinctus* Lesser Prairie-chicken	6. *Pipilo chlorura* Green-tailed Towhee
7. *T. phasianellus* Sharp-tailed Grouse	7. *Passerculus sandwichensis* Savannah Sparrow
8. *Centrocercus urophasianus* Sage Grouse	8. *Ammodramus savannarum* Grasshopper Sparrow
9. *Bartramia longicauda* Upland Sandpiper	9. *A. henslowii* Henslow's Sparrow
10. *Athene cunicularia* Burrowing Owl	10. *Pooecetes gramineus* Vesper Sparrow
11. *Asio flammeus* Short-eared Owl	11. *Chondestes grammacus* Lark Sparrow
	12. *Amphispiza belli* Sage Sparrow
	13. *Spizella breweri* Brewer's Sparrow
	14. *S. pallida* Clay-colored Sparrow

plains becoming fragmented also. Cattle numbers on the western range in 1890 were estimated at 45 million, plus about that many domestic sheep (Fedkiw 1989). The ultimate consequence of fencing that many animals was to reduce the natural variability in grazing behavior of herding ungulates and, ultimately, to standardize grazing intensities across broad landscapes (Knopf 1993).

The well known destruction of the bison on the shortgrass prairie was immediately followed by an equally intensive effort to eradicate the other major herbivore, the prairie-dog. Prairie-dogs historically occupied an estimated 404,858 km², compared to only 6073 km² in 1980 (Summers and Linder 1978). This 98% reduction has been attributed to the potential competition between prairie dogs and cattle for grass forage, claims which are neither supported by data (O'Meilia et al. 1982) nor by indications that ungulates and prairie dogs are actually symbiotic foragers (Krueger 1986). Most significantly, prairie-dogs are ecological "keystone" species (Gilbert 1980, Terborgh 1986). Keystone species are those that (by their presence) provide appropriate habitat conditions or prey for the continued existence of other species. In the case of prairie dogs and birds, such species include the endemics Ferruginous Hawk and Mountain Plover, and more widespread species as the Burrowing Owl.

Cultivation

The second major change in the Great Plains landscape has been the plowing of grasses, primarily for cereal grain production. The eastern plains have been virtually obliterated for grain (primarily corn) production, as evidenced by data available from Illinois and Iowa (Table 2). Only 10.4 km² of the original 103,600 km² of native prairie survives in the state of Illinois (Mlot 1990), although the structurally similar tame-grass hayfields provide acceptable habitats for some birds of the historic landscape. Where locally grown on the shortgrass and transition prairie zones, corn generally requires irrigation. These latter regions are sown mostly to dryland (winter) wheat. Unlike the eastern plains, however, the proportion of native grasslands on the western Great Plains (Colorado, Montana, Wyoming) that have remained in a grassland landscape is comparatively high. In addition, 15,436 km²

TABLE 2.   RELATIVE AREA (KM² × 10³) OF PRIVATE LANDS IN CROPLAND, INTRODUCED PASTURE GRASSES, AND NATIVE GRASS RANGELANDS ON THE GREAT PLAINS OF THE UNITED STATES (ADAPTED FROM U.S.D.A. 1987)

	Cropland	Pasture-land	Rangeland
Tallgrass prairie			
Illinois	100.07	12.78	0.0
Iowa	107.00	18.36	0.0
Total	207.07	31.14	0.0 (0%)
Mixed prairies			
Kansas	117.84	9.07	68.43
Nebraska	82.06	8.60	93.47
North Dakota	109.43	5.15	44.31
Oklahoma	46.82	28.89	60.95
South Dakota	68.58	10.94	92.02
Total	424.72	62.65	706.65 (59.2%)
Shortgrass prairie			
Colorado	42.91	5.10	98.03
Montana	69.59	12.29	153.12
Wyoming	10.39	3.05	108.92
Total	122.89	20.44	360.07 (71.5%)

remain in 19 National Grasslands (USDA 1990), with 17 of those on the Great Plains, predominantly in the shortgrass prairie. Compared to the eastern grassland landscape, the western is merely fragmented rather than obliterated.

The historical decline in native grasslands has slowed with additional losses of only 17.75 km² occurring from 1982 to 1987 (USDA 1989). The first four years of the Conservation Reserve Program prompted the reseeding of 21,697 km² to native grasses through 1989 (S. Brady, Soil Conserv. Serv., pers. comm.). The reseeding represented 5.3% of cropland in the three shortgrass prairie states and 3.4% of cropland in the transition prairie states. The program has had negligible impact on restoring taller grass sites to the east.

Loss of wetlands

The drainage of wetlands during cultivation practices has profoundly altered the phytogeography of grasslands locally (Dahl 1990). Losses in Illinois and Iowa have equalled 86.3% of an estimated 49,421 km² historical wetland area. Comparable values for Colorado, Wyoming, and Montana show only a 40.0% loss of 20,838 km². Losses in the mixed-grass states have been an intermediate 56.6% of 70,478 km². These numbers support the intuitive relationship between the loss of wetlands and intensity of cultivation across the Great Plains.

Woody development

The vertical structure of the grassland landscape is fragmented also. Fire control has enabled woody vegetation to encroach on the northern and southern grasslands (Bird 1961, Pulich 1976). In addition, almost 3% of the Great Plains is now forested by shelterbelts planted to reduce wind erosion (Baer 1989). Trees are currently being planted on the Great Plains at the rate of 20.7 × 10⁶/year (Griffith 1976).

On the shortgrass prairie, woody vegetation has also increased through ecological processes. Shrub and small tree encroachment occur along the entire periphery of the Great Plains due to control of natural fires. Equally significant has been the ecological development of streamside forests of alien and exotic tree species across the western landscape. These forests appeared in response to 20th-century water-management practices that favor woody colonization and secondary succession (Knopf and Scott 1990, Johnson 1993).

THE CONTEMPORARY AVIFAUNA

Of the 435 bird species breeding in the United States, 330 have been documented as breeding on the Great Plains (Johnsgard 1979). Whereas many species such as the Passenger Pigeon (Grinnell 1875) and Eskimo Curlew (Sutton 1967) historically appeared on the grasslands, a review of changes by species, genus, or even ecological guild is beyond the scope of this paper. Rather, I proffer that avian assemblages on the grasslands reflect two broad patterns of change that have occurred in the last century: native endemic species have declined in numbers while simultaneously (and rather independently) alien and exotic species have increased immeasureably.

TABLE 3. BIOME AND GUILD COMPARISONS OF CONTINENTAL TRENDS IN BIRD ASSEMBLAGES BASED ON BREEDING BIRD SURVEY DATA, 1966–1991 (ADAPTED FROM DROEGE AND SAUER 1993)

Group	No. species	No. (%) increasing	P
Grassland Nesters[1]	18	3 (17)	0.008
Wetland Nesters	41	26 (63)	0.117
Waterfowl	15	10 (67)	0.302
Woodland Nesters	60	37 (62)	0.092
Deciduous Woodland Nesters	15	9 (60)	0.607
Coniferous Woodland Nesters	26	17 (65)	0.169
Scrub Nesters	60	19 (32)	0.006
Urban Nesters	12	4 (33)	0.388
Permanent Residents	48	20 (42)	0.312
Neotropical Migrants	90	53 (59)	0.113
Short-distance Migrants	83	37 (45)	0.380
Primary Cavity Nesters	11	6 (55)	1.000
Secondary Cavity Nesters	27	17 (63)	0.248
Open-Cup Nesting Passerines	103	50 (49)	0.844
Ground Nesters	33	15 (46)	0.728
All birds	302	153 (51)	0.863

[1] Bird species defined at the Breeding Bird Survey include only upland, grass-nesting species that were recorded on ≥ 50 routes in 1966 and 1991. Of the endemics defined by Mengel, Long-billed Curlew, Sprague's Pipit, Lark, Baird's, Cassin's sparrows, and McCown's and Chestnut-collared longspurs met these criteria. Of the more widespread species, Greater Prairie-chicken, Upland Sandpiper, Horned Lark, Eastern and Western meadowlarks, Dickcissel, Savannah, Grasshopper, and Vesper sparrows met inclusion criteria. Two grassland-nesting species included in this guild that did not appear on Mengel's list include Ring-necked Pheasant (*Phasianus colchicus*) and Bobolink (*Dolichonyx oryzivorus*).

Declines in grassland endemic species

During the last quarter of the century, grassland species have shown steeper, more consistent, and more geographically widespread declines than any other behavioral or ecological guild of North America species, including neotropical migrants (Table 3). Not surprising, the geographic pattern of these declines (Fig. 1) is polarized to the eastern and western provinces to which the grassland endemics are primarily adapted. More surprising, most of the species that breed on the grasslands also spend the winter on the continent (MacArthur 1959: Fig. 8-4). The problems of declines in grassland species is associated almost entirely with North American processes.

Population declines of individual species are often difficult to detect due to the in-

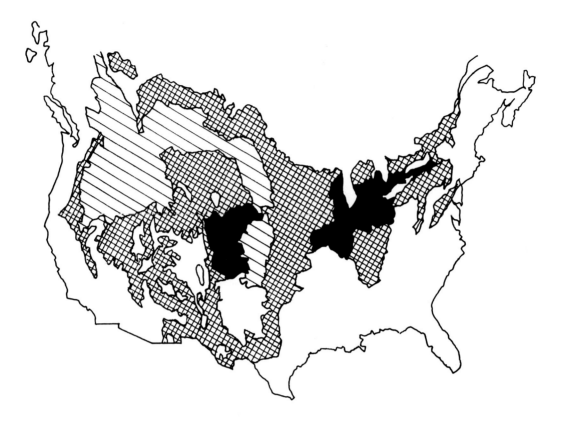

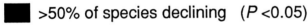

■ >50% of species declining   (*P* <0.05)

▨ >50% of species declining   (*P* >0.05)

▨ ≥50% of species increasing (*P* >0.05)

FIGURE 1. Geographical patterns of population changes for grasslands birds of North America based on analyses of Breeding Bird Survey data within physiographic strata. (Figure adapted from Droege and Sauer 1993).

herent variability in geographic distribution of a species population as illustrated for Dickcissel (Robbins and Van Velzen 1969, Fretwell 1986). However, continental population trends for individual species within the native grasslands avifauna (Table 4) generally support the decline seen for the grassland-nesting guild. Excluding the wetland-associated Marbled Godwit and Wilson's Phalarope, seven of the ten endemic species showed population declines during the last 26 years, with declines of four (Mountain Plover, Franklin's Gull, Cassin's Sparrow, Lark Bunting) being statistically significant. Similarly, 16 of the 25 more widespread species declined during this time period with six (Eastern Meadowlark, Grasshopper, Henslow's, Lark, Brewer's, and Clay-colored sparrows) being statistically significant. Across all grassland species, populations of only the Upland Sandpiper and McCown's Longspur have increased significantly since 1966.

Reasons for population declines among species within the grassland avifauna are difficult to assess. Examining trends for those species where declines are supported statistically, the declines appear to be localized

TABLE 4.   ANNUAL RATES OF CHANGE IN CONTINENTAL POPULATIONS OF GRASSLAND BIRD SPECIES 1966–1991 (BREEDING BIRD SURVEY DATA)

Species	No. of routes	Percentage[1]		Population trend[2]
		Increasing	Decreasing	
Endemics				
Ferruginous Hawk	242	51.7	42.6*	+0.4
Mountain Plover	40	45.0	50.0	−3.6*
Long-billed Curlew	222	45.5	50.0	−0.6
Marbled Godwit	181	54.7	43.1	+1.0
Wilson's Phalarope	339	41.3	54.6	+0.8
Franklin's Gull	225	35.1	60.4*	−7.4*
Sprague's Pipit	136	38.2	55.9	−3.1
Cassin's Sparrow	169	49.7	48.5	−3.4*
Baird's Sparrow	132	39.4	56.8	−1.6
Lark Bunting	344	39.8	57.6*	−3.3*
McCown's Longspur	66	45.5	47.0	+7.9*
Chestnut-colored Longspur	151	42.4	54.3	+0.6
Secondary species				
Mississippi Kite	163	58.9	40.5*	+0.4
Swainson's Hawk	607	48.8	46.6	+1.2
Northern Harrier	1075	43.7	52.5	−1.0
Prairie Falcon	261	47.1	43.7*	+0.2
Greater Prairie-chicken	47	40.0	53.2	−10.3
Lesser Prairie-chicken	8	25.0	62.5	+8.1
Sharp-tailed Grouse	180	41.7	52.8	+0.9
Sage Grouse	103	52.4	46.6	+6.2
Upland Sandpiper	668	51.5	45.8*	+3.5*
Burrowing Owl	349	43.3	51.6	−0.2
Short-eared Owl	268	38.1	57.5*	−0.7
Horned Lark	1708	40.6	56.8*	−0.7
Sage Thrasher	230	53.0	44.8	+1.4
Eastern Meadowlark	1714	30.5	68.6*	−2.2*
Western Meadowlark	1304	38.0	59.7*	−0.6
Dickcissel	780	37.6	60.9*	−1.7*
Green-tailed Towhee	207	43.0	51.2	+0.3
Savannah Sparrow	1418	42.9	54.4*	−0.6
Grasshopper Sparrow	1446	37.6	58.8*	−4.6*
Henslow's Sparrow	249	30.9	61.8*	−4.2*
Vesper Sparrow	1473	38.5	58.2*	−0.6
Lark Sparrow	909	44.7	52.6	−3.4*
Sage Sparrow	205	38.0	58.5*	−2.4
Brewer's Sparrow	359	39.8	55.7*	−4.1*
Clay-colored Sparrow	441	43.8	52.4	−1.5*

[1] Percentages totaling <100% include some routes with no change in numbers of birds detected. Asterisk indicates trend significantly ($P < 0.05$) different from no difference between number of surveys with increasing vs. decreasing species populations.
[2] Annual rate (expressed as a percentage) of change in population numbers. Asterisk indicates a statistically significant ($P < 0.05$) rate of population change.

for Franklin's Gull, Dickcissel, Henslow's and Grasshopper sparrows, Lark Bunting, and Eastern Meadowlark in that these species show a significant difference in the proportion of surveys with increasing vs. decreasing populations. This pattern of significant local declines for species that also are declining continentally reflects a pattern of loss of local breeding habitats.

Declines in populations of Mountain Plover, and Cassin's and Clay-colored sparrows were universal across their respective geographic ranges (not varying among surveys). The seasonal distributions and ecology of the sparrows are poorly understood. The plover is now rare on its former wintering areas in southern Texas and has a highly fragmented wintering distribution in California. Based upon the plover example, declines in this group of birds appear attributable to decline or degradation in the quality of habitats available for wintering.

Population trends for a third group of grassland species (Ferruginous Hawk, Mississippi Kite, Upland Sandpiper, Short-eared Owl, Horned Lark, Western Meadowlark, Vesper, Savannah, and Henslow's sparrows) show significant changes in relative abundance among surveys even though continental numbers are stable. The geographic distributions of these species appear to be changing at present.

Whereas wetlands-associated species have certainly declined since settlement of the grasslands in the mid 1800s, BBS data indicate that populations of the endemic Marbled Godwit and Wilson's Phalarope are stable. Wetland conservation actions to benefit waterfowl have apparently stabilized populations of these latter species.

Increases in cosmopolitan species

The negative consequences of landscape fragmentation to local and regional avian assemblages are well known (Robbins et al. 1989b) and have real implications to the conservation of grassland birds (Samson 1980, Johnson and Temple 1986). Fire control and woody plantings on the grasslands have had such an effect by favoring many species that can colonize the newly created forest patches. Regional responses of bird assemblages to a century of fire control are not available, but can be inferred from studies (e.g., Dixon 1989) of individual species populations.

A large percentage of breeding bird species on the central Great Plains appear restricted to sites of artificial woody plantings (Martin 1981). Most shelterbelt species are forest-edge inhabitants historically present in midwestern oak (*Quercus* spp.) savannas and eastern deciduous forests. Yahner (1983) reported that only three (Western Meadowlark, Savannah and Vesper sparrows) of the 47 most abundant species using shelterbelts on his study area were typical of the historic grasslands of western Minnesota.

Although forest-bird species historically occurred west of their general habitats and into streamside forests of the eastern grasslands (Coues 1874), the development of riparian forests along streambeds of the shortgrass prairie has effectively created linear forests that have favored the movement of many species farther onto (and even across) the grasslands. At one location, Crook, Colorado, 83 species of birds in the riparian vegetation during the early breeding season included only three representatives (Cassin's, Clay-colored, and Harris' sparrows) of the Great Plains avifauna, and none of those bred locally (Knopf 1986). That riparian forest developed since 1900, and >90% of the native birds currently at that site have colonized in recent times. The proportion is >95% if exotic species are included.

As a consequence of the riparian forest development on the western Great Plains, some of the invading species established secondary contact with closely related congeners. Such species include representatives of flickers, jays, buntings, grosbeaks, towhees, and orioles (Sibley and West 1959, West 1962, Sibley and Short 1959, 1964; Short 1965, Rising 1970, Williams and Wheat 1971, Emlen et al. 1975, Moore and Buchanan 1985); there are so many species, in fact, that the region has been ornithologically identified as the Great Plains Hybrid Zone (Rising 1983). Further north, western riparian species such as the Yellow-breasted Chat (*Icteria virens*) and American Goldfinch (*Carduelis tristis*) were historically hypothetical or accidental in Wyoming (Knight 1902), yet breed state-wide today. Enhanced deciduous forests on the grasslands have also favored movements of reptiles and mammals (Knopf and Scott 1990) and have, in part, been fundamental in defining faunal mixing as a conservation issue (Knopf 1992).

CONSERVATION INTO THE NEXT CENTURY

Just as grasslands are avifaunistically simple, so too appear the challenges facing conservation of these birds. Unquestionably, faunal invasions of the central grasslands are wildlife enhancements. Such enhancements have positive public-awareness benefits for conservation issues in general and, thus, seem desirable except where aliens and exotics degrade habitats of endemic species. The U.S. Department of Agriculture's Conservation Reserve Program promises to reverse the decline in breeding habitats for some species, much as waterfowl conservation programs have had some secondary benefits for wetlands species. The Western Governor's Association is currently discussing a political template for regionalizing conservation action, which will be the first step towards aligning conservation action with biogeographic provinces (Knopf 1992). That international action, the Great Plains Initiative, holds great promise for a proactive and more cost-effective approach to conservation by focusing conservation on the floral and faunal integrity of the Great Plains (Knopf and Samson 1995).

Ecological processes driving population trends of North American grassland birds are currently undescribed. As a group, grassland birds have declined more than birds of other North American vegetative associations. Unlike neotropical migrants which have experienced declines primarily in the northeastern deciduous forests (Robbins et al. 1989a), however, declines in grassland species are occurring at a continental scale. The decline in the Mountain Plover, Cassin's Sparrow, and Lark Bunting are major conservation concerns. The lack of understanding of the wintering ecology of grassland birds precludes optimistic projections for especially these species experiencing widespread, geographic declines.

ACKNOWLEDGMENTS

I thank J. R. Jehl, Jr. and N. K. Johnson for the opportunity to develop this manuscript and S. Droege for his insights.

LITERATURE CITED

ALLEN, J. A. 1871. Notes of an ornithological reconnaissance of portions of Kansas, Colorado, Wyoming, and Utah. Harvard Bulletin of the Museum of Comparative Zoology 2:130–183.

ALLEN, J. A. 1874. Notes on the natural history of portions of Dakota and Montana territories, being the substance of a report to the Secretary of War on the collections made by the North Pacific Railroad Expedition of 1873, Gen. D. S. Stanley, Commander. Proceedings of the Boston Society of Natural History 17:33–86.

BADARACCO, R. J. 1971. An interpretive resource analysis of Pawnee Buttes, Colorado. Ph.D. Dissertation. Colorado State University, Fort Collins.

BAER, N. W. 1989. Shelterbelts and windbreaks in the Great Plains. Journal of Forestry 87:32–36.

BIRD, R. D. 1961. Ecology of the aspen parkland of western Canada in relation to land use. Canadian Department of Agricultural Research Branch Publication 1066, Ottawa.

COUES, E. 1874. Birds of the Northwest. U.S. Government Printing Office, Washington, D.C.

COUES, E. 1878. Field-notes on birds observed in Dakota and Montana along the forty-ninth parallel during the seasons of 1873 and 1874. U.S. Department of Interior, Bulletin of U.S. Geological and Geographical Survey of The Territories IV. No. 3, Article 25:545–661.

DAHL, T. E. 1990. Wetlands losses in the United States 1780's to 1980's. U.S. Department of Interior Fish and Wildlife Service, Washington, D.C.

DIXON, K. L. 1989. Contact zones of avian congeners on the southern Great Plains. Condor 91:15–22.

DROEGE, S., AND J. SAUER. 1993. Geographic patterns of population trends among guilds of North American landbirds. Proceedings of the International Bird Census Commission.

EMLEN, S. T., J. D. RISING, AND W. L. THOMPSON. 1975. A behavioral and morphological study of sympatry in the Indigo and Lazuli buntings of the Great Plains. Wilson Bulletin 87:145–179.

FEDKIW, J. 1989. The evolving use and management of the nation's forests, grasslands, croplands, and related resources. U.S. Department of Agriculture, Forest Service General Technical Report RM-175.

FRÉMONT, J. C. 1845. Report of the exploring expedition to the Rocky Mountains in the year 1842 and to Oregon and North California in the years 1843–44. U.S. Army Corps of Topographical Engineers. Blair and Rives, Washington, D.C.

FRETWELL, S. 1986. Distribution and abundance of the Dickcissel. Current Ornithology 4:211–242.

GILBERT, L. E. 1980. Food web organization and conservation of neotropical diversity. Pp. 11–34 *in* M. E. Soulé and B. A. Wilcox (eds.), Conservation biology. Sinauer Associates, Inc., Sunderland, Massachusetts.

GRIFFITH, P. W. 1976. Introduction to the problems. Pp. 3–7 *in* R. W. Tinus (ed.), Shelterbelts on the Great Plains. Proceedings of the Great Plains Agricultural Council No. 78, Denver, Colorado.

GRINNELL, G. B. 1875. Zoological report. Pp. 79–84 *in* W. Ludlow (ed.), Report of a reconnaissance of the Black Hills of Dakota made in the summer of 1874. U.S. Army Department of Engineers, Washington, D. C.

HAYDEN, F. V. 1862. On the geology and natural history of the Upper Missouri; with a map. Transactions of the American Philosophical Society 12:1–218.

HOBBS, R. J., AND L. F. HUENNEKE. 1992. Disturbance, diversity, and invasion: implications for conservation. Conservation Biology 6:324–337.

HORNADAY, W. T. 1887. The extermination of the American Bison. Smithsonian Institution Report of the U.S. National Museum 1887:367–548, plus XXII plates.

HYDE, G. E. 1974. The Pawnee Indians. University of Oklahoma Press, Norman.

IRVING, W. 1835. A tour on the prairies. J. Murray, London.

JOHNSGARD, P. A. 1979. Birds of the Great Plains. University of Nebraska Press, Lincoln.

JOHNSON, R. G., AND S. A. TEMPLE. 1986. Assessing habitat quality for birds nesting in fragmented tallgrass prairies. Pp. 245–249 in J. Verner, M. L. Morrison, and C. J. Ralph (eds.), Wildlife 2000. University of Wisconsin Press, Madison.

JOHNSON, W. C. 1993. Woodland expansion in the Platte River, Nebraska: patterns and causes. Ecological Monographs.

KIRSCH, L. M. 1974. Habitat management considerations for prairie chickens. Wildlife Society Bulletin 2:124–129.

KNIGHT, W. C. 1902. The birds of Wyoming. University of Wyoming Experiment Station Bulletin 55.

KNOPF, F. L. 1975. Spatial and temporal aspects of colonial nesting of the White Pelican, *Pelecanus erythrorhynchos*. Ph.D. Dissertation, Utah State University, Logan.

KNOPF, F. L. 1986. Changing landscapes and the cosmopolitism of the eastern Colorado avifauna. Wildlife Society Bulletin 14:132–142.

KNOPF, F. L. 1988. Conservation of steppe birds in North America. International Council for Bird Preservation Technical Publication 7:27–41.

KNOPF, F. L. 1992. Faunal mixing, faunal integrity, and the biopolitical template for diversity conservation. Transactions of the North American Wildlife and Natural Resources Conference 57:330–342.

KNOPF, F. L. 1993a. Perspectives on grazing nongame bird habitats. In press in P. R. Krausman (ed.), Rangeland wildlife. Society for Range Management.

KNOPF, F. L., AND F. B. SAMSON. 1995. Conserving the biotic integrity of the Great Plains. In S. Johnson and A. Bouzaher (eds.), Conservation of the Great Plains Ecosystems: Current science, future options. Kluwer Academic Press, Dordrecht, The Netherlands.

KNOPF, F. L., AND M. L. SCOTT. 1990. Altered flows and created landscapes in the Platte River headwaters, 1840–1990. Pp. 47–70 in J. M. Sweeney (ed.), Management of dynamic ecosystems. North Central Section of the Wildlife Society, West Lafayette, Indiana.

KRUEGER, K. 1986. Feeding relationships among bison, pronghorn, and prairie dogs: an experimental analysis. Ecology 67:760–770.

MACARTHUR, R. H. 1959. On the breeding distribution pattern of North American migrant birds. Auk 76:318–325.

MARTIN, T. E. 1981. Limitation in small habitat islands: chance or competition? Auk 98:715–734.

MATTES, M. J. 1988. Platte River Road narratives. University of Illinois Press, Chicago.

MENGEL, R. M. 1970. The North American Central Plains as an isolating agent in bird speciation. Pp.

280–340 in W. Dort and J. K. Jones (eds.), Pleistocene and recent environments of the central Great Plains. University of Kansas Press, Lawrence.

MLOT, C. 1990. Restoring the prairie. BioScience 40: 804–809.

MOORE, W. S., AND D. B. BUCHANAN. 1985. Stability of the Northern Flicker hybrid zone in historical times: implications for adaptive speciation theory. Evolution 39:135–151.

O'MEILIA, M. E., F. L. KNOPF, AND J. C. LEWIS. 1982. Some consequences of competition between prairie dogs and beef cattle. Journal of Range Management 35:580–585.

PULICH, W. M. 1976. The Golden-cheeked Warbler. Texas Parks and Wildlife Department, Austin.

RISING, J. D. 1970. Morphological variation and evolution in some North American orioles. Systematic Zoology 19:315–351.

RISING, J. D. 1983. The Great Plains hybrid zones. Current Ornithology 1:131–157.

ROBBINS, C. S., AND W. T. VAN VELZEN. 1969. Breeding bird survey 1967 and 1968. U.S. Bureau of Sport Fisheries and Wildlife Special Scientific Report 124, Washington, D.C.

ROBBINS, C. S., J. R. SAUER, R. S. GREENBERG, AND S. DROEGE. 1989a. Population declines in North American birds that migrate to the neotropics. Proceedings National Academy of Science 86:7658–7662.

ROBBINS, C. S., D. K. DAWSON, AND B. A. DOWELL. 1989b. Habitat area requirements of breeding forest birds of the middle Atlantic States. Wildlife Monographs 103:1–34.

ROE, F. G. 1951. The North American buffalo. University of Toronto Press, Canada.

SAMSON, F. B. 1980. Island biogeography and the conservation of prairie birds. Pp. 293–305 in C. L. Kucera, (ed.), Seventh North American Prairie Conference, Springfield, Missouri.

SHORT, L. L., JR. 1965. Hybridization in the flickers (*Colaptes*) of North America. Bulletin of the American Museum of Natural History 129:309–428.

SIBLEY, C. G., AND L. L. SHORT, JR. 1959. Hybridization in the buntings (*Passerina*) of the Great Plains. Auk 76:443–463.

SIBLEY, C. G., AND L. L. SHORT, JR. 1964. Hybridization in the orioles of the Great Plains. Condor 66: 130–150.

SIBLEY, C. G., AND D. A. WEST. 1959. Hybridization in the Rufous-sided Towhees of the Great Plains. Auk 76:326–338.

STANSBURY, H. 1852. Exploration and survey of the valley of the Great Salt Lake of Utah, including a reconnaissance of a new route through the Rocky Mountains. U.S. Army Corps Topographical Engineers. Lippincott, Grambo & Coi, Philadelphia, Pennsylvania.

SUMMERS, C. A., AND R. L. LINDER. 1978. Food habits of the black-tailed prairie dog in western South Dakota. Journal of Range Management 31:134–136.

SUTTON, G. M. 1967. Birds of Oklahoma. University of Oklahoma Press, Norman.

TERBORGH, J. 1986. Keystone plant resources in the tropical forest. Pp. 331–344 in M. R. Soulé (ed.), Conservation biology. Sinauer Associates, Inc., Sunderland, Massachusetts.

TOWNSEND, J. K. 1839. Narrative of a journey across the Rocky Mountains to the Columbia River. H. Perkins, Philadelphia.

UDVARDY, M. D. F. 1958. Ecological and distributional analysis of North American birds. Condor 60: 50–66.

U.S.D.A. 1987. Basic statistics 1982 National Resources Inventory. U.S. Department of Agriculture Soil Conservation Service Bulletin No. 756.

U.S.D.A. 1989. Summary report 1987 National Resources Inventory. U.S. Department of Agriculture Soil Conservation Service Bulletin No. 790.

U.S.D.A. 1990. Land areas of the National Forest System as of September 30, 1990. U.S. Department of Agriculture Forest Service. FS-383.

WEST, D. A. 1962. Hybridization in grosbeaks (*Pheucticus*) of the Great Plains. Auk 79:399–424.

WIENS, J. A. 1974. Climatic instability and the "ecological saturation" of bird communities in North American grasslands. Condor 76:385–400.

WILLIAMS, O., AND G. P. WHEAT. 1971. Hybrid jays in Colorado. Wilson Bulletin 83:343–346.

YAHNER, R. H. 1983. Seasonal dynamics, habitat relationships, and management of avifauna in farmstead shelterbelts. Journal of Wildlife Management 47:85–104.

ZIMMERMAN, J. L. 1992. Density-dependent factors affecting the avian diversity of the tallgrass prairie community. Wilson Bulletin 104:85–94.

Studies in Avian Biology No. 15:258–272, 1994.

CHANGES IN SALINE AND ALKALINE LAKE AVIFAUNAS IN WESTERN NORTH AMERICA IN THE PAST 150 YEARS

JOSEPH R. JEHL, JR.

Abstract. I use biological, historical and limnological data to consider how changes at some of the major saline and alkaline lakes in the western United States may have affected their ability to support breeding and migratory birds in the past 150 years. I emphasize hypersaline lakes (salinities >50‰), where the birdlife is dominated by a few species, principally California Gull, Wilson's Phalarope, Red-necked Phalarope, and Eared Grebe, that can exploit the abundant invertebrate prey resources. Of eight lakes treated in detail, two have been irretrievably lost, and the long-term survival of another is questionable. Major engineering modifications are planned or in effect at three others. Only two or three lakes seem likely to be able to support their current avifaunas well into the next century.

Key Words: Pyramid Lake, NV; Winnemucca Lake, NV; Carson Sink, NV; Great Salt Lake, UT; Lake Abert, OR; Mono Lake, CA; Owens Lake, CA; Salton Sea, CA; Eared Grebe; *Podiceps nigricollis*; Wilson's Phalarope; *Phalaropus tricolor*; Red-necked Phalarope; *P. lobatus*; California Gull; *Larus californicus*.

Scattered through the aridlands of the western United States and southwestern Canada, the saline and alkaline lakes of North America constitute an important but generally unappreciated resource for migratory birds (Behle 1958, Winkler 1977, Boula 1985, Jehl 1988 and references therein). They are often characterized by high rates of annual production, which provides the food resources for the migrants. Their fresh water input is seasonal, mostly deriving from winter precipitation that will evaporate during the following summer. The majority are shallow, and all but the largest undergo important annual and seasonal fluctuations in size and salinity. Indeed, lakes that have been productive for years can disappear in a short time. This means that their biota must either be physiologically flexible and able to withstand long periods of highly variable and sometimes harsh conditions, or, like birds, be opportunistic and able to disperse when conditions require (Jehl 1988).

Limnologists consider a lake to be saline when its salinity (or total dissolved solids) attains 3‰ (Hammer 1986). Biotic diversity varies inversely with concentration. Many bird species tolerate salinities up to 10–12‰, then drop out. Concentrations of ≈15‰ are a barrier to reproduction in waterfowl (e.g., Moorman et al. 1991). Most fish cease to breed at 40–45‰, and at 50–60‰, in the absence of these and other predators (e.g., corixids, copepods) the invertebrate fauna becomes a biculture of brine shrimp (*Artemia* sp.) and brine flies (*Ephydra* sp.). Those invertebrates can become an almost unlimited food resource for the few bird species that can exploit tiny prey without ingesting the noxious water (e.g., Mahoney and Jehl 1985). Prominent avian species in or around hypersaline lakes (>50‰) include American Avocets (*Recurvirostra americana*), Black-necked Stilts (*Himantopus himantopus*), Snowy Plovers (*Charadrius alexandrinus*), and California Gulls (*Larus californicus*), which are common breeders, and the migrant Wilson's (*Phalaropus tricolor*) and Red-necked (*P. lobatus*) phalaropes and Eared Grebes (*Podiceps nigricollis*), which seem inured to almost any level of salinity, so long as prey persist.

In this paper I supplement the meager biological data with limnological and historical records to consider how conditions at some of the major Great Basin lakes, especially those with hypersaline environments, may have affected their ability to support birdlife in the historical period (1840–present). Information on the geological histories of many of these lakes and basins can be found in Hubbs and Miller (1948).

FIGURE 1. Aerial view of Pyramid Lake, NV. The dry, white alkali basin to the east is the remains of Winnemucca Lake. Both lakes were fed by the Truckee River, which enters from the south and bifurcates before entering Pyramid Lake. Pyramid Lake received water first, because of its lower elevation, and then spilled in Winnemucca Lake, which became "extinct" in the late 1930s.

PYRAMID LAKE, NEVADA

Pyramid Lake, discovered by Capt. John Charles Frémont in 1844, is a meager remnant of Pleistocene Lake Lahontan, which once covered 22,000 km² of western Nevada to a maximum depth of 157 m. Even so, Pyramid remains the largest (444 km²), deepest (103 m), and limnologically perhaps the most stable of the major saline lakes in North America (Hammer 1986; Fig. 1). It is slightly saline (≈5‰) and sustains amphipods, fish, (including the endangered cui-ui, [*Chamistes cujus*]), and other potential prey for aquatic birds. In the prehistoric period it was a major site for aboriginal people, who made extensive use of waterfowl in migration (Knack and Stewart 1984).

Like other Great Basin lakes, Pyramid reached peak elevations in the late 19th century, but then began to decline, owing to the diversion of the Truckee River and the completion of the Newlands Irrigation Project (1903); between 1890 and 1980 it dropped by 21 m (Fig. 2). This probably had little effect on the birdlife, because the salinity was low and changes were slight.

This lake's most important avian resources are the colonial birds breeding on Anaho Island National Wildlife Refuge (established in 1913). Baseline historical data come from periods when the lake was relatively high and include reports by Robert Ridgway (1877) and E. R. Hall (1924). The latter spent the summer of 1924 there, noting 14 species of waterbirds, of which only the White Pelican (*Pelecanus erythrorhynchos*), California Gull, and Double-crested Cormorant (*Phalacrocorax auritus*) were common. Through most of this century the pelican colony has been among the largest in the United States, typically holding 3000–

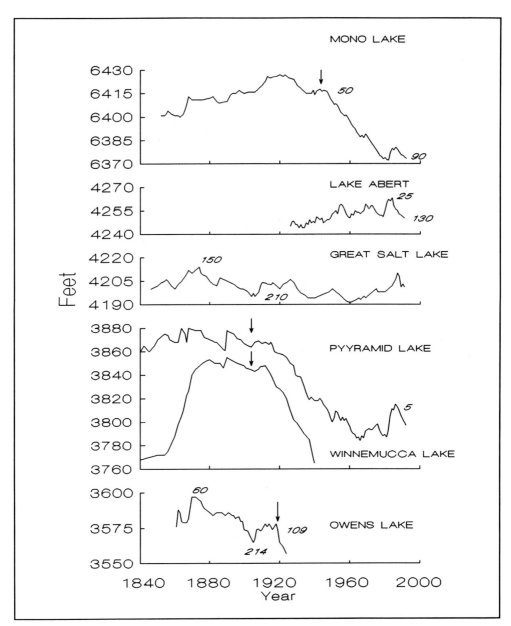

FIGURE 2.   Changes in the surface elevations of some major saline lakes in western North America. Approximate salinities are indicated in italics. Arrows indicate the start of diversion projects.

5000 nests (A. Janik, pers. comm.; Marshall and Giles 1953). Colony size (range—50 pairs in 1988 to 10,700 pairs in 1986) and productivity are influenced by foraging conditions in the Lahontan Basin, 96 km to the south. In good years productivity averages nearly 1 chick/pair, but in the recent drought (e.g., 1988–1992) virtually no young fledged.

Gull populations have also fluctuated, but seem to have shown little overall change. They were exploited by native people and miners before the refuge was created (Hall 1924), but from 1986–1992 counts have averaged about 2600 pairs (maximum 4240 in 1992; R. Anglin, pers. comm.), which is about the size of the colony described by

Ridgway in 1877 (Yochem et al. 1991). Cormorants are likely to have increased after the refuge was created. Hall (1924) reported "several hundred and perhaps a thousand" adult birds; this can be compared to 1330 nests in 1951, and an average of 1700 nests (maximum 5400) from 1986–1992 (R. Anglin, pers. comm.).

At one time the potential landbridging of Anaho Island was a concern (Marshall and Giles 1953), but resolution of the water rights of native peoples at Pyramid Lake, coupled with regulations to preserve the cui-ui, has resulted in increased inflow, making it likely that the integrity of the island and the colonies will be maintained.

WINNEMUCCA LAKE, NEVADA

Winnemucca Lake, 8 km to the east of Pyramid Lake, was not mentioned by Frémont, and may have barely existed at that time (Hardman and Venstrom 1941), owing to a long dry spell. It first appeared on maps as Mud Lake, a very small body of water, in 1850. With the return of wet conditions in 1859–1860 lakes throughout the Great Basin began to fill, and by 1882–1889 Winnemucca was 42 km long, 6 km wide, and 26 m deep. A subsequent dry period and the diversion of the Truckee River (1903) led to the lake's terminal decline.

The Winnemucca basin is steep-sided and lacks fringing mudflats or marshes. Archaeological evidence suggests that it was probably more productive and attractive to native people at relatively low stands, when marshes at the southern end attracted numerous migrating waterfowl (Hattori 1982). The wildlife values were recognized in 1936, when President Roosevelt created the Winnemucca Lake National Wildlife Refuge, but too late. The President's signature had barely dried when, in 1938, the lake followed suit. Subsequently, even under the best spring runoff conditions, it was never more than an ephemeral sheet of water. With no possibility of obtaining water, the Fish and Wildlife Service abandoned the refuge in 1962.

FIGURE 3. The Swesey family of Nevada boating on (ostensibly) Lake Winnemucca about 1911–1914. Courtesy of Special Collections, University of Nevada, Reno.

Little information about wildlife populations has been preserved. In June 1889, Keeler (1889) compiled a list of 51 bird species, which included all of the expected waterbirds, none in notable quantity. His report is likely incomplete because the lake was high and he would have needed a boat to visit open-water habitats (Fig. 3). However, he did note that a grebe (probably *Aechmophorus* sp., though listed as *Colymbus holboellii*) was very common, and that Eared Grebes were fairly common in the slough. Also common were California Gulls and White Pelicans, visitors from Pyramid Lake.

Because Winnemucca Lake did not have its own source of water, but was fed by the Truckee River via overflow from Pyramid Lake (Fig. 1), it was subject to large limnological changes. At its high point it was alkaline and brackish; yet, at the low levels of the 1920s it was still sufficiently fresh to accommodate a commercial fishery (Hattori 1982). Accordingly, it could not have maintained significant brine fly or brine shrimp populations or been an important concentration point for bird species that require more saline habitats.

THE CARSON SINK AREA, NEVADA

Many pioneers through the Great Basin followed the Humboldt River southwesterly for 500 km across Nevada, before it ended in the Humboldt Sink. Adjacent to this in the south they found the Carson Sink, which captures the outfall of the Carson River as it enters from the west.

The Carson Sink once consisted of 190,000 acres of wetlands (R. Anglin, pers. comm.), and held enormous concentrations of waterfowl (Thompson 1986). The completion of the Newlands Project diverted additional water into the area, which wound up being used by industry, homes, and farms, so that only agricultural runoff of questionable quality was left for the marshes. Even so, enough drizzled through that 23,000 acres became the Stillwater National Wildlife Refuge and Game Management Area in 1948.

The existence of these Lahontan Valley wetlands played a mitigating role in the abandonment of the Winnemucca Lake refuge. In 1960 the Fish and Wildlife Service considered that the "relatively new Stillwater Wildlife Management Area ... appears to adequately provide for the segment of the Pacific Flyway waterfowl which pass through the area." Presciently, it added that Stillwater lacked a secure water supply and that its adequacy "to serve waterfowl needs may not always be thus" (USFWS 1960).

Stillwater, like other interior basin wetlands, is an oasis for transient waterfowl that winter in the Central Valley of California (see also Banks and Springer 1994). In 1988, for example, it attracted 400,000 ducks, including 25% of the Pacific Flyway population of Canvasbacks (*Aythya valisneria*). At other times it has been a major breeding area for Redheads (*Aythya americana*), White-faced Ibis (*Plegadis chihi*), and Canada Geese (*Branta canadensis*). In spring and fall migrating Avocets, Black-necked Stilts, Wilson's Phalaropes, and Long-billed Dowitchers (*Limnodromus scolopaceus*) can occur by the tens of thousands.

The problem of a secure water supply remains. The wetlands still fluctuate with rainfall and runoff, but unpredictably and unreliably. In 1983–1984 they were flooded

and fresh, encompassing >100,000 acres. But the drought returned—and with it high salinity—and the marshes dried out.

The value of the Carson Sink was finally acknowledged in 1988, when funds to purchase water rights and marginal agricultural land in the Fallon area were made available by Congress and local bond issues. Unfortunately, the drought persisted, undermining this artificial, economic "solution" to a problem caused by too many people. After providing water to Reno, farms near Fallon, and Pyramid Lake (partly to sustain a *single* fish species under the uncompromising mandate of the Endangered Species Act), there was nothing left in the Truckee to support *large and diverse populations* of wetland-requiring birds! (In this case, application of the ESA could result in the creation of additional endangered species or populations). In 1992 only 550 acres of marsh remained, and Stillwater, like its precursor Winnemucca Lake, could no longer be managed for the resources it was established to preserve (R. Anglin, pers. comm.). The wet winter of 1992–1993 barely ameliorated the situation, and Stillwater's long term ability to support breeding and migratory birds is problematical.

GREAT SALT LAKE, UTAH

Wildlife, specifically beaver pelts, was central to the exploration of Great Salt Lake in the 1820s. Birds, attracted by uncountable populations of alkali flies and brine shrimp, were also noted by early explorers. Ogden reported thousands of gulls in Cache Valley in 1825 (evidently California Gulls, which should then have been called "Utah Gulls", but the species was not described until 1854). Frémont in 1843–1844 described "enormous concentrations of waterfowl" and "flocks of screaming plover" at the deltas of the Bear and Weber rivers, and Stansbury in 1850 discovered the California Gull colonies that have so greatly influenced local lore (see Behle 1990 for a masterly treatment of the history of Utah ornithology).

As a salt lake, Great Salt Lake is relatively young, having attained its current size and conditions about 11,000 years BP (Arnow 1984). Its precursor was Pleistocene Lake Bonneville, a freshwater lake that covered 52,000 km^2 of Utah, Nevada, and Idaho to a maximum depth of 1600 m. In the brief historical period Great Salt Lake has undergone large fluctuations in size (from 2600–6500 km^2) and salinity (150–210‰, prior to 1960; Arnow 1984). The changes, which can be rapid, affect birdlife by land-bridging or drowning nesting islets, affecting food supply, and creating or eliminating freshwater habitats. Between September 1982 and July 1984, a 3 m rise inundated and salt-burned major waterfowl nesting areas at Bear River National Wildlife Refuge, causing its closure for several years.

Behle (1958) reviewed changes in the avifauna and noted the expansion and shifting of the gull colonies. From the early 1930s through the 1980s the population showed little change at 75,000–80,000 birds (Paul et al. 1990:301), then jumped to 134,000–156,000 in 1990–1993 (fide Utah Division of Wildlife Resources). Behle (1958) also reported decreases in White Pelicans, herons, and Double-crested Cormorants, but these seem to have been short-term responses to fluctuating lake levels and have been reversed (Utah Division of Wildlife Resources). More recent studies have established Great Salt Lake as North America's largest fall staging area for Wilson's Phalaropes and the second largest for Eared Grebes (Jehl 1988). Up to one million Red-necked Phalaropes have been alleged in fall (Kingery 1982), but recent estimates have been much lower (100,000–240,000; D. Paul, pers. comm.). All estimates, however, need reevaluation, because (like those for most nonbreeding birds at this immense lake) they are based on extrapolation. Until thorough aerial surveys can be made over open-water habitats in late August, when Red-necked Phalaropes peak, the true abundance of this species will remain unknown. White Pelican colonies on Gunni-

son Island sometimes surpass those at Pyramid Lake (maximum 9000 pairs; D. Paul, pers. comm.). The basin also holds the world's largest breeding assemblage of California Gulls, Snowy Plovers (Paton *in* Page and Gill 1994) and White-faced Ibis.

The lake today is a far different place from that seen by Ogden in 1825, or even by Behle in 1958. It is the most modified—and most diversified—of our salt lakes. Wildlife habitat along the east and south shores has been lost to industry and agriculture, although this has been tempered by the creation of fresh and brackish impoundments of wetlands for state and federal refuges and private duck clubs. The extensive dike systems of commercial salt works contribute nesting areas for gulls and waterfowl. The most profound change limnologically has resulted from the construction of a trans-lake causeway for the railroad in 1957–1959. This separated the lake into a highly saturated ($\approx$250‰) and often sterile North Arm, and a more productive South Arm (100–120‰; Butts 1980). (Note that conditions within these two broad areas are rarely uniform. Subareas with different salinity regimes in the South Arm include the Bear River marshes, Farmington Bay, Ogden Bay, and Stansbury Bay). When the lake underwent a major rise in 1984, salinity in the South Arm dropped to $\approx$50‰ and the invertebrate fauna changed from one dominated by brine shrimp to an assemblage in which brine shrimp were made rare by corixid predation (Wurtsbaugh and Smith-Berry 1990). The North Arm, which had been sterile, was quickly repopulated by shrimp (Fig. 4), and Wilson's Phalaropes and Eared Grebes shifted out of the fresher areas and followed their prey north, not returning to the South Arm until salinity increased in 1988 (76‰).

If proposed today, the separation of Great Salt Lake into two halves, one of which was sterile, would likely be ridiculed as being environmentally damaging. Yet, the building of the causeway, which reduced salt loads in the South Arm, and other man-made

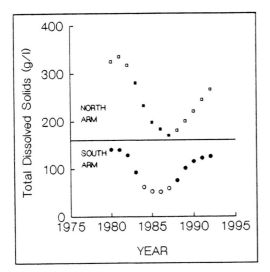

FIGURE 4. Changes in salinity and in the location of commercial brine shrimp harvesting activities (solid figures) in the North and South arms of Great Salt Lake, Utah. Brine shrimp are a major prey for aquatic species occupying hypersaline lakes.

modifications have enhanced habitat diversity, such that Great Salt Lake is ornithologically the most impressive salt lake on the continent. On the other hand, the biological justification of a current proposal to create a freshwater enclosure ("Davis Lake") within the lake—by impounding the flow of the Jordan River behind Antelope Island—is questionable. While this would create additional large areas of fresh or brackish water, it would also eliminate a major source of fresh water, and thus change salinity regimes in the South Arm. If diversions cause salinity to rise beyond the tolerance of the prey populations, as in the North Arm, the lake's habitat for halophilic species of invertebrates and birds would be effectively lost.

LAKE ABERT, OREGON

Lake Abert (Fig. 5), in south-central Oregon, is by far the state's largest salt lake. It was named by Frémont in 1843 for his boss, Colonel J. J. Abert, Chief of the U.S. Topographical Engineers (and father of J. W. Abert, the inspiration for the towhee's patronym; McKelvey 1955). At its high point

(in 1984) it covered 155 km^2, was 5 m deep, and had a salinity $\approx 25\%$. Its shallow basin results in highly variable limnological conditions, and in some years (most recently 1937) the lake has been dry.

In the past decade, at least, the lake's abundant although variable populations of brine flies and brine shrimp (commercial harvest ≈ 20 tons in 1990) have attracted bird populations that have sometimes been impressive. Except for perhaps 1000 pairs of American Avocets and 100 pairs of Snowy Plovers, which occupy alkali flats, few birds breed (Keister 1992). Yet it attracts thousands of migrating shorebirds (avocets, stilts, peep), gulls, and waterfowl (Boula 1985); it is a major staging and molting area for southbound Wilson's Phalaropes in July–August (Fig. 6), and has sometimes held the second-largest concentration of that species in the U.S. (150,00 in 1981). Up to 15,000 Eared Grebes molt and stage there into September (Boula 1985, Jehl 1988). Several thousand Ruddy Ducks (*Oxyura jamaicensis*) and Shovelers (*Anas clypeata*) are sometimes present (Boula 1985) and may use it as the destination for a molt migration (Jehl, unpubl.).

Lake Abert is fed by the Chewaucan River, which "before 1915 flowed through Chewaucan Marsh . . . . After the marsh was drained, between 1884 and 1915, some of the water was used to irrigate the newly-formed agricultural land" (Keister 1992). In 1993 plans were approved to dam the river to create a freshwater marsh, as well as to impound 8 km^2 on the west side for mineral extraction. While the impact on bird populations may not be significant (Keister 1992), such an action would inevitably lead to an increase in mean salinity and more frequent intervals of desiccation.

For stable bird populations it might seem desirable, then, to manage the lake for higher levels. However, periodic drying is required to maintain the viability of shallow lakes (Van Denburgh 1975), because this precipitates salts, which can be removed by deflation. While desiccation can cause short-

FIGURE 5. Lake Abert, Oregon.

term challenges for the biota (Keister 1992), the alternative is a build-up of salts to concentrations that no longer support prey populations.

Over the long term, Keister (1992) concluded that the hydrology of Lake Abert was probably close to that found before the advent of modern agriculture. By extension, it would seem that the bird populations have not changed much because of local anthropogenic actions, but the paucity of historical data precludes any firm conclusions.

MONO LAKE, CALIFORNIA

Mono Lake, the fourth largest (178 km^2) saline lake in North America, is also probably the oldest and most reliable habitat for hypersaline lake birds, as it has been in existence for 750,000 years and saline for at least 100,000 years (NAS 1987, Newton 1991). It was discovered in 1852, and for most of the historical period salinity has approximated 45–60‰ (NAS 1987). Sub-

stantial water has been diverted from streams feeding Mono Lake for most of this century. After the City of Los Angeles began to divert feeder streams in 1940 lake level began to decline and by 1982 salinity approximated 90‰. Increased salinity, per se, probably had little effect on bird populations, as the salinity was already at or above the threshold for most invertebrates, other than brine shrimp and brine flies (see also Wurtsbaugh and Smith-Berry 1990 for changes in Great Salt Lake). However, physical changes associated with changing water levels were significant. At high stands there were freshwater marshes, which attracted abundant and diverse migrating waterfowl said to number in the hundreds of thousands. Today, annual waterfowl populations approximate 15,000 and are dominated by Ruddy Ducks (which use the area for a molt migration; Jehl, unpubl.), Shovelers, and Green-winged Teal (*Anas carolinensis*).

FIGURE 6. Adult female Wilson's Phalaropes staging at Abert Lake, Oregon in early July. Other major concentration points are Mono Lake, Great Salt Lake, and, in some years, the Carson Sink.

The world's second-largest assemblage of California Gulls breeds on a series of islands in Mono Lake. First reported by Wm. Brewer in 1863, this colony has become symbolic of environmental values in efforts to stop water diversion (e.g., NAS 1987). While many hypersaline lake birds probably have a long history at Mono Lake, the gulls' occurrence as nesters must be relatively recent, because the oldest island dates only to 1700 BP (S. Stine, pers. comm.). The first quantitative estimates of colony size are 2000–3000 birds in 1916–1919 (Jehl et al. 1984). Now (1992), in spite of a half-century of water diversions, there are 65,000. Court rulings requiring that the lake be maintained high enough to insure the presence of some islands insures that the persistence of a large gull colony is no longer in doubt.

Mono Lake is the continent's (world's?) largest molting and staging area for Eared Grebes, with fall populations thought to approximate 750,000–1,000,000 birds. We know that numbers were sufficiently large to attract commercial hunters in the 19th century (Denton 1949). Whether they matched current numbers is unknowable,

but perhaps unlikely for two reasons: 1) the destruction for agriculture of wetland breeding areas in the interior of the continent; and 2) the presence of a similar site nearby, Owens Lake, which held immense numbers, at least in some years. Wilson's Phalaropes also use Mono Lake as a molting and staging area before migrating to South America, and thousands of Red-necked Phalaropes pass through in the fall. In the period 1980–1993 peak numbers of both of these migratory species were variable, owing to conditions elsewhere in the range. In the early 1980s, for example, peak numbers of Wilson's averaged 50,000–70,000 individuals, making Mono second to Great Salt Lake as a staging area; later in that decade numbers dropped, concurrent with a major drought in the western and central U.S. and Canada. The historical record is too vague to determine changes in status, except to indicate that both species have long been present (Jehl 1986, 1988).

OWENS LAKE, CALIFORNIA

Owens Lake, which like Mono Lake lies in the rainshadow of the Sierra Nevada, has been hypersaline for the last 6000 years (Newton 1991). It was discovered by Joseph Reddiford Walker in 1834, and named by Frémont in 1834 for Richard Owens, a member of his expedition. In 1864 Brewer (1966) called it "the color of coffee . . . nearly a saturated solution of salt and alkali." After the wet winter of 1867–1868 it deepened by 3 m (9 m by 1872), yet remained hypersaline (68‰). In 1872 it covered 285 km² and was home to an 85-foot steamboat that carried silver bullion across the lake for shipment by mule train to Los Angeles.

Some of the Owens River was diverted for agriculture in the late 1800s, but this was only a minor cause of the lake's decline to 1905, when "bicarbonate of soda precipitates during the winter months without evaporation" (Newton 1991). The lake must have been intermittently sterile then (214‰). It eventually rose about 3 m but in 1917 the Owens River was diverted for Los Angeles and the lake died (Fig. 7).

Scanty but critical data establish the lake's attractiveness to birdlife before diversions. Dawson (1922:50) wrote that he had been "lured to this section [in 1919] by extravagant accounts of extensive swamps where ducks bred by thousands; but what we found, instead, was a few decadent sloughs, which were being sucked dry by the feeders of the great Los Angeles aqueduct." Kahrl (1982: 35) quotes an early settler that "the lake was once 'alive with wild fowl, from the swift flying Teel to the honker goose . . . . Ducks were by the square mile, millions of them. When they rose in flight, the roar of their wings . . . could be heard on the mountaintop at Cerro Gordo, ten miles away . . . .'" While estimates of bird numbers and sound transmission are easily exaggerated (the loudest thunder clap can be heard only six miles away; F. Awbrey, pers. comm.), the abundance of waterfowl (most probably the salt-tolerant Ruddy Ducks and Shovelers) seems evident.

The lake's enormous alkali fly populations, which were also used as food by Paiute Indians, were the major and perhaps sole attraction for phalaropes and grebes. In late July or early August 1859, Davidson (Wilkie and Lawton 1976:24) reported "whole navies of Aquatic birds . . . about the size of jack snipe, have a sharp, straight bill, and the Indians represent them as half-webbed and having a small fleshy paddle projecting from the outer toe." While this description could loosely apply to either the Wilson's or Red-necked phalaropes, it may pertain mainly to Wilson's, which migrate earlier than the Red-necked (Jehl 1988).

The lake's use by molting and staging Eared Grebes was established by the local press (also Fisher 1893), which reported "legions upon legions of a so-called 'duck . . .'" which "have no real wings or feathers and consequently cannot fly . . ." (*Inyo Register,* 4 April 1882). Two years later the *Inyo Independent* (20 June 1874), was still bemused, but entirely accurate in its observations:

"*A query for Ornithologists*

On Owens Lake there are at all seasons of the year myriads of small waterfowl, considerably smaller than the common diver for which they are often taken by casual observers. "The bird is of the diver species doubtless, since it is a good diver and swimmer, but in other physical abilities it is different from any other we have ever heard of. If what we are told about it is true . . . it can neither walk nor fly. Thousands . . . are thrown on the shore and there perish . . . . At such times the Indians would reap a good harvest in stripping them of feathers and down; these products being finer then (sic) the same from any geese, and command as ready a market . . . . The feathers can be obtained in any quantity at a dollar a pound in San Francisco. Here, with Indian help, ought to be a chance for a profitable business.

A specimen . . . was sent to Washington for classification but, Agassiz being dead, it does not appear that anyone there could tell anything about it . . . .

FIGURE 7. Top: A photograph taken from the western side of Owens Lake, CA, between 1904–1916. Photo by A. A. Forbes, Courtesy of the Eastern California Museum, Independence, CA. Bottom: The situation in August 1993—a dry playa.

Its bill is long, sharp, and easily broken; something on the snipe order. The pedal appendages are more like flippers than feet, standing at such angles to the body, they are useless for any purpose except swimming.

Of its habitat little is known, other than its food consists of the billions of worms, the only other indigenous creature in those acrid waters.

Some think it is propagated from spawn like a fish, since its breeding places have never yet been discovered."

The lake must have been very attractive, but several reports of large-scale mortality (botulism?) strike a disquieting note. These include "fully two million dead 'ducks' piled around the lake" (*Inyo Register,* 4 April 1882).

In summary, for most of the historical period, from the 1840s (and perhaps as far back as 6000 BP) Owens Lake was a small analog of Great Salt Lake. Its demise left Mono Lake, 190 km to the north, as the closest alternative habitat for grebes and phalaropes.

THE LAKE THAT WASN'T THERE

The third largest saline lake in North America, unlike others in this report, did not exist when the Forty-niners reached California, and no one is credited with its discovery. The Salton Sea was created when an irrigation canal ruptured in 1905 and allowed the Colorado River to flow into the Salton Trough. By the time repairs were made in 1907 a nearly-fresh lake 60 km long remained. Enhanced by the proximity of irrigated agricultural fields, the area attracted sufficient waterfowl to be designated a National Wildlife Refuge in 1930.

The Sea's position as a northern extension of the Gulf of California places it on the flyway for many migrants, as well as for trapped vagrants trying to exit the Gulf of California (McCaskie 1970). It is a wintering area for 30,000 Canada and Snow geese

FIGURE 8. Eared Grebes staging in spring migration at the Salton Sea, California. Major fall staging areas include Mono Lake, California, Great Salt Lake, Utah, and Abert Lake, Oregon.

(*Anser caerulescens*), and 140,000 ducks (including half of the Pacific Flyway population of Ruddies; Setmire et al. 1990), and is a migration stop for thousands of shorebirds. In January–March most of the New World population of Eared Grebe may pass through on its return trip to the nesting grounds (Fig. 8). Great concentrations of phalaropes have not been reported, however, probably because the Sea is too fresh and the food base is not suitable.

Problems with water supply and quality have given the Sea an unsavory reputation. Much of its inflow derives from agricultural and industrial runoff and municipal waste (Setmire et al. 1990). Massive dieoffs of fish (some from temperature changes) and shorebirds and waterfowl (from avian cholera and botulism) are not unusual, and in 1992 an estimated 150,000 Eared Grebes died from undetermined causes.

When the Sea formed its salinity was 3.5‰, and it would have attracted a great diversity of birdlife. Today it hovers at 40–43‰ and waterbird diversity on the sea itself is likely to be much reduced. Current salinities approach the upper limit for reproduction by some of its aquatic inhabitants (mainly, a rotifer, barnacle, cyclopoid copepod, nereid worm, and several fish, all but one of which were introduced). At 50‰, which could be realized within a decade (Hagar and Garcia 1988), a new community—perhaps based on brine flies and brine shrimp—might result, which could shift the composition of the avifauna toward that of Mono Lake.

Plans to maintain the Sea's environment (e.g., by controlling inflows, diking off segments) involve interests ranging from homeowners with beachfront property to irrigation districts and electrical utilities, as well as international concerns (some of the inflow is from Mexico). Inherently, they also involve a morass of agencies with overlapping and conflicting responsibilities. Whatever action (or no action) is taken, the Salton Sea, of all the lakes considered here, is the most likely to undergo massive changes in the 21st century.

DISCUSSION

The saline and alkaline lakes of the Great Basin are important breeding grounds and, especially, migratory stopover points for species that can tolerate their harsh and varied conditions. This is best evidenced by the fact that national wildlife refuges have been established at five of the eight lakes discussed in this report (Pyramid Lake, Carson Sink, Winnemucca Lake, Great Salt Lake, Salton Sea), and Western Hemisphere Shorebird Reserve Sites at three (Mono Lake, Carson Sink and Carson Lake, Great Salt Lake).

Scanty historical records over the past century and a half preclude detailed analyses of faunal changes in most areas. Even if these existed, they would be poor indices to changes at the population or species level, because the interior lakes constitute a series of disjunct and intermittently-available oases, whose users must be semi-nomadic and capable of shifting as environmental conditions require (e.g., Jehl 1988, Alberico 1993). In this regard, data on the Whiteface Ibis, a ground-nesting species of alkali marshes, are instructive. A survey in 1979–1980 revealed 24,500 breeding birds, 79% of which nested in Utah (Voeks and English 1981). When Great Salt Lake flooded in 1983–1989 and traditional nesting areas were submerged, numbers increased in the Malheur and Summer lakes areas of Oregon, southern Idaho, and the Stillwater/Carson Lake area (Ivey et al. 1988, Henny and Herron 1989, G. Keister, pers. comm.). When those areas dried in 1987–1992 (in 1992 there was virtually complete nesting failure at Stillwater and Malheur) the ibis again became common at Great Salt Lake (V. Roy, pers. comm.). Despite these shifts, there is no indication that the total population has undergone any appreciable change (D. E. Manry, pers. comm.).

The health of bird populations that use unstable habitats is to a large extent dependent on the availability of back-up sites that can be used when conditions change. Unfortunately, there is not much redundancy left in the saline and alkaline lakes of the west. Owens and Winnemucca lakes have been lost to demands of increasing human populations and will never be restored. The adequacy of long-term water supplies for the Carson Sink area is questionable. Engineering modifications to the water balance at Lake Abert are imminent, and others are being considered for the Salton Sea and Great Salt Lake. The Salton Sea is near a salinity threshold that could lead to its ecological reorganization. Of the lakes considered here only Mono, Pyramid, and perhaps Great Salt seem likely to remain largely unchanged in their ability to support current populations of migratory birds into the foreseeable future.

ACKNOWLEDGMENTS

I am indebted to the following for comments and assistance in the preparation of this paper: S. I. Bond, W. Radke, R. McKernan, D. Babb, R. Anglin, V. Roy, B. Henry, A. Janik, D. Manry, G. Keister, G. Ivey, D. Paul, P. White, K. Robinette, C. Henny, N. Johnson, and L. Neel.

LITERATURE CITED

ALBERICO, J. 1993. Drought and predation cause avocet and stilt breeding failure in Nevada. Western Birds 24:43–51.

ARNOW, R. 1984. Rise of Great Salt Lake. U.S. Geological Survey, Water Supply Paper No. 2275, pp. 31–33.

BANKS, R. C., AND P. F. SPRINGER. 1994. A century of population trends of waterfowl in Western North America. Pp. 134–146 in J. R. Jehl, Jr., and N. K.

Johnson (eds.), A century of avifaunal change in Western North America. Studies in Avian Biology 15.

BEHLE, W. H. 1958. The bird life of Great Salt Lake. University of Utah Press. Salt Lake City, UT.

BEHLE, W. H. 1990. Utah birds: historical perspectives and bibliography. Utah Museum of Natural History Occasional Publication No. 9.

BOULA, K. M. 1985. Foraging ecology of migrant waterbirds, Lake Abert, Oregon. M. S. Thesis, Oregon State University, Corvallis, OR.

BREWER, W. H. 1966. Up and down California in 1860–1864. (Ed. by F. H. Farquhar). University of California Press.

BUTTS, D. S. 1980. Factors affecting the concentration of Great Salt Lake brines. Utah Geological and Mineral Survey Bulletin 116:163–167.

DAWSON, W. L. 1922. The season of 1919. Journal of the Museum of Comparative Oology 2:45–54.

DENTON, S. W. 1949. Pages from a naturalist's diary. V. Denton, ed. Alexander Printing Co., Boston, MA.

FISHER, A. K. 1893. Report on the ornithology of the Death Valley Expedition of 1891, comprising notes on the birds observed in southern California, southern Nevada, and parts of Arizona and Utah. Pp. 7–158 *in* The Death Valley Expedition. Part. II. North American Fauna No. 7. U.S. Department of Agriculture.

HAGAR, J., AND J. GARCIA. 1988. Appendix G. A review of the potential biological response to salinity changes in the Salton Sea. Report J-347. BioSystems Analysis Inc., Sausalito, CA.

HALL, E. R. 1924. Birds of Pyramid Lake. May 15–Aug. 3, 1924. Smithsonian Institution Archives, Record Unit 7176, U.S. Fish and Wildlife Service, 1860–1961. Field Reports, Box 70, Folder 1.

HAMMER, U. T. 1986. Saline lake ecosystems of the world. Dr. W. Junk Publishers, Dordrecht. The Netherlands.

HARDMAN, G., AND C. VENSTROM. 1941. A 100-year record of Truckee River runoff estimated from changes in levels and volumes of Pyramid and Winnemucca lakes. Transactions American Geophysical Union, 1941, pp. 71–90.

HATTORI, E. M. 1982. The archaeology of Falcon Hill, Winnemucca Lake, Washoe County, Nevada. Nevada State Museum Anthropological Papers No. 18.

HENNY, C. J., AND G. B. HERRON. 1989. DDE, selenium, mercury, and White-faced Ibis reproduction at Carson Lake, Nevada. Journal of Wildlife Management 53:1032–1045.

HUBBS, C. L., AND R. R. MILLER. 1948. The zoological evidence/correlation between fish distribution and hydrographic history in the desert basins of Western United States. *In* The Great Basin, with emphasis on Glacial and Postglacial times. Bulletin of the University of Utah 38:17–166.

IVEY, G. L., M. A. STERN, AND C. G. CAREY. 1988. An increasing White-faced Ibis population in Oregon. Western Birds 19:105–108.

JEHL, J. R, JR. 1986. Biology of the Red-necked Phalarope (*Phalaropus lobatus*) at the western edge of the Great Basin in fall migration. Great Basin Naturalist 46:185–197.

JEHL, J. R., JR. 1988. Biology of the Eared Grebe and Wilson's Phalarope in the nonbreeding season; a study of adaptations of saline lakes. Studies in Avian Biology 12.

JEHL, J. R., JR., D. E. BABB, AND D. M. POWER. 1984. History of the California Gull colony at Mono Lake, California. Colonial Waterbirds 7:94–104.

KAHRL, W. 1982. Water and power. University of California Press, Berkeley, CA.

KEELER, C. A. 1889. An annotated list of the birds observed [Pyramid Lake and Winnemucca Lake, Nev,]. June 1889. Smithsonian Inst. Archives, Record Unit 7176, U.S. Fish and Wildlife Service, 1860–1961. Field Reports, Box 10, Folder 10.

KEISTER, G. P., JR. 1992. The ecology of Lake Abert: analysis of further development. Oregon Department of Fish and Wildlife Special Report, 34 pp.

KINGERY, H. 1982. Mountain West. American Birds 36:202.

KNACK, M. C., AND O. C. STEWART. 1984. As long as the river shall run. University of California Press, Berkeley, CA.

MAHONEY, S. A., AND J. R. JEHL, JR. 1985. Adaptations of migratory shorebirds to highly saline and alkaline lakes: Wilson's Phalarope and American Avocet. Condor 87:520–527.

MARSHALL, D. B., AND L. W. GILES. 1953. Recent observations on birds of Anaho Island, Pyramid Lake, Nevada. Condor 55:105–116.

McCASKIE, G. 1970. Shorebird and waterbird use of the Salton Sea. California Fish and Game 56:87–95.

McKELVEY, S. D. 1955. Botanical exploration of the Trans-Mississippi West, 1790–1850. Arnold Arboretum, Harvard, Cambridge, MA.

MOORMAN, A. M., T. E. MOORMAN, G. A. BALDASSARRE, AND D. M. RICHARD. 1991. Effects of saline water on growth and survival of Mottled Ducks in Louisiana. Journal of Wildlife Management 55:471–476.

NATIONAL ACADEMY OF SCIENCES. 1987. The Mono Basin Ecosystem. National Academy Press, Washington, D.C.

NEWTON, M. 1991. Holocene stratigraphy and magnetostratigraphy of Owens and Mono lakes, eastern California. Ph.D. Thesis, University of Southern California.

PAGE, G. W., AND R. E. GILL, JR. 1994. Shorebirds in Western North America: late 1800s to late 1900s. Pp. 147–160 *in* J. R. Jehl, Jr., and N. K. Johnson (eds.), A century of avifaunal change in Western North America. Studies in Avian Biology 15.

PAUL, D. S., J. R. JEHL, JR., AND P. K. YOCHEM. 1990. California Gull populations nesting at Great Salt Lake, Utah. Great Basin Naturalist 50:299–302.

RIDGWAY, R. 1877. United States geological exploration of the 40th Parallel, Clarence King (geologist-in-charge). Part III. Ornithology, pp. 303–669.

SETMIRE, J. G., J. C. WOLFE, AND R. STROUD. 1990. Reconnaissance, investigation of water quality, bottom sediment and biota associated with irrigation drainage in the Salton Sea area, California 1986–87. U.S. Geological Survey Water Resources Investigative Report 89-4102.

THOMPSON, S. 1986. Migratory bird populations and habitat relationships in the Lahontan Valley, Nevada (1986–1990). Unpublished MS. Stillwater Wildlife Management Area, Fallon NV.

U.S. FISH AND WILDLIFE SERVICE. 1960. Letter from G. L. Wiseman, Regional Director, Portland, OR, to Refuge Manager, Stillwater Refuge. 24 May 1960.

VAN DENBURGH, A. S. 1975. Solute balance of Abert and Summer lakes, south-central Oregon. Geological Survey Professional Paper 502-C.

VOEKS, R., AND S. ENGLISH. 1981. White-faced Ibis (*Plegadis chihi*) populations and distribution in the western United States: 1979–1980. Unpublished report, U.S. Fish and Wildlife Service, Portland, OR.

WILKIE, P. J., AND H. W. LAWTON (EDS.). 1976. The expedition of Capt. J. W. Davidson from Fort Tejon to the Owens Valley in 1859, Ballena Press Publications in Archaeology, Ethnology and History, No. 8.

WINKLER, D. W., (ED.). 1977. An ecological study of Mono Lake, California. Institute of Ecology Publication 12, University of California, Davis.

WURTSBAUGH, W. A., AND T. SMITH-BERRY. 1990. Cascading effect of decreased salinity on the plankton, chemistry, and physics of the Great Salt Lake (Utah). Canadian Journal of Fisheries and Aquatic Sciences 47:100–109.

YOCHEM, P. Y., J. R. JEHL, JR., B. S. STEWART, S. THOMPSON, AND L. NEEL. 1991. Distribution and history of California Gull colonies in Nevada. Western Birds 22:1–12.

Studies in Avian Biology No. 15:273–285, 1994.

THE EFFECTS OF HUMAN-INDUCED CHANGES ON THE AVIFAUNA OF WESTERN RIPARIAN HABITATS

ROBERT D. OHMART

Abstract. Western riparian habitats have suffered significant degradation and loss from human activities. I estimate that 95% of the riparian habitats in the west have been either altered, degraded, or destroyed in the past 100 years. Riparian habitats represent about 1% of the total western landscape, yet support avian values equal to or in excess of the richest avian habitats in the continental United States. Many agents have degraded or destroyed riparian habitats but the most important are water management, agriculture, and domestic livestock grazing. The first two have run their course and their future impacts will be minimal. The latter is significant and is the most insidious threat to riparian habitats and their avifauna. Where short stream reaches have been given better management or where livestock have been excluded, the recovery has been phenomenal. Many endangered species and neotropical migrants in the west are only found in riparian habitats. Data are lacking to clearly tie the degradation and loss of these habitats to declining numbers of neotropical migrants except in well-studied examples, e.g., the lower Colorado River. If the western avifauna is to remain intact, public agencies must improve their conservation and land management practices.

Key Words: Agriculture; domestic livestock grazing; riparian degradation; riparian habitats; riparian restoration; water management.

This paper examines avifaunal habitat changes caused by major human-induced environmental modifications of riparian habitats in the 11 western states. By major induced changes, I include water management activities (dams, reservoirs, instream flow reductions, flood control and dewatering of rivers), domestic livestock grazing, and agriculture. Others are recreational activities, mining, and timber harvesting, but because of space limitations they are not considered. Not all of these activities have had equal impacts, but all have been significant. Some losses may be offset with revegetation efforts, some are near or beyond rectification, and, in some cases, reversal is possible with simple management changes. If the western North American avifauna, as we know it, is to be conserved for future generations then wise use of riparian habitats is essential. A minimum of 95% of the riparian habitats in the west have been lost, altered, or degraded by human-induced change. Along the lower Colorado River alone over 95% of the native gallery forest has been extirpated and the existence of many bird species is in jeopardy (Rosenberg et al. 1991).

Riparian habitat refers to the alluvial floodplain along either side of the channel (permanent or intermittent flow) and the vegetation growing there. Arid-adapted upland species are prevented from encroaching into the floodplain because of intermittent flooding, high water table levels, and high available soil moisture. Riparian vegetation is prevented from entering the uplands because of lack of available soil moisture. In arid environments, the transition between riparian and upland habitats is usually less than a meter.

Riparian plant species have their roots located in the capillary fringe just above the water table and generally are confined to floodplain habitats. Mesquites (*Prosopis* spp.) are located on higher or second terraces where flooding does not occur annually, and when it does its duration is less than two weeks. Mesquites may also occur in the upland, where its stature is that of a small shrub. Cottonwoods (*Populus* spp.) and willows (*Salix* spp.) occupy lower or first terraces along the stream. They normally occur along permanent streams but will occasionally grow along intermittent streams, if the water table is near the channel surface, even though the channel is dry. Depth to the water table is critical to the occurrence of a number of riparian trees and shrubs.

Most riparian trees and shrubs do poorly in soil or water where the salinity approaches or exceeds 3 electroconductivity units (ECs). There are some exceptions, and most of those species are in the Chenopodiaceae. Most riparian plants evolved with low salinity water and melting spring snow pack generally producing annual floods.

Annual floods are a key element to healthy, functioning riparian systems. Floods deposit new alluvial soils, cover or wash away organic material, irrigate and bring new soil nutrients onto the floodplain, and leach accumulated salts toward the stream and eventually out of the system. If the flood event is heavy the channel may move by eroding on one side and depositing new materials on the other. Riparian vegetation is adapted to pioneering into new soils with rhizomes, stolons, and wind- and water-disseminated seeds. Seedlings quickly become established on wet soils with high water tables and begin stabilizing newly deposited soils.

RIPARIAN VEGETATIVE COMPONENTS MOST IMPORTANT TO BIRDS

In our studies of riparian habitats along the lower Colorado River in western Arizona, my colleagues and I attempted to determine the vegetative components most important to birds. We hoped to build habitats that possessed all necessary components, yet transpired less water and had less resistance to flow during floods than native or natural communities.

To achieve this we sampled bird species composition and densities along 800-m or 1600-m lines three times each monthly for more than ten years. More than 100 census lines were located in relatively homogeneous plant communities between Davis Dam and the U.S.–Mexico boundary (443 km). We also quantified numerous vegetation variables in each censused area, so that we could test vegetation variables with avi-

an use values. We counted trees and shrubs in belts along each entire census line, including data on height, species, and if parasitized by mistletoe (*Phoradendron californicum*).

We were able to identify the most important plant community components for birds in general, and in many instances specific components for individual species. These components, in approximate order of importance, are tree species and densities, foliage height diversity, foliage volume, patchiness, habitat patch size, shrubs and shrub densities, and mistletoe.

Importance of specific tree species and their densities is a component that has not been examined in other avian community studies. We documented the importance of this variable by comparing tree species' influence on horizontal and vertical patchiness and foliage volume. Bird species responded with greater frequency to number of particular tree species than any other variable (Rice et al. 1984). This is not surprising, since the avifauna evolved with specific tree species, which provide nest sites, forage areas, and cover. Exotic trees such as athel tamarisk (*Tamarix aphylla*) may have similar vertical profiles, foliage volumes, and horizontal patchiness but never attain the same avian values as forests of cottonwoods (*Populus fremontii*) and willows (*Salix gooddingii*). Although I specifically reference desert riparian tree species, other species in the genera *Populus* and *Salix* are also extremely important to birds (Thomas 1989, Winternitz 1980, Winternitz and Cahn 1983).

The vertical foliage profile comprises the horizontal layers of vegetation in a particular plant community. Each layer tends to have a cadre of species associated with it (Ohmart and Anderson 1982), and if that layer is missing ten or more species of birds will generally not be found. In our Colorado River studies we found that birds responded to four layers of vegetation. Nineteen species are associated with the canopy or overstory layer (≥7.6 m), 10 species with the

4.6–7.6 m layer, 13 species with the 1.5–4.6 m layer, and 11 species with the 0.15–1.5 m layer. The overstory was composed of foliage specialists that were generally missing when this layer was absent or poorly represented (Ohmart and Anderson 1982).

Foliage volume is the amount of surface area of vegetation per cubic volume of space. Because it is related to insect abundance (Anderson and Ohmart, unpubl. data) the greater the amount of vegetation in each of the vertical layers, the higher the density of most birds. Some species appear to need dense vegetation to create suitable habitat. This appears to be most critical in the overstory layer in desert riparian habitats, where many of the visiting insectivorous breeding birds nest in the hottest summer months. This dense canopy layer appears to be vital in ameliorating summer temperature extremes (Hunter 1988).

Intracommunity patchiness or the differential height of tree tops in a mixed-tree species forest creates high patchiness values. Exactly why this attracts more bird species is conjecture, but patchy environments support more species than monocultures with low patchiness values (Ohmart and Anderson 1982).

Habitat patch size is an important avian component in continuous forest habitats (Blake and Karr 1984, Temple and Cary 1988, Faaborg et al. 1989) and it appears to be as well in riparian habitats, with large blocks containing higher avian values than those of 0.5 ha or less (Anderson and Ohmart 1985).

Many shrubs play important roles in attracting birds. Quail bush (*Atriplex lentiformis*) attains heights of 3–4 m and a mature plant may cover a 10-m² area. The dense evergreen foliage disallows light penetration and drying of the litter accumulated under the shrub. Thrashers, towhees, quail, and other ground-foraging birds feed on the insects in the litter and use the dense foliage as escape cover and shade (Anderson et al. 1978, Anderson and Ohmart 1985). Foliage-gleaning insectivores are heavily attracted to the abundant insect fauna on the leaves, which are retained in winter. The litter and foliage insects are important food resources for wintering birds, while the dense foliage provides roosting cover. Wolfberry (*Lycium* spp.) has similar values to birds except that it is a much smaller plant. The berries produced in the spring are relied on heavily by frugivorous birds. Moderate densities of quail bush and wolfberry greatly enhance riparian values for birds (Anderson and Ohmart 1985).

Infestations of mistletoe in honey mesquite (*Prosopis glandulosa*) communities along the lower Colorado River may add as many as seven or eight species to this community type (Anderson and Ohmart, unpubl. data). Phainopepla (*Phainopepla nitens*), Northern Mockingbird (*Mimus polyglottos*), Cedar Waxwing (*Bombycilla cedrorum*), Western Bluebird (*Sialia mexicana*), American Robin (*Turdus migratorius*), and Sage Thrasher (*Oreoscoptes montanus*) rely on the fruit of this plant during the winter months. Mistletoe and other berries make up ≥90% of the above species' winter diet.

IMPORTANCE OF RIPARIAN HABITATS TO BIRDS

Riparian habitats, though tiny in area, have been reported to support as many breeding pairs of birds/unit area as the best avian habitats in the United States (Carothers et al. 1974, Stamp 1978). Johnson et al. (1977) reported that of 166 breeding species in west Texas, southern New Mexico, and southern Arizona 51% were completely dependent on riparian habitats, while another 20% were partially dependent on it. In California, Gaines (1977) reported that 43% of the species breeding in cottonwood-willow-dominated habitat had "a primary affinity" to this habitat type. The cottonwood-willow habitat along the Verde River in central Arizona provided the only breeding habitat for over 50% of the total species breeding in that riparian environment. Across an altitudinal cline between 1200 m and 2750 m, Knopf (1985) reported in a two-year study which examined over 100 species that 82% of all species were observed in riparian sites. In southeast Oregon riparian areas were of principal importance for 62% of the birds (Kindschy 1978).

More impressive than citing literature is to ask yourself, where have I gone birding in the west and seen the greatest number of species at highest densities? In Arizona that is easily answered with Cave Creek in the Chiricahua Mountains, Sonoita Creek near Patagonia, Ramsey Canyon in the Huachuca Mountains, the San Pedro River in southeastern Arizona, or the Verde River in central Arizona. Flycatchers, trogons, many hawks, hummingbirds, becards, and others are found primarily along our riparian habitats in Arizona.

Has riparian habitat loss and degradation been so severe that the future of this large segment of birds that are dependent on this habitat is in jeopardy? An honest answer is that we are not sure, but many riparian species are in trouble. For example, the Summer Tanager (*Piranga rubra*) and Yellow-billed Cuckoo (*Coccyzus americanus*) have been virtually extirpated from the west coast and the lower Colorado River (Rosenberg et al. 1991), and the latter is declining throughout the west (W. C. Hunter, pers. comm.). The *extimus* race of the Willow Flycatcher (*Empidonax traillii*) is a Candidate 1 Species on the endangered species list and soon to be listed. Most state game and fish agencies have listings of birds they consider endangered (Atwood 1994). In Arizona, 40% of the birds on the list are riparian species (T. Corman, pers. comm.) and in New Mexico over 50% of the species are aquatic or riparian (J. Hubbard, pers. comm.).

Recently, much concern has been expressed over declining populations of neotropical migratory birds (Morton and Greenberg 1989, Askins et al. 1990), which have been linked to human-induced activities such as tropical deforestation, forest fragmentation, and general habitat loss. In the west there are two major habitats that support the main breeding populations of these migrants—riparian habitats and montane forests. Riparian habitats have suffered dramatically from the above activities and continue to do so. Desert riparian forests are tropical deciduous woodlands with subtropical affinities (Lowe and Brown 1982). The Arizona Nature Conservancy (1987) listed the cottonwood-willow forest as the rarest forest community type in North America.

CHANGES INDUCED BY WATER MANAGEMENT TECHNIQUES

A constant supply of water is essential to human survival in the arid west. The most successful settlements have been built along riparian systems that provide a dependable water source. The vegetation along the streams is generally viewed as a nuisance or food for domestic livestock.

Reservoirs

Exploitation of the west began slightly before the turn of the century. Because agriculture expanded on rich alluvial soils, the problems of a constant water supply and the annual threat of floods were resolved with storage reservoirs; virtually every major stream in the west has one or more. Most in the west were built in large bowl-like settings, and have large surface areas that promote high annual evaporative water losses. Fradkin (1984) reports that almost a million acre-feet of water is lost annually from Lake Mead. This water exits as distilled water, leaving the salts behind. The higher salinity water is released for downstream use, impairing the survival of most riparian plants.

Dams create a multitude of problems for riparian habitats and are essentially the death knell for two of the most valuable avian habitat components—cottonwoods and willows and vertical profile. Initially the backed-up water floods and kills all the vegetation and the dam itself stops natural flooding, which is essential to cottonwood and willow reproduction. If floods (now termed controlled-releases from dams) do occur they are usually 1) too late for successful reproduction of trees or 2) of such long duration that native vegetation drowns in the process (Hunter et al. 1987, Rosenberg et al. 1991).

Water releases are generally predicated on downstream needs for irrigation, cities, or power generation. Because floods that watered the alluvial floodplain have been stopped, minimum releases cause the water table to be lowered, which further stresses the downstream vegetation. With time a high vertical profile forest of ≥30 m cottonwoods and willows will be reduced to tree species seldom exceeding 10 m and with lower foliage volumes.

An example of the effects of water management activities can be seen in a number of neotropical migrants on the lower Colorado River. Dams eliminated cottonwood-willow reproduction, increased salinities, reduced instream flows, and allowed many mature tree communities, which were robbed of floods that wash litter away, to succumb to fires. The steamboat era in the late 19th century significantly reduced mature soft-wood species for fuel use, but historical photographs and written testimony demonstrate abundant cottonwood-willow regeneration all along the river up until Hoover Dam was operational in 1936 (Ohmart et al. 1977). Bird census data collected monthly from over 10 years in the 1970s and 1980s spell out the rapid demise of many avian species (Rosenberg et al. 1991).

Swarth (1914) reported the Yellow-billed Cuckoo as fairly common along the Gila and lower Colorado River drainages. The Yellow-billed Cuckoo showed a 93% decline from 242 birds in 1976 to 18 in 1986. The breeding race of the Willow Flycatcher had already been extirpated when our work began. The breeding habitat in which I have observed this species consists of dense and patchy mature willows with very moist, even boggy soil conditions. These habitats probably disappeared from the Colorado River

in the 1950s and 1960s, when there was intensive dredging and channel straightening. Vermilion Flycatchers (*Pyrocephalus rubinus*) were reported by Grinnell (1914) as common and he predicted this species would become more common as patches of forest were opened. He failed to realize either the extent to which the forest would be cleared or the drying that would occur from channelization. This species now numbers about ten pairs from Yuma, Arizona, to Needles, California. In 1976, we recorded 203 Bell's Vireos (*Vireo bellii*); in 1988 the population was down to 88. The prolonged water releases in the mid-1980s led to very high water tables, which killed much of the preferred habitat for this species.

As habitats are modified, the results are negative for some species but positive for others. Grinnell (1914:72–73) observed, "the little open water sometimes attracted a few transient ducks and mudhens, but so far as known no water birds outside the Ardeidae remain to breed anywhere along the Colorado River." From his notes in 1910 and our river census data in 1978 we were able to compare waterfowl changes that occurred in that period. A selected few that Grinnell did not report but that we found in relatively high numbers were 620 American Wigeon (*Anas americana*), 276 Bufflehead (*Bucephala albeola*), 1743 Common Goldeneye (*B. clangula*), and 591 Common Merganser (*Mergus merganser*). Grinnell observed eight species, whereas we observed 19, whose total population was 5238 individuals (Anderson and Ohmart 1988, Ohmart et al. 1988). There are numerous other waterbirds, both wading and deep-water, that are attracted to the reservoirs that now dot the Colorado River (Rosenberg et al. 1991). Also, as marsh habitats developed along canals and in deltas behind dams, a race of Clapper Rail (*Rallus longirostris yumanensis*) spread north from the Colorado River Delta in Mexico (Ohmart and Smith 1973). The secretive Black Rail (*Laterallus jamaicensis*) also found habitat created by water storage seeps near Imperial Dam

(Repking and Ohmart 1977). Unfortunately, the zenith of waterfowl numbers has passed, as recreational and homesite development reduce the habitat availability of these species. The Clapper Rail may be at the beginning of its decline as selenium values approach and exceed safe reproductive levels (Radtke et al. 1988, Kepner, unpubl. data).

Once a dam was in place, more sophisticated water managers sought channelization to straighten the river, which more expeditiously lowered the water table. The next step was stripping the bank of vegetation, then shaping the sloughing banks, and finally riprapping or cementing the soil to reduce dredging costs. Dredge spoil material was generally placed in low wet areas, frequently old oxbows or backwaters that supported emergent vegetation.

In the 1960s, engineers began viewing large trees along rivers as wasting or transpiring large quantities of water. The theory, for which there are no definitive data, was that by removing the tree or wick, water would be saved for beneficial use downstream. For the next 20 years many trees were removed by federal agencies. Even today, thousands of hectares along the Pecos River in New Mexico are cleared of riparian vegetation to conserve or salvage water (Hildebrandt and Ohmart 1982).

Dewatering of rivers very quickly eliminates native trees and favors the shorter-statured exotic saltcedar (*Tamarix chinensis*). Fortunately, this activity has not been widespread, but portions of the Gila River in western Arizona and >443 km of the Rio Grande in west Texas are dewatered. Even in a highly deteriorated state these barely surviving riparian habitats support more species and higher bird populations than adjacent uplands (Engel-Wilson and Ohmart 1978).

Groundwater pumping, which lowers water tables and kills riparian vegetation, has been localized but its effects are quick and dramatic (Minckley and Brown 1982). Large mesquite bosques in Arizona that supported huge breeding colonies of White-winged Doves (*Zenaida asiatica*), large populations of Lucy's Warbler (*Vermivora luciae*), Abert's Towhees (*Pipilo aberti*), and a multitude of other species are now gone (Phillips et al. 1964).

Federal and state flood control dikes are commonplace throughout the west to protect those who built in floodplains. Bulldozers scraped the channel free of vegetation before dirt dams were built. In most of these activities riparian vegetation above the dam has returned, but that below has died as water tables dropped.

DOMESTIC LIVESTOCK GRAZING

Most people do not think of this human-induced change to riparian habitats until they see a stream that has not been grazed. Carothers (1977:3) stated "the most insidious threat to the riparian habitat today is domestic livestock grazing." I concur and the following data illustrate the magnitude of the problem just on public lands in the west, where the Bureau of Land Management (BLM) and the U.S. Forest Service administer vast areas for domestic livestock grazing. BLM reported that on 0.52 million ha of riparian-wetland habitats and 78,400 km of streams from 10 of the 11 state offices, only 7% were meeting management objectives, 8% were not meeting them, and 85% were unknown (GAO 1992). From over 20 years' experience I contend that the 85% unknown can be added to the 8% not meeting objectives. The U.S. Forest Service reported that 93,339 km of riparian habitats within grazing allotments in western rangelands were not meeting forest objectives (GAO 1992).

A brief history will give the reader a feel for the evolution of domestic livestock grazing on public lands. Early in the 1700s the Spanish brought all classes of domestic livestock to the arid southwest, but cattle and horses were most important. Their presence ensured transportation, a food supply, and leather in a harsh, unpredictable environment. In the 1860s and well into the 1900s there was no management of public lands and everything was there for the taking. Grass was free and those who controlled the water controlled the forage. The cattle industry expanded rapidly in the 1880s as new railroads carried beef east to a new market. A $5 calf brought $60 a few months later after running on free pasture. In Arizona, by 1833–1884 the Governor wrote "every running stream and permanent spring were settled upon, ranch houses built, and adjacent ranges stocked" (Report of the Governor 1896:21). By 1891, it was estimated that 1.5 million head were on Arizona ranges (Report of the Governor 1896:22).

Three years of drought then ensued. Cattle began dying in the hot dry months of May and June of 1892 and by late spring 1893 losses were "staggering" (Report of the Governor 1896:22). Land (1934) stated, "Dead cattle lay everywhere. You could actually throw a rock from one carcass to another." Arizona rangelands were left barren and unprotected to wind and water erosion (Hastings and Turner 1965). The timing and consequences of such resource damage was similar in all 11 western states (Adams 1975, Behnke 1978, Meehan and Platts 1978, GAO 1988). Overgrazing continued into the 20th century and although better management was begun in the 1930s, many grazing allotments are overstocked today (GAO 1988).

Cattle are strongly attracted to riparian areas, where water, forage, and shade are all close at hand, and will spend 5 to 30 times longer there than in adjacent uplands of similar areal extent (Skovlin 1984). They congregate in riparian habitats during the summer months or plant growing season (Severson and Boldt 1978). In a study with light-to-moderate stocking rates, cattle removed 20% of the vegetation in the upland compared to almost 45% of the vegetation along the stream (Goodman et al. 1989). Where ranges are overstocked, herbage removal approached 100% in riparian habitats (Platts and Nelson 1985). Cottam and Evans (1945) examined vegetational differences between Red Butte and Emigration canyons near Salt Lake City, Utah. Both were privately owned and grazing began shortly after 1847. The U.S. Government purchased Red Butte in 1888 and began protecting it from grazing to insure a clean water supply. In 1945, total density of vegetation in Red Butte Canyon was twice that in Emigration Canyon. Ten native perennial grasses were found in Red Butte and not in Emigration Canyon. "These facts would seem to emphasize the danger of complete extermination of rare and highly palatable species in overgrazed areas" (Cottam and Evans 1945:178).

The effects of unmanaged cattle grazing on riparian habitats that have never been grazed before are very perceptible within ±5 years. Subsequent changes are hardly noticeable until about a century later, when the last overmature forest begins dying and falling. When cattle first graze a system they trample the banks which, when combined with erosion, widens the stream. (A stream protected from grazing for 50 years showed a 94% reduction in channel width [Clifton 1989]). All palatable vegetation from the ground to about 1.5 m is consumed, and this occurs annually, encouraging the spread of vegetation less valuable to cattle and wildlife. As the channel widens it carries more of the floodwater, whose increased scouring force further widens the banks, as well as deepening the channel bottom, which can be scoured away until the stream flows over either bedrock or large cobble. The lowered channel bottom reduces the water table level in the floodplain, and upland species such as juniper (*Juniperus* spp.) and big sage (*Artemisia tridentata*) begin extending into the floodplain terrace. Upper Black Canyon in the Aldo Leopold Wilderness Area, Gila National Forest, New Mexico, typifies many streams at mid-elevations in the west (Fig. 1).

The process of riparian degradation exceeds a human life span and, to my knowledge, there are no pristine areas to use as yardsticks. Little concern was expressed for

FIGURE 1. Upper Black Canyon in the Aldo Leopold Wilderness Area in the Gila National Forest in New Mexico. Note the size and degraded condition of the channel, the lack of herbaceous ground cover, down cottonwoods, the few live cottonwoods remaining, and the invasion of upland conifers onto the dry floodplain. Photograph by R. D. Ohmart on August 30, 1992.

riparian habitats until about 15 years ago (Johnson and Jones 1977). Since then numerous symposia have highlighted these habitats, and conservation groups have begun to pressure legislators for stricter laws. Better management must come soon or the next 20 years will show the accelerated collapse of the last forest trees. Elmore (1992) reports the elimination of extensive willow stands in Oregon from grazing, and the same holds true in much of Arizona and New Mexico (Ohmart, pers. obs.).

Much research has been conducted on western riparian habitats in the past 10–15 years (Skovlin 1984), and agencies have been forced into protecting stream reaches for endangered native trout. The resiliency of riparian habitats is remarkable after only eight years of cattle exclusion (see examples in GAO 1988, Chaney et al. 1991). In Grand Gulch, southeastern Utah, prior to 20 years of rest, the stream was entrenched to bedrock (in places over 20 m), the floodplain

terraces were covered with annuals, and the stream was dominated by saltcedar. Today, the stream is agrading, coyote willow (*Salix exigua*) stems equal or exceed 30/m², sedges and grasses mat the alluvial soils preventing erosion and trapping sediment, and all age classes of cottonwoods abound (Ohmart, pers. obs.).

Elmore (1992) argues that riparian habitats can heal with better management of cattle in riparian systems and, in general, that is true. Yet, in experience the healing process is extended at least three or four times what it would be with total exclusion. For example, on Mahogany Creek in Nevada bank stabilization with narrowing of the channel, return of the understory, and the proliferation of young cottonwoods and willows has been amazing in ten years. Stream flow after recovery was increased by 400% (GAO 1988). Such a rapid response would never have occurred with any cattle use, regardless of the season. Along Date

FIGURE 2.   Date Creek near Wickenburg, Arizona. Cattle graze year-round in the foreground and only in the nongrowing season on the other side of the fence. Photograph by J. Feller on October 3, 1992.

FIGURE 3.   Date Creek near Wickenburg, Arizona. Stream grazed only in the nongrowing season for 24 years. At flood stage the alluvial soils are covered by the grasses and sedges to disallow erosion and trap sediment. Photograph by J. Feller on October 3, 1992.

Creek in Arizona, where the growing season is eight months or longer, stream gradient is moderate and the sediment loads are high for bank building; after 24 years of only winter grazing this reach is just now in the stage of rapid recovery (cf. Figs. 2 and 3). Vegetative conditions along Date Creek and other streams under grazing protection by The Nature Conservancy are far superior to most Arizona streams.

A time of crisis is rapidly approaching for most riparian habitats. This could have been prevented if permittees and federal agencies had used better management as little as a decade ago. We now know that unless heavily degraded streams receive total rest for eight to ten years the seed source for riparian trees may be eliminated (GAO 1988). Unfortunately, permittees and agencies are reluctant to change and this, in many instances, has slowed or stopped management improvement. Ironically, where riparian management has been improved, permittees have reported reduced feed costs, the regeneration of permanent water supplies where streams were intermittent, better use of upland forage by cattle, and generally better livestock health and higher calving rates (GAO 1988, Ohmart, pers. obs.).

A classic example of how dramatically some neotropical species can respond with the exclusion of cattle comes from the San Pedro River in southeastern Arizona. Approximately 64 km of grazed riparian habitat were obtained by BLM in the 1980s and cattle were removed by 1 January 1987, when the river supported good mature stands of cottonwood-willow forests. Census lines (see Riparian Vegetative Components Most Important to Birds), were established in 1985 and data were collected three times monthly each year to present. The birds listed in Table 1 demonstrate how a rapid response is possible as the understory returns.

RIPARIAN HABITAT RESTORATION

Revegetation

Because of the high value of riparian habitats to all forms of wildlife and especially

TABLE 1. INCREASES IN AVIAN DENSITIES/40 HA AFTER CESSATION OF DOMESTIC LIVESTOCK GRAZING IN JANUARY 1987 (D. KRUEPER, UNPUBL. DATA)

Species (densities are birds/40 ha)	Years						Increase
	1986	1987	1988	1989	1990	1991	
Western Wood-Pewee (*Contopus sordidulus*)	8	16	22	38	28	29	3.6×
Yellow Warbler (*Dendroica petechia*)	29	84	99	227	131	176	6.1×
Common Yellowthroat (*Geothlypis trichas*)	7	24	39	115	110	149	21.0×
Yellow-breasted Chat (*Icteria virens*)	26	44	47	95	100	110	4.1×
Summer Tanager (*Piranga rubra*)	44	84	73	167	94	108	2.4×
Song Sparrow (*Melospiza melodia*)	Trace	11	14	38	36	61	50.0×

birds, there have been numerous efforts to revegetate portions of rivers either as mitigation or enhancement. Anderson and Ohmart (1982) designed the first such effort on the lower Colorado River in 1978, and have since attempted numerous others.

In our efforts we have always planted those species with the highest value to wildlife. Prior to any revegetation effort, which is expensive, a number of biotic factors must be examined if the effort is to succeed. Soil salinity should be sampled throughout the site, not only on the soil surface but at 0.5 m deep; salinity of the groundwater should be sampled as well. Many native trees cannot tolerate high salinity levels and will only grow to about 10–12 m tall at maturity should they survive at all.

Depth to groundwater is also important, since most native riparian trees are normally shallow rooted. If the roots are not established just above the water table when irrigation is terminated the tree cannot survive. Augering of large holes and back filling these for planting sites is also important. This loosens the soil and destroys any clay or silt layers that would prevent the roots from reaching water. Unless large holes are augered to the water table the probability of success is low.

There is a high risk element in attempting revegetation efforts on large rivers below dams. Most dams have the function of water storage and in periods of exceptionally high rainfall, engineers attempt to maintain the reservoir at maximum storage. Subsequent heavy rains and runoff into the res-

ervoir must be control-released to avoid spilling, which could destroy property and lives. These controlled releases may last for weeks or months. Long releases raise water tables, drown native plant communities, and also elevate the salts near the soil surface. The last two actions are highly detrimental to survival of revegetated communities.

Shallow reservoirs in arid climates evaporate large quantities of water annually. Salts are left behind, and water drained from agricultural crops increases the salt load as well. Two years of high controlled releases on the lower Colorado River in the mid-1980s drowned much of the little remaining native vegetation highly important to birds, and increased salt concentrations near the soil surface has rendered about 75% of the floodplain unsuitable for cottonwood and willow revegetation (Anderson 1988).

Agriculture

This habitat change is primarily manifested along larger rivers with rich alluvial soils. Reservoirs provide a constant water supply and seemingly never ending canals, which allow agriculture to expand over the entire floodplain. The lower Colorado River is the pinnacle of this industry in the west. Cottonwood-willow, honey mesquite, and all other represented communities are root plowed and the dead vegetation is piled and later burned. Hectare after hectare of riparian habitat is treated in this fashion until available land or water becomes a limiting factor. Not only is avian habitat destroyed, but this farming practice has consequences on the vegetation that was not cleared. For example, the water used in irrigation drains from the field carrying leached salts, pesticides, and herbicides, and returns to the river—and eventually the water table—to become the supply for the remaining vegetation.

With this habitat conversion a breeding passerine fauna is eliminated and waterfowl, shorebirds, and other mostly nonpasserine species are attracted to this more open habitat. Virtually all of the species enhanced by the habitat change on the lower Colorado River were wintering birds, with few remaining in the valley to breed. For details of these changes see Anderson and Ohmart (1982), Ohmart et al. (1985), and Rosenberg et al. (1991).

ACKNOWLEDGMENTS

I am extremely grateful to C. D. Zisner for her help in typing and preparing the manuscript. J. Feller kindly provided black-and-white photographs of Date Creek. Finally, to D. Krueper for allowing me to cite his unpublished data.

LITERATURE CITED

ADAMS, S. N. 1975. Sheep and cattle grazing in forests: a review. Journal of Applied Ecology 12:143–152.

ANDERSON, B. W. 1988. Soil and salinity conditions in the Colorado River floodplain. California Department of Fish and Game, Sacramento, CA.

ANDERSON, B. W., AND R. D. OHMART. 1982. Revegetation for wildlife enhancement along the lower Colorado River. Bureau of Reclamation, Lower Colorado Region, Boulder City, NV.

ANDERSON, B. W., AND R. D. OHMART. 1985. Riparian revegetation as a mitigating process in stream and river restoration. Pp. 41–79 in J. A. Gore (ed.), The restoration of rivers and streams: theories and experience. Butterworth Publishers, Boston, MA.

ANDERSON, B. W., AND R. D. OHMART. 1988. Ecological relationships among duck species wintering along the lower Colorado River. Pp. 191–263 in M. Weller (ed.), Waterfowl in winter. University of Minnesota Press, Minneapolis, MN.

ANDERSON, B. W., R. D. OHMART, AND J. DISANO. 1978. Revegetating the riparian floodplain for wildlife. Pp. 318–331 in R. R. Johnson and J. F. McCormick (tech. coords.), Strategies for protection and management of floodplain wetlands and other riparian ecosystems. USDA Forest Service General Technical Report WO-12. Washington, D.C.

ASKINS, R. A., J. F. LYNCH, AND R. GREENBERG. 1990. Population declines in migratory birds in eastern North America. Current Ornithology 7:1–57.

ATWOOD, J. L. 1994. Endangered small landbirds of the western United States. Pp. 328–333 in J. R. Jehl, Jr. and N. K. Johnson (eds.), A century of avifaunal change in western North America. Studies in Avian Biology No. 15.

BEHNKE, R. J. 1978. Grazing and the riparian zone: impact on aquatic values. Pp. 126–132 in Lowland river and stream habitat in Colorado: a symposium. Colorado Chapter of the Wildlife Society and Colorado Audubon Council, Greeley, CO.

BLAKE, J. G., AND J. R. KARR. 1984. Species composition of bird communities and the conservation benefit of large versus small forests. Biological Conservation 30:173–187.

CAROTHERS, S. W. 1977. Importance, preservation and management of riparian habitat: an overview. Pp. 2–4 in R. R. Johnson and D. A. Jones (tech. coords.), Importance, preservation and management of riparian habitat: a symposium. USDA Forest Service General Technical Report RM-43, Rocky Mountain Forest and Range Experiment Station, Fort Collins, CO.

CAROTHERS, S. W., R. R. JOHNSON, AND S. W. AITCHISON. 1974. Population structure and social organization of Southwestern riparian birds. American Zoologist 14:97–108.

CHANEY, E., W. ELMORE, AND W. S. PLATTS. 1991. Livestock grazing on western riparian areas. Produced for U.S. Environmental Protection Agency by the Northwest Resource Center, Inc., Eagle, ID.

CLIFTON, C. 1989. Effects of vegetation and land use on channel morphology. Pp. 121–129 in R. E. Gresswell, B. A. Barton, and J. L. Kershner (eds.), Practical approaches to riparian resource management: an educational workshop. U.S. Bureau of Land Management, Billings, MT.

COTTAM, W. P., AND F. R. EVANS. 1945. A comparative study of the vegetation of grazed and ungrazed canyons of the Wasatch Range, Utah. Ecology 26:171–181.

ELMORE, W. 1992. Riparian responses to grazing practices. Pp. 442–457 in R. J. Naiman (ed.), Watershed management: balancing sustainability and environmental change. Springer-Verlag, New York, NY.

ENGEL-WILSON, R. W., AND R. D. OHMART. 1978. Assessment of vegetation and terrestrial vertebrates along the Rio Grande between Fort Quitman, Texas and Haciendita, Texas. Final report, U.S. Section, International Boundary and Water Commission, El Paso, TX.

FAABORG, J., R. L. CLAWSON, J. GIBBS, D. WENNY, R. GENTRY, M. VAN HORN, R. O'CONNOR, AND K. KARLSON. 1989. Islands within islands: problems facing forest warblers in a highly fragmented landscape. Symposium abstract. Ecology and conservation of neotropical migrant landbirds. Manomet Bird Observatory, Woods Hole, MA.

FRADKIN, P. L. 1984. A river no more: the Colorado River and the West. University of Arizona Press, Tucson, AZ.

GAINES, D. 1977. The valley riparian forests of California: their ecology and conservation. Institute of Ecology, University of California, Davis, CA.

GENERAL ACCOUNTING OFFICE (GAO). 1988. Public rangelands: some riparian areas restored but widespread improvement will be slow. GAO/RCED-88-

105. U.S. General Accounting Office, Resources, Community, and Economic Development Division, Washington, D.C.

GENERAL ACCOUNTING OFFICE (GAO). 1992. Response to Congressional Requesters. Rangeland management: assessment of Nevada consulting firm's critique of three GAO reports. GAO/RCED-92-178R. U.S. General Accounting Office, Resources, Community, and Economic Development Division, Washington, D.C.

GOODMAN, T., G. B. DONART, H. E. KIESLING, J. L. HOLCHEK, J. P. NEEL, D. MANZANARES, AND K. SEVERSON. 1989. Cattle behavior with emphasis on time and activity allocations between upland and riparian habitats. Pp. 95–102 in R. E. Gresswell, B. A. Barton, and Jeffrey L. Kershner (eds.), Practical approaches to riparian resource management: an educational workshop. Printed by U.S. Bureau of Land Management, Billings, MT.

GRINNELL, J. 1914. An account of the mammals and birds of the lower Colorado Valley with especial reference to the distributional problems presented. University of California Publications in Zoology 12: 51–294.

HASTINGS, J. R., AND R. M. TURNER. 1965. The changing mile. University of Arizona Press, Tucson, AZ.

HILDEBRANDT, T. D., AND R. D. OHMART. 1982. Biological resource inventory (vegetation and wildlife)—Pecos River Basin, New Mexico and Texas. Bureau of Reclamation, Amarillo, TX.

HUNTER, W. C. 1988. Dynamics of bird species assemblages along a climatic gradient: a Grinnellian niche approach. Unpublished Master's thesis, Department of Zoology, Arizona State University, Tempe, AZ.

HUNTER, W. C., B. W. ANDERSON, AND R. D. OHMART. 1987. Avian community structure changes in a mature floodplain forest after extensive flooding. Journal of Wildlife Management 51:493–500.

JOHNSON, R. R., AND D. A. JONES (tech. coords.). 1977. Importance, preservation and management of riparian habitat: a symposium. USDA Forest Service General Technical Report RM-43, Rocky Mountain Forest and Range Experiment Station, Fort Collins, CO.

JOHNSON, R. R., L. T. HAIGHT, AND J. M. SIMPSON. 1977. Endangered species versus endangered habitats. Pp. 68–79 in R. R. Johnson and D. A. Jones (tech. coords.), Importance, preservation and management of riparian habitat: a symposium. USDA Forest Service General Technical Report RM-43, Rocky Mountain Forest and Range Experiment Station, Fort Collins, CO.

KINDSCHY, R. R. 1978. Rangeland management practices and bird habitat values. Pp. 66–69 in Proceedings of the workshop on nongame bird habitat management in the coniferous forests of the western United States. USDA Forest Service General Technical Report PNW-64. Pacific Northwest Forest and Range Experiment Station, Portland, OR.

KNOPF, F. L. 1985. Significance of riparian vegetation to breeding birds across an altitudinal cline. Pp. 105–111 in R. R. Johnson, C. D. Ziebell, D. R. Patton, P. F. Ffolliott, and R. H. Hamre (tech. coords.), Riparian ecosystems and their management: reconcil-

ing conflicting uses. USDA Forest Service General Technical Report RM-120, Fort Collins, CO.

LAND, E. 1934. Reminiscences. Manuscript in Arizona Pioneers' Historical Society, Tucson, AZ.

LOWE, C. H., AND D. E. BROWN. 1982. Introduction. Desert Plants 4:8–16.

MEEHAN, W. R., AND W. S. PLATTS. 1978. Livestock grazing and the aquatic environment. Journal of Soil and Water Conservation 33:274–278.

MINCKLEY, W. L., AND D. E. BROWN. 1982. Wetlands. Desert Plants 4:223–287.

MORTON, E. S., AND R. GREENBERG. 1989. The outlook for migratory songbirds: "future shock" for birders. American Birds 43:178–183.

OHMART, R. D., AND P. M. SMITH. 1973. North American Clapper Rail literature survey. Bureau of Reclamation, Lower Colorado Region, Boulder City, NV.

OHMART, R. D., AND B. W. ANDERSON. 1982. North American desert riparian ecosystems. Pp. 433–479 in G. L. Bender (ed.), Reference handbook on the deserts of North America. Greenwood Press, Westport, CT.

OHMART, R. D., W. O. DEASON, AND C. BURKE. 1977. A riparian case history: the Colorado River. Pp. 35–47 in R. R. Johnson and D. A. Jones (tech. coords.), Importance, preservation and management of riparian habitat: a symposium. USDA Forest Service General Technical Report RM-43, Fort Collins, CO.

OHMART, R. D., B. W. ANDERSON, AND W. C. HUNTER. 1985. Influence of agriculture on waterbird, wader, and shorebird use along the lower Colorado River. Pp. 117–122 in R. R. Johnson, C. D. Ziebell, D. R. Patton, P. F. Folliott, and R. H. Hamre (tech. coords.), Riparian ecosystems and their management: reconciling conflicting uses. USDA Forest Service General Technical Report RM-120, Fort Collins, CO.

OHMART, R. D., B. W. ANDERSON, AND W. C. HUNTER. 1988. The ecology of the lower Colorado River from Davis Dam to the Mexico-United States International Boundary: a community profile. U.S. Fish and Wildlife Service Biological Report 85(7–19).

PHILLIPS, A. R., J. T. MARSHALL, AND G. MONSON. 1964. The birds of Arizona. University of Arizona Press, Tucson, AZ.

PLATTS, W. S., AND R. L. NELSON. 1985. Stream habitat and fisheries response to livestock grazing and instream improvement structures, Big Creek, Utah. Journal of Soil and Water Conservation 40:374–379.

RADTKE, D. B., W. G. KEPNER, AND R. EFFERTZ. 1988. Reconnaissance investigation of water quality, bottom sediment, and biota associated with irrigation drainage in the lower Colorado River Valley, Arizona-California, and Nevada, 1986–1987. Department of the Interior, U.S. Geological Survey Water-Resources Investigation Report 88:4002.

REPKING, C. F., AND R. D. OHMART. 1977. Distribution and density of Black Rail populations along the lower Colorado River. Condor 79:486–489.

REPORT OF THE GOVERNOR OF ARIZONA TO THE SECRETARY OF THE INTERIOR. 1896. Government Printing Office, Washington, D.C.

RICE, J., B. W. ANDERSON, AND R. D. OHMART. 1984. Comparison of the importance of different habitat attributes of avian community organization. Journal of Wildlife Management 48:895–911.

ROSENBERG, K. V., R. D. OHMART, W. C. HUNTER, AND B. W. ANDERSON. 1991. Birds of the lower Colorado River Valley. University of Arizona Press, Tucson, AZ.

SEVERSON, K. E., AND C. E. BOLDT. 1978. Cattle, wildlife and riparian habitats in the western Dakotas. Pp. 94–103 *in* Management and use of Northern Plains rangeland. Regional Rangeland Symposium, Bismarck, ND.

SKOVLIN, J. M. 1984. Impacts of grazing on wetlands and riparian habitat: a review of our knowledge. *In* Developing strategies for rangeland management. National Research Council/National Academy of Sciences. Westview Press, Boulder, CO.

STAMP, N. E. 1978. Breeding birds of riparian woodlands in southcentral Arizona. Condor 80:64–71.

SWARTH, H. S. 1914. A distributional list of the birds of Arizona. Pacific Coast Avifauna 10:1–133.

TEMPLE, S. A., AND J. R. CARY. 1988. Modeling dynamics of habitat-interior bird populations in fragmented landscapes. Conservation Biology 2:340–347.

THOMAS, J. W. (tech. ed.) 1989. Wildlife habitats in managed forests—the Blue Mountains of Oregon and Washington. USDA Agricultural Handbook 553, Washington, D.C.

WINTERNITZ, B. L. 1980. Birds in aspen. Pp. 247–257 *in* Management of western forests and grasslands for nongame birds. USDA Forest Service General Technical Report INT-86, Rocky Mountain Forest and Range Experiment Station and Intermountain Region, Ogden, UT.

WINTERNITZ, B. L., AND H. CAHN. 1983. Nestholes in live and dead aspen. Pp. 102–106 *in* Snag habitat management: proceedings of the symposium. USDA Forest Service General Technical Report RM-99, Rocky Mountain Forest and Range Experiment Station, Fort Collins, CO.

Studies in Avian Biology No. 15:286–292, 1994.

Case Histories

EVIDENCE OF CHANGES IN POPULATIONS OF THE MARBLED MURRELET IN THE PACIFIC NORTHWEST

C. John Ralph

Abstract. The Marbled Murrelet (*Brachyramphus marmoratus*) occurs along the coasts of the North Pacific. It is unique among the Alcidae in its tree nesting habits. Recent research has revealed that in forested areas it is closely associated with old-growth coniferous forests, most of which have been harvested over the past 100 years. All historical accounts, although fragmentary, indicate a previously higher population of the bird throughout its North American range. Several reasons for the decline have been advanced, including habitat removal, mortality due to capture in fishing nets, and increased predation during nesting. The current population is estimated at about 360,000 birds.

Key Words: Marbled Murrelet; *Brachyramphus marmoratus*; Alcidae; population; mortality; predation; demography; old-growth forests.

The Marbled Murrelet (*Brachyramphus marmoratus*) is an alcid breeding along the coasts of the North Pacific (Fig. 1). The better known race (*B. m. marmoratus*), breeds from Alaska south to central California. The other race (*B. m. perdix*) occurs from the Russian Far East south to northern Japan. Although the species is fairly abundant in some areas, it has largely escaped ornithological study until recently, because of its secretive nesting habits and its frequenting of nearshore waters, where oceanic bird surveys miss it.

Increasing concern about its apparent decline has resulted in its being listed as "threatened" in the states of Washington, Oregon, and California by the U.S. Fish and Wildlife Service in 1992, and also by the Province of British Columbia in 1990. I will examine the life history traits of the species that put it at potential risk, the present population size, evidence of habitat affinities, and evidence for decline.

HABITS OF THE MARBLED MURRELET

Knowledge of the habits of the Marbled Murrelet is essential for understanding the reasons for its population changes over the past century. Many of its habits make it vulnerable to predation on the nest and difficult to study.

On the ocean, the murrelet usually occurs in pairs as it dives for small fish and invertebrates. It does occur in flocks of up to a dozen birds, or even several hundred, especially in Alaska and British Columbia. Such aggregations can occur in tidal rips, the often food-rich boundary between the tidal flow and calmer waters of a channel, fjord, or estuary.

Marbled Murrelet nests are difficult to find and observe because they are high above the ground in large trees, widely scattered, often far inland, involve no nest construction, and are usually visited only once a day. In most of its range the species nests in solitary pairs (or perhaps loose associations) on the wide, upper branches of old conifers, primarily within 50 km of the coast. These habits resulted in its nest being the last to be discovered (in 1974) of a widespread, North American breeding bird (Binford et al. 1975). All of the 38 tree nests found through 1992 have been in coniferous "old-growth" forests, which I define here as those unmodified by timber harvesting, and whose larger trees average over 200 years old. At a few sites in Alaska the bird does nest on the ground above the local tree line, in low-lying mat vegetation (see Mendenhall 1992).

Some aspects of the species' breeding biology reflect its vulnerability to predation, and others result in a low reproductive rate. Birds usually visit the breeding stands within a half hour of dawn at most latitudes, calling and flying through and over the forest. During these periods the birds may relieve nest duties, feed the young, or merely visit the stand. This is the only time observers can estimate numbers of murrelets in a stand. The breeding plumage, in contrast to its winter plumage of dark above and white below, is the "marbled" plumage, completely mottled dark brown, which provides effective camouflage in a forest environment. Murrelets lay but a single egg per clutch (Sealy 1974). The incubation and nestling periods are about 30 days each (Simons 1980, Hirsch et al. 1981), allowing a long exposure to forest predators, such as jays and ravens. Both parents alternate care of the egg and young chick on a 24-hr rotation. When a nest exchange occurs, the relieving bird flies directly to the nest site, and the incubating bird departs with little or no ceremony. After the chick is a few days old, it is usually left alone while both adults forage, bringing it food once to several times a day.

POPULATION TRENDS AND PRESENT SIZE

Nowhere in its range has there been a report of an increase in numbers of Marbled Murrelets. All accounts note fewer birds.

Asia

There is no information on trends of *B. m. perdix* offshore of its breeding grounds in the Russian Far East and south to the northern Japanese islands. Russian biologists (e.g,. N. Konyukhov, pers. comm.) have found the race to be quite uncommon.

Alaska

Data from Christmas Bird Counts in a few areas showed an overall decline of at least 50% in absolute abundance from the early 1970s to the late 1980s, despite a 50% increase in observer effort (J. Piatt and N. Naslund, pers. comm.). The species reaches its greatest densities in Alaska, occurring sparsely in the western Aleutian Islands, and more commonly along the coasts of central

FIGURE 1. The North American range (outlined) of the Marbled Murrelet showing known areas of concentration (stippled).

and southeastern Alaska (Kessel and Gibson 1978, Piatt and Ford 1993). Mendenhall (1992) reported an estimate of 250,000, based on ocean surveys by M. McAllister. Piatt and Ford (1993) estimated the population at around 200,000, based on other extensive surveys.

British Columbia

Historical accounts suggest an overall decline. Brooks (1926) noted, without details, that wintering murrelets had declined between 1920 and 1925 along the east coast of Vancouver Island. Pearse (1946) reported a decline in the Comox area between 1917 and 1944, which he attributed to the removal of old-growth forests. Finally, Kelson et al. (in press) surveyed an area in 1992 and found a decline of 40% from a 1982 survey. Rodway et al. (1992) stated that the bird occurs today in most coastal areas, and they estimated the population at 45,000–50,000 birds.

Washington

Whereas previous observers (Rhoads 1893, Edson 1908, Rathbun 1915, Miller et al. 1935) described the murrelet as common, abundant, and numerous, Speich et al. (1992) felt that it was "now only locally common." They suggested a breeding population of about 5000, distributed mainly in northern Puget Sound.

Oregon

Nelson et al. (1992) noted that since 1970 murrelet distribution has been similar to historic accounts (e.g., Gabrielson and Jewett 1940), but the density was lower. For instance, Nelson noted that "large numbers are now rarely reported from the mouth of Columbia River, at Yaquina Bay, and Tillamook County," where they were formerly more common. The statewide population was estimated at "less than 1000 pairs" from a variety of sources (Nelson et al. 1992).

California

Evidence of declines has accumulated in the state. Carter and Erickson (1992) noted three specific areas in Del Norte, Humboldt, and Santa Cruz counties where birds largely disappeared from probable breeding sites after timber harvesting. This includes the observation by Joseph Grinnell (field notes of July 1923 at the Museum of Vertebrate Zoology at the University of California, Berkeley) that "Mr. Wilder says that he has not himself heard these birds since the redwoods were lumbered off the hillsides back of his place." Another observation is that of Dawson (1923), who was camping in June 1916 about a kilometer from the coast in Trinidad, Humboldt County, and noted that "some birds passed quite low over our camp," a behavior typical of birds nesting nearby. Today, no murrelets are heard in the forests near Trinidad (Paton and Ralph 1990). Additional evidence of a decline comes from a 1937 oil spill, when Aldrich (1938) found 14 dead Marbled Murrelets on San Francisco and Marin county beaches. Today the species is rare in this area (Carter and Erickson 1988, Paton and Ralph 1990), and in more recent spills, only a very few were found (e.g., Stenzel et al. 1988, Page et al. 1990).

The state's population has been estimated at 1600–2000 (Sowls et al. 1980, Carter and Erickson 1992), based on some coastal surveys in the two regions of concentration. From more extensive work in recent years, we now estimate the population in excess of 5000 individuals (Ralph and Miller, unpubl. data).

HABITAT ASSOCIATIONS

Prior to the 1970s, the only reference to the species' actual nesting habitat was an Indian account, reported and discounted by Dawson (1923), that murrelets nested inland in "hollow trees." Today, this seems interpretable as large, old trees containing hollows.

Evidence has accumulated recently that the species requires old-growth forests for nesting. In the 1970s observers began to note that its offshore range was contiguous with inland old-growth (Sowls et al. 1980, Carter and Erickson 1992, Nelson et al. 1992). From anecdotal observations several authors have also associated this species' presence inland with older forests (see summaries in Marshall 1988 and in Carter and Morrison 1992). Systematic surveys have confirmed this in California (Paton and Ralph 1990), Oregon (Nelson 1990), Washington (T. Hamer, pers. comm.), British Columbia (Rodway et al. 1991), and Alaska (K. Kuletz, pers. comm.). Despite extensive observations by numerous observers in forests of various ages, all forest nests have been found in old-growth.

Old-growth coniferous forests were formerly continuous in much of the species' present range. By all estimates, at least 80% of the old-growth forests have been removed in California, Oregon, and Washington (e.g., Morrison 1988). In British Columbia and Alaska, less has been harvested, although the rate is increasing. In southeast Alaska, although probably less than 10% of the former forest cover has been harvested, much of this includes the largest trees which occur within a few kilometers of shore, where they are more easily harvested (C. Iverson, pers. comm.).

BREEDING SUCCESS

A low or declining reproductive rate could have contributed to the historical reduction of the species' population. The reproductive rate has several components. The proportion of the population breeding has only been documented by Sealy (1974), who found that about 85% of the birds in a large sample collected from the ocean in British Columbia had brood patches (both sexes incubate). This is within the normal range for other alcids (Hudson 1985). In contrast, the fledging success appears to be low. Data compiled by K. Nelson (pers. comm.) revealed that of the 43 nests found through the 1992 season, the outcome of 17 (including all the Alaskan ground nests) was unknown, 19 nests failed, and only seven fledged a young bird. Of these 26 with a known outcome, the success rate was then only 27%, as compared to about 70% in other alcids (Hudson 1985).

Another measure of reproductive success is the proportion of young in the offshore population. In the past five years off the California coast during late July and early August, murrelets in juvenal plumage were usually less than 3% of the population (Ralph et al., unpubl. data). Similarly, C. Strong (pers. comm.), off Oregon, found 1.2–3.5% in 1992. Surveying at three headlands on the Oregon coast from 1988–1991, Nelson and Hardin (pers. comm.) found young averaging 3.2% (range 2–5%) of the population. However, we do not know when birds molt into a plumage similar to an adult in winter. If this occurs rapidly, perhaps half of the young would be overlooked. Even so, this would only double the percentage to a maximum of 10%, still quite low. In a variety of other alcids normal production would result in 25–30% young (Hudson 1985, Ainley and Boekelheide 1990), with the early fledging Ancient Murrelet (*Synthliboramphus antiquus*) at more than 40% (Gaston 1992). It is of interest that a demographic model based on the average of 27% nest success discussed above predicts a very low proportion of young on the water, after dilution with non-breeders and some early mortality (S. Beisinger, pers. comm.). This lends corroboration to the offshore ratio of less than 5%. It seems very likely that the current recruitment rate is not adequate to maintain the population and that it was much higher in the past.

POSSIBLE CAUSES OF POPULATION DECLINES

Habitat removal

The absence of murrelets in areas that have lost their old-growth forests, and their occurrence today only in the remaining old-growth, are presumptive evidence that declines have occurred due to the extensive removal of these forests. The most direct evidence of the effect of habitat loss is the 40% decline of a British Columbia population reported by Kelson et al. (in press), coinciding with the removal of about 5–10% of the old-growth between 1982 and 1992. This followed a decade in which approximately 7–10% of the old-growth had been harvested. Since alcids commonly live 10 years or more (Hudson 1985), the population's response to the removal of nesting habitat might well have been delayed.

Fishing activities

In parts of its range, incidental catch of murrelets in nets set by fishermen can be a significant source of mortality. Carter and Erickson (1992) summarized gill-net deaths in central California. They estimated that 150–300 murrelets were lost between 1979 and 1987 from a population at present estimated to be a few hundred birds. In British Columbia, Carter and Sealy (1984) found that 6% of the breeding adults in a population were caught in a year's gill-net operation in Barkley Sound. In addition, Sealy and Carter (1984) reported hundreds of birds killed over several years by gill-netting in Prince William Sound, Alaska, and probably also in southeast Alaska, based on information from P. Isleib. Commercial fishermen in Alaska have told me that they have at times netted several murrelets a day in gill and purse seine nets. This, multiplied by the many hundreds of fishing boats within the murrelet's range, could have had significant effects. J. Piatt and N. Naslund (pers. comm.) found in Prince William Sound that net mortality was 923 in 1990 and 714 in 1991. Based on netting permits throughout Alaska, they estimated that some 3300, or about 2.1%, of the population, dies each year from this cause. The many years of netting in Alaska waters in this century could have resulted in a substantial loss, especially in recent years with the advent of the less visible monofilament nets.

Oil spills

Historically, the species has been a common victim of oil spills (e.g., Racey 1930, Burger in press), probably due in part to its nearshore distribution. It has been estimated that the *Exxon Valdez* spill in Prince William Sound resulted in a loss of approximately 6500 individuals, or a toll of about 3% of the total Alaskan population (Piatt et al. 1990, Piatt, pers. comm.).

Predation

Unlike most burrow and crevice-nesting alcids, Marbled Murrelets suffer high rates of nest predation, at least in recent years. Of the 19 documented failures, 14 (74%) were due to avian predators (Nelson, pers. comm.), including Steller's Jay (*Cyanocitta stelleri*), Common Raven (*Corvus corax*), and possibly Great Horned Owl (*Bubo virginianus*). (Of the other failures, chicks fell out of three nests, one chick suffered a burst aorta just prior to fledging, and one was abandoned by the adults.) Of the 26 nests with a known outcome, then, 54% were lost to predation: a rate that is almost unmatched in other alcids (e.g., Hudson 1985; but for exceptions see Murray et al. 1983, Gaston 1992). I suspect that this reflects a recent development in the species' life history. It seems unsustainable given the murrelets low intrinsic rate of reproduction.

There is, of course, the possibility that the nests located by investigators are in sites easily located by predators. Many of the nests have been on the edges of older stands or in stands fragmented by timber harvest, where predators are possibly more abundant than in continuous old-growth. However, low numbers of young at sea indicate that the low reproductive rate probably applies to all nests.

DISCUSSION

Three lines of evidence indicate that Marbled Murrelet populations are declining. 1) All historical, anecdotal, or quantitative reports are of declines; none of increases. 2) Nest records and habitat surveys find a close association of the species with old-growth forests, which have been reduced by more than 80% over the past 150 years. 3) Current rates of recruitment do not appear to be high enough to sustain the species.

Even though no one has reported increases in murrelet populations, we must consider the possibility that murrelets disappearing from one area have merely moved to another. It seems likely that a long-lived bird, finding its nesting grove destroyed, would move elsewhere, aggregating in the remaining nest stands. In extreme northern California, relatively large stands of old-growth redwoods in parks are islands amidst oceans of clear cuts and young second growth. There, in the Lost Man Creek area of Redwood National Park, we (Paton and Ralph 1990) found the highest rate of murrelet activity anywhere in the species' range, with an average of 150–250 detections per morning during the breeding season. The seasonal peaks usually exceeded 350, and we recorded 399 on one morning in July 1991. This concentration could: 1) be due to especially favorable offshore resources; 2) represent once-common densities on the north coast of California; or 3) be an aggregation of birds displaced by harvesting. It is not yet clear which of these alternatives (or combination of alternatives) is correct, but I think that the first two are much more probable.

It seems likely that the species now has a very low reproductive rate, by the measure of fewer than 5% of juvenile birds offshore. This is very troubling for the species' long-term survival. Even if this is an underestimate, it is unlikely that even a rapid passage through juvenal plumage could account for the difference between this and the proportion of juveniles in most alcids (25–30%).

The high predation on nests seems unsustainable, given the apparent low intrinsic reproductive rate. It is possible that increased fragmentation of the historically more continuous old-growth forests has resulted in increased numbers of predators, such as ravens, crows, and jays. If so, predation is likely a very pervasive factor that cannot be easily reversed. The effect of predation would be greatly compounded by a constant drain at sea of young, and especially adults, in fishing nets.

The evidence strongly suggests that over the past century Marbled Murrelet populations have declined throughout their entire range. Their nesting areas have been much reduced, and they are suffering high mortality from predation and fishing nets. The identification and protection of critical nesting and foraging habitats is essential for the long term maintenance of the species as a part of the avifauna of the Pacific Northwest.

ACKNOWLEDGMENTS

I thank the members of the interagency Marbled Murrelet Conservation Assessment Team who have contributed many ideas and data to our ongoing appraisal of the species. K. Nelson shared her compilation of the known nests of the species. J. Piatt and H. Carter were especially helpful in contributing their experiences and insights. I am also grateful to Mike Horton, J. R. Jehl, Jr., N. K. Johnson, K. Nelson, M. McAllister, S. Miller, and especially Carol Pearson Ralph for their helpful comments on drafts of the manuscript.

LITERATURE CITED

AINLEY, D. G., AND R. J. BOEKELHEIDE (eds.). 1990. Seabirds of the Farallon Islands. Stanford University Press, Stanford, CA.

ALDRICH, E. C. 1938. A recent oil pollution and its effects on the waterbirds of the San Francisco Bay Area. Bird Lore 40:110–114.

BINFORD, L. C., B. G. ELLIOTT, AND S. W. SINGER. 1975. Discovery of a nest and the downy young of the Marbled Murrelet. Wilson Bulletin 87:303–319.

BROOKS, A. 1926. Scarcity of the Marbled Murrelet. Murrelet 7:39.

BURGER, A. E. In press. Effects of the Nestucca oil spill on seabirds along the southwest coast of Vancouver Island in 1989. Technical Report Series, Canadian Wildlife Service, Pacific and Yukon Region, Delta, British Columbia.

CARTER, H. R., AND R. A. ERICKSON. 1988. Population status and conservation problems of the Marbled Murrelet in California, 1892–1987. Unpublished final report, California Department Fish and Game, Sacramento, CA.

CARTER, H. R., AND R. A. ERICKSON. 1992. Status and conservation of the Marbled Murrelet in California, 1892–1987. Pp. 92–108 in H. R. Carter and M. L. Morrison (eds.), Status and conservation of the Marbled Murrelet in North America. Proceedings of the Western Foundation of Vertebrate Zoology 5.

CARTER, H. R., AND M. L. MORRISON (eds.). 1992. Status and conservation of the Marbled Murrelet in North America. Proceedings of the Western Foundation of Vertebrate Zoology 5.

CARTER, H. R., AND S. G. SEALY. 1984. Marbled Murrelet mortality due to gill-net fishing in Barkley Sound, British Columbia. Pp. 212–220 in D. N. Nettleship, G. A. Sanger, and P. F. Springer (eds.), Marine birds: their feeding ecology and commercial fisheries relationships. Special Publication, Canadian Wildlife Service, Ottawa.

DAWSON, W. L. 1923. The birds of California. South Moulton Company, San Diego, CA.

EDSON, J. M. 1908. Birds of the Bellingham Bay region. Auk 25:425–439.

GABRIELSON, I. N., AND S. G. JEWETT. 1940. Birds of Oregon. Oregon State University Press, Corvallis, OR.

GASTON, A. J. 1992. The Ancient Murrelet: a natural history in the Queen Charlotte Islands. Academic Press, San Diego, CA.

HIRSCH, K. V., D. A. WOODBY, AND L. B. ASTHEIMER. 1981. Growth of a nestling Marbled Murrelet. Condor 83:264–265.

HUDSON, P. J. 1985. Population parameters for the Atlantic Alcidae. Pp. 233–261 in D. N. Nettleship and T. R. Birkhead (eds.), The Atlantic Alcidae. Academic Press, Inc., Orlando, FL.

KELSON, J., I. MANLEY, AND H. CARTER. In press. Assessment of change in population size for Marbled Murrelets in Clayoquot Sound, British Columbia: 1982 to 1992. Northwestern Naturalist.

KESSEL, B., AND D. D. GIBSON. 1978. Status and distribution of Alaska birds. Studies in Avian Biology 1.

MARSHALL, D. B. 1988. The Marbled Murrelet joins the old-growth forest conflict. American Birds 42: 202–212.

MENDENHALL, V. M. 1992. Distribution, breeding records, and conservation problems of the Marbled Murrelet in Alaska. Pp. 5–16 in H. R. Carter and M. L. Morrison (eds.), Status and conservation of the Marbled Murrelet in North America. Proceedings of the Western Foundation of Vertebrate Zoology 5.

MILLER, R. C., E. D. LUMLEY, AND F. S. HALL. 1935.

Birds of the San Juan Islands, Washington. Murrelet 16:51–65.

MORRISON, P. H. 1988. Old-growth in the Pacific Northwest: a status report. The Wilderness Society, Washington, D.C.

MURRAY, K. G., K. WINNETT-MURRAY, Z. A. EPPLEY, G. L. HUNT, JR., AND D. B. SCHWARTZ. 1983. Breeding biology of the Xantus' Murrelet. Condor 85:12–21.

NELSON, S. K. 1990. Distribution of the Marbled Murrelet in western Oregon. Unpublished report, Nongame Program, Oregon Department of Fish and Game, Publication Number 89-9-02.

NELSON, S. K., M. L. C. MCALLISTER, M. A. STERN, D. H. VAROUJEAN, AND J. M. SCOTT. 1992. The Marbled Murrelet in Oregon, 1899–1987. Pp. 17–41 in H. R. Carter and M. L. Morrison (eds.), Status and conservation of the Marbled Murrelet in North America. Proceedings of the Western Foundation of Vertebrate Zoology 5.

PAGE, G. W., H. R. CARTER, AND R. G. FORD. 1990. Numbers of seabirds killed or debilitated in the 1986 Apex Houston oil spill in central California. Pp. 164–184 in S. G. Sealy (ed.), Auks at sea. Studies in Avian Biology 14.

PATON, P. W. C., AND C. J. RALPH. 1990. Distribution of the Marbled Murrelet at inland sites in California. Northwestern Naturalist 71:72–84.

PEARSE, T. 1946. Notes on changes in bird populations in the vicinity of Comox, Vancouver Island— 1917 to 1944. Murrelet 27:4–9.

PIATT, J. F., AND R. G. FORD. 1993. Distribution and abundance of Marbled Murrelets in Alaska. Condor 95:662–669.

PIATT, J. F., C. J. LENSINK, W. BUTLER, M. KENDZORIAK, AND D. R. NYSEWANDER. 1990. Immediate impact of the "Exxon Valdez" oil spill on marine birds. Auk 107:387–397.

RACEY, K. 1930. Effect of fuel oil on seabirds. Murrelet 11:22.

RATHBUN, S. F. 1915. List of water and shore birds of the Puget Sound region in the vicinity of Seattle. Auk 32:459–465.

RHOADS, S. N. 1893. The birds observed in British Columbia and Washington during spring and summer, 1892. Proceedings of the Academy of Natural Sciences Philadelphia 1893 (Part I):21–65.

RODWAY, M. S., J.-P. L. SAVARD, AND H. M. REGEHR. 1991. Habitat use and activity patterns of Marbled Murrelets at inland and at-sea sites in the Queen Charlotte Islands, British Columbia. Technical Report Series No. 122. Canadian Wildlife Service, Pacific and Yukon Region, British Columbia.

RODWAY, M. S., H. R. CARTER, S. G. SEALY, AND R. W. CAMPBELL. 1992. Status of the Marbled Murrelet in British Columbia. Pp. 17–41 in H. R. Carter and M. L. Morrison (eds.), Status and conservation of the Marbled Murrelet in North America. Proceedings of the Western Foundation of Vertebrate Zoology 5.

SEALY, S. G. 1974. Breeding phenology and clutch size in the Marbled Murrelet. Auk 91:10–23.

SEALY, S. G., AND H. R. CARTER. 1984. At-sea distribution and nesting habitat of the Marbled Murrelet in British Columbia: problems in the conservation of a solitarily nesting sea-bird. Pp. 737–756 in J. P. Croxall, P. G. H. Evans, and R. W. Schreiber (eds.), Status and conservation of the world's seabirds. International Council of Bird Preservation Technical Publication Number 2.

SIMONS, T. R. 1980. Discovery of a ground-nesting Marbled Murrelet. Condor 82:1–9.

SOWLS, A. L., A. R. DEGANGE, J. W. NELSON, AND G. S. LESTER. 1980. Catalog of California seabird colonies. United States Department of Interior, Fish and Wildlife Service, Biological Service Program, FWS/OBS-80/37.

SPEICH, S. M., T. R. WAHL, AND D. A. MANUWAL. 1992. The numbers of Marbled Murrelets in Washington marine waters. Pp. 48–60 in H. R. Carter and M. L. Morrison (eds.), Status and conservation of the Marbled Murrelet in North America. Proceedings of the Western Foundation of Vertebrate Zoology 5.

STENZEL, L. E., G. W. PAGE, H. R. CARTER, AND D. G. AINLEY. 1988. Seabird mortality in California as witnessed through 14 years of beached bird censuses. Unpublished report, Point Reyes Bird Observatory, Stinson Beach, CA.

Studies in Avian Biology No. 15:293–300, 1994.

CHANGES IN THE DISTRIBUTION AND ABUNDANCE OF SPOTTED OWLS DURING THE PAST CENTURY

R. J. Gutiérrez

Abstract. The Spotted Owl (*Strix occidentalis*) occurs from southwestern British Columbia, Canada south to Michoacán, México. Approximately 12,127 Spotted Owls are known to exist in the United States. Throughout its entire range one can infer that the species has declined over the past century due to a rapid decline in its habitat, mature and old growth conifer forests. Most habitat loss is due to logging of original forests, but other factors (e.g., urbanization) also have contributed. The inference of decline is supported by observed gaps in the owl's original geographic distribution, trends in habitat loss, declining demographic trends, and differences in owl densities among and between populations. Where owls are found in previously logged forests, those forests almost always contain residual elements of the original forests.

Key Words: *Strix occidentalis*; Spotted Owl; distribution; abundance.

The Spotted Owl (*Strix occidentalis*) is distributed from southern British Columbia, Canada south through the Pacific coast states and the southwestern United States to the highlands of central México (Dunbar et al. 1991; USDI 1992a, 1993; Verner et al. 1992) Because of past decline and expected future decline in habitat, primary (mature and older) forests, both Northern and Mexican Spotted Owls (*S. occidentalis caurina* and *S. occidentalis lucida,* respectively) have been declared threatened subspecies in the United States (USDI 1990, 1993).

In this paper I examine changes in Spotted Owl populations and their habitat north of Mexico during the past century. Since historic surveys are not available, I will use information on current owl distribution, changes in habitat or habitat characteristics, and population trends based on intensive demographic studies to infer how populations have been affected.

METHODS

DISTRIBUTION AND ABUNDANCE

Distribution and abundance of Northern Spotted Owls were estimated using a Geographic Information System (GIS) established by the Northern Spotted Owl recovery team (USDI 1992a). The data supporting the GIS were derived from extensive owl surveys conducted by the U.S. Forest Ser-

vice, Bureau of Land Management, National Park Service, California Department of Fish and Game (CDFG), university researchers, and private timber companies. Although these surveys were not exhaustive they can be used to infer relative differences in distribution and abundance of Northern Spotted Owls within geographic provinces of the Pacific Northwest.

Distribution and abundance of California (*S. o. occidentalis*) and Mexican Spotted Owls were taken from databases maintained by the CDFG (G. Gould, Jr., pers. comm.) and Region 3 (i.e., southwestern United States) of the U.S. Forest Service (K. Fletcher, pers. comm.). The proportion of pairs and of single owls at sites (a location where an owl was detected at least once) in the Sierra Nevada and southwestern United States (Arizona and New Mexico) were estimated from average territory occupancy by pairs and individuals measured at thoroughly surveyed sites.

CHANGES IN HABITAT

Three sources of information were used to assess changes in habitat: 1) U.S. government forest inventory data (loss of habitat characteristics associated with areas of owl use was used to infer changes in owl distribution and abundance); 2) egg records (Western Foundation of Vertebrate Zoology); and 3) distribution of owls within hous-

TABLE 1. DISTRIBUTION AND ABUNDANCE OF NORTHERN SPOTTED OWLS AND THEIR HABITAT IN THE UNITED STATES

Area	Acreage			Number of owls		Federal lands[2]	
	Federal	Nonfederal	Total	Pairs[1]	Singles[1]	Potential habitat	Suitable habitat
CA Cascades	1,042,800	1,449,100	2,491,900	40	23	696,100	73,500
CA Coast	467,700	5,214,400	5,682,100	482	112	279,800	14,200
CA Klamath	4,518,600	1,568,200	6,086,800	589	246	2,316,700	1,075,600
Eastern OR Cascades	1,512,500	710,500	2,223,000	181	39	964,600	410,400
Western OR Cascades	4,532,200	2,149,300	6,681,500	1,081	308	3,177,000	2,113,800
OR Coast	1,385,000	4,408,600	5,793,600	303	77	1,338,000	478,200
OR Klamath	2,120,000	1,893,600	4,013,600	402	74	1,591,400	839,900
Willamette Valley	13,900	2,628,300	2,642,200	4	0	13,900	3,600
Eastern WA Cascades	3,405,200	2,203,600	5,608,800	218	12	1,114,900	697,300
Western WA Cascades	3,762,100	2,445,700	6,207,800	290	45	1,435,500	1,403,400
Olympic Peninsula	1,530,300	1,500,200	3,030,500	157	40	449,400	507,700
Western WA Lowlands	86,000	6,394,900	6,480,900	6	4	65,900	0
Total	24,376,300	32,566,400	56,942,700	3,753	980	13,443,200	7,608,800

[1] Northern Spotted Owls verified between 1986–1991 (1992 data used for State of Oregon, California, Crater Lake National Park lands, and Western Washington Lowlands).
[2] Suitable habitat = current habitat potentially used by nesting, roosting, or foraging owls; potential habitat = land that would be capable of producing suitable habitat if trees were allowed to grow to old age (this habitat is currently unsuitable due to logging and other impacts).

ing developments. Sources two and three were used to infer the effects of urbanization on owls.

DEMOGRAPHY

Throughout the range of each subspecies current trends in population dynamics and density of owls have been estimated from data gathered during long-term studies (Gutiérrez and Pritchard 1990, Anderson and Burnham 1992, Noon et al. 1992, Gutiérrez et al. 1993, LaHaye et al. 1992). Age specific estimates of survival and fecundity as well as density estimates have been derived from thousands of observations of color-banded birds. These studies all followed the design outlined in Franklin et al. (1990). Herein, demographic information is used to exemplify recent changes in Spotted Owl populations across its range.

RESULTS

DISTRIBUTION AND ABUNDANCE

The exact numerical decline of Spotted Owls cannot be calculated because the relationship between habitat loss (and habitat fragmentation) and owl desertion or death is unknown. However, it is apparent that

dramatic declines in owl populations have occurred throughout the Pacific Northwest due to habitat loss (Table 1). The majority (56%; 4772 individual birds) of the known Northern Spotted Owl population occurs within only 29% of its range (Table 1, Fig. 1). Spotted Owls also have declined during the past century in British Columbia, Canada primarily as a result of extensive logging and perhaps because of the invasion of Barred Owls (*Strix varia*; Dunbar et al. 1991).

Variation in observed number of owls among geographic provinces can be attributed to differences in completeness of surveys, demographic trends, natural variation in habitat distribution and quality, human caused habitat loss (e.g., logging, water development, urbanization), and natural environmental changes (e.g., fire, volcanic eruptions). However, logging has caused the greatest decline in habitat for all three subspecies (USDI 1992a, 1993; Verner et al. 1992). Declines in primary forest range from 51–100% on federal lands in the Pacific Northwest (Table 1). On private land, primary forest has declined by 95–100% (Table 1, USDI 1992a). The most striking examples have occurred in the Western Washington Lowlands and Oregon Coast Range

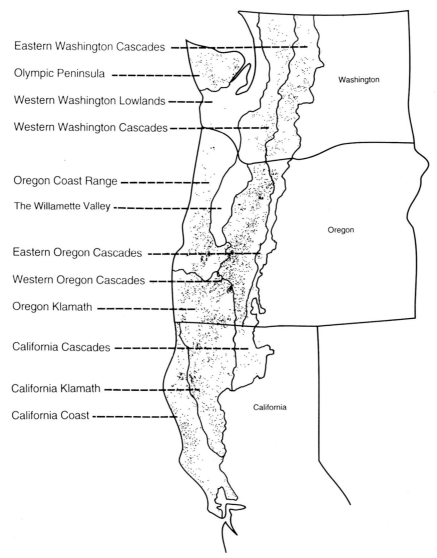

FIGURE 1. Distribution of Northern Spotted Owls by geographic province in the United States. Each dot represents the location of pairs or single owls reported in Table 1.

provinces (Table 1, Fig. 1, USDI 1992a). Only six pairs and four single owls could be found in 1992 on what was once approximately 2,400,000 ha of primary forest in the Western Washington Lowlands Province.

In the Sierra Nevada of California, Spotted Owls are widely distributed on public land, but apparently are not as numerous on private land. There are a minimum of 2452 (1008 pairs and 436 single) owls known

to occur in the Sierra Nevada as of 1992 with approximately 5% occurring on private land (CDFG data base).

In southern California, Spotted Owls are distributed as an archipelago of isolated populations (LaHaye et al. 1994). Approximately 598 individuals are known in 15 populations ranging from 3–270 individuals (CDFG data base; see also LaHaye et al. 1994). Loss of habitat and early resource exploitation in southern California is similar to that of the Sierra Nevada, although not as intensive (McKelvey and Johnston 1992).

Of particular interest is the apparent absence of Spotted Owls from the Santa Cruz Mountains and forests north of Monterey Bay, California. Spotted Owls currently occur in both conifer and hardwood forests within the Santa Lucia Range, south of Monterey Bay. Their absence to the north could be a historic anomaly, a natural extinction event, or a result of the almost complete logging of primary conifer forests in the Santa Cruz Mountains. If logging is responsible owls may recolonize the Santa Cruz Mountains as forests mature.

The Mexican Spotted Owl, the least known of the subspecies, is found throughout forested canyons and conifer regions of the southwest and is known from 725 sites (Fletcher, pers. comm.). I estimated that 579 of these sites would be occupied by pairs and 117 by single owls, based on data from New Mexico and Arizona (Gutiérrez et al. 1993). Most locations are from mixed conifer and pine-oak zones of Arizona and New Mexico with <20% of locations from canyons and riparian forests (Fletcher, pers. comm.).

TRENDS IN HABITAT LOSS

Impacts of logging

Rapid loss of primary forests has occurred since 1960 on public land in the Pacific Northwest (USDI 1990, Table 1). By 1992, suitable habitat remaining on public lands ranged from 0–46% (Table 1). Clearcutting has led not only to habitat loss but also to a high degree of forest fragmentation (Harris 1984). Fragmentation has been shown to be detrimental to Spotted Owls (Bart and Forsman 1992, Carey et al. 1992, Johnson 1992).

McKelvey and Johnston (1992) traced historic trends in forest conditions in the Sierra Nevada which were different than the Pacific Northwest. Sierran forests, although strongly influenced by fire, were a mosaic of stands with different structure (i.e., open

to dense). Areas with diverse forest structure probably formed the core of Spotted Owl habitat in presettlement days.

In the Sierra Nevada it is possible that Spotted Owls could have undergone as many as three periods of decline resulting from the activities of Europeans. First, extensive and intensive livestock grazing in conjunction with human-set fires during the 1800s (McKelvey and Johnston 1992) may have removed much of the habitat for some major owl prey species (e.g., *Neotoma fuscipes*). Next, in the 1870s logging removed many of the basic elements of owl habitat over large areas, potentially rendering them temporarily unsuitable. However, with wildfire control and prevention, ingrowth of conifers and hardwood trees was prevalent both in relict old stands and residual stands (McKelvey and Johnston 1992). This process resulted in the present forest structure that is used by owls (i.e., stands dominated by large, old trees with an uneven diameter distribution of smaller trees forming secondary canopy layers, Verner et al. 1992). Thus, regrowth of the secondary forest beneath the original or remnant stands probably resulted in a recolonization of disturbed areas of the Sierra Nevada. The current trend in removal of key habitat elements (see below) during logging may precipitate another decline in the Sierran owl population (Bias and Gutiérrez 1992, McKelvey and Weatherspoon 1992, Verner et al. 1992).

Many key elements (e.g., nest trees, coarse woody debris) associated with Spotted Owl habitat in the Sierra Nevada were remnants of original forests (Verner et al. 1992). Because of lower intensity logging in the Sierra, these key habitat elements were still widely distributed in 1992 (Verner et al. 1992). However, their removal had dramatic effects on nesting owls in some areas. For example, "sanitation" logging, which removes old trees that often are used as nest sites apparently caused abandonment of an area (e.g., Bias and Gutiérrez 1992). This area was a patchwork of alternating public

(60%) and private (40%) land. Since 1986 20 nests representing 20 different pairs have been found on public land (Gutiérrez et al., unpubl. data) and none on private land where "sanitation" logging was practiced. The probability that none of the nests would be found on private land was extremely low ($P = 0.6^{20} = 0.00004$).

Mexican Spotted Owls primarily use three kinds of habitat: montane conifer (over 80% of the owls are found in this habitat, USDI 1993), riparian, and steep, rocky canyons. Between 6–36% of the owl's conifer habitat has been lost on national forests in Arizona and New Mexico because of logging and other events such as wildfire (Fletcher, pers. comm.). Riparian habitat also has decreased substantially since Bendire (1882) first collected a nesting owl in this habitat type. Canyon habitats probably have not changed as extensively as conifer and riparian habitats.

Two additional sources of information gathered from field studies indicated owl populations have declined in the southwest. First the difference in density between study populations in Arizona and New Mexico (0.106 and 0.172 owls/km^2, respectively; Gutiérrez et al. 1993) may have been the result of more intensive tree cutting in Arizona. Second, within the New Mexico study area, two adjacent canyons of similar size were censused repeatedly and equally during 1991 and 1992; one contained six pairs and one single owl while the other contained three pairs of owls. Approximately half of the canyon with the lower density had been logged in the recent past.

Declines due to urbanization and other factors

Although rarely considered a major impact, urbanization and agriculture have had a significant effect on the distribution and abundance of Spotted Owls. Urban expansion and agricultural development have claimed at least 224,000 and 392,000 ha, respectively, of formerly suitable habitat from south Tacoma to Everett, Washington

since the turn of the century (D. Hays, pers. comm.). No resident owls have been reported in this area in the past decade (D. Hays, pers. comm.). In the San Bernardino Mountains of southern California 6700 ha of dispersed housing (houses and developments scattered throughout otherwise suitable owl habitat) have been surveyed for owls since 1987 (LaHaye and Gutiérrez, unpubl. data). Although the area surrounding the developed forest contained dense and productive owl populations, residential areas did not contain owls. Further, egg and nest records from southern California between 1900 and 1930 indicated Spotted Owls were nesting in relatively low elevation evergreen/riparian forests within canyons. Most of these habitats have been eliminated by urban expansion.

Dispersed housing and suburban development is increasing rapidly in the Sierra Nevada, southern California, and in some areas of the southwest (McKelvey and Weatherspoon 1992). The mid-elevation counties in the Sierra Nevada are among the fastest growing in California (McKelvey and Weatherspoon 1992). Although current impacts are unknown, this development probably is affecting the distribution and abundance of Spotted Owls.

Owls in previously logged forests

Spotted Owls may occur in forests that have been previously logged (Forsman et al. 1977, Forsman 1988), primarily on private lands within the California coast province (Table 1, USDI 1992a). The fact that Spotted Owls occur in forests other than in primary forests has been used as evidence that owls are either adaptable or compatible with timber harvesting (e.g., USDI 1992b). Since they have been observed in a variety of habitats throughout their range (e.g., Forsman et al. 1984, Carey et al. 1992, Verner et al. 1992, USDI 1993), occupation of some previously logged forests does not conflict with the general inference that Spotted Owls are declining where even-aged forest management occurs.

In almost all cases in which Spotted Owls occur in forests with prior logging, these sites contain remnants from the original forests. These forests are heterogeneous in structure and often contain elements similar to natural, unlogged forests (Bart and Earnst 1992). In addition, coastal redwood (*Sequoia sempervirens*) forests can achieve tree size typical of Spotted Owl habitat within 80 years following logging. When these forests also contain an understory of tanoak (*Lithocarpus densiflorus*), they are frequently used. Nevertheless, the ability of these forests to sustain owl populations is unknown.

In assessing possible changes over the past century in previously logged forests, I judge (from early photographs [see McKelvey and Johnston 1992 for examples of Sierra Nevada logging]) that partial logging probably resulted in temporary displacement of Spotted Owls. In order to predict future changes in Spotted Owl populations in recently recolonized areas scientists need to know if future harvest patterns and methods will perpetuate conditions that currently attract owls. If owls are found only in heterogeneous or uneven-aged forests, then clearcutting (a primary method of harvest on private and public land), which results in even-age forests, probably will lead to their extirpation.

Demographic trends

Spotted Owl densities vary from 0.105–0.273 owls/km^2 across the species range (USDI 1992a, Noon et al. 1992, Gutiérrez et al. 1993). The finite rate of annual population change (λ) derived from estimates of fecundity and survival from territorial populations throughout the Pacific Northwest show that all study populations are declining at annual rates of 6–12% (Anderson and Burnham 1992). Forsman et al. (1984) estimated an empirical rate of decline of approximately 1.1% per year based on observations of territorial birds. Forsman et al. (1987:54) also reported a decline in one population of 18–29% over a 10-year period, presumably due to logging. Differences

between empirical and projected rates of decline could be accounted for by bias in the estimates of the vital rates used to calculate λ and/or to the stabilizing effect of floaters on the territorial population (Franklin 1992). Anderson and Burnham (1992) also reported that the rate of decline was accelerating over the period each population was studied. This was related to an increasing rate of adult female mortality, suggesting a changing source of bias if one existed or an accelerating response to continued disturbance. Noon and Biles (1990) demonstrated that adult female survival was the most important parameter affecting estimates of λ for Northern Spotted Owls.

Of the two Spotted Owl populations studied in the Sierra Nevada neither could be demonstrated to be declining (Noon et al. 1992). However, two other populations were declining in southern California. LaHaye et al. (1992) projected an annual decline of 14% in the San Bernardino Mountains, while I (unpubl.) estimated an empirical decline of 16% on Mount San Jacinto. Empirical changes in the San Bernardino population did not show the same rate of decline predicted by estimates of λ (e.g., LaHaye et al. 1992). However, changes in numbers of territorial birds may be buffered by the presence of floaters (nonterritorial birds; see Franklin 1992).

DISCUSSION

SPOTTED OWL POPULATIONS: THE NEXT CENTURY

Documenting the decline of a species is an odious task for an ecologist. However, in the case of the Spotted Owl, there is hope that its populations can be stabilized and will recover in the next century. Both the Northern and Mexican races are listed as threatened, not only because of their current and past population trends but also because of projected declining trends in their habitat (USDI 1990, 1992a, 1993). In fact, the habitat of all three subspecies is expected to decline substantially under projected U.S.

Forest Service (the primary steward of Spotted Owl habitat) harvest scenarios (USDI 1990, 1993; McKelvey and Weatherspoon 1992). However, conservation plans have been developed to arrest the decline of the Northern and Californian races and their habitat (Thomas et al. 1990, USDI 1992a, Verner et al. 1992), and one plan is being developed for the Mexican Spotted Owl. Their implementation is essential for the owl, species that share its habitat, and stable local economies. Because these are only plans formulated on the best available information, they should be considered "conservation hypotheses." Their test, through monitoring population trends, will be stabilization and recovery of Spotted Owl populations.

ACKNOWLEDGMENTS

I thank M. Bias, A. Franklin, W. LaHaye, D. Lutz, C. Moen, D. Olson, and M. Seamans who led the various field studies. R. Holthausen, R. Anthony, E. Starkey, J. Bart, D. Hays, D. Johnson, G. Gould, J. Verner, B. Noon, K. McKelvey, and T. Beck formed the scientific cores of the Northern Spotted Owl Recovery Team and the California Spotted Owl Technical Team; their work greatly aided the development of this paper. P. Carlson and F. Seavey helped compile data. K. Fletcher and G. Gould provided current owl information for the southwest and California, respectively. J. Palmer provided support throughout the study. J. Dunk, A. Franklin, L. George, J. Jehl, N. Johnson, W. LaHaye, K. McKelvey, K. Westcott, and J. Verner reviewed the paper. The following grants supported this research: U.S. Forest Service (PSW-92-0021CA); California Department of Fish and Game (FG1510); Bureau of Land Management (8950-A2-0028); Rocky Mountain Forest and Range Experiment Station (53-82FT-1-04); U.S. Fish and Wildlife Service (RWO14-16-0009-1547 no. 28); and Southern California Edison Corporation. In addition, PSW Research Station, Arcata provided logistic support.

LITERATURE CITED

ANDERSON, D. R., AND K. P. BURNHAM. 1992. Demographic analysis of Northern Spotted Owl populations. Pp. 319–328 *in* Draft Recovery Plan for the Northern Spotted Owl. U.S. Fish and Wildlife Service Regional Office, Portland, OR.

BART, J., AND S. EARNST. 1992. Suitable habitat for Northern Spotted Owls: an update. Pp. 281–317 *in* Draft Recovery Plan for the Northern Spotted Owl. U.S. Fish and Wildlife Service Regional Office, Portland, OR.

BART, J., AND E. D. FORSMAN. 1992. Dependence of Northern Spotted Owls *Strix occidentalis caurina* on old-growth forests. Biological Conservation 62:95–100.

BENDIRE, C. E. 1882. The spotted owl. Ornithologist and Oologist 7:99.

BIAS, M. A., AND R. J. GUTIÉRREZ. 1992. Habitat associations of California Spotted Owls in the central Sierra Nevada. Journal of Wildlife Management 56:584–595.

CAREY, A. B., S. P. HORTON, AND B. L. BISWELL. 1992. Northern spotted owls: influence of prey base and landscape character. Ecological Monographs 62:223–250.

DUNBAR, D. L., B. P. BOOTH, E. D. FORSMAN, A. E. HETHERINGTON, AND D. J. WILSON. 1991. Status of the Spotted Owl, *Strix occidentalis,* and Barred Owl, *Strix varia,* in southwestern British Columbia. Canadian Field-Naturalist 105:464–468.

FORSMAN, E. D. 1988. A survey of Spotted Owls in young forests in the northern Coast Range of Oregon. Murrelet 69:65–68.

FORSMAN, E. D., E. C. MESLOW, AND M. J. STRUB. 1977. Spotted Owl abundance in young versus old-growth forests, Oregon. Wildlife Society Bulletin 5:43–47.

FORSMAN, E. D., E. C. MESLOW, AND H. M. WIGHT. 1984. Distribution and biology of the Spotted Owl in Oregon. Wildlife Monographs 87:1–64.

FORSMAN, E. D., C. R. BRUCE, M. A. WALTER, AND E. C. MESLOW. 1987. A current assessment of the Northern Spotted Owl population in Oregon. Murrelet 68:51–54.

FRANKLIN, A. B. 1992. Population regulation in Northern Spotted Owls: theoretical implications for management. Pp. 815–827 *in* D. R. McCullough and R. H. Barrett (eds.), Wildlife 2001: populations. Elsevier Press, Essex, England.

FRANKLIN, A. B., J. P. WARD, R. J. GUTIÉRREZ, AND G. I. GOULD. 1990. Density of northern Spotted Owls in northwest California. Journal Wildlife Management 54:1–10.

GUTIÉRREZ, R. J., AND J. PRITCHARD. 1990. Distribution, density, and age structure of Spotted Owls on two southern California habitat islands. Condor 92:491–495.

GUTIÉRREZ, R. J., D. R. OLSON, AND M. E. SEAMANS. 1993. Demography of two Mexican Spotted Owl (*Strix occidentalis lucida*) populations in Arizona and New Mexico: Final Report, 1993. Unpubl. Report. Rocky Mountain Forest and Range Experiment Station, U.S. Department of Agriculture, Flagstaff, AZ.

HARRIS, L. D. 1984. The fragmented forest. University of Chicago Press, Chicago, IL.

JOHNSON, D. H. 1992. Spotted Owls, Great Horned Owls, and forest fragmentation in the central Oregon Cascades. MS Thesis, Oregon State Univ., Corvallis, OR.

LAHAYE, W. S., R. J. GUTIÉRREZ, AND D. R. CALL. 1992. Demography of an insular population of Spotted Owls (*Strix occidentalis*). Pp. 803–814 *in* D. R. McCullough and R. H. Barrett (eds.), Wildlife 2001: populations. Elsevier Press, Essex, England.

LAHAYE, W. S., R. J. GUTIÉRREZ, AND H. REŞIT AKÇAKAYA. 1994. Spotted Owl metapopulation dynamics in southern California. Journal of Animal Ecology.

McKELVEY, K. S., AND J. D. JOHNSTON. 1992. Historical perspectives on forests of the Sierra Nevada and the Transverse Ranges of southern California: forest conditions at the turn of the century. Pp. 225–246 *in* J. Verner et al. (tech. coords.), The California Spotted Owl: a technical assessment of its current status. Pacific Southwest Research Station, Forest Service, U.S. Department of Agriculture, Albany, CA.

McKELVEY, K. S., AND C. P. WEATHERSPOON. 1992. Projected trends in owl habitat. Pp. 261–273 *in* J. Verner et al. (tech. coords.), The California Spotted Owl: a technical assessment of its current status. Pacific Southwest Research Station, Forest Service, U.S. Department of Agriculture, Albany, CA.

NOON, B. R., AND C. M. BILES. 1990. Mathematical demography of Spotted Owls in the Pacific Northwest. Journal of Wildlife Management 54:18–27.

NOON, B. R., K. S. McKELVEY, D. W. LUTZ, W. S. LAHAYE, R. J. GUTIÉRREZ, AND C. A. MOEN. 1992. Estimates of demographic parameters and rates of population change. Pp. 175–186 *in* J. Verner et al. (tech. coords.), The California Spotted Owl: a technical assessment of its current status. Pacific Southwest Research Station, Forest Service, U.S. Department of Agriculture, Albany, CA.

THOMAS, J. W., E. D. FORSMAN, J. B. LINT, E. C. MESLOW, B. R. NOON, AND J. VERNER. 1990. A conservation strategy for the Northern Spotted Owl. Interagency Science Committee to address the Conservation of the Northern Spotted Owl, Portland, OR.

USDI. 1990. Endangered and threatened wildlife and plants; determination of threatened status for the Northern Spotted Owl. Federal Register 55:26114–26194.

USDI. 1992a. Draft recovery plan for the Northern Spotted Owl. U.S. Fish and Wildlife Service Regional Office, Portland, OR.

USDI. 1992b. Final environmental assessment for proposed issuance of a permit to allow incidental take of Northern Spotted Owls on the California timberlands of Simpson Timber Company. U.S. Fish and Wildlife Service, Portland, OR.

USDI. 1993. Endangered and threatened wildlife and plants; final rule to list the Mexican Spotted Owl as a threatened species. Federal Register 58:14248–14271.

VERNER, J., K. S. McKELVEY, B. R. NOON, R. J. GUTIÉRREZ, G. I. GOULD JR., AND T. W. BECK. 1992. Assessment of the current status of the California Spotted Owl, with recommendations for management. Pp. 3–26 *in* J. Verner et al. (tech. coords.), The California Spotted Owl: a technical assessment of its current status. Pacific Southwest Research Station, Forest Service, U.S. Department of Agriculture, Albany, CA.

Studies in Avian Biology No. 15:301–315, 1994.

THE COWBIRD'S INVASION OF THE FAR WEST: HISTORY, CAUSES AND CONSEQUENCES EXPERIENCED BY HOST SPECIES

STEPHEN I. ROTHSTEIN

Abstract. No other native bird species has increased in distribution and abundance in the Far West over the last century as much as the Brown-headed Cowbird (*Molothrus ater*). Its remarkable colonizing ability is associated with its brood parasitism, which allows it to commute daily between widely disjunct feeding and breeding sites. Consequently, cowbirds use a wider range of habitats than other birds. When the western invasion began around 1900, the Dwarf Cowbird (*M. a. obscurus*) occurred along the Colorado River and farther east in the Southwest, while the much larger Nevada Cowbird (*M. a. artemisiae*) occurred east of the Sierran-Cascade axis. The former rapidly colonized southern California, the Central Valley and the Bay Region by 1922, eventually reaching western Washington and British Columbia in 1955. The advance northward, at a rate of 20–35 km/yr in California and 70–78 km/yr in Oregon and Washington, was facilitated by anthropogenic habitat changes. As they spread, cowbirds parasitized new host populations some of which declined. Cowbird removal is probably necessary to save the remnants of two taxa, Least Bell's Vireo (*Vireo bellii pusilus*) and Southwestern Willow Flycatcher (*Empidonax traillii extimus*), which would probably have survived coexistence with cowbirds had not most of their riparian habitat also been destroyed. Habitat restoration, not cowbird control, holds the most promise for the long term management of these hosts.

Key Words: Brood parasitism; colonization; cowbird; endangered species; *Molothrus*; range expansion.

Parasitic birds are significant for the basic evolutionary and ecological questions they provoke (Rothstein 1990) and for their potential effect on host species (Mayfield 1977). Among the most well-studied parasitic birds is the Brown-headed Cowbird whose parasitism makes it perhaps the most unpopular native bird in North America. It has often been condemned, e.g., Dawson (1923: 77) referred to the female cowbird as ". . . the unchaste mother of a race gone wrong . . . a blight upon the flower of Progress." whose existence means that "Evolution is at a standstill." No wonder Wheelock (1904: 412) wrote that ". . . Californians are to be congratulated that as yet the Cowbird is only an irregular winter visitant to the southeastern corner of their state." But only 29 years later, cowbirds had become so common that Willett (1933:156) called their increase ". . . remarkable; in fact unparalleled by any other of our native birds." Here I present an overview of the history and causes of the cowbird's colonization of the Far West. I also discuss the consequences experienced by some host taxa that were once abundant but are now imperiled.

GENERAL COWBIRD CHARACTERISTICS THAT ENHANCE COLONIZING ABILITY

Because cowbirds are free of parental duties they do not need to base their daily activities around a particular location, namely a single nest. Thus they can uncouple vital activities such as maintenance and reproduction by carrying them out in disjunct areas. Cowbirds in the Sierra Nevada of California, for example, "commute" up to 6.7 km between large home ranges, where they carry out breeding activities such as courtship and egg laying in the morning while alone or in small groups, and localized sites where large flocks forage in the afternoon (Rothstein et al. 1980, 1984, 1987). Cowbirds prefer and may require areas of short grass or bare ground for foraging (Friedmann 1929) and prefer to forage among large grazing mammals. Sierran feeding sites are anthropogenic, e.g., horse corrals, pastures with livestock, bird feeders, or campgrounds. The commuting behavior seems to be unique: many nonparasitic birds nest and feed in widely separated

TABLE 1. Incidence of Cowbirds (BHCO) and the Next Five Most Commonly Listed Species on Breeding Bird Censuses in Volumes 60–64 of *The Journal of Field Ornithology*. Forest Censuses Are Done Completely within Forests, with Censuses in Mixed Habitats Excluded. Full Names of Bird Species, Represented by Standard Four Letter Codes, Are Given Below[1]

				Year					
	1988		1989		1990		1991		1992
Total censuses:	87		96		98		126		132
Forest censuses:	54.0%		54.2%		58.2%		67.5%		59.1%
BHCO	60.9%	BHCO	62.5%	BHCO	61.2%	BHCO	61.9%	BHCO	56.1%
AMRO	48.3	AMRO	55.2	AMRO	48.0	REVI	56.3	YETH	48.5
NOFL	43.7	REVI	47.9	REVI	48.0	EWPE	50.8	REVI	47.7
YETH	43.7	EWPE	45.8	YETH	48.0	AMRO	50.8	AMRO	47.0
EWPE	40.2	NOFL	44.8	DOWO	46.9	BCCH	46.8	DOWO	41.7
BLJA	39.1	WOTH	44.8	EWPE	46.9	BLJA	46.8	EWPE	40.2
BCCH	39.1			BLJA	46.9	YETH	46.8		
REVI	39.1								
RSTO	39.1								

[1] AMRO: American Robin (*Turdus migratorius*), BCCH: Black-capped Chickadee (*Parus atricapillus*), BHCO: Brown-headed Cowbird (*Molothrus ater*), BLJA: Blue Jay (*Cyanocitta cristata*), DOWO: Downy Woodpecker (*Picoides pubescens*), EWPE: Eastern Wood-pewee (*Contopus virens*), NOFL: Northern Flicker (*Colaptes auratus*), REVI: Red-eyed Vireo (*Vireo olivaceus*), RSTO: Rufous-sided Towhee (*Pipilo erythrophthalmus*), WOTH: Wood Thrush (*Hylocichla mustelina*), YETH: Yellowthroat (*Geothlypis trichas*).

places but they disperse from communal breeding sites to feed at scattered sites; cowbirds by contrast disperse from communal feeding sites to scattered breeding sites (Rothstein et al. 1984).

Most or all cowbird populations show at least some degree of commuting behavior. This uncoupling of breeding and feeding activities enhances colonization in two ways. First, the tendency to fly relatively large distances on a daily basis predisposes cowbirds to disperse large distances. Even without commuting, cowbirds move large distances as their morning breeding ranges (Dufty 1982, Rothstein et al. 1984) alone are 7–68 times larger than the 1–3 ha ranges of passerines of similar body sizes (Schoener 1968).

Second, the uncoupling allows cowbirds to occur in regions with habitats that meet breeding and feeding needs in separate places. Most passerines must meet both of these needs in a single place. Indeed, my tabulations of the 1988–1992 breeding bird surveys (*The Journal of Field Ornithology*, vols. 60–64) done throughout North America show that the percentage of censuses that included cowbirds as breeders was consistently much higher than for any other species (Table 1). This result is especially impressive because most censuses were in forests, where cowbirds are not abundant. The "forest effect" can be seen in the high prevalence in Table 1 of such woodland species as the Eastern Wood-pewee (*Contopus virens*), Red-eyed Vireo (*Vireo olivaceus*), and Wood Thrush (*Hylocichla mustelina*).

Other factors that facilitate colonization are: 1) a propensity to parasitize almost every passerine with which cowbirds are sympatric (Friedmann 1963); 2) high fecundity (females lay 30–40 or more eggs per season; Rothstein et al. 1986) which gives cowbird populations an enormous growth potential; 3) a possible relative lack of defenses in host populations not previously sympatric with a brood parasite (e.g., Briskie et al. 1992).

A HISTORY OF THE COWBIRD'S INCREASE IN WESTERN NORTH AMERICA

Willett's suggestion that the cowbird has increased to a greater extent than any other native bird applies also to all of North America. Before the widespread forest clearing and agriculture brought about by the European colonization, the cowbird's favored foraging conditions of short grassy areas with grazing mammals were widespread only in the Great Plains and the Great

Basin. Cowbirds began a dramatic increase in the heavily forested East in the mid- to late 1700s (Mayfield 1965). That increase has continued into recent years as cowbirds first colonized Newfoundland in 1957 (Baird et al. 1957) and began to breed in Florida in the 1950s (Weston 1965). What is not clear, however, is whether the cowbird is completely new to all of eastern North America as Mayfield (1965) suggested. Even upon their arrival in North America, the first European colonists found some obligate grassland birds such as the Heath Hen (*Tympanuchus cupido cupido*) nesting along the East Coast. Given their daily mobility patterns (above) and tendency to disperse from one population to another (Fleischer and Rothstein 1988), it seems likely that cowbirds were originally found in small numbers in the east.

Because it occurred more recently, the cowbird's increase in the west is better documented. Around 1900, cowbirds were widespread throughout the Great Basin and adjoining parts of Oregon and Washington east of the Cascades. These birds are referable to the "Nevada Cowbird" (*M. a. artemisiae*). In addition, the "Dwarf Cowbird" (*M. a. obscurus*) was common along the Colorado River (Brown 1903, Grinnell 1914) and in the Tucson area (Bendire 1895) and presumably occurred farther east to Texas (Friedmann 1929). Cowbirds bred along the Colorado River as early as the 1860s (Cooper 1974), but even then the lower Colorado River valley was not pristine, as Spaniards brought in livestock in the late 1600s (Rosenberg et al. 1991). This could have enabled the Dwarf Cowbird to colonize the area. The Nevada Cowbird's ancient status in the west is similarly uncertain. Grinnell (1909) argued that it must have been present in the Great Basin for a long period to have evolved its large size and other distinctive features. However, Bishop (1910) described a new subspecies (*M. a. dwighti*), which later proved to be identical to *M. a. artemisiae,* from the northern Great Plains. Thus, the Nevada

Cowbird could have been a recent arrival in the west as Coues (1874) reported that every wagon train passing over the prairies in summer was accompanied by cowbird flocks.

In any case, cowbird abundance in the Great Basin and adjoining areas east of the Cascades has increased greatly since the late 1800s. During extensive travels through the intermountain states in the late 1800s, Bendire (1895) noted cowbirds on "but very few occasions," and Ridgway (Baird et al. 1874) only saw cowbirds twice. Especially instructive are records from eastern Oregon. Bendire (1877) found no cowbirds in Harney County in 1875 and 1876, although he visited localities such as Malheur Lake where they are now abundant (Littlefield 1990). The first Oregon records (Woodcock 1902) were from central and northern Baker County, roughly 160 km northwest of Bendire's area. Other early Oregon records are summarized by Gabrielson and Jewett (1940). Cowbirds became common around Malheur Lake by 1918 (Willett 1919), perhaps aided by an increase in agriculture since the 1870s. A contemporaneous increase appears to have occurred in eastern Washington as Dawson (1909:44) wrote that ". . . the Cowbird is no longer rare east of the Cascades . . . ," and that "the earlier writers make no mention of it . . ." in Washington.

Cowbirds probably did not breed west of the Cascade-Sierra axis or the Colorado River prior to about 1890, except in coastal southwestern British Columbia, where small numbers may have bred sporadically (Kermode 1904, Brooks and Swarth 1925). An 1862 record from San Diego County (Cooper 1874) was early enough in spring to have been a wintering flock. Rothstein et al. (1980) and Laymon (1987a) briefly summarized the cowbird's colonization of California and here I present a more detailed account (summarized in Fig. 1 and Table 2) for the region from California to British Columbia based on all of the original literature, numerous museum specimens, *Audubon Field Notes* (1947–1965) and compilations of host use

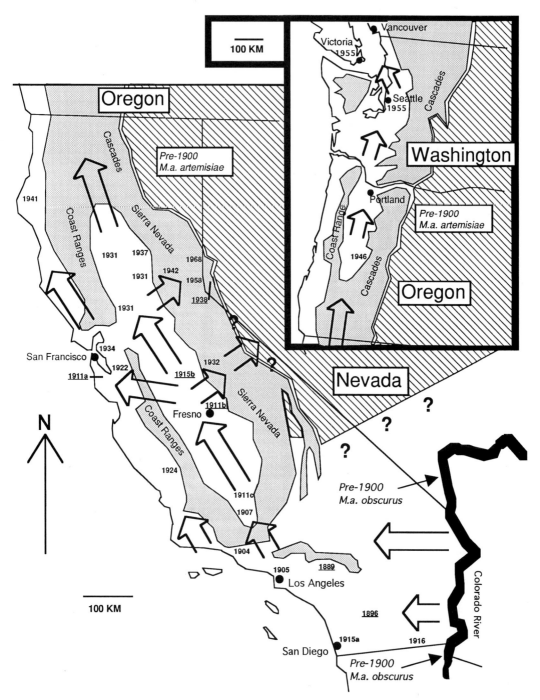

FIGURE 1.　The pre-1900 distribution of *Molothrus ater artemisiae* and *M. a. obscurus,* and the subsequent spread of the latter throughout most of California and the Pacific Northwest. Shaded areas represent major mountain ranges. Question marks reflect uncertainty about the range of *artemisiae* in southern Nevada and the Eastern Sierra before 1900. Large arrows show likely movement patterns of *obscurus* and indicate the first dates that it reached various locations, most of which are mentioned in the text. Underlined years represent records that may not reflect the arrival of the advancing wave of *obscurus* because of uncertain reliability, a lack of evidence of breeding or a clear indication that a case reflects an isolated breeding episode. The locality and reference for each year are listed in Appendix I.

by H. Friedmann and his colleagues. Data from the latter are cited as "Friedmann compilations" (contact me for exact citations) unless given in major summaries (Friedmann 1963, Friedmann et al. 1977, Friedmann and Kiff 1985).

The earliest indication of breeding west of the Colorado River is Wall's (1919:209) vague reference to a cowbird egg found ". . . somewhere about thirty years ago . . ." in San Bernardino County, prompted by Hanna's (1918) claim to have found the first local breeding records in 1918. Thus cowbirds may have bred sporadically in southern California before their large scale colonization began around 1900. Similarly, two specimens collected on 30 April, 1896, at Borrego Springs, San Diego County (Unitt 1984) may have been breeders. The first wholly reliable breeding records are of single parasitized nests from Santa Paula, Ventura County, in 1904 and Los Angeles in 1905 (Willett 1912). By 1912, Willett (1912) called cowbirds "fairly common" in the lowland willow regions of Los Angeles County, but the first breeding adult was not collected until 1915 (Miller 1915). These and other records (see Willett 1933), indicate that cowbirds occurred locally in coastal California from Santa Barbara County south by 1915, although some areas were not colonized until later, e.g., Buena Park, Orange County in 1923. Rowley (1930) noted that cowbirds went from uncommon to abundant between 1920 and 1926 along the San Gabriel River and nearby areas, and Willett (1933) wrote that they were "well established" throughout southern California west of the deserts.

Cowbirds reached the southern end of the Central Valley by 1907, when Linton (1908) found their eggs in Bell's Vireo (*Vireo bellii*) nests at Buena Vista Lake. Four years later, cowbirds were common near Bakersfield, 35 km to the northeast (Swarth 1911) and one was seen farther north near Fresno (Tyler 1913). In 1915, an adult male was collected at Snelling, Merced County (Grinnell and Storer 1924), 300 km north of Buena Vista Lake.

The first records for the Bay Region were assumed to be La Jeunesse's (1923) 1922 discovery of ten cowbird eggs in nests near Irvington, Alameda County. New records for various parts of the Bay Region occurred both north and south of Irvington over the next decade (Sibley 1952), suggesting that this represented a disjunct colonization rather than an advancing wave from southern California. It is possible that this colonization originated from the Central Valley as cowbirds seemed to move northward more rapidly there than along the coast (Fig. 1, Table 2). Even as late as 1935, Miller (1935) referred to Irvington as the cowbird's center of abundance in the Bay Region. Cowbirds were not noted at Berkeley, only 50 km north of Irvington until 1934 (Benson and Russell 1934). Remarkably, the first breeding adult specimens for the Bay Region were not taken until 1934 (Grinnell 1934), despite the presence of locally active collectors from U.C. Berkeley. Curiously, a parasitized Song Sparrow (*Melospiza melodia*) clutch collected in 1911 by M. S. Ray (U.C. Berkeley, MVZ no. 12929) at Palo Alto escaped the notice of these Bay Area ornithologists (e.g., Grinnell and Wythe 1927). This may have been an isolated cowbird intrusion rather than the forerunner of the population La Jeunesse discovered 11 years later. The earliest record between southern California and the Bay Area, and outside of the Central Valley, is a parasitized Song Sparrow clutch taken in 1924 at Paso Robles (MVZ no. 11893).

The first breeding season records for the northern part of the Central Valley are from 1931, when Neff (1931) saw cowbirds at scattered localities in Yuba, Sutter and Glenn counties. Cowbirds were apparently abundant in the area by May 1937, when 99 were trapped at Oroville, Butte County (Behle 1937). Presumably, cowbirds moved rapidly northward through the Valley, which has no obstacles to dispersal and contains widespread agriculture.

Cowbirds were first noted on the west slope of the Sierra Nevada in 1932 (Friedmann compilations) and 1934 (Michael

TABLE 2. THE RATE OF NORTHWARD ADVANCE AS COWBIRDS COLONIZED AREAS WEST OF THE SIERRAN-CASCADE AXIS. DATA PRESENTED ARE THE YEARS AND DISTANCES BETWEEN THE FIRST RECORDS OF COWBIRDS DURING THE BREEDING SEASON (APRIL–JULY) FOR VARIOUS REGIONS. REFERENCES FOR EACH RECORD ARE IN THE TEXT

Site and year for each record (regions)	Years	km	km/yr
Santa Paula to Irvington, 1904–1922 (S. Coastal Calif. to Bay Region)	18	275	25
Irvington to Fernbridge, 1922–1941 (Bay Region to N. Coastal Calif.)	19	383	20
Buena Vista Lk. to Snelling, 1907–1915 (S. to mid Central Valley)	8	270	34
Fernbridge to Eugene, 1941–1946 (NW. Calif. to Oregon)	5	390	78
Eugene to Vancouver Is., 1946–1955 (Oregon to British Columbia)	9	630	70

1935) in Yosemite Valley at an elevation of 1200 m. Gaines (1988) traced their subsequent spread in the Central Sierra and showed that they reached sites as high as 2130 m by 1935. By 1961, they were "numerous" at Tuolumne Meadows at 2620 m. However, abundance may be true only for Sierran areas strongly affected by man as even in the early 1980s cowbirds were rare or absent from West Slope sites 10 km or more from human influence (Verner and Rothstein 1988). Because the colonization of the West Slope progressed from low to high elevations, the birds probably came from the Central Valley.

On the East Slope of the Sierra, parasitism records show cowbirds in Mono County at elevations above 2130 m in the early 1920s (Friedmann 1963). But they apparently largely died out by the late 1920s, as Rowley (1939) saw no adults and found only one parasitized nest from 1926 to 1939. There are additional parasitized nests from Mono County in the 1930s (Friedmann compilations). Extensive field work from 1978 to the present shows that cowbirds are now common at sites Rowley often visited (Rothstein et al. 1980, 1984). Another Eastern Sierran area that has received a relatively large amount of attention is the Tahoe

Basin, where early workers found no cowbirds (Barlow 1901, Ray 1903, Bryant 1928). Orr and Moffitt (1971) give 1959 as the first year of its occurrence although G. McCaskie (pers. comm.) first noted them in 1957. In addition, N. K. Johnson (pers. comm.) noted cowbirds on rare occasions on the Nevada side of Lake Tahoe between 1948 and 1954 and they made occasional forays into the area as early as 1938, when a parasitized MacGillivray's Warbler (*Oporornis tolmiei*) nest was found (Friedmann et al. 1977). Remarkably, cowbirds did not reach the Sage Hen Valley, only 25 km north of Lake Tahoe, until 1968 after about 20 years of observations there (J. M. White, pers. comm.). Today, cowbirds occur commonly all around Lake Tahoe and in the Sage Hen Valley (pers. obs.). Cowbirds occurred nearby along the Truckee River, which drains Lake Tahoe, in the late 1800s (Baird et al. 1874) so it is not clear why it took them so long to become well established in the Tahoe area. Perhaps the dense, widespread forests of the Tahoe region retarded the cowbird's local advance.

The last major region of California to be colonized was the heavily forested northwestern corner. In 1941, Talmadge (1948) found three parasitized nests about 10 km apart in Humboldt County, and later (1947–1948) found parasitism over a much wider area. The next areas to be colonized were west of the Cascades in Oregon, Washington and British Columbia. The first breeding record for western Oregon occurred in 1946 at Eugene (Gullion 1947). In western Washington and in British Columbia, the first confirmed breeding records occurred in 1955 at Seattle and Victoria (Flahaut and Schultz 1955); by 1957, cowbirds had become "numerous" (Schultz 1957) and were still increasing in 1960 (Boggs and Boggs 1960). There are few cowbird references in *Audubon Field Notes* from 1961 to 1965, indicating that cowbirds were then widespread and common in the Pacific Northwest as confirmed by Crowell and Nehls (1971). Today, cowbirds are still common throughout western Oregon and Washington (Alcorn

TABLE 3. MALE COWBIRD WING LENGTHS. DATA FROM NORTHWESTERN NEVADA AND THE COLORADO RIVER INCLUDE NEARLY ALL SPECIMENS FROM GRINNEL (1909 AND 1914). DATA FROM THE SACRAMENTO, SAN JOAQUIN AND IMPERIAL VALLEYS INCLUDE MOST OF THE SPECIMENS CITED IN DICKEY AND VAN ROSSEM (1922) AND BEHLE (1937) AND OTHERS IN VARIOUS MUSEUMS. DATA IN THE LAST FOUR ROWS ARE FROM FLEISCHER AND ROTHSTEIN (1988)

Region, period	Adult		Yearling	
	Mean ± SE	(N)	Mean ± SE	(N)
Northwestern Nevada, 1909[1]	115.4 ± 1.00	(7)	112.3 ± 0.44	(3)
Lower Colorado River, 1910[1]	102.9 ± 0.55	(7)	100.8 ± 0.45	(23)
Sacramento Valley, pre-1940[1]	105.5 ± 0.72	(6)	102.8 ± 0.48	(11)
San Joaquin Valley, pre-1940[1]	105.4 ± 0.57	(15)	102.9 ± 0.56	(11)
Imperial Valley, pre-1940[1]	104.3 ± 0.80	(13)	—	
Western Sierra, 1981	103.7 ± 0.28	(68)	101.7 ± 0.35	(33)
Eastern Sierra—min., 1981–1985[2]	104.4 ± 0.25	(152)	102.3 ± 0.17	(264)
Eastern Sierra—max., 1981–1985[2]	105.9 ± 0.16	(283)	103.7 ± 0.17	(183)
Eastern Sierra, 1912–1922[1]	109.1 ± 0.75	(7)	104.9 ± 1.15	(4)

[1] Data for these samples are from museum specimens measured by me. Data for the remaining samples were collected in the field by my collaborators.
[2] The two Eastern Sierra, 1981–1985 samples are from the sites with the smallest and largest birds (with N's of at least 20 individuals) among five sites along a 90 km north–south transect.

1978) and at least southern coastal British Columbia (Godfrey 1986, pers. obs.). The northward range expansion proceeded at an accelerating pace when it reached Oregon and British Columbia (Table 2), "fueled" perhaps by increasing populations to the south.

WHERE DID THE COLONIZING COWBIRDS COME FROM?

The two western subspecies of the cowbird are well differentiated in areas far from potential contact zones. Grinnell's 1910 *obscurus* sample from the lower Colorado River was 11.5 to 12.5 mm smaller in male wing length than his 1909 type series for *artemisiae* from northwestern Nevada (Table 3). In addition, the rictal flanges of nestling *obscurus* are yellow whereas they are white in *artemisiae* (Rothstein 1978). The cowbirds of southern California are close in size to *obscurus* (Table 3) and have yellow flanges and evidently originated from the Colorado River, the nearest area where this subspecies bred before 1900. A Colorado River origin is also indicated by flight whistle variation. In most of California west of the Sierran crest and north of a line through the Los Angeles Basin this song type (Rothstein et al. 1988) conforms to the "coastal type" of whistle (Rothstein et al. 1986). While coastal flight whistles show dialect variation as regards certain details, they all possess a characteristic final syllable which rises gradually in frequency, then drops suddenly and ends in a brief high frequency sweep (examples in Rothstein et al. 1986, 1988). Cowbirds along the northern part of the lower Colorado River have whistles with this characteristic syllable but it is absent in dialects east of the crests of the Sierra and Cascades (Rothstein and Fleischer 1987; O'Loghlen and Rothstein 1993; SIR unpubl.). Because cowbirds south of the Los Angeles Basin in Orange and San Diego counties do not do coastal whistles, they may be *obscurus* from the southern part of the Lower Colorado River. It is unlikely that cowbirds spread from Baja California as they were found there only as wintering birds in the late 1800s (Bendire 1895).

The cowbirds of northern California west of the Sierran-Cascades axis could be the Colorado River *obscurus* continuing an advance northward, *artemisiae* from the Great Basin, or a mixture of both subspecies. The first of these possibilities is indicated by the occurrence of coastal flight whistles throughout the Central Valley and along the coast at least as far north as the Bay Region (Rothstein et al. 1986). Similarly, the chronology of the colonization suggests that *artemisiae* had little or no role in it as the more northern parts of the state were colonized only after *obscurus* was established in the south (Fig. 1). Furthermore, specimens from the Bay Region, the northern Central Valley and west slope of the Sierra (Table 3; see also Grinnell 1934, Miller 1935, Grinnell and Miller 1944) are close in size to Colorado River *obscurus* and much smaller than *artemisiae*. Similarly, 95% of young cowbirds on the Sierran west slope have yellow flanges, versus 12–28% on the east slope (Fleischer and Rothstein 1988).

The only hint that *artemisiae* colonized areas west of the Sierran crest is Dickey and van Rossem's (1922) report that males from the southern end of the Central Valley were larger than typical *obscurus*. Behle (1937) reported that cowbirds from Oroville, 520 km to the north of Dickey and van Rossem's site, were closer to *obscurus* (wing lengths of 101.2 mm versus 103.5 mm) and suggested that *artemisiae* colonized the extreme southern Central Valley via the Kern River gap. I have located 14 of 15 of Behle's male specimens and 11 of 18 of Dickey and van Rossem's; 79% of the former but only 36% of the latter are yearlings, which could by itself explain the wing length difference because male cowbirds average a 2.7 mm increase in wing length between their yearling and subsequent years (Rothstein et al. 1986). My measurements of known age males from the northern and southern parts of the Central Valley show that wing lengths were virtually identical before 1940 (Table 3) and negate Behle's *artemisiae*-Kern River gap hypothesis.

The most surprising aspect of the wing length data (Table 3) is the similarity between birds from the west slope of the Sierra at Dinkey Creek and from southern California. The former are only 65 km from known populations of *artemisiae*, whereas the latter are 320–500 km away. Analyses of body size, colorimetric characters and mitochondrial DNA (Fleischer and Rothstein 1988, Fleischer et al. 1991) show that

there has been recent and extensive gene flow eastwards across the Sierran crest from *obscurus* to *artemisiae* in the Mammoth Lakes area of Mono County. The wing length data (Table 3) indicate that there has been little or no gene flow in the reverse direction. The trans-Sierran gene flow could not have occurred prior to the 1930s–1940s because there were no cowbirds on the west slope before then. But it has proceeded at such a rapid rate that today's cowbirds from the eastern Sierra are closer in size to *obscurus* from the Central Valley than to eastern Sierran *artemisiae* collected between 1912–1922 (Table 3). A similar shift of cowbird populations from *artemisiae* toward *obscurus* occurred in northern Arizona sometime after 1935 (Phillips 1968) and in north–central Colorado after 1943 (Ortega and Cruz 1992). All of these data indicate that *obscurus* is more vagile or outcompetes *artemisiae* and that the latter is undergoing a general decline in size.

There are too few wing length data available to indicate the origin and subspecies status of the cowbirds that colonized western Oregon, Washington and British Columbia in the 1940s and 1950s, but this area's northern location apparently led workers to assume that the colonizers were *artemisiae* (AOU 1957). However, the timing of critical events (i.e., colonization of the Bay Area of California by 1922, coastal northwestern California by 1941, western Oregon by 1946 and western Washington in 1955) suggests that these birds are *obscurus* continuing their advance up the Pacific Coast.

The characteristics of cowbirds currently breeding west of the Cascades all but confirm that these birds are comprised mostly or exclusively of the *obscurus* stock that originated along the Colorado River. The "coastal" flight whistle that is widespread in California west of the Sierra occurs west of the Cascades in Oregon and Washington (pers. obs.). There are occasional pockets of differently structured flight whistles in this region, but this is also the case in California where this flight whistle type occurs. The coastal form of the flight whistle is unlikely to have come from *artemisiae* populations east of the Cascades because cowbirds there have numerous highly divergent local flight whistle dialects, all different from the coastal type, as in the eastern Sierra (Rothstein and Fleischer 1987). In addition, each of 15 nestling cowbirds from Mandarte Island in southwestern British Columbia had yellow flanges (J. N. M. Smith, pers. comm.), whereas only four of 23 had yellow flanges east of the Cascades in Adams and Grant counties, Washington (E. Stevens, pers. comm.).

Unlike the present birds in the coastal Northwest, those that occasionally occurred there early in this century were probably *artemisiae*, as the nearest *obscurus* were then at least 1000 km to the south. A June 1922 adult male specimen from Clallam County on the Olympic Peninsula (Jewett et al. 1953) (UCLA no. 22-271) has a wing length of 108 mm, which is much closer to the mean size of *artemisiae* than of *obscurus* (Table 3). The small numbers of cowbirds that have occurred regularly during the breeding season in southeastern Alaska since the 1940s (Kessell and Gibson 1978) are probably a westward extension of *artemisiae* because this subspecies ranged that far north in inland Canada even in the 1920s (Friedmann 1929).

WHY DID THE COLONIZATION OCCUR?

The cowbird range extensions in the far west since 1900 are due largely or completely to a very rapid colonization by *obscurus* that originated along the Colorado River around 1900 and reached western Washington and British Columbia, 1600 km to the north, by 1955. It occurred because most anthropogenic changes (except for outright urbanization), improved or created feeding, and to lesser extent breeding habitat, for cowbirds. These changes involve irrigation and agriculture in the Southwest and forest clearing in the Sierra Nevada,

Cascades and the Pacific Northwest. The ever growing suburban areas of the west also provide prime habitat. Even in the inland Northwest, increased agriculture may explain the increase that *artemisiae* underwent in the late 1800s (Dawson 1909).

But human activity does not explain all of this increase. In particular, the Central Valley of California had vast marshes and riparian zones in its pristine state which would have provided numerous hosts (Gaines 1974). It also had extensive grasslands, and the widespread tule elk (*Cervus nannodes*) would have provided a mammalian foraging associate. If cowbirds had long been present along the Colorado River, the dispersal abilities shown since 1900 suggest that they could have colonized the Valley centuries ago. That they did not do so indicates that *obscurus* may be a relative newcomer to the Colorado River. If *artemisiae* is similarly a newcomer to areas between the Sierra-Cascade axis and the Rocky Mountains (above), both subspecies may have colonized areas west of the Great Plains in the last several hundred years, with *artemisiae* coming from the north and *obscurus* from the south. The former possibility is supported by Bendire's (1895) observation that cowbirds were abundant in Saskatchewan and Alberta in 1894 whereas he and others found them to be rare in the late 1800s farther to the south in areas such as the Great Basin and eastern Washington.

IMPACT OF THE COWBIRD'S WESTERN INCREASE ON HOST SPECIES

Given its abundance and fecundity, the cowbird has a potential to lower the recruitment rate of host species. At least 10 songbird species have declined since the cowbird's spread in California and it is often suggested that these declines are due partly or mainly to parasitism (e.g., Gaines 1974, Garrett and Dunn 1981). Below, I discuss two case species (see also Rothstein and Robinson 1994).

Least Bell's Vireo
*(*Vireo bellii pusillus*)*

The Least Bell's Vireo was initially common in riparian woodland primarily in the Central Valley and coastal slopes of southern California. A decline was noticed by 1930 (Grinnell and Miller 1944), and it was extirpated from the Central Valley by the early 1970s (Goldwasser et al. 1980). It was designated as an endangered species by the U.S. Fish and Wildlife Service in 1982 (Franzreb 1989). In 1987, about 440 territorial males remained in the United States in southern California counties from Santa Barbara to San Diego.

The vireo's decline occurred within 20 to 30 years of the cowbird's invasion of California and many of the earliest cowbird records consisted of parasitized vireo nests. Within a decade or two of the cowbird's arrival most nests in southern California seemed to be parasitized (Franzreb 1989). When studies of the remnant vireo populations began in the late 1970s, most had parasitism rates of about 50% (Goldwasser et al. 1980, Franzreb 1989). Because Bell's Vireos that accept cowbird eggs generally raise only a cowbird (Pitelka and Koestner 1942, Mumford 1952), it is obvious that cowbirds can have an enormous effect on vireo recruitment. Vireos may have persisted in Southern California but not in the Central Valley because they begin to breed earlier in the former region thereby enabling many early nests there to escape parasitism.

However, parasitism is not the only factor in the vireo's decline. The Central Valley has lost 95% of its riparian vegetation in this century (Smith 1977) and the loss in southern California's has also been massive. Even where riparian habitat remains, flood control programs may keep it from regenerating seral stages that are optimal for vireos (Rosenberg et al. 1991). Thus, habitat loss is at least as important as cowbird parasitism in the vireo's near extinction. Nevertheless, it is likely that parasitism will cause the current remnant populations to go extinct without human intervention (Laymon 1987a). Removal of cowbirds (Beezely and Rieger 1987) from vireo habitat has greatly increased productivity (Franzreb 1989) and the Least Bell's Vireo is much more numerous now than when its near extinction was first recognized in the late 1970s.

Willow Flycatcher
*(*Empidonax traillii*)*

Although Grinnell and Miller (1944) described the Willow Flycatcher as common in lowland parts of California and sporadic in montane localities up to 2440 m, the entire California population had less than 150 pairs in the mid-1980s (Harris et al. 1987). Unitt (1987) reported that the Southwestern Willow Flycatcher (*E. t. extimus*) was absent from numerous southern California to western Texas sites where it once occurred and suggested that no more than 500 pairs were left. Many early California records of cowbirds were of parasitized Willow Flycatcher nests, so parasitism was a likely factor in this species' decline. But as with Bell's Vireo, both cowbird parasitism and habitat destruction appear to be the major problems.

The California Fish and Game Commission listed the Willow Flycatcher as endangered in 1990. This listing includes *extimus* and the two other subspecies in California, *brewsteri* and *adastus*. The latter two subspecies have also been virtually extirpated from California but may be maintaining reasonable healthy populations farther north from Oregon and British Columbia and east to the Rocky Mountains. Flycatcher populations west of the Cascades in Oregon to British Columbia should be closely monitored. Unlike California, this mesic region has widespread suitable habitat, so if Willow Flycatchers decline there, it may be due largely to cowbird parasitism.

The overall effect of parasitism on the Southwestern Willow Flycatcher is unclear. Cowbirds have been present in the eastern part of this bird's range throughout recorded history and some samples show little parasitism there (data in Unitt 1987, but see also Brown 1988). Although it is likely that both habitat destruction and cowbird parasitism are factors, it is probable that the latter will cause the extirpation of many remnant populations if left unchecked. A cowbird control program was initiated in 1993 along the South Fork of the Kern River where the largest California population of *extimus* experiences about a 50% rate of parasitism (Whitfield 1990). However, a cowbird control program to aid Least Bell's Vireos along the Santa Margarita River in San Diego County may explain an increase from five territorial flycatchers in 1981 to 17 in 1986 (Unitt 1987).

Parasitism at elevations above 1000–1500 m, where the race *brewsteri* still breeds in California, is absent to slight, even where cowbirds occur (Stafford and Valentine 1985, Flett and Sanders 1987). Suitable montane habitat was probably always limited, occurring in patchily distributed moist meadows and streams with stands of willows surrounded by forest or sagebrush. These moist areas are heavily used by range cattle which knock over nests and degrade the habitat by consuming the lower foliage of willows. Limiting cattle grazing is effective in boosting flycatcher productivity (Valentine et al. 1988). Although cowbird parasitism may not now be a major factor in high elevation parts of California, the situation may be different in the Rocky Mountains (Sedgwick and Knopf 1988). Furthermore, cowbird parasitism is the most likely cause of the flycatcher's complete extirpation from Yosemite Valley (Gaines 1988), which is at an intermediate elevation of 1200 m.

A key difference between the vireo and flycatcher is the late breeding of the latter, which usually begins about 1 June and peaks in mid-June even in the warm climate of lowland southern California (Unitt 1987). Although cowbird activity in California begins to decline by late June (Payne 1973), cowbirds show signs of breeding, such as courtship and male-male aggression, until mid- to late July (pers. obs.). This complete overlap in the breeding seasons of the cowbird and flycatcher may explain why the latter has declined even more drastically than the vireo, some of whose early nests escape parasitism.

IS COWBIRD PARASITISM THE PRIMARY REASON FOR THE DECLINE OF ANY WESTERN BIRD SPECIES?

The two hosts profiled above are obligate riparian breeders in much or all of their range, as are most of the other land birds that have declined seriously in the west (De Sante and George 1994, Ohmart 1994). While cowbirds are implicated in some changes, they are not the only factor. The Yellow-billed Cuckoo (*Coccyzus americanus*) has declined to a greater extent than any other riparian species (Laymon 1987b), yet experiences virtually no cowbird parasitism (Friedmann et al. 1977). I suggest that most or all of the cowbird hosts that have declined to near extirpation would have maintained self-sustaining populations had large expanses of riparian habitat remained.

Bell's Vireos (*V. b. arizonae*) experienced heavy parasitism along the Colorado River at least as early as 1900, yet did not decline until the 1950s when dam construction made it worthwhile to convert large riparian tracts to agriculture (Rosenberg et al. 1991). Today, they are virtually gone from this region. Another heavily-used host, the Yellow Warbler (*Dendroica petechia*), also did not begin to decline along the Colorado until the 1950s. Both Bell's Vireos and cowbirds bred in the Owens Valley early in this century and the former's disappearance (Goldwasser et al. 1980) seems wholly due to the loss of riparian habitat. Some of the largest extant populations of the Southwestern Willow Flycatcher occur in the eastern parts of its range, where it has been sympatric with cowbirds longer than in California, but where more riparian habitat remains (Unitt 1987). In addition, these and other riparian species that have declined in the west breed in the east and Midwest, where they have survived cowbird parasitism for at least hundreds of years. The key difference is that in these latter regions mesic habitats are widespread and not limited to watercourses. Although cowbirds may be involved in recent declines of these species in the east and Midwest, which are moderate to slight compared to those in the west, habitat destruction in North America and in the Neotropics may be far more important.

Thus habitat destruction and not cowbird parasitism seems to be the primary cause of host declines in the west. This conclusion does not mean that cowbirds are blameless: it is probably no coincidence that these two species—the only once widespread riparian hosts in California that are virtually extirpated—are ones in which acceptance of a cowbird egg nearly always results in the loss of the host's entire brood. I suggest, however, that if extensive riparian habitat were still widespread, these hosts would be able to survive in the presence of cowbirds. Such habitat needs to be as broad as possible because there is often an edge effect, with cowbird parasitism dropping off towards the interior of densely wooded habitat (Gates and Gysel 1978, Brittingham and Temple 1983). An edge effect may explain why vireos and flycatchers in California and along the Colorado River persisted so long after early workers (Brown 1903, Friedmann compilations) remarked that nearly all of their nests were parasitized. Had this really been the case, these two birds would have been extirpated in only a few years. Perhaps these early rates of nearly 100% parasitism applied mainly to the nests most easily found, i.e., on the edge of dense riparian growth.

Cowbird control programs are needed to sustain the few vireos and flycatchers that remain in California. However, undue emphasis on this open-ended management technique should not deter recovery efforts from concentrating on the more long term but more difficult solution of restoration of riparian habitat.

ACKNOWLEDGMENTS

I thank J. R. Jehl, Jr. and N. K. Johnson for their numerous constructive comments, which greatly improved this paper. Preparation of this manuscript was supported by UCSB Faculty Research and Intercampus Travel Grants. NSF grants BNS 82-16778 and BNS 86-16922 supported the work, much of it done jointly with R. C. Fleischer, on cowbird vocalizations, morphological variation and distribution. Any overview of cowbird biology and host impacts, such as mine, rests on the remarkable foundation of information and insights arising from the nearly 70 years of cowbird research by the late H. Friedmann.

LITERATURE CITED

ALCORN, G. D. 1978. Northwest birds, distribution and eggs. Western Media, Tacoma, WA.

AMERICAN ORNITHOLOGISTS' UNION. 1957. Checklist of North American birds. Fifth ed. American Ornithologists' Union, Baltimore, MD.

BAIRD, S. F., T. M. BREWER, AND R. RIDGWAY. 1874. A history of North American birds. Little, Brown and Company, Boston, MA.

BAIRD, J., R. I. EMERY, AND R. EMERY. 1957. Northeastern Maritime Region. Audubon Field Notes 11: 387–390.

BARLOW, C. 1901. A list of the land birds of the Placerville-Lake Tahoe stage road. Condor 3:151–184.

BEEZLEY, J. A., AND J. P. RIEGER. 1987. Least Bell's Vireo management by cowbird trapping. Western Birds 18:55–61.

BEHLE, W. H. 1937. The cowbirds of the Sacramento Valley, California. Condor 39:227–228.

BENDIRE, C. 1877. Notes on some birds found in southeastern Oregon. Proceedings Boston Society Natural History 19:109–141.

BENDIRE, C. 1895. The cowbirds. Report of the U.S. National Museum for the year ending June 30, 1893, pp. 589–624.

BENSON, S. B., AND W. C. RUSSELL. 1934. The cowbird breeds in Berkeley. Condor 36:219.

BISHOP, L. B. 1910. Two new subspecies of North American birds. Auk 27:59–63.

BOGGS, B., AND E. BOGGS. 1960. Northern Pacific Coast Region. Audubon Field Notes 14:472–474.

BRISKIE, J. V., S. G. SEALY, AND K. A. HOBSON. 1992. Behavioral defenses against avian brood parasitism in sympatric and allopatric host populations. Evolution 46:334–340.

BRITTINGHAM, M. C., AND S. A. TEMPLE. 1983. Have cowbirds caused forest songbirds to decline? BioScience 33:31–35.

BROOKS, A., AND H. S. SWARTH. 1925. A distributional list of the birds of British Columbia. Pacific Coast Avifauna No. 17.

BROWN, B. T. 1988. Breeding ecology of a Willow Flycatcher population in Grand Canyon, Arizona. Western Birds 19:25–33.

BROWN, H. 1903. Arizona bird notes. Auk 20:43–50.

BRYANT, C. A. 1928. Some bird notes from Boca. Gull 10:10–11.

COOPER, J. G. 1874. Animal life of the Cuyamaca Mountains. American Naturalist 8:14–18.

COOPER, J. G. 1974. Ornithology, Volume 1, Land birds. Arno Press, New York, NY.

COUES, E. 1874. Birds of the Northwest: a hand-book of the ornithology of the region drained by the Missouri River and its tributaries. Government Printing Office, Washington, DC.

CROWELL, J. B., JR., AND H. B. NEHLS. 1971. Northern Pacific Coast Region. American Birds 25:787–793.

DAWSON, W. L. 1909. The birds of Washington. Occidental Publishing, Seattle, WA.

DAWSON, W. L. 1923. The birds of California, Vol. 1. South Moulton, Co., San Diego, CA.

DE SANTE, D. F., AND T. L. GEORGE. 1994. Population trends in the landbirds of western North America. Pp. 173–190 *in* J. R. Jehl and N. K. Johnson (eds.), A century of avifaunal change in western North America. Studies in Avian Biology No. 15.

DICKEY, D. R., AND A. J. VAN ROSSEM. 1922. Distribution of *Molothrus ater* in California with the description of a new race. Condor 24:206–210.

DUFTY, A. M., JR. 1982. Movements and activities of radio-tracked Brown-headed Cowbirds. Auk 99:316–327.

FLAHAUT, M. R., AND Z. M. SCULTZ. 1955. Northern Pacific Coast Region. Audubon Field Notes 9:395–397.

FLEISCHER, R. C., AND S. I. ROTHSTEIN. 1988. Known secondary contact and rapid gene flow among subspecies and dialects in the Brown-headed Cowbird. Evolution 42:1146–1158.

FLEISCHER, R. C., S. I. ROTHSTEIN, AND L. S. MILLER. 1991. Mitochondrial DNA variation indicates gene flow across a zone of known secondary contact between two subspecies of the Brown-headed Cowbird. Condor 93:185–189.

FLETT, M. A., AND S. D. SANDERS. 1987. Ecology of a Sierra Nevada population of Willow Flycatchers. Western Birds 18:37–42.

FRANZREB, K. E. 1989. Ecology and conservation of the endangered Least Bell's Vireo. U.S. Fish Wildlife Service, Biological Report 89(1).

FRIEDMANN, H. 1929. The cowbirds, a study in the biology of social parasitism. C. C. Thomas, Springfield, IL.

FRIEDMANN, H. 1963. Host relations of the parasitic cowbirds. US National Museum Bulletin No. 233.

FRIEDMANN, H., AND L. F. KIFF. 1985. The parasitic cowbirds and their hosts. Proceedings Western Foundation Vertebrate Zoology 2:225–304.

FRIEDMANN, H., L. F. KIFF, AND S. I. ROTHSTEIN. 1977. A further contribution to knowledge of the host relations of the parasitic cowbirds. Smithsonian Contributions Zoology No. 235.

GABRIELSON, I. N., AND S. G. JEWETT. 1940. Birds of Oregon. Oregon State College, Corvallis, OR.

GAINES, D. 1974. A new look at the nesting riparian avifauna of the Sacramento Valley, California. Western Birds 5:61–80.

GAINES, D. 1988. Birds of Yosemite and the east slope. Artemisia Press, Lee Vining, CA.

GARRETT, K., AND J. DUNN. 1981. Birds of southern California. Los Angeles Audubon Society, Los Angeles, CA.

GATES, J. E., AND L. W. GYSEL. 1978. Avian nest dispersion and fledging success in field-forest ecotones. Ecology 59:871–883.

GODFREY, W. E. 1986. The birds of Canada. National Museums of Canada, Ottawa.

GOLDWASSER, S., D. GAINES, AND S. R. WILBUR. 1980. The Least Bell's Vireo in California: a de facto endangered race. American Birds 34:742–745.

GRINNELL, J. 1909. A new cowbird of the genus *Mol-*

othrus. University California Publications in Zoology 5:275–281.

GRINNELL, J. 1914. An account of the mammals and birds of the Lower Colorado Valley. University California Publications in Zoology 12:51–294.

GRINNELL, J. 1934. The race of cowbird in the San Francisco Bay region. Condor 36:218–219.

GRINNELL, J., AND A. H. MILLER. 1944. The distribution of the birds of California. Pacific Coast Avifauna No. 27.

GRINNELL, J., AND M. W. WYTHE. 1927. Directory to the bird-life of the San Francisco Bay region. Pacific Coast Avifauna No. 18.

GRINNELL, J., AND T. I. STORER. 1924. Animal life in the Yosemite. University California Press, Berkeley.

GULLION, G. W. 1947. Cowbird young in western Oregon. Condor 64:145.

HANNA, W. C. 1918. First occurrence of the Dwarf Cowbird in the San Bernardino Valley, California. Condor 20:211–212.

HARRIS, J. H., S. D. SAUNDERS, AND M. A. FLETT. 1987. Willow Flycatcher surveys in the Sierra Nevada. Western Birds 18:27–36.

JEWETT, S. G., W. P. TAYLOR, W. T. SHAW, AND J. W. ALDRICH. 1953. Birds of Washington State. University Washington Press, Seattle, WA.

KESSELL, B., AND D. D. GIBSON. 1978. Status and distribution of Alaskan birds. Studies in Avian Biology No. 1.

KERMODE, F. 1904. British Columbia birds. Provincial Museum, Victoria.

LA JEUNESSE, H. V. 1923. Dwarf Cowbird nesting in Alameda County, California. Condor 25:31–32.

LAYMON, S. A. 1987a. Brown-headed Cowbirds in California: historical perspectives and management opportunities in riparian habitats. Western Birds 18:63–70.

LAYMON, S. A. 1987b. Can the western subspecies of the Yellow-billed Cuckoo be saved from extinction? Western Birds 18:19–25.

LINTON, C. B. 1908. Notes from Buena Vista Lake, May 20 to June 16, 1907. Condor 10:196–198.

LITTLEFIELD, C. D. 1990. Birds of Malheur National Wildlife Refuge, Oregon. Oregon State University Press, Corvallis, OR.

MAYFIELD, H. 1965. The Brown-headed Cowbird with old and new hosts. Living Bird 4:13–28.

MAYFIELD, H. 1977. Brown-headed Cowbird: agent of extermination? American Birds 31:107–113.

MICHAEL, C. W. 1935. Cowbirds appear in Yosemite. Condor 37:178.

MILLER, A. H. 1935. Further comments on the cowbirds of the San Francisco Bay region. Condor 37:217–218.

MILLER, L. H. 1915. Dwarf Cowbird in the San Diegan region. Condor 17:165.

MUMFORD, R. 1952. Bell's Vireo in Indiana. Wilson Bulletin 64:224–233.

NEFF, J. A. 1931. Cowbirds in the Sacramento Valley. Condor 33:250–252.

O'LOGHLEN, A. L., AND S. I. ROTHSTEIN. 1993. An extreme example of delayed vocal development: song learning in a population of wild Brown-headed Cowbirds. Animal Behaviour 46:293–304.

OHMART, R. D. 1994. The effects of human-induced

changes on the avifauna of western riparian habitats. Pp. 273–285 *in* J. R. Jehl, Jr. and N. K. Johnson (eds.), A century of avifaunal change in western North America. Studies in Avian Biology No. 15.

ORR, R. T., AND J. MOFFITT. 1971. Birds of the Lake Tahoe region. California Academy of Sciences, San Francisco, CA.

ORTEGA, C. P., AND A. CRUZ. 1992. Gene flow of the *obscurus* race into the north-central Colorado population of Brown-headed Cowbirds. Journal Field Ornithology 63:311–317.

PAYNE, R. B. 1973. The breeding season of a parasitic bird, the Brown-headed Cowbird, in central California. Condor 75:80–99.

PHILLIPS, A. R. 1968. The instability of the distribution of land birds in the Southwest. Pp. 129–162 *in* A. H. Schroeder (ed.), Collected papers in honor of Lyndon Lane Hargrave. Archaeological Society New Mexico, Santa Fe, NM.

PITELKA, F. A., AND E. J. KOESTNER. 1942. Breeding behavior of Bell's Vireo in Illinois. Wilson Bulletin 54:97–106.

RAY, M. S. 1903. A list of the land birds of Lake Valley, Central Sierra Nevada mountains, California. Auk 20:180–193.

ROSENBERG, K. V., R. D. OHMART, W. C. HUNTER, AND B. W. ANDERSON. 1991. Birds of the Lower Colorado River Valley. University Arizona Press, Tucson, AZ.

ROTHSTEIN, S. I. 1978. Geographical variation in the nestling coloration of parasitic cowbirds. Auk 95: 152–160.

ROTHSTEIN, S. I. 1990. A model system for coevolution: avian brood parasitism. Annual Review Ecology and Systematics 21:481–508.

ROTHSTEIN, S. I., AND R. C. FLEISCHER. 1987. Vocal dialects and their possible relation to honest status signalling in the Brown-headed Cowbird. Condor 89: 1–23.

ROTHSTEIN, S. I., AND S. K. ROBINSON. 1994. Conservation and coevolutionary implications of brood parasitism by cowbirds. Trends in Ecology and Evolution 9.

ROTHSTEIN, S. I., J. VERNER, AND E. STEVENS. 1980. Range expansion and diurnal changes in dispersion of the Brown-headed Cowbird in the Sierra Nevada. Auk 97:253–267.

ROTHSTEIN, S. I., J. VERNER, AND E. STEVENS. 1984. Radio-tracking confirms a unique diurnal pattern of spatial occurrence in the parasitic Brown-headed Cowbird. Ecology 65:77–88.

ROTHSTEIN, S. I., J. VERNER, E. STEVENS, AND L. V. RITTER. 1987. Behavioral differences among sex and age classes of the Brown-headed Cowbird and their relation to the efficacy of a control program. Wilson Bulletin 99:322–337.

ROTHSTEIN, S. I., D. A. YOKEL, AND R. C. FLEISCHER. 1986. Social dominance, mating and spacing systems, female fecundity, and vocal dialects in captive and free-ranging Brown-headed Cowbirds. Current Ornithology 3:127–185.

ROTHSTEIN, S. I., D. A. YOKEL, AND R. C. FLEISCHER. 1988. The agonistic and sexual functions of vocalizations of male Brown-headed Cowbirds, *Molothrus ater*. Animal Behaviour 36:73–86.

ROWLEY, J. S. 1930. Observations on the Dwarf Cowbird. Condor 32:130–131.

ROWLEY, J. S. 1939. Breeding birds of Mono County, California. Condor 41:247–254.

SCHOENER, T. W. 1968. Sizes of feeding territories among birds. Ecology 58:636–643.

SCHULTZ, Z. M. 1957. Northern Pacific Coast Region. Audubon Field Notes 11:372–373.

SEDGWICK, J. A., AND F. L. KNOPF. 1988. A high incidence of Brown-headed Cowbird parasitism of Willow Flycatchers. Condor 90:253–256.

SIBLEY, C. G. 1952. The birds of the South San Francisco Bay region. Unpubl. ms in collections of The Western Foundation of Vertebrate Zoology, Camarillo, CA.

SMITH, F. 1977. A short review of the status of riparian forests in California. Pp. 1–2 *in* A. Sands (ed.), Riparian forests in California: their ecology and conservation. Institute Ecology Publications No. 15.

STAFFORD, M. D., AND B. E. VALENTINE. 1985. A preliminary report on the biology of the Willow Flycatcher in the central Sierra Nevada. Cal-Neva Wildlife Transaction 1985:66–77.

SWARTH, H. S. 1911. Field notes from south-central California. Condor 8:160–163.

TALMADGE, R. R. 1948. The cowbird moves northward in California. Condor 50:273–274.

TYLER, J. G. 1913. Some birds of the Fresno District, California. Pacific Coast Avifauna No. 9.

UNITT, P. 1984. The birds of San Diego County. San Diego Society Natural History, San Diego, CA.

UNITT, P. 1987. *Empidonax traillii extimus*: an endangered subspecies. Western Birds 18:137–162.

VALENTINE, B. E., T. A. ROBERTS, S. P. BOLAND, AND A. P. WOODMAN. 1988. Livestock management and productivity of Willow Flycatchers in the central Sierra Nevada. Transactions Western Section Wildlife Society 24:105–114.

VERNER, J., AND S. I. ROTHSTEIN. 1988. Implications of range expansion into the Sierra Nevada by the parasitic Brown-headed Cowbird. Pp. 92–98 *in* D. Bradley (ed.), Proceedings, State of the Sierra Symposium 1985–86. Pacific Publications Co., San Francisco, CA.

WALL, E. 1919. The Wilson Snipe nesting in southern California. Condor 21:207–209.

WHEELOCK, I. G. 1904. Birds of California. A. C. McClury, Chicago, IL.

WHITFIELD, M. J. 1990. Willow Flycatcher reproductive response to Brown-headed Cowbird parasitism. Master's thesis. California State University, Chico, CA.

WESTON, F. M. 1965. A survey of the bird life of northwestern Florida. Bulletin Tall Timbers Research Station 5:1–147.

WILLETT, G. 1912. Birds of the Pacific Slope of Southern California. Pacific Coast Avifauna No. 7.

WILLETT, G. 1933. A revised list of the birds of southwestern California. Pacific Coast Avifauna No. 21.

WILLETT, G. 1919. Bird notes from southeastern Oregon and northeastern California. Condor 21:194–205.

WOODCOCK, A. R. 1902. Annotated list of the birds of Oregon. Bulletin No. 68, Oregon Agricultural Experiment Station, Corvallis, OR.

APPENDIX I.   Localities and references for each year listed in Figure 1. 1889—Colton-San Bernardino area (Wall 1919); 1896—Borrego Springs (Unitt 1984); 1904—Santa Paula and 1905—Los Angeles (Willett 1912); 1907—Buena Vista Lake (Linton 1908); 1911a—Palo Alto (MVZ no.12929); 1911b—Fresno (Tyler 1913); 1911c—Bakersfield (Swarth 1911); 1915a—San Diego (Unitt 1984); 1915b—Snelling (Grinnell and Storer 1924); 1916—Calexico (Friedmann compilations); 1922—Irvington (La Jeunesse 1923); 1924—Paso Robles (MVZ no. 11893); 1931—Yuba, Sutter and Glenn counties (Neff 1931); 1932—Yosemite Valley (Friedmann compilations); 1934—Berkeley (Benson and Russell 1934); 1937—Oroville (Behle 1937); 1938—Lake Tahoe (Friedmann et al. 1977); 1941—Humboldt County (Talmadge 1948); 1942—Nevada City (Friedmann compilations); 1946—Eugene (Gullion 1947); 1955—Seattle and Victoria (Flahaut and Schultz 1955); 1958—Lake Tahoe (G. McCaskie, pers. comm.); 1968—Sage Hen Valley (J. M. White, pers. comm.).

Studies in Avian Biology No. 15:316–327, 1994.

ENDEMIC SONG SPARROWS AND YELLOWTHROATS OF SAN FRANCISCO BAY

Joe T. Marshall and Kent G. Dedrick

Abstract. Three field-identifiable subspecies of the Song Sparrow (*Melospiza melodia*) still occupy remnants of the original 302.7 square miles (784 sq. km) of tidal marsh vegetation in the San Francisco estuary. They are the Alameda Song Sparrow (*M. m. pusillula*), Samuel's Song Sparrow (*M. m. samuelis*), and the Suisun Song Sparrow (*M. m. maxillaris*). Their areas and their numbers are 15.1% of 1850s size due to man-made hindrance to tidal flow. The breeding range of another bay area bird, the San Francisco Common Yellowthroat (*Geothlypis trichas sinuosa*), is undefined. It could be determined by netting molting birds from July through September, before they migrate.

Key Words: Song Sparrow; Common Yellowthroat; San Francisco Bay; tidal marsh; habitat loss; endemic subspecies.

The three subspecies of the Song Sparrow (*Melospiza melodia*) and the three San Francisco Bay estuaries whose tidal marshes they inhabit are among the great, unappreciated, natural wonders of California. They are the Alameda Song Sparrow (*Melospiza melodia pusillula*) in South San Francisco Bay, Samuel's Song Sparrow (*M. m. samuelis*) in San Pablo Bay, and the Suisun Song Sparrow (*M. m. maxillaris*) of Suisun Bay. Field identification characters of the birds and their original distributions of about one hundred square miles (259 sq. km) each are shown in Figure 1. Requirements for the small territory of each pair are met by frontage upon a tidal slough, the banks of which support rich growth of *Grindelia, Salicornia, Spartina foliosa,* or *Scirpus*. By obstructing tidal flow, mankind has reduced this habitat by 84.9 percent to 45.8 mi^2 (118.7 km^2; Table 1). Priceless tidal marshes have become monotonous salt evaporation ponds (hereafter called salt ponds), pastures, cities, factories, and game refuges for fresh-water ducks.

In 1986, S. Gregory advised J. Marshall that fresh water from sewage treatment was eliminating salt marsh plants from the south end of San Francisco Bay, jeopardizing the Alameda Song Sparrow. Marshall found Song Sparrows still at Dumbarton Point, in South San Francisco Bay, that June. In the fall of 1986, when the birds had just acquired their new, distinctive earth colors, L.

R. Mewaldt, J. and E. Marshall, M. Rippey, and R. Leong netted Song Sparrows in all three estuaries, with results detailed below.

Fearing that the Suisun Song Sparrow, *M. m. maxillaris,* was the most vulnerable, we who netted, joined by H. Cogswell, K. Dedrick, S. Gregory, H. T. Harvey, R. F. Johnston, and S. Senner, petitioned the Department of Interior on 20 November 1987 to give *maxillaris* protection under the Endangered Species Act. But federal action was "precluded" because of lack of personnel to evaluate the petition. In the spring of 1990, J. Marshall, R. Johnston, J. Collins, M. Rippey, and S. Hadley joined in slogging and boating through the Suisun marshes so as to present the State with a better population estimate, the subject of this paper. The petition, presented by Mewaldt, was unanimously rejected by the California Fish and Game Commission.

OBJECTIVE

This paper aims to compare present tidal marsh acreage with the original areas in which the San Francisco Bay Song Sparrows lived in the 1850s. The present fragments are not all in the position of former marsh. Some, especially those in Suisun Bay, are accretions to the former shore, due to the heavy sediment load from Sierra Nevada hydraulic mining following the 1849 gold rush.

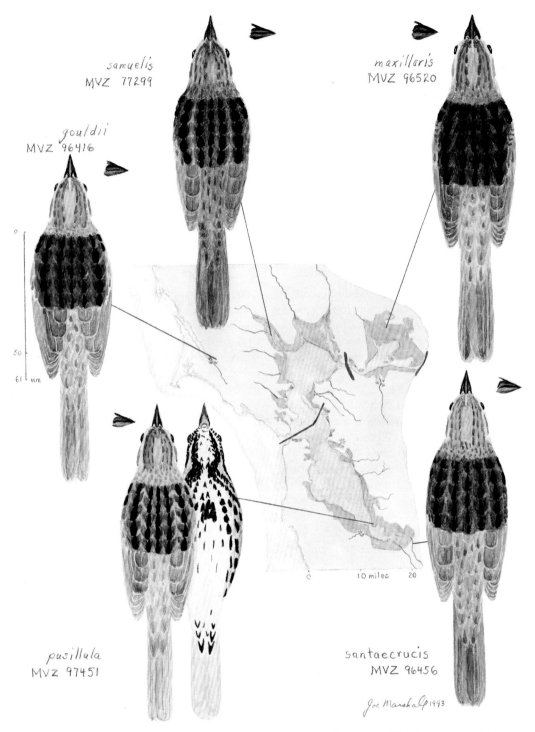

FIGURE 1. Song Sparrow subspecies of the San Francisco Bay. Another, reddish-brown race with blurry streaks, *P. m. rufina* from the northwest coast of North America, winters here.

TABLE 1.   Historic and Present Tidal Marshland Habitat Acreages, San Franciso Bay, California

Song Sparrow subspecies	Historic habitat area:[1] acres (sq. km)	Present habitat area:[2] acres (sq. km)	Per cent of historic habitat
Alameda Song Sparrow (*M. m. pusillula*)	65,811.0 (266.3)	6677.6 (27.0)	10.2%
Samuel's Song Sparrow (*M. m. samuelis*)	63,690.5 (257.8)	14,060.2 (56.9)	22.1%
Suisun Song Sparrow (*M. m. maxillaris*)	64,254.9 (260.0)	8585.7 (34.8)	13.4%
Totals	193,756.4 (784.1)	29,323.5 (118.7)	15.1%

[1] Planimeter results by KGD of map by Nichols and Wright (1971).
[2] Revision by Dedrick (1993) of results by Dedrick (1989).

We can state precisely what percent of former habitat remains for today's sparrows. From there we tackle the murky problem of estimating current populations, in number of pairs or singing males (= territories).

METHODS

Hydraulic mining debris from the Sierra Nevada in the late 1800s poured into the San Francisco estuary, and threatened Bay navigation by shoaling and loss of tidal prism. The marshlands contribute to the tidal prism, and Gilbert (1917) gave us an early breakdown of historic marsh areas for various portions of the Bay. Later, Nichols and Wright (1971) and others independently determined historic acreages (Dedrick 1989). For this paper, we needed detailed acreages for small marsh segments; we thus planimetered the Nichols and Wright map at scale 1/62,500 to obtain the results in Table 1; these areas correspond to the subspecies distributions given in Figure 1.

Recent estimates of Bay marsh acreages vary excessively according to author, for reasons that remain a mystery. Because of this, Dedrick (1989) performed a detailed planimeter study of 1980 aerial photos taken at scale 1/24,000 for the California State Lands Commission. Recently, over 540 individual Bay marsh tracts from the 1989 study have been traced onto USGS quadrangle maps (Dedrick 1993). These results are also used in Table 1 and in Figures 2–4 along with the Nichols and Wright (1971) historical marsh maps. The 540 parcels show how fragmented the marsh has become, with continuity destroyed among groups of Song Sparrow territories.

Population estimates herein for pristine marsh (acres × 1.11 territories per acre) are based on a mapped census of color-banded Song Sparrows on 100 acres (40.5 ha) at Richmond (San Pablo Marsh) by Johnston (1956:255, table 2). The average number of territories during his four years of total counts is 111, with 80% to 90% of the higher marsh unoccupied because it is more than a territory's width from a slough. This density is entirely different from the theoretical maximum, not applicable here, of 9.45 territories per acre (23.4 per ha) if all the sloughs were 30 feet apart and lined with territories 30 by 153.6 feet (9.1 m by 46.8 m) (Johnston 1956:255, table 1). Collins and Resh (1985) studied a similar but much older marsh along the Petaluma River, where they found territory size and territory alignment along sloughs to be the same as Johnston's. Thus, our estimate of original populations is 71,000 pairs of each subspecies, each of which had an original area of 100 mi² (259 km²).

Marshall netted Song Sparrows in fall of 1986 in order to identify subspecies in the hand, then released them. In the 1940s and in spring 1990 he mapped pairs and singing males on Geological Survey topographic sheets, with best results from a kayak, to which the birds were oblivious. Birds hidden because of undercover nesting or foraging duties were called up, if needed, by imitating the song. We inspected habitats from kayak, rowboat, outboard, Baykeeper patrol yacht, airplane, car, and on foot.

Definitions

We mainly use the English system for terrain measurements because it is the standard on all charts, maps, and documents pertaining to the San Francisco Bay and its wildlife (metric in parentheses). Names of triangular-stemmed *Scirpus* from Marshall (1948) are changed: *Scirpus campestris* is now *S. robustus* and *Scirpus olneyi* becomes *S. americanus* (Rice et al. 1982).

Our scientific trinomials apply to field-identifiable subspecies (Marshall 1964) except that for convenience we also recognize the Santa Cruz Song Sparrow (*M. m. santaecrucis,* Grinnell 1901b), easily identified in the hand during banding operations (Fig. 1). The three San Francisco Bay Song Sparrows were defined by their original describers (Baird 1858, Ridgway 1899, Grinnell 1909). Marshall (1948) quantified their colors and measurements, and Allan Brooks (Grinnell and Miller 1944, frontispiece) painted them in realistic side view.

ALEMEDA SONG SPARROW
(*M. m. pusillula*)

Mewaldt and Marshall netted 11 Song Sparrows in fresh fall plumage on 25–26 October 1986 at Dumbarton Point salt marsh. Nine were buffy gray-brown on the back, yellow beneath; two were plainer gray, white beneath. Wing chords averaged 56.2 mm and five weights averaged 18.06 grams. These hand-held birds proved that *M. m. pusillula* still exists in its classic colors and proportions, the smallest and yellowest subspecies in the species.

The marsh of 906.1 acres (366.7 ha) at Dumbarton Point includes luxuriant *Salicornia* with *Grindelia* lining the branchlets of Newark Slough, more of that habitat just southeast of the Refuge Headquarters hill, and a great tract of native *Spartina foliosa* at the shore. Song Sparrows are dense there; we estimated the population as 1006 pairs. We saw excellent tidal habitat at Hoffmann Marsh (30.2 acres = 12.2 ha), beside Albany Hill. At Redwood Point, across the Bay northwest from Dumbarton, are other pristine remnants of *Salicornia* marsh, enriched with *Jaumea, Distichlis,* and *Spartina* at Bird

Island (89.3 acres = 36.1 ha) and Corkscrew Slough (75.2 acres = 30.4 ha). Greco Island (730.6 acres = 295.7 ha) reverted to salt marsh decades ago; since a 1976 levee break, part of Bair Island (475.5 acres = 192.4 ha) is rapidly reverting to marsh.

We also saw the tame Song Sparrows in extensive *Scirpus californicus* and *Typha* at the Alviso Marina and heard two good singers at Emeryville Marina, with no natural habitat. Mewaldt and Marshall banded 11 breeding birds at Triangle Marsh, north of Alviso, on 3 April 1987. The entire Alviso area had been *Salicornia* and *Grindelia* marsh during an earlier study (Marshall 1948). Now 167,000,000 gallons a day of treated fresh water effluent from San Jose-Santa Clara Water Pollution Control Plant (CH2M-HILL 1987) emerges at Artesian Slough, converting Triangle Marsh to brackish-loving *Scirpus robustus*. The Alameda Song Sparrow is adapted to salty intake (Basham and Mewaldt 1987); nevertheless, it remains abundant in Triangle Marsh. Six of our banded birds were buffy gray-brown with yellow belly; five were more grayish on the back, with white or cream underparts. Wings of these seven males and four females averaged 57.1 mm, weights 19.30 g. At Artesian Slough, a band of freshwater *Scirpus californicus* several miles long and 100 yards wide yielded only one Song Sparrow, heard and not seen. Mewaldt and Marshall also examined several hundred yards of *Typha* emanating along a leak of the Hetch-Hetchy Aqueduct at the Tri-City Animal Shelter just off Thornton Road. No Song Sparrows occurred along that freshwater habitat; it connects to a *Salicornia* ditch where *pusillula* is common. For unknown reasons, the upland, brown Song Sparrow of the East Bay and Peninsula hills (*M. m. santaecrucis,* Fig. 1) is not yet invading fresh-water habitats on the bayshore. Were it to do so in numbers, made possible by its huge population relative to the remnants of *pusillula,* it could easily hybridize the Alameda Song Sparrow out of existence.

At Coyote Creek Riparian Station, also near Alviso and 2.2 miles (3.5 km) upstream from the salt marsh, Song Sparrows being banded are the plain brown of East Bay *santaecrucis*. One adult near headquarters, however, had a yellow belly.

Dedrick planimetered 102.8 mi² (266.3 km²) of 1850s habitat and 10.4 mi² (27.0 km²) for the present area of the Alameda Song Sparrow (Fig. 2). Our past and present population estimates are 73,050 and 7412 pairs, respectively.

SAMUEL'S SONG SPARROW
(*M. m. samuelis*)

In 1986 E. Marshall, J. Marshall, M. Rippey, and R. Leong netted Song Sparrows at the north rim of San Pablo Bay: three at Lower Tubbs Island, 28 October 1986; four under and south of the bridge on Skaggs Island Road, 1 November 1986; and nine at Dutchmans Slough off the Napa River on 2 November 1986. These small, blackish-olive birds all typify *M. m. samuelis*, the blackest population of the species. Wings and weights of 15 average 58.2 mm and 18.31 g; 13 bill depths average 6.56 mm.

Birds were established along a stagnant ditch beside Tubbs Island. None of the verdant marsh on Tubbs is inhabited, except for two males singing in *Spartina* by the pond and "plenty of Song Sparrows" along the one little slough, which receives some water through a tide gate. At Dutchman Slough, the birds utilize *Baccharis pilularis* on the levee next to the marsh. Most remaining salt marshes in the range of *samuelis*, even the rims of salt ponds, look good for Song Sparrows. We found none while crossing the ditched *Spartina* bay front of Sears Point Road (2416.5 acres = 977.9 ha). Marshall's field notes at the Museum of Vertebrate Zoology state that in fall 1947 this bay-side habitat along the Sears Point Cutoff was tall *Salicornia* with a fringe of *Spartina*, whose seeds the abundant Samuel's Song Sparrows were eating. At the head of Richardson's Bay, Marin County, is good salt marsh (12.1 acres = 4.90 ha) northeast

of Tamalpais High School, with no Song Sparrows. On 26 June 1987, when this marsh should have been swarming with juvenile *samuelis*, we saw only two singing males, in peripheral weeds; one of them, however, did go out to sing from a *Grindelia*. The largest present home of *samuelis* is the magnificent Petaluma Marsh (3196.2 acres = 12.94 km², upstream from the mouth of San Antonio Creek), with at least 3548 pairs.

The former area of Samuel's Song Sparrow (Fig. 3) was 99.5 mi² (257.7 km²) with 70,696 pairs. Currently 22.0 mi² (56.9 km²) of tidal marsh are available, with 15,607 pairs (optimistic, considering that we could not find the species on the Sears Point Road shore, Solano County).

SUISUN SONG SPARROW
(*M. m. maxillaris*)

On 30 October 1986, M. Rippey and J. Marshall netted five Song Sparrows in the dense population at Pelican Point, near the west end of Roaring River Slough. These birds had chocolate back color, average wing of 60.0 mm, weight 19.10 g, and bill depth of 7.52 mm. Bills flared laterally at nostril level as viewed from above. These attributes typify the isolated subspecies, *M. m. maxillaris*.

The original range of the Suisun Song Sparrow was in brackish marsh from Southampton Bay and Martinez east to Collinsville and Pittsburg (Fig. 4) for a total of 100.4 mi² (260.0 km²) and at least 71,323 pairs. Because the easternmost remnants at Collinsville (7.0 acres = 2.8 ha) and mouth of Montezuma Slough (9.8 acres = 4.0 ha) may be too small and too isolated by fields to support the birds, we draw present limits farther up Montezuma Slough and on Van Sickle Island opposite Pittsburg. Apparently the Song Sparrow is absent from the Delta, where Marshall found none in fall of 1942; in the nesting season M. Josselyn found no Song Sparrows on Lower Sherman Island (pers. comm. to S. Hadley) and J. Collins notes that only a few exist at Browns

(b) Present Marsh

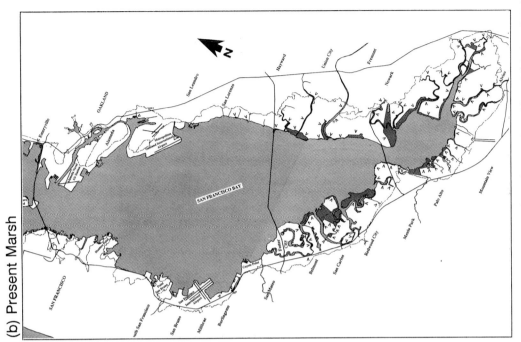

(a) Historical Marsh

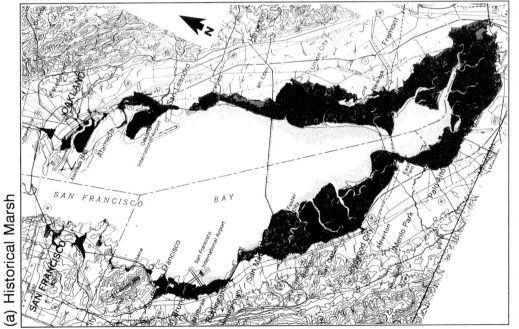

FIGURE 2.   Historical and present tidal marshlands of Southern San Francisco Bay. Historical marsh is darkened area in (a); adapted from Nichols and Wright (1971). Present marsh is shaded area in (b); the apexes of letters "v" point to marsh parcels in Dedrick (1989, 1993).

(b) Present Marsh

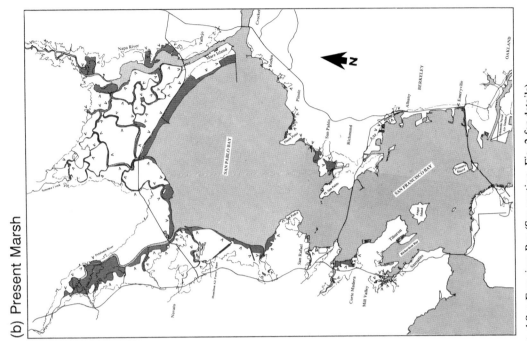

(a) Historical Marsh

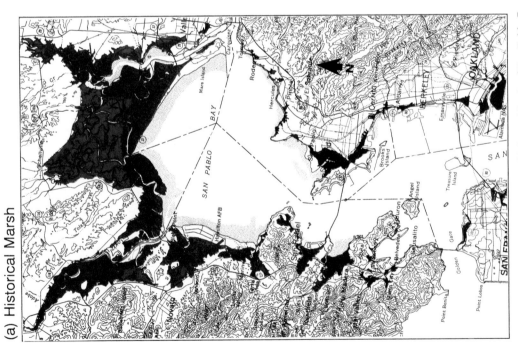

FIGURE 3. Historical and present tidal marshlands of San Pablo Bay and central San Francisco Bay (See caption, Fig. 2 for details).

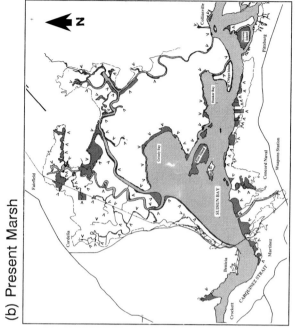

(b) Present Marsh

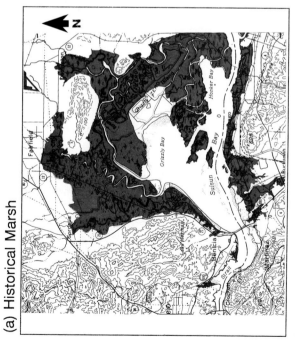

(a) Historical Marsh

FIGURE 4. Historical and present tidal marshlands of Suisun Bay and Carquinez Strait (See caption, Fig. 2 for details).

Island (at its west end, pers. comm.), where fresh-water marsh plants hold sway.

Suisun Marsh is in three separate pieces. First is Southampton Bay, with the richest variety of brackish plant species and densest population of Song Sparrows that Marshall has seen. The unique, isolated genotype is doomed because the marsh is turning fresh and the first Marin Song Sparrow (*M. m. gouldii*) has appeared in Benicia (summer 1992, R. Leong, pers. comm.). Originally 168.6 acres (68.2 ha) and 187 pairs, by 1947 it was 158 acres (63.9 ha) and 176 pairs (Marshall 1948), accessed by way of Spenger's famous houseboat restaurant. In 1990 Marshall and R. Johnston found several birds in *Salicornia, Lepidium,* and a central area of *Salix* and *Typha* springing up due to freshwater runoff from the adjacent suburb. The lower half is still brackish marsh of high quality (M. Rippey, pers. comm.). Therefore the present 134.0 acres (54.2 ha) should support 149 pairs.

The second portion of Suisun Marsh is the South Side, formerly 7768.2 acres (31.4 km²) supporting an estimated 8623 pairs. J. Collins, R. Johnston, and J. Marshall examined Point Edith on 25 May 1990 and in the thick *Baccharis* on the levee of the old shore heard more Song Sparrows singing simultaneously than we could count. There were also birds on large territories in the great arc of *Scirpus robustus* growing into the Bay, a spectacular accretion from the gold rush. Collins studied the South Suisun marshes and its Song Sparrows using sophisticated technology not only in analyzing cores 18 feet deep containing the same plants as present, but in mapping territories by flipping driftwood at each male to press it around its territorial perimeter. He found tightly-packed territories along some *Scirpus acutus* shores. We eagerly await his publication, but for the present estimate the population as 1945 pairs on 1752.0 tidal acres (7.09 km²).

Estimating the present numbers of the Suisun Song Sparrow in its third and major enclave is so complicated by differences in habitat quality that we now realize it would have been best to count every pair rather than to sample. Historic brackish marshes of North Suisun Bay (88.0 mi² = 227.9 km²) present a graded series of habitats from tall *Scirpus acutus* at the bay shore and banks of larger sloughs upward to broad expanses of *Salicornia* with smaller species of *Scirpus* down in the narrowing sloughs and *Grindelia* in a row up on their banks. Such are conditions at the Rush Ranch at the upper reaches of First Mallard Branch. Though it is the best surviving example of a complete marsh, its upper dendrites, where Song Sparrows should be densest, have been ruined by a series of parallel mosquito abatement ditches that bleed the tidal force just as in a human case of shock, where one bleeds to death into one's own capillary bed. The dendrites have become overgrown and filled in. This is offset by marked abundance of Song Sparrows in the devious windings of Spring Branch and in the broad borders of *Scirpus acutus* along First Mallard Branch (99 pairs in 36 acres = 14.6 ha), such that our mapped census of about 154 acres (62 ha) on the Rush Ranch is 159 pairs, nearly the same as San Pablo Marsh. J. Marshall, R. Johnston, and M. Rippey made this census during 12 days from 1 to 28 May 1990 by plotting the birds and keeping track of simultaneous singers day after day so as to divide up territories.

The coterminous Rush Ranch with Second Mallard Branch, 1241.5 acres (502.4 ha), is the largest tidal marsh remaining in North Suisun, with about 1378 pairs. Along with the islands, it is a two-dimensional habitat. The rest of North Suisun habitat is mostly linear, consisting of the rich *Scirpus acutus* fringe of beach and levee. It supports large populations at Nurse, Hastings, Luco, and Hill Sloughs. Marshall's sum of counts in the fringe is 207 pairs in single file along 11.32 miles (18.2 km) of slough border, 18 to the mile.

The linear and two-dimensional tidal populations are not the whole story. The oval, concentrated shape of the marsh en-

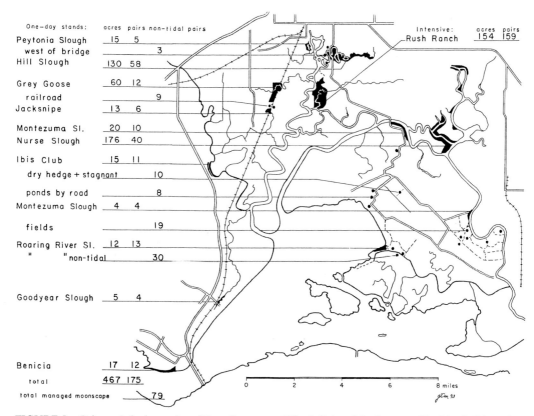

One-day stands:	acres	pairs	non-tidal pairs		Intensive:	acres	pairs
Peytonia Slough	15	5			Rush Ranch	154	159
west of bridge			3				
Hill Slough	130	58					
Grey Goose	60	12					
railroad			9				
Jacksnipe	13	6					
Montezuma Sl.	20	10					
Nurse Slough	176	40					
Ibis Club	15	11					
dry hedge + stagnant			10				
ponds by road			8				
Montezuma Slough	4	4					
fields			19				
Roaring River Sl.	12	13					
" "non-tidal			30				
Goodyear Slough	5	4					
Benicia	17	12					
total	467	175					
total managed moonscape			79				

FIGURE 5.   Pairs and singing males of Song Sparrows of North Suisun Marsh mapped by Marshall in spring 1990 with help in the field from J. Collins, S. Hadley, R. Johnston, J. Richardson, and M. Rippey. Based on Marshall's unbound field notes with sketch maps in Library, Bird Division, Smithsonian Institution. The numbers show that Marshall actually mapped 334 pairs on 9.3% of the tidal marsh, for an estimate of 3603 pairs on the 6699.7 tidal acres plus 200 on the scorched earth of Grizzly Island = 3803 *maxillaris* pairs in North Suisun.

courages dispersing Song Sparrows to spill into the center from dense peripheral populations of the duck clubs and shores. That non-tidal center, mostly dry and behind levees, is Grizzly Island, a moonscape devoted to obscene monocultures (elk, pheasant, and mallard). Here the Song Sparrows swarm in *Baccharis pilularis* and roses on perimeter levees close to a tidal slough, and a few establish on large, dangerously open territories in dry fields that have scattered clumps of unsubmerged tules. J. Richardson heard some in a hedge of giant *Atriplex,* alerting Marshall to find seven territories along 2800 feet (853 m) of hedge in the dry grass back of Fish and Game Headquarters (ditch between E and F in field 13), with surface water only at the two ends. Dots on Figure 5

show where these situations, unusual for the species, were found.

Our tentative count for North Suisun's 6699.7 tidal acres × 1.11 pairs per acre, plus 200 spilled-over, non-tidal territories is 7637 (but see Fig. 5 for a different approach). The total for the subspecies, *M. m. maxillaris* is thus 13.4 mi^2 (34.8 km^2) and 9530 pairs.

SAN FRANCISCO COMMON YELLOWTHROAT
(*Geothlypis trichas sinuosa*)

Much of the habitat of the San Francisco Common Yellowthroat is also lost when tidal flow is blocked. Grinnell (1901a, 1913) distinguished this endemic, partly migratory, west-central California representative of the Common Yellowthroat by its dark colors and small size. Its exact breeding area was never delimited. We offer a suggestion as to how that can be done.

The subspecies *sinuosa* is identified by its dark back and brown flank feathers of fall. Its breeding distribution is mapped from molting birds, because they do not wander or migrate until the fall molt is complete. So, net the birds from July through September and map those dark ones that are obviously molting or that still have sheaths or sheath duff on the auriculars, which are the last feathers replaced.

When museum specimens of the Common Yellowthroat in molt from California are looked at under north light, age and sexual differences disappear, and racial differences are enhanced, if attention is directed only upon the back and flanks. Marshall searched for such examples among all summer and fall California specimens of the Common Yellowthroat in the collections of the California Academy of Sciences, Los Angeles County Museum, Museum of Vertebrate Zoology, San Jose State University, and Smithsonian Institution. He found the following handful of specimens that illuminate our problem. They are so rare in collections that they must be listed. They enable us to begin a sketchy map of fresh fall plumages: dark in scattered localities around the San Francisco Bay; pale in remote, peripheral counties.

The Bay Area group of 14 museum specimens and one live bird are the molting *G. t. sinuosa* with dark back and brown flanks, from just four localities: Museum of Vertebrate Zoology 37787, 37790–37793, collected by Joseph Grinnell from 29 August to 6 September in 1900 and 1901 at the mouth of San Francisquito Creek, Palo Alto; California Academy of Sciences 15016 and 15028 also from Palo Alto, 22 July 1901 and 8 August 1899, and 54808 from Daughters, Alameda County on 18 August 1881; Smithsonian Institution 476255–476260, collected by Tom Burleigh on 14 and 19 August 1960 at Martinez, Contra Costa

County. A live bird netted in *Salicornia* marsh at Dumbarton Point, Alameda County, 25 October 1986, was an immature molting to adult female that was dull, dark olive on back and crown, wing 54 mm.

The remote group of 16 molting specimens from seven counties represents *G. t. occidentalis* (also called *arizela*) with pale back and flanks: Museum of Vertebrate Zoology, 11 July to 23 September and one from 13 October, in various years, Humboldt County (16984, 87652, 87654–87656), Lassen County (44432), Mono County (28651), Lake County (126344), Sacramento County (Courtland, 51649), San Joaquin County (41100, 41103), and Monterey County (31167–31169, 37798, 92389). Thus is *sinuosa* hemmed in on the north, east, and south by pale birds from as close as Lake, Sacramento, and Monterey counties. The color of Point Reyes, Marin County, birds on the west should be determined!

CONCLUSIONS AND RECOMMENDATIONS

Intergradation between Bay Area Song Sparrows of the salt marshes with those in the uplands (Marshall 1948), due to crowding against the Bay by hills with their riparian connections (such as Walnut Creek contacting the marsh at Avon), decrees that the racial traits are diluted in the marshes of Marin and Contra Costa Counties. On the other hand, those marshes sequestered from the hills by broad, grassy plains are archives of the supreme flourishing of the subspecific characteristics. This adds a new dimension to conservation. If future generations are to savor these unique examples of diversity, then we must recognize the importance of subspecies and their exemplary populations: Dumbarton Point (*pusillula*: 906 acres = 366.7 ha) in the San Francisco Bay National Wildlife Refuge, Petaluma Marsh (*samuelis*: 3196 acres = 1293.4 ha) administered by the California Department of Fish and Game, and Rush Ranch (*maxillaris*: 1241.5 acres = 502.4 ha) managed by

Solano County Farmlands and Open Space Foundation. This is simple triage: write off Alviso and Southampton Marshes going fresh, and all the little marshes of intergrades to be wiped out in one marine accident. Add restored acres to the populations at Dumbarton, Petaluma, and Rush Ranch. Rehabilitate Rush Ranch Marsh to full capacity. Secure and conjoin Redwood Point Marshes (Greco Island and Corkscrew Slough) as back-up to pitifully small, strung-out Dumbarton. Enlarge upper Newark Marsh to protect *pusillula* from spills that would destroy the Bay edge; fix the Hetch-Hetchy leak and burn the offending cattails to protect the genotype from *santaecrucis*. Place oil booms to be flung across the mouths of Newark Slough, Sonoma Creek, and Suisun Slough in an emergency.

We have proved a reduction of San Francisco Bay tidal marshes to less than a sixth of former extent, which prompts serious concern about future prospects for their Song Sparrows. We have not even mentioned dangers from Norway rats (*Rattus norvegicus*), red foxes (*Vulpes vulpes*), house cats (*Felis cattus*), toxic spills, and exotic *Phragmites* and eastern *Spartina alterniflora,* because it is so obvious that the main threats are fresh water and levees. The three subspecies of Song Sparrows could be saved merely by knocking down a few levees and filling some mosquito ditches. The timidity and paralysis of those capable of carrying out this simple feat, which could be done with a hand shovel, is beyond belief!

ACKNOWLEDGMENTS

We thank the Coyote Creek Riparian Station, the California Department of Fish and Game's Grizzly Island Headquarters, the San Francisco Bay National Wildlife Refuge, N. Havlik and the Rush Ranch, and the University of California's Department of Entomology for access to natural habitats under their control and for permission to net (and release) representative birds. M. Rippey and S. Hadley (Bay Institute) arranged boat and air travel. The Bay Institute, International Council for Bird Protection, and State Lands Commission donated grants for Marshall's travel and museum research. J. N. Collins, R. F. Johnston, L. R. Mewaldt, and M. Rippey advised us from their profound knowledge of the tidal ecosystem.

LITERATURE CITED

BAIRD, S. F. 1858. Description of a new sparrow collected by Mr. Samuels in California. Proceedings of the Boston Society of Natural History 6:379–380.

BASHAM, M. P., AND L. R. MEWALDT. 1987. Salt water tolerance and the distribution of South San Francisco Bay song sparrows. Condor 89:697–709.

CH2M-HILL. 1987. Informational brochure: San Jose-Santa Clara Water Pollution Control Plant. San Jose, CA.

COLLINS, J. N., AND V. H. RESH. 1985. Utilization of natural and man-made habitats by the salt marsh song sparrow, *Melospiza melodia samuelis* (Baird). California Fish and Game 71:40–52.

DEDRICK, K. G. 1989. San Francisco Bay tidal marshland acreages: recent and historic values. Pp. 383–398 *in* O. T. Magoon et al. (eds.), Proceedings Sixth Symposium Coastal and Ocean Management (Coastal Zone–89). American Society of Civil Engineers, New York, NY.

DEDRICK, K. G. 1993. Atlas of present tidal marshland, San Francisco Bay, California. Pp. 2451–2463 *in,* O. T. Magoon et al. (eds.), Proceedings Eighth Symposium Coastal and Ocean Management (Coastal Zone–93). American Society of Civil Engineers, New York, NY.

GILBERT, G. K. 1917. Hydraulic mining debris in the Sierra Nevada. Professional Paper 105, U.S. Geological Survey, Department of the Interior. Government Printing Office, Washington, DC.

GRINNELL, J. 1901a. The Pacific Coast yellowthroats. Condor 3:65–66.

GRINNELL, J. 1901b. The Santa Cruz song sparrow, with notes on the salt marsh song sparrow. Condor 3:92–93.

GRINNELL, J. 1909. Three new song sparrows from California. University of California Publications in Zoology 5:265–269.

GRINNELL, J. 1913. Note on the palustrine faunas of west-central California. University of California Publications in Zoology 10:191–195.

GRINNELL, J., AND A. H. MILLER. 1944. The distribution of the birds of California. Pacific Coast Avifauna 27:1–608.

JOHNSTON, R. F. 1956. Population structure in salt marsh song sparrows. Condor 58:24–44, 254–272.

MARSHALL, J. T. 1948. Ecologic races of song sparrows in the San Francisco Bay region. Condor 50:193–215, 233–256.

MARSHALL, J. T. 1964. R. W. Dickerman, The song sparrows of the Mexican plateau. Auk 81:448–451.

NICHOLS, D. R., AND N. A. WRIGHT. 1971. Preliminary map of historic margins of marshland, San Francisco Bay, California. U.S. Geological Survey, Open File Map.

RICE, W. E., S. F. SMITH, AND D. C. WASSHAUSEN. 1982. National list of scientific plant names. U.S. Soil Conservation Service, Washington, DC, Vol. 1, 416 pp.; Vol. 2, 438 pp.

RIDGWAY, R. 1899. New species, etc., of American birds.—iii. Fringillidae (continued). Auk 16:35–37.

Studies in Avian Biology No. 15:328–339, 1994.

ENDANGERED SMALL LANDBIRDS OF THE WESTERN UNITED STATES

JONATHAN L. ATWOOD

Abstract. Lists of small western landbirds that have been recognized by federal or state wildlife agencies as endangered, threatened, or of special conservation concern are compared with the results of recent analyses of population trends based on literature surveys, the North American Breeding Bird Survey, and migration counts. There is little concordance between species officially "listed" by wildlife agencies and those determined by professional ornithologists to be showing widespread population declines. In part these differences are explained by limitations in population monitoring techniques. However, the absence from official lists of 27 species that appear to be declining in the western United States suggests an urgent need to improve the current process by which wildlife agencies identify species that warrant special conservation concern.

Key Words: Endangered species; conservation; population trends; wildlife agencies.

At present, seven species or subspecies of small landbirds that occur primarily or entirely in the western United States have been listed as threatened or endangered under the U.S. Endangered Species Act (ESA). Additionally, 16 species, subspecies, or populations of small western landbirds have been identified by the U.S. Fish and Wildlife Service (FWS) as possibly warranting protection under the ESA, or have been formally petitioned for addition to the U.S. List of Endangered and Threatened Wildlife and Plants. One hundred thirty-three species of small landbirds have been listed by the wildlife agencies of at least one of the 17 western states under various categories indicating special conservation concern.

Federal and state lists of endangered or sensitive species may provide some index of declines in western bird populations that have transpired since the early 1900s. More importantly, however, lists of birds that have been or are being considered for legal designation as threatened or endangered classifications may indicate whether or not regulatory protection of bird populations is effectively incorporating current scientific information. In other words, do lists of endangered, threatened, and sensitive bird species compiled by federal and state wildlife agencies accurately reflect known or suspected population declines?

In this paper I identify the small, western landbirds currently included on federal or state lists of endangered or sensitive species, and compare these lists with the results of three recent studies (Sauer and Droege 1992, DeSante and George 1994, Pyle et al. 1994) that assessed regional trends in western bird populations. Finally, I discuss the implications of these comparisons on the listing process currently used by federal and state wildlife agencies.

DEFINITIONS AND METHODS

The following summary is geographically restricted to the United States west of approximately 95° longitude, excluding Alaska and Hawaii. Birds belonging to the orders Columbiformes, Cuculiformes, Caprimulgiformes, Apodiformes, Trogoniformes, Coraciiformes, Piciformes, and Passeriformes are here referred to as "small landbirds."

Species (as defined below) considered to be in danger of extinction throughout all or a significant portion of their range may be classified as "endangered" under the ESA; "threatened" species are those that are "likely to become [endangered] within the foreseeable future." Any of five factors may legally qualify a species for designation as "endangered" or "threatened," including "(a) the present or threatened destruction, modification, or curtailment of its habitat or range; (b) overutilization for commercial, recreational, scientific, or educational purposes; (c) disease or predation; (d) the inadequacy of existing regulatory mechanisms; [and] (e) other natural or manmade factors affecting its current existence." Candidacy lists under the ESA include Category 1 species, defined as taxa for which legal protection appears to be biologically warranted, but which have not yet been formally listed as threatened or endangered, and Category 2 species, for which "conclusive data on biological vulnerability and threat" are currently lacking. Although legal protection is not given to candidate species under the ESA, such species are sometimes afforded special considerations during environmental review and planning, and often are the focus of research aimed at clarifying their current status.

Most western states have also enacted various forms of endangered species legislation. In general, state laws use definitions of the words "threatened" and "endangered" that parallel those given by the ESA. However, terms used to describe declining species or those of potential conservation concern, roughly equivalent to the Category 1 and Category 2 species listed under federal regulations, are highly variable. Because of these pronounced inconsistencies, I combine all of the various categories used by the FWS and the 17 western state wildlife agencies; the limited detailed information that is available concerning definitions used by each state is provided in footnotes to Table 1. I refer to this combined category, which includes taxa that range from being fully protected as endangered to those which are merely listed as being of unknown status or in need of further monitoring, as "species of conservation concern."

The ESA broadly defines the word "species" to include "any subspecies of fish or wildlife or plants, and any distinct population segment of any species of vertebrate, fish, or wildlife which interbreeds when mature." However, the analyses of population trends provided by Sauer and Droege (1992), DeSante and George (1994), and Pyle et al. (1994) did not, in general, refer to taxa below the species level. Consequently, to fa-

cilitate comparison of these two data sets, I use the more traditional, biological definition of "species" in cases where wildlife agencies have described particular subspecies or populations as endangered, threatened, or sensitive. For example, I refer to Song Sparrow (*Melospiza melodia*) as a "species of conservation concern" based on the fact that three subspecies (*maxillaris, samuelis,* and *pusillula*) are listed as Category 2 candidates by the FWS.

RESULTS

One hundred thirty-five species of small, western landbirds are currently indicated as species of conservation concern on lists prepared by the FWS or at least one of 17 state wildlife agencies (Table 1). Seventy-eight (58%) occur either peripherally in the western United States, or as peripheral populations in those states where they appear on official lists of sensitive or threatened species (American Ornithologists' Union 1957). Of the 252 total "listings" (including species, subspecies, and populations) provided among all of the agency lists, 115 (46%) refer to peripheral populations. Three species (Scrub Jay, California Towhee, and Song Sparrow) are included solely by virtue of listed subspecies with highly restricted geographic distributions.

Of the remaining 54 species characterized by relatively widespread distributions in the western United States, population trend information was provided by Sauer and Droege (1992), DeSante and George (1994), or Pyle et al. (1994) for 37 (Table 2). Significant population declines were noted by one of these sources in 22 cases (59%). None of the 54 species exhibited declining population trends that were detected by two or more of the sources. Fourteen (26%) of these 54 species nest primarily in arid woodlands or scrub habitats, 12 (22%) in coniferous forests or oak woodlands, 11 (20%) in riparian habitats, marshes, or streamside areas, 10 (18%) in grassland habitats, and 7 (13%) in miscellaneous habitat types (Table 2).

TABLE 1. SMALL LANDBIRDS CLASSIFIED AS ENDANGERED, THREATENED, OR OF SPECIAL CONSERVATION CONCERN IN THE WESTERN UNITED STATES (EXCLUDING ALASKA AND HAWAII)

Common name[a]	Scientific name	US[b]	WA[c]	OR[d]	CA[e]
Common Ground-Dove	*Columbina passerina*	—	—	—	—
*Black-billed Cuckoo	*Coccyzus erythrophthalmus*	—	—	—	—
Yellow-billed Cuckoo	*Coccyzus americanus*	—	C	C	—
Yellow-billed Cuckoo (Western)	*C. a. occidentalis*	—	—	—	E
Greater Roadrunner	*Geococcyx californianus*	—	—	—	—
Lesser Nighthawk	*Chordeiles acutipennis*	—	—	—	—
Common Nighthawk	*Chordeiles minor*	—	—	—	—
*Common Poorwill	*Phalaenoptilus nuttallii*	—	—	—	—
*Buff-collared Nightjar	*Caprimulgus ridgwayi*	—	—	—	—
*Whip-poor-will	*Caprimulgus vociferus*	—	—	—	—
Black Swift	*Cypseloides niger*	—	M	R	SC
Vaux's Swift	*Chaetura vauxi*	—	C	—	—
*Broad-billed Hummingbird	*Cyanthus latirostris*	—	—	—	—
*White-eared Hummingbird	*Hylocharis leucotis*	—	—	—	—
*Violet-crowned Hummingbird	*Amazilia violiceps*	—	—	—	—
*Lucifer Hummingbird	*Calothorax lucifer*	—	—	—	—
*Costa's Hummingbird	*Calypte costae*	—	—	—	—
*Elegant Trogon	*Trogon elegans*	—	—	—	—
*Belted Kingfisher	*Ceryle alcyon*	—	—	—	—
Lewis' Woodpecker	*Melanerpes lewis*	—	C	C	—
Acorn Woodpecker	*Melanerpes formicivorus*	—	—	U	—
*Gila Woodpecker	*Melanerpes uropygialis*	—	—	—	(E)
*Red-bellied Woodpecker	*Melanerpes carolinus*	—	—	—	—
Williamson's Sapsucker	*Sphyrapicus thyroideus*	—	—	U	—
*Ladder-backed Woodpecker	*Picoides scalaris*	—	—	—	—
*Red-cockaded Woodpecker	*Picoides borealis*	(E)	—	—	—
White-headed Woodpecker	*Picoides albolarvatus*	—	C	C	—
Three-toed Woodpecker	*Picoides tridactylus*	—	M	C	—
Black-backed Woodpecker	*Picoides arcticus*	—	M	C	—
*Northern Flicker (Gilded)	*Colaptes auratus chrysoides*	—	—	—	(E)
Pileated Woodpecker	*Dryocopus pileatus*	—	C	C	—
*N. Beardless-Tyrannulet	*Camptostoma imberbe*	—	—	—	—
*Western Wood-Pewee	*Contopus sordidulus*	—	—	—	—
*Alder Flycatcher	*Empidonax alnorum*	—	—	—	—
Willow Flycatcher	*Empidonax traillii*	—	—	—	E
Willow Flycatcher (Southwestern)	*E. t. extimus*	P	—	—	—
Gray Flycatcher	*Empidonax wrightii*	—	M	—	—
*Buff-breasted Flycatcher	*Empidonax fulvifrons*	(P)	—	—	—
Vermilion Flycatcher	*Pyrocephalus rubinus*	—	—	—	SC
*Ash-throated Flycatcher	*Myiarchus cinerascens*	—	(M)	—	—
Brown-crested Flycatcher	*Myiarchus tyrannulus*	—	—	—	SC
*Tropical Kingbird	*Tyrannus melancholicus*	—	—	—	—
*Thick-billed Kingbird	*Tyrannus crassirostris*	—	—	—	—
*Rose-throated Becard	*Pachyramphus aglaiae*	—	—	—	—
Horned Lark (California)	*Eremophila alpestris actia*	C2	—	—	—
Horned Lark (Streaked)	*E. a. strigata*	—	M	U	—
Purple Martin	*Progne subis*	—	C	C	SC
*Tree Swallow	*Tachycineta bicolor*	—	—	—	—
Bank Swallow	*Riparia riparia*	—	—	U	T
Scrub Jay (Eagle Mtn.)	*Aphelocoma coerulescens cana*	C2	—	—	—
*Black-billed Magpie	*Pica pica*	—	—	—	—
Chihuahuan Raven	*Corvus cryptoleucus*	—	—	—	—
*Black-capped Chickadee	*Parus atricapillus*	—	—	—	(SC)
*Boreal Chickadee	*Parus hudsonicus*	—	(M)	—	—
*Red-breasted Nuthatch	*Sitta canadensis*	—	—	—	—
Pygmy Nuthatch	*Sitta pygmaea*	—	—	V	—
Cactus Wren	*Campylorhynchus brunneicapillus*	—	—	—	—
Cactus Wren (Coastal population)	*C. b. couesi* (in part)	P	—	—	SC
Canyon Wren	*Catherpes mexicanus*	—	—	—	—
*California Gnatcatcher	*Polioptila californica*	—	—	—	(SC)

TABLE 1. EXTENDED

ID[f]	NV[g]	UT[h]	AZ[i]	MT[j]	WY[k]	CO[l]	NM[m]	ND[n]	SD[o]	NE[p]	KS[q]	OK[r]	TX[s]
—	—	—	—	—	—	—	E1	—	—	—	—	—	—
(SCC)	—	—	—	—	—	—	—	—	—	—	—	—	—
SCB	—	T	T	—	—	U	—	(P)	—	—	—	—	—
—	—	—	—	—	—	—	—	—	—	—	—	—	—
—	P	—	—	—	—	—	—	—	—	—	U	—	—
—	P	—	—	—	—	—	—	—	—	—	—	—	—
—	P	—	—	—	—	U	—	—	—	—	—	—	—
—	—	—	—	—	—	—	—	(P)	—	—	—	—	—
—	—	—	—	—	—	—	(E1)	—	—	—	—	—	—
—	—	—	—	—	—	—	—	—	—	—	(SC)	—	—
—	—	—	—	—	—	—	—	—	—	—	—	—	—
—	—	—	—	—	—	—	(E2)	—	—	—	—	—	—
—	—	—	—	—	—	—	(E2)	—	—	—	—	—	—
—	—	—	(C)	—	—	—	(E2)	—	—	—	—	—	—
—	—	—	—	—	—	—	(E2)	—	—	—	—	—	—
—	—	—	—	—	—	—	(E2)	—	—	—	—	—	—
—	—	—	(C)	—	—	—	(E1)	—	—	—	—	—	—
—	—	—	(C)	—	—	—	—	—	—	—	—	—	—
—	—	S12	—	—	—	U	—	—	—	—	—	—	—
—	—	—	—	—	—	—	—	—	—	—	—	—	—
—	—	—	—	—	—	—	(E2)	—	—	—	—	—	—
—	—	S12	—	—	—	—	—	(P)	—	—	—	—	—
—	—	—	—	—	—	—	—	—	—	—	(SC)	—	—
—	—	—	—	—	—	—	—	—	—	—	—	(E)	(E)
SCC	—	—	—	—	—	—	—	—	—	—	—	—	—
SCC	—	S1	—	—	—	—	—	—	—	—	—	—	—
—	—	—	—	—	—	—	—	—	—	—	—	—	—
—	—	—	—	—	—	—	—	—	—	—	—	—	—
—	—	—	—	U	—	—	—	(P)	—	—	—	—	—
—	—	—	—	—	—	—	(E1)	—	—	—	—	—	(T)
—	—	—	—	—	—	—	—	(P)	—	—	—	—	—
—	—	—	—	—	—	—	—	(P)	—	—	—	—	—
—	—	S12	E	—	—	—	—	—	—	—	—	—	—
—	—	—	—	—	—	U	E2	—	—	—	—	—	—
—	—	—	(E)	—	—	—	—	—	—	—	—	—	—
—	—	—	—	—	—	—	—	—	—	—	—	—	—
—	—	—	—	—	—	—	—	—	—	—	—	—	—
—	—	—	(C)	—	—	—	—	—	—	—	—	—	—
—	—	—	(C)	—	—	—	(E1)	—	—	—	—	—	—
—	—	—	(C)	—	—	—	—	—	—	—	—	—	(T)
—	—	—	—	—	—	—	—	—	—	—	—	—	—
—	—	—	—	—	—	—	—	—	—	—	—	—	—
—	—	S2	—	—	—	—	—	—	—	—	—	—	—
—	—	—	—	—	—	—	—	—	—	—	(U)	—	—
—	—	—	—	—	—	—	—	—	—	—	—	—	—
—	—	—	(C)	—	—	—	—	—	—	—	—	—	—
—	—	—	—	—	—	U	—	—	—	—	—	—	—
—	—	—	—	—	—	—	—	—	—	—	—	—	—
—	—	—	—	—	—	—	—	(P)	—	—	—	—	—
SCC	—	—	—	—	—	—	—	—	—	—	—	—	—
—	—	(S2)	—	—	—	—	—	—	—	—	—	—	—
—	—	—	—	—	—	—	—	—	—	—	—	—	—
—	—	—	—	—	—	U	—	—	—	—	—	—	—
—	—	—	—	—	—	—	—	—	—	—	—	—	—

TABLE 1. CONTINUED

Common name[a]	Scientific name	US[b]	WA[c]	OR[d]	CA[e]
California Gnatcatcher (Coastal)	P. c. californica	T	—	—	—
*Black-capped Gnatcatcher	Polioptila nigriceps	—	—	—	—
Eastern Bluebird	Sialia sialis	—	—	—	—
Western Bluebird	Sialia mexicana	—	C	V	—
Mountain Bluebird	Sialia currucoides	—	—	—	—
*Veery	Catharus fuscescens	—	—	—	—
*Wood Thrush	Hylocichla mustelina	—	—	—	—
*Gray Catbird	Dumetella carolinensis	—	—	—	—
*Northern Mockingbird	Mimus polyglottos	—	—	—	—
Sage Thrasher	Oreoscoptes montanus	—	C	—	—
Bendire's Thrasher	Toxostoma bendirei	—	—	—	SC
*Curve-billed Thrasher	Toxostoma curvirostre	—	—	—	—
Crissal Thrasher	Toxostoma crissale	—	—	—	SC
LeConte's Thrasher	Toxostoma lecontei	—	—	—	SC
Sprague's Pipit	Anthus spragueii	—	—	—	—
Loggerhead Shrike	Lanius ludovicianus	C2	C	—	—
Loggerhead Shrike (Migrant)	L. l. migrans	—	—	—	—
Loggerhead Shrike (San Clemente)	L. l. mearnsi	E	—	—	—
Bell's Vireo	Vireo bellii	—	—	—	—
Bell's Vireo (Arizona)	V. b. arizonae	—	—	—	E
Bell's Vireo (Least)	V. b. pusillus	E	—	—	E
Black-capped Vireo	Vireo atricapillus	E	—	—	—
Gray Vireo	Vireo vicinior	—	—	—	SC
*Solitary Vireo	Vireo solitarius	—	—	—	—
*Philadelphia Vireo	Vireo philadelphicus	—	—	—	—
* Blue-winged Warbler	Vermivora pinus	—	—	—	—
*Golden-winged Warbler	Vermivora chrysoptera	—	—	—	—
*Orange-crowned Warbler	Vermivora celata	—	—	—	—
*Virginia's Warbler	Vermivora virginiae	—	—	—	(SC)
*Colima Warbler	Vermivora crissalis	—	—	—	—
*Tropical Parula	Parula pitiayumi nigrilora	(C2)	—	—	—
*Yellow Warbler (Sonora)	Dendroica petechia sonorana	—	—	—	(SC)
*Chestnut-sided Warbler	Dendroica pensylvanica	—	—	—	—
*Yellow-rumped Warbler	Dendroica coronata	—	—	—	—
Black-throated Gray Warbler	Dendroica nigrescens	—	—	—	—
Golden-cheeked Warbler	Dendroica chrysoparia	E	—	—	—
*Yellow-throated Warbler	Dendroica dominica	—	—	—	—
*Prairie Warbler	Dendroica discolor	—	—	—	—
*Cerulean Warbler	Dendroica cerulea	(C2)	—	—	—
*American Redstart	Setophaga ruticilla	—	—	—	—
*Worm-eating Warbler	Helmitheros vermivorus	—	—	—	—
*Northern Waterthrush	Seiurus noveboracensis	—	—	—	—
*Mourning Warbler	Oporornis philadelphia	—	—	—	—
Common Yellowthroat	Geothlypis trichas	—	—	—	—
Common Yellowthroat (Brownsville)	G. t. inseperata	C2	—	—	—
Common Yellowthroat (Saltmarsh)	G. t. sinuosa	C2	—	—	SC
*Hooded Warbler	Wilsonia citrina	—	—	—	—
Yellow-breasted Chat	Icteria virens	—	—	—	SC
*Hepatic Tanager	Piranga flava	—	—	—	(SC)
Summer Tanager	Piranga rubra	—	—	—	SC
*Scarlet Tanager	Piranga olivacea	—	—	—	—
*Western Tanager	Piranga ludoviciana	—	—	—	—
*Northern Cardinal	Cardinalis cardinalis	—	—	—	(SC)
Blue Grosbeak	Guiraca caerulea	—	—	—	—
*Varied Bunting	Passerina versicolor	—	—	—	—
Dickcissel	Spiza americana	—	—	—	—
*Olive Sparrow (Texas)	Arremonops r. rufivirgatus	(C2)	—	—	—
*Green-tailed Towhee	Pipilo chlorurus	—	(C)	—	—
California Towhee (Inyo)	Pipilo crissalis eremophilus	T	—	—	E
*Abert's Towhee	Pipilo aberti	—	—	—	—
*Bachman's Sparrow	Aimophila aestivalis	(C2)	—	—	—

TABLE 1. EXTENDED (CONTINUED)

ID[f]	NV[g]	UT[h]	AZ[i]	MT[j]	WY[k]	CO[l]	NM[m]	ND[n]	SD[o]	NE[p]	KS[q]	OK[r]	TX[s]
—	—	—	—	—	—	—	—	—	—	—	—	—	—
—	—	—	(C)	—	—	—	—	—	—	—	—	—	—
—	—	—	—	(SC)	—	—	—	W	—	—	—	—	—
—	—	S12	—	—	—	—	—	—	—	—	—	—	—
—	—	—	—	—	—	U	—	—	—	—	—	—	—
—	—	—	(T)	—	—	—	—	—	—	—	—	—	—
—	—	—	—	—	—	—	—	(P)	—	—	—	—	—
—	—	—	(T)	—	—	—	—	—	—	—	—	—	—
—	—	—	—	—	—	—	—	(P)	—	—	—	—	—
—	—	—	—	—	—	—	—	—	—	—	U	—	—
—	—	—	—	—	—	—	—	—	—	—	(SC)	—	—
—	—	(S12)	—	—	—	—	—	—	—	—	—	—	—
—	—	—	—	—	—	—	—	—	—	—	—	—	—
—	—	—	C	—	—	—	—	W	—	—	—	—	—
—	—	S1	—	—	—	U	E1	W	—	—	—	—	—
—	—	—	—	—	—	—	—	—	—	—	—	—	SU
—	—	S12	—	—	—	—	E2	(P)	—	—	—	SC	—
—	—	—	—	—	—	—	—	—	—	—	—	—	—
—	—	—	—	—	—	—	—	—	—	—	(E)	(E)	E
—	—	—	—	—	—	—	E2	—	—	—	—	—	—
—	—	—	—	—	—	—	—	(P)	—	—	—	—	—
—	—	—	—	—	—	—	—	(P)	—	—	—	—	—
—	—	—	—	—	—	—	—	—	—	—	(U)	—	—
—	—	—	—	—	—	—	—	(P)	—	—	—	—	—
—	—	—	—	—	—	—	—	(P)	—	—	—	—	—
—	—	—	—	—	—	—	—	—	—	—	—	—	—
—	—	—	—	—	—	—	—	—	—	—	—	—	(S1)
—	—	—	—	—	—	—	—	—	—	—	—	—	(T)
—	—	—	—	—	—	—	—	(P)	—	—	—	—	—
—	—	—	—	—	—	—	—	(P)	—	—	—	—	—
—	—	—	—	—	—	U	—	—	—	—	—	—	—
—	—	—	—	—	—	—	—	—	—	—	—	—	E
—	—	—	—	—	—	—	—	—	—	—	(SC)	—	—
—	—	—	—	—	—	—	—	—	—	—	(U)	—	—
—	—	—	—	—	—	—	—	—	—	—	(SC)	—	(SU)
—	—	—	(T)	—	—	—	—	—	—	—	—	—	—
—	—	—	—	—	—	—	—	—	—	—	(U)	—	—
—	—	—	—	—	—	—	—	(P)	—	—	—	—	—
—	—	—	—	—	—	—	—	(P)	—	—	—	—	—
—	—	S1	—	—	—	—	—	—	—	—	—	—	—
—	—	—	—	—	—	—	—	—	—	—	—	—	SU
—	—	—	—	—	—	—	—	—	—	—	—	—	—
—	—	—	—	—	—	—	—	—	—	—	(U)	—	—
—	—	—	—	—	—	—	—	W	—	—	—	—	—
—	—	—	—	—	—	—	—	—	—	—	—	—	—
—	—	—	—	—	—	—	—	(P)	—	—	—	—	—
—	—	—	—	—	—	—	—	(P)	—	—	—	—	—
—	—	—	—	—	—	—	—	(P)	—	—	—	—	—
—	—	—	—	—	—	U	—	(P)	—	—	—	—	—
—	—	—	—	—	—	—	(E2)	—	—	—	—	—	—
—	—	—	—	SC	—	—	—	—	—	—	—	—	—
—	—	—	—	—	—	—	—	—	—	—	—	—	(SU)
—	—	—	—	—	—	—	—	—	—	—	—	—	—
—	—	—	—	—	—	—	(E2)	—	—	—	—	—	—
—	—	—	—	—	—	—	—	—	—	—	—	—	(T)

TABLE 1. CONTINUED

Common name[a]	Scientific name	US[b]	WA[c]	OR[d]	CA[e]
*Botteri's Sparrow (Texas)	*Aimophila botterii texana*	(C2)	—	—	—
Rufous-cr. Sparrow (S. Calif.)	*Aimophila ruficeps canescens*	C2	—	—	—
*Brewer's Sparrow	*Spizella breweri*	—	—	—	—
Vesper Sparrow (Oregon)	*Pooecetes gramineus affinis*	—	M	—	—
Sage Sparrow	*Amphispiza belli*	—	C	—	—
Sage Sparrow (Bell's)	*A. b. belli*	C2	—	—	—
Sage Sparrow (San Clemente)	*A. b. clementeae*	T	—	—	—
Lark Bunting	*Calamospiza melanocorys*	—	—	—	—
Savannah Sparrow (Belding's)	*Passerculus sandwichensis beldingi*	C2	—	—	E
*Savannah Sparrow (Large-billed)	*P. s. rostratus*	C2	—	—	(SC)
Baird's Sparrow	*Ammodramus bairdii*	C2	—	—	—
Grasshopper Sparrow	*Ammodramus savannarum*	—	M	U	—
*Grasshopper Sparrow (Arizona)	*A. s. ammolegus*	—	—	—	—
*Henslow's Sparrow	*Ammodramus henslowii*	(C2)	—	—	—
*LeConte's Sparrow	*Ammodramus leconteii*	—	—	—	—
*Sharp-tailed Sparrow	*Ammodramus caudacutus*	—	—	—	—
Song Sparrow (Alameda)	*Melospiza melodia pusillula*	C2	—	—	SC
Song Sparrow (San Pablo)	*M. m. samuelis*	C2	—	—	SC
Song Sparrow (Suisun)	*M. m. maxillaris*	C2	—	—	SC
*Swamp Sparrow	*Melospiza georgiana*	—	—	—	—
*White-throated Sparrow	*Zonotrichia albicollis*	—	—	—	—
*Dark-eyed Junco (Gray-headed)	*Junco hyemalis caniceps*	—	—	—	(SC)
*Yellow-eyed Junco	*Junco phaeonotus*	—	—	—	—
McCown's Longspur	*Calcarius mccownii*	—	—	—	—
Bobolink	*Dolichonyx oryzivorus*	—	—	V	—
Tricolored Blackbird	*Agelaius tricolor*	C2	—	(R)	SC
*Hooded Oriole (Mexican)	*Icterus cucullatus cucullatus*	(C2)	—	—	—
*Hooded Oriole (Sennett's)	*I. c. sennettii*	(C2)	—	—	—
*Audubon's Oriole	*Icterus graduacauda audubonii*	(C2)	—	—	—
*Rosy Finch (Black)	*Leucosticte arctoa atrata*	—	—	(R)	—
*Pine Grosbeak	*Pinicola enucleator*	—	—	—	—
*Lesser Goldfinch	*Carduelis psaltria*	—	(M)	—	—

Totals

Endangered or threatened, non-peripheral		7	0	0	7
Miscellaneous categories, non-peripheral		16	17	16	16
Endangered or threatened, peripheral		1	0	0	2
Miscellaneous categories, peripheral		10	4	2	8

[a] Taxa are identified to subspecies only if so indicated on a particular list. Asterisks indicate peripheral taxa (a) distributed primarily in Mexico, Canada, or the eastern United States, or (b) of peripheral occurrence west of 95° longitude in the state(s) in which they are officially listed. Listing designations shown in parentheses indicate populations considered to be peripheral to the taxon's primary area of distribution.

[b] US: United States. E = endangered; T = threatened; P = petitioned; C1 = Category 1; C2 = Category 2—USFWS, Endangered and Threatened Wildlife and Plants (Aug 1992) and 56 FR 58804 (Nov 1991).

[c] WA: Washington. C = candidate species (under review for possible listing as threatened or endangered); M = monitor (limited habitat availability, unresolved taxonomic problems, or unknown population status)—Washington Dept. of Wildlife, Nongame Program, Wildlife Management Division (Summer 1991).

[d] OR: Oregon. C = sensitive species (critical); V = sensitive species (vulnerable); R = sensitive species (peripheral or naturally rare); U = sensitive species (undetermined status)—Oregon Dept. of Fish and Wildlife (Dec 1991).

[e] CA: California. E = endangered; T = threatened; SC = species of special concern—Calif. Dept. Fish and Game (Mar 1990).

[f] ID: Idaho. SCB = species of special concern, Category B (peripheral species); SCC = species of special concern, Category C (undetermined status)—Natural Heritage Section, Nongame and Endangered Wildlife Program, Idaho Dept. of Fish and Game (Aug 1991).

[g] NV: Nevada. P = protected (limited or vulnerable distribution)—Nevada Dept. of Wildlife (date not specified; pers. comm. received Feb 1992).

[h] UT: Utah. T = threatened; S1 = sensitive species (declining population); S2 = sensitive species (limited range or habitat); S12 = sensitive species (declining population and limited range or habitat)—Utah Division of Wildlife Resources (May 1992).

[i] AZ: Arizona. E = endangered; T = threatened; C = candidate—Arizona Game and Fish Dept. (Jul 1988).

[j] MT: Montana. SC = species of special interest or concern; U = additional data needed on status or population trend—Montana Dept. of Fish, Wildlife and Parks (Jan 1991).

[k] WY: Wyoming. No small landbirds listed—Wyoming Game and Fish Dept. (pers. comm., Feb 1992).

[l] CO: Colorado. U = undetermined—Colorado Division of Wildlife (Jan 1992).

[m] NM: New Mexico. E1 = endangered, group 1 (any species or subspecies whose prospects of survival or recruitment are in jeopardy); E2 = endangered, group 2 (any species or subspecies whose prospects of survival or recruitment are likely to be in jeopardy in the foreseeable future)—Endangered Species Program, New Mexico Dept. of Game and Fish (Feb 1992).

[n] ND: North Dakota. T = threatened; P = peripheral (small populations limited by habitat availability); W = watch (declines suspected but unconfirmed)—North Dakota Game and Fish Dept. (Aug 1986).

[o] SD: South Dakota. R = rare—South Dakota Dept. of Wildlife, Parks and Forestry (date not specified; pers. comm. received Feb 1992).

[p] NE: Nebraska. No small landbirds listed—Nebraska Game and Parks Commission (pers. comm. received Mar 1992).

[q] KS: Kansas. E = Endangered; SC = species in need of conservation; U = unclassified (additional data needed)—Investigation and Inventory Office, Kansas Wildlife and Parks (date not specified; pers. comm. received Feb 1992).

TABLE 1. EXTENDED (CONTINUED)

ID[f]	NV[g]	UT[h]	AZ[i]	MT[j]	WY[k]	CO[l]	NM[m]	ND[n]	SD[o]	NE[p]	KS[q]	OK[r]	TX[s]
—	—	—	—	—	—	—	—	—	—	—	—	—	(T)
—	—	—	—	—	—	—	—	(P)	—	—	—	—	—
—	—	—	—	SC	—	—	—	—	—	—	—	—	—
—	—	—	—	—	—	—	—	—	—	—	—	—	—
—	—	—	—	—	—	—	—	—	—	—	—	—	—
—	—	S12	—	—	—	—	—	—	—	—	—	—	—
—	—	—	—	—	—	—	—	—	—	—	—	—	—
—	—	—	T	SC	—	—	(E2)	W	R	—	—	—	SU
—	—	—	—	—	—	—	(E2)	—	—	—	—	—	—
—	—	—	—	—	—	—	—	—	—	—	(SC)	—	(SU)
—	—	—	—	(SC)	—	—	—	(W)	—	—	—	—	—
—	—	—	—	—	—	—	—	(W)	—	—	—	—	—
—	—	—	—	—	—	—	—	—	—	—	—	—	—
—	—	—	—	—	—	—	—	—	—	—	—	—	—
—	—	—	—	—	—	—	—	—	—	—	—	—	—
—	—	—	—	—	—	—	—	(P)	—	—	—	—	—
—	—	—	—	—	—	—	—	(P)	—	—	—	—	—
—	—	—	—	—	—	—	—	—	—	—	—	—	—
—	—	—	—	—	—	—	(E2)	—	—	—	—	—	—
—	—	—	—	—	—	—	—	T	—	—	—	—	—
—	—	S1	(E)	—	—	—	—	—	—	—	SC	—	—
—	—	—	—	—	—	—	—	—	—	—	—	—	—
—	—	—	—	—	—	—	—	—	—	—	—	—	(SU)
—	—	—	—	—	—	—	—	—	—	—	—	—	(SU)
—	—	—	—	—	—	—	—	—	—	—	—	—	(SU)
—	—	—	—	—	—	—	—	—	—	—	—	—	—
—	—	—	(C)	—	—	—	—	—	—	—	—	—	—
—	—	—	—	—	—	—	—	—	—	—	—	—	—
0	0	1	3	0	0	0	5	1	0	0	0	0	2
4	3	11	1	4	0	10	0	5	1	0	3	1	3
0	0	0	5	0	0	0	15	0	0	0	1	2	6
1	0	2	9	2	0	0	0	27	0	0	11	0	7

[r] OK: Oklahoma. E = endangered; SC = species of special concern, Category 2 (data suggests declining population, but inadequate to support listing)—Oklahoma Dept. of Wildlife Conservation, Nongame Section (Sep 1990).
[s] TX: Texas. E = endangered; T = threatened; species of special concern, Rank 1 (critically imperiled in state, extremely rare, very vulnerable to extirpation); SU = species of special concern, uncertain ranking—Texas Parks and Wildlife Dept. (Jan 1992).

Using a conservative interpretation of trends described by Sauer and Droege (1992), DeSante and George (1994), and Pyle et al. (1994), I found that 27 species of small western landbirds that exhibit evidence of population declines are absent from federal or state lists of species of conservation concern (Table 3). Six (Band-tailed Pigeon, Olive-sided Flycatcher, Swainson's Thrush, Wilson's Warbler, Chipping Sparrow, and Black-throated Sparrow) were found to be declining by at least two sources. Thirteen (48%) of these 27 species nest in a variety

of miscellaneous habitats, 6 (22%) in arid woodlands or scrub habitats, 4 (15%) in coniferous forests or oak woodlands, 3 (11%) in grasslands, and 1 (4%) in riparian habitats or streamside vegetation.

DISCUSSION

A comparison of small landbird species listed by federal or state wildlife agencies as being of conservation concern with recent analyses of population trends in the western United States demonstrates a substantial lack of concordance. Some differences are

TABLE 2. POPULATION TRENDS OF SMALL WESTERN LANDBIRDS IDENTIFIED AS SPECIES OF CONSERVATION CONCERN ON OFFICIAL WILDLIFE AGENCY LISTS

Common name[a]	Scientific name	Habitat[b]	Trend and source			
			LIT[c]	BBS1[d]	BBS2[e]	MIG[f]
Common Ground-Dove	*Columbina passerina*	M				
Yellow-billed Cuckoo	*Coccyzus americanus*	R	−			
Greater Roadrunner	*Geococcyx californianus*	S	−			
Lesser Nighthawk	*Chordeiles acutipennis*	S		+	ns	
Common Nighthawk	*Chordeiles minor*	F		ns	ns	
Black Swift	*Cypseloides niger*	M		ns		
Vaux's Swift	*Chaetura vauxi*	F	−	ns		
Lewis' Woodpecker	*Melanerpes lewis*	F	−			
Acorn Woodpecker	*Melanerpes formicivorus*	F				
Williamson's Sapsucker	*Sphyrapicus thyroideus*	F	−			
White-headed Woodpecker	*Picoides albolarvatus*	F				
Three-toed Woodpecker	*Picoides tridactylus*	F				
Black-backed Woodpecker	*Picoides arcticus*	F				
Pileated Woodpecker	*Dryocopus pileatus*	F				
Willow Flycatcher	*Empidonax traillii*	R	−	ns		ns
Gray Flycatcher	*Empidonax wrightii*	S		ns	ns	
Vermilion Flycatcher	*Pyrocephalus rubinus*	R	−			
Brown-crested Flycatcher	*Myiarchus tyrannulus*	R		+		
Horned Lark	*Eremophila alpestris*	G	−			
Purple Martin	*Progne subis*	M	−	ns	ns	
Bank Swallow	*Riparia riparia*	R		ns	ns	
Chihuahuan Raven	*Corvus cryptoleucus*	S	−			
Pygmy Nuthatch	*Sitta pygmaea*	F				
Cactus Wren	*Campylorhynchus brunneicapillus*	S	−			
Canyon Wren	*Catherpes mexicanus*	M				
Eastern Bluebird	*Sialia sialis*	M				
Western Bluebird	*Sialia mexicana*	F		ns		
Mountain Bluebird	*Sialia currucoides*	F		ns		
Sage Thrasher	*Oreoscoptes montanus*	S		ns		
Bendire's Thrasher	*Toxostoma bendirei*	S		ns		
Crissal Thrasher	*Toxostoma crissale*	R				
LeConte's Thrasher	*Toxostoma lecontei*	S				
Sprague's Pipit	*Anthus spragueii*	G	−			
Loggerhead Shrike	*Lanius ludovicianus*	M		ns		
Bell's Vireo	*Vireo bellii*	R	−	ns	ns	
Black-capped Vireo	*Vireo atricapillus*	S				
Gray Vireo	*Vireo vicinior*	S	−			
Black-throated Gray Warbler	*Dendroica nigrescens*	S	−			ns
Golden-cheeked Warbler	*Dendroica chrysoparia*	S				
Common Yellowthroat	*Geothlypis trichas*	R		ns	+	+
Yellow-breasted Chat	*Icteria virens*	R	−	+	ns	
Summer Tanager	*Piranga rubra*	R				
Blue Grosbeak	*Guiraca caerulea*	M		+	+	
Dickcissel	*Spiza americana*	G				
Rufous-crowned Sparrow	*Aimophila ruficeps*	S				
Vesper Sparrow	*Pooecetes gramineus*	G	−			
Sage Sparrow	*Amphispiza belli*	S		ns		
Lark Bunting	*Calamospiza melanocorys*	G		ns		
Savannah Sparrow	*Passerculus sandwichensis*	G		ns		ns
Baird's Sparrow	*Ammodramus bairdii*	G	−	+		
Grasshopper Sparrow	*Ammodramus savannarum*	G	−	ns		
McCown's Longspur	*Calcarius mccownii*	G	−	+		
Bobolink	*Dolichonyx oryzivorus*	G	−		ns	
Tricolored Blackbird	*Agelaius tricolor*	R				

[a] Excluding: (a) species occurring peripherally in the western United States, (b) species occurring as peripheral populations in the state(s) where they are listed as being of conservation concern, and (c) species represented solely by listed subspecies with highly restricted distributions. See text for further discussion.

[b] Habitat categories: G = grassland, F = coniferous forest/oak woodland, S = arid woodlands and miscellaneous scrub, R = riparian, marsh, and streamside, M = miscellaneous.

[c] LIT. Based on results of literature survey presented by DeSante and George (1994). Increasing trends (+) defined as those where "major increases

TABLE 3. SMALL WESTERN LANDBIRDS WITH REPORTEDLY DECLINING POPULATIONS THAT ARE ABSENT FROM OFFICIAL WILDLIFE AGENCY LISTS OF SPECIES OF CONSERVATION CONCERN

Common name	Scientific name	Habitat	Trend and source			
			LIT	BBS1	BBS2	MIG
Band-tailed Pigeon*	*Columba fasciata*	F	−	−		−
Mourning Dove	*Zenaida macroura*	M		ns		−
Black-chinned Hummingbird	*Archilochus alexandri*	M		−		
Anna's Hummingbird	*Calypte anna*	M	+	−		
Rufous Hummingbird	*Selasphorus rufus*	M		−		
Allen's Hummingbird	*Selasphorus sasin*	M		−		
Olive-sided Flycatcher*	*Contopus borealis*	F		−		−
Say's Phoebe	*Sayornis saya*	M		−	−	
Rock Wren	*Salpinctes obsoletus*	M		−		
Swainson's Thrush*	*Catharus ustulatus*	F		−	ns	−
Cedar Waxwing	*Bombycilla cedrorum*	M		ns		−
Lucy's Warbler	*Vermivora luciae*	S		−		
Townsend's Warbler	*Dendroica townsendi*	F	+	ns		−
MacGillivray's Warbler	*Oporornis tolmiei*	M		−		ns
Wilson's Warbler*	*Wilsonia pusilla*	R		−	ns	−
Rufous-winged Sparrow	*Aimophila carpalis*	S	−			
Chipping Sparrow*	*Spizella passerina*	M		−		−
Black-chinned Sparrow	*Spizella atrogularis*	S		−		
Black-throated Sparrow*	*Amphispiza bilineata*	S	−	−		
Fox Sparrow	*Passerella iliaca*	M		−		ns
Chestnut-collared Longspur	*Calcarius ornatus*	G	−	+		
Eastern Meadowlark	*Sturnella magna*	G		−		
Western Meadowlark	*Sturnella neglecta*	G	+	−		ns
Brewer's Blackbird	*Euphagus cyanocephalus*	M		−		ns
Northern Oriole	*Icterus galbula*	M		ns	−	ns
Scott's Oriole	*Icterus parisorum*	S		−	+	
Lawrence's Goldfinch	*Carduelis lawrencei*	S		−		

* Declines indicated by two or more sources.

trivial, and merely reflect limitations in population monitoring techniques. Broad-scale analyses based on methods such as the Breeding Bird Survey or migration counts are unlikely to accurately detect trends characterizing taxa with geographically limited distributions. For example, even though Sauer and Droege (1992) and DeSante and George (1994) found no significant declines for Willow Flycatcher or Bell's Vireo based on data collected throughout the western United States, there is little doubt that two subspecies of these birds that are frequently included on official agency lists (South-western Willow Flycatcher, *Empidonax traillii extimus*; Least Bell's Vireo, *Vireo bellii pusillus*) are both highly threatened due to loss and degradation of riparian habitat (Phillips 1948, Unitt 1987, U.S. Fish and Wildlife Service 1986, Franzreb 1989).

Such factors may excuse the absence of some officially "listed" taxa from summaries of declining species based on analyses of population trends, but they do not explain the failure of public wildlife agencies to incorporate into official lists the results of recent scientific findings concerning the status of bird populations. For example, the

←
(>50% population increase)" were cited in at least one western state; decreasing trends (−) as those where "major decreases (>50% population decrease)" were cited in at least one western state.
d BBS1. Based on analysis of Breeding Bird Survey data (1966–1991) presented by DeSante and George (1994). Increasing trends (+) include those defined as "Strong increasing" by DeSante and George; decreasing trends (−) include those defined as "Strong decreasing" by DeSante and George. Non-significant or less pronounced trends indicated by "ns".
e BBS2. Based on analysis of Breeding Bird Survey data (1966–1988) presented by Sauer and Droege (1992); + = significantly increasing trend (P < 0.05), − = significantly decreasing trend (P < 0.05), ns = non-significant.
f MIG. Based on linear regression analysis of weather-adjusted spring migration captures (1968–1992) presented by Pyle et al. (1994); + = significantly increasing trend (P < 0.05), − = significantly decreasing trend (P < 0.05), ns = non-significant.

existence of at least 27 declining species of small, western landbirds—none of which have been officially recognized by federal or state wildlife agencies—casts obvious doubt on the effectiveness of the present process.

Furthermore, official lists of species of conservation concern are frequently inflated by inclusion of peripheral species that are "threatened" only by virtue of their occurrence as small, often isolated populations located "on the wrong side" of a political boundary line. The frequent inclusion of such species on official lists, although perhaps understandable from the standpoint of local conservation concerns, may ultimately threaten the public credibility of the overall endangered species listing process, and divert research and management attention that should be given to truly threatened populations. For instance, Sauer and Droege (1992) and DeSante and George (1994) found significant population increases for Ash-throated Flycatcher in the western United States. Nonetheless, the state of Washington lists Ash-throated Flycatcher as of conservation concern ("Monitor" status), even though the species' normal range barely extends north of Oregon (Jewett et al. 1953, American Ornithologists' Union 1957). Furthermore, Washington also applies the "Monitor" designation to Three-toed Woodpecker, which, at least based on its appearance on the official lists of Oregon, Idaho, and Utah, may well be a species for which there is a legitimate cause for concern. Similarly, New Mexico ascribes the same listing category ("Endangered, group 2") to White-eared Hummingbird, which occurs only as a peripheral species in the United States (American Ornithologists' Union 1957), as it does to the Southwestern Willow Flycatcher, for which the state represents a major portion of the subspecies' range (Phillips 1948, Unitt 1987).

Similar inconsistencies characterize virtually every agency list examined in this analysis. In perhaps the most inexplicable case, the FWS lists the Mexican Hooded Oriole (*Icterus cucullatus cucullatus*) as a Category 2 candidate, even though the subspecies only occurs as an occasional migrant in western Texas (American Ornithologists' Union 1957).

There is little evidence that lists compiled by federal or state wildlife agencies provide a comprehensive and accurate picture of threatened or declining bird populations in the western United States. This fact should especially concern conservationists. The existing environmental review processes used by most local or state planning authorities often depend on official lists of protected or sensitive species as the primary biological criterion by which to evaluate potential impacts of proposed projects. Also, lists of sensitive species compiled by wildlife agencies may be important in shaping land-use decisions associated with ecosystem or multispecies conservation planning (U.S. Fish and Wildlife Service 1993). Finally, official lists frequently direct research attention (and needed funding) toward studies aimed at clarifying the population status of these species.

Current lists of species of conservation concern that have been compiled by federal and state agencies leave much to be desired. Inconsistent and poorly defined terminology, failure to systematically incorporate current scientific data, and over-emphasis on protection of peripheral populations that show no evidence of widespread declines have created a vague and confusing system that has minimal value to scientists or conservationists. Given the increasing threats faced by bird populations throughout the United States, there is an urgent need to improve the process by which species are officially identified as being in need of special conservation attention.

ACKNOWLEDGMENTS

L. Nagy assisted with initial compilation of data, which were provided by representatives of the U.S. Fish and Wildlife Service and western state wildlife agencies. M. Kasprzyk and D. Lahaise helped with preparation of the final manuscript, which was improved by the editorial comments of J. Jehl. B. Atwood gave needed encouragement. This work was supported financially by the trustees and members of Manomet Bird Observatory.

LITERATURE CITED

AMERICAN ORNITHOLOGISTS' UNION. 1957. Checklist of North American birds, 5th ed. American Ornithologists' Union, Baltimore, MD.

DeSANTE, D. F., AND T. L. GEORGE. 1994. Population trends in the landbirds of Western North America. Pp. 173–190 *in* J. R. Jehl, Jr. and N. K. Johnson (eds.), A century of avifaunal change in western North America. Studies in Avian Biology No. 15.

FRANZREB, K. E. 1989. Ecology and conservation of the endangered Least Bell's Vireo. Biological Report 89. U.S. Fish and Wildlife Service, Washington, DC.

JEWETT, S. G., W. P. TAYLOR, W. T. SHAW, AND J. W. ALDRICH. 1953. Birds of Washington State. University of Washington Press, Pullman, WA.

PHILLIPS, A. R. 1948. Geographic variation in *Empidonax traillii*. Auk 65:507–514.

PYLE, P., N. NUR, AND D. F. DeSANTE. 1994. Trends in nocturnal migrant landbird populations at Southeast Farallon Island, California, 1968–1992. Pp. 58–74 *in* J. R. Jehl, Jr. and N. K. Johnson (eds.), A century of avifaunal change in western North America. Studies in Avian Biology No. 15.

SAUER, J. R., AND S. DROEGE. 1992. Geographic patterns in population trends of Neotropical migrants in North America. Pp. 26–42, *in* J. M. Hagan III and D. W. Johnston (eds.), Ecology and conservation of neotropical migrant landbirds. Smithsonian Institution Press, Washington, DC.

UNITT, P. 1987. *Empidonax traillii extimus*: an endangered subspecies. Western Birds 18:137–162.

U.S. FISH AND WILDLIFE SERVICE. 1986. Endangered and threatened wildlife and plants: determination of endangered status for the Least Bell's Vireo. Federal Register 51:16474–16482.

U.S. FISH AND WILDLIFE SERVICE. 1993. Endangered and threatened wildlife and plants; proposed special rule to allow take of the threatened coastal California Gnatcatcher. Federal Register 58:16758–16759.

Studies in Avian Biology No. 15:340–348, 1994.

Prospects

PRESERVING AND RESTORING AVIAN DIVERSITY: A SEARCH FOR SOLUTIONS

J. Michael Scott

Abstract. I describe a strategy for maintaining avian biodiversity into the 22nd century that uses the tools of avian ecology and conservation biology. Underlying it are ten assumptions: 1) many of the present and past causes of avian jeopardy will be factors in the future; 2) the effects of a limiting factor cannot be eliminated or significantly ameliorated by actions taken at a scale that is finer grained than the scale at which the limiting factor operates; 3) high quality, well distributed habitat is the key to healthy bird populations; 4) the area of concern must be the entire historical range of a species; 5) restoration of habitat is critical; 6) faunal mixing resulting from anthropogenic habitat alteration is a threat to the integrity of avian communities; 7) alien non-avian species are threats as predators, competitors, habitat modifiers and disease vectors; 8) survival chances are enhanced if metapopulations exist; 9) research and management efforts should be conducted in a biological, rather than political, context and 10) the time to save a species is when it is common. This plan calls us to think globally and act locally, to consider proximate and ultimate factors affecting populations, to place more emphasis on research and conservation in biological rather than political contexts, and to acknowledge that growth of human population size is the driving force behind the loss of avian diversity.

Key Words: Conservation; neotropical migrants; management; research; scale.

"To Keep Every Cog and Wheel Is The First Precaution Of Intelligent Tinkering"—Aldo Leopold

In this volume authors have reviewed and synthesized our knowledge about population trends and effects of human-induced environmental change, and presented case histories for many of the birds in the western United States. I provide a view of what might be done to help restore and maintain the viability and integrity of these avian populations. I will repeatedly refer to the need for an approach based on systems and a better understanding of the issues of scale, temporal, spatial, and biological, for designing research and recovery efforts. I emphasize the theme of building bridges among groups and working across political boundaries. My basic assumption is there exists an urgent need to proactively rather than reactively address conservation issues in biological rather than political contexts.

In seeking strategies to save, restore, and maintain avian diversity, I have looked to the past for solutions and guidance. The dramatic rebound of the peregrine falcon *Falco peregrinus* (Cade et al. 1988) with the banning of DDT and large scale reintroduction efforts shows the possibility of even eliminating pervasive threats from the environment. The recovery of the Aleutian Canada Goose (*Branta canadensis leucopareia*) following the removal of alien foxes from the breeding grounds and reduction in take by hunters is equally impressive (Rees 1989, Anonymous 1991). These are excellent examples of the need to address both proximate and ultimate factors limiting a population's size and distribution. In both cases, the proximate cause of decline was reproductive failure. But it was only when the ultimate causes were removed that populations recovered.

As an insight to changes in western birds, Linsdale's (1930:105) review of the problems of bird conservation in California is instructive. He stated that "An examination of available information bearing upon population numbers in California birds reveals no single species which can be designated certainly on the verge of extinction. However, several species, or groups of species within the state are low in numbers and need watching and possibly, help in maintaining their statuses." He listed 17 species

TABLE 1. STATUS ATTRIBUTED TO BIRDS IN CALIFORNIA BY LINSDALE (1930) AND EHRLICH ET AL. (1992)

Species	In jeopardy Linsdale	In jeopardy Erlich et al.
Common loon (*Gavia immer*)[a]	no	yes
Brown Pelican (*Pelecanus occidentalis*)	no	yes
Least Bittern (*Ixobrychus exilis*)	no	yes
Reddish Egret (*Egretta rufescens*)	no	yes
Black-crowned Night-Heron (*Nycticorax nycticorax*)	no	yes
White-faced Ibis (*Plegadis chihi*)	no	yes
Aleutian Canada Goose (*Branta canadensis leucopareia*)	yes	yes
Fulvous Whistling Duck (*Dendrocygna bicolor*)	yes	yes
Canvasback (*Aythya valisineria*)	yes	yes
Harlequin Duck (*Histrionicus histrionicus*)	yes	yes
California Condor (*Gymnogyps californianus*)	yes	yes
White-tailed Kite (*Elanus leucurus*)	yes	no
Bald Eagle (*Haliaeetus leucocephalus*)	yes	yes
Northern Harrier (*Circus cyaneus*)	no	yes
Harris Hawk (*Parabuteo unicinctus*)	no	yes
Red-shouldered Hawk (*Buteo lineatus*)	yes	no
Swainson's Hawk (*Buteo swainsoni*)	no	yes
Golden Eagle (*Aquila chrysaetos*)	yes	no
Prairie Falcon (*Falco mexicanus*)	yes	no
Peregrine Falcon (*Falco peregrinus*)	yes	yes
Sharp-tailed Grouse (*Tympanuchus phasianellus*)	yes	yes
Black Rail (*Lateralus jamaicensis coturniculus*)	no	yes
Clapper Rail (*Rallus longirostris yumanensis*)	yes	yes
Clapper Rail (*Rallus longirostris obsoletus*)	yes	yes
Clapper Rail (*Rallus longirostris levipes*)	yes	yes
Snowy Plover (*Charadrinus alexandrinus*)	yes	yes
Long-billed Curlew (*Numenius americanus*)	yes	yes
Elegant Tern (*Sternus elegans*)	no	yes
Least Tern (*Sterna antillarum*)	no	yes
Marbled Murrelet (*Brachyramphus marmoratus*)	no	yes
Black Tern (*Chlidonias niger*)	no	yes
Yellow-billed Cuckoo (*Coccyzus americanus*)	no	yes
Common Barn-Owl (*Tyto alba*)	no	yes
Burrowing Owl (*Athene cunicularia*)	no	yes
Spotted Owl (*Strix occidentalis caurina*)	no	yes
Short-eared Owl (*Asio flammeus*)	no	yes
Willow Flycatcher (*Empidonax traillii*)	no	yes
Whip-poor-will (*Caprimulgus vociferus*)	no	yes
Purple Martin (*Progne subis*)	yes	yes
Sage Sparrow (*Amphispiza belli clementeae*)	no	yes
California Gnatcatcher (*Polioptila californica*)	no	yes
Western Bluebird (*Sialia mexicana*)	no	yes
Yellow-billed Magpie (*Pica nuttalli*)	yes	no
Loggerhead Shrike (*Lanius ludovicianus mearnsi*)	no	yes
Yellow Warbler (*Dendroica petechia*)	no	yes
Common Yellowthroat (*Geothlypis trichas sinuosa*)	no	yes
Song Sparrow (*Melospiza melodia samuelis*)	no	yes
Song Sparrow (*Melospiza melodia maxillaris*)	no	yes
Song Sparrow (*Melospiza melodia pusillula*)	no	yes
Tricolored Blackbird (*Agelaius tricolor*)	no	yes
Bell's Vireo (*Vireo bellii pusillus*)	no	yes
Inyo California Towhee (*Pipilo crissalis eremophilus*)	no	yes
Savannah Sparrow (*Passerculus sandwichensis beldingi*)	no	yes

Lindsdale Yes; Ehrlich et al. No	5
Lindsdale No; Ehrlich et al. Yes	34
Lindsdale Yes; Ehrlich et al. Yes	14

[a] Names used are those in American Ornithologists' Union checklists, 5th and 6th editions (AOU 1957, 1983). In some instances, only the California population or subspecies is in jeopardy.

and shorebirds, ducks, and geese as groups with problems. Five of these species were not listed by Ehrlich et al. (1992). However, 34 California taxa listed by Ehrlich et al. (1992) were not identified by Linsdale as having problems (Table 1).

The west is usually defined as the area west of the 100th meridian exclusive of Mexico (Peterson 1969), including the Hawaiian Islands; 750 bird species occur there. Using floristic provinces, ecoregions, (e.g., Bailey 1980) or physiographic regions that occur in whole or part west of the Meridian rather than political boundaries would allow full consideration of the birds of the Gulf and Pacific islands off Baja California, and of the Sonoran ecoregion that extends into Northern Mexico (Fig. 1). A recent survey of the avifauna of the North American continent exclusive of Mexico, but including Hawaii, found 92 species or subspecies that occur in the west, to be in jeopardy (Ehrlich et al. 1992, see also Atwood 1994). Of 33 extinctions of species and subspecies in the United States since European settle-

FIGURE 1. Spatial distribution of the ten floristic provinces of the continental United States and Canada (after Gleason and Cronquist 1964). Used with permission of Fritz Knopf. Taken from Knopf 1992.

ment, 25 (78%) have occurred in the west. The loss of populations has been much greater but undocumented. Add to this a minimum of 50 species extinct in the Hawaiian Islands as a result of the 1500 year influence of Polynesians before the arrival of Europeans (Olson and James 1991, James and Olson 1991).

The reasons for loss and placing in jeopardy of species have been varied and changing. In a worldwide review, King (1978) found that in the period 1600–1980, 91%

of extinctions were due, at least in part, to the impact of introduced species: in 25% human take was a factor; while for 32% habitat loss or change was a consideration. There is currently a different mixture. Temple (1986) found that for currently endangered species, habitat modification was the single most important factor for 82% of the taxa, followed by excessive human take (44%), and introduced species (36%).

The ultimate cause of extinction and jeopardy is a human population whose de-

mands on the global ecosystem are greater than the planet can sustain on a long-term basis (Daily and Ehrlich 1992). The United States population increased from 3.9 million in 1790 to 249 million in 1990, with a projected population of 349 million by 2025 (U.S. Department of Commerce 1991). Because of the settlement patterns, rates of increase have been greater in the west in the past 150 years. With increased human populations and increased consumption of resources and goods (Daily and Ehrlich 1992) has come increased habitat loss, fragmentation, and loss of community integrity. Future wildlife losses can be anticipated to be greatest in those areas still having the greatest extent of intact native habitats (Knopf 1992).

In this section, I discuss specific issues that affect the avian populations in the west and lay out a plan for conserving them. I make ten assumptions:

1) Many of the factors that have resulted in the loss of bird species or reduction in their ranges and abundance will continue to be factors in the future.

2) Thriving avian populations require abundant, well distributed, high quality habitat.

3) The effects of a limiting factor cannot be eliminated or significantly ameliorated by actions taken at a scale that is finer grained than the scale at which the limiting factor operates. As an example, if regional lead accumulation leading to poisoning is a significant factor in the decline of California Condors (*Gymnogyps californianus*) (Wiemeyer et al. 1988, Pattee et al. 1990), then treatment of individual birds and provision of contaminant-free carcass at specific sites will not be enough to save the species. The sources of lead must be significantly reduced throughout the range of the species.

←

(*Toxostoma redivivum*), and Tricolored Blackbird (*Agelaius tricolor*). The Least Bell's Vireo (*Vireo bellii pusillus*) is an endangered subspecies in the southwest. Used with permission of Fritz Knopf. Taken from Knopf 1992.

FIGURE 2. Top to bottom: Continental distributions of Bell's Vireo (*Vireo bellii*), California Thrasher

4) Conservation, research, and management efforts must nearly always transcend political boundaries (Figs. 1, 2) and perhaps more importantly, the mental boundaries that we create.

5) Restoration of habitats will frequently be necessary (see Ohmart 1994). If recovery or management efforts are restricted to the present range of a species, they may unnecessarily limit the long term viability of a species. An example is the recovery efforts for Hawaiian forest birds that focus on less than 25% of their historical ranges (Scott et al. 1986). Efforts throughout a species' historical range, not necessarily just its current range (Verner 1992), will be frequently necessary to restore avian populations fully.

6) Faunal mixing resulting from human induced habitat loss, fragmentation, and change may affect the integrity of avifaunas (Knopf 1992). Faunal mixing may occur as the direct result of introductions by man or as the result of habitat alteration, e.g., creation of riparian corridors, urbanization of an area (Emlen 1974), or habitat loss and fragmentation which can result in the expansion of a species range. Change is a natural process, but we need to minimize the human induced changes if we are to maintain our native avifauna.

7) Alien non-avian species are a threat as predators, competitors, habitat modifiers, and disease vectors. The most harmful impacts of introduced species usually occur on islands.

8) The survival chances of species are greatly enhanced if a metapopulation structure can be maintained or reestablished (Sabelis et al. 1991, Gilpin and Hanski 1991).

9) Restoration efforts should be placed in a context of physiographic region, ecoregion, a species range, or some other biologically meaningful framework.

10) The time to save a species is when it is common.

GENERAL ACTION PLAN

What can we do to make a difference?

1) "Think globally, act locally." Most of the species that occur in the west spend a portion of their time elsewhere, some as far away as the polar seas. Thus, efforts to maintain the numbers as well as the genetic diversity and population structure of shearwaters should consider conditions throughout their range to include oil pollution, gill netting, competition from commercial fisheries in their wintering areas, as well as the sanctity of their southern hemisphere breeding grounds. The importance of cooperative international efforts in bird conservation has been realized since passage of the Migratory Bird Treaty Act. It has been more recently augmented by several recent programs, particularly efforts to establish hemisphere reserves for migrant shorebirds (Myers et al. 1987), the North American Waterfowl Management Plan (U.S. Department of the Interior and Environment Canada 1986) and The Partners in Flight project (Stangel and Eno 1992), which involves international programs to protect or restore populations of neotropical migrants. Similar efforts are needed to make ecosystems and species ranges the common currency guiding conservation and development decisions.

2) Consider both the proximate and ultimate factors. Proximate causes are those that are acting to cause the immediate decrease of a species. Ultimate causes are those that were responsible for the original decline to a point of jeopardy. The proximate cause may be decreased reproductive success, as in the case of the Peregrine Falcon, but simply increasing reproductive success through brood augmentation or release of captive-reared offspring was only a partial solution to the problem. Reducing DDT in the environment was the solution, as it was the ultimate cause of reproductive failure (Cade et al. 1988). Similarly, recovery efforts for Masked Bobwhite Quail (*Colinus virginianus ridgwayi*) were not successful despite supplementing wild populations with thousands of captive reared birds. The problem was poor habitat, and only when a long-term drought was broken and grazing

pressure reduced or eliminated, did the population begin to show signs of recovery (Gabel and Drobrott 1989).

3) Clearly and loudly articulate the relationship between the increase in human populations and the natural world (Daily and Ehrlich 1992, Ehrlich and Ehrlich 1991).

4) Emphasize research and conservation efforts in biological rather than political contexts (Knopf 1992). Species do not recognize political borders (Fig. 2). In a review of 5 years of *The Condor,* fewer than 5% of the published papers were appropriately extrapolative to a biologically defensible unit. Our arguments for the protection of species would be more forceful if we could defensibly make inferences beyond our study sites and coherently link the hierarchical levels of biological organization.

SPECIFIC ACTIVITIES FOR SOCIETIES

1) Fund the visit to annual meetings of active foreign scientists. Collaborative research is born out of partnerships, mutual respect, and friendship.

2) Sponsor and publish proceedings of symposia that address critical areas in conservation biology or particularly sensitive species of birds. In doing so, involve managers and devote a significant portion of the proceedings to management issues. Examples of this type of effort include:

Ecology and Management of the Spotted Owl in the Pacific Northwest (Gutiérrez and Carey, eds. 1985)

Conservation of Marine Birds of North America (Bartonek and Nettleship 1979)

Ecology and Conservation of Neotropical Migrant Landbirds (Hagan and Johnston 1992)

Endangered Birds (Temple 1978)

3) Conduct research in foreign countries, applying the suggestions of Short (1984) and Verner (1992) in tropical areas.

4) Publish in Spanish the titles and abstracts of articles appearing in ornithological journals.

5) Provide ornithological journals for foreign libraries, establish biological documentation centers in Latin America and Pacific Island countries, and sponsor individual subscriptions to foreign scientists (Duffy 1988, Strahl 1992, and Foster et al. in press).

6) Encourage development and funding of a network of bird observatories in this hemisphere (New World Bird Observatory Network, NEWBORN). In addition to their research efforts, they can be a source of inspiration for conservation. An excellent model is the Point Reyes Bird Observatory, with its strong scientific program, involvement in conservation issues, and commitment to public participation and education (Salzman 1989).

7) Encourage publication of more conservation-oriented manuscripts by ornithological journals. Possible incentives include: a) awards for the best conservation-oriented papers; b) direct assistance for research.

8) Initiate an Adopt-An-Island Program. Individual islands would be adopted by individuals, groups of individuals, small bird clubs, and private companies. These groups would play active roles in eliminating alien plants and animals from North Pacific Islands (Harrison 1992). There are many examples of alien predator species having devastating impacts on island birds (terrestrial and marine) (see Temple 1986 and Loope et al. 1988). Equally devastating are the effects of introduced ungulates and other herbivores (Bailey 1956). While there have been efforts to control these species on some islands and some impressive successes, e.g., foxes were eliminated from many of the breeding islands of the Aleutian Canada Goose, the elimination efforts have not been systematic, and the losses continue. New Zealanders have pioneered effective programs to remove alien predators and herbivores from small islands (Towns et al. 1990).

9) When papers presented at society meetings have particular significance to avian conservation, ask the local committee to invite the media. Provide them with ab-

stracts, contact names, and numbers. Getting issues into the public eye can make a difference.

10) As a society, have a fund-raiser for a specific conservation activity. One possibility is fully stocking libraries at several Pacific Island research facilities that have a policy of lending to other libraries in the region. This effort could augment the establishment of biological documentation centers in Latin America by the U.S. Fish and Wildlife Service (Duffy 1988). Explore a joint venture with the U.S. Information Agency to translate key articles and monographs to Spanish and Portuguese and to make additional literature available through the USIS Network of overseas libraries.

INDIVIDUAL ACTIONS

1) In maintaining species we must seek to maintain self-sustaining metapopulations that retain their full evolutionary potential, rather than a single population that may be no more than a living museum exhibit with a low probability of long-term survival.

2) Write letters to newspapers and our elected representatives. Scientists are well respected by the public and by political leaders.

3) Participate in breeding bird surveys or initiate a breeding bird census. Be part of the loose network of people monitoring our birds.

4) For westerners in particular, get to know your nearby National Forest or Bureau of Land Management district. Meet with the staffs of these public agencies when you see things that displease you, and compliment them when they do something right. Participate in the planning process, and alert managers to any problems.

5) Take a business person to lunch or in the field. Share your knowledge of and enthusiasm for the resource.

Effective conservation requires that we examine issues on scales larger than individuals and breeding seasons (Scott et al. 1993). We must define our sampling uni-

verses by biological criteria and draft our findings so that they can be extended to larger biological, temporal, and spatial scales (Wiens 1989, Landres 1992). We need to think hierarchically, for the scale at which we ask questions and initiate management actions affects the answers and responses we obtain (Wiens 1989). Think in terms of landscapes and ecosystems that birds perceive, rather than political boundaries. We are fortunate in the west, for we still have vast tracts of unpeopled lands. With the exception of the Hawaiian Islands, most of the historic avifauna is still with us, but times are changing and changing fast. For a window to the future, one needs to look no further than the coastal sage community of Southern California. Once widespread and considered a nuisance habitat, it now occupies but a fraction of its historical range. One bird species associated with it, California Gnatcatcher (*Polioptila californica*), is threatened, and more than 80 plants and animals are at risk. If we are to be even marginally successful in our efforts to maintain bird species as self-sustaining metapopulations in natural environments, then we must increase our research, management, and restoration efforts at the systems level of organization. The best time to save a species is when it is still common.

ACKNOWLEDGMENTS

I thank D. Wilcove, M. Jennings, J. Jehl, N. Johnson, L. Kiff and R. Banks for comments and thoughtful discussion of the information presented in this chapter. Thanks to F. Knopf who graciously provided permission to use previously published figures. K. Bennett and K. Merk patiently and graciously worked with me to translate my draft manuscript into acceptable journal form.

This contribution is no. 701 of the Idaho Forest Wildlife and Range Experiment Station, and was funded in part by the Idaho Cooperative Fish and Wildlife Research Unit and Idaho Department of Fish and Game.

LITERATURE CITED

AMERICAN ORNITHOLOGISTS' UNION. 1957. Checklist of North American birds, 5th edition. Lord Baltimore Press, Baltimore, MD.
AMERICAN ORNITHOLOGISTS' UNION. 1983. Checklist of North American birds, 6th edition. Allen Press, Inc., Lawrence, KS.

ANONYMOUS. 1991. Aleutian Canada Goose reclassified from endangered to threatened. Endangered Species Technical Bulletin 16:10–12.

ATWOOD, J. L. 1994. Endangered small landbirds of the western United States. Pp. 328–338 *in* J. R. Jehl, Jr. and N. K. Johnson (eds.), A century of avifaunal change in western North America. Studies in Avian Biology No. 15.

BAILEY, A. M. 1956. Birds of Midway and Laysan islands. Denver Museum Pictorial No. 12.

BAILEY, R. G. 1980. Descriptions of the ecoregions of the United States. U.S. Forest Service, Miscellaneous Publication No. 1391. 77 pp.

BARTONEK, J. C., AND D. N. NETTLESHIP. 1979. Conservation of marine birds of northern North America. U.S. Dept. of the Interior Fish and Wildlife Research Report No. 11. Washington, DC.

CADE, T. J., J. H. ENDERSON, C. G. THELANDER, AND C. M. WHITE (eds.). 1988. Peregrine falcon populations. The Peregrine Fund, Boise, Idaho.

DAILY, G. C., AND P. R. EHRLICH. 1992. Population sustainability and earth's carrying capacity. BioScience 42:761–771.

DUFFY, D. C. 1988. Ornithology in Central and South America: cause for optimism. Auk 105:395–397.

EHRLICH, P. R., AND A. H. EHRLICH. 1991. Healing the planet. Addison-Wesley Publishing Co., Inc., New York, NY.

EHRLICH, P. R., D. S. DOBKIN, AND D. WHEYE. 1992. Birds in jeopardy. Stanford University Press, Stanford, CA.

EMLEN, J. T. 1974. An urban bird community in Tucson, Arizona: derivation, structure, and regulation. Condor 76:184–197.

FOSTER, M. S., M. A. JENKINSON, AND A. ALLEN. In press. The Tools of the Trade Library Enhancement in Developing Countries. Bioscience.

GABEL, R. R., AND S. J. DROBROTT. 1989. Saving the masked bob white. Endangered Species Technical Bulletin 13:6–7.

GILPIN, M., AND I. HANSKI (eds.). 1991. Metapopulation dynamics: empirical and theoretical investigations. Academic Press, London, England.

GLEASON, H. A., AND A. CRONQUIST. 1964. The natural geography of plants. Columbia University Press, New York, NY.

GUTIERREZ, R. J., AND A. B. CAREY (eds.). 1985. Ecology and management of the spotted owl. U.S. Forest Service General Technical Report Pacific Northwest-185.

HAGAN, J. M. III, AND D. W. JOHNSTON. 1992. Ecology and conservation of neotropical migrant landbirds. Smithsonian Institution Press, Washington, DC.

HARRISON, C. S. 1992. A conservation agenda for the 1990's: removal of alien predators from seabird colonies. Pacific Seabird Group Bulletin 19:5.

JAMES, H. F., AND S. L. OLSON. 1991. Description of thirty-two new species of birds from the Hawaiian Islands. Part II. Passeriformes. Ornithological Monographs No. 46.

KING, W. B. 1978. Endangered birds of the world and current efforts toward managing them. Pp. 9–18 *in* S. A. Temple (ed.), University of Wisconsin Press, Madison, WI.

KNOPF, F. L. 1992. Faunal mixing, faunal integrity and the biological template for diversity conservation. Pp. 330–342 *in* R. McCabe (ed.), Transactions of the 57th North American Wildlife and Natural Resources Conference. Wildlife Management Institute, Washington, DC.

LANDRES, P. B. 1992. Temporal scale perspectives in managing biological diversity. Pp. 292–307 *in* R. McCabe (ed.), Transactions 57th North American Wildlife and Natural Resources Conference. Wildlife Management Institute, Washington, DC.

LINSDALE, J. M. 1930. Problems of bird conservation in California. Condor 32:105–115.

LOOPE, L. L., O. HARMANN, AND C. P. STONE. 1988. Comparative conservation biology of Oceanic Archipelagoes. BioScience 38:272–282.

MYERS, J. P., M. DOOHERTY, K. HEINZEL, R. JUNG, AND M. STEIN. 1987. Scarce resources and common species. Endangered Species Technical Bulletin 12:1.

OHMART, R. D. 1994. The effects of human-induced changes on the avifauna of western riparian habitats. Pp. 273–285 *in* J. R. Jehl, Jr. and N. K. Johnson (eds.), A century of avifaunal change in western North America. Studies in Avian Biology No. 15.

OLSON, S. L., AND H. F. JAMES. 1991. Description of thirty-two new species of birds from the Hawaiian Islands. Part I. Non-passeriformes. Ornithological Monographs No. 45.

PATTEE, O. H., P. H. BLOOM, J. M. SCOTT, AND M. R. SMITH. 1990. Lead hazards within the range of the California condor. Condor 92:931–937.

PETERSON, R. T. 1969. A field guide to western birds. Houghton Mifflin Co., Boston, MA.

REES, M. D. 1989. Aleutian Canada Goose proposed for reclassification. Endangered Species Technical Bulletin 14:8–9.

SABELIS, M. W., O. DIEKMANN, AND V. A. A. JANSEN. 1991. Metapopulation persistence despite local extinction: predator-prey patch models of the Lotka Volterra type. Pp. 267–283 *in* M. Gilpin and I. Hansk (eds.), Metapopulation dynamics: empirical and theoretical investigations. Academic Press, London, England.

SALZMAN, J. E. 1989. Scientists as advocates: the Point Reyes Bird Observatory and gill netting in central California. Conservation Biology 3:170–180.

SCOTT, J. M., F. DAVIS, B. CSUTI, R. NOSS, B. BUTTERFIELD, C. GROVES, H. ANDERSON, S. CAICCO, F. D'ERCHIA, T. EDWARDS, J. ULLIMAN, AND R. G. WRIGHT. 1993. Gap analysis: a geographic approach to protection of biological diversity. Wildlife Monographs No. 123.

SCOTT, J. M., S. MOUNTAINSPRING, F. L. RAMSEY, AND C. B. KEPLER. 1986. Forest bird communities of the Hawaiian islands: their dynamics, ecology and conservation. Studies in Avian Biology No. 9.

SHORT, L. L. 1984. Priorities in ornithology: the urgent need for tropical research and researchers. Auk 101:892–893.

STANGEL, P., AND A. ENO. 1992. Conservation on a grand scale. Pp. 648–656 *in* R. McCabe (ed.), Transactions of the 57th North American Wildlife and Natural Resources Conference, Wildlife Management Institute, Washington, DC.

STRAHL, S. D. 1992. Furthering avian conservation in Latin America. Auk 109:680–682.

TEMPLE, S. A. (ed.). 1978. Endangered birds: management techniques for preserving threatened species. University of Wisconsin Press, Madison, WI.

TEMPLE, S. A. 1986. The problem of avian extinctions. Pp. 453–485 *in* R. F. Johnston (ed.), Current ornithology. Volume 3. Plenum Press, New York, NY.

TOWNS, D. R., C. H. DAUGHERTY, AND I. A. E. ATKINSON (eds.). 1990. Ecological restoration of New Zealand Islands. Conservation Sciences Publication No. 2. Wellington (Department of Conservation). P. 11.

U.S. DEPARTMENT OF COMMERCE. 1991. Statistical abstract of the United States. The National Data Book. United States Department of Commerce, Economics and Statistical Administration Bureau of Census. United States Government Printing Office, Washington, DC.

U.S. DEPARTMENT OF THE INTERIOR AND ENVIRONMENT CANADA. 1986. North America Waterfowl Management Plan. U.S. Fish and Wildlife Service, Washington, DC.

VERNER, J. 1992. Data needs for avian conservation biology: have we avoided critical research? Condor 94:301–303.

WIEMEYER, S. N., J. M. SCOTT, M. P. ANDERSON, P. H. ANDERSON, AND C. J. STAFFORD. 1988. Environmental contaminants in California condors. Journal of Wildlife Management 52:238–247.

WIENS, J. A. 1989. The ecology of bird communities. Volume 2. Cambridge University Press, New York, NY.